Nations of the Modern World

Brazil: A Political Analysis

Peter Flynn

Brazil:
a Political Analysis

London · Ernest Benn
Boulder · Westview Press

First published 1978 by Ernest Benn Limited
25 New Street Square, Fleet Street, London EC4A 3JA
& Sovereign Way, Tonbridge, Kent, TN9 1RW
and Westview Press
5500 Central Avenue, Boulder, Colorado 80301

Distributed in Canada by
The General Publishing Company Limited, Toronto

Printed in Great Britain by The Anchor Press Ltd
and bound by Wm Brendon & Son Ltd
both of Tiptree, Essex

A Nations of the Modern World Book

British Library Cataloguing in Publication Data

Flynn, Peter
Brazil. – (Nations of the modern world).
1. Brazil – History 2. Brazil – Politics and government
I. Title II. Series
981 F2521

ISBN 0–510–38100–6

Library of Congress Cataloging in Publication Data

Flynn, Peter.
Brazil, a political analysis.
(Nations of the modern world)
Bibliography: p. 576
Includes index.
1. Brazil—Politics and government—1954– 2. Brazil—Economic conditions—1918– 3. Brazil—Politics and government—1930–1954.
I. Title. II. Series.
F2538.2.F55 320.9′81′06 77–16243

ISBN 0–89158–747–0

for Judith, Catherine, Sarah and Peter

Contents

1937–45

1945–55

1956–61

1961–64

List of Illustrations

Inserted between pages 276 *and* 277

Map

Acknowledgements

Acknowledgements are due to the following copyright-holders for permission to reproduce the illustrations:

Mike Andrews: 4
Brazilian Embassy, London: 19, 23
The *Brazilian Gazette*, London: 25
Camera Press Limited: 7, 10, 16, 20, 21, 29
J. Allan Cash: 11, 12
Companhia Melhoramentos, São Paulo: 6
Dr J. P. Dickenson: 22, 26
O Estado de São Paulo: 8, 9, 14, 15
Marcel Gautherot, Rio de Janeiro: 13
Anthony Hall: 27, 28, 30
Paul Popper Limited: 3, 17, 18
Realidade, São Paulo: 5

1 Introduction

One of the most beautiful sambas to have appeared in Brazil in recent years is *Pedro Pedreiro*, the story of a poor workman from the north-east, waiting and waiting in vain, for the sun, for a train, for a rise in wages, and for a son who in his turn will wait. Another, by the same author, Chico Buarque de Hollanda, tells in *Construção* of the death of a worker on a building site, who falls exhausted from scaffolding and dies in the street, holding up the traffic. Improbable themes, one may think, for popular songs, whistled, sung, and danced all over Brazil, yet they, and other songs like them, have immense success, and not just for the beauty of the music. The themes are those regularly found in Brazilian music, not just sun, sea, and beauty, of which, happily, there is plenty, but suffering, sadness, loss, and exploitation, which is no less common. *Pedro Pedreiro* touches one of the most intractable problems of modern Brazil, the disparity in wealth and opportunity between the north-east, once the heart of Brazil's economy, and the booming prosperous centre-south, the centre of economic growth since the coffee boom of the nineteenth century, and now the hope of thousands of north-eastern migrants, looking for work and a better life, and too often finding neither. *Construção*, in part, hints at why this is: the social, economic, and political priorities enshrined in the so-called 'Brazilian development model', source of the once bright, though now somewhat tarnished, 'Brazilian miracle'. The workman, dying in the street, another victim of the headlong pursuit of growth, both physical and economic, simply holds up that other symbol and pivot of economic success, the motor car.

This book tries to offer some explanation of the condition of Pedro Pedreiro, of why a young middle-class musician from São Paulo should satirize the 'Brazilian miracle', why his work so often fails to appear, and why, when it does appear, it is sung so enthusiastically. This is not a history of Brazil. It is an attempt at political analysis, presented chronologically. The difference is important. The aim of this book is not to enter into the *cruces* of Brazilian history in the nineteenth and twentieth centuries. Detailed monographs are seeking to do that, especially the work of Brazilian historians, who over the last decade, in particular, have transformed the historiography of modern Brazil. But this analysis is presented historically for several reasons. One is the belief that the issues most hotly debated in contemporary Brazilian politics have deep historical roots, forming part of a long continuous process. Brazil is not just a nation recently arrived on the world scene. It was independent, proud of its liberal constitution and achievement as a nation well before many European states had yet taken shape. The pattern of regional and local politics found even in the twentieth century can often be traced back to the nineteenth or even the eighteenth century, as the following chapter argues. So, too, can many of Brazil's most pressing problems in recent years, affected, for instance, by the fact that Brazil only ended slavery as late as 1888, or that already well before then the most dynamic sector of the economy, that of coffee exports, was fully integrated into the international capitalist system of trade and investment. The pattern of land tenure, too, was long established, leaving problems not only in the north-east, but all over Brazil, which still have not been solved. The strong wave of European immigrants, especially from Italy and Germany, made an important contribution, but was overlaid on social formations already long formed, and was to be reconciled with a population already freely mixed, to which one of the most important contributions had come from the large African population, seeking after emancipation to find, without notable success, a role in the development of Brazil's capitalist economy.

These are some of the issues discussed, though not in detail, in the earlier chapters of this book. But always the historical discussion is aimed at throwing light on more recent development, to trace the roots of current problems and help towards an understanding of contemporary Brazil, especially in the period after 1945. The long historical sweep is chosen partly to provide background for those who may want it, but essentially to explain the continuities, often very tangled, of politics in the modern period. This is, of course, particularly important from 1930 onwards, the period in which Brazil's modern state was formed and the personalities and problems of its contemporary politics clearly appeared. One central emphasis in this study is on the essential continuity of Brazilian politics from 1930 onwards. More than any single politician, Getúlio Vargas shaped Brazilian politics, with much of the subsequent story being a form of support for or opposition to Vargas. But, even more important than the contribution of able politicians or eminent statesmen, like Vargas or Oswaldo Aranha, was the fact that from at least 1930 onwards there came into play social and economic forces moulding Brazilian politics over the next four decades. There is a shift in weight from the coffee bourgeoisie, the dominant class of the 'Old Republic', to a new industrializing bourgeoisie, still centred in São Paulo, often made up of the same families, but as a class significantly different in economic aims and political programme. It was this class, still being formed, which not only urged forward Brazil's industrialization, but moulded and controlled a new centralized state apparatus to serve its needs, including the new centralized federal army, at last stronger than the armed forces of Brazil's constituent states.

As political analysis this study takes comparative themes and issues debated not only in relation to Brazil, but more widely in political sociology and political economy. It is concerned to understand political process, not just political process in Brazil. It asks, at the level of what sometimes is called middle-range theory, about the political role of the armed forces, about how this relates to political parties, to trade unions, the working class generally, and to other groups actively involved in politics, students, intellectuals, and the Church. These are matters of comparative political debate and the discussion which follows offers some comment on why, for example, soldiers intervene in politics and what—a less frequently debated topic—they do with government once power has been won

Behind this book, too, it must frankly be said, is a preoccupation with, and a certain stand on, general theory. Elsewhere that theory is made explicit. Here it can remain implicit, scarcely needing to be worked out in detail when the facts of recent political experience in Brazil speak so loudly for themselves. It is these facts, the weight of empirical evidence rather than *a priori* theory, which have shaped the central theme of this present study, that the main issue in modern Brazilian politics, as elsewhere, is contending class interests, the demands of certain social groups as opposed to others; a struggle expressed as much by a military *coup* as by noisy demonstrations in the streets.

Some of the issues discussed here, again, regretfully, of comparative international concern, are at the very least distasteful. They include the use of torture for political purposes and the creation of a state apparatus ready to repress opposition whenever it may appear. But again these are features of contemporary politics which have not only besmirched the reputation of Brazil, but of many other countries, and as such have to be examined. One inescapable question in this context is how far the need for coercion and repression springs from the very nature and dynamic of international capitalism, especially as expressed through enormously rich and powerful transnational corporations. In Brazil these groups even helped to finance one of the most repressive elements of the security apparatus, the notorious OBAN (Operação Bandeirantes). How far transnational or multinational corporations distort the pattern of national development is an inescapable theme of this book. So, too, is the question of how far a regime such as that created in Brazil after 1964, widely regarded as the efficient tool of multinational interests, can challenge or reject those interests, perhaps by means of those very armed forces whose intervention originally helped to form Brazil's authoritarian, dependent capitalism and the state apparatus which sustains it.

The problem of the state emerges as perhaps the most vitally important in this whole discussion. What is the nature of the bourgeois state which was built up from at least 1930 onwards in Brazil? How does the state prior to 1964 relate to the authoritarian state developed after the *coup*? What general, theoretical conclusions can be derived from a study of the Brazilian state, on such hotly debated issues as the nature of 'Bonapartism' or the relative autonomy of the state? Conclusive answers, quite evidently to anyone involved in this debate, will not be found here. But it is hoped that some pointers at least will lead to further work and discussion.

And it is here, more than anywhere, that acknowledgement must be made to the enormous debt owed to friends and colleagues in Brazil, and elsewhere in Latin America. One of the striking features of Latin America is not only its wide range of social and political experience, often very painful, but the wealth and depth of Latin American reflection on that experience. Often that reflection is part of the most mature, most realistic discussion in social science circles, so that the debt owed to friends and colleagues such as Florestan Fernandes, Regis de Castro Andrade, Herbet de Souza, and René Dreifuss, is great indeed, even though they are likely to disagree sharply with many of the arguments and conclusions presented here. In Brazil, deepest thanks are owed to Dona Alzira Vargas do Amaral Peixoto, Dr Euclydes Aranha Neto, and Dr Emmanuel Waissmann, for friendship, kindness, and help over many years. Sometimes the most perceptive reflection on the nature of Brazilian politics comes from quite a different source, a fisherman in Paraíba or a young woman in a *favela* in Fortaleza, cutting through in a sentence a whole fog of mystification. Many friends in Brazil will choose to disagree strongly with much of what is argued here. One knows they will not disagree with the conclusion, that any lasting political solution for Brazil, as for any other country, must require not only care for, but the active participation of, the people of Brazil, including Pedro Pedreiro.

Finally, sincere thanks are owed to John Collis, whose careful comments and attention to detail were a very great help. Also to Mrs Isabel Ovenstone and Mrs May Townsley, who typed the manuscript, with great good humour and patience. A special word of thanks to Elizabeth Allen, who prepared the map and compiled the index. Above all, the deepest debt of thanks is owed to my wife, Judith, and to our children Catherine, Sarah, and Peter. Those who know best the progress of this study, best know how much is owed to Judith.

Glasgow **P.F.**
September 1977

2 From Empire to Republic: the End of the Slave Economy

The Historical Roots

Having stressed the need to set recent Brazilian development in an explicitly comparative theoretical framework, it is equally important to underline the features of that process which are specific to Brazil and shaped by its particular historical formation, from the period of Portuguese colonialism, throughout the continuing slave economy of the nineteenth century, into the period of the 'Old Republic', with the emerging dominance of the coffee magnates and the political elite of São Paulo. Brazil may, indeed, be a fast-changing, 'modernizing' society, but it is easy to be misled by some of the more dramatic features of population growth and shift, the manifold problems of recent industrialization and the growth of modern technology. Brazil is not just a 'new nation' recently arrived on the world scene, but an old society with deeply set roots, enjoying political independence and a considerable measure of autonomy long before some European nations, let alone those of the 'Third World'. Like most countries of Latin America, Brazil has been politically independent for only a few decades less than the United States and has possessed a sophisticated liberal democratic constitution and a national framework of government much longer than more 'developed' European nation states, such as, for example, Germany or Italy. Apart, therefore, from those features of rapid social and economic change which are so evident in contemporary Brazil, one must constantly bear in mind those elements of society, which do not change, or change only more slowly, and which are often among the most important political determinants.[1]

One feature of nineteenth-century politics reflected till recently in twentieth-century development was the intense energy, passion and, bitterness of political activity at the local level—in the *município*, the township, and the region—and the consequent weakness, and superficiality, of much national politics. The pattern is a familiar one which can be found in most large, and many not so large, countries which have bad communications, a low level of national integration, and a predominance of local cultures and regionally rooted social structures. In nineteenth-century Brazil, as in nineteenth-century Italy or Germany, or as often still in present-day Latin America, life was tied very closely, often exclusively, to the immediate locality, the farm or the township, extending at most to the confines of the neighbourhood or region. Important decisions were, therefore, often made locally not nationally, with resources allocated on the spot rather than in some remote capital. Local politics had more real blood in them, often quite literally. National politics, and national rulers, were by comparison anaemic, unreal, of little day-to-day consequence or interest, as the political patterns followed closely the lines of social and economic life. It was largely this which made national politics in Brazil seem relatively peaceful and gentle, providing the basis for a myth of political tolerance which still persists. But for anyone willing to penetrate local political infighting the story is substantially different, a long, bitter catalogue of family quarrels and rivalry, of blood-feuds determining politics over generations, of unforgiving political vendettas and ready recourse to violence. At the local level there is less talk of tolerance. It is here where issues most impinge and where, in consequence, knives are often drawn.

The local character of much political activity is, then, one determining feature of nineteenth-century politics and a persistently important legacy to the recent and present scene. But other features, too, must be remembered as giving a particular, sometimes specific, quality to politics in modern Brazil. They include institutional features, such as the preservation of the monarchy till 1889 and the much more important socio-economic determinants—the growth of São Paulo's power, based on coffee and its modern economy, the late ending of legal slavery and a slave mode of production, the exclusion of most of the population from even primary education or any share in national life, and the general hardening, largely in consequence, of a tight, exclusive political system operating for the benefit of a relatively narrow social stratum. Of more direct and immediate political importance was to be the emergence from the 1860s onwards of the armed forces as a major national pressure-group offering a growing, though still feeble, challenge to the established political class.

The Monarchy

Compared with Spanish America certainly the most conspicuous, if not the most important, of these features is the persistence of the monarchy in Brazil till as late as November 1889, a factor within the nineteenth-century Brazilian system to which much importance has been attached and which figures largely in all descriptions of nineteenth-century Brazilian politics. Its significance does, however, very much depend on whether one focuses primarily on the façade and panoply of national politics played out in Rio de Janeiro or on the substance and pith of political activity at the grass-roots level in the provinces. Too often, unfortunately, historians have taken emperors and statesmen at their own evaluation and paid too much attention to their claims to power, their speeches, their programmes, and their paper-thin constitutions. The nineteenth-century political history has, therefore, mostly been written in terms of Pedro I and Pedro II and the ephemeral ministries which came and went in Rio de Janeiro.

The monarchy was of some political importance in nineteenth-century Brazil: but how significant was it and what really was its role, especially in relation to the power exercised instinctively by the landed magnates on their plantations and *fazendas*? First, it has to be remembered just how limited was the monarchy's real power as distinct from its legal claims and formal pretensions. This was to remain true of Brazilian central governments much later than the Empire, but in the case of the monarchy the difference between the claim to and the reality of power was the more sharply contrasted precisely because of the loudness and formality of the claim. Its very weakness was, indeed, one clue to the successful persistence of the monarchy, that for much of the time its central government had little direct impact on the daily lives and, therefore, on the vested interests of those who held control in the countryside. The Emperor might rule in Rio de Janeiro, his government might make large claims and politicians might loudly complain of his repression,[2] but for the *fazendeiro* and his dependents on his estate, often weeks away from the capital, politics remained essentially a local issue, for most of the time untroubled by central intervention.[3] The Brazilian monarchy therefore, as in many other countries, could survive as long as it had some function and did not consistently or seriously offend a major vested interest. When by the 1880s it did so offend, in the case of São Paulo and of the officer corps in the army, it collapsed without a struggle, almost without a trace. Meanwhile, nineteenth-century politics remained, as they were long to continue, intense and really vital only at the local level. Like the Tsar in Russia or the kings of medieval Europe the Brazilian Emperor made a claim to power which fell mercifully short of reality.[4]

What, then, was the importance of the monarchy in the shaping of modern Brazil? First, undoubtedly, it helped the independence movement to proceed smoothly and peacefully as compared with the upheavals in the rest of Latin America. That process was, in fact, to remain free from persisting rancour and limited, more than perhaps any other independence movement in history, in the degree of social and political upheaval it produced. The continuity of the Portuguese royal house gave some immediate legitimacy to the new regime and helped to preserve the existing administrative framework at a time when elsewhere in Latin America the old structures were being generally broken. This, in turn, was an important factor in maintaining national territorial integrity and preventing that fragmentation of Brazil into smaller units which occurred in post-independence Spanish America.[5] Brazil, however, loosely united, or disunited in practice, continued as a political concept and a recognized independent nation. Credit for this cannot be given solely, even largely, to the monarchy, since the relatively smooth process of Brazilian independence was a mixture, in ascending importance, of wisdom, inertia, and historical accident. It did, however, act as one of the agents of the change, primarily because of the fortuitous presence of the Portuguese royal family in Brazil from 1808 till the eve of independence.

After having been virtually ignored by Portugal, except in so far as it could be exploited,[6] Brazil or, more strictly, Rio de Janeiro, had suddenly in March 1808 to adjust to the arrival of the Portuguese court in flight from Napoleon, and the influx of about 15,000 comparatively sophisticated and demanding people into a small colonial capital of less than 60,000. The Portuguese court stayed for thirteen years till D. João VI returned to Portugal in 1821, leaving some few, usually exaggerated, improvements in the condition of the country.[7] The arrival of the court, it has been said, ended the colonial period in Brazil.[8] It is true, that, under strong British pressure, D. João in 1808 opened Brazilian ports to friendly nations with import duties of 24 per cent.[9] He also in 1810 gave Britain a virtual trading monopoly with a tariff duty of 15 per cent *ad valorem*, a situation which lasted till 1844, laying the foundations of that British penetration of the Brazilian economy which was to last until the twentieth century. Again, it is true, he established the Bank of Brazil in 1808 and removed restrictions on manufacturing in Brazil imposed in 1785. Medical and law schools and a military college were opened. The royal library came to Rio de Janeiro and even a printing press was allowed. But all these were only small beginnings with little immediate impact on the bulk of Brazilian society. They represented no real change of heart on the part of Portugal,[10] but were responses to growing, mainly British,[11] pressures. The main thrust from within Brazil itself came later, taking advantage of the enlarged opportunities, but stemming above all from coffee in the vigorous state of São Paulo.

Meanwhile, the bulk of the population, it should be remembered, remained outside the political system, many still living in slavery,[12] most of them illiterate,[13] cut off, not only from the outside world, but from any effective communication with the rest of the country. With the exception of the one interior state of Minas Gerais, the population of which had grown in the eighteenth-century mining boom,[14] most Brazilians were strung along the coast, as indeed they continue to be even after the building of Brasília and the Trans-amazonian highway system. The overwhelming majority were, therefore, poor and ignorant, weakened by disease,[15] generally undernourished, severely limited in terms of physical mobility, deprived of almost any hope of social mobility, and debarred from participation in the new political system of the Empire.[16] It was a situation which, by any standard, presented a low base for national development.

Not that the new Emperor, Pedro I, proved himself greatly concerned to pursue developments or to follow liberal principles. Right from the start of his reign he showed an authoritarian petulance in the treatment of his ministers, and a harsh disregard for Brazilian feelings.[17] Having been astute enough to accept leadership of a movement he could not resist, he soon quarrelled with his principal advisers and forced into exile the main architect of Brazilian independence, José Bonifacio de Andrada e Silva. His arbitrary behaviour caused great anger in the capital as he came generally to be seen as continuing his family's exploitation of Brazil and representing the interests of Portugal rather than of a genuinely independent new nation. He was finally forced to abdicate, returning unlamented to Portugal in 1831. His departure, more than his accession, took Brazilian independence a faltering step ahead.

The very fact that Brazil could survive such a disastrous reign is again a clue to the function of the monarchy at this, though not in a later, period. The primary need was for the Emperor to provide some form of legitimate authority at the top, a useful piece of constitutional cement. The Portuguese royal house provided helpful formal continuity and little more was really needed of it.

The 1824 Constitution

The wide gap between formal claims and genuine exercise of power was the more vividly revealed by the new imperial constitution of March 1824, a document which, like most subsequent Brazilian constitutions, was based on foreign legal theory, with a strong dash of wishful thinking, but with little attention to the hard, sharp facts of Brazilian political practice. It was a relatively advanced document for its time, much influenced by the writing of the Swiss French constitutional theorist Henri Benjamin Constant de Rebecque.[18] Much emphasis was laid on a 'moderating power', distinct from the legislative, executive, and judicial, which was to be vested in the Emperor alone, giving him a watching brief over all other branches of government and preserving the supremacy of the monarchic as distinct from the aristocratic and popular element.[19] The Emperor was to share executive power with his ministers and besides his Council of State there was a Senate, life members of which were again to be selected by the Emperor from three lists of nominees submitted by provincial legislatures. The judiciary was to be independent, and legislative, budgetary, and fiscal powers were to be given to an Assembly, the deputies being indirectly elected for four years. The principal emphasis, however, was on the role of the Emperor, the key figure in the highly centralized theoretical system, able to appoint and dismiss his ministers, veto bills, dissolve the Assembly, and exercise his moderating power as 'supreme head of the nation and its first representative' that he might 'ceaselessly maintain the independence, balance and harmony of the other political powers'.[20]

Constitutional emphasis on strong central government only underlined the difficulty in practice of imposing central control and the strong, persistent tendency to division within the sprawling new Empire. Inertia helped to keep it together, whereas any activity always threatened to break it. Pedro I, after a war with Argentina from 1825 to 1828, had already had to acknowledge the independence of disputed territory in the south, which now became the new state of Uruguay. But there were strong pressures for further secession on the frontiers, a force which was to remain especially powerful in the southernmost area of Rio Grande do Sul, proud of its distinctive culture and traditions and jealous of its own political control. These and similar demands came to a head after the Emperor left for Portugal, in the period of Regency from 1831 to 1840. There was a revolt in Pará in 1831, in Minas Gerais in 1833, in Matto Grosso and Maranhão in 1834, and the most serious movement in the north-east, the so-called Insurreição Praieira in Pernambuco from 1848 to 1849.[21] Most dangerous of all was a bitter running war of secession in Rio Grande do Sul lasting from 1835 to 1845, a movement which was to continue at intervals until well into the twentieth century, being finally defeated only in the mid-1930s, and then by a politician who was himself a *gaúcho*.

As can be seen from the continuing revolts, the accession in 1840 of a fifteen-year-old boy, crowned in 1841 as Emperor Pedro II, did little to unite the country more effectively. The position remained much as before, with the central government too weak to impose full control and the provinces in the last analysis really too weak to break away. Effectively, power remained, as it was to continue, in the hands of the rural landowners, untroubled by government decree.

Land Tenure

The basis of that control was, as generally throughout Latin America, that most important of all legacies of the colonial period, the system of landholding, which divided most of the country into *latifundia*, or very large estates, so giving the land to a small fraction of the country's population and reducing the majority to a condition of dependence. When land was the primary source of wealth, the great majority of the population worked that land for others, first as slaves, later as, at best, tenant farmers, but more often as sharecroppers with no security of tenure. The nature of this landholding system will be discussed in more detail from a political viewpoint in the analysis of the Peasant Leagues of the north-east in the 1950s and 1960s. It is impossible to find accurate statistics for the nineteenth century, but already by independence most of the land was assigned to some owner, even though he was usually incapable of exploiting it fully.[22] The size of holdings and their underutilization was, indeed, one of the features of rural Brazil which most impressed nineteenth-century travellers and increasingly provoked Brazilian and foreign critics, as when James Henderson argued that:

> . . . It is a great misfortune to the Brazil, that extensive tracts of land have been granted to donatories, who do not possess the means of cultivating one-hundredth part of it, but hold it on under the expectation that the gradual improvement of the country will render it daily more valuable . . .[23]

John Luccock, similarly, noted the underutilization of land, especially in Minas Gerais, and reported in amazement the size of cattle farms in Rio Grande do Sul, the smallest, he said, being about 20,000 acres and the largest near to 600,000.[24] Other travellers, too, commented on the low standards of cultivation and the enormous size of many estates.[25] Nor was this just a nineteenth-century phenomenon. As late as the census of 1940 nearly three-quarters (74·83 per cent) of those classified as landholders held only 11 per cent of the total area, while 73·1 per cent of the land was in the hands of only 7·8 per cent of proprietors, all of them being large landowners with holdings of more than 200 hectares.[26] More recently still, it has been pointed out, the concentration of large estates has been increasing, especially in the north-east, with the growth, in particular, of large sugar *usinas*, financed by powerful consortia,[27] while, as a parallel development, there has also been an increase in the number of small *minifundia* holdings. Inequality in the distribution of land and key resources, such as water, is reinforced, as commonly in the *latifundia* system, by unequal distribution of educational opportunities[28] and medical services, and exacerbated, for most of the rural population, by primitive agrarian techniques. In a survey in 1967 in north-eastern Brazil, undertaken by Professor Charles Slater of Michigan State University, more than 50 per cent of the farmers interviewed had never heard of chemical fertilizers.[29] The overall picture, therefore, throughout the modern period is one of extremes, with a few men holding enormously large estates, often not worked efficiently, while in some areas, especially in the north-east, the great bulk of the rural population remain landless, dependent, and without security on the land they work for others. Even in the mid-twentieth century the figures reveal a situation for the most part of rural poverty, dependence, and deprivation.

Political Control

How the rural landowners exercised control is the main key to politics throughout the nineteenth century and, indeed, well beyond. It is the basis of Brazilian political life, the core of a system which, though modified, still survives and which explains in large part many of the issues which the nation still faces. It can best be seen in its later forms in the Old Republic from 1889 to 1930, but some mention of it is also needed when considering the Empire. The Brazilian name for the system is *coronelismo*, literally, the rule of 'colonels', a name deriving from the fact that in many *municípios* of the interior the local landowner or political boss was usually, too, the 'colonel' of the National Guard in the area.[30] Essentially it is the system of clientage politics commonly found in rural areas when a representative system of government is imposed on an impoverished, widely scattered, largely illiterate, and highly dependent electorate. In this sense, therefore, it is not exclusive to Brazil, since it is a function of early attempts at representation in a developing society, being found in, for example, eighteenth- and much of nineteenth-century England, in Italy at least till the time of Giolitti, and in Spain and throughout Latin America. *Coronelismo* in Brazil is an example of the system known as *caciquismo* in Spain and Spanish America, the dominance by rural bosses, or *caciques*, within the electoral system at the local level.[31]

While leaving till later a closer analysis of *coronelismo*, one aspect of the overall system under the Empire should be noted, since it reveals perhaps the most important direct function of the monarchy and the way in which the 'poder moderador' of the constitution was made a political reality. With the elections controlled by the political *chefes* in the interior and the central government being based in Rio de Janeiro, a key issue, as always in such situations, was how to articulate the system, so as to link the infrastructure in the countryside with the formal machinery of government in the capital. In particular, the problem was, in eighteenth-century English terms, how to 'make' a government and how also to establish some peaceful process generally acknowledged as legitimate for providing, when necessary, an alternative government. It was a question already faced in England and one which was especially to trouble politicians in nineteenth-century Spain and Italy as they, too, needed to resolve the tensions arising from a controlled system of elections. It was a felt need in political practice rather than a question made explicit to the politicians themselves, a demand of the system within which, in their various countries, they found themselves working. In Brazil, as elsewhere, the response was a system of political bargaining, a variation of the politics of agreement among friends, based on an established working consensus rather than explicit conflict. In practice this demanded bargaining between representatives of the central government and the heads of the political clans in the interior, an arrangement by which the *coroneis* co-operated with politicians in the province and they, in turn, with the central government. The local *chefes*, after due arrangements had been made, could always deliver the vote and could, therefore, when the system was working smoothly, always guarantee that the government of the day would win the election. Spoils at both the local and national levels could then be shared between all interested parties without the need to resort to violence or a descent into political anarchy.

This system as it operated under the Empire, and later under the Republic, demanded, however, that certain political facts should be acknowledged by all parties and that—most important—all should accept the rules of the game. The first such fact was the political pre-eminence within their own territory of the interior of the heads of the political clans. They might fight among themselves, but, once the important issue of local control was settled, that fact had to be accepted within the chain of political bargaining. No one must any longer rock the boat. In this respect it should be remembered how tight a control the heads of the landowning families kept locally. The electorate remained very small throughout the whole period of the Empire. It has been estimated at only 142,000 out of a population of 15 million even after an extension of the suffrage in 1881.[32] The 1881 reform, the Lei Saraiva, introduced direct suffrage, but left different classes of elector, depending on income. An elector of the first grade, *eleitor de paróquia*, had to have an annual income of 100 milreis, one of the second grade, *eleitor de província*, 200 milreis. Eligibility for election was also tied to income, 400 milreis for the Chamber, 800 milreis for the Senate. The elector had to be over twenty-five, unless married, or a military officer over twenty-one, or a graduate, or a cleric in holy orders. Among those still excluded were sons living at home, unless they held public office, most servants and members of religious orders living in enclosed community. Illiterates (about 90 per cent of the population) could in theory vote, but most lacked the financial qualification.[33] The local powerful families could always manipulate the vote and even when, with the growth of the law schools of São Paulo and Olinda, there appeared a new group of *bachareis*, young graduate lawyers, who often represented their families in the provincial assemblies, the real power lay with the heads of those families in every area. The local assemblies might discuss high points of law and constitutional theory, but, when major decisions were to be taken, the decisive voice was that of the landowner, able to break the career of anyone injudicious enough to challenge him.[34] The rural families, in practice if not in law, decided the lists of electors and in the last analysis, therefore, the provincial assemblies had to act in accord with the views of those few families in every region who controlled and ruled the province. The family alliances created wider municipal and regional groupings, those large political clans to which a man's first loyalty was due. These were the real power in every region. Nor, as Morazé emphasizes, would they easily allow interlopers from outside, however resounding their title or imposing their wealth, as when in the town of Bananal one of the richest but recently arrived landowners, the Baron Bela Vista, was not even allowed to be on the list of electors. In the province of Espírito Santo the richest landowner, the Baron Itapemirim, could not break the grip of the long-entrenched Bittencourt family, so that, even when the Emperor made Baron Itapemirim the president of the province of Espírito Santo, the ranks remained closed. Baron Itapemirim always lost the election in Itapemirim.[35]

As the century progressed, the political clans in the regions also formed the basis for the two political parties represented in Rio de Janeiro, parties which, as in so many countries, took the names of Liberal and Conservative. The names meant little, without clear distinction of ideology or class or economic basis. Nor did the two parties have, as so commonly elsewhere in Latin America, sharply divided attitudes over the Church and anticlericalism. The Brazilian Church was never a major landowner, as it was in Mexico, and did not become a focus of hostility between the two political parties. These were rather more the expression at the national level, at the apex of the system, of local divisions in the provinces, two arbitrary groupings distinguished mainly by the fact that they opposed each other. There was strong emotional commitment, loyalties ran deep and rivalries were fierce, above all at the local level, where spoils were fought over and divided; but as the system tapered to the top, as it appeared in the Assembly in Rio de Janeiro, there was little to choose between the parties or the ministries they formed, a further reflection of the weakness of national as opposed to local political life. It was a situation which was to continue for many decades to come with the persistent failure of political mobilization at the national level and the continuing lack of genuinely national political parties with a coherent programme or distinctive basis.

Within this system the Emperor came to play an important role, acting in effect as the highest *coronel*, the ultimate grand *cacique*. Pedro II had few illusions about the political system, possessing a saving sense of realism which sharply distinguished him from his predecessor and allowed him to succeed where Pedro I had failed. Like Getúlio Vargas in the twentieth century he knew how to reconcile conflicting interests and maintain a careful balance between rival forces and pressures. Frequently, therefore, when serious conflict seemed likely, he would dissolve the Assembly and refer the decision to the political chiefs in their territory, avoiding as far as possible direct confrontation between the central government and the provinces, so exercising, in effect, a 'moderating power'. But, equally important, the Emperor by shrewd use of his authority to dissolve the Chamber was also able to maintain the formalities of two-party government with alternating ministries from the two political parties. In a situation where the government in office could always guarantee to win the election this was, clearly, an important function, allowing the Emperor in Brazil to fulfil the role which Canovas with his *turno pacífico* performed in Spain[36] and providing a peaceful method, accepted as legitimate and valid by the interest groups concerned, for producing alternative ministries to satisfy party demands. The Emperor's use of his dissolving power also helped to defuse party politics and resolve that struggle for political supremacy, as politicians in Italy sought to do with their policy of *transformismo*.[37] Even more important still, perhaps, the working consensus between *coroneis* and their followers in the interior, the politicians at the provincial level, and the Emperor and politicians in Rio de Janeiro created a viable, relatively stable system of *civilian* politics and avoided the descent either to extreme political violence, even civil war, or, alternatively, to military take-over and the extinction of civilian government.

'King Coffee'

The system could, however, only be maintained when all the elements were in at least reasonable balance. In this sense it would always be endangered when any one group risked upsetting it, perhaps by being too ambitious and breaking those rules on which consensus depended, or when some new, extraneous factor intervened. When eventually this happened, the result was a crisis which, without basically changing the system, was severe enough to end the monarchy. There were two new factors which grew steadily in importance throughout the period of the Empire and which subsequently were to dominate and determine political development over many decades. These were the growing power of São Paulo, based on coffee, and the rising political ambition of the officer class in the army. Of the two the first factor was the more fundamental and substantial, representing a change in the dominant mode of production within the Brazilian economy, which was to lead to the end of slavery and, subsequently, to the shaping of a political system expressing the new priorities of the coffee exporters, mostly centred in São Paulo. Throughout the years since independence coffee had been emerging as the new, challenging, element in Brazilian society and politics, centred first in the Paraíba valley and later in São Paulo. It represented the definitive shift of wealth, population, and power to the southern and eastern states of Brazil, eventually creating São Paulo as the commercial and financial capital of the nation.[38] Coffee was by the middle of the century the latest in the series of Brazilian monopoly economies,[39] increasingly exported from São Paulo as the railways were built from 1852 to 1868. When by 1868 the railway link was completed between the coffee plantations of the interior over the difficult, wooded mountain range to Santos, the autonomy and power of São Paulo were further guaranteed. By the end of the century, at a period (1895–99) when Brazil had 66·8 per cent of the world production of coffee, and coffee made up to 50 per cent of the nation's exports, the coffee of Brazil was both produced and exported by São Paulo. The wealth of Brazil was coffee and coffee was São Paulo.[40]

This dramatic growth in wealth and status also produced in São Paulo rising demands for greater autonomy and wider control by the *paulistas* over their own affairs. There was a growing belief in the province, later to harden into a repeatedly expressed conviction, that São Paulo was being held back by the rest of Brazil, hampered by the outworn structures and economies of declining areas further north and severely hamstrung by the centralized framework of the Empire. How much substance there was in such charges was irrelevant as long as *paulista* politicians themselves believed them. The rallying cry of 'autonomy' was increasingly used in *paulista* political writing, debate, and conversation, accompanying the steady growth of the São Paulo Republican Party.[41] So it was argued, for example, by one of the leading Republican apologists that a federal republic with marked local autonomy would allow each region to 'employ resources as best it thought',[42] that São Paulo was 'incontestably the only one giving to the imperial government without receiving', and that some form of separatism was necessary, since São Paulo, together with southern Brazil, would advance more rapidly once freed from the 'regime of the despotic centralization of the empire'.[43]

One major issue in particular seemed to justify the *paulista* charge that the development of Brazil was being hampered by outworn economic and social systems. This was the controversial question of slave emancipation. The ending of the slave trade, under British pressure,[44] had been promised at the time of independence, but repeatedly postponed till finally the trade was ended in 1850. Prices of slaves then rose swiftly from 1850 onwards and *paulista* coffee-growers, hit by rising costs, began to feel acutely the shortage of manpower for the expanding coffee economy. Demand, therefore, grew for new immigrant labour, but this, too, was scarce as immigrants remained understandably reluctant to enter a country where the workman was identified with a slave. The Emperor, on the other hand, could not, it seemed, end slavery without seriously offending many landowners. Many *paulistas* also felt that slavery was a persistent reproach to a modernizing nation and now believed that the progress of their region was being hindered by the centralized imperial system and the political influence of less prosperous areas.[45] São Paulo, therefore, led the way in the encouragement of immigrants, who, having numbered in all before 1850 only about 19,000, began with the prosperity of coffee to enter Brazil at a rate of 15,000 a year.[46] São Paulo private enterprise led the way with 60,000 immigrants in over sixty colonies from 1847 to 1857 and, as the coffee booms continued, the immigrants, especially northern Italians, flowed steadily to São Paulo, transforming the ethnic and social structure of southern Brazil, developing the coffee areas, and providing the energy and skills for nascent industrialization. São Paulo had won its way, but only, as many *paulistas* believed, against the influence of other more conservative groups in the country, who still preserved too great a degree of control within the political system.[47]

More important still, the emancipation issue also helped further to mobilize the other new force in Brazilian politics, which had been growing in strength and influence in recent decades, the only element in the political system which could rival, and which would eventually outstrip, the political strength of the *paulistas*. This was the officer corps of the then imperial and later the federal army, already the most important single pressure group in Brazilian politics and the most decisive in ending the Empire and creating the Republic. The influence of the army had been growing steadily ever since the war against Paraguay from 1865 to 1870, which, like the two world wars of the next century, had an important catalytic effect on the army's political development and on the nation generally.[48] Poppino describes the war as 'the major stimulus to the modernization of the empire', especially in terms of communications, transportation, and industry, accelerating, for example, the spread of the telegraph and the building of railways.[49] Before the war the army had been small, badly trained, and severely lacking in status. The Minister of War was usually a civilian, a fact resented by many army officers, who also complained persistently of civilian ignorance, neglect, and lack of appreciation of the army's role in society.[50] The Paraguayan War brought rapid expansion in numbers, new prestige, higher salaries, and better conditions of service, but only to be followed by an apparent return to pre-war conditions and attitudes as numbers and money were sharply cut.[51] The officers at once turned on the defensive, an insecure, threatened elite, hurt both in their pride and in their prospects for advancement. They were angry that their services should be forgotten or disparaged by civilians for whom, in general, they had a low regard[52] and they were consequently more ready than before the war to join in national politics, first on the issue of slave emancipation, then in alliance with republican leaders.[53]

Few of the high-ranking officers were, in fact, convinced republicans, most of them insisting that they supported the monarchy. But they found themselves carried along by events, continuously involved in defending the 'honour' of the officer class[54] and increasingly compromised with the republican movement. The Clube Militar, founded in 1887, became involved in republican activity, as republican politicians, especially in São Paulo, sought the army's support, which they believed was indispensable for their success.[55] Some prominent republicans, such as the leading São Paulo politician Bernardino de Campos, strongly warned against the dangers of invoking military support, but most, including such influential figures as Rui Barbosa and Júlio de Castilhos,[56] thought army backing was absolutely necessary. The press in general exaggerated the imperial government's hostility towards the army, including such influential papers as *Correio do Povo, País, Diário Popular*, and *Província de São Paulo*, seeking to win army sympathy, spreading such rumours as the government's intention to build up a strong rival police force and to disperse army officers throughout Brazil to curb their political activity. Military opposition and resentment steadily hardened, expressed most forcibly in meetings in the Clube Militar, where, for example, on 9 November 1889 one of its leading spokesmen, Benjamin Constant, demanded 'full powers to free the military from a state of affairs incompatible with its honour and its dignity'.[57] For most officers, however, this 'freeing' of the military, with which they were in full agreement, meant not the removal of the Emperor, but only of the current ministry headed by the Viscount Ouro Preto, a man generally regarded as hostile to army interests.[58] Much the most important army leader, Marshal Deodoro da Fonseca, president of the Clube Militar, had, like most of his colleagues, no clear aims or political programme, being concerned to defend army interests and military honour rather than stage a republican *coup*. Even after he had been persuaded, largely by Benjamin Constant and Rui Barbosa, to lead the movement against the government, he hesitated over removing the Emperor. It was only after the swift, bloodless *coup* had been successful and Marshal Deodoro heard that an old rival from Rio Grande do Sul, Gaspar Silveira Martins, might be called on to form a new ministry that he finally agreed to the declaration of the Republic.[59]

That the Empire fell so easily was largely because its support had already been eroded. By the late 1880s the Emperor had already quarrelled with the Church,[60] had aroused the suspicions of the armed forces, had antagonized some landowners over abolition,[61] and had generally failed to meet the challenge of growing republican feeling, a particularly important failure, since there were widespread misgivings over the chance of finding a suitable successor to Pedro II. When, therefore, in November 1889 the army leaders in the capital decided to declare the Republic, there was virtually no protest, opposition, or monarchist reaction. The two political groupings who had come to dominate national politics, the army command and the *paulista* coffee-growers, had together decided that the continued existence of the Empire was not in their best interests. There was no other group strong enough, or perhaps sufficiently concerned, to oppose them, and the monarchy fell silently and without resistance once pressure was applied.[62] At the national, as opposed to local, level a new phase was beginning, as the political struggle between soldiers and civilians really began in earnest.

Notes

1 See the perceptive article by David Maybury Lewis, who stresses that considerable growth may be accompanied by little change, 'Growth and change in Brazil since 1930: an anthropological view', in *Portugal and Brazil in transition*, ed. Raymond S. Sayers (London, 1968), 159–72.
2 Nelson de Sousa Sampaio, 'O "parlamentarismo" no Brasil império', *Revista de Direito Público e Ciência Política*, 7 (1964), 85–6.
3 See below for the important articulating function of the monarchy in later years, linking local, regional, and national politics in one coherent system and providing a mechanism for the peaceful change of government in Rio de Janeiro.
4 Richard William Southern, *The Making of the Middle Ages* (London, 1953), 146.
5 Alan Krebs Manchester, 'The Growth of bureaucracy in Brazil, 1808–1821', *JLAS*, 4, No. 1 (May 1971), 77–83. Also, for the importance of such continuity, though in another context, see Hamza Alavi, 'The State in post-colonial societies', 59–81.
6 Kenneth Robert Maxwell, *Conflicts and conspiracies: Brazil and Portugal, 1750–1808* (London, 1973). Surveys of the colonial period now available in English translation include Caio Prado Júnior, *The Colonial Background of modern Brazil*, trans. Suzette Macedo (Berkeley and Los Angeles, 1969); Celso Furtado, *The Economic Growth of Brazil*, trans. Ricardo W. de Aguiar and Eric C. Drysdale (Berkeley and Los Angeles, 1963); and the still valuable João Pandia Calógeras, *A History of Brazil*, trans. and ed. Percy Alvin Martin (Chapel Hill, 1939). The standard economic history is Roberto Cochrane Simonsen, *História econômica do Brasil, 1500–1820*, 3rd ed. (São Paulo, 1957), which shows the heavy dependence of the Portuguese economy on Brazil. The most important recent study of the colonial period, up to the mid-19th century, is in Sérgio Buarque de Holanda, ed., *História geral da civilização brasileira*, 4 vols. in 2 (São Paulo, 1963–67), I (A época colonial), II (O Brasil monárquico).
7 One of the few indisputable benefits of this sudden incursion is the beautiful detailed record of Brazilian society made by the court painter, Jean Baptiste Debret, who arrived with the Portuguese court, stayed in Brazil fifteen years, then published his perceptive text and superb paintings of Brazil after his return to Paris. The most readily available edition is now *Viagem pitoresca e histórica ao Brasil*, trans. with notes Sérgio Milliet, 3rd ed., 2 vols. in 1 (São Paulo, 1954). A similar early 19th-century record was made by Johann Moritz Rugendas. The collection unfortunately was scattered in the 1920s, but it is partly to be found in Rugendas, *Viagem pitoresca através do Brasil*, trans. Sérgio Milliet, 5th ed. (São Paulo, 1954). Other artists, too, left invaluable pictorial evidence for the social historian, notably Thomas Ender.
8 Simonsen, op. cit., 391 quoting Robert Southey, *History of Brazil*, 3 vols. (London, 1817–22). The same point, in only slightly different terms, is argued by Hélio Jaguaribe, *Economic and Political Development: a theoretical approach and a Brazilian case study* (Cambridge, Mass., 1968), 113–19, 'a government and administration bereft of a Kingdom' found a Kingdom which 'wanted a government and administration'.
9 Manuel de Oliveira Lima, *O Império Brasileiro, 1822–1889*, 2nd ed. (São Paulo, n.d.), 461.

10 Brazilian development was D. João's primary concern, as shown by Dorival Teixeira, 'Política financeira: o primeiro Banco do Brasil', in Buarque de Holanda, op. cit., I, 100–18.

11 The main demands were from commercial interests in the capital. João Camillo de Oliveira Torres, *O Presidencialismo no Brasil* (Rio de Janeiro, 1962), 30. The British role is emphasized by Nelson Werneck Sodré, *História da burguesia brasileira*, 2nd ed. (Rio de Janeiro, 1967), 42–8; and especially in Buarque de Holanda, op. cit., II, 64–99. The wider role of Great Britain in independence and in the ending of the slave trade is examined in Leslie Bethell, *The Abolition of the Brazilian slave trade* (London, 1970), 27–61; see also, Alan Krebs Manchester, *British Preeminence in Brazil, its rise and decline* (Chapel Hill, 1933).

12 The population of Brazil at independence in 1822 was still, of course, very small. Caio Prado Júnior, *História econômica do Brasil*, 9th ed. (São Paulo, 1965), appendix, estimates the total population in 1823 as 3,960,866 divided into 2,813,351 free and 1,147,515 slaves; he also calculates an annual inflow of slaves at that time of about 40,000.

13 Richard Graham, *Britain and the Onset of Modernization in Brazil, 1850–1914* (London, 1968), 17, says that even as late as 1877 only 1,563,000 free persons knew how to read and write, while 5,580,000 free persons over five years old did not. The population was then over 10 million (10,112,061 in 1872, with 8,601,255 free and 1,510,806 slave). Slave literacy was, as might be expected, extremely low. On proposals for education of slaves see Robert Conrad, *The Destruction of Brazilian slavery, 1850–1888* (Berkeley and Los Angeles, 1972), 158–9; Robert Brent Toplin, *The Abolition of slavery in Brazil, 1880–1888* (New York, 1972), pp. 170–3; Florestan Fernandes, *The Negro in Brazilian society*, trans. Jacqueline D. Skiles, A. Brunel, and Arthur Rothwell, ed. Phyllis B. Eveleth (New York, 1969).

14 Charles Ralph Boxer, *The Golden Age of Brazil, 1695–1750* (Berkeley and Los Angeles, 1962).

15 Much evidence and further reference with regard to public health in colonial Brazil is in Gilberto Freyre, *The Masters and the Slaves*, trans. S. Putnam, 2nd English lang. ed. rev. (New York, 1956). See 71–5 on syphilis and, on the deficiencies of diet, 60ff., where he suggests that the best nourished were probably the negro slaves. See also his *Mansions and the Shanties*, trans. and ed. Harriet de Onís (New York, 1963), 185–90. Yellow fever, in particular, remained a severe scourge, even in Rio de Janeiro, till the turn of the century, when Dr Oswaldo Cruz rid the city of it. Dietary deficiency is also discussed in Josué de Castro, *The Geography of Hunger* (Boston, 1952), and more generally in Thomas Lynn Smith, *Brazil: people and institutions*, rev. ed. (Baton Rouge, 1954), 302–9. Freyre also emphasizes how a foolish aping of European habits in food and dress often harmed the health of a pretentious Brazilian 'elite'. The persistence till well into the 20th century of advertisements in Brazilian newspapers for patent medicines to cure the most startling range of diseases both reflects their prevalence and the lack of adequate means of treatment for most of the population.

16 On this last point see Oliveira Lima, *O Império Brasileiro*, 36 who describes a painting by Pedro Américo of the Brazilian proclamation of independence, being watched in uncomprehending astonishment by the workman driving his oxen. One of the features in many 19th-century paintings—in Debret, Rugendas, Ender—is the marginal negro or *caboclo*, who, like figures in an Elder Breughel, is at the mercy of forces outside his comprehension.

17 There is a good study of Pedro I in Alan Krebs Manchester, 'The paradoxical Pedro, first emperor of Brazil', *HAHR*, 12 (1932), 176–97, which contains

further references. See also his *British Preeminence in Brazil*; Sérgio Corrêa da Costa, *Every inch a king, a biography of Dom Pedro I, first emperor of Brazil* (New York, 1950); and Pedro Calmon, *Vida de d. Pedro I, o rei cavaleiro*, 3rd ed. (Porto, 1952).

18 Parts of his *Cours de politique constitutionelle* were reproduced almost verbatim in this imperial constitution, which is analysed in Sousa Sampaio, 'O "parlamentarismo" no Brasil'. See also João Camillo de Oliveira Torres, *A democracia coroada* (*teoria política do Império do Brasil*), 2nd ed., rev. (Petrópolis, 1964).

19 The theory is set out in Articles 98 to 101 which explain the idea of a 'moderating power', a concept which Constant says he derived from Clermont-Tonnerre. This 'moderating power' is here described as the 'key of the whole political organization'.

20 Brazil, Constitution, Article 98. Herman Gerlarch James, *The Constitutional System of Brazil* (Washington, DC, 1923).

21 They were all regional revolts mostly arising out of local issues. On the Pernambuco rising see Edison Carneiro, *A insurreição praieira, 1848–49* (Rio de Janeiro, 1960). He stresses how a few powerful families, such as the Rego Barros and Cavalcanti, controlled the social and political life of the region and sees the revolt as, essentially, a regional reaction against increased centralization under the Empire. It seems, however, to have been caused largely by growing alarm over a declining regional economy, like so many other regional revolts. The leaders merely blamed the central government as a scapegoat, so exaggerating the impact, for good or ill, of the central administration. The decline stemmed from structural factors outside the government's control. Even today the administration, for all its planning, finds it difficult to make significant changes in the economy of the north-east. On the other hand, the political mythology, what local leaders believed and their perceptions of the imperial government's role, was important. Other regional revolts reflected at varying times, severe racial tensions and a growing conflict of interest between rural and urban society.

22 The process of granting land in the colonial period is well described in Lynn Smith, op. cit., 369–410. For the more general problem as it affects Spanish America, see Keith Broadwell Griffin, *Underdevelopment in Spanish America* (London, 1969), 75–86, where he examines the economic consequences of the *latifúndio* system. The implications for Brazil are examined in Alberto Passos Guimarães, *Quatro séculos de latifúndio* (São Paulo, 1963); and Raymundo Faoro, *Os donos do poder: formação do patronato político brasileiro* (Rio de Janeiro, 1958). See also the very useful article by Warren Dean, 'Latifundia and land policy in 19th century Brazil', *HAHR*, 51, No. 4 (1971), 606–25.

23 James Henderson, *A History of Brazil* (London, 1821), quoted in Lynn Smith, op. cit., 373.

24 John Luccock, *Notes on Rio de Janeiro and the southern parts of Brazil* (London, 1820), 216, 415.

25 They include Maria Graham, *Journal of a voyage to Brazil* (London, 1824); Henry Koster, *Travels in Brazil* (London, 1816); John Mawe, *Travels in the interior of Brazil* (London, 1812); Robert Walsh, *Notices of Brazil in 1828 and 1829*, 2 vols. (London, 1830); George Gardner, *Travels in the interior of Brazil, 1836–1841* (London, 1846); James Wetherwell, *Brazil: Stray notes from Bahia* (Liverpool, 1860); Sir Richard Francis Burton, *Explorations of the highlands of the Brazil*, 2 vols. (London 1869); Thomas Plantagenet Bigg-Wither, *Pioneering in South Brazil*, 2 vols. (London, 1878); Hastings Charles Dent, *A Year in Brazil* (London, 1886). These travel

accounts, together with some of those mentioned elsewhere, form a most valuable, and highly readable, source for 19th-century Brazil.

26 See Sinopse do censo agrícola, Dados Gerais in *Recenseamento Geral do Brasil 1940* (Rio de Janeiro, 1940). Lynn Smith, op. cit., 377–422 points out that, although as many as two rural families in three fell outside the terms of reference of the census, still the figures show that of the remainder in 1940 85·7 per cent of farmers had the use of only 18·2 per cent of land, while 0·5 per cent of operators with holdings of over 2,500 hectares controlled the use of 24·5 per cent of land in farms or estates.

27 Guimarães, op. cit., 159 quotes examples taken from Manuel Correia de Andrade, *A terra e o homen no Nordeste* (São Paulo, 1963). They include the Bezerra de Melo group, controlling over 70,000 hectares of continuous lands, the Costa Azevedo group (45,000), and the Ermírio de Morais group (40,000). Working from 1960 census data Guimarães also lists the states in terms of the number of holdings over 1,000 hectares. Only five have a low concentration (under 20 per cent) of such holdings; eight have a high one (50–60 per cent) and six a very high one (over 60 per cent). Guimarães, op. cit., 187–8.

28 Griffin, op. cit., 72.

29 Montague Yudleman and Frederic Howard, *Agricultural Development and economic integration in Latin America* (London, 1970), 78.

30 The National Guard was founded in August 1831, providing a local militia which could be called upon in an emergency. Its main function, however, soon became ceremonial, with its uniformed officers lending colour to religious and civic occasions and enjoying some legal privileges, such as not being sent to the common gaol if convicted of a criminal offence. It carried considerable status with landowners and later with local professional men or successful business people, eager to be 'colonel' or among its officers. See the note in what is the best treatment of *coronelismo* and one of the most seminal books on Brazilian politics, Victor Nunes Leal, *Coronelismo, enxada e voto* (Rio de Janeiro, 1948), 7–10.

31 How the system worked in Brazil is discussed in more detail in the next chapter. For *caciquismo* more generally see Raymond Carr, *Spain: 1808–1939* (Oxford, 1966), 366–79. Carr emphasizes that in Spain, as will later be stressed here with regard to Brazil, *caciquismo* 'was not a parliamentary regime with abuses: the abuses were the system itself . . . a natural growth'. For Latin American *caciquismo* generally, see the brief comment in Jacques Lambert, *Latin America: social structure and political institutions*, trans. Helen Katel (Berkeley and Los Angeles, 1967), 153–5. The Italian case is noted in passing by Dennis Mack Smith, *Italy: a modern history* (Ann Arbor, 1959), who does not, unfortunately, present it as directly functional to the social and economic system, but rather in terms of 'corruption'.

32 Richard Graham, op. cit., 21.

33 Sousa Sampaio, op. cit., 87.

34 Charles Morazé, *Les Trois Ages du Brésil: essai de politique* (Paris, 1954), 79.

35 Morazé, op. cit., 85. There is a parallel here with the attitude of many of the English squirearchy to *arrivistes*, even when some of these 'newcomers' had received their honours long ago from 18th-century Hanoverian kings. In Brazil, as in England, it is a mistake to equate local status with wealth.

36 Carr, op. cit., 356.

37 For *transformismo* in Italy, especially under Depretis, see Mack Smith, op. cit., 110–11.

38 See João Frederico Normano, *Brazil, study of economic types* (Chapel Hill,

1935). The economic cycles are well described in Rollie E. Poppino, *Brazil: the land and people* (New York, 1968), 113–56.

39 Normano, op. cit., 40.

40 Richard Graham, op. cit., 30. Also Stanley J. Stein, *Vassouras, a Brazilian coffee country, 1850–1900* (Cambridge, Mass., 1957); and Pierre Monbeig, *Pionniers et planteurs de São Paulo* (Paris, 1952). The shift of coffee exports from Rio de Janeiro to São Paulo proceeded slowly but surely, Poppino, op. cit., 151. The figures are set out in Affonso de E. Taunay, *Pequena história do café no Brasil* (Rio de Janeiro, 1945), op. cit., 279.

41 Calls for autonomy were, for example, regularly made in the influential newspaper *Diário Popular* (SP). Republican demands had been growing, especially in São Paulo and Rio Grande do Sul, marked by the proclamation of an important republican manifesto on 3 December 1870. Some of the background can be found in the memoirs of one of the most eminent *paulista* republicans, Manuel Ferraz de Campos Salles, *Da Propaganda á Presidéncia* (São Paulo, 1908).

42 Alberto Salles, 'Catecismo republicano', in *Alberto Salles, ideológo da República*, ed. Luis Washington Vita (São Paulo, 1965), 193, quoted in June Edith Hahner, *Civilian–Military Relations in Brazil, 1889–1898* (New York, 1969), 127.

43 Alberto Salles, *A pátria paulista* (Campinas, 1887), 184, quoted in Hahner, op. cit., 127; See also George C. A. Boehrer, *Da monarquia á república*; *história do Partido Republicano do Brasil* (*1870–1889*), trans. Berenice Xavier (Rio de Janeiro, 1954); and José Maria dos Santos, *Bernardino de Campos e o Partido Republicano Paulista* (Rio de Janeiro, 1960).

44 The British motives were not altruistic. See Bethell, *The Abolition of the Brazilian slave trade.*

45 This is not to suggest, of course, that landowners in the coffee areas mostly, or even largely, opposed the continuance of slavery. Much of the pro-emancipation feeling was urban rather than rural.

46 Jaguaribe, op. cit., 133; Calógeras, op. cit., 243.

47 J. A. Rios, 'Italianos em São Paulo', in *São Paulo, espírito, povo, instituições*, ed. J. V. Freitas Marcondes and Osmar Pimentel (São Paulo), 1968, 75–91. On the immigrants and early industrialization, see Manuel Diegues Júnior, *Imigração*; *urbanização e industrialização* (Rio de Janeiro, 1964), 133–4. On the situation in the north-east, see Jaime Reis, 'Abolition and the economics of slaveholding in north-east Brazil', University of Glasgow, Institute of Latin American Studies, *Occasional Papers*, No. 11 (Glasgow, 1974).

48 For the war see Pelham Horton Box, *The Origins of the Paraguayan War*, 2 vols. (Urbana, 1939).

49 Poppino, op. cit., 205.

50 For the army in the earlier period see Nelson Werneck Sodré, *História militar do Brasil* (Rio de Janeiro, 1965); Oliveira Lima, op. cit., 424–35; and Buarque de Holanda, op. cit., II, 1, 265–77; II, 4, 235–314. The issue of civilians in the War Ministry went on until well into the 20th century, when J. Pandia Calógeras, the historian, was one of the most able men to hold the post. See Theodorico and Gentil Torres, *Ministros da guerra do Brasil, 1808–1950*, 4th ed. (Rio de Janeiro, 1950).

51 From an estimated 23,000 at the end of the Paraguayan War the army was reduced to about 15,000 by 1880, then stayed between 11,000 to 13,000. These figures, compiled from the *Relatórios* of Ministers of War, are quoted in Hahner, op. cit., 92. See also Charles Willis Simmons, *Marshal Deodoro and the fall of Dom Pedro II* (Durham, N.C., 1966), 27–8, who says that at the start of the war Brazil had less than 17,000 men in the armed forces. He

suggests that by 1865 the army numbered 35,698 officers and men and by October 1867, 42,873.

52 Francisco José de Oliveira Vianna, *O ocaso do império*, 3rd ed. (Rio de Janeiro, 1959), 129–30; José Maria Bello, *A History of modern Brazil, 1889–1964*, trans. James L. Taylor with a new concluding chapter by Rollie E. Poppino (Stanford, 1966), 42–3.

53 Abolitionist feeling among army officers was in part expressed by their refusal to catch runaway slaves, though this was also because they felt that slave-catching was not their job and beneath their dignity. For a discussion of abolition and further references see R. Graham, 'Causes for the abolition of negro slavery in Brazil: an interpretive essay', *HAHR*, 46 (1966), 123–37; W. Dean, 'The planter as entrepreneur: the case of São Paulo', *HAHR*, 46 (1966), 138–52, where he emphasizes the *paulista* concern for abolition as labour became scarce and their desire for political control. Also Simmons, op. cit., 54; Hahner, op. cit., 11–12.

54 There was a whole series of incidents in the 1880s involving alleged slurs on military honour. See Raymundo Magalhães Júnior, *Deodoro, a espada contra o império*, 2 vols. (São Paulo, 1957, 207); Simmons, op. cit., 48–56.

55 The Clube Militar was to remain very important in army politics. See Gerardo Majella Bijos, *O Clube Militar e seus presidentes* (Rio de Janeiro, 1961); Magalhães Jr, op. cit., I, 218–19; and Heitor Lyra, *História da queda do Império*, 2 vols. (São Paulo, 1964), I, 138–44.

56 Rui Barbosa, one of Brazil's most eminent statesmen and jurists, was by 1889 editing the influential newspaper *Diário de Notícias* (Rio), in which he regularly defended military interests. Later he became the foremost opponent of military involvement in politics. See Luis Viana Filho, *A vida de Rui Barbosa*, 6th ed. (São Paulo, 1960); and Raymundo Magalhães Júnior, *Rui, o homen e o mito*, 2nd ed., rev. (Rio de Janeiro, 1965). Júlio de Castilhos led, and firmly ruled, the powerful Republican Party of Rio Grande do Sul, using its newspaper *A Federação* (Pôrto Alegre), to support the army. See Othello Rosa, *Júlio de Castilhos* (Pôrto Alegre, 1928).

57 Hahner, op. cit., 28. Benjamin Constant Botelho de Magalhães, not to be confused with the Swiss French politicial theorist mentioned already, taught in the military college, where he urged the then fashionable mélange of Comtean positivism.

58 Some officers, certainly, were prepared to go further, a view urged by Benjamin Constant on 22 October 1889 in a speech at the Military College of Praia Vermelha. Speaking to the officers of the visiting Chilean cruiser *Almirante Cochrane* and to an audience which included the War Minister, Cándido de Oliveira, he claimed: '. . . the undeniable right of the armed forces to depose the legitimate powers constituted by the nation when the military understands that its honour requires that this be done, or judges it necessary and convenient for the good of the country . . .'. See Max Fleiuss, *História administrativa do Brasil*, 2nd ed. (Rio de Janeiro, 1923), 425, quoted in Simmons, op. cit., 107.

59 Details of the *coup* and events leading to it can be found in what is still the best study of Pedro II, Mary Wilhelmine Williams, *Dom Pedro the Magnanimous, second emperor of Brazil* (Chapel Hill, 1937), 327–82. See also the clear accounts in Simmons and Hahner and there are further references in P. A. Martin, 'Causes of the collapse of the Brazilian empire', *HAHR*, 4 (Feb. 1941), 4–48, and G. C. A. Boehrer, 'The Brazilian Republican Revolution: old and new views', *Luso-Brazilian Review*, 3 (Winter 1966), 43–57.

60 The row with the Church arose from the maladroit activities of the new twenty-eight-year-old bishop of Olinda, who from his appointment in 1872

began to attack Masonry and its involvement in the *irmandades*, the civil and religious brotherhoods in the north-east. The importance of the case has been much exaggerated, since the church never played a key role in the political system. Petty rancour on both sides did, however, lead to a wider Church–State confrontation. See Williams, op. cit., 173–85; Simmons, op. cit., 66–72. There is an excellent study of the lay brotherhoods of the north-east in Anthony John Russell-Wood, *Fidalgos and philanthropists: the Santa Casa da Misericordia of Bahia, 1550–1755* (London, 1968).

61 The importance of abolition has also been exaggerated: See Lyra, op. cit., 228–33. The vital factor was the decision of the army leadership in the capital, especially since by 1889 out of a total of 13,152 men in the army, 1,911 were stationed in Rio de Janeiro; Hahner, op. cit., 29–30.

62 The confused, uncertain origins of the Republic are brought out in Bello, op. cit., 46–57, who quotes the interesting, but inevitably partial, reminiscences of the deposed prime minister, the Viscount Ouro Preto, Affonso Celso de Assis Figueiredo, *Advento da dictadura militar no Brasil* (Paris, 1891). In the next few years much political capital was made of a 'monarchist threat', especially during the naval revolt of 1893–94, but there was never any serious monarchist movement. See Hahner, op. cit., 66, 98–109. A major source of monarchist views, including those of Ouro Preto, is the large anti-republican collection *A década republicana*, 8 vols. (Rio de Janeiro, 1899–1901).

1899-1930

3 The Coffee Oligarchy and the Old Republic

Civilian–Military Tensions

Like many so-called 'revolutions' in modern Brazilian history the change from Empire to Republic had no immediate, certainly no radical, effect on society. Mainly it showed more clearly than before the growing power of the armed forces and the tensions which were likely to build up between them and the civilian politicians, especially in São Paulo. Such tension, indeed, merely followed the logic of the two groups' essential loyalties, with the *paulista* and other state politicians principally committed to their regional interests, so to a high degree of state autonomy, and the armed forces already representing, at however elementary a level, an involvement in national issues which must necessarily transcend state loyalties, and which, in turn, demanded greater central control of most national resources. Already, therefore, the Old Republic was to see a move towards a rudimentary economic nationalism among some, especially the younger, army officers, countered by civilian politicians inextricably entangled in regional loyalties. This issue, however, was only to emerge more clearly as the politics of the Old Republic developed and really only to an important degree after 1930.

A more immediately striking feature of the civilian–military *coup* which deposed Pedro II was the way in which at so many points it closely parallels that other civilian–military *coup* which in April 1964 removed President João Goulart. The similarity again reflects the persistent structural problems of Brazilian politics in the intervening seventy-five years and underlines, in particular, the continuing failure to maintain a viable system of party politics at the national level. On both occasions, in 1889 as in 1964, the civilians believed that they could use the army for their own purposes, only realizing their mistake too late as the army command tightened its grip and governed with only the façade of constitutional rule. Again the differences between the two cases are equally instructive. In 1889 the armed forces were disunited, ill-organized, lacking confidence and political experience. They had no clear ideology or concept of their role. They had come to power almost unawares and proceeded fumblingly, without conviction. Above all, they were faced by a powerful civilian group, especially in São Paulo, so that after five years the civilians were able to regain control and rule, virtually without interruption, till 1964. By April 1964, however, the situation was substantially different with the roles sharply reversed. The armed forces were now both more united and more ready to take over, while the civilian politicians, in contrast, were weaker, generally discredited, and less capable of resisting military pressure. Instead, therefore, of a relatively quick return to civilian rule, as after 1889, all the signs pointed to a prolonged, ever more tenacious military administration, confident in its ability and convinced of the righteousness of its self-appointed mission. The differences, therefore, as much as the similarities require explanation, part of which lies in the nature of politics in the Old Republic from 1889 to 1930.

If they had few ideas and even less preparation for government, the army leaders, once in power in 1889, certainly showed strong determination to retain control and take advantage of their new opportunities for spoils. There was a swift increase in the number of officers appointed to government jobs, to obvious posts, such as the War and Navy Ministries, but also to positions in the states, where the Clube Militar organized its own pressure groups to safeguard army interest and influence policy. Civilian politicians were soon dismayed at the strong grip which the first president, Marshal Deodoro da Fonseca, kept on government and at the stern military reaction to any criticism, even from their former allies, the republican press.[1] There was growing fear of arbitrary military rule, especially as yet another soldier, Marshal Floriano Peixoto, succeeded to the presidency in 1891. Even some civilians who had at first tolerated military rule as being necessary, they believed, for preserving order, now had second thoughts. These included the young Baron Rio Branco, later to become one of Brazil's most eminent statesmen, who in the early days of the Republic, on 28 December 1889, had written to Rui Barbosa from his position in the consulate in Liverpool: 'the question today is no longer between monarchy and republic, but between republic and anarchy'.[2] Now, like many others, he grew uneasy over military control, agreeing with the highly respected and influential Joaquim Nabuco, who charged that the 'Paraguayan tyranny' had been brought back to Brazil 'at the points of the same bayonets and lances which had overthrown it',[3] a point echoed by Rui Barbosa, who refused to believe that 'politics could be demilitarized while the nation's government was in the hands of an armed dictator'.[4]

Despite such criticism, it was not the growing disenchantment with military rule, a reaction again found after 1964, which most seriously or immediately affected the army's control, but rather the divisions among the armed forces themselves. Many officers, for example, genuinely felt that they should withdraw from political involvement, preserving at most that 'moderating power' previously attributed to the Emperor, merely acting as arbitrator or watchdog of the constitution. The army, they thought, was, or should be, above day-to-day political squabbles.[5] Others, in contrast, thought national politics too important to be left to inept or corrupt politicians, who cared at best only for their local or regional interests, so they urged that the duty of soldiers to defend the honour and institutions of Brazil demanded a direct, overt political commitment, which could no longer be shelved.[6] Much the most weakening disputes, however, came on an altogether less elevated and less cerebral plane, over the relative roles of the different services in running the country and, particularly, in inter-service rivalry between the army and the navy. There was a growing swell of complaint from naval officers, strangely similar to that previously heard from the army, not this time against civilian neglect and disparagement, but over the inordinate favour shown to army officers with the change in regime. Such resentment grew steadily all through the presidency of Deodoro da Fonseca, who finally in November 1891 was forced out of office after navy leaders in Rio de Janeiro had resisted arrest and provoked a military crisis.[7] Still the divisions widened and the bitterness increased, culminating in a major naval revolt from 1893 to 1894 in which the rebels joined with dissident regional politicians in Rio Grande do Sul in a movement which now seriously threatened the unity of the new Republic.[8] This naval revolt, combined with the challenge in the south, gave the civilian politicians, especially in São Paulo, the chance to regain lost ground. The military president was forced to ask for their help, especially for the support of their state armed forces, with the result that in November 1894 a civilian *paulista* president, Prudente de Moraes, was able to take over the government, followed by two more *paulista* presidents, Campos Salles (1898–1902) and Rodrigues Alves (1902–08), in a pattern of political domination which continued unbroken until 1930.[9]

While such military divisions were the principal factor in ending the military regime, again providing a point of comparison for the period after 1964, equally significant, and in sharp contrast with the post-1964 situation, was the civilians' confident ability to seize their opportunity and build strongly upon it. The economic basis for the political pre-eminence of São Paulo and the south is discussed in other chapters, as is the increasing *paulista* demand for autonomy,[10] but one crucially important element in their success in 1893 must be appreciated. This was the emergence of a powerful new factor in the political equation in the form of the state armed forces, now backing growing economic power and political ambition with a matching military force. Throughout the whole period of the Old Republic and into the Vargas era this was to remain one of the most important elements in the relations between the federal government and the states, limiting, especially, the federal president's power to intervene in the richest or most influential states and always weighting the scales in tight political bargaining. Already under the Empire the *paulista* leaders had stressed both the need for state autonomy and guaranteed political stability. Keenly aware at a time of rapid economic expansion of the importance of their standing abroad, they were especially afraid that political violence or a series of military *coups* and revolts might seriously damage their credit, as well as making Brazil, and São Paulo in particular, less attractive to European immigrants. Such fear was, indeed, according to Campos Salles, a man later to be federal president, one of the principal causes of *paulista* distaste for military intervention, since armed movements '. . . disturbed the normal functioning of national life, causing the destruction of our credit abroad'.[11] Army officers, after all, so the *paulistas* and other civilian politicians argued, were not trained for financial administration. Their involvement must, therefore, cause great alarm as to 'the credit of the Republic, so seriously jeopardized by the incapacity of the officers who have been governing us'.[12] One reaction in São Paulo and other major states was to work harder to build up their own state militia, so as to prevent civil disturbance and political violence and at the same time to limit the federal army's power within their states. State police forces had already existed under the Empire, but were of little military consequence. Now, working under the new federal constitution of 1891, which gave much enlarged power to the states,[13] the *paulistas* in particular developed a bigger, better equipped, well-trained Força Pública, the military expression, as well as the guarantee, of São Paulo's economic and political supremacy. In 1888 the São Paulo force numbered less than 500 men. By 1893 and the naval revolt there were about 3,000, three infantry battalions with modern equipment, one cavalry regiment, and one battalion of armed 'firemen', numbers which were steadily increased in the following years.[14] By promising the help of these forces to the federal government São Paulo's politicians were consequently able to take advantage of the political and military crisis of 1893 and further assert their control in November 1894 under the first civilian president, Prudente de Moraes. But it was, it should be noted, this effective military backing rather than, for example, any deep concern for a tradition of civilian politics which allowed the re-emergence of the civilian politicians. This again was to be one of the most significant differences between the politicians of the 1890s and their successors after 1964, who had, of course, no such military force to which they could appeal.

The Constitution of 1891

Again, however, it was not just this local military capacity which allowed the *paulista* success. Their strength and influence had already been reflected in the new republican constitution of 1891, which clearly expressed the growing confidence of the state politicians and their strong dislike of central control. Some state leaders within the Constituent Assembly had, indeed, so far favoured extreme state autonomy as to want simply a confederation of twenty nations, a policy especially favoured in Rio Grande do Sul, where the separatist tendencies expressed in earlier revolts were still so strong.[15] The *gaúcho* political leader, Júlio de Castilhos, who urged this radical federalism, was backed not only by others from the south, but by such prominent republican spokesmen as Campos Salles from São Paulo, João Barbalho of Pernambuco, and Leopoldo de Bulhões from Goiás, men for whom 'the states were the reality, the Union . . . the fiction . . .'.[16] They opposed a draft constitution which had carefully sought to reconcile state autonomy and central control, especially in such matters as public order and finance, so that the resulting compromise went even further in guaranteeing the autonomy of the former provinces, now become the twenty states of the Republic.[17] Executive power was to be in the hands of the president, with his ministers responsible to him. The legislature was to be composed of a Chamber of Deputies, chosen by a limited electorate of property-holding, male citizens over twenty-one, who must be literate, and a Senate, in which three senators came from each state and the Federal District, so making sixty-three in all. But among all the provisions of the constitution two were of special political significance. The first, intended to preserve an adequate degree of central control, were the clauses permitting the federal government to intervene in the states, especially by imposing a 'state of siege' under Articles 6 and 48, a power which presidents were always ready to invoke, especially in their relations with weaker states which lacked a powerful state militia. Tougher-minded presidents, such as the *mineiro* Artur Bernardes (1922–26), governed most of their term under a 'state of siege', so provoking fierce resentment among state politicians jealous of their rights.[18] Still more important, however, in terms of allocation of resources and the real exercise of power were the fiscal clauses. These granted the states wide rights in the levying of taxes, above all of export taxes, which belonged solely to the states.[19] This, as always, was one of the acid tests in terms of local versus central control, and one of the key factors in preserving the vitality of local as opposed to national politics. Political configurations inevitably traced the pattern of fiscal control in a system where, to such a significant extent, resources—and consequently patronage and power—were allocated locally rather than at the national level. Export taxes, in particular, were tenaciously defended, as in for example a series of fierce debates up till 1930 between the president of Rio Grande do Sul, Borges de Medeiros, and the various federal presidents.[20] Their importance can be judged from the fact that by 1933 export taxes accounted on average for 35 per cent of state revenues from taxation and in some states were over 50 per cent, an explanation, too, of how important in terms of increased central power was their subsequent extinction by Vargas.[21] The states of Brazil were, indeed, in a stronger position with regard to taxation than were their equivalents in the United States.

> . . . Not only are the same limitations imposed there [Brazil] as we find in our constitution, viz., prohibition on export taxes, requirement of uniformity throughout the states, prohibition of preferences to the ports of one state over those of another . . . but in addition, by article 9 of the Brazilian constitution, certain important sources of revenue are assigned exclusively to the states which in the United States are not denied to the Union. Whereas the federal government with us is limited in regard to direct taxes only by the requirement that they shall be laid in proportion to population of the states, and not even that with regard to income taxes since the adoption of the sixteenth amendment, in Brazil the states are given exclusive power to tax not merely exports, but also real property, transfer of property rights, and industries and professions . . . the federal government in Brazil is deprived of the possibility of using important sources of revenue that are open to the Union under our constitution . . .[22]

They were, too, always trying to enlarge their powers at the expense of the federal government, a point noted by Prudente de Moraes in his presidential *Mensagem* to Congress of 1895:

> . . . The tendency of the states to invade the taxing sphere reserved for the Union demands on your part the most careful vigilance

in order to prevent embezzlement in the collection of its revenue, which, as you know, were deprived of abundant sources by constitutional provision.[23]

The states were always eager to assume control of indirect taxation, especially of import duties, which were the most important source of national revenue, providing nearly 50 per cent of the budget in 1889 (48·3 per cent), 56·4 per cent in 1911, and still as much as 42·3 per cent in 1928.[24] The federal government, on the other hand, tried persistently to control and develop direct taxation, with an *imposto de renda* law in 1892 and new legislation on income tax in 1924 and 1926. One problem here was, however, the severe difficulty of assessment and collection, problems persisting long after 1930, so that income tax produced only 0·6 per cent of the budget in 1910 and still only 3·1 per cent in 1928.[25]

The Superstructure of Political Control

This fiscal struggle was only one aspect of that deeper political issue, already emphasized, of state versus federal control, as well as a reflection of the already greatly enlarged powers of the major states, especially São Paulo. While the Ministry of Finance was the real testing ground for ministers and the fiscal issue was always a dominant one,[26] the struggle over taxation should be seen as essentially only one point of tension in the wider, difficult process of national and political integration and the overall shaping of the Brazilian state. As the Republic progressed, it became increasingly obvious that all the more specifically political problems still remained unsolved: how to provide a legitimate national government and means for its peaceful change; how to run such a huge country effectively; and how, in particular, to link the administration in Rio de Janeiro with the now even stronger political forces in the states and the interior. None of these issues, clearly, had been solved by the mere change from Empire to Republic and after the early years of uncertainty, revolt, and military control the new civilian presidents were more than ever aware of the need to reach solutions.

Electoral Corruption

Faced with the same problem as the Emperor and his ministers the new republican presidents found, as might be expected, similar answers, frequently expressed in the phrases *política dos governadores* (the politics of the governors) or, more pejoratively, *café com leite*, the politics of *café au lait*. The second phrase drew more attention in its popular usage to the *source* of political control, the economic dominance of the coffee-rich state of São Paulo and the cattle state of Minas Gerais.[27] The term 'política dos governadores' emphasized rather more the superstructure, the *means* of control and the ways in which power was expressed. Essentially, although its detailed workings were extremely complex, the *política dos governadores* 'was a means of political control, particularly of elections, by which the federal president was able to put pressure on the 'president' or governor of a state, who in turn used his influence on the local *chefes* and his supporting *coroneis*, or colonels, who then passed on the message to the voters under them. It was a vertical chain of control, the expression of the patron-client relationship at the level, first of local, then of state, eventually of national politics, as the *coronel* duly delivered his votes to the state governor, who in turn supported the national president. The president, therefore, when the system worked smoothly, could never fail to win an election and see his nominee succeed him. Nor was it usually difficult to find support for people and policies he favoured or to exclude men or movements which challenged his position, since the men returned to Congress, grouped in state blocks or *bancadas*, could swiftly be brought to heel by a president wishing to impose control. This was especially true from the time that Campos Salles was president (1898–1902), since in preparation for the elections of 1900 he significantly changed the rules of the game, quite genuinely, it seems, to minimize electoral fraud.[28]

Unfortunately, no matter what steps Campos Salles or others might take, it was extremely difficult, granted the system within which they were working and the general conditions of late nineteenth-century Brazilian society, to avoid well-founded charges of collusion and fraud in the interests of a narrow, regional socio-economic group. Only a small proportion of the population was, after all, directly involved in politics and the mechanisms of control were very effective.[29] In the last analysis, too, a government had to be 'made' and it was difficult to see how this could be done without recourse to what formally would be classed as 'corruption'.[30] In this respect, one simple point was made by the *tenente* leader Juarez Távora, giving evidence to the Constituent Assembly of 1933–34:

> . . . We are a country in which, as a rule, the elector hasn't the means to travel from his home to the polling station where he has to vote. If any of you wants to take a pencil and work out the cost of transporting over a million electors in the interior . . .[31]

Another witness, Domingos Velasco, made the same point:

> . . . It would be impossible to have an electorate at all if the chefe in the município did not bring them and pay their expenses . . . They organize the transport, lodging and food for hundreds, often thousands of electors. Such hospitality is expensive, because in the interior the electors come on the evening before polling and only return the day after the election. And during this time they spend not a penny, not even on the entertainments which must always be provided on election day . . .[32]

Kinship and Ritual Kinship Ties

The whole process, whether understood as fraud or corruption or in other terms, began at the most local level, rooted, especially in the more traditional, rural areas, in the kinship and class system of which *coronelismo* was, in one sense, only the political expression. The degree of dependence of the rural population on the landowner, as a direct result of the landholding system, has already been stressed. At the same time social anthropologists have persistently emphasized the importance of such structures as the extended family (*parentela*) and the ties of ritual kinship (*compadrio*) resulting from religious or socio-religious relationships. Just how important these factors were, and still are, in Brazilian politics is controversial, but they should at least be remembered, to underline that *coronelismo* and its electoral 'corruption' was only one, the political, aspect of a much wider, coherent social system, functioning, and so to be judged, only as part of that total system.[33]

There is widespread agreement as to the importance of the family in Brazilian social development[34] and, in particular, of the *parentela*, the extended family or 'clan', so prominent in rural areas. This group was made up not only of all recognized relatives on one's father's and mother's side and all those of one's husband or wife—a bilateral extension of relatives—but also of the members of what has been called the 'ancestor-oriented family', a wider group related to some prominent person in the past and usually bearing his name.[35] The *parentela* has been described as 'traditionally the most important single institution in Brazil',[36] with due emphasis on the role of the *parentela* in the political system:

> . . . at the beginning of the century, state politics were spoken of as oligarchies dominated by one or two large parentelas. In each state certain well-known parentelas or ancestor-oriented families dominated local political parties, which were but reflections of family interests. The families who were politically dominant in the state depended upon local political leaders in the small towns

> and rural zones, whose power, in turn, depended upon their own parentela. . . . Even national politics operated in terms of coalitions between large regional parentelas.[37]

In state after state all through the Old Republic, and well beyond, politics were a reflection of the interests and rivalries of these dominant 'clans', controlling the electoral system, bartering their blocks of votes to state and national leaders.[38] The *parentela* was especially strong, so politically significant, among the dominant elite groups in every state,[39] but less so among the poorer members of society, to whom recognition of kinship ties could often be a disadvantage.[40]

While, however, the *parentela* linked the elite groups horizontally with each other, rather than with those below them, the mechanism of political control was reinforced vertically by yet another element, *compadrio.* This in Brazil, as in varying degrees in other Catholic cultures, was the social aspect of the duties accepted by the godfather and godmother in a child's baptism. The godparents were now bound not only to the child, but equally to the child's parents, as *compadre* and *comadre*, relationships which could be further extended through confirmation and other religious ceremonies or quasi-religious rituals. Since these new duties were often taken very seriously, it was clearly the parents' concern to acquire for their child the best-placed godfather and godmother they could find, a guardian who would provide some protection and security in what was for most poorer Brazilians a very insecure world. In a society where education did not provide a vehicle of social mobility and the influence of the state was still small, such structures had real, direct significance. But the political implications were equally clear, since a man was bound to his kin and to his *compadre*, who, often, too, might be his *patrão.* If, therefore, he were qualified to vote, he would scarcely do so against his patron's interests, especially when, as in the Old Republic, the vote was not even secret.

Such structures obviously reinforced *coronelismo*, as described already, so leading to such pejorative descriptions of the electoral system under the Old Republic as *voto do cabresto*, the herd vote. But other elements, too, strengthened that system, including, what is often overlooked, that it provided some however limited advantages for the rural voter. It is not really enough, if one is to understand the system fully, simply to condemn it as a form of electoral coercion, since one important feature of its persistence was that whatever, admittedly few, benefits came to the rural voter were owed to the *coronel.* This is well brought out in the classic study of *coronelismo* by Victor Nunes Leal, already quoted, as when he notes, for example, that among the terms popularly used for the *coronel* was 'o indivíduo que paga as despesas' (the one who pays the bills)[41] and when he lists some of the duties which a good *coronel* was expected to perform and which, sometimes at least, he had to undertake if he were to keep his position unchallenged. These included, for example, to arrange work, lend money, witness documents, obtain credit in local shops, provide the services of a lawyer or a doctor, sometimes hospital care, help with a journey, fix railway passes, give food and shelter, prevent the police taking one's clients' arms or see they were restored. The *coronel* would have to assist at weddings, perhaps even enforce them, where necessary, help in all legal and fiscal matters, and, in short, provide an endless variety of personal service, 'which depended on him directly or on his followers, friends and chefes . . .'[42] So, too, it is

> . . . through his interest and on his insistence that the major improvements come. The school, the road, the telegraph, the railway, the church, the clinic, the hospital, the club, the football pitch, electric light, drainage, piped water—all demand his energy and attention . . .[43]

Eventually it was this aspect of the system—the indirect benefits the voter might expect—which led to an increase of political bargaining at the local level, especially as Brazilian society became less static and a new *coronel* could more often arise to challenge the current one.[44] This same process of political bargaining was then transferred with modifications to the cities, with voters in the *favelas*, for example, bartering their votes in a very similar manner through the *cabo eleitoral*, or electoral chief.

In part at least, then, *coronelismo* survived and persisted because it provided some limited benefits for the *caboclo* voter of the interior, arising at first, perhaps, from the *chefe*'s paternalistic concern for his clients, later from the need to maintain his position against the challenge of a rival political leader or even, indeed, of the growing influence of the central government.[45] In this sense the *coronelismo* system was both an obstacle to and a substitute for reform and revolution, providing not just a system of coercion and corruption, but, more insidiously, corruption tempered by humanity.[46]

Violence

If, on the other hand, the system was, as argued, supported by services to the voters, it was also firmly backed by violence or the threat of violence, again a feature of all such political systems.[47] The *coronel*, in other words, made very sure that he could not lose, since defeat was the ultimate disgrace, involving his personal honour, quite apart from direct personal losses to himself and his followers. To indulge in political 'corruption' brought no disgrace within the system as it then worked, but to lose, an affront to his local status, even to his *machismo*, was disgraceful. He therefore took every precaution to ensure that self-interest and kinship and ritual kinship ties were adequately reinforced by political mechanisms, backed, if necessary, by the threat of violence.[48] While, therefore, on the one hand his duty was to look after his own people (*filhotismo*), he had the converse duty to persecute his enemies and make life difficult for them (*mandonismo*), a duty summed up in the phrase 'negar pão e agua ao adversário' (to deny bread and water to one's opponent).[49] Hence, for example, the phrase 'para os amigos, pão, para os inimigos, pau' (for friends, bread, for opponents, the stick),[50] or, as still more tellingly expressed in a neat distinction in Minas Gerais, 'aos amigos se faz justiça, aos inimigos se aplica a lei' (for friends, justice: for enemies, the law).[51] Local society was, therefore, split by political rivalries at every level, with separate clubs and cafés, with ceaseless disparagement and scorn of opponents, and deliberate neglect or prosecution when in office. So, for instance, there would be minor nuisances, such as the roadway outside an opponent's house not being laid or going unmended, while, more substantially, the tax and other laws would be rigorously imposed on him by police and officials controlled by the group in power and he would constantly be troubled and harassed. But these were the rules of the game, acknowledged by all concerned, each in turn taking advantage of his electoral victory, rewarding friends at the expense of opponents. This in practice was the adaptation at the local level of the representative system to the hard realities of Brazilian rural society, just as it was, in strikingly similar ways, for example, in Spain, Italy, or Greece, or more generally in Latin America. But it was a total system, a coherent framework of rules and conventions, rooted in direct, immediate, personal loyalties rather than in an acceptance of abstract principles of political theory. It was not just a corruption of the 'democratic' process, but, rather, the 'corruption' was the system itself, a response to the structures of rural Brazil, only fully to be understood at this grassroots level.[52]

The 'Levels' of Fraud

From another point of view, of course, the politics of the Old Republic were open to every conceivable charge of corruption, collusion, and intimidation, presenting a breadth and variety of fraud which again help to explain later developments, including the low status and reputation of politicians, men who too often in popular opinion were engaged not in *política* (politics), but in *politicagem*, the corrupt manipulation of politics. The *first* stage of fraud began with the electoral lists and the voting, since the lists were shamelessly rigged by the *chefes*, excluding opponents and calling even dead men to vote on their behalf. The vote was not secret, remaining open throughout the whole period, so that political leaders could easily check how their followers voted. The ballot papers, printed locally, did not have on them the names of all rival candidates (*cédula única*), but simply one name (*cédula avulsa*). Often the political leaders and their friends would seal these slips in envelopes, passing them among their supporters before the election, who would then deposit them without even knowing for certain for whom they had voted.[53] When the voter went to the poll itself, there were no cabinets, just tables presided over by two officials (*fiscães*) appointed by the party currently in control. The voter would give his name, publicly deposit his vote, then sometimes go to do the same in another poll elsewhere.

Once the voting was finished, the judge had to seal the urns. This began the *second* stage of fraud, since, if the judge thought there were still some danger to his party, he could for example open the urn at his house, or get supporters to do it overnight, substituting a new set of votes, carefully keeping the same number as the number of names on the list, so that they might be checked at the *apuração*, the checking of votes. But this was the *third* stage of fraud, the *apuração*. It was supposed to take place in the *município* as soon as possible, with a representative of the other party present. He, however, would often be kept out, at gunpoint if necessary, as votes for an opponent were then read as votes for the candidate of the party in office, or as the actual records of the votes—the official *actas*—were sometimes replaced by other lists prepared beforehand. Sometimes, indeed, the presiding judge would dispense with elections altogether, substituting the notorious *bico de pena* (literally, pen-nib) for the longer, time-consuming, expensive process of the vote.[54]

Finally, there was still a *fourth* level at which control could be exercised, the last stage of the process in the recognition by Congress. Again this was meant as a safety mechanism to weed out earlier fraud, but in practice it allowed the party in power, especially from the time of Campos Salles onwards, to reject unwanted members. Occasionally, even, as in the notorious case of the Liberal Alliance members from Paraíba in 1930, the government would brazenly reject all opposition members elected, on the grounds that their elections had been irregular.

The Opposition

Civilian Opposition

Such an electoral system, however much it may be understood, was clearly open to the severest criticisms, particularly of those who were excluded from most of its benefits.[55] The whole political system of Brazil seemed to be organized by and for those relatively few men, centred in São Paulo and the south, who controlled the riches of the nation in terms of coffee and seemed cynically to be manipulating the political mechanisms to increase their wealth and power still further. Criticism grew stronger and more vehement, stemming especially from those states of the Republic, principally Rio Grande do Sul and the states of the north-east, which were excluded from that inner circle which controlled the system, and from certain increasingly disaffected members of the army officer corps, especially a young group who came to be called the *tenentes*, or lieutenants.

One particular focus of fierce resentment was what many regarded as an excessive dependence on coffee, the distortion, as they felt, of the nation's overall development by allocating too many resources to this one, however important, product. This feeling became stronger as the federal government took over the 'defence' of coffee as a major national policy, causing representatives of other states to feel that even more of the nation's wealth would be channelled in that direction.[56] This reaction was especially strong in the southernmost state of Rio Grande do Sul, too far south to benefit from the coffee boom, but capable, as it especially demonstrated during the First World War, of developing its other nascent industries, such as cattle, *charque* (jerked beef), and wine,[57] and starved, as many felt, of federal aid and credit at the expense of São Paulo. After the 1893 rising Rio Grande do Sul, with its relatively sophisticated political system and its long military experience, was always a thorn in the side of successive federal governments, always a source of instability within the delicately balanced federal system. Up to the First World War, however, this problem was contained, largely by allowing Rio Grande do Sul both greater autonomy and a larger share in national politics than was enjoyed by other states. In particular, this revolved around two men, the *gaúcho* political leader, Borges de Medeiros, and a *gaúcho* spokesman in Rio de Janeiro, who for years acted as political broker and kingmaker, Pinheiro Machado. Medeiros remained in the south, organizing and controlling his powerful Riograndense Republican Party.[58] Pinheiro Machado stayed in the capital, at the centre of the political web, vetting possible candidates for the federal presidency, watching over *gaúcho* interests, and exercising more than any other republican politician that 'moderating' role, the function of grand *cacique*, previously carried out by the Emperor.[59]

In this way the system was able to survive the only major crisis between the start of the century and the war, the lively, hard-fought campaign of 1910 in which the liberal statesman from Bahia, Rui Barbosa, scathingly attacked the corruption of Brazilian politics and warned of the dangers of encroaching militarism, only to be overwhelmingly defeated by the political machine supporting its pedestrian army candidate, Marshal Hermes da Fonseca.[60] But the 1910 campaign was important. It was the first major frontal attack on the established system, delivered in brilliant, memorable speeches in an unprecedentedly energetic campaign by an apparently honest politician appealing, for the first time in Brazilian politics, directly to the people. The shabby election of his unworthy opponent shocked many Brazilians for the first time into a realization of the widespread reforms required.

As always the war was a great political catalyst.[61] It brought in the major cities a quickening of workers' demands, an increase in early political organization, and the first major industrial strikes, especially in São Paulo.[62] It also stimulated a mushroom industrialization, an early short-lived experience of import substitution, especially in Rio Grande do Sul, which was to leave bitterness and anger in post-war years as European supplies were renewed, federal help was refused, and early hopes were sacrificed, unnecessarily as many *gaúchos* believed, in the continuing interests of coffee. The war also saw the death of Pinheiro Machado, murdered in 1915, leaving a major gap which no one was to fill and changing the whole delicate balance between Rio Grande do Sul and the dominant states of the Republic. Equally important, the war brought, as so often, growing national pride, leading in turn to a more refined sense of frustration, especially among the young, over Brazil's backwardness, low national standing, and notoriously corrupt electoral system.[63] Finally, it brought greater status to the army, a new prestige and increase of confidence. This in the long run was a dangerous inflation of corporate pride, since here, too, in the post-war years there was to be the familiar regression and consequent sense of grievance leading to more ambitious political demands.

More specifically, Brazil emerged from the war into a political crisis over the presidency. Rodrigues Alves, the *paulista* president designated under the *café com leite* agreement, died before taking office for the second time. This led eventually to the administration of Epitácio Pessoa, who found himself to his enormous surprise chosen as a compromise candidate to be Brazil's first north-eastern president, the only north-easterner till Castello Branco in 1964. But the crisis over Pessoa's election was nothing compared to that which built up in terms of his succession and culminated in the dramatic, bloodstained events of 1922. This marked the beginning of the end for the Old Republic and the start of a process which was to lead to 1930 and the accession of Getúlio Vargas.

Military Opposition: 'Tenentismo'

1922 brought the first centenary celebrations of independence, marked by a successful international exhibition and the return to Brazil of the remains of Pedro II and his Empress, Teresa Cristina. It also saw a milestone in Brazilian cultural history with the holding of the Semana de Arte Moderna, the week of modern art, in São Paulo, reflecting the growing nationalist concern of writers and artists to find a genuinely Brazilian expression for Brazilian themes rather than the derivative, often poor imitations of foreign models, which many felt had distorted Brazilian artistic achievement.[64] But July 1922 also saw the sudden, violent emergence of a new political force, still weak, undefined, and uncertain of its aims, but which almost overnight in early July was to enter Brazilian mythology as one of its most colourful, heroic elements. This was the political protest movement of young army officers, later to be known as *tenentismo*, which in July 1922 found expression and tragic glory in an ill-conceived, badly-executed barracks revolt, centred principally in the fort of Copacabana in Rio de Janeiro. The origins of the revolt were in every sense undistinguished, involved in a squalid, highly personal, bitter struggle over the presidential succession.[65] The official candidate was this time a *mineiro*, Artur Bernardes, who was strongly opposed by the president of the state of Rio de Janeiro, Nilo Peçanha, heading a movement called the *Concentração Conservadora* (Conservative Concentration).[66] This was the open confrontation between rival state leaders, especially provoked by Rio Grande do Sul, which had been avoided in 1919 by the choice of the compromise candidate, Pessoa. Now again in 1922 the crisis revealed all the tensions within the system of elite consensus. This time the challenge was more serious, since the opposition, by winning the support of Rio Grande do Sul, led by Borges de Medeiros, was threatening to upset the whole balance of power on which the political conventions of the Old Republic rested. Such an alliance was immediately interpreted as a betrayal by the official candidate, Bernardes, who was angered and alarmed still further when his opponents won the backing of the former president, Marshal Hermes da Fonseca, who had great influence in the army. Marshal Hermes, nephew of the first president of the Republic, had been an unimpressive president and had wisely retreated to Europe for a few years on leaving office. He was, consequently, extremely surprised to find himself warmly welcomed on his return by the political opposition seeking his support.[67]

It was at this point that 'army honour', always inflammable, was said to have been insulted in letters allegedly written by Bernardes.[68] The authenticity of these letters now became a subject of fierce controversy and, though they were later shown to be forgeries, their effect in the circumstances was highly explosive. Army feeling, especially in the Clube Militar, ran very high, with mounting resentment against the federal president, Epitácio Pessoa, for permitting, even encouraging it seemed, insults to the army, a controversy which became so public and bitter that eventually Epitácio Pessoa closed the Clube Militar and ordered the arrest of its hot-headed president, Marshal Hermes. This immediately provided the spark for a sudden, conspicuously ill-prepared revolt in the military college and barracks in and around the capital, particularly in the fort of Copacabana, the revolt breaking out on 5 July 1922. This fort, poised on one horn of the beautiful crescent of Copacabana beach, was commanded by a son of Marshal Hermes da Fonseca, for whom insulted military honour was now, of course, mingled with affronted family pride. He and a handful of other officers and men defied the federal government for two days, ineffectively at one point shelling the district of Copacabana. They had no clear idea of their aims, beyond their desire to oppose the president and assuage their injured military feelings, but they ended their stand with a vivid, heroically defiant gesture. Pinning fragments of the Brazilian flag on their chests, they marched out along the sun-filled promenade and then, joined by at least one civilian in the watching crowd, were shot down and bayoneted with only a few survivors as they bravely resisted arrest.[69]

The deaths of the young *tenentes* of Copacabana far transcended the intellectual weakness of their movement or the narrow political origins of their protest.[70] Their sacrifice had an immediate symbolic quality, providing instant heroes and martyrs at a crucial time in a political tradition which previously had lacked them, just as their defiance expressed for many Brazilians their own growing disquiet over the corruption and manipulation of national politics. The survivors were heroes whose picture was carried by patriotic Brazilians of all ages and classes as a symbol of a fresh spirit of renewal in national life. More important still, there was now new impetus to the *tenente* movement as it was joined by other young officers and as some found in prison after the revolt time to think and talk and clarify their political positions.[71] There were also other connections formed, with dissident politicians in every state—in Rio Grande do Sul, which in 1923 was again torn apart by a fierce political civil war,[72] in São Paulo, where the newly formed Democratic Party became a rallying-point for opposition, and throughout the north-east, especially in Paraíba and Pernambuco, where resentment increased as the north-eastern president left office and resources again dried up, redirected to the already prosperous states further south.[73]

Hardly had this excitement died down when the next important outburst came in 1924, this time in São Paulo, its start marking the second anniversary of the Copacabana revolt on 5 July 1924, as *tenente* rebels now joined members of the *paulista* opposition. This new revolt, led by a retired army colonel, Isidoro Dias Lopes, was more serious than in 1922. The rebels, though numbering at their peak only about 5,000 in all as against a government force of over 20,000, included most of the well-trained Força Pública of São Paulo, some members of the federal army, and many European immigrants who already had military experience. The city of São Paulo was in rebel hands from 9 July till 27 July when, after the federal forces had already shelled the city, the rebels were forced to withdraw westwards towards the Paraná river.[74] There was never, it seems, any real chance of the revolt in São Paulo provoking a widespread rising against President Bernardes. Nor, even in São Paulo, did it ever have the character of a popular or radical revolution. But the seizure of Brazil's major commercial city and the movement's limited success was again a measure of the strong regionalist feeling in São Paulo and a warning of the potential danger should *paulista* leaders be able, as again they were to try in 1932, to win the active support of other states. More important still, the 1924 revolt showed the growing capacity for organization on the part both of dissident state politicians and disaffected members of the armed forces, especially the *tenentes*, an alliance which eventually in 1930 was to have more success, leading to the end of the Old Republic.[75]

'The Long March'

Ironically, it was the failure of the 1924 revolt which brought in the long run perhaps its most important contribution to Brazilian political development, since it led directly to one of the most far-reaching and, again, one of the most colourful episodes in the politics of the 1920s. This was the 'Long March' of the so-called 'Prestes Column' or, more accurately, the Miguel Costa–Prestes Column,[76] an experience of great subsequent importance in the development and thinking of the radical left in Brazil.

Again, like the Copacabana revolt, the Long March, a two-year trek of about 14,000 miles through the Brazilian wilderness, has all the vivid, arresting qualities of exciting cinema.[77] Retreating from São Paulo at the head of about 3,000 men, one of the rebel leaders, Juarez Távora, a north-easterner of great personal charm, whose brother had just been killed in the revolt, eventually reached what is now one of Brazil's main tourist attractions, the wild, beautiful Iguaçu Falls in south-west Paraná, near the Argentine–Paraguay border. Távora was then sent to Rio Grande do Sul to help start a rising there, a revolt which, if it were to have had any chance of success, should have coincided with that in São Paulo. The leaders in the south were again two *tenentes*, Luís Carlos Prestes, then aged twenty-six, later to be the leader of Brazilian communism,[78] and Siqueira Campos, another heroic figure who in 1930 was to be tragically drowned in the River Plate after unsuccessfully trying to persuade Prestes, then in Buenos Aires, to join the Vargas revolt.[79] These started the rising in Rio Grande do Sul, centred in the old Missões territory, in October 1924: but they were again opposed by strong federal forces and by state militia and irregulars loyal to the state president, Borges de Medeiros, who this time also supported the federal president Bernardes.[80] Faced with such troops, hardened and experienced in the bloody fighting of 1923, the rebels were soon defeated. Prestes and another rebel leader later to be prominent as a *tenente* leader, João Alberto Lins de Barros, then managed to escape with about 2,000 men, but half their force defected at the Argentine border late in 1924 and it was March 1925 before they could join the other *paulista* rebels in Paraná. These, too, had just been defeated by federal forces, so that the total strength of the rebels was about 1,600, most of them badly armed, against almost 15,000 federal troops. Despite these odds it was decided to march through Paraguay and re-enter Brazil. The force was split into two brigades and there then began the 14,000-mile march which was only to end in March 1927, when Bernardes had left office and the remnants of the rebel column were to reach Bolivia and Paraguay.

This march of the 'Prestes Column' is a vivid story full of action set against some of the most colourful, dramatic background in the world. In over two years the rebel force marched and counter-marched from the Paraguayan jungles through the whole length of Brazil as far as the north-eastern states of Paraíba and Ceará, then back again through Alagoas, Bahia, Goiás, Matto Grosso, and eventually into Bolivia.[81] At every point the story seems larger than life, as when João Alberto, right at the start, found himself among the smoke of Alegrete having to direct artillery towards a church, near which were, he knew, his wife and his newly-born child whom as yet he had not seen.[82] There were encounters not only with pursuing federal forces, but, more bloody and fearsome, with the bandits, or *cangaçeiros*, of the north-east, gunmen hired by landowners to harass the weary column. There were internal quarrels involving violent rebels drunk with *cachaça*, the Brazilian cane spirit, and severe instant punishments for those found guilty of stealing from the peasantry. There were lesser dramas, too, as women followed their men into the interior, one reportedly giving birth to three children before the march was ended.[83] And throughout the whole painful journey was the mounting frustration of being unable to mobilize the peasantry.

When possible the rebel leaders printed a broadsheet, *O Libertador*, carrying the message of the *tenentes*, advocating land reform and urging the peasants to action, but the people of the interior were often illiterate and all such efforts were forlorn. There was colourful publicity for the column in the cities and widespread but covert support among the upper classes, many of whom at this time even called their infant sons Luís Carlos after the now legendary Prestes. There was, too, some success merely in surviving and defying Bernardes till the end of his term and, again, the column served to focus Brazilian attention away from the coast towards the acute problems of the interior. It helped, as had the Canudos revolt and the work of Euclides da Cunha,[84] to underline the issues of Brazil as a whole and remind the coastal, urban elite of the poverty, degradation, and despair of the interior. But as an attempt to provoke the support of the Brazilian peasantry and win their active co-operation in the stirrings of a national revolution the long guerrilla march was a mournful, deeply depressing failure. Yet it was here that it was perhaps most important, since Prestes, now disillusioned over the revolutionary potential of the *caboclo* of the interior, was after 1930 to become the most influential leader of Brazilian communism and one of the most powerful figures in the whole Latin American movement, turning its Brazilian development firmly away from guerrilla activity in the countryside towards long-term strategies of mass working-class activity in the towns. It was a policy which the Brazilian Communist Party was never subsequently to relinquish except for a few tragic months in 1935.[85]

Over the next two years or more, throughout the administration of Washington Luís, the decline of revolutionary activity, whether of civilian politicians or of *tenentes*, was reinforced by a period of economic prosperity as Brazil enjoyed an easing of credit and benefited from a general upturn in the world economy. The new president ended the unpopular 'state of siege' enforced by his predecessor and in 1927 balanced his budget. He was able to raise new loans from

London and Wall Street to push ahead with his plans for developing communications, especially the arterial roads. He also moved further towards restoring a currency backed by gold, following the then approved financial orthodoxy, and seemed to be showing that the policies and energies which had been so successful in São Paulo could equally well be applied to the whole of Brazil. Throughout 1927 and 1928 there was, consequently, a growing despondency among all revolutionary groups as Washington Luís further consolidated his position, a depression and pessimism clearly reflected in both civilian and *tenente* diaries and correspondence. The only apparent advances were in Minas Gerais, where the state president, Antônio Carlos de Andrada, introduced limited liberal reforms, including a secret vote and the suffrage for women. In São Paulo the recently created Democratic Party was only advancing slowly, seeming to many to be little different from the entrenched São Paulo Republican Party it was seeking to displace. This group, on the sudden death in 1927 of the president of São Paulo, hastily responded to pressure from Washington Luís and elected as state president his protégé, Júlio Prestes de Albuquerque.[86] But even in these relatively prosperous, peaceful times the political system was still held in only delicate balance, always able to fall apart should the working consensus between the major states ever be seriously disturbed, and in 1929 that consensus was deliberately broken, rejected by the man who seemed to have most interest in its preservation, the federal president, Washington Luís.

The Political Crisis

Like so many successful heads of government Washington Luís became the victim of his own success. Always conscious, as were most Brazilian presidents, of the need to push through his programme quickly before his successor might reverse it,[87] he became increasingly inclined towards a policy of *continuismo*, especially since he had a deep suspicion and mistrust of the man who under the *café com leite* system should be his successor, the president of Minas Gerais, Antônio Carlos de Andrada. He disliked him personally, but, more seriously, was alarmed by repeated criticism which Antônio Carlos had made of those very financial policies which Washington Luís regarded as the cornerstone of his administration.[88] Eventually, therefore, the federal president determined that he would not give his official backing to the presidential candidacy of Antônio Carlos, but would break the 'Golden Rule' and throw all his weight in support of another *paulista*, the president of the state of São Paulo, Júlio Prestes.

The details of the political crisis which built up throughout 1929 until the presidential election of March 1930, or of how the situation was affected by the international financial crisis, or how events after March 1930 eventually led to the October revolution and the accession to the presidency of Getúlio Vargas, are clearly described elsewhere.[89] Only the more salient points need be stressed in so far as they further reveal the nature of the political system as it then operated and as they influenced the development of politics after 1930.

Perhaps the first point to emphasize is that the crisis was primarily a political one. The system, as already seen, had always been under strain, in 1910 during the Rui Barbosa campaign, in 1919 at the time of Epitácio Pessoa's election, and, most seriously, when Bernardes in 1922 was faced with the combined opposition of state politicians and hostile army officers. At the same time, a challenge, either by armed rebellion, as in São Paulo in 1924 and throughout the time of the Prestes Column, or through an electoral opposition alliance as in March 1930, could easily be defeated. Armed conspiracies were usually too localized, as the *paulistas* found in 1924, and again in 1932, while the president, controlling the electoral machine, could always win the elections, as Washington Luís clearly showed in 1930, when the results, except in Minas Gerais, Rio Grande do Sul, and Paraíba, were a disaster for the opposing Liberal Alliance headed by Vargas. What, however, the system could not sustain, and what the army leaders could not tolerate, was a major split in the ruling class, with one side stubbornly refusing to make the usual concessions, even at the risk of civil war, which was the situation in October 1930.

The fatal mistake of Washington Luís was his refusal to reach the settlement which, time and again, was offered to him by Vargas and other opposition leaders, hoping at least to find an alternative candidate to Júlio Prestes.[90] A more adroit, flexible politician, such as Vargas himself, could almost certainly have weathered the storm, but Washington Luís remained intransigent, even when the armed forces' command in October 1930 urged him to avoid direct confrontation. Then the whole system of the Old Republic, founded and depending on the politics of class coherence and consensus, showed its essential incapacity to survive serious conflict. The marriage of convenience, the arrangement between friends, was over.

The Old Republic, in this sense, was mined from within, the political crisis preceding and being always more important than the financial and economic problems induced by the Wall Street crash, which acted as an important catalyst. The refusal of Washington Luís to grant emergency credits to the coffee magnates lost him much support in São Paulo,[91] but it was not their resentment which defeated him in October. Nor was it the armed opposition of the pro-Vargas forces moving from the north-east,[92] since there was no important conflict to compare with, for example, the fighting in São Paulo in 1924. The revolution which was started on 3 October represented a most serious challenge to the government, uniting state leaders in Rio Grande do Sul and Minas Gerais with important elements in São Paulo and the north-east and dissident garrisons of the federal army. But the president was still justified in feeling that such opposition could be contained as long as the armed forces as a whole remained loyal. Certainly it seems that even at this late hour a compromise settlement could have been reached, preserving the Old Republic in some form. Vargas himself had always been reluctant to oppose the federal president, still showing some hesitation as late as mid-October when the revolution was already well advanced, and his movement contained many whose primary aim was to prevent the succession of Júlio Prestes.[93]

But there was, above all, one vital factor, the attitude of the armed forces' command. They finally decided that civil war could only be avoided by removing Washington Luís, hence their take-over under the title of *Junta Pacificadora.* The *Junta* were right in their estimation of the degree of popular support for the revolution and the fighting which would result from Washington Luís's stubbornness. Nevertheless, it was their intervention and their decision not to resist the rebels which finally determined the outcome, as they now put aside Washington Luís as swiftly and easily as their predecessors had dealt with Pedro II and as their successors were to remove João Goulart. It was the armed forces in 1930 as in 1889 and 1964 who were determining events, including their subsequent decision to hand over power to Vargas.

The role of the army in ending as in starting the Old Republic is, then, one important feature in terms of subsequent developments. Another important factor, already mentioned, was the breaking of the working political agreement between the dominant states of the centre-south, since 1930 marked the success of those previously excluded states of the far south and the north-east, in part reflecting and in part determining the greater unity of Brazil, a start to a long, slow period of national integration under Vargas, ending the extreme autonomy of the states as seen in the constitution and politics of the Old Republic.[94]

Finally, it is again worth remembering that Vargas was coming to power at the head of a divided movement, formed as an *ad hoc* electoral alliance, then scrambled together again later in 1930 by Oswaldo Aranha as a hesitant, doubtful military challenge which most of its leaders hoped would not be taken up. The Liberal Alliance had no clear programme or distinct ideology. This was a short-term disadvantage but partly, too, a source of strength, allowing Vargas great political flexibility and opportunism, well-suited to a political system in which personal patronage and local loyalties always far exceeded explicitly ideological commitment.

The Old Republic was ended. Getúlio Vargas was in office, heading a provisional government and expected by many to be replaced soon, perhaps within months. Instead he held unbroken control till 1945, then again, after only a short absence, till his tragic death in 1954. Here now coming to power was the man who, more than any other single statesman, shaped modern Brazil and helped to fashion the Brazil ian state.

Notes

1 The most notorious case in this respect was the attack in November 1890 by officers and men in civilian dress on the presses of *Tribuna*, a paper which had printed criticism of the president, who was also said to have known of plans for the attack. See M. F. de Campos Salles, *Da propaganda á presidéncia* (São Paulo, 1908), 54–60.

2 J. E. Hahner, *Civilian-military relations in Brazil, 1889–1898* (New York, 1969), 102.

3 ibid., 105.

4 *Jornal do Brasil* (17 June 1893); Hahner, op. cit., 112.

5 On the army inheriting this role see Gilberto Freyre, *Ordem e progresso*, 2 vols. (Rio de Janeiro, 1959), I, 50–1.

6 Hahner, op. cit., 76.

7 Bello, op. cit., 87–8.

8 The Federalist revolt of 1893 in Rio Grande do Sul was only one of a series of conflicts which threatened secession in Brazil's most southern state. It had been preceded by the *Farrapos* revolt of 1835–45, already mentioned, in which Garibaldi played a part, and was followed by other risings, continuing till 1932, all reflecting the extreme regionalist feeling in the south. The 1893 revolt was a furiously fought regional conflict, in which the Federalists, led by a prominent monarchist, Gaspar Silveira Martins, were accused of seeking a monarchist restoration and secession. Essentially, however, it was a local power struggle. Bello, op. cit., 107–30 gives a clear account of it, as of the naval revolt. See, too, Glauco Carneiro, *História das revoluções Brasileiras*, 2 vols. (Rio de Janeiro, 1965) and Dunshee de Abranches, *A Revolução da Armada e a Revolução Rio Grandense* (Rio de Janeiro, 1955). For Garibaldi in Brazil see Lindolfo Collor, *Garibaldi e a Guerra dos Farrapos*, 2nd ed. (Rio de Janeiro, 1938).

9 Direct *paulista* control was finally broken in 1932, since when, significantly, the state has provided only one federal president, for the few colourful

months in 1961 under Jânio Quadros. Minas Gerais, too, the other dominant state till 1930, has since then produced only one president, Juscelino Kubitschek.

10 For São Paulo's development see R. M. Morse, *From community to metropolis* (Gainesville, 1958). W. Dean, *The Industrialization of São Paulo 1880–1945* (Austin, 1969), and, more generally, the review article by J. T. Winpenny, 'Industrialization in Brazil' in *Journal of Latin American Studies*, vol. 2, part 2 (November 1970), 199–208.

11 Campos Salles, op. cit., 52–3; Hahner, op. cit., 130.

12 Guimarães Natal to Prudente de Moraes, 20 June 1894, quoted Hahner, op. cit., 130.

13 See above, pp. 32–4.

14 These figures are from Hahner, op. cit., 133. The state forces become more formidable in later years, trained by foreign military missions. Usually better equipped and enjoying better pay, conditions, and status than the federal army garrison, they were a continual cause of discontent among jealous army officers, a significant factor in the growth of *tenentismo*. Throughout this period the *paulistas* insisted that one of their number should command the Força Pública and it was especially important in the early days of the Vargas regime, when commanded by Miguel Costa. Much the best study of a state's armed forces is that of the São Paulo Força Pública: Heloisa Rodrigues Fernandes, *Política e segurança Força Pública do Estado de São Paulo: Fundamentos histórico—sociais* (São Paulo, 1974). See, too, the useful discussion in the unpublished Paris doctoral thesis by Paul Manor, 'La place et le rôle de militaires dans la société brésilienne sous la première république (1889–1919)'.

15 Bello, op. cit., 79.

16 ibid.

17 See K. Loewenstein, *Brazil under Vargas* (New York, 1942), 9; and A. Marchant: 'Politics, government and the law', in T. L. Smith and A. Marchant, *Brazil: portrait of half a continent* (New York, 1951), 356ff.

18 For an analysis of the 'state of siege' from 1891 onwards and a detailed bibliography see *Revista Brasileira de Estudos Políticos* (17 July 1964), 193–210.

19 See especially Articles 5, 7, 9, 10, 11.

20 For an analysis of such political rivalries and their impact on party formation see: Maria do Carmo Campbello de Souza, 'O Processo Político—Partidário na Primeira República', in M. Nunes Dias *et al*, *Brasil em Perspectiva* (São Paulo, 1968), 185–252.

21 Already in 1891 the aggregate of such revenues was the equivalent of about £2 million, so that their loss to the federal government meant a drop from 9$998 to 8$059 per head—E. Hambloch, *His Majesty the President* (London, 1935). The standard of currency was the *milreis*, written 1$000. This was divided into 1,000 *reis* (singular, *real*). Larger sums were expressed in *contos*, one *conto* equalling 1,000 *milreis*, written as 1:000$000. In 1942 the *milreis* was renamed the *cruzeiro*, though that unit had first been introduced in the 1920s. At the turn of the century the *conto* was worth about US$333. The *conto* of 1,000 *cruzeiros* has more recently been replaced by the New Cruzeiro. See F. dos Santos Trigueiros, *Dinheiro no Brasil* (Rio de Janeiro, 1966), 131–5.

22 H. G. James, *The constitutional system of Brazil* (Washington, 1923), 20–1, quoted Normano, op. cit., 122.

23 *Mensagens Presidenciaes, 1891–1910*; Normano, op. cit., 123. Also ibid., 123: 'The republican period came to be characterized by a tariff war between

the states themselves and between them and the union . . .'

24 ibid., 135.

25 ibid., 135, 149.

26 There were 74 Ministers of Finance in the 67 years of the Empire and 28 in the 41 years of the Old Republic. They included some of Brazil's most able statesmen—Rui Barbosa, Rodrigues Alves, Bernardino de Campos, Leopoldo de Bulhões, David Campista, João Pandiá Calógeras, Antônio Carlos de Andrada, and Getúlio Vargas. See Augusto de Bulhões, *Ministros de Fazenda do Brasil. 1808–1954* (Rio de Janeiro, 1954).

27 A glance at the list of presidents again shows how apt was the name, since of the ten presidents from 1894 to 1930 five were from São Paulo and three from Minas Gerais. The only exceptions were Hermes da Fonseca, an army candidate (1910–14) and Epitácio Pessoa (1919–22), from Paraíba, a compromise choice of the political king-makers. There was no other north-eastern president until Castello Branco (1964–67), who has been followed by three *gaúchos*. An important source for this period is Epitácio Pessoa, *Pela Verdade*, 2 vols. (Rio de Janeiro, 1957) and his *Na Política da Paraíba* (Rio de Janeiro, 1962).

28 Details can be found in Campbello de Souza, op. cit., 206–9. Very simply, the changes affected a Congressional committee, the 'comissão reconhecedora de diplomas', which judged whether or not candidates had been validly elected. By altering the rules for the appointment of the head of that committee the new legislation virtually allowed those already in Congress to choose their successors, or at least veto those they disliked.

29 In the most bitterly contested and most seriously organized election of the Old Republic, that of March 1930, fewer than 2 million men voted, out of a population of over 40 million. The campaign was marked by all the usual violence and coercion, so that, for example, in Vargas's state of Rio Grande do Sul he received 298,627 votes as against, officially, only 982 for Júlio Prestes. In all, Prestes received rather more than 1,100,000 votes as against Vargas's total of about 700,000. See Barbosa Lima Sobrinho, *A Verdade sôbre a Revolução de Outubro* (S. Paulo, 1933), 145–8 and other details below.

30 This leads into the important, but involved, discussion of the nature and function of 'corruption' in developing societies and, particularly, of electoral corruption in a society on which a representative electoral system has only recently been imposed. Of the large bibliography see, for example, Samuel P. Huntington, *Political Order in Changing Societies* (New Haven, 1968), 59–71 on the relation between corruption and 'modernization'. More generally, see R. Wraith and E. Simpkins, *Corruption in Developing Countries* (London, 1963) and the most useful discussion in J. Scott, *Comparative Political Corruption* (Englewood Cliffs, 1972). See, too, P. Flynn, 'Class Clientelism and Coercion: some Mechanisms of Social Control', *Journal of Commonwealth and Comparative Politics* (July 1974).

31 Nunes Leal, op. cit., 198.

32 ibid., 199.

33 In this sense Huntington seems to miss the mark (op. cit., 71) in arguing: 'In Brazil . . . the weakness of political parties has been reflected in a "clientalistic" pattern of politics in which corruption has been a major factor', basing his judgement, it seems, on N. Leff, 'Economic Development through Bureaucratic Corruption', *American Behavioral Scientist*, 8 (Nov. 1964), 10–12. A better argument can be made that the weakness of political parties at the national level is rather the reflection of the robust persistence of patron-client structures in the locality.

34 See G. Freyre, *The Masters and the Slaves* (New York, 1956), 26–7: 'The

family and not the individual, much less the State or any commercial company was . . . the great colonizing factor in Brazil, the productive unit . . . and in politics it was the social force that set itself up as the most powerful colonial aristocracy in the Americas. . . .'

35 The terms are clearly explained in Charles Wagley's highly readable *An Introduction to Brazil* (New York, 1963).

36 ibid., 186.

37 ibid., 197–8. While this point is broadly valid, it perhaps needs to be qualified partly because of its tendency to equate *parentela* and clan. One difficulty, in particular, is in determining, as it were, the margins of the *parentela*, since it is in functional terms an ego-oriented category. There is need of much more detailed research on the patterns of recruitment and the political role of *parentela* and other associated structures.

38 Wagley quotes, for example, Luis Augusto da Costa Pinto, *Lutas de famílias no Brasil* (S. Paulo, 1949), on the feud between the Pires and the Camargos, which started about 1640. Usually the family struggles over a particular *município* determined party membership, as in the case of Barbaçena in Minas Gerais, split between the Andrades and the Bias Forte family, or the rivalry between the Vargas and the Dorneles families in São Borja, Rio Grande do Sul. Marvin Harris reports political divisions in a small town in Bahia, where 'One barber cuts only UDN hair, another only PSD hair . . .' M. Harris, *Town and Country in Brazil* (New York, 1956), 197–8. For a reflection of this in literature see the trilogy on Rio Grande do Sul, Erico Verissimo, *O Tempo e o Vento*, translated as *Time and the Wind* by L. L. Barrett (New York, 1951).

39 See, for example, the cases quoted in a most useful study of the Old Republic by Edgard Carone, especially *A Primeira República* (*1889–1930*) (S. Paulo, 1969), 89–95, on the Acioli family in Ceará, who held virtually every post worth having, as did the Neira family in Paraíba.

40 Recognition of relatives often imposed extra burdens on poor people whose resources were already severely stretched, so that there seems some correlation between strong *parentela* links and higher socio-economic status. See C. P. Kottak, 'Kinship and Class in Brazil', *Ethnology* vol. 6. No. 4 (October 1967), 427–43, who suggests modifications to earlier views and gives further references. The political importance of *parentela* lay, of course, mainly at the elite level.

41 Nunes Leal, op. cit., 11.

42 ibid., 199–200.

43 ibid., 21. See, too, Edgard Carone: *A República Velha* (*Instituições e Classes Sociais*) (S. Paulo, 1970), especially 249–84 on *coronelismo* and oligarchy.

44 Nunes Leal particularly emphasizes increased physical mobility after the Second World War and the spread of the transistor radio in encouraging new demands. The challenge of a newcomer to the power of the entrenched *coronel* is vividly and amusingly described by Jorge Amado in his Bahian novel *Gabriela, Cravo e Canela*, translated by W. L. Grossman and J. L. Taylor as *Gabriela, Clove and Cinnamon* (New York, 1962), a novel which can throw more light on local politics than many articles of political science.

45 The process of 'modernization' and the growing influence of central government can, of course, often be a stimulus to 'corruption', sometimes because there are more spoils to be shared with relatives and associates, partly because of the *chefe*'s need to counteract the increasing role of the government or perhaps of a political party organized nationally and with a strong ideological base. See in this respect Huntington, op. cit., 61 and the discussion in J. R. B. Lopes, 'Some Basic Developments in Brazilian Politics

and Society', in E. N. Baklanoff (ed.), *New Perspectives of Brazil* (Nashville, 1966), 59–77. The political use of clientelism as a mechanism of social control is discussed in some detail in Flynn, op. cit.

46 Huntington again makes a similar point from a slightly different angle: '. . . Like machine politics or clientalistic politics in general, corruption provides immediate, specific, and concrete benefits to groups which might otherwise be thoroughly alienated from society. Corruption may thus be functional to the maintenance of a political system in the same way that reform is. Corruption itself may be a substitute for reform and both corruption and reform may be substitutes for revolution . . .'; op. cit., 64.

47 Carone, op. cit., 68–84.

48 Nunes Leal stresses this point that the only dishonour was to lose. He also (op. cit., 200–1) examines the conventions covering political violence, especially on election day, and the refined gradations from the usual *threat* of violence to its much rarer *use* against a *chefe*.

49 ibid.

50 ibid., 23–4.

51 Nunes Leal, op. cit., 200.

52 As argued already, Brazilian politics *can* be read from the top down, in terms of national policies or groups, but only by imposing at times a coherence which the material itself lacks. Hence the acute need for good local history and local political studies. One of the few exceptions is perhaps the study of the army, since it has, exceptionally in the Brazilian context, a national identity and character.

53 Much of the information on how the elections were rigged comes from charges made by critics of the system, especially in the campaign of 1930. Some of it comes from friends in Brazil who as young children sealed such envelopes for distribution to voters.

54 Again in the circumstances this was fairly logical, since the voters would, in any case, vote as directed should they be brought to the polls: Nunes Leal notes this obliquely when he says how *bico de pena* was at least one practical answer to the problem of soaring electoral expenses: '. . . the rural element . . . is wretchedly poor. It is then the *fazendeiros* and *chefes* who have to bear the expenses of making the electoral lists and holding the elections. Without money and without direct interest the *roceiro* [in this context a poor peasant; strictly, one holding land in return for clearing it] would not make the least sacrifice in this respect. Papers, transport, lodging, meals, lost days of work, even clothes, shoes, a hat for the election, all must be paid for by political organizers concerned for his qualification and appearance. . . . The old process of *bico de pena* greatly reduces the electoral expenses. The new codes, increasing the electorate and demanding the effective presence of voters, increase these expenses. . . .' (op. cit., 20).

55 It may be noted in passing that such electoral fraud did not stop with the introduction of the secret ballot after the 1930 revolution. So, for example, in later years one stratagem among many to ensure control of the vote was for the local party leaders to gather their men in a bar near the polling station. The first man was then sent in. Once in the booth, he carefully pocketed his voting slip and deposited a blank sheet of paper in the urn. He then returned to the bar and gave the official voting slip to the second man, who marked his vote there and then under the scrutiny of the party agents. Then this second man went to the poll, left the vote he had already cast, and returned to the bar with another blank voting slip for the third voter. This could go on all day with the vote being carefully controlled, and

at the end of the day there would be only one null vote—the first blank sheet left by the first man to vote.

56 There is a particularly useful account of coffee 'defence' in Carone, *A República Velha*, 27–51.

57 Such resentment is very clear in the correspondence of *gaúcho* politicians as revealed in the papers of one of Rio Grande's, and Brazil's, most distinguished statesmen, Oswaldo Aranha.

58 Especially see João Neves da Fontoura, *Memórias*, vol. I: *Borges de Madeiros e seu Tempo* (Rio de Janeiro, 1958).

59 See especially on Pinheiro Machado the perceptive remarks in Morazé, op. cit., 87–9, where he quotes Clemenceau, who, visiting Brazil, remarked that it was governed by one man, Pinheiro Machado.

60 On this election see Viana Filho, op. cit., 366–92 and the account in Bello, op. cit., 211–15.

61 See below, pp. 76–7.

62 See below, pp. 76–7; also Paulo Nogueira Filho, *Ideais e Lutas de um Burgûes Progressista. O Partido Democrático e a Revolução de 1930*, 2nd ed. (Rio de Janeiro, 1965), I, 71.

63 This is well brought out in ibid., 54–5, 73–83.

64 M. da Silva Britto, *Antecedentes da Semana de Arte Moderna* (Rio de Janeiro, 1964). Also J. Cruz Costa, *A History of Ideas in Brazil* (Berkeley and Los Angeles, 1964), 250–71 and T. Skidmore, 'Brazil's Search for Identity in the Old Republic' in R. S. Sayers ed., *Portugal and Brazil in Transition* (London, 1969), 127–44.

65 A coherent account of the 1922 rising and of politics throughout the Vargas period is in J. W. F. Dulles, *Vargas of Brazil. A Political Biography* (Austin, 1967). Dulles also provides very useful references to many secondary sources.

66 Nilo Peçanha had served as federal vice-president, taking over the executive from 1909–10 when the president died. He had also been Foreign Minister. His challenge was the most serious threat since the 1910 campaign of Rui Barbosa. See Brígido Tinoco, *A Vida de Nilo Peçanha* (Rio de Janeiro, 1962). Peçanha and Marshal Hermes da Fonseca were in 1921–22 used as rather reluctant leaders of the civilian/military opposition, much as Getúlio Vargas was cast in that role in 1929–30.

67 He was especially used to express armed services' resentment at the appointment by Epitácio Pessoa of civilian Ministers of War and the Navy, the only such use of civilians during the Republic. As after the Paraguayan War and the Second World War these post-war years were times of acute military sensitivity to any hint at a cutback in their role or status.

68 H. Silva, *O Ciclo de Vargas*, vol. I: *1922. Sangue na Areia de Copacabana* (Rio de Janeiro, 1964), 1–21.

69 Though they became popularly known as the 'Eighteen of the Fort', there were, in fact, less than eighteen, the only survivor now being Brigadier Eduardo Gomes, who ran as presidential candidate after 1945. The revolt was very much a family affair, in that the only outbreak at any distance from Rio was a short-lived gesture in Matto Grosso, again led by a relative of Marshal Hermes da Fonseca. See G. Carneiro, *História das Revoluções Brasileiras*, 2 vols. (Rio de Janeiro, 1965), I, 244–5.

70 The revolt had many of the features of some contemporary student protests, generous, impulsive, and unclear in its aims. So, too, had the repression, a grotesque over-reaction by the regime, later justified by Epitácio Pessoa as being necessary to stop subversion. See his statement of 15 November 1922; ibid., I, 248.

71 See, for example, João Alberto Lins de Barros, *Memórias de um Revolucionário*, 2nd ed. (Rio de Janeiro, 1954), 18–22. João Alberto joined his companions in the revolt out of a sense of comradeship, then began discussing politics in prison with Joaquim Távora, later to be killed in the São Paulo revolt of 1924. Again there is the parallel with later student activity. See, too, Juarez Távora (Joaquim's brother), *A Guisa de Depoimento sôbre a Revolução Brasileira de 1924*, vol. I (São Paulo, 1927): vol. III (Rio de Janeiro, 1928): vol. I, passim.

72 Dulles, op. cit., 23–7. The war started with an electoral attempt to unseat Borges de Medeiros, but quickly became a bloody civil war with no quarter given on either side.

73 Another important source of reform demand at this time was the newly-formed Brazilian Communist Party, officially started in 1922; but this is discussed in the next chapter.

74 Silva, op. cit., 363–430; Carneiro, op. cit., I, 263–84; Dulles, op. cit., 27–31. Also Nelson Tabajara de Oliveira: *1924: A Revolução de Isidoro* (São Paulo, 1956).

75 The whole period, with its intrigues, revolts, and changing political fortunes, is captured in novel form by Rosalina Coelho Lisboa, *A seara de Caim*, 2nd ed. (Rio de Janeiro, 1952).

76 The first force of revolutionaries to take to the interior were the rebels pulling out of São Paulo, led by a commander of a Força Pública regiment, Miguel Costa. Costa was later made a revolutionary general, when the various rebel groups joined forces at the end of March 1925. Two brigades were then formed, the Rio Grande Brigade, led by Prestes, and the São Paulo Brigade under Juarez Távora. But the popular name is the 'Prestes Column', despite Miguel Costa's role. Costa was to be very important in *paulista* politics in the early 1930s.

77 The classic, highly readable account is by Lourenço Moreira Lima, who was a member of the column, recording its wanderings in personal detail, *A Columna Prestes* (*Marchas e Combates*), 2nd ed. (São Paulo, 1945). Also João Cabanas, *A Columna da Morte*, 6th ed. (Rio de Janeiro, 1927). Also Juarez Távora, op. cit., vol. III; Carneiro, op. cit., I, 285–308; and H. Silva, *1926. A Grande Marcha* (Rio de Janeiro, 1965). The most complete study of the Column is Neill Macaulay, *The Prestes Column. Revolution in Brazil* (New York, 1974).

78 See Jorge Amado, *O Cavaleiro da Esperança: Vida de Luiz Carlos Prestes*, 10th ed. (Rio de Janeiro, 1956).

79 See the account in Lins de Barros, op. cit., 226–34. João Alberto was travelling with Siqueira Campos when their plane crashed into the river. João Alberto survived while Siquiera Campos, a powerful swimmer, was drowned, a severe blow and great personal loss to the revolutionary movement. Also see G. Carneiro, *O Revolucionário Siqueira Campos*, 2 vols. (Rio de Janeiro, 1966). Campos was one of the '18' of the Fort.

80 Medeiros had burned his fingers in 1922 in supporting Peçanha against the federal president and was now anxious not to provoke reprisals against his state.

81 There is a series of small maps in Lins de Barros, op. cit., which are conflated in Dulles, op. cit., and Silva, op. cit. There is a more detailed map in Moreira Lima, op. cit., 44 and again a detailed map, also showing some of the engagements, in Juarez Távora, op. cit., vol. III.

82 Lins de Barros, op. cit., 29–30.

83 Dulles, op. cit., 37.

84 The Canudos revolt of 1896–97 is described in one of the most famous of

Brazil's sociological novels: Euclides da Cunha, *Os Sertões*, translated as *Rebellion in the Backlands* (Chicago, 1944). The story of the fanatical resistance to the death of the zealots of the Bahian interior, costing the government forces nearly 5,000 men, brought to many coastal Brazilians a revelation of another Brazil, again brought home to them during the march of the Column. For the bare details of the Canudos affair see Bello, op. cit., 149–55 and Carneiro, *História das Revoluções Brasileiras*, I, 96–117.

85 There was, from 1967 onwards, some change of strategy with Marighela and the urban guerrilla movement, but his was a breakaway group from the official party. Prestes, it can be argued, had by 1927 learned most of the lessons which others in Latin America were only to appreciate fully after the failure of Ché Guevara forty years later.

86 For details of these developments see A. J. Barbosa Lima Sobrinho, *A Verdade sôbre a Revolução de Outubro* (São Paulo, 1933); V. A. de Melo Franco, *Outubro 1930*, 2nd ed. (Rio de Janeiro, 1931); Maurício de Medeiros, *Outras Revoluções Virão* (Rio de Janeiro, 1932).

87 This has been a constant problem for any president anxious to get things done. Washington Luís had recently seen how Epitácio Pessoa's work for the north-east had been stopped by his successor. See A. O. Hirschman, *Journeys Towards Progress* (New York, 1963), 30–7. The same problem occurred under Kubitschek in relation to Brasília.

88 Neves da Fontoura, op. cit., II, 25; Lima Sobrinho, op. cit., 23–35.

89 There is a clear account in Dulles, op. cit. and the other sources already quoted.

90 Vargas, again, was afraid of reprisals should his bid fail, of being 'another Nilo Peçanha', as he said. He, like any *coronel* of the interior, knew that failure was the ultimate disgrace, a point also to remember when assessing the events of August 1954.

91 Lima Sobrinho, op. cit., 105–15.

92 R. J. Alexander, 'Brazilian Tenentismo', *HAHR* XXXVI (May 1956), 239–42; J. D. Wirth, 'Tenentismo in the Brazilian Revolution of 1930', *HAHR* XLIV (May 1964), 161–79; and J. Young, *The Brazilian Revolution of 1930 and its Aftermath* (New Brunswick, 1967), 55–69, which should also be consulted for the coffee crisis, 70–80.

93 On Vargas's hesitancy see Young, op. cit., 64. This continuing irresolution and the divided nature of the Vargas movement is also discussed in P. Flynn, 'The Revolutionary Legion and the Brazilian Revolution of 1930' in R. Carr, ed., *Latin American Affairs*, St Antony's Papers, No. 22 (London, 1970), 63–105.

94 The contrast between these 'two Brazils' in 1930 is vividly seen in two photographs juxtaposed in Hélio Silva, *1931. Os Tenentes no Poder* (Rio de Janeiro, 1966), 66–7. One shows Júlio Prestes leaving for exile, every inch the *paulista* financier, in well-cut suit and homburg, raincoat over his arm, carrying a cane and accompanied by the British consul in formal white uniform. The other photograph is of members of the Paraíba police, small dark men, sitting with feet dangling over the back of a lorry, wearing loose sandals, *vaqueiro* hats, and spotted neckerchiefs. Here was the 'other Brazil' making its claim, just as did the *gaúcho* horsemen from Rio Grande do Sul, tethering their horses at the top of the fashionable Avenida Rio Branco in Rio de Janeiro.

1930–37

4 Getúlio Vargas: from Liberal Alliance to *Estado Novo*

Continuing Class Control

In 1930, for the first time in Brazilian history, a political movement had caught the popular imagination and as Vargas moved to Rio de Janeiro his journey became a triumphal procession, his train mobbed and cheered at every station by excited crowds waving red flags and banners and cheering for the revolution.[1] Never before or since did any Brazilian head of state come to office with such widespread support, backed by men of all classes, from Rio Grande do Sul in the south to Pernambuco and Paraíba in the north-east. The army leaders, it soon became clear, had judged well in choosing the defeated presidential candidate and sending Washington Luís to the Fort of Copacabana.

Unfortunately, for many of those who cheered so loudly for the victory of the democratic candidate the years after 1930 brought only disappointment and disillusion. The early euphoria soon faded, the revolutionary chanting died away, and as the decade progressed, Brazil moved further than ever from genuinely representative popular government. Instead, by the end of the 1930s Vargas was governing the country under a corporatist constitution, which formally denied the principles of representative democracy and, as he left office under army pressure in 1945, Brazil was to start a new era of party politics built on only shallow foundations. Political parties by 1945 were being hastily and artificially assembled, but the opposition was only starting to be vocal again, student groups only just recovering, and the trade union movement was already cast in a non-aggressive role, its militancy curbed and its bargaining power very low. The working class, whether rural or urban, still had no real power and a whole generation had grown up without experience of open political debate. Only the state, the centralized machinery of government, and, above all, the armed forces were emerging politically stronger and more confident from the first fifteen years of Vargas's rule.

That the victory of the democratic candidate of 1930 should have ended in this way is only one of the many contradictions of Brazilian politics, but, looking at the overall pattern of the country's development, this failure to move more closely towards the promised democratic government, based on mass political parties and an effective Congress, is the most evident feature of this decade and a half. It also helps to explain the relative ease with which after another two decades the armed forces could intervene and re-establish an authoritarian, strongly centralized regime even less inclined towards popular participation than the *Estado Novo* which had ended in 1945. The reason is that the twenty years of formally democratic, multiparty politics were, in one sense, only a variation of the norm of authoritarian control which preceded and followed it, making the major theme of the period since 1930 not one of a move towards participation and a more open system, but, rather, of a persistent underlying pattern of class control. The central problem, in other words, is *not* one of 'an experiment in democracy',[2] but, rather, of the regular repression of popular efforts to challenge the existing system of class control. The *forms* of that control changed, as did the alignment of forces within the ruling class, but there is an essential continuity, throughout the *Estado Novo* to 1945, the period of 'bourgeois democracy' to 1964, and the military-led authoritarianism of subsequent years.[3] Why this control should have persisted, and how, is, therefore, one of the most fascinating, and controversial, questions not just for Brazil, but for many contemporary societies, the answer to which lies in the nature and particular shaping of the Brazilian state, a process which now was to accelerate under the government of Getúlio Vargas.

The paradox of the failure of the democratic candidate to provide democratic government was, in any case, more apparent than real. Vargas, as already suggested, was not a radical or popular revolutionary leader, even in the limited sense that he aimed to base his power on mass acclaim or support. Nor was his movement, in class terms, really a popular one. Those who hoped for radical revolution, still more those who envisaged popular participation in government and cheered Vargas as their champion, were bound to be disappointed, since, with all its apparent heterogeneity of aims and interests, the new Vargas regime was still essentially made up of those same social classes who had been important before 1930, even though it was eventually to open the door to new social forces, above all, the industrial bourgeoisie eager for import-substitution industrialization.[4] The regional emphasis quickly changed to some degree, with more prominence given to men from Rio Grande do Sul and the north-east, but the class composition and dominant interests remained very similar. This was a point which Luís Carlos Prestes, the *tenente* leader of the 1920s, now moving towards communism, had been quick to make and which became increasingly clear as the decade progressed. The 1930 revolution, judged as a class phenomenon, was predominantly a bourgeois movement which would, in time, turn increasingly to defend the interests of a growing urban, industrializing middle class; but despite its early promises, it had still, in the short term, to defend the primary source of the nation's wealth, the coffee economy centred in São Paulo. This was made all the more necessary and urgent by the swelling economic crisis internationally and the collapse of coffee prices, so that Vargas in his early years had little chance to introduce substantial changes in the social and economic structure of the country.

More important still, in terms of how these new challenging social forces could find expression through the political system, he had not yet sufficient power to make such changes. Right from the start, despite his apparent bland calm, Vargas was embroiled in a bitter, irreconcilable struggle for power, challenged both within his own winning, but always brittle, alliance and by regional groups, especially in São Paulo, who deeply resented the success of the *gaúcho* politician and rightly calculated the threat to their own previously dominant position. Vargas's only means to offset this threat was increasingly, but especially after the defeat of São Paulo in 1932, to move more completely into the shadow and control of the leaders of the armed forces, above all, the federal army, a move which required the build-up of this most important element of the state apparatus. In this sense, his whole fifteen years in power was a dangerous, difficult balancing act between resentful state politicians, looking over their shoulders to their period of power before 1930, and army leaders, suspicious of all politicians and watchful of every move Vargas made. Both groups were, essentially, hostile to the growth of genuinely popular participation, so that it is, in large part, a tribute to Vargas's political skill that Brazil in these years neither slipped back towards the state-controlled, oligarchic politics of before 1930 nor moved abruptly towards the style of military government which increasingly threatened, but did not arrive till ten years after Vargas's death. Of these two alternatives, however, the first was always more likely until the armed forces were sufficiently strong, and politically prepared, to take over direct control, a situation which only arose after 1945.

The first, most serious challenge came from the regionalist politicians who previously had controlled the national system in the way already described. The constitution of the Old Republic had been designed to give the fullest autonomy to the states, especially

São Paulo. The whole system had been geared to give maximum benefit and control, in an ostensibly democratic framework, to that small group of men, mostly in São Paulo and Minas Gerais, who controlled the country, working, as far as possible, in smooth collaboration with political leaders in other states, of which the most important was Rio Grande do Sul. These were the small elite group who ran the country in their own and their regions' interest, which, in their eyes, neatly coincided with the national interest. It was this system which the young *tenentes* of the 1920s described as 'oligarchic' and which, now in power with Vargas, they were determined should be destroyed.[5] This was the hard basis of their repeated demand that 'constitutional' rule and new elections for Congress should only come after a thorough process of 'cleansing' (*saneamento*). Otherwise, they argued, they would merely be handing back the country to those very men they had fought against in the 1920s and for whose removal they had joined the revolution in 1930. 'Constitutional' demands in their view were merely a pious cloak to cover a return to power and control by regionalist oligarchic politicians and the men they represented, especially in São Paulo. On the other hand, such *tenente* neglect of constitutional rule was easily interpreted as the first step towards military dictatorship, similar to that which they had successfully opposed in the first years of the Republic. So the *paulistas* soon began to talk of 'military soviets'[6] and they were quick to accuse Vargas of recklessly imposing on Brazil a *caudilho* style of dictatorship more commonly found in Spanish America, but understandable, they scornfully acknowledged, in a *gaúcho* from Rio Grande do Sul.

The São Paulo Revolt: 1932

Within days, even hours, of Vargas taking office this argument was being fiercely carried on, inflamed at once by the failure of Getúlio to appoint as governor of São Paulo a member of the São Paulo Democratic Party, whom the *paulistas* claimed they had been promised. Instead he imposed, as they alleged, a young *tenente*, a north-easterner, João Alberto Lins de Barros, instantly and vigorously opposed by the São Paulo ruling class as an alien nominee of a hostile central government.[7] Their regionalist resentment grew intense, but, even when João Alberto was finally forced to resign in July 1931, the *paulistas* were unable to have their way in naming his successors. Relations steadily worsened till in July 1932 São Paulo openly defied the central government in an armed revolt which lasted three months and which even led some *paulistas* seriously to demand secession from the federation and their recognition as an independent sovereign state.

This revolt of São Paulo from July till October 1932 was the most serious crisis Vargas faced throughout the 1930s and one of the major turning-points in contemporary Brazilian history.[8] As a military operation it was a sad failure, a chapter of accidents punctuated by moments of idealism and heroism; but as a direct political confrontation between the central government and Brazil's richest, most powerful state it was a crucial, acid test of strength. The essence of the opposition plan, hatched throughout 1931 and 1932, was, in fact, not for military engagement, but for a political *coup* involving the political leaders of São Paulo, Rio Grande do Sul, and Minas Gerais, the idea being that Vargas could quickly be deposed and the *tenente* influence destroyed. But this plan backfired at every point, partly through the premature, ill-judged action of one of the plotters, an army commander in Matto Grosso, General Bertoldo Klinger. Klinger's too early defiance, leading to his immediate dismissal, then forced the *paulistas* to move earlier than they had intended. Unfortunately, their allies in Rio Grande do Sul, notably the old *gaúcho* republican leader, Borges de Medeiros, and the Libertador leader Raul Pilla, found that they could not live up to their promises, and failed to swing the state behind them in opposition to Vargas. They had powerful backing among former Vargas supporters, who had now left him on the 'constitutional' issue, but, fatally, they had failed to win over Vargas's representative and old friend in Rio Grande do Sul, Flores da Cunha, who controlled the powerful, well-equipped state forces, the *Brigada* and the *provisórios*, without whose support all opposition was hopeless.[9] In Minas Gerais, too, there was only at best a promise not to help the federal forces against São Paulo and there was no significant help from other states. Above all—by far the most important factor—the federal army remained loyal to Vargas and his provisional government.

There had been some, but only marginal, provision for armed opposition by the *paulistas*, but all had really depended on the political *coup*. São Paulo was now left with its fists clenched, offering defiance, but with no real hope of victory, a situation the *paulista* leaders soon recognized, even before General Klinger arrived in São Paulo on 12 July, not with his army from Matto Grosso, as promised, but with much less panache and military circumstance, coming by train, accompanied only by his wife and a few aides. Despite this failure of their plans, the *paulistas* determined to continue their opposition. Again, unfortunately, they lost whatever little chance of early success they might have had. They failed to launch an immediate bold attack on Rio de Janeiro, using their highly trained Força Pública against an unprepared federal army, but, instead, allowed the campaign to settle down into a defensive trench warfare around São Paulo's frontiers, making defeat only a matter of time.

The political nature of the *paulista* opposition can in part be seen from the different reaction of social classes in the state. There was widespread support for the revolt from the middle and upper classes, who found new solidarity in, for example, their 'campaign of gold', in which women sold their jewellery and men their academic rings to provide fighting funds against the 'dictatorship'.[10] Society ladies quickly offered their services in nursing, and poets and orators sang the praises of São Paulo's resistance, if sometimes with much exaggeration and at too great a length. There was, more substantially, a renewed stimulus to industry[11] as it, too, was put on a war footing and considerable imagination and ingenuity were shown in the manufacture of munitions, drawing especially on the experience of European immigrants.[12]

In contrast to this enthusiasm of the middle and upper classes the working class of São Paulo was markedly cool in its support, shrewdly, and rightly, judging that the quarrel was one for the bourgeoisie of São Paulo. If anything, its sympathy was more with the central government or rather with *tenente* leaders such as João Alberto[13] and the former commander of the São Paulo Força Pública, Miguel Costa. Costa, who had jointly led the Miguel Costa–Prestes Column in the 1920s, was a popular figure, who in the months preceding the revolt had tried to organize in São Paulo a Revolutionary Legion, which he later tried to turn into a workers' party. He had aimed directly at mobilizing the industrial workers politically and was one of the first people arrested by the São Paulo rebels, much concerned about *tenente* involvement in popular politics.[14]

In October 1932 the revolt was ended, with the *paulistas*, heavily outnumbered and out-gunned, accepting the military defeat which had been inevitable once the federal army had remained loyal to Vargas. Politically, however, the failure of the revolt was very important. It illustrated clearly the need for a successful *coup* in Brazil to win not only the political leaders of the major states, but, above all, the leaders of the federal army, a lesson forgotten again in several later *coup* attempts, but fully understood by those who in 1964 aimed to remove President João Goulart. Clearly, if São Paulo, Brazil's most powerful, richest state, could not successfully defy the central government, no other state had the remotest chance. Nor had any combination of states unless they could carry the army behind them, a factor made even more cogent from the 1930s onwards, when state forces were considerably reduced and the federal army vastly strengthened and better trained and equipped.

October 1932, rather than October 1930, marked the end of the Old Republic, representing the last effort by the *paulista* dominant groups and their allies to regain control of the state apparatus as they had managed to do after 1889. From 1932 onwards the most striking feature of Brazilian politics was now to be an increasing central control and direction, with the states' and regional powers steadily eroded. In the next few years the local politicians were to lose financial control by removal of those inter-state 'export' taxes, so carefully cherished in the 1891 constitution. The states' constitutional powers were to be reduced, their flags burned, and, above all, the state armed forces were to be brought firmly under the control of the federal army. The process of national integration, so feeble until the 1930s, was now to go on apace, headed by Vargas, already so used to central control within his own state of Rio Grande do Sul, but always carried out under the watchful suspicious eye of the federal army command.

The defence of civilian political control had been the positive element in the *paulista* 'constitutional' case, however spurious and narrowly elitist this had been in other respects. The defeat of São Paulo, despite Vargas's ostentatious magnanimity and constitutional gestures, severely weakened the fabric of civilian politics, making easier the way to authoritarian government and increased military influence. It also underlined more sharply the acute need for viable political organizations at the national level to replace the essentially local structure of power which now had been broken. There was need, too, as was fully realized, for new administrative machinery to bear the greatly increased load thrust upon the central government, again a demand which could not be shelved.

Unfortunately, it was easier to see the need than to satisfy it, especially as every attempt at popular political mobilization cut across the system of class control, which remained so strong after as before 1930, just as it also challenged and threatened the newly acquired power and prestige of the military command. The 1930s were, therefore, to see several notable attempts at mass political organization on a national level, but with all of them failing, or being destroyed, by the time the *Estado Novo* was imposed on the country.

The Constituent Assembly and Continuing Crisis

Even before the defeat of São Paulo, Vargas had promised to restore constitutional rule, a promise the *paulistas* had mistrusted and ignored. He had issued an electoral code in February 1932 and had authorized funds for a new system of electoral courts. According to this new code literacy was still to be a condition for voting, but the vote was now to be secret and the electorate was to be greatly extended, in theory at least, by the grant of the vote to women and a reduction of the voting age from twenty-one to eighteen. A commission was appointed to draw up the new constitution and already there was provision for direct representation of professional groups and classes. This was an early indication of the corporatist influence from Europe, later to be so strong, but also a genuine attempt to counter the excessive strength of the state-based political machines.

After the 1932 revolt Vargas, making generous concessions to conciliate São Paulo and reintegrate the state into national life,[15] also quickened the move towards constitutional rule. Elections were fixed for 3 May 1933 with the Constituent Assembly to meet the following November. Political groups and new political parties quickly began to form, but far the most important element was still the old state political cliques. This was clear even in São Paulo, where, although many of its leaders were now in exile, the strongest force was an alliance between the Republican and the Democratic parties, further reflecting the class identity of which the *tenentes* and others had accused them. The new alliance was most ably led by Armando de Salles Oliveira, a brother-in-law of Júlio de Mesquita Filho, editor of the influential newspaper owned by his family, *O Estado de São Paulo*. Mesquita Filho, who had played an important role in the 1932 revolt, was now in Portugal, but the persistent strength and influence of the class he and his paper represented were clearly seen in the backing they were able to give to Salles Oliveira now and in later years. They far outweighed the fragmented groups led by *tenentes*, even the new São Paulo Socialist Party headed by Miguel Costa.

Elsewhere, too, the state parties remained strong, while radical mobilization was everywhere relatively weak. The Communist Party was still illegal and the *tenentes* were badly split in their attitude towards the elections, making only feeble attempts to organize workers' parties of which the most important initiative was Costa's in São Paulo, An *ad hoc* Catholic organization, the Liga Eleitoral Católica, urged the relevance of Catholic social teaching, but much the most important new movement was, significantly, the Ação Integralista Brasileira (AIB), founded in 1932 by Plínio Salgado, a prolific littérateur, who had drafted the manifesto of the Revolutionary Legion in São Paulo and now was to become the leader of the Brazilian variant of European fascism.

The election of the new assembly, on 3 May 1933, went off quietly, confirming in the men returned the hold of the old political class, a fact which Vargas acknowledged when, for example, he now appointed as his personal representative, or *interventor*, in São Paulo the leader of *paulista* bourgeois liberalism, Armando de Salles Oliveira. But even as he tried to conciliate São Paulo, another crisis broke, again illustrating the highly personal nature of local and national politics and the way in which they were interwoven. The new crisis concerned the interventorship of Minas Gerais, still the most heavily populated state and a key factor in national politics. It was the only state whose governor had not been changed after 1930, because of the support which the elderly Olegário Maciel had given to the Vargas movement, and to avoid a confrontation over his succession. In September 1933 that choice had to be faced on the death of Olegário Maciel, at once producing another of the most serious political crises of the decade, the *caso mineiro*, the case of Minas Gerais.

Already in Minas Gerais there had been serious political violence in the months following Vargas's success, with two groups, the PRM (Minas Republican Party) and the newly created Legion of Minas Gerais, both claiming to have supported Vargas, so entitled to his support.[16] Maciel's death brought this rivalry to a head, presenting Vargas with an embarrassing choice between personal friends. The crucial issue was that the Minas affair was not just a question of local political control, but an important element in a long-term bid for the federal presidency involving two of Vargas's closest friends and supporters, Oswaldo Aranha and Flores da Cunha. Aranha had worked ceaselessly to get Vargas into power in 1930 and Flores da Cunha, by refusing to back the *paulistas*, had saved Vargas in 1932: but each was now supporting a different candidate in Minas Gerais, in 1933, as part of his network of clientage and support to help his aims of succeeding Vargas in the presidency the next time round. Flores da Cunha urged the claim in Minas Gerais of the current state Secretary of the Interior, Gustavo Capanema, while Aranha backed Virgílio de Melo Franco, one of the leading *mineiro* plotters in the 1930 revolution and a member of an influential political family, son of Afrânio de Melo Franco, Vargas's Minister of External Affairs. Vargas, clearly, could not satisfy both demands, but to offend either could jeopardize his own chances in the Constituent Assembly's election for the federal presidency and breed dangerous resentment. His answer was to seek a compromise solution, trying to get an alternative candidate acceptable to both parties in the person of Benedicto Valladares, then a relatively unknown *mineiro* politician. The result in later years was to bind Valladares, like many others, directly to Vargas as part of his powerful spreading net of personal patronage and control, but it was also to leave bruised feelings and dangerous rancour among the rival parties.[17]

There is inevitably in clashes such as this *caso mineiro*, with its bitter interchange of caustic notes, charges and counter-charges, and hurried compromises patched up over extended lunches, a strong flavour of parish-pump politics: but the importance of such apparently trivial issues can scarcely be exaggerated, as the bitterness, still so strong in the correspondence, makes clear. There was, it must be repeated, no sharp distinction between local and national politics, with national politics being largely, even in the mid-1930s, a tissue of local alliances built on direct personal relationships. No national issue could provoke the bitterness, passion, and violence of these struggles in São Paulo, Minas Gerais and elsewhere, so that to neglect local politics for the national scene is often to leave the substance for the shadow. The 'cases' of São Paulo and Minas Gerais in these years are, therefore, not just guides to national politics. In a very real sense they are national politics.

Nor, equally important, were they merely short-lived crises, since, despite Vargas's charm and skill and his carefully calculated mollifying gestures, the affair of Minas Gerais left deep resentment. Aranha felt passed over and was hurt, while, on the other side, the Melo Franco family nurtured a sense of being wronged,[18] which was to be an important factor in their siding with the growing opposition to Vargas, as it eventually built up towards 1945 in the form of the UDN (National Democratic Union). The UDN, though ostensibly a democratic opposition to Vargas, was in large measure a heterogeneous coalition of anti-Vargas forces, often, as in this case, based on personal resentment and anger at missing the benefits of patronage.

While this row was brewing, the Constituent Assembly met on 15 November 1933, joined by forty 'class representatives',[19] eighteen from workers' syndicates, seventeen from employers', two from the civil service, and three from the liberal professions. These now came to help the 214 constituent members already elected on 3 May to decide on the constitution and choose a new president, the draft constitution being debated and modified till in July 1934 a compromise document was at last agreed. The version finally promulgated greatly extended the power of the federal government, with much enlarged responsibilities for social and economic policies, but it also tried to limit the personal power of the president by comparison with the constitution of 1891. States' power was, therefore, curbed while providing defences against personalist ambitions of the president, who was, for example, forbidden to sit for a second consecutive term. There was also an attempt to reduce the powers of the major states, providing federal deputies for every 150,000 inhabitants, but only one for every 250,000 after a total of twenty deputies from any one state. In all it was a mixed, eclectic constitution, perhaps most notable for the important new responsibilities it gave to the federal government to intervene on social and economic matters and for its early evidence of the growing corporatist influences from Europe. It was not a constitution of which Vargas much approved, giving less power to the president than the strongly positivist constitution of Rio Grande do Sul to which he was accustomed. In any case the constitution of 1934 was to be short-lived and untested in practice, soon set aside in the general polarization of politics in the next few years and Brazil's move towards authoritarianism and the corporate state.

National Mobilization: Attempts and Failure

In the overall shaping of Brazilian politics much more important than these new constitutional forms were the continuing attempts by various groups to build a genuinely national political force cutting through those family and regional loyalties which, as the cases of Minas and São Paulo showed, were still so all-important. The defeat of São Paulo had left Vargas both stronger and weaker, stronger in his ability to impose terms on the regional politicians, as the Minas crisis showed, but weaker in his growing dependence on the leaders of the federal army, and the army leaders were now from the middle of the decade to become even stronger and more important as political parties of both left and right failed to take hold at the national level. The failure of the left, whether democratic or revolutionary, was particularly important in this respect, since it also marks Brazil off from other countries, such as, for example, Chile in this period, again illustrating the strength and tenacity of the Brazilian ruling class.

The three most important attempts at national organization were the effort immediately after Vargas came to power to form a Revolutionary Legion or National Revolutionary Party, the related, but slightly later, growth of the *Integralista* movement, and the search for an effective socialist solution for Brazil's problems, whether peacefully or by revolutionary action. The failure of all three attempts by the end of the decade illustrates, and largely explains, much of the country's subsequent political development or lack of development.[20]

The Legion

The idea of the Legion was carefully discussed in the early months after Vargas came to power, the debate being chiefly carried on by

Oswaldo Aranha, the brilliant, energetic *gaúcho* politician who had planned the armed conspiracy in 1930, and other civilian and *tenente* leaders.[21] Essentially these represented those elements in the 1930 revolution who wanted not merely a change of government, but a new social and political order. Their discussions also, however, reflected a general disenchantment with representative democracy as it had been practised, or abused, in Brazil, combining a reaction against the corruption and coercion of the Old Republic with the swelling international criticism of parliamentary democracy. So in planning the Legion much use was made of Italian formulations advocating a corporatist state and the programmes and projects elaborated throughout 1931 all reveal the strongly authoritarian, even fascist, tendencies of *tenentismo*. The emphasis is on finding some genuinely Brazilian solution for Brazil's development problems, solving them *brasileiramente*, in a Brazilian way, a reflection of that nationalism which over the last two decades had been finding stronger, more aggressive, expression, as seen in the cultural sphere in modernism and its rejection of derivative imitations and now, increasingly, in economic and political thinking. The Legion, in this respect, is one of the early political expressions of the 'slavophile' tradition in Brazil, and elsewhere in Latin America, resentful of foreign control of the coffee economy and, as was argued, the distortion of Brazil's overall economic development in the interest of a narrow group at home and their allies abroad, concerned, too, with the imposition of unsuitable foreign political models on a country so different in every way from the societies from which they were derived.

One result of this thinking was a strongly elitist, even condescending, strain in the Legion's formulae, rejecting ideas of participation in favour of an authoritarian, fascist-style ideal of mobilization, emphasizing discipline, order, hierarchy, and a closely-knit cell organization, with provision for training and indoctrination at every level, with encouragement of informers and an intelligence network to keep the purity of the movement. But there was, too, a genuine concern for social reform and national regeneration, demanding wider social services and more government responsibility and even renewing earlier *tenente* demands for land reform and the nationalization of land, all part of what Aranha called the 'new era of the moral and material reconstruction of Brazil'.

It is important to appreciate initiatives such as this attempt to build the Legion in order to understand the long authoritarian tradition in Brazil, already so clear in these formulations of the early 1920s, dominant in the *Estado Novo* and more powerful than ever after 1964. The roots of contemporary Brazilian authoritarianism partly spring from nationalist authors of the late nineteenth and twentieth centuries, and these programmes of the first Vargas years. It is, overall, perhaps the most coherent most persistent political tradition in Brazil in so far as it also reflects the stern, paternalistic control of the upper and middle classes. Profoundly concerned, even when it does not use the terminology, with issues of national development and foreign influence, it is, at the same time, convinced that liberal democracy has no real solutions for the nation's problems. In this respect the controversy between the *tenentes* and the *paulista* middle-class liberals is of far more than historical interest. The constitutionalism of the liberals was merely, the *tenentes* believed, a smug phrase to cover a system of narrow class and regional control, their criticism, in this respect, also coming close to much current, and later, criticism, on the left of the allegedly spurious character of liberal democracy in a country like Brazil.

In any case, the Legion was short-lived. It grew strongly for a short time in Rio de Janeiro, São Paulo, and Minas Gerais, with rather less success elsewhere. In Minas Gerais it most closely followed the model of European fascism, its members dressed in khaki shirts and even organizing a 'March on Belo Horizonte'. In São Paulo, under the leadership of Miguel Costa, it had a much more radical tone, appealing to industrial workers and claiming membership of 17,000 at its peak in 1931. Everywhere, however, the story was the same as the Legion, now openly assuming the role of a new National Revolutionary Party, clashed with entrenched local interests and provoked fierce reaction from regional politicians. By late 1931, certainly by the start of the São Paulo revolt, the Legion was a spent force, its leaders and membership going in different directions, absorbed again into the state machine politics from which they had sought to escape. But this sharp failure of the Legion was itself instructive. Once again it revealed the bitter antagonism to any effort to organize a national political movement, while already indicating the facile attraction of fascist models for many of the middle class and their supporters in the armed forces.

Integralism

For many Legionaries the logical move seemed to be towards what was to prove one of the most successful political groupings of the decade, the newly formed *Integralista* movement, the Ação Integralista Brasileira (AIB), formed in 1932 by Plínio Salgado, mainly responsible for the manifesto of the São Paulo Legion. He always claimed great originality for Integralism, emphasizing its indigenous origins, but in many important respects the movement directly aped contemporary European fascism both in its trappings and its content. The AIB adopted the sigma, the sign of the integral, as its emblem, dressed its followers in green shirts, and used a derivative Tupi greeting—'Anaué'. As the movement grew, its strength was demonstrated in mass meetings and well-organized marches through the cities and towns of Brazil, all to underline the discipline, order, and authority of this new national political force, so different, its admirers claimed, from the weakness, corruption, and unprincipled opportunism of previous Brazilian politics.[22]

Highly critical of liberal democracy as a flaccid, inefficient artefact implanted on Brazil and far too easily manipulated, the AIB emphasized organic unity and the strict hierarchical organization of society, demanding radical reform of the whole social, political, and economic system, an integral change based on Salgado's analysis of Brazilian reality. In crusading nationalist tones it attacked international capitalism, but mainly because it was international rather than because it was capitalist. So one of its leading theorists, Gustavo Barroso, in his manual *What the Integralist should know*, demanded nationalization of key industries, the strict control of immigration, and a curbing of the power of foreign bankers. But Barroso also linked his attack to anti-semitism, in works such as *Brazil, Colony of Bankers, The São Paulo Synagogue,* and *Roosevelt is Jewish.*[23] This anti-semitism was for the most part, however, untypical. Barroso, whose mother, called Dodt, came from Würtemburg, was much more anti-semitic than most of his fellow Integralists, more inclined to look to Hitler's Germany rather than to Italy or Portugal for his model. Salgado, by contrast, was altogether more eclectic, admitting influence from Haya de la Torre, Oliveira Salazar, Gil Robles, Charles Maurras and, of course, Mussolini, even though he insisted on the essentially indigenous character of his theories. The anti-semitism of the AIB can, therefore, too easily be exaggerated by accepting the Academician Barroso as its spokesman.

The economic nationalism, on the other hand, found a more responsive audience, quick to blame foreign capitalism for Brazil's current troubles. There was wide support, too, for the plan to create a new centralized banking system and for demands for wider credit for agriculture through a new Ministry of Agriculture and for reform of education, improved public health, and an honest, effective system of public administration. Such calls, constantly repeated in the AIB's publication *A Offensiva,* were its main source of support, far outweighing its relatively marginal anti-semitism, and the programme was publicized with unprecedented efficiency in scores of newspapers linked to the AIB's National Secretariat for Propaganda.

Another very important source of support, associated with the demands for reform, was the insistence on the 'integralization' of all aspects of national life, this being tied to the persistent emphasis on discipline, authority, and clear hierarchical organization. The stern calls for rigorous discipline, order, and dedication to the national cause won wide support among many intellectuals, officers of the armed forces, some of the Brazilian hierarchy, and many prominent laymen. Here, they felt, was an honest, reforming movement, a viable alternative to the Marxist philosophy which they may not have understood, but readily condemned.

One source of support for Integralism was those who reacting against the corruption of the Old Republic and its dependence on foreign financial interests and markets, wanted a party of reform, even of radical change, but who, often out of Catholic sentiment rather than practice or conviction, were unable to accept the atheism associated with communism. Among the more distinguished early supporters of Integralism who later moved to a critical position on the left of the political spectrum was Dom Helder Câmara, subsequently archbishop of Recife and Olinda. The genuine concern for reform and social change among many who in the 1930s looked hopefully to Integralism should not be underestimated.

Based on a cell organization, which linked groups at the district, municipal, state, regional, and national levels, the AIB grew steadily till by late 1937 it had over 4,000 organized cells in about 700 districts and 130 urban districts. An Integralist Chamber of 400 sat at national level, coming under the chief administrative unit, the Chamber of Forty, all personally chosen by Salgado. Despite its claim to appeal to all classes and interests the whole *Integralista* movement was markedly middle class in its composition and tone. There were, for example, no working men in the Chamber of Forty, nor even much indication that the leadership saw working-class involvement as a high priority.[24] Most of the forty were professional men, including government officials, seven members of the armed forces, and nine from commerce and industry. Analysis of its cell membership also shows it to have been a notably elitist organization, appealing, despite its social reform programme, to the interests and prejudices of the middle class or those who perceived themselves as being middle class. There was a large concentration of white-collar workers, professional men, intellectuals, and army officers and the movement also seemed to attract the middle-aged rather than the young, having, for example, little following among university students.[25] Nevertheless, its smartly goose-stepping demonstrations appealed to those who looked for order and discipline, and its motto 'For family, for country and for God' found a ready response among the officer class of the armed forces, many of these being attracted by the AIB's nationalism and its promise to defend that Western Christian civilization with which many officers, then as in later years, strongly, if vaguely, identified. So General Pantaleão Pessoa, chief of staff of the armed forces till 1935, spoke in its favour, as did other army leaders, ordering that Barroso's *Brazil, Colony of Bankers* should be put in the Military Academy library. The always conservative navy was especially favourable to Integralism, so that by late 1937 and the start of the *Estado Novo* the AIB commanded among the officer class of the armed forces far more support than any other political grouping.[26]

Estimates of the Integralists' strength vary greatly. They themselves claimed 180,000 members by late 1934 and 400,000 a year later. Even allowing for wild exaggeration, membership by the end of 1937 seems to have been not less than 250,000 out of a national population of over 40 million.[27] At first sight such numbers seem small, till one again remembers the very small percentage of Brazilians actively engaged in politics, that, for example, less than 2 million men had voted in the crucial election of 1930. Integralism, in other words, essentially, after all the qualifications have been made, a fascist movement, had by late 1937 much the most appeal for the active political elite of Brazil, both civilian and military. Very soon the formal organization was to be broken, as Vargas in 1938 outwitted Salgado and dissolved the AIB together with all other political parties. A little later, by 1945, it was difficult to find anyone willing to admit he had been an Integralist, as the war ended and Allied success instantly made liberal democracy as fashionable as it was opportune. But the influence and the ideas of the AIB still persisted all through the decades of the 1940s and 1950s, nurtured by 'Cold War' propaganda and stirred anxiously by the apparent strength of mass political movements based on popular participation and its alleged 'subversive' challenge to law and order as perceived by many middle-class former Integralists. As late as the mid-1960s Salgado could point to scores of federal deputies and senators who had once been his followers, while in the statements and analysis of Brazil's new, mostly elderly, military rulers there were direct echoes of the AIB's appeal of the 1930s.[28]

The very success of fascist mobilization in this decade and later partly explains the relative failure of the other most notable attempt at political organization in the same years, the effort to build a socialist movement and organize the working class for political action. This again is a highly controversial issue, but fundamental for understanding the shaping of contemporary Brazilian politics. The whole controversy over the degree of class consciousness of the

Brazilian working class and the alleged tension between mere mass consciousness and genuine class consciousness is discussed below (pp. 141–9). So, too, is the concept of social and political control exercised in the interests of a narrow class and the mechanisms by which this is normally brought about. Having, however, already stressed the persistent strength of patronage and clientelism and the strong ties of kinship and local allegiance, and while accepting the negative effect this has, as later argued, on class formation, it is vital to probe deeper. Essentially, these features of Brazilian politics, as of many other societies, are merely the expression of class control, only explicable in terms of social class as the primary political factor. Here, too, in the last analysis is the explanation for the relative failure of popular mobilization in Brazil, a failure clearly underlined and largely determined in the middle years of the 1930s and the advent of the *Estado Novo*.

The ANL

The most important attempt to build a mass political movement of the left before the clamp-down of the *Estado Novo* was the ANL, the Aliança Nacional Libertadora organized in March 1935 as Brazil's first Popular Front movement in accordance with the new policy of the Comintern, as it was to be expressed at the Comintern's 7th International Congress in Moscow in July and August 1935.[29] The Brazilian attempt at Popular Front organization, was, however, short-lived, largely because of a disastrous reversal of policy demanding direct revolutionary action, but, more substantially, because of the strength of opposition which it provoked, a growing reaction which, even without the premature revolt in November 1935, threatened to stifle the move to unite the various forces on the left. This again, however, is a controversial issue, since, for various reasons, it is difficult to estimate how successful might have been a longer effort at popular mobilization.[30]

A major problem bedeviling careful estimates of the capacity of the Brazilian working class to organize politically is that the history of the working class in Brazil, as in so many countries, has not yet been written. The poor rarely leave records of the kind historians seek, and under a system of control and institutionalized coercion they are notoriously reluctant to express class or other grievances directly, often preferring to play the game on the terms dictated to them, however much they resent it. Great care, consequently, must be taken with theories elaborated on the supposed lack of class-consciousness among the Brazilian poor, arguing, in effect, the inevitable weakness of popular radical mobilization. It is true, as often argued, that the Brazilian working class was by the 1930s still relatively small and ill-organized. It was estimated in the 1920 census that the urban working class numbered only about 275,000 and it had only grown to about 700,000 by the middle of the next decade. The slow pace of industrialization and the relatively slack demand for labour also meant that militants could easily be removed, replaced by blackleg workers from the endless supply of cheap labour from the north-east. But such explanations for the failure of the working class to organize and produce its own leaders are insufficient and too easily ignore the many efforts of workers in all parts of Brazil to organize on a class basis from the first years after emancipation and even earlier.

Only now are such early challenges being noted and examined,[31] but it should be remembered that there had been minor strikes in Rio de Janeiro as early as 1858 and increasing signs of unrest in the following years. There was an important rail strike on the Central do Brasil in 1891 and in Recife the stevedores, who with the railwaymen were among the most militant of workers, first organized their union in 1894, staging a serious strike the next year. There were more rail strikes in the north-east and elsewhere in the same year and again in 1901, when factory workers in São Paulo also demanded better pay and conditions. Such stoppages became common, leading in 1901 to the founding in Recife of the Centro Operário (Workers' Centre), which now helped to organize workers' protest more effectively. In 1903 came the biggest demonstration of strength so far with a strike of 25,000 textile workers in São Paulo for twenty days, leading the federal government to pass a law the following year allowing the expulsion of foreign agitators, who were largely blamed for the trouble. That there was some basis for this charge was shown by the forming of the Socialist Party in São Paulo in 1902 with its newspaper in Italian, *Avanti!* It is important to note, however, that the early organization in the north-east was *not* anarchist or encouraged by foreigners, but a much more indigenous development.

In the far south, too, workers were being organized. Five hundred workers in Pôrto Alegre went on strike for thirty-five days in 1905. The movement was spreading, and in 1906, after a further stevedores' strike, there was held the first Brazilian Workers' Congress, marked by fierce argument between anarchists and socialists. Copying the French CGT, socialists now formed the Brazilian Workers' Confederation, with its paper at first again in Italian, *La Parola dei Socialisti*, but issuing the first Portuguese-language socialist paper in 1912, *A Voz do Trabalho*. The Confederation was soon claiming fifty member groups across the country and the growing sophistication of workers' protest was clearly seen in a major railway strike in 1909 against the British-owned Great Western railway, a strike involving 8,600 workers, which paralysed the north-east. The strike was well organized, with effective picketing, collection of funds for strikers' families, and widespread support for the cause of the Brazilian workers against the British owners.

Already, too, the working class was producing its own leaders, dedicated, able to organize their fellows, and, even at this stage, showing considerable class-consciousness in their analysis of the causes of the misery and poverty of so many working people in Brazil. In 1917 came the most serious confrontation so far, with a general strike in São Paulo and other important strikes in Recife, Rio de Janeiro, and other major centres. But such growing activity also brought swift reaction, especially after 1917, when the Russian Revolution quickened the fears of many of the controlling classes, who previously had seemed almost tolerant of growing working-class demands. So in 1922, for example, workers' leaders in Recife were imprisoned and killed, union offices were closed, and everything was done to break the new labour movement, the reaction in the north-east being mainly associated, it seems, with the entry into office of a new state governor in Pernambuco determined to curb workers' militancy.

Such examples serve to qualify the common tendency to dismiss the Brazilian working class as somehow more lacking in class awareness or dedication than their counterparts elsewhere, a view which also too easily allows some theorists to speak of a consequently weak political organization at the popular level as explaining eventual military intervention. This argument is examined later,[32] but it is at least important to notice that even by the 1920s, and even more by the late 1930s, there was already some tradition of working-class activity and an appreciable degree of genuine class-consciousness among Brazilian workers across the country, from Pernambuco to Rio Grande do Sul.

One important feature, however, of the weakness of the left by 1937, as compared, for example, with the influence of the Integralists, was the gap between the working class and the groups which most sought to represent them, most notably the PCB, the Brazilian Communist Party. Here, again, is one of the guides to subsequent political fortunes in Brazil, though still a controversial one, confused by current debate on the role of the PCB and other orthodox Communist parties in Latin America and by lack of hard evidence on certain issues. Before the founding of the Brazilian Communist Party in 1922 there had already been attempts to start a socialist movement. Much of the impetus, as elsewhere in Latin America, came from European groups, especially, as already seen, from the Italians. (The Socialist Party in Italy, founded in 1892, had 33 members in parliament by the turn of the century.) But even as early as 1918 some Communists had met in Rio de Janeiro and in November 1921 a group there accepted the principles of the 3rd International and called a Congress for March 1922, so leading to admission to the Comintern. Several newspapers were produced, including *Movimento Communista, Voz Cosmopólita,* and *A Classe Operária.* By 1925 the party claimed between 350 and 500 members, but it remained largely neglected by the Comintern and had only feeble contacts with the Iuyamtorg Corporation (Prima S/A), the centre for Soviet activities in South America, based first in Buenos Aires, then, after its expulsion in 1931 by the Uriburu government, in Montevideo. After the third National Congress in December 1928 and January 1929 the party began organizing the General Labour Confederation and showed some interest in mobilizing rural workers with a Workers' and Peasants' Bloc. Despite these efforts, however, progress among the mass of workers was slow, with the party split on ideological grounds from other groups on the left.

The most important single gain for the PCB in the early 1930s was its winning of the then most charismatic and popular figure in Brazilian politics, the *tenente* leader, Luís Carlos Prestes. Prestes was still for most, especially younger, Brazilians the legendary, romantic hero who had successfully defied the Bernardes government as he led his Column through the length and breadth of Brazil. In exile in Bolivia and Argentina since 1927 he had read hard and spent long hours debating and analysing the nature of Brazil's problems. While refusing to support the Liberal Alliance, even when his friends João Alberto Lins de Barros and Siqueira Campos flew to Buenos Aires to persuade him, he also was slow in his move towards communism. After the tragic drowning of Siqueira Campos on his return flight from Buenos Aires, Prestes released a manifesto in May 1930, urging his reasons for refusing to help Vargas; but still his position failed to satisfy the PCB, who attacked him in *A Classe Operária* as a 'bourgeois caudillo opportunist'.[33]

By 1935 and the start of the ANL, Prestes had taken the plunge and joined the party. He had already spent time in Moscow and in 1934 was named as head of the movement in Brazil, in the obvious hope that his fame would attract the mass support which previously had been missing. In thrusting Prestes so rapidly into the lead the PCB was, in fact, only underlining what was already, and was to continue, one of its most severe problems, the wide gap between the leadership of the Communist movement and the mass of Brazilian workers whom it sought to represent. Some of the new men, like Carlos Marighela, had roots among the people;[34] others, like Prestes, could communicate with and lead working men; but too many had little or no experience of the lives and condition of the working class with which they sincerely identified and whose interests they sought to advance. One early leader, Honório de Freitas Guimarães, had been educated at Eton during the First World War, disliking it intensely,[35] and others came from similarly privileged backgrounds, which, if they at times helped to provoke reaction, made it extremely difficult to communicate across class boundaries to the Brazilian poor, long schooled in mistrust and suspicion for members of another class, especially when bearing gifts.

The organization of a Popular Front policy in 1935 was, of course, determined less by conditions in Brazil than by the changing demands of Comintern policy derived almost exclusively from Europe. On the other hand, it seemed a more viable alternative than a direct revolutionary strategy, so that the leaders of the ANL ignored the lack of preparation across the country and spoke too lightly of a solidarity of interests of rural and urban workers which had never previously been apparent. Still, there was some hope of success in pulling together all the forces on the left against the growing threat from the right, so apparent in Brazil as elsewhere. In March 1935 the Popular Front movement was launched, the ANL holding its first public rally in Rio de Janeiro on 30 March, during which a young law student, Carlos Lacerda, nominated Luís Carlos Prestes as the honorary leader of the new movement. Several thousand people present roared their approval, but within days the Vargas government showed its reaction by issuing a National Security Law, which later was used against the ANL. The law reflected the popular identification of the ANL with the Communist Party, even though most of its leaders and officials were not Communists and were emphatic in making clear that the ANL was a movement to unite all elements on the left. Of its six main organizers three were civilians and three military officers associated with *tenentismo*, none of them a Communist,[36] but Prestes's statement accepting the honorary presidency, published on 3 May, caused renewed alarm:

> . . . Every honest Brazilian has the profound feeling that national liberation is impossible without the annulment of foreign debts, without the confiscation and nationalization of the imperialist factories, and without the expulsion of the emissaries of imperialist capital from Brazil . . .[37]

The main theme of the ANL, however, was to combat fascism, especially appealing to many middle-class liberals who were alarmed at the growth of the Integralist movement. Its programme, in general terms, was similar to that of other Popular Front movements, especially the Chilean Popular Front, which was formed the following year. It was anti-imperialist and anti-capitalist and urged the need for radical social and economic reforms; but it also sought, like all such movements, to appeal as widely as possible, to be comprehensive rather than radically exclusive. So, for example, Prestes reassured politicians, such as Virgílio de Melo Franco, who nursed grievances against Vargas, but who disliked radicalism even more. To these he emphasized the reformist aims of the ANL, stressing, too, the hostility to foreign imperialists rather than to their allies among the bourgeoisie and landowners in Brazil. But the programme of the ANL made clear its aim to end the *latifúndio* system and introduce genuine agrarian reform, including redistribution of large holdings to the peasantry. It demanded higher wages and better conditions for rural as well as urban labour and constantly, and cogently, attacked the exploitation of Brazil by foreign interests. For most of its short existence, however, the primary aim of the ANL was to win widespread support and build up a national movement capable of winning the political power it needed to put its programme into action.

Like the AIB the ANL sought to build cells across the country, with secretariats at the municipal, regional, and national levels. Cells, each of ten members, were organized locally or along occupational lines, so that by July 1935 and its swift suppression the movement was claiming around 400,000 members. This was certainly an exaggeration, but even a much more conservative estimate of perhaps 100,000 still represents a major leap forward in only a few short months. Most of the membership, as might be expected in the early stages, was middle class or from among white-collar workers, but already, by contrast with the Integralists, for example, there is evidence of increasing working-class support and of working men at times among the leadership of the cells. Predictably, too, it was at the time of its suppression still predominantly an urban movement, but by no means exclusively, and there is again evidence that it was quite rapidly expanding in rural areas and among the rural population.

As earlier with the Legion, and indeed to some extent with the AIB, the ANL varied considerably in different parts of the country, making a somewhat different appeal as circumstances demanded. So in São Paulo it built on the work and organization of the Legion seeking to mobilize working-class support under the leadership of Miguel Costa, who previously had led the *paulista* Legion and now shared the leadership of the ANL in São Paulo with Caio Prado Júnior, one of several radical intellectuals who never compromised despite bitter opposition over long years. Caio Prado Júnior was also an example of the way rich men gave their support, though far more helped the AIB, and some families, like the Guinles, were said to have backed both horses by at the same time contributing to the ANL and the Integralist movement. In Rio de Janeiro there was rather more appeal to middle-class intellectuals and students, while in the south the ANL remained weak, greatly outweighed by the support given to the Integralists. Most of the ANL's success was in the major towns and cities, with particularly marked support in the north-east, both in the towns and the interior. Members of the national directorate toured the north-east from May to July, cheered by large crowds in the coastal cities, as ANL speakers attacked the *latifúndio* system and the inordinate power of foreign financial interests in the region's economy. There were also the first signs of rural guerrilla organization, stimulated by the Communist Party, showing how ready were some of the rural population to respond to the call for political action once they thought there was some chance of success.[38]

It may, ironically, have been these brief signs of support which encouraged the Communist leaders in the ANL to overplay their hand, change their strategy, and lead the movement to disaster, though largely, too, they were reacting to increased repression by the government and to directives from abroad. There always had been those within the PCB who had urged the need for revolutionary action on the grounds that peaceful challenge and change would not be allowed, a view apparently confirmed in the weeks after the ANL was launched, as the government began to enforce its National Security Law to prevent workers' mobilization on the left, while ignoring the activities of the Integralists. The Communist members of the ANL now urged more strongly than ever the need for a more effective, more militant strategy.

The clearest, most dramatic sign of this new line was a manifesto issued by Prestes on 5 July 1935, the anniversary of the *tenentes*' revolt at Copacabana. It had been widely publicized before its release and, amidst a blaze of comment and controversy, pushed the ANL towards confrontation. Previously the programme had been deliberately comprehensive and conciliatory, avoiding the language of class war, concentrating its attacks on Brazil's heavy foreign debt burden and foreign control. Now, under the ringing slogan of 'All power to the National Liberation Alliance', Prestes, with growing pressure from the Comintern, produced a radical programme under nine headings. These included such items as the immediate redistribution of land, without compensation, to peasants and workers. The battle was on, he said, between 'those who would consolidate . . . the most brutal kind of fascist dictatorship' and those who sought 'the national liberty of Brazil with bread, land, and liberty for its people'.

Prestes's awareness of the real issues was, it soon turned out, clearer in important respects than that of the more optimistic and cautious members of the ANL. His manifesto, echoed in the increasingly aggressive columns of the left-wing press, was a defiant challenge to the government repression which he had rightly foreseen. On 12 July, only a week after the manifesto appeared, and the day for which a general strike had been called, police occupied the ANL's offices and the movement was suppressed, once again repeating the now familiar pattern of crushing any class-based challenge as soon as it threatened to become strong. Here, as Prestes had predicted, was the government showing its true colours, still protecting the interests of the old controlling classes and the growing bourgeoisie, being ever more dependent on their goodwill and that of the leaders of the armed forces, who, while favouring the economic nationalism and authoritarianism of the Integralists, deeply feared any genuinely radical challenge.

This persistent apprehension and reaction is the key to understanding why a legal, constitutionally based radical challenge failed both in 1935 and in later years. The most that could be allowed was the formal existence of a radical movement, but never one which seriously threatened the existing order. At any hint of such challenge controls were immediately reimposed, usually with a swift appeal to military power, the pattern in the mid-1930s as again in the early 1960s. But, on the other hand, a direct, violent attack on the system was never really possible, since the working class and their supporters, in the 1930s as in the 1960s, could never effectively counter the institutionalized force commanded by the government, a point strongly underlined as Prestes and his group now swung to their new strategy of direct action.

Support for such strategy soon proved to be very small. Almost the only notable reaction to the repression of the ANL was a march of five hundred men in São Paulo led by Caio Prado Júnior, while Prestes received swift refusals from former *tenente* comrades when now he asked for their help. He and a small group of Comintern agents quickly tried to reshape ANL and PCB cells into revolutionary groups, but there was no firm foundation of training, no adequate provision of equipment, none of the long, careful preparation required to present a realistic challenge. Agents were busy throughout the country, but there was little evidence of popular support. In these circumstances any attempt at revolutionary action was bound to be immature, ill-conceived, and certain of disaster, playing directly into the hands of a government anxious to impose further controls.

In November 1935 that excuse came, in the form of three short-lived, unco-ordinated military risings between Saturday, 23 and Wednesday 27 November in Rio de Janeiro, Recife, and Natal.[29] Both then and in later years the significance of these risings was much exaggerated, with lurid, unsubstantiated accounts of rape and pillage and the vicious murder of fellow officers sleeping in their beds; but such propaganda was more useful to the government than hard analysis of what really occurred. Subsequent evidence suggests that, though made in the name of the ANL, the support for the few Communist and ANL leaders involved stemmed mainly from local issues and immediate, concrete grievances, rather than from commitment to revolutionary strategy. Certainly there was never any serious threat even to local, let alone national, government control, with the risings soon suppressed and the leaders scattered or arrested. But these short outbreaks were more than enough to justify swift government repression not only of ANL members, but, more widely, of anyone alleged to be involved in subversive activity.

It is impossible to calculate accurately the number of those arrested and imprisoned. Communist spokesmen put it as high as 20,000 in the months following the revolts, but even the most sober estimates suggest that the number of political prisoners was at times half this number. In January 1936 was formed the National Commission for the Repression of Communism and as late as mid-1937 it has been calculated that one hundred arrests a month were being made in and around Rio de Janeiro for alleged participation in the events of 1935. Heavy sentences were imposed on the leaders of the revolts and prominent members of the ANL. Agildo Barata, the *tenente* leader, who played the most prominent part in the revolt in Praia Vermelha barracks in Rio de Janeiro, was only released, broken in health, in 1945. Prestes was sentenced to sixteen years and eight months, plus another thirty years for his alleged part in a political murder. Others, too, were given heavy sentences and many PCB members and sympathizers spent long years in gaol or on the prison island of Fernando de Noronha. The radical movement in Brazil was crushed and scattered, driven underground for the next ten years, during the course of which all parties were to be suppressed under the authoritarian constitution of the *Estado Novo*.

Such repression, censorship, and control were the most important result of the fiasco of 1935, a disaster for radical, or even popular, reformist politics, largely provoked by inexperience, miscalculation, and in part by ill-informed directives from the Comintern. But equally important, on the other side, was the mythology born of the 1935 'Communist' risings. The myth of the Communist threat was now immeasurably strengthened, especially in the armed forces, who now celebrated the repression of the revolt with an annual parade and a special decoration for loyal officers involved. Over the years this myth was to grow rather than fade, cultivated in the post-war years of the Cold War, and nurtured by those who, nearly thirty years later, were to repeat the pattern when intervening in 1964 to save Brazil once more from a 'Communist threat'.

The March of Authoritarianism: 1935–37

The swift suppression of the ANL was only one measure of the growing strength, control, and patronage of the state and central government under Getúlio Vargas, a control both tested and further increased at this time by yet another confrontation with regional politicians. Having weathered the crises in São Paulo and Minas Gerais, Vargas was again being faced with a direct challenge, this time from his own state of Rio Grande do Sul, led by Flores da Cunha, its *interventor* from 1930 to 1934 and now, under the new constitution, its governor. Here again the apparently local nature of the crisis should not be allowed to mask the profound importance of this test of strength within the national power structure. Flores da Cunha had saved the provisional government by staying loyal to Vargas in 1932, so preventing Rio Grande do Sul from siding with the *paulistas*. He had been disappointed when his candidate had not been made governor of Minas Gerais in 1933 and he was now working feverishly to build up support across the country for his own candidature to succeed Vargas as federal president in 1938. A strong element in his basis of support in Rio Grande do Sul was his share in the large gambling profits in the state, but much more important was the backing he had as *interventor*, then governor, from the state armed forces. These consisted of the state force, the *Brigada*, about 6,000 men, and over 20,000 *provisórios*, or provisionals. Together these formed the strongest, best-equipped armed force in Brazil until the federal army increased in strength in the *Estado Novo*, and Flores da Cunha was busy buying arms from abroad to establish his military base still more strongly while, at the same time, enlarging his net of clientage and political connection.

While spreading his supporters throughout the country Flores came up against one of the other major national figures to emerge from the 1930 revolution, General Góes Monteiro,[40] the Chief of Staff of Vargas's forces in 1930 and another who had stayed loyal, after some hesitation, in 1932. Góes Monteiro, later to be one of the chief architects of the *Estado Novo* and of the new, more politically conscious and articulate federal army, had recently been appointed Minister of War. He was implacably hostile, like many army officers, to the state armed forces and determined to reduce them to the control of the federal army as a necessary part, as he believed, of the unifying thrust of the new regime. Within a few years he was to come out on top, but early in 1935 he lost the first round when, faced by an obstructionist congressional group controlled by Flores da Cunha, he was forced to resign as Minister of War.

By late 1935 Vargas was grateful for the excitement and confusion arising from the armed revolts in the name of the ANL, since he was already being hard pressed on the succession question and was receiving renewed reports about Flores's buying of arms. In every respect the *gaúcho* leader had the appearance of an 'overmighty subject' poised to make his bid. Appearances, however, were deceiving, since beneath all the byzantine shifts of taut, personal allegiances and bitter recriminations which marked the run-up to the election, the pattern of political power was moving steadily, as it had done ever since 1932, towards the federal government and its allies in the federal army command.

The details of the political manoeuvring in preparation for the presidential election are complex, but in terms of understanding subsequent political developments and the changing distribution of real power between all the groups involved it is most important to note how slowly, but steadily, throughout 1936 and 1937 the federal army leaders managed to strip away the armed support of the state politicians, above all Flores da Cunha in Rio Grande do Sul. The concept of the Brazilian politicians' *dispositivo militar* is discussed below (pp. 295–7, 310), when emphasizing that civilian and military politics can never be separated throughout the country's modern history, since every civilian politician of any importance has had his *dispositivo militar*, a military group to which he can turn for patronage and support when necessary. It is, therefore, a fatal, though quite common, exercise to separate models of civilian and military political behaviour. Briefly, in this case, the army leaders managed to deprive the state politicians of their armed support, winning the most effective single round in the struggle between the centralizing aims of Vargas and the military leaders and the entrenched regionalism of the state politicians.

A key victory was in achieving the replacement in December 1936 of the Minister of War, João Gomes, an officer who in the 1920s had hunted the *tenentes*, and who could not be brought into line with the strategy being urged by Góes Monteiro. Now he was replaced by a man who shared the belief in the need to curb state armed forces and impose army control. This new minister was Eurico Gaspar Dutra, later to succeed Vargas as president in 1945, when, significantly, the other contestant was also to be a military officer. The new appointment was a signal breakthrough for Góes and his group, clearly indicating that, under pressure from the contending presidential candidates, Vargas was already moving more closely under the wing of the army and was more ready to listen to authoritarian, anti-democratic recommendations. Already rumours of *continuismo* filled the air, a continuation only possible under military protection.

The ideology behind the army's demand for greater centralization and control is also discussed elsewhere, as in the class interest which such ideology represented. In 1937, however, the issues were made particularly poignant for the army leaders in the growing danger, as they perceived it, of a victory either to an apparently reformist, demagogic, perhaps even radical candidate, José Américo de Almeida, or to the representative of São Paulo, Armando de Salles Oliveira. Still always in the background, too, was the possible military challenge led by Flores da Cunha and Rio Grande do Sul. The alarming possibility of a joint challenge from Rio Grande do Sul, headed by Flores da Cunha with the *Brigada* and the *provisórios*, and from São Paulo, with all its military and economic power, raised all over again the spectre of 1932, but this time with the states working together. The candidature of José Américo de Almeida, on the other hand, the north-eastern writer dramatically campaigning as the 'people's candidate' and criticizing the class structure and distribution of wealth in Brazilian society, provoked different, but even stronger, fears. Here it seemed was a genuine demand to open up and radically reform society, a move which the army then, as later, was determined to resist.

Early in 1937 Vargas and the army leaders began their move. Already by February it was known that Francisco Campos was preparing an authoritarian constitution on Vargas's request. Campos, leader of the fascist-style Legion in Minas Gerais, was notorious for his doctrinaire authoritarian views and his admiration for European fascism. Much later, in 1964, he was to be joint author of Institutional Act No. 1 after the military *coup*. Now he was preparing a blueprint for another authoritarian regime to be imposed on Brazil. In May, under the pretext of an imminent plot, a 'state of war' was declared and, as one of the first necessary precautions, the powerful armament of the *provisórios* in Rio Grande do Sul was transferred to the federal arsenals, in one move drawing the teeth of the most powerful armed force in Brazil. Swiftly at the same time Vargas and his army allies won command of one of the few other crucial political heights, appointing Góes as Chief of Staff to join his friend, Eurico Gaspar Dutra, Minister of War. The lines were now drawn for the final round, the curbing of the state forces and the control achieved by Góes Monteiro and Dutra being of fundamental political importance in shaping the pattern of state control in subsequent years.

Badly hit by these sudden moves, the states' leaders were caught yet again within a few months. A specious Communist plot, the 'Cohen Plan', which had been drawn up by an *Integralista* army officer, Olímpio Mourão Filho, was announced to the nation on 30 September. Mourão Filho, who again in 1964 was to be one of the leaders of the *coup*, was in 1937 an army captain and, like many others, an ardent admirer of Plínio Salgado. His plan had been devised as part of a theoretical exercise, a scenario for resisting a Communist plot: but now it was announced to the nation by the press and radio as a genuine, bloodcurdling threat to society. Vargas and other leaders solemnly played their part, recalling in particular the horrors so narrowly averted in the 'Communist' risings of 1935. Even allowing, as one must, for the 'imitation effect' engendered in the military and the conservative classes everywhere at this time, as they watched the progress of fascism in Europe and the conflict in Spain, the 'Cohen Plan' still remains a startling piece of duplicity. It was enough, however, to allow another declaration of a 'state of war' and in the key states of Rio Grande do Sul, São Paulo, Pernambuco, and Bahia the job of administering this 'state of war' was carefully entrusted to the regional army commanders. From now on, the government hurriedly declared, the state forces of São Paulo, Rio Grande do Sul, and Pernambuco must be incorporated into the federal armed forces.

In all the excitement and confusion of these years it is easy to miss the significance of these immensely important moves in the real power relations within Brazil. Neither the ANL nor the Communist Party was a real threat to the security and constitutional order of the country. The working class was not yet in a position to offer effective challenge to the entrenched power of the rural oligarchy and the growing urban and industrial bourgeoisie. Nor were the Integralists, despite all their noise, a direct challenge, since they never built up a serious paramilitary force comparable to that which was formed in Germany. Rather, in so far as power grew out of the barrel of a gun, the more immediate confrontation was between different factions of the controlling class. It expressed itself in this period in the struggle between Vargas and his army allies and the state politicians backed by their powerful armed forces, most notably Flores da Cunha. Amidst all the excitement of Integralist goose-stepping and 'Communist' plots this struggle had continued since 1930. The issue was essentially decided in 1932, but not finally determined till 1 October 1937 and the Congressional decision to support the military request for effective powers to counteract the threat of the 'Cohen Plan'. But already the victory had been won, as the states' leaders rightly recognized in refusing to offer any opposition. The extraordinary regional and state power of the Old Republic was now finally broken and the strength of the regional politicians greatly reduced.

Most important of all, in class terms, the defeat of the regional politicians both reflected, and was now itself to accelerate, the growing power and interests of the centralizing, urban, industrial bourgeoisie. The rule of coffee was still long to continue, but the way was now open for that enormous strengthening and enlarging of the central government and the Brazilian state apparatus which was to characterize the *Estado Novo*. Working within the military ideology of development and economic nationalism, under the strict control of an authoritarian regime, new interests were now to emerge, nurturing the rising industrial bourgeoisie at the expense of other classes. Working-class mobilization had been crushed in 1935 and the rural oligarchy brought to heel by the end of 1937. The way was now open for the *Estado Novo*, directed by Vargas and the handful of civilian supporters of authoritarian rule who had recently gathered around him. They, in turn, were dependent on the goodwill of the men who really controlled the system, Góes Monteiro, Eurico Gaspar Dutra, and their military colleagues, who, as will be seen, consciously or otherwise were now to defend and promote the interests of Brazil's new industrial bourgeoisie.

The Coup

Once the real issues of power had been decided the formal moves towards authoritarian government came quickly and easily, with no more than a token protest. The constitutional changes already prepared by Francisco Campos were ushered in with a predictable show of unanimity by the heads of the army and navy. Plínio Salgado, moving in a daze of self-congratulation at the apparent success of his own ideas, agreed to give Integralist support. He found himself rather startled in being, it seemed, outflanked on the right by Campos and by figures such as Filinto Müller, the chief of police, who like Campos overtly favoured fascism and who was to play a prominent role in politics over three decades later in another military-led regime. Salgado spoke with Vargas, was reassured by him and by General Newton Cavalcanti over the future role of the Integralists, and on 1 November headed the march of '50,000 Greenshirts' from Praça Mauá through the city. Reports from across Brazil confirmed the support available for a continuation by Vargas, including the report from the north-east by yet another man to figure prominently after 1964, the later governor of Guanabara, Negrão de Lima.

It was then only a matter of pulling the levers, as Góes Monteiro openly advocated a change of regime and the Minister of Justice, Macedo Soares, resigned, to be replaced on 9 November by Francisco Campos. Campos was accompanied by, among others, his young protégé and fellow *mineiro* Carlos Medeiros Silva, who had already worked with Campos in 1936, when Campos was Secretary of Education in the Federal District. Again, almost three decades later the wheel was to come full circle as Medeiros Silva was in his turn to become Minister of Justice under the Castello Branco government, again introducing an authoritarian, centralizing constitution in January 1967.[41] Already, in other words, the pattern was being shaped and the seeds of future authoritarian control were being sown.

The *coup* was all set for 15 November, the anniversary, ironically, of the Brazilian Republic, but, under pressure from Filinto Müller, Vargas agreed to jump the gun and bring in the *Estado Novo* on the wet dismal morning of 10 November 1937. For the next seven and a half years Brazil was to experience the first of its periods of markedly authoritarian government, conducted increasingly on behalf of the industrial bourgeoisie, eager for expansion. It was to be a period, as again in the later years of military-dominated government, of coercion and repression by a regime anxious for 'modernization' and 'development', but understanding these aims in terms of narrow class interest. The new apparatus of the Brazilian state was now to be further shaped and, at the same time, tightly controlled by the industrial bourgeoisie in close collaboration with the armed forces' leaders, eager for import substitution and fully aware of the need to control all other social forces, above all the urban industrial working class.

The pendulum had now swung completely, from the revolution of 1930, to bring in the people's candidate, to the *coup* of 1937, to exclude the electorate, squash the presidential election, destroy political parties, and impose an authoritarian corporatist constitution backed by the force of the greatly strengthened federal army and an ever more powerful state machine. Here, in the subdued silence which accepted the *Estado Novo*, rather than in the popular, street-backed enthusiasm which had hailed the Liberal Alliance, was the pointer to the political future of modern Brazil.

Notes

1 On the popularity of the Vargas movement see Nogueira Filho, op. cit., II, 403–7, 438; Silva, *A Grande Marcha*, 401–7; and the references in Flynn, op. cit., ed. Carr, 69 note 19.
2 The subtitle of Skidmore's valuable study, T. E. Skidmore, *Politics in Brazil 1930–1964. An Experiment in Democracy* (New York, 1967).
3 See, in this respect, R. Miliband, *The State in Capitalist Society* (London, 1969), 21. 'Capitalism . . . can produce, or . . . can accommodate itself to, many different types of political regime'. Also ibid., 8, note 1, 'the forms of the bourgeois state are extremely varied, but in essence they are all the same. . . .'
4 See on this the discussion in Boris Fausto, 'A Revolução de 1930' in Nunes Dias *et al*, op. cit., 255–84. Having noted the dominance of the coffee-exporting interests, Fausto stresses the relative lack of coherent opposition from the industrialist camp in a social system which was reflected in the Liberal Alliance. The Alliance failed to give clear expression to industrialists' and others' demands. But the industrialist lobby was strong within the heterogeneous coalition and was to find more confident expression later.
5 Fausto, among others, sees the period from 1930 to 1934 as characterized principally by a struggle between the *tenente* group and those who previously had held power, with Vargas balancing in between both.
6 See Flynn, op. cit., ed. Carr, 90.
7 ibid., 89–90.
8 On the São Paulo revolt see the account in English in Dulles, op. cit., 83–116. Also Carneiro, *História das Revoluções Brasileiras*, II, 396–413; Hélio Silva, *1932: A guerra paulista* (Rio de Janeiro, 1967); Nogueira Filho, op. cit.; and Euclydes Figueiredo: *Contribuição para a História da Revolução Constitucionalista de 1932* (São Paulo, 1954).
9 It is easy to exaggerate the capacity of the *Brigada*, but they were *relatively* well-equipped, and were previously under the direction of the Riograndense Republican Party leaders. Estimates of the provisional forces put them as high as 20,000. Flores da Cunha was later to have his political ambitions frustrated and was to quarrel with Vargas. His removal from the head of Rio Grande do Sul in October 1937 was an important step towards the centralization of power which was pursued under the *Estado Novo*.
10 The revolt brought together all sectors and factions of the *paulista* bourgeoisie, both those involved in the coffee export economy and those who favoured industrial development. The explicitly class constitution of the revolt is therefore rather confused, with a quasi-nationalist sentiment temporarily overriding divisions within the *paulista* bourgeoisie. Fausto, op. cit., 278, stresses how the revolt brought together *all* elements of the *paulista* bourgeoisie on essentially *political* grounds. The rallying cry against 'dictatorship' had little objective foundation, since Vargas had already made promises of 'constitutional' government, which, as his private correspondence reveals, he intended to keep. The *paulistas* refused to believe him.
11 On the role of industry see especially Clovis de Oliveira, *A Indústria e o Movimento Constitucionalista de 1932* (S. Paulo, 1956).
12 One of the most ingenious, if scarcely the most lethal, of these contributions was that of a rather droll Englishman, who produced a modification of the rattle (*matraca*) used by more exuberant soccer supporters. This produced a reasonable imitation of machine-gun fire and was, it seems, used with

enthusiasm by poorly armed *paulista* troops to keep their federal counterparts cowering within their trenches.

13 João Alberto introduced a number of measures favouring the working class of São Paulo. See details in Flynn, op. cit., ed. Carr, 89–90 and Fausto, op. cit., 280. Part of the reaction against him was because of the bourgeois perception of him as inclining towards socialism, and even tolerating Communists. See Nogueira Filho, op. cit., II, 587.

14 Flynn, op. cit., 93. Miguel Costa was one of the foremost representatives of the more radical wing of *tenentismo*. His combination of head of the Revolutionary Legion of São Paulo with command of the Força Pública deeply alarmed the controlling groups among the *paulista* bourgeoisie, causing them to join ranks against him and against Vargas. It is here that the class nature of the *paulista* reaction is most clearly seen.

15 He had to protect the 'interests of São Paulo', including those of the coffee-exporters. See Fausto, op. cit., 278–9. See, too, Vargas's statement to the *paulistas* even before the fighting had ended, 20 September 1932, in Getúlio Vargas, *A Nova Política do Brasil*, 11 vols. (Rio de Janeiro, 1938–47), II, 90–1.

16 For some details of the Minas crisis and the tension between the PRM and the Legion, with further references, see Flynn, op. cit., 98–105.

17 For one account of how Valladares was chosen see his own memoirs, Benedicto Valladares, *Tempos Idos e Vividos, Memórias* (Rio de Janeiro, 1966), 36–60. See, too, Lourival Coutinho, *O General Góes Depõe . . .*, 2nd ed. (Rio de Janeiro, 1956), 252; Carolina Nabuco, *A Vida de Virgílio Melo Franco* (Rio de Janeiro, 1962), 87–8; and Alzira Vargas do Amaral Peixoto, *Getúlio Vargas, Meu Pai* (Pôrto Alegre, 1960), 96.

18 See Alfonso Arinos de Melo Franco, *Um Estadista da República*, 3 vols. (Rio de Janeiro, 1955), III, 1505–6.

19 Vargas laid great stress on these 'class representatives'. See his speech at the opening of the constituent assembly, 15 November 1933. Vargas, op. cit., III, 33.

20 Fausto, op. cit., 276–84, argues cogently that the particular shaping of the Brazilian state and its relationship to the working class required the suppression of all other attempts at political expression, whether through *tenentismo*, Integralism, or the National Liberation Alliance.

21 See, in particular, Flynn, op. cit., 63–105.

22 The best analysis in English of the Integralist movement is in R. M. Levine's meticulously researched study, *The Vargas Regime. The Critical Years, 1934–1938* (New York, 1970), especially 81–100. The most enlightening source for Integralist ideology is still Salgado's own writings, particularly *O Integralismo perante a Nação*, 3rd ed. (Rio de Janeiro, 1955) and *Enciclopédia do Integralismo*, 11 vols. (Rio de Janeiro, 1957–61). See, too, the writings of other Integralist theorists, such as Gustavo Barroso. There is useful information in the work of Olbiano de Melo, himself once an Integralist, *A marcha da revolução social no Brasil* (Rio de Janeiro, 1957). Also see Hélgio Henrique Trindade, 'Plínio Salgado e a revolução de 30: antecedentes', in *Revista Brasileira de Estudos Políticos*, 38 (1974), 9–56, and 'A Ação Integralista Brasileira: aspectos históricos e ideológicos', *Dados*, No. 10 (1973), 25–56.

23 Levine, op. cit., 89.

24 This second point is the more important. Lack of working-class membership at the top was to be expected, but the main emphasis in Integralist mobilization always remained among more middle-class groups. There was some appeal to a certain section of the urban working class, but the official member-

ship figures, implying wider support, were inflated. Despite the claims based on the marches in Rio de Janeiro and elsewhere, the main support for Integralism remained among the professional classes and the bourgeoisie. See Levine, op. cit., 99.

25 It did, however, attract a substantial number of university teachers and intellectuals.

26 The links with Integralism are therefore an important part of the history of authoritarianism and corporatism among the officer corps of the armed forces.

27 Levine, op. cit., 95.

28 There was a striking number of ex-Integralists or sympathizers in, or associated with, the post-1964 regime, especially in ARENA, where men such as Filinto Müller and Raimundo Padilha survived as prominent political figures.

29 Levine, op. cit., 61. He provides a good analysis of the ANL and the insurrections of November 1935, but seems to make unnecessarily heavy weather of '. . . what prompted the PCB to act largely unprepared . . .' The Popular Front strategy, as initially conceived, was the only feasible one at the time. The main puzzle, as Levine also acknowledges, is why there was the sudden switch, within such a short time, to revolutionary insurrection.

30 On the ANL and the PCB (Brazilian Communist Party) more generally, see the account in Dulles, op. cit., and, in particular, Ronald H. Chilcote, *The Brazilian Communist Party. Conflict and Integration. 1922–1972* (New York, 1974). Also, Astrojildo Pereira, *A formação do P.C.B.* (Rio de Janeiro, 1962); Oswaldo Peralva, *O Retrato* (Rio de Janeiro, 1962); Agildo Barata, *Vida de um Revolucionário: Memórias* (Rio de Janeiro, n.d.); Affonso Henriques, *Vargas, o Maquiavélico* (S. Paulo, 1961) and *Ascensão e Queda de Getúlio Vargas*, 3 vols. (Rio de Janeiro, 1966); Leôncio Basbaum, *História Sincera da República*, vol. III (São Paulo, 1962).

31 One interesting reminder of this is the account based on the reminiscences of Manoel do Ó, a militant worker in Pernambuco, who died in 1969 aged one hundred: Manoel do Ó, *100 Anos de Suor e Sangue. Homens e Jornadas da Luta Operária do Nordeste* (Petrópolis, 1971). See, more generally, M. Vinhas, *Estudos sôbre o Proletariado Brasileiro* (Rio de Janeiro, 1970); E. Dias, *História das Lutas Sociais no Brasil* (Rio de Janeiro, 1962); Edgard Leuenroth, *Anarquismo Roteiro da Libertação Social* (Rio de Janeiro, 1963); José Oiticica, *Ação Direta* (*Meio Século de Pregação Libertaria*) (Rio de Janeiro, 1970).

32 See P. Flynn, 'Class and Politics in Brazil', *New Society*, vol. 21, No. 518 (August 1972) and 'Class Clientelism and Control . . .'. Also see, in particular, Florestan Fernandes, *Sociedade de Classes e Subdesenvolvimento* (Rio de Janeiro, 1968) and *The Negro in Brazilian Society* (New York, 1969). The work currently being done in São Paulo, especially in CEBRAP (Brazilian Centre for Analysis and Planning), is throwing important new light on the development of the Brazilian working class and its incorporation into the political system.

33 Levine, op. cit., 60. For the sources on the early shaping of the PCB see the works already cited (above, notes 30–1).

34 For Carlos Marighela see below (pp. 409, 412–18, 443). He was the son of a negress mother and an Italian immigrant father.

35 Levine, op. cit., 63–5.

36 ibid., 66–7.

37 ibid., 68.

38 The appeals, in the north-east, and their allegedly disappointing response,

are well worth further investigation. ANL speakers emphasized the degrading conditions in which so many north-easterners lived and worked, contrasting them with the wealth and power of the landowners. Levine speaks of the relative failure of such appeals (op. cit., 78), but the tour was only a very short one. It was perhaps premature to dismiss it by referring simply to renewed federal government interest in the north-east and the traditional 'political apathy' of the population. The more puzzling issue still, however, is why Sissón and other ANL leaders, after this experience, should have called for armed revolution.

39 Levine again provides the best account in English: op. cit., 100–24.

40 See his reminiscences as set out in Lourival Coutinho, *O General Góes depõe,* 2nd ed. (Rio de Janeiro, 1956). A careful study of the political career of Góes Monteiro, both in military and civilian politics, is badly needed.

41 See below, p. 354.

1937–45

5 The *Estado Novo:* Corporatism and the Industrial Bourgeoisie

The Political Watershed

One of the more bizarre ceremonies which marked the start of the *Estado Novo* was the solemn public burning in Rio de Janeiro of the flags of the twenty states of the federation. It was a self-conscious performance in which Francisco Campos proudly proclaimed the virtues of the new regime and underlined his own authoritarian views and the firm centralizing priorities of the constitution which he had drafted. The wheel, it seemed, had now turned fully, from the politics of the Old Republic, designed to give maximum autonomy to the states, to this unified, tightly organized Brazil, which Campos in 1937, as again in 1964, was the first to introduce in new legislation. But the smouldering flags, though few people realized it at the time, marked one of the major watersheds of modern Brazilian politics, more important than the noisy, dramatic arrival of Vargas in 1930, even if his success had seen the start of the change which now was accelerating, and more important than the apparently major switch to party government in 1945. This latter marked a change in style rather than content, whereas the *golpe* of 1937, like that of 1964, expressed a major, qualitative change in the substance of politics, introducing new priorities and heralding the arrival of new political forces.

In part the *Estado Novo* was, as already argued, an *ad hoc* political device to prevent the success of either the *paulista* candidate, Salles Oliveira, or the more demagogic José Américo de Almeida. Partly, too, in this sense, it represented the growing alarm of leaders of the armed forces at the possible return to power of *paulista* civilian groups who had been defeated in 1932. It also reflected the general international disenchantment with democratic forms and the growing commitment to authoritarian corporatism, especially, many believed, as a viable alternative to communism. For many, again, it was a happy solution to the uncertainties of politics at a time when the Western world was moving rapidly towards confrontation and war.

All these interpretations can be defended, as can the view that the new regime was the logical outcome of those centralizing tendencies evident in Brazil from at least 1930 and now made possible by the success of Góes Monteiro and other army leaders in curbing the power of the state armed forces, a victory clearly seen in the humbling of Flores da Cunha in Rio Grande do Sul. But the real importance of the *Estado Novo* went beyond these factors, though all in varying degrees contributed to it.[1] Its significance was, rather, that through the new centralized machinery which was being created, through the political power of the strengthened federal army, and through the enlarged personal role of Getúlio Vargas, a social class was now trying to establish an hegemony which was to be central to the whole formation of the Brazilian state in the next three decades. That class, essentially the industrializing bourgeoisie centred in São Paulo, was too weak to maintain control by means of a liberal democratic political system. Its answer, notably successful until 1945, was to exert its influence through state-directed corporatism, combining tight ideological control with a pervasive net of corporatist labour and social legislation, requiring for this purpose the vigorous strengthening and development of the Brazilian state apparatus.[2]

Despite his promises to diversify the economy after 1930 and to break the stranglehold of coffee, Vargas had not been able to introduce such changes. Coffee had remained the core of Brazil's wealth, with the liberal democratic framework retained, despite its evident weakness and flaws, as the political expression of a laissez-faire economic liberalism which resisted the calls for tighter controls and protection, which grew stronger as the decade advanced. The heart of the problem, as so often in modern Brazilian politics, lay in São Paulo, producing a tension which still has been insufficiently explored. Briefly, this was that ever since 1930 and indeed for longer, there had been growing disagreement between those elements in São Paulo who demanded continuing government support for the coffee-based export economy and those who vigorously urged the need to push Brazil further and faster towards industrialization, a road which would require firm government intervention in the economy, therefore, greatly increased central control with all the means necessary to impose it.[3] What, in short, was being demanded was an abrupt, decisive shift in economic policy, dictated from above, enforced by a central government willing to embark on a degree of state control which could only be possible by abandoning the form of liberal democracy practised and enjoyed by the *paulista* coffee magnates and their allies in the Old Republic.[4]

The paradox, in other words, was that an apparent defeat of São

Paulo or, in effect, of the coffee interests reflected in that old liberal democratic system championed in 1937 by Salles Oliveira, was in reality a victory for a vigorous new social class, again centred in São Paulo and championed by new men such as the industrialist Roberto Simonsen.[5] The *Estado Novo* was a major watershed in that it now saw the full emergence in Brazil of an industrial bourgeoisie, both creating and seizing in the next few years a modern, centralized bourgeois state, which they were to continue to control and use for their own purposes.[6] 1945 saw a change of style, with the dropping of Vargas and a response to new pressures, mostly from the United States;[7] but essentially the system after 1945, though in new forms, continued unchanged. In this sense, the *Estado Novo*, though much under-estimated and often passed over by historians eager to reach the more 'normal' years of multi-party government, was the kernel of modern Brazil and one of the guides to the years following that other major *coup* of 1964, again to be introduced by the pro-fascist Francisco Campos, and again leading eventually to a major political shift, this time of power not to the 'national', but much more explicitly to the international, interests of multinational companies and their political support groups in Brazil.

Some of the struggles and intra-elite rivalries have already been indicated. In terms of the political shaping of modern Brazil, however, it is important to note that the economic crisis which arose in 1937 was not in itself enough to explain the *coup* of 10 November.[8] The *Estado Novo* resulted, rather, from that conjuncture of changing economic circumstances and the new political possibilities allowed by those shifts in power already described, above all the signal victory of the federal army in controlling for the first time the armed power of the state forces and the fact that there was in Getúlio Vargas precisely the man needed to direct this new political experiment.

The Role of Getúlio Vargas

It is vital to understand this conjuncture in order to appreciate the full significance of the *Estado Novo* and how, in particular, it relates to the formation of the bourgeois state in Brazil's more recent corporatist experience. It is especially necessary to understand the key personal role of Vargas, as one who fitted in both with the centralizing aims of the industrial bourgeoisie and the newly dominant federal army, but who also retained elements of positivist concern for the working class in a political tradition which he was to develop towards the end of the *Estado Novo* and beyond.

All accounts of Vargas, except the best, that of his daughter

Alzira,[9] present him as a phlegmatic figure of opaque inscrutability, a cold, calculating manipulator strangely lacking in what are perceived to be the more typically Brazilian qualities of spontaneity and fiery enthusiasm. But this is not the picture which emerges from a careful reading of his correspondence and it is an image still harder to reconcile with the passion of his death note or, still more, with the manner of his dying. How then does one square the public image with the man who emerges in his letters, conversations, and the deep affection of his life-long friends such as Oswaldo Aranha?

Much of Vargas's apparent deviousness obviously arose from political necessity, particularly, in the early years, from the need to conciliate rival elements among his own supporters, who could all claim to have helped him to victory.[10] It was a difficult, often perilous, balancing trick which could easily leave both sides embittered, as it did conspicuously in the Minas Gerais succession in 1933. Eventually the strain became too great even for Vargas; but for years he managed to hold together an intensely personal system based on clientage and direct loyalties, while managing to contain both civilian and military pressures. In so successfully riding the political storms no other Brazilian politician has yet shown such skill and adroitness.

One clue to this ability, which both helps in understanding the *Estado Novo* and in demythologizing the enigmatic Vargas so often presented, is always to remember that when Vargas came to power in 1930 he was already forty-seven years old, a mature politician formed in Rio Grande do Sul, where political allegiances were intense, politics were fierce and bloody, and survival extremely difficult. Unfortunately, almost all interpretations of Vargas discuss him in terms of his experience after 1930,[11] or even present him almost exclusively as the 'populist' politician of his last years in office, comparing 'Getulista' populism with that of, say, Perón in Argentina or Gaitán in Colombia, an emphasis which makes much of Vargas's career all the more difficult to analyse.

Starting, instead, at the other end, one should remember that in Brazil, as in many federal systems, one of the severest challenges for politicians is always the transition from local and state politics to the wider, altogether different, demands of national government. Local success, prestige, and a soundly established local base are a necessary springboard to the national level, but often in Brazil, as, for example, in the United States, the consummate local or regional politician finds himself floundering when cut off from this base, perhaps discovering that the qualities, skills, and techniques so necessary in regional politics have little appeal, are irrelevant, or even a positive disadvantage, once he has stepped outside his own environment.

Conspicuous examples in Brazil in later years were Jânio Quadros, full of panache and vigour in São Paulo, but stumbling and uncertain in Brasília, or Francisco Julião, perfectly attuned to the tone and mood of the north-eastern Peasant Leagues, but so far identified with that region as never to have been credible as a genuinely national figure. The two outstanding successes, on the other hand, were Juscelino Kubitschek, moving with ease from Belo Horizonte to Rio de Janeiro, fitting happily both in style and content the political demands of the 1950s, and, above all, Getúlio Vargas. Both Vargas and Kubitschek were examples of that frequent, but insufficiently noted, phenomenon, politicians who drive, albeit often unconsciously, with their eyes in the rear-view mirror,[12] and in the case of Vargas in the late 1930s, as of Kubitschek in the 1950s, it was important that their early experience so closely fitted current national demands. By the start of the *Estado Novo* these were effectively the call from the industrial bourgeoisie and the more important army leaders for an authoritarian, quasi-paternalist, centralized system to defend and promote specific interests, a call which Vargas, with his long experience in Rio Grande do Sul, could easily echo.

The politics of Rio Grande do Sul were both similar to and markedly different from those of the rest of Brazil,[13] producing an intensity of involvement and a sophistication of party organization and control not found elsewhere. Other states had one dominant republican party, but Rio Grande do Sul was split between the Republican Party, headed by the state boss, Borges de Medeiros, and the rival Aliança Libertadora, under Assis Brasil. Factional and party loyalties were fierce and the state's recent history was stained by bitter political feuds and savage civil wars in 1835–45, 1893–95, and, more recently, throughout 1923. In the bloody struggle of 1893–95 conservative estimates of casualties listed about 12,000, or about 12 per cent of the total state population.[14] The state's politics, in particular, had been sharply influenced from the last years of the Empire by a determined political leader, Júlio de Castilhos, who later dominated the Rio Grande Republican Party, laying down an unequivocal party line as editor of the official paper, *A Federação*. This reflected the strong Comtean positivist influence on Castilhos and the whole Republican movement in Rio Grande, bringing to its politics an authoritarian centralist structure more inflexible than that of other states. Under Castilhos's influence, largely drawing on Comte's *Appel aux conservateurs*, a state constitution was developed under which the single legislative chamber was limited to approving the budget, while the state president had wide executive powers to pass decrees on all non-financial matters and could be re-elected indefinitely, provided he won three-quarters of the total vote. This indefinite re-election provided an opportunity for *continuismo* and a concentration of power and patronage which other states' constitutions aimed to limit, and was to be the immediate cause of the *gaúcho* civil war in 1923, when Borges de Medeiros, the successor to Júlio de Castilhos as state political boss, had himself re-elected for the fifth time.

One of the central features of *gaúcho* politics was this strong centralized system controlled by one man, enjoying wide executive power and only loosely responsible to the legislature, a system which sought to enshrine the Comtean aims of elitist conservatism combined with a narrowly defined concern for 'progress'. It was this tradition into which Vargas was born in 1883 and which his family and their friends, such as the Aranhas, fought fiercely to protect. This was the political philosophy he absorbed through the skin as a young *gaúcho* politician and affirmed in later years as a loyal supporter of Borges de Medeiros, whom in 1928 he succeeded as president of Rio Grande do Sul.[15] It was, moreover, to this tradition that he referred, however implicitly, after arriving in Rio de Janeiro in 1930 as a mature, seasoned politician. Vargas never stopped learning all through his career, but, equally, he never forgot his early formation in Rio Grande do Sul.[16] Here was a political model eminently suited to the needs of the new centralizing bourgeoisie after 1937 and fully endorsed by the leaders of the armed forces, the most important of whom had themselves been shaped in part by that same *gaúcho* tradition.

The two most important army leaders were those already mentioned, Góes Monteiro and Eurico Gaspar Dutra.[17] Both grew steadily in stature and influence throughout the 1930s till Dutra succeeded Vargas as federal president in 1945, largely through the help of Góes Monteiro, and both had strong links with Vargas and other prominent *gaúcho* politicians, including the members of the so-called 'Generation of 1907'. The name of the group derives from the fact that four of its members had graduated from the law school in Pôrto Alegre in 1907 and 1908, Vargas, João Neves da Fontoura, Firmino Paim Filho, and Maurício Cardoso, and had started their careers in 1907 as members of the 'Castilhista Student Bloc'.[18] The others in the group were Flores da Cunha, the oldest, born in 1880, who saved Vargas in 1932, Oswaldo Aranha, the youngest, born in 1894, who stayed close to Vargas at every point in his career, despite their many disagreements, and Lindolfo Collor, the first Minister of Labour after 1930, who laid down the guidelines for the new social and labour legislation.[19] The early association of these young men, who were to be so important in national politics under Vargas, was widened in their contact within the 'Castilhista Student Bloc', an electoral grouping formed in 1907, to which also belonged two young cadets at the recently established military academy in Pôrto Alegre, Pedro Góes Monteiro and Eurico Gaspar Dutra. There was in all of the debate of these young men a strongly nationalist reformist strain, clearly evident, for example, in the elegant speeches of Aranha from his student days on. The persistent contact between Vargas, this *gaúcho* civilian group, and some of the most able military leaders should, therefore, be remembered when examining the shaping of politics in the Vargas years, particularly in the *Estado Novo*. The broadly 'Castilhista' model to be followed by Vargas was, in other words, already well known and attractive to those who now guided the nation's politics.

In discussion of these early, persistent influences on Vargas it has sometimes been pointed out that, while Vargas started after 1930 with a government heavy with *gaúchos*, he soon spread his patronage more widely, so that by 1934, for example, there was only one *gaúcho* in the cabinet.[20] But this, it should be noted, was the direct result of a specific crisis, the resignations preceding the São Paulo revolt of 1932, losses which Vargas fought fiercely to prevent. Meanwhile *gaúchos* continued to hold many of the lesser, but still vitally important, posts and Vargas's personal correspondence throughout the 1930s, and beyond, shows how closely he maintained contact with his native state and how strong were its influences. The *gaúcho* tradition is seen both in the authoritarian concentration of power in the executive and, at a different level, in the concern for 'progress' and a consciousness of the so-called 'social question', both of which, in varying forms, were to be important in the political system headed by Vargas.

Lindolfo Collor and the Incorporation of the Working Class

In terms of this second element in the shaping of politics after 1930 one of the most important *gaúcho* influences was undoubtedly Lindolfo Collor, appointed by Vargas as the country's first Minister of Labour. It was he who began to impose the pattern of industrial relations and labour control which was to characterize the relations between the working class and the state over the next three decades, introducing the process of the incorporation or 'co-optation' (*cooptação*) of the urban, and later rural, working class into a system where conflict was carefully damped down and control effectively imposed under the ostensible guise of class consensus.[21] The need for such control in relation to their own class interests was early seen by the leaders of those industrialists who were to come out on top by 1937, men such as Roberto Simonsen, or the self-made Italian immigrant tycoon Francisco Matarazzo,[22] so that, while they preached the virtues of inter-class harmony and consensus, some *paulista* employers operated a blacklist against workers thought to be 'fermenters of indiscipline', and used intimidation, backed by police action, to break any attempt at a strike.[23] Despite his sound intentions Collor after 1930 had begun to provide just the kind of controlled system the industrialists and employers required, and the process was now to be speeded up from 1937 under the much more explicitly corporatist constitution of the *Estado Novo*.

The origins of Brazilian corporatism still have not been studied sufficiently, but, again, an important part of the answer lies in Rio Grande do Sul and the translation of its experience to the national level, in large measure through Collor.[24] There was already in that state considerable experience in the control not only of the rural, but also of the urban, vote, with already a concern for the political behaviour of the urban working class hardly paralleled even in São Paulo or Rio de Janeiro.[25] Electoral turn-out was consistently high in sharply contested elections and *gaúcho* politicians were already developing for the urban electorate 'populist' appeals of the kind that were to be so strongly developed later. Collor, as principal author of the Liberal Alliance programme of 1929–30, was fully aware that the 'social question' could not be left to the police. It is difficult to assess his position accurately, since he left office in March 1932 together with other *gaúcho* politicians who broke with Vargas, but he had already in important respects pointed the way to the pattern of industrial relations of later years. Collor was an educated, cosmopolitan figure and the only member of the 'Generation of 1907' who was not a lawyer, having been trained first in pharmacy, then in social science. He had already written a study of Garibaldi and his time in Brazil[26] and was co-founder of the Instituto Histórico e Geográfico do Rio Grande do Sul in 1921 and from 1923 onwards the editor of *A Federação*. He was a protestant, the son of German parents,[27] and his knowledge of German, his background in the social sciences, and his time as a federal deputy on the Foreign Relations Committee of the Chamber have all been cited as in part explaining his unusual knowledge of European corporatism and his concern for social and labour issues.[28] He was the obvious choice for heading in 1930 the new Ministry of Labour, Commerce and Industry, popularly known as the 'Ministry of the Revolution', and he quickly introduced new labour legislation, which, while often ineffective in practice as a means of protecting workers' rights, was a most important move towards federal government involvement in this sphere and, more significantly, towards greater government control of the working class. In December 1930, for example, retirement pension institutes were officially created for particular groups of state, municipal, public utility, and transport workers. In March 1931 earlier legislation on workers' holidays was strengthened and in May 1932, after Collor's resignation, laws were passed regulating the working hours of both men and women. Later that year provision was made for emergency treatment for workers and the employment of minors was officially controlled, while over the next two years there was legislation on industrial accident insurance and maternity benefits, followed in 1936 by the formation of commissions to fix minimum wages.

Unfortunately, most of these decrees were never effectively operated and employers often found it easy to go directly contrary to their spirit and purpose. The decree of 1932, for instance, enforcing an eight-hour day, also allowed an extra two hours to be worked by mutual agreement, an agreement not difficult to reach for employers ready to take stern measures against dissenters.[29] The law on holidays was also turned against the workers, since to claim his holiday pay the worker had to present a passbook, which among other things showed where he had worked previously and why he had left his last job, so providing easy recognition of anyone involved in strikes or labour activity. Other legislation demanded further identification and attempted to impose further control, since by the end of 1932 the Brazilian worker already had to carry several pass cards.[30] The new union legislation also severely hindered any self-generated action from the working class, again pointing the way to the fuller corporatist experience of the *Estado Novo*. Under the new legislation only one union was allowed for each trade, so that out of the 1,494 unions which existed before 1930 only 364 were now recognized by the new Ministry, reflecting, as Collor said of Decree No. 19770 of March 1931, the government's determination 'to incorporate the trade union movement into the state and the laws of the Republic'.[31] Steadily from this time on the militancy of the organized working class was to be blunted, as the unions were brought still further under direct state control, with the introduction of, for example, a trade union levy (*impôsto sindical*), by which the worker had to pay the equivalent of one day's wage every year into a fund which was administered through the Ministry of Labour to the unions. Such bureaucratization of the unions was to be developed more strongly in later years, making many union leaders representatives of the government or the bosses rather than the workers, but the basis of the whole paternalist structure of labour relations was laid by Collor, producing a system which again closely fitted the needs of the industrial class after 1937 in its eager pursuit of import substitution.[32]

Examining the results in practice of this new legislation the contradiction and real significance of Collor's work are sharply underlined, namely that, while he genuinely aimed to resolve social tensions and improve the conditions of the working class, his whole concept of this process was paternalistic and essentially corporatist, producing an interlocking system of social control which was to be consciously strengthened and refined under the *Estado Novo*. Coming on top of the purges of working-class organizations already described which followed the collapse of the ANL in 1935, later legislation still further weakened the organizing capacity of the urban workers, while strengthening the grip of those groups seeking wider and more authoritarian state control. The eventual result was that the trade unions, rather than being seen as having some autonomous existence *vis-à-vis* the state, are, from this time on, better understood as part of the state apparatus.

Estado Novo Constitution

Francisco Campos, who had secretly drafted the constitution of the new regime, firmly believed in the need for such enlarged state power.[33] The executive power of the president was to be greatly strengthened, especially in the current state of emergency, which was also declared in the constitution. It was he who must decide when indirect elections for a national assembly should take place, the members of which would play a diminished role, similar to that of deputies in the state assembly of Rio Grande do Sul. He would also choose one of the two candidates for election to the presidency, the other being chosen by a large electoral college, and, despite the earlier crises over presidential re-election, this was not explicitly forbidden in the new constitution. There was also to be a Federal Council of sixty, of which ten would again be chosen by the president, with two others from each state, and a National Economic Council was to oversee the organization of the economy.[34]

Article 139 of the new constitution explicitly forbade strikes and lockouts, while only those trade unions recognized by the state were to be allowed to represent the interests of their members. Strikes were defined as anti-social, as being seen part of that 'class struggle' which the preamble to the constitution explicitly rejected, and 'incompatible with the superior interests of national production'. The promise of a progressive labour policy (Article 137), with reference to minimum-wage legislation and measures to protect women workers and improve working conditions, were all couched in the same paternalist language, while the proposed National Economic Council, with its members to be selected on the basis of a simply defined occupational representation, again echoed the formulae of fascist Italy. The nationalist inspiration of the *Estado Novo* was seen in proposals to nationalize banks, mines, insurance, and essential industries (Articles 145–153) and the new concern for tighter controls was clearly reflected in Article 122, which provided for censorship of press, theatre, cinema, and radio, 'in order to guarantee the peace, order, and safety of the public' and 'to protect the public interest of the people and the security of the state', a constitutional provision which led to the much-enlarged Department of Press and Propaganda (DIP).

It has often been argued that the essence of the new constitution was the sanctioning under Article 180 of sweeping powers to the president of the Republic until the national parliament could meet after the end of the current crisis,[35] and the newly enlarged role of the president did, undoubtedly, represent a formidable concentration of power, extending to his succession, too, since his nominee would be in a much stronger position than the one chosen by the electoral college, if only because that college was to meet only three weeks before the election. But the more significant aspect of all these provisions was the degree to which they directly reflected the commanding position of the small dominant group who inspired and pushed them through. All the constitutional provisions, from those on executive power, to those on economic planning, economic nationalism, trade union organization, labour conditions, and censorship of the media, were directly and deliberately geared to enlarge and confirm the political control of the industrial bourgeoisie.

Bureaucracy

In the formation of this apparatus of a bourgeois state the only element still conspicuously missing was a strong, coherent bureaucracy, a gap which Vargas and his colleagues at once sought to fill, since there was general agreement that the much-enlarged responsibilities of the federal government, as expressed through the new ministries[36] and the recently created planning bodies, would require a professional highly trained civil service. So Article 67 of the *Estado Novo* constitution proposed a new administrative department, which was to introduce reforms and take on extensive powers, including preparing the annual budget. This was to be known as the Departamento Administrativo do Serviço Público, or DASP, and was intended to have direct influence on every branch of government.

Here again, as seen throughout the new constitution, the *Estado Novo* was to a large degree giving greater force to earlier attempts at change, since there had already been, for example, after 1934 a report of a Congressional sub-committee, headed by Maurício Nabuco, which had proposed, among other things, a division between federal and regional civil services. This was followed by another sub-committee under Luís Simões Lopes, who was long to influence subsequent debate on administrative reform. The main difference between the two proposals turned on the thorny problem of patronage, which Nabuco believed should be tolerated, though controlled, but which Simões Lopes, with a 'purer' approach influenced by North American theory, was determined to eradicate.[37] The report of this Simões Lopes commission was then embodied in the 'Law of Readjustment' of October 1936, which has been described as 'one of the major revolutions in thinking about the civil service in Brazil . . . the Brazilian equivalent of the Northcote Trevelyan Report'.[38] Strongly influenced by foreign administrative theory, the report proposed major changes with regard to recruitment, training, and classification of civil servants and in the whole organization of government departments. It aimed to create a professional civil service based on merit and tested in examination, to replace the existing system linked to family or political patronage, and it was this same reforming thrust which was now summarized and strengthened in the *Estado Novo* constitution.

As a model of administrative reform these proposals were far-sighted and in line with the best contemporary theory, but it was a model difficult to apply, since it cut so sharply across the vested interests of many already in government service and made excessively high demands in relation to the educational calibre of many candidates. Despite these and subsequent reforms most entry into the civil service was not through examination, and personal patronage continued important long after the end of the *Estado Novo*, or even after the death of Vargas.[39] Many civil servants continued to be, in effect, part time, often carrying on one or more other jobs, and there was conspicuous overstaffing in many departments, sustaining the popular charge that the civil service was largely a system of patronage for the middle classes. But, at the same time, the changes under the *Estado Novo* had real political importance. They reinforced the general consensus that the powers of the federal government should be extended, so that the debate now centred on how such powers should best be exercised. More substantially, though ironically in terms of the reforming ideals involved, the changes introduced, especially DASP, greatly increased the personal patronage of Vargas and his close associates. DASP never took over some of the more technical functions envisaged for it, but it did become 'an unofficial "super-ministry" ',[40] used by Vargas to carry through policies or initiatives which he particularly favoured, and, since the ministers and *interventores* in the various states, all men bound to Vargas, were also able to choose their own personal staff, the overall result of the attempts at reform was, in practice, to weaken still further those groups who had previously controlled Brazil and to strengthen the position of Vargas and those interests now dominant in the *Estado Novo*. This extended influence also helped to establish the basis for the Vargista political machine which was eventually to be built on the double foundation of the *interventores*, through the PSD, and the trade unions, through the PTB. Here again, in other words, the attempts at civil service reform, like the other measures already analysed, increased the power of the new dominant class, provided more efficient machinery for its exercise, and pointed the way to future tensions and changes within the structure of the Brazilian state.

The Concentration of Power

Before examining those tensions and conflicting demands, which by 1942 were already clearly apparent, it is necessary to appreciate the greatly increased concentration of political power in these early years of the *Estado Novo*, as Vargas and those who backed him removed any threat to their control. The sharpest example was in his handling of the Integralists, but they were only the most conspicuous of the groups thrust aside. The AIB, taking this first example, had grown steadily in the three years since its only rival mass organization, the ANL, had been suppressed in 1935. There had been strong reaction to it from state political leaders, alarmed at its challenge to their position, but it had been well received by the Italian and German communities in the south and had widespread middle-class support.[41] Military officers continued to give it their backing and the movement seemed poised for much greater success when Salgado and his followers helped the *Estado Novo coup* in 1937.[42] Vargas was characteristically ambiguous in his public attitudes, but showed sympathy with the anti-communism of the Integralists, especially in the period of febrile persecution of the left after the suppression of the 1935 risings. He knew of estimates that the Integralists had the support of perhaps 500,000 voters out of a total electorate of about 3 million[43] and he had reports of their following in the armed forces' leadership. But, once the *coup* of November 1937 was over, he had no hesitation in taking measures which must strike at them. The Integralists were deeply dismayed by Decree-

Law 37 of 3 December 1937, which forbade all political parties, civilian militias, and similar organizations, as well as the use of uniforms, flags, and insignia, a measure which caught the AIB in its own demands for the suppression of factional groupings. Salgado was surprised and alarmed, but had to be content with a minor role in the new administration, while seeing his party reorganized as the Brazilian Cultural Association. There was growing depression, panic, and anger among the leadership, especially among some Integralist army officers, with a rising demand for direct action while it might still have a chance of success, a call which led on the night of 10 May 1938 to a half-hearted attempt at a *coup* in an attack on Guanabara Palace in Rio de Janeiro.

The events of that evening, which at once allowed the suppression of the Integralist movement, are still unclear. All accounts of the attack against Vargas, his daughter Alzira, and a handful of his staff, underline the ineptitude and peculiar hesitancy on both sides, suggesting that neither the attackers nor some of those who should have defended the president were ready to commit themselves too soon.[44] There had been haphazard, careless plotting for months, with all the old opponents of Vargas ready to join forces against him. Flores da Cunha, now regretting his support in 1932, was bitterly critical and ready to supply arms, as were *paulista* politicians such as Armando de Salles Oliveira and the former leader of the rebel forces in 1932, Euclides Figueiredo. Figueiredo was one of several conspirators arrested in March 1938, but the plotting went on, coming to a head on the night of 10 to 11 May. But the night attack was bungled, with the truck containing the attackers' few arms being driven off by mistake just as the attack on Guanabara Palace should have been pressed home. There was no co-ordination among the different groups of rebels, with leaderless men wandering the streets and bars of the city, many wearing green and white kerchiefs marked 'Avante!', but doing anything but respond to their own call. The confusion of the assault was, on the other hand, only equalled by those officially charged with the defence of the palace, as the police chief, Filinto Müller, promised help which never arrived and Dutra, warned of the attack at only 1 a.m., had to rush round the city to gather reinforcements. It was 5 a.m. before Cordeiro de Farias and a handful of men were able to get into the palace from the adjoining Fluminense Football Club, their entry having been further delayed until Vargas's secretary could find a porter with a key.

Despite its comic-opera qualities the Integralist attack could have been serious, and Vargas and his daughter Alzira came out of the incident well, having bravely resisted what might have been a well-planned assault. But the main lesson of the failed *coup* was precisely to underline the lack of cohesion among opposition groups and the fatal lack of that armed support already noted among the Integralists. The assault only served as an opportunity for Vargas to move vigorously against Salgado and his supporters, till in June 1939 Salgado left for a comfortable refuge in Portugal. Other opposition groups, too, were broken, including the *paulistas,* as Armando de Salles Oliveira and Júlio de Mesquita Filho were again forced to leave for Europe, and other critics, such as Artur Bernardes and Lindolfo Collor, were silenced, then encouraged to leave the country.

Most of Vargas's opponents were, in any case, deeply divided among themselves and much of their resentment was personal rather than ideological. After two years of the *Estado Novo* all opposition seemed effectively silenced, with the government in full control. The opponents of Vargas were to gather again as new political forces, particularly outside Brazil, brought stronger pressure for change and rallied the heterogeneous opposition in the form of the UDN (National Democratic Union). But for the next few years the opposition was vituperative rather than effective, essentially powerless as long as the army leaders and the industrial interests they supported remained firmly behind Vargas in the tightly unified system they had introduced in November 1937.

The Political Catalyst: the War

Despite this apparent strength and its stern monopoly of power, the *Estado Novo* carried within it the seeds of its own decay. It was, in a sense, almost too successful in its exclusive representation of the narrow social forces which had shaped it, so that it only needed a shift in the balance of those forces to crack open the foundations on which it stood. There were, in particular, severe tensions within the system, some of which have still not been fully resolved. One of these was between the more nationalist elements of the bourgeoisie, strongly advocating state intervention to accelerate the move towards import substitution, and others more open to the demand for the involvement of foreign finance and technology in that process, a controversy which was linked, in turn, to the argument over the need for strict authoritarian political control or for the expediency of a return to some form of liberal democracy reflected in a party system of government through Congress. This, once again, was linked to two strategies concerning the role of the organized working class, which, if not substantially different in practice, were, in terms of class control, sufficiently different in political form. These tensions were to remain and the controversy was to intensify as the *Estado*

Novo progressed and, above all, as Brazil was to enter the war on the Allies' side, commit itself to the defence of democracy against fascism, and open its economy to large United States and other foreign aid.[45]

It was partly these unresolved tensions which prevented Vargas in the early years of the *Estado Novo* from shaping a strong political movement or even a national political party to institutionalize his control, an omission which has often been noted. Partly, too, this reflected the waning of effective opposition and his deep involvement with his five-year plan for infrastructural development, including the foundation of Brazil's steel industry. But a more important reason seems to have been the clear inadvisability of too sharply defining his position at a time when a changing foreign situation could quickly bring new pressures to bear on Brazil and when, in the meantime, it was an advantage for Vargas to remain as ambivalent as possible. Vargas well knew that the basis of his *Estado Novo* government lay not in popular support, but in the continued backing of the leaders of the armed forces and the industrialist interests which were profiting from the new economic policies. Both groups were markedly uncertain in their attitude towards Germany and the United States, so that Vargas had to feel his way carefully, without too sharply defining a position.[46] He was not really free to build a political movement linked to a clearly stated position or programme, even had he wished to do so.

In this respect as in so many others, the war brought rapid changes, acting as an important political catalyst. Once Brazil had decided to support the Allied cause and had defined, at least in the short term, the direction of its foreign interests, there was no longer room for such painful fence-sitting. Instead, there was a felt need to adjust the *Estado Novo*, not only to a much enlarged foreign, mostly United States, element in the industrial process, but to accommodate a corporatist political framework, as expressed in the *Estado Novo* constitution, to a rapidly changing context, in which the values for which Brazil was now fighting were ostensibly democratic. Such tensions help to explain why, even as early as 1942, Vargas was changing direction and laying greater emphasis on establishing the bases of *trabalhismo*, his political strategy linked to the trade unions. The change has often puzzled analysts of Vargas's political development, seeking to understand why he introduced such changes well before the Allied victory was at all certain, but the answer seems to be in the fact that the primary impetus came not from the approach of victory, but from the logic of the initial commitment to the Allied side and the economic and political implications that choice contained.

Vargas, as has been seen, was heading till 1942 a political and economic system which had been shaped deliberately to push forward a basically nationalist, protectionist industrialization process, reinforced by a centralized, authoritarian political system, willing to use new forms of censorship and propaganda to maintain control and acknowledging the need to curb the political power of the working class. But by 1942 the situation had changed radically, as he himself was among the first to realize. Already the door was again opening to a greater foreign share in Brazil's industrialization, and pressure was rapidly mounting for a less overtly authoritarian political system, with a new, enlarged, if still controlled, role for at least the urban working class. It was, once again, a measure of Vargas's immense political skill that he was so quick to assess that change and take steps to meet it, certainly long before those army leaders who by 1945 had also read the same signals, and who decided on abrupt action to remove Getúlio Vargas, the one man, ironically, who might have effected the smooth political transition required.

The Shaping of Trabalhismo

The extraordinary flexibility of Vargas's response to these new demands has often brought further charges of cynicism, opportunism, and lack of political principle in what seemed to many then, and since, an anxious, undignified scramble onto the democratic bandwaggon. Such accusations could certainly be levelled against others, especially by 1945, but they do less than justice to Vargas and, more importantly, they distort the whole origins and shaping of *trabalhismo*, the powerful political system linked to the trade unions, which Vargas was now starting to build. If, therefore, one is to understand Vargas and his contribution to the whole political process of modern Brazil, it is important to realize that this new strategy was by no means entirely new, that it was not simply an *ad hoc* response to the closer enmeshing of Brazilian industrialization with United States capitalism and the concomitant demand for a liberal democratic framework, but that, rather, it formed an important part of the political tradition from which he sprang and the concept of national politics to which he was committed.

Apart from the emphasis on centralized, authoritarian control there was also in the positivist *gaúcho* tradition that other element, already noted, of a narrowly defined, elitist concern for 'progress' and a pragmatic awareness of the potential importance of the working class. This concern had been reflected in Vargas's formal programme since 1930 and had been further developed, though in limited form, by Collor, so that the administration, despite its assiduous support, in practice, of the industrialists and employers since the start of the *Estado Novo*, also had within it elements which could now rapidly be developed to conciliate and woo a revitalized urban electorate.[47]

Vargas had always kept the door open for such a move, most notably in his annual Labour Day addresses in the Vasco da Gama stadium, as when on 1 May 1940, introducing the minimum wage, he stressed the dignity of labour and the contribution which the workers made to national development, while also contrasting the neglect of the working class by the previously elected governments with the concern shown by the *Estado Novo* and its Minister of Labour, Valdemar Falcão.[48] Stressing the government's aim to establish minimum living standards for all the population, he promised to raise the indices of health and productivity 'to solve the important problems which slow down our progress . . .' and a Labour Code to bring together all social and labour legislation, noting that other 'older civilizations', so often offered as models to Brazil, had not yet solved their labour problems. But he also warned against 'evil influences', who sought to poison the Brazilian sense of brotherhood with 'the exoticism of class struggle'. Brazilian society, he said, would never tolerate extremism: its happiness could only be achieved by productive work, within a legal system providing peace and justice for all, owners and employees, heads of industry and workers of all kinds. Like many of his speeches, as will be seen, this emphasis on class harmony and the rejection of class struggle clearly reveals the strongly conservative corporatist features of Vargas's thinking. Like many of his class he believed that the class struggle was alien to Brazil, an import from Europe to a society whose traditions were more harmonious and where 'extremism' was to be shunned. It was a view he had later to modify as he saw the fierce strength of class interests, above all in the rejection of any substantial share of national wealth and power for the mass of the working population and the poor; but many of his speeches at this time stress the integrative rather than the divisive features of politics, as well as a mythology of class collaboration which was to be one of the main characteristics of *trabalhismo*.[49]

In moving towards greater emphasis on a political strategy which gave a more positive, but still controlled, role to the working class, and which represented for that class, as already argued, a change of style rather than of substance in class relations, Vargas again showed his ability to appoint the right man at the right time. In a cabinet reshuffle of June 1941 Alexandre Marcondes Filho had been appointed to the Ministry of Labour. He was a *paulista* lawyer, who had already expressed warm support for Vargas[50] and who had seen in São Paulo the possible force of the organized urban workers. He, like Collor before him, was to develop strongly the political links between Vargas and the government-controlled trade unions in an attempt to harness their political power, and he worked energetically to produce the massive Labour Code, which Vargas had promised. In May 1942 Vargas missed his usual demonstration in Rio de Janeiro, when he was involved in a serious motor-car accident on his way down from Petrópolis, but by the following year the consolidated legislation was almost ready and Vargas was able to announce a wide range of new plans, including those for 'model restaurants', especially in the interior and, for tackling the problem of workers' education, partly through a system of factory schools.[51] There were already, too, new signs of a direct appeal to the mass of the Brazilian workers, with renewed attacks on the old 'democratic' politicians. Vargas urged all workers to join the government-sponsored trade unions, telling the worker:

> . . . to integrate himself more closely in the organization of the State and free himself completely from the parasitical exploitation of political operators [*politiqueiros*] and demagogues, always ready to promise what they cannot give in return for that to which they have no right.

The renewed vigour of these attacks also reflected the increasing pressure on all sides for a return to electoral politics. Such pressure was not in itself sufficient to explain Vargas's early turn towards *trabalhismo*, but could be seen in his increasingly frequent public justification of his policies and his reiterated scorn for calls for democracy from men who in the past had shown little regard for it, or who used such demands to pay off old personal scores. In a speech of 10 November 1943, the sixth anniversary of the *Estado Novo*, when inaugurating the beautiful new Ministry of Finance building, Getúlio again returned to the attack, while making further direct appeals to his audience. He was speaking less than a month after a group of prominent *mineiros* had publicly demanded the restoration of democracy and, it is worth noting, within a month of Juan Perón's assumption of the Ministry of Labour in Argentina. Praising the new building, Getúlio stressed how right it was that the state should give an example to private industry of the need to provide adequate workplaces for employees. He announced a rise in salaries and wages, then warned against the distractions of debating the advantages of the electoral process and of involvement in political agitation 'simply to satisfy the demagogic yearnings of a few miserable pettifogging lawyers with time on their hands',[52] especially when they were 'troublemakers, suddenly turned reformers always known in political circles for their reactionary tendencies'.

Such attacks have provided easy ammunition for those who see Vargas as essentially anti-democratic and determined to hang on greedily to power: but again this does him less than justice. His scorn for critics echoed that of the earlier *tenentes* and many others, both military and civilian, who saw Brazil's earlier liberal experience as largely a sham, operated in the interests of a small ruling class. Vargas was genuine in his belief that his regime had done more, and would do more, for the mass of the Brazilian people than those which had preceded him, which was certainly true, and he was equally genuine in his fear that elections called at the demand of the political class whose hold he believed had been broken after 1930 would merely put back the clock. But he also knew that changes had to come and that he could not stand in their way.

As the *Estado Novo* progressed, his position became increasingly vulnerable and difficult to maintain. He deeply mistrusted, as he made clear in his speeches, a return to the old system, and he would have preferred, as he also made clear, some new form of representation based on occupational groupings and working closely with the trade unions. But he came to see that the demand for immediate elections was too strong and could not be resisted. Grudgingly, but sincerely, he promised such elections, but, as in 1932, he was not believed or trusted by opponents who were more anxious to get rid of Vargas than to introduce genuinely democratic processes. It was a dilemma which was to face not only Vargas, but most of his successors, most notably his political protégé Goulart, who also was to be removed in the name of democracy by groups whose understanding of it was at best idiosyncratic.

The shape of the debate can be seen in his speech of 10 November 1943. After the war, he said, 'with the fullest guarantees for freedom of opinion, we shall readjust the political structures of the Nation and we will consult fully and completely the Brazilian people . . .'

> . . . And it will be from the organized working classes [*das classes trabalhadoras organizadas*] that we shall prefer to draw the elements required for national representation: employers, workers, tradesmen, farmers—new people, full of energy and hope, able to build and carry forward the work of progress. The primacy in the positions of authority, control and consultation will go to those who work and produce, not to those who corruptly cultivate public office as a means of livelihood and personal advantage. There will be opportunity, too, for the young to make themselves heard, who now in the schools, the factories and the barracks

are making ready, eager . . . to build the future of the country.[53]

This was not, it should be emphasized, in any sense an exclusive appeal to the working class. Quite the contrary. The 'organized working classes' and 'those who work and produce' are all those engaged in productive labour, so that the basic concept is again integrative and opposed to the idea of class struggle. There is already, too, that deliberate looseness in political vocabulary to soften the force of the appeal and make it as comprehensive as possible, as in the use of *agricultores* rather than peasants or rural workers. Already the vocabulary of later populism is being shaped as Vargas again starts to cultivate his earlier image as the people's candidate.

But at the same time, as will be stressed when discussing the mass populist mobilization of later years, it is easy to react too disparagingly to these appeals, dismissing them too readily as another form of mystification, perhaps a more subtle and dangerous pattern of class control, corrosive of more authentic radical moves. Such judgements may, indeed, be justified and necessary, but they should not miss the significant shift in emphasis implied in Vargas's new approach to the mass of the people, or the potential, albeit limited, for genuine class challenge which it ultimately contained. It marked, for example, at the very least, an acceptance of the need to pay more attention to the redistribution of resources and to give a wider, if still limited, share of political influence to classes which previously had been almost entirely excluded. Vargas, as he himself may well have realized, was opening a Pandora's box, raising aspirations and demands which would not easily be satisfied by the old-style politicians who loudly demanded a return to democratic political forms which previously had suited their class so well.

How Vargas would have liked to see the system changed is still not clear, since, in the event, his hand was forced, so that his preference for a direct mandate became irrelevant and his personal direction was interrupted, while his repeated assurances to honour the election programme were mistrusted. But even these limited appeals to new political forces were enough to bring out again in stark relief the underlying class configurations of Brazilian politics, tracing a pattern which was to be followed over the next three decades. Pressure began to build up from early 1942, intensified in May after Vargas's motor accident, which brought swiftly to a head the constant preoccupation over who might succeed him as president. In the resulting crisis various rows flared up, including one over the staging in Rio de Janeiro of a pro-United States parade on the fourth of July, which in turn led to the resignations of the Minister of Justice, Francisco Campos, the acting Minister of Justice, Leitão da Cunha, the chief of police, Filinto Müller, and the head of the Department of Press and Propaganda, Lourival Fontes. Marcondes Filho now took on even wider responsibilities with the Ministry of Justice, emphasizing the growing importance of the build-up of *trabalhismo*, while a minor but notable result of the resignations was that the censorship and control exercised by the DIP never seemed to be as effective after the resignation of Fontes.

The tight structure of the *Estado Novo* seemed to be cracking at many different points, with new forces pressing on it from every angle. One of these was the Society of the Friends of America, founded in January 1943, which drew together many disparate elements critical of Vargas.[54] It was regarded with deep suspicion by Dutra and other army leaders because of its many left-wing members, but became a strong pressure-group for a return to democratic institutions.

Another similar call came in the Manifesto of the *mineiros*, of October 1943. This was a rambling, sententious document, signed by *mineiros* of all political shades, many of whose memories when calling for democracy seemed, as in the case of Artur Bernardes, conveniently short.[55] But the Manifesto was a straw in the wind, showing how easily the enemies of Vargas could settle their differences and how quickly, in particular, they could react in alarm at any hint of a new alliance with the Brazilian working class similar to that which was being achieved by Perón in Argentina. Other protests were drafted, producing the reaction from Vargas seen above (p. 112), and a claim from Marcondes Filho that the declaration of war suspended the six-year presidential term, so allowing a constitutional extension of Vargas's presidency for another fourteen months after the war ended.[56] Such proposals brought howls of protest against *continuismo*, which were not silenced by Vargas's repeated promises that, once war was ended, the people '. . . in full freedom . . . will choose their leaders and representatives democratically, within the framework of law and order'.[57] Such promises were regarded as constrained and ambiguous, especially when set against the attacks on the Society of Friends of America and the resignation of Aranha.

By mid-1944 with the FEB on its way to the Italian front, tension was running high and, behind the shouting for liberalism and democracy, the lines were being drawn around the issues of class confrontation, with the characteristic call to guarantee law and order in a situation which, Vargas's critics alleged, was rapidly deteriorating. Their alarm was exaggerated, despite the growing signs of popular, often noisy, support for Getúlio in the streets of Rio de Janeiro: but it was in the interest of his opponents to heighten middle-class anxiety both among civilians and in the armed forces.

It was the latter who were the crucial factor. The critics of Vargas could issue wordy manifestos and his supporters could yell support outside his windows, but the real decision rested, as in all the earlier crises, with the heads of the armed forces, and by the end of August 1944 the two firmest cornerstones of the *Estado Novo*, Góes Monteiro and Eurico Gaspar Dutra, had both come round to the view that Brazil should return to democratic elections as soon as reasonably possible. Góes listened to Marcondes Filho's proposal for an election based on the unions, but disagreed, believing the unions should: '. . . simply look after their class interests and not turn themselves into political parties'.[58] After Aranha resigned, Góes returned from Montevideo, where he had gone earlier in the year, and at once began to discuss with Dutra the changes that were necessary. Both were convinced that the *Estado Novo* was, as Góes put it, 'démodé' and both knew of growing dissatisfaction in the armed forces, among the officers in Italy, the air force in the north-east, and, as Góes had found on his journey from Uruguay, in the garrisons in the south.[59] Dutra argued that, since Góes and he had been primarily responsible for starting the *Estado Novo*, they had a continuing responsibility for seeing to its modification,[60] and Góes discovered that there was already talk of a military initiative to depose Vargas, with Eduardo Gomes as the most likely substitute.[61] Góes claims that he then told Vargas that he had come back from Montevideo 'to put an end to the *Estado Novo*', and the president agreed to discuss with Góes, Dutra, and Marcondes Filho how best this could be done. The accounts may be questionable in detail, but the essential point remains that, once this decision had been made, Vargas had no real alternative but to accept it. Marcondes Filho could continue to work at shaping the political movement based on the trade unions, but there was no effective counter-force to resist the will of the military leaders. Góes Monteiro claimed in all sincerity that he was not anybody's man, but, in effect, he had now put the weight of the armed forces behind those who opposed Vargas and who, more significantly for the future, strongly resisted the whole concept of *trabalhismo* and a new role, as they perceived and feared it, for the Brazilian working class. Despite his denials, Góes Monteiro and the army had unequivocally taken sides, just as their successors were to do nearly twenty years later.

The Dismantling of the Estado Novo

If Vargas had ever doubted that he would soon have to call elections, all those doubts were now ended, as he made even clearer in a series of speeches around Brazil, in which he also underlined more strongly than ever the achievements of the last few years in the field of social and labour legislation and the rapid advances in basic industries and the possession of Brazil by Brazilians. In this sense the last months of his government were among the most important in defining his political position, sometimes, it seemed, even for himself, and in turning the forces of *trabalhismo* and the patronage exercised by the *interventores* into a formidable machine for mass political mobilization and wide electoral support.[62]

He continued to acknowledge the need for political change, while denying the totalitarian nature of his regime, which was rather, he said, a strong regime with marked concentration of power. But the government, he insisted, had no official candidate and he had no personal ambitions in this direction.[63] Such protests, however, hardly squared with the work which Marcondes Filho was putting in to turn the support generated by the labour legislation into an organized political movement, and the reforming people's candidate again seemed to be revived as Vargas, who had harshly suppressed the ANL, now talked of amnesty for Communists, new links with the Soviet Union, and a government based on direct popular appeal.[64] Here already was the foundation of the political style and organization which was to continue in Brazil after 1945, until the armed forces, who were to depose Vargas within a few months, again intervened, this time to remove his political successor, Goulart.

On 28 February 1945 Vargas issued an Additional Act, or Constitutional Amendment No. 9, promising that an election date would be announced for the presidency and for federal and state legislatures; but the opposition still continued to mistrust such promises, gathering in a heterogeneous coalition which brought together people of widely differing positions who wanted Vargas out. One much-publicized demand had come in January 1945 from the First Brazilian Writers' Congress in São Paulo, which included a number of Communists, who continued to oppose Vargas until Prestes and the Party later decided to give him their support, and by April 1945 the main opposition movement, mostly composed of middle-class civilians and army officers who opposed Vargas and feared his popular support, had gathered under the heading of the UDN.

Many of the UDN made uneasy bedfellows, but they were held together by their hostility to Vargas, often springing from personal resentment as much as ideological disagreement. They included, for instance, the excluded candidate of 1937, José Américo de Almeida, the defeated *gaúcho* rival and former friend, Flores da Cunha, the rejected *mineiro* presidential successor of 1933, Virgílio de Melo Franco, and the sternly anti-Vargas *paulista* journalist, Júlio de

Mesquita Filho. While, however, the UDN membership read like a roll-call of those who had been defeated or disappointed by Vargas throughout the 1930s, or earlier, there was also, it should be stressed, a strong class connotation to the opposition movement. This is especially worth noting, since many accounts of post-war Brazilian parties underplay this element, by drawing attention, for example, to the often remarkable similarity in the social origins of their leaders and the lack of sharply defined social or economic divisions on many issues. This is discussed later, but it is important to realize that, right from the start, a common thread binding the diverse interests of the UDN was not just personal opposition to Vargas, nor, certainly, a deep unswerving commitment to democratic processes, but, rather, a generally shared fear of the organized working class and the threat contained, as they perceived it, in *trabalhismo*. The UDN was from the beginning a party of class solidarity, rallying to close the ranks against any challenge from below. The PSD and even the PTB, as argued later, might have elitist leaders and an inadequate concept of the forces of social change, but both were inextricably linked to the new Vargista movement which was now being shaped, which the UDN rightly feared as a threat to the interests it represented. The UDN was always to be against any substantially enlarged popular participation in politics, seeing the workers as at best a source of electoral support, and it was a party which in its policies and priorities was persistently to support middle- and upper-class interests, being mostly neglectful of distributionist policies, except, again, in so far as those might serve narrow electoral purposes.

The fear of Vargas winning mass support was further increased when Luís Carlos Prestes, now freed from prison, gave his and the PCB's backing to Getúlio,[65] and was not much quietened by the decree of 28 May 1945, fixing the presidential election for 2 December 1945.[66] The Vargas movement was now forming in two blocs, partly as a matter of strategy and partly as the result of mutual distrust between Marcondes Filho and General Dutra,[67] who was now generally seen as the most suitable Vargista candidate. Marcondes Filho had been replaced in the Ministry of Justice by a friend of Dutra, Agamemnon Magalhães, who helped to launch Dutra's candidacy in March 1945, and Vargas then began the official organization of *two* parties, one stemming from Marcondes Filho's labour machine, the other mobilizing the wide patronage system attached to the federal *interventores* in all the states. The first, to harness the vote of organized labour, was to be the PTB, the Brazilian Labour Party, while the other was to be inappropriately named the PSD, the Social Democratic Party:

> . . . He added [says Góes Monteiro of an interview with Vargas] that he would found two parties—one from the working class ['do proletariado'] with the help of Srs. Marcondes Filho and Segadas Viana: the other from the middle classes and the bourgeoisie, a typically government party . . . whose foundations would be laid by the state interventors . . .[68]

The unprecedented choice of two prominent military officers, General Dutra and Brigadier Eduardo Gomes, as the presidential candidates of the PSD and UDN respectively, further underlined both the new role of the armed forces in national politics and the degree to which this was now accepted. But Vargas was conspicuously slow in backing Dutra and there was even talk of a new arrangement, perhaps bringing in General Góes Monteiro, who had succeeded Dutra as Minister of War.[69] Vargas's hesitancy reflected that of many workers, especially in the centre-south and the country, who saw in Dutra, indeed in both military candidates, a threat to the advances contained in the social and labour policies of the *Estado Novo*, however limited they might be.[70] The popular cry was not for Dutra, but for Getúlio: 'Queremos Getúlio!' (We want Getúlio!), so that many, both in the Vargas-sponsored PSD, as well as in the UDN, began to suspect that Vargas might still reject the election plans and appeal directly to the people to keep him in office. Getúlio vigorously denied such intentions, but often with an additional ambiguous clause, as when speaking on 1 May 1945 in the Vasco da Gama stadium, he said the election results would be upheld, that he did not want to be a candidate, but added that '. . . The Brazilian people have the political maturity to choose whoever suits them best'.[71] He knew that the armed forces, and in particular General Góes Monteiro, would have to approve any change, whether of presidential candidate or of a move to elect a constituent assembly, which would later decide the terms of the presidential election.[72]

The call for a constituent assembly to precede the elections was now being made loudly by the *Queremistas*, in an excited, noisy rally in Rio de Janeiro on 13 August and, even more insistently, in a mass turn-out on 3 October, the fifteenth anniversary of the start of the Vargas revolution of 1930. As the enthusiastic crowds filled the streets and marched, cheering and yelling for Vargas on Guanabara Palace, Getúlio was obviously moved and elated by a demonstration of support which no other presidential candidate could hope to equal. But he also well knew the constraints of his position. He agreed that a constituent assembly would be a 'genuinely democratic process', with precedents in Brazilian history, but he also repeated to the crowd his intention to uphold elections and not to stand as candidate.[73] Then, however, came an appeal and an attack which seemed once again to open up new possibilities, bringing cheers from the crowd and whipping up the fears of his opponents:

> . . . The calling of a constituent assembly is a profoundly democratic act, which the people has the right to demand. When the people's will is not satisfied it is always stirred to disorder and revolt. And we need to solve our political problems within a framework of law and order. I must tell you that there are powerful reactionary forces, some hidden, others visible, totally opposed to the calling of a constituent assembly. I can promise you that, in so far as it depends on me, the people can count on my support . . .[74]

Here, already fully fledged, was the populist style of later years, urging the themes of hidden foreign interests working through political groups at home, inimical to the true interests of the mass of the Brazilian people, interests which could so easily be twisted and thwarted in an ostensibly free, democratic process, which was, in reality, no more than a sham, a new way of exerting class control. But such charges were much more than windy rhetoric. The pressures for a return to a liberal democratic framework, with which every anti-Vargas group had now identified itself, had largely sprung, as seen already, from the opening of the Brazilian economy to increased foreign influences during the war, especially from the United States, and Vargas clearly perceived that either of the presidential candidates would be more acceptable to United States businessmen and their government than his own form of economic nationalism, associated, as it now was, with mass support. He knew perfectly well that many in the United States, and elsewhere, were greatly alarmed by the shaping of politics in Argentina and were drawing parallels with his own campaign in Brazil,[75] and, more specifically, he was now speaking less than a week after the United States ambassador in Brazil, Adolf Berle, had intervened in the Brazilian debate by siding with the opposition. Speaking in the Hotel Quitandinha in Petrópolis on 29 September, Berle had sided with those who were demanding elections, so, in effect, supporting Vargas's opponents and aligning the government he represented with one political group.[76] Berle had discussed his speech with Spruille Braden, who was passing through Brazil on his return to the United States to take up the post of Under-Secretary of State, coming from Argentina, where he had been ambassador and where recently he too had been involved in a political row. It was later claimed that Berle had cleared his speech with Vargas, who subsequently, according to one report, said he had paid little attention as it was read out, since Berle had presented it in such 'badly mumbled Portuguese'.[77] The facts are still not clear, but it was, at the very best, a partisan involvement in a delicate political situation, which at once strengthened nationalist charges that outside interests were bringing pressure on Brazilian politicians and soldiers.[78]

Vargas still insisted that he would support the elections, urging Brazilian workers to join the PTB, which he described as the workers' party, though warning them against being duped in an electoral game in which promises would soon be forgotten:[79] but suddenly he seemed to play right into the hands of his enemies in a series of abrupt political moves.

The first was a decision to bring forward the date of state elections to coincide with those of 2 December, so apparently making sure that his *interventores* would be able to use their influence to the full. This allowed his critics to argue that, if Vargas could once change the electoral rules, he might do so again, even to cancel the election arrangements,[80] and their case seemed further strengthened when Vargas suddenly moved João Alberto Lins de Barros, the former *tenente* and *interventor* in São Paulo, who had co-ordinated economic planning during the war, from his current post as police chief of Rio de Janeiro to become mayor of the city. This seemed a crude device to allow pro-Vargas and pro-constituent rallies, which previously had been forbidden as a threat to public order, and there seemed even clearer evidence of a swift move to personal control when Vargas named his brother Benjamim (pejoratively referred to as 'o Beijo', 'the Kiss') as the new chief of police. Benjamim, who had formed a personal guard for Getúlio after the attack on the Guanabara Palace in May 1938, was mistrusted by many senior officers as well as by his opponents in the UDN. There was now increased speculation that Vargas was trying to follow a path similar to that of Perón, who on 17 October 1945 had been recalled to power by mass popular support,[81] and there were reports of increased military readiness to help Vargas to follow the same path to stay in office.[82]

None of these suspicions ever passed beyond apparently inspired rumour, and many of the allegations come from anti-Vargas groups or those who were eventually led to move against him, and who subsequently needed to justify their action. But in 1945, as again in 1964, political rumour, combined with heightened middle-class anxiety over the threat to law and order and property, was enough to make senior military officers side with the opposition in a move to depose the president. Vargas consistently maintained that he did not wish to continue in office, but the crisis reached a head with the resignation of Góes Monteiro as Minister of War on 29 October.[83] Góes immediately alerted military commanders throughout the country and put into operation a contingency plan already prepared, which allowed Góes himself to take command of all military forces.

Dutra, too, now joined in these moves and João Alberto and the Minister of Justice, Agamemnon Magalhães, agreed to try to persuade Vargas not to appoint his brother as chief of police. The leaders of the armed forces accepted the need for joint action and used tanks in a show of force: but Vargas showed he was determined to carry through his nomination. With the gauntlet thus thrown down, Góes Monteiro appointed another former *tenente*, Cordeiro de Farias, to carry a formal ultimatum to Vargas, meanwhile arranging for the temporary presidential appointment of the Chief Justice, José Linhares. There was now no escape for Getúlio, since he had no alternative force in the working class or the *Queremistas* and he could not continue in office after having been, in effect, publicly accused of plotting to stay in power by a direct appeal to the people. Quietly and with dignity he accepted the ultimatum. Linhares was swiftly brought in to replace him on 30 October and next day Vargas left without fuss for Rio Grande do Sul, leaving Rio de Janeiro in 1945, as he had entered it in 1930, on the immediate decision of the leaders of the armed forces.

The parallels between the expulsion of Vargas in 1945 and that of João Goulart in 1964 are clear and strong. Both were removed by a bloodless *coup* after they had appeared to have massive popular support. In both cases the move against them was spearheaded by the leaders of the armed forces in close collaboration with politicians of the UDN, on both occasions using the plea that law and order and constitutional government made their action necessary. Góes Monteiro says in his memoirs that, commenting to Vargas in October 1945 on the events in Argentina, he forcefully stressed that it was *not* the power of the masses which had guaranteed the success of Perón, but the support of the military high command.[84] It was he, Góes, he later insisted, who kept Vargas in office and who could as easily remove him.[85] Essentially, Góes was right. There was no military or organized political force in the country which could resist the federal army, certainly not the noisy pro-Vargas demonstrators in the streets of Rio de Janeiro. Again, as will be seen, this position had not substantially altered by 1964.

An even more important parallel lies in why the military intervened on the two occasions two decades apart. Emphasis has already been placed on the *dispositivo militar*, the military support required by all ambitious politicians in Brazil. Góes Monteiro, much like

Castello Branco, was not consciously or explicitly tied to any faction, but prided himself, rather, on his aloofness from political quarrels. But in both cases this was a delusion. It is difficult to argue that either Vargas in 1945 or Goulart in 1964 were in any sense radical politicians. Both allowed their political rhetoric to outstrip by far its radical content. Both failed even to show the axe to the root of class exploitation and social inequality, let alone to use it. At the same time, however, both were involved in movements which could perhaps have been transformed into more authentic, self-generating radical attacks on the established order—a debate to be taken up later—and both, which was of more immediate political importance, were *perceived* by conservative forces in Brazil to represent a genuine class challenge based on a new role for the working class. *Queremismo*, like the 'populism' of nearly twenty years later, seemed to many middle-class politicians, their military supporters, and their associated interests in the United States and elsewhere, as likely to lead to a radical challenge, even though, on both sides, radicalism was too easily identified with inchoate protest and emergent nationalism.

It is still difficult to chart with certainty the changes in Vargas's own position, moving from full support of the elitist authoritarian model demanded by the industrialists and the soldiers after 1937, in the full flush of import substitution, to a position which was still authoritarian, but which by 1945 could envisage a fuller role for the working class and could even accommodate the demands for formally democratic institutions, however much he mistrusted and disliked them. The argument here has been that, apart from being a highly subtle, flexible politician, Vargas sprang from a political tradition which was genuinely ambivalent in its attitude to the working class and that he believed, with much justification, that he was more finely attuned to the needs of the majority of the Brazilian people than the politicians who opposed him or the soldiers who kept him in power only as long as they chose. In any case, he was never fully a free agent from the time he reached Rio de Janeiro till the time he returned to his ranch in São Borja, so that it is impossible to know how differently, in other circumstances, he might have shaped his policies.

Many of the opponents who ousted Vargas may not have understood him or the phenomenon with which they were dealing, but they were sufficiently alarmed to band together with the army leaders to impose a new form of government on Brazil. The country was now to have two decades of formal party politics till, once again, the soldiers would step in to call another tune.

Notes

1 The most complete study of the *Estado Novo* is Edgard Carone, *O Estado Novo (1937–1945)* (Rio de Janeiro, 1976) and *A Terceira República (1937–1945)* (Rio de Janeiro, 1976), the latter being a collection of source material for the period.

2 For general discussion of corporatism, which, unfortunately, severely underplays the elements of class interest and ideological control, see James M. Malloy (ed.), *Authoritarianism and Corporatism in Latin America* (Pittsburgh, 1977). For analysis which gives more emphasis to class interests in Brazilian corporatism see Luciano Martins, *Pouvoir et développement économique: formation et évolution des structures politiques au Brésil* (Paris, 1976), especially 114–20.

3 W. Dean, *The Industrialization of São Paulo 1880–1945* (Austin, 1969), 128–48, 181–206. Also Carlos Manuel Pelaez, *História da Industrialização Brasileira* (Rio de Janeiro, 1972), 33–64, 165–73; and Werner Baer and Annibal Villela, 'Industrial Growth and Industrialization: Revisions in the Stages of Brazil's Economic Development', *Journal of Developing Areas*, 7 (January 1973), 217–34. After substantial earlier moves towards industrialization the pace slowed down in the 1920s and accelerated after 1930. ibid., 225–6: '. . . in 1931 industrial production had fully recovered from a decline which had started in 1928 and in the following eight years it more than doubled. . . .'

4 Similarly Joseph L. Love, *Rio Grande do Sul and Brazilian Regionalism, 1882–1930* (Stanford, 1971), 250: 'By 1937 national industrial output was double the output of the mid-1920s, and the phenomenon of industrialization and urbanization were facilitating, and, indeed, making mandatory, a modernization of the state . . .'. Also Dean, op. cit., 209: 'The *Estado Novo* abandoned economic as well as political liberalism'.

5 This is not to suggest that Salles Oliveira in any narrow sense directly represented the interests of coffee, but rather that he was by 1937 the leader of that old *paulista* liberalism which previously had been sustained by the coffee magnates and which did not fit the political economy represented by Simonsen. On the background to these demands and the economic crisis which led to this change in strategy see Dean, op. cit., 207–9.

6 This control was, as usual, exercised indirectly, at first through Vargas, supported by the army; then, after 1945, through the more usual framework of liberal democracy in the party system of mass politics, a form substantially different from that of the Old Republic, and one more difficult to control than that old elitist system or that of the *Estado Novo*.

7 There is, of course, substantial controversy over whether Brazil really had a 'national' bourgeoisie, since it was always supported by foreign finance, being closely tied, even when most nationalist in tone, to the structure of international capitalism. See, for example, Celso Furtado, *Analise do 'Modelo' Brasileiro* (Rio de Janeiro, 1972). There is certainly, however, a much sharper nationalist edge to industrialists' demands in the late 1930s and up to about 1943 than in the years immediately preceding and following, a point discussed below. For the distinction between 'national' and 'comprador' bourgeoisie see André Gunder Frank, *Capitalism and Underdevelopment in Latin America* (London, 1971), who also sees Vargas in this period as 'identified . . . more and more with the national industrial bourgeoisie', 209. For wide-ranging reflection on the changing role of the Brazi-

lian bourgeoisie see Florestan Fernandes, *A Revolução Burguesa no Brasil. Ensaio de Interpretação Sociológica* (Rio de Janeiro, 1975).

8 While describing that crisis Dean seems (op. cit., 207–9) to exaggerate the reaction from political liberalism within the Republican Party, since many had already been calling for tighter controls. While many industrialists, too, did not at first realize the significance of the changes, they soon came to see the advantages of a process which so directly benefited them. Levine, op. cit., 155.

9 Vargas do Amaral Peixoto, op. cit.

10 See Flynn, op. cit., ed. Carr, 100.

11 In this respect one of the most useful books on Vargas is the relatively little-known study by Barros Vidal, *Um Destino à Serviço do Brasil* (Rio de Janeiro, 1945). I am most grateful to D. Alzira Vargas do Amaral Peixoto for drawing my attention to this work, which especially emphasizes Vargas's early experience in Rio Grande do Sul.

12 A tempting British comparison in this respect is Joseph Chamberlain, working out his Birmingham experience at the national level, then trying to impose it on a worldwide empire, arguing that what Uganda needed was what Birmingham had, a development scheme. Another, though different, case is perhaps Anthony Eden, acting in the Suez crisis with his eyes firmly turned towards Munich, determined that this time there would be no appeasement.

13 The best account in English of *riograndense* politics in this period is Love, op. cit.

14 Levine, op. cit., 51.

15 In 1916 Borges offered Vargas the job of state chief of police, which he declined. He was made leader of the state legislature a year later, then chosen as head of the important committee to count the votes in the controversial state presidential election which led to the bloodshed of 1923. After election as federal deputy he became in 1924 head of the *gaúcho bancada* in the federal chamber and in 1926 he served as President Washington Luís's Minister of Finance till he was recalled as state president in succession to Borges de Medeiros in 1928. Love, op. cit., 217–18.

16 ibid., 218, 289 rightly qualifies the direct influence of positivism on Vargas. Certainly he did not consciously look to Comtean positivism as a guide, as Castilhos had done; but the paternalist authoritarianism he favoured squares easily with the Rio Grande model. Similarly, although Vargas broke completely with the heavy-handed, abrasive *style* of Borges de Medeiros, such difference in style, marked by Vargas's bland capacity for compromise, should not distract from the similarity in *substance* of the overall political model in terms of how power was essentially seen to work.

17 On Góes see especially his memoirs: Coutinho, op. cit., and on Dutra: José Caó, *Dutra: O Presidente e a Restauração Democrática* (São Paulo, 1949) and José Teixeira de Oliveira, *O Govêrno Dutra* (Rio de Janeiro, 1956). The continuing influence of some of these men on Brazilian politics should be borne in mind. Dutra, for example, was to remain influential long after he left the presidency in 1950. He was regularly consulted in the years following the 1964 *coup*, and only died in June 1974, aged ninety-two.

18 Love, op. cit., 84.

19 The important contribution of Collor is discussed later, together with that of Marcondes Filho. One of the notable features of Vargas's personal success as a politician was his capacity for choosing the right man at the right time and for inspiring a high degree of personal loyalty. These qualities are evident in most contemporary accounts of Vargas, which also stress his

smiling imperturbability. See, for example, Cláudio de Araujo Lima, *Mito e Realidade de Vargas*, 2nd ed. (Rio de Janeiro, 1955), 39. Also Luiz Vergara, *Fui Secretário de Getúlio Vargas* (Rio de Janeiro, 1960), 121. The same perception of an amiable, good-humoured personality is also reflected in the very Brazilian collection of jokes and anecdotes about Getúlio: José Queiroz Júnior, *222 Anedotas de Getúlio Vargas* (Rio de Janeiro, 1955).

20 Love, op. cit., 251.

21 This emphasis on class harmony and consensus goes back a long way in Brazilian social thinking, with the frequently repeated assertion that the class war is 'un-Brazilian', an alien import from Europe. This seems to spring in part from paternalist patterns of thought among the governing classes and in part is influenced, if often indirectly, by Catholic social teaching on class harmony. Vargas's own speeches, as seen later, are full of references to the need for such harmony. The *pelego* trade union leadership, namely one serving the bosses and the government rather than the workers, is discussed below.

22 Dean in his well-documented study of entrepreneurs in São Paulo says of Simonsen: 'For him the workers were "good and simple souls", who needed to be bought off with better wages in order to avoid the introduction into Brazil of the class struggle. He agreed with Ortega y Gasset's estimate of mass man and preferred to see society controlled by an educated elite', op. cit., 144, and of Matarazzo's view of the workers: '. . . acquired skills or diligence are not recognised as means of achieving success, hence the ordinary worker cannot hope to improve his station. The ideal society would be that which provided the proletarian with security in his fated role and at the same time discouraged him from futile aspirations', ibid., 176.

23 ibid., 164. Employers were very concerned to keep their workers from 'militant influences', preferring to provide paternalistic services rather than higher wages, since these 'would be frittered away' by their irresponsible employees. This background of conscious social control, including the use of paternalism and patronage, has already been stressed, to offset the frequent description of the Brazilian political process as one in which class interest and class consciousness are of relatively little importance. See for a brief statement Flynn, 'Class and politics in Brazil'.

24 Describing how in March 1931 Collor drew up a decree providing for government sponsorship of 'qualified' unions, Love (op. cit., 249–50) notes: '. . . This meant the regime would exercise tutelage over union organization, membership, and financing. Collor emphasized that class cooperation rather than class struggle was the government's objective. Though no doubt influenced by corporativism, the bureaucratic apparatus for organizing and controlling unions may have had a more direct source of inspiration in Rio Grande do Sul. The labour sindicato was analogous to the commodity syndicates of the late 1920s in the use of bargaining power. The union, having a monopoly on its service, could theoretically drive up prices [i.e., wages], just as the charcque and rice syndicates did for their commodities'. The more substantial links seem, however, to be in his overall perception of the controlled role of labour, as of other political forces.

25 The Aranha papers, for example, contain sophisticated breakdowns of the electoral qualifications of all employees on the Rio Grande do Sul railway for 1926 and 1929, including the number of illiterates, foreigners, women and minors, with equally detailed analyses of electoral statistics for most of the *municípios*. The fiercely contested political struggles of that state had underlined the importance of both getting out and controlling the vote and there are early signs of direct 'populist' appeal to an urban electorate which

could not be directly coerced.

26 Lindolfo Collor, *Garibaldi e a Guerra dos Farrapos*, 2nd ed. (Rio de Janeiro, 1958). Garibaldi is said to have adopted his red shirts in imitation of the Brazilian federalists or *libertadores* (*maragatos*) in the Farrapo war of 1835–45.

27 He was the son of João Boeckel and Leopoldin Schreiner, but after his father's death was brought up by his stepfather, João Collor, and subsequently signed himself Lindolfo Leopoldo Boeckel Collor. See *Pasta Lindolfo Collor*. *Estado de São Paulo* archive.

28 Love, op. cit., 291. While emphasizing the role of Collor and the experience of Rio Grande do Sul in the development of corporatism, one should note that corporatist-style control was found more generally in Brazil, including the north-east. The influence of Catholic social teaching, as expressed in the social encyclicals, seems especially important in this respect.

29 Dean, op. cit., 191.

30 ibid., 189. The value of such identification for controlling militant workers was explicitly acknowledged by the employers. It is not clear how far these requirements were followed in practice, though Dean says that '. . . Mass identification came to absorb the efforts of growing numbers of the middle-class bureaucracy'.

31 See Leôncio Martins Rodrigues, *Conflito Industrial e Sindicalismo no Brasil* (São Paulo, 1966), 159. For this same process of union control see too R. J. Alexander, *Labor Relations in Argentina, Brazil and Chile* (New York, 1962) and Jover Telles, *O movimento sindical no Brasil* (Vitória, 1962). The bitter personal experience of one labour leader is expressed in Manoel do Ó, op. cit., while the early shaping of the labour movement is described in Edgar Rodrigues, *Socialismo e Sindicalismo no Brasil* (Rio de Janeiro, 1969).

32 The wider significance of this process is discussed in the next chapter, but see Azis Simão, 'Industrialisation et syndicalisme au Brésil' and Alain Touraine, 'Industrialisation et Conscience Ouvrière à São Paulo', in *Sociologie du Travail*, 3 (1961), 66–95.

33 See his book *O Estado Nacional, sua estructura, seu conteúdo ideológico* (Rio de Janeiro, 1940). Also Azevedo Amaral, *O estado autoritário e a realidade nacional* (Rio de Janeiro, 1938).

34 For an overall analysis of the constitution see Karl Loewenstein, *Brazil under Vargas* (New York, 1942), 45–58.

35 ibid., 48.

36 Apart from the Ministry of Labour, Industry, and Commerce already mentioned, the most important change was the emergence from the Ministry of Justice and the Interior of the new Ministry of Education and Public Health in 1931 and the reorganization of the Ministry of Finance in 1934.

37 G. B. Siegel, *The Vicissitudes of Government Reform in Brazil: the Rise and Fall of DASP* (Los Angeles, 1966), quoted in F. D. Lambert, 'Trends in Administrative Reform in Brazil', *Journal of Latin American Studies*, I, 2, 167–88. Lambert gives a most useful survey of the debate, highlighting this crucial issue of how patronage should be approached, which ties in with the general problem of clientelism as discussed above.

38 Lambert, op. cit., 173.

39 It has been estimated that even three decades after these reforms only 10 per cent of officials had entered the civil service by examination, and Lambert, op. cit., shows in particular the clamour for public office under Kubitschek and the continuing problems of reform. These have still not been solved under the post-1964 military regime, though the direction of patronage may have changed.

40 ibid., 176.

41 Levine, op. cit., and Dulles, op. cit., for general accounts. Also Stanley E. Hilton, '*Ação Integralista Brasileira*—Fascism in Brazil, 1932–1938', *Luso-Brazilian Review*, IX, No. 2 (1972), 3–29, especially on the reaction in the states.

42 Salgado offered Vargas the support of 100,000 men, adding: 'We do not have arms or transportation, but we have sufficient patriotism to place national defence above everything else'. Hilton, op. cit., 17, quoting *Jornal do Brasil* (27 November 1937). Such rhetoric without the capacity for action was typical of the AIB. The lack of arms, transport, and organization to resist suppression was to prove fatal over the next few months.

43 Hilton, op. cit., 20.

44 See the description in Dulles, op. cit., 183–8 and Hélio Silva, *1938—Terrorismo em campo verde* (Rio de Janeiro, 1971).

45 For the general debate on economic nationalism and industrialization see below, pp. 425ff. Also, for example, Roberto Simonsen, *A indústria em face da economia nacional* (São Paulo, 1937); Nelson Werneck Sodré, *História da Burguesia Brasileira* (Rio de Janeiro, 1964); Octavio Ianni, *Estado e Capitalismo: Estrutura Social e Industrialização no Brasil* (Rio de Janeiro, 1965). Some of the debate on planning and economic liberalism came to a head in 1945 in a controversy between Simonsen and Eugênio Gudin, see Eugênio Gudin, *Rumos de Política Econômica* (Rio de Janeiro, 1945) and Roberto Simonsen, *O Planejamento da Economia Brasileira* (São Paulo, 1945).

46 The army leadership was undecided on the international situation. Góes Monteiro was welcomed in Germany, then as assiduously courted by General Marshall. Many military officers were sympathetic to Germany and many were understandably alarmed at the possibility of being involved in a conflict by the United States without receiving adequate arms help. Both the industrialists and the coffee-exporters were conscious of the rapid increase in German trade, even if much of this was in blocked marks, which, it was argued, allowed Germany to retrade Brazilian goods at a profit.

47 An analogy, again relevant for contemporary Brazil, is perhaps the chameleon political quality of the Catholic Church, able to draw from its political tradition both arguments to justify hierarchical authority and a rigid class system and, with equal ease, those which demand greater equality and the end of such a system. The positions are not so much contradictory as drawing, rather, on different elements in a broad tradition. In both cases the authoritarian pattern was immediately stronger, but the other was there, when necessary.

48 Vargas, op. cit., VII, 291–5.

49 Much of the thinking on class harmony in Brazil and the alien quality of the idea of class interest and tension, a view frequently urged by Brazilians with more access to power and privilege, is also redolent of much Catholic social teaching in the post-*Rerum Novarum* period. Unfortunately, the influence of such teaching in Brazil, both direct and indirect, has not yet been much examined. But for one attempt at an overall analysis of conservative thinking and perceptions see Paulo Mercadante, *A Consciência Conservadora no Brasil* (Rio de Janeiro, 1965), which makes much of the idea of 'conciliation' and the idea, as Vargas here proposes, of not going to 'extremes'.

50 Marcondes Filho, *Um Estadista como ainda não surgira no Brasil* (Rio de Janeiro, n.d.).

51 Vargas, op. cit., X, 31–7.

52 ibid., X, 175–9, 178.
53 ibid., 178–9.
54 Its president was Manoel Rabelo, who had been *interventor* in São Paulo during the crisis of 1931. Oswaldo Aranha was chosen as its vice-president, but police closed the meeting in Rio de Janeiro in October 1943 at which he was installed. By 1944 the Society seemed to be pushing Aranha as a presidential successor to Vargas, which was partly behind a confrontation in August 1944 in which Aranha resigned as Minister of Foreign Affairs.
55 A partisan pro-*mineiro* account of the genesis of the Manifesto is in Carolina Nabuco, *A Vida de Virgílio Melo Franco* (Rio de Janeiro, 1962), 132–53, including the full text. It is worth noting that this 'democratic' manifesto, signed by many notorious reactionaries, was started over a long lunch during a discussion of the recent deplorable events in Argentina and Perón's recent appeals to the working class. Fear of such an alliance between Vargas and the Brazilian workers was as strong a motive in this elitist group as was love of democracy. See, too, Virgílio A. de Mello Franco, *A campanha da U.D.N. (1944–1945)* (Rio de Janeiro, 1946), 103–11.
56 Marcondes Filho, echoing Vargas's distrust of the 'liberal' politicians, proposed, among other things, a plebiscite and an election based on the trade unions. Such discussion was now intense, as seen, for instance, in a meeting described by General Góes Monteiro between himself, Marcondes Filho, and Vargas's son-in-law, Ernâni do Amaral Peixoto. Góes was opposed to such proposals, seeing them, as he said later, as the start of a proposed 'República Sindicalista', which he thought was continued under Goulart, See Coutinho, op. cit., 396.
57 Vargas, op. cit., X, 277–82. Speech to Brazilian Press Association, 15 April 1944.
58 Coutinho, op. cit., 397.
59 The most prominent air force officer and critic was Brigadier Eduardo Gomes, the last survivor of the 1922 *tenente* rising, who in 1945 became the air force candidate of the UDN in opposition to Dutra in the presidential election. Góes Monteiro lists the officers he spoke with on his journey. ibid., 403.
60 ibid., 404.
61 ibid. For Dutra's side see José Caó, *Dutra: O Presidente e a Restauração Democrática* (São Paulo, 1949), 215–16.
62 See his speech in Belo Horizonte, 1 July 1944, where he already began to define his position more closely, especially on economic nationalism: '. . . The fight against economic colonialism is precisely one of the basic doctrines on which all Brazilians agree. . . .' Vargas, op. cit., XI, 38. Also two speeches to the armed forces: 10 November 1944 (ibid., 49) and his stress on national issues and industrialization on 31 December 1944 (ibid., 73–80).
63 ibid., 93–112. Interview to journalists, 2 March 1945.
64 ibid., 110–11. Among the most influential voices urging diplomatic links with the Soviet Union was Oswaldo Aranha. The loss to the Vargas government of this highly respected statesman, resigning as Minister of Foreign Affairs, was a severe blow.
65 Not all party members agreed with this. See, for example, the severe strictures of Agildo Barata, who saw Prestes's release as part of a bargain in which he would support Vargas's ambitions towards *continuismo*. Prestes had, however, probably gauged the situation better than Barata, who says that he eventually 'set his watch by Prestes's', as did many others. Agildo

Barata, *Vida de um Revolucionário* (Rio de Janeiro, n.d.), 321–4.

66 This was to be the date for the presidential and Congressional elections. Elections for state assemblies and governors were to follow on 6 May 1946 and this later date seemed to lessen the chances of Vargas's *interventores* carrying as much influence as they might in an earlier election.

67 Coutinho, op. cit., 411.

68 ibid., 413.

69 Góes emphasizes how strong were Vargas's reservations over Dutra. This was not just a matter of personal dislike, since Vargas suspected how little sympathy or understanding Dutra had of the strategy of *trabalhismo*, and how limited his public appeal: ibid., 413–17.

70 ibid., 416.

71 Vargas, op. cit., XI, 149–50.

72 Coutinho, op. cit., 417–18. Góes was meeting every day in the Ministry of War the generals currently in Rio de Janeiro, discussing all aspects of national politics and reporting these discussions, he says, faithfully to Getúlio. ibid., 421–2.

73 Vargas, op. cit., XI, 191: 'Before God . . . and the Brazilian people . . . I reaffirm that I am not a candidate and I only want to preside over elections . . . handing over the government to my substitute legally chosen by the nation . . .'

74 ibid.

75 The importance of the success of Perón in increasing alarm among anti-Vargas groups is generally underestimated, yet the Argentine example was regularly brought up, as seen in the start of the Manifesto of the *mineiros* (above, p. 115). It also much influenced Góes Monteiro's thinking, both during and after his time in Montevideo, and certainly was important in the thinking of the State Department. More generally, there is a tendency to neglect the impact of the experience of one Latin American country in the political thinking of another. In more recent years this has been particularly important, most obviously in the influence of the Cuban experience, but also of the military in Peru and, most recently, in the moralizing over the difficulties of Chile under Allende or Argentina under Campora, or Perón, by defenders of the current 'Brazilian model'.

76 Góes Monteiro later said that Berle's speech was 'probably inspired by the opposition'. Coutinho, op. cit., 431.

77 ibid., 432.

78 For a forceful nationalist interpretation of the role of the United States in ousting Vargas see Adyr Pontes Sette, *A verdade sôbre a deposição de Getúlio Vargas* (Juiz de Fora, 1947). Pontes Sette says Vargas had refused to approve Berle's speech, so disagreeing with Góes Monteiro's later evidence and his accusation that Vargas and his colleagues were deliberately provoking a crisis. Coutinho, op. cit., 432–3.

79 Vargas, op. cit., XI, 197–9. Speech of 10 October.

80 The alarm and excitement are described by Góes Monteiro in Coutinho, op. cit., 437–8, as many saw a repetition of the cancelled elections of 1938.

81 ibid., 438–9.

82 ibid., 440–1.

83 Góes gives a scarcely credible account of how he was only told by João Alberto on the morning of 29 October, after picking up João Alberto on the way to work, that the latter was to move from the office of Chief of Police to that of mayor, with the current mayor, Henrique Dodsworth, moving as ambassador to Lisbon. Góes says he only heard the details as he drove

along Avenida Atlántica and through Botafogo, since Vargas had instructed João Alberto not to tell Góes of the changes till the last minute. Coutinho, op. cit., 441–3.

84 ibid., 438–9.

85 ibid., 442, 445.

1945–55

6 Liberal Democracy and Social Tensions

A Political Artefact?

Even as Vargas left Rio de Janeiro on the last day of October 1945, there were clearly apparent tensions, even contradictions, in the new political order which was being hurriedly thrown together. There were good grounds to doubt, for example, the strength of the commitment to popular representative democracy of many of the civilian politicians, such as those who had signed the Manifesto of the *mineiros*, who were now gathering in the anti-Vargas coalition of the UDN. Could their understanding of democracy, many now asked, ever go far beyond the old, narrow, elitist pattern of politics they had known under the Old Republic? Representative, at most, of a small social group, they had never yet shown a readiness to open up the social and political system to genuine participation by the mass of the Brazilian people. Were they now really committed to wider participation, and how would they react if political power ever seemed to be shifting from them? There were similar doubts about the sudden change of heart of men such as Góes Monteiro and Eurico Gaspar Dutra, who only a few years earlier had fully accepted the corporatist authoritarianism of the *Estado Novo* and whose rejection of Vargas in the name of democracy smacked too sharply of political opportunism rather than of a reasoned, deep-seated commitment to participatory democracy and far-reaching social and political freedoms. How, again, would they, and other leaders of the armed forces, react to substantial shifts of power towards those groups who previously had been excluded?

These, and many other, questions were made sharper by the fact that recent political changes clearly had been influenced as much by the changing international context as by demands within Brazil for a more open, participatory system. Some moves towards a democratic political framework had been contained in the logic of Brazil's choice to side with the Allies, as Vargas himself realized, but there were good grounds to doubt whether the changes now being effected implied much more than a dropping of the pilot, rather than turning the ship in a new direction or, still less, radically changing the relations between those who manned the ship. If, too, the changes accelerated by the war and the wider role of the United States could so substantially affect Brazil, what might be the continuing impact of foreign, especially United States, interests, not least on military officers who now, more than ever before, were closely involved with colleagues in the United States, and whose contacts were likely to grow even stronger in the years ahead? Not all these issues were fully or clearly perceived as Vargas first left office, but all were seen and discussed to some degree, not least by those groups on the left and among working-class organizations who previously had felt the main brunt of political repression and who now hoped that at least some limited advances might come in the wake of the noisy political excitement of 1945.

Other, more fundamental and more substantial, questions were less fully discussed or perceived, especially the structural and institutional issues implied in the sudden change from corporatist to liberal democratic politics. By 1945 political crisis, especially a general crisis of hegemony, had become the norm in Brazil, with nothing yet found to replace the relatively stable system of the Old Republic, designed to express and safeguard the interests of an agrarian export-based bourgeoisie, but which already had been creaking well before 1930. The *Estado Novo* had provided tighter centralized control and a much-strengthened state apparatus to support the needs of industrial groups, still mostly centred in São Paulo. Neither system, however, had aimed to develop other priorities, such as a well-organized, sufficiently autonomous trade union movement, a viable pattern of social reforms for the majority of Brazil's people, or a political system designed to protect and strengthen popular liberties and genuinely popular representation. How easily, then, could corporatist structures and institutions be rejected or changed in terms of the very different priorities contained in the alleged new commitment to democratic politics? How far, for example, would the content, as well as the whole spirit, of corporatist legislation relating to the labour movement be changed, and how far would that movement, and all organizations and groups on the left of Brazilian political life, perceive and respond to the changing, or perhaps relatively little changing, pattern of national politics? How, too, would all these issues be affected by other related factors, especially changes in both the national and international economies, such problems, for example, as the already mounting inflation and the widening role of the United States both in Brazil and in Latin America as a whole?

It was to take two decades for most of these questions to be resolved, and even then not fully. At the level of social and political analysis they are still fiercely debated, and will be even more so in the future as more evidence becomes available and as the body of relevant social theory is further refined both by Brazilian and other experience of the relations between social tensions, rising demands for change, and the capacity in particular of liberal democracy to accommodate and satisfy such tensions and demands. The ten years after 1945, to the death of Vargas and the succession, after further political crisis, of Juscelino Kubitschek, were to make all these issues sharper and more urgent, if still no nearer solution.

Electoral Politics

A further irony of Brazilian politics in late 1945 was that, even though Vargas had been removed to Rio Grande do Sul, his influence and prestige seemed to grow rather than diminish, just as almost a decade later his political stature was to be enormously increased by the tragic circumstances of his death and the issues which he underscored in his final message to the Brazilian people. It was largely fear of Vargas's popular appeal which had precipitated the *coup* in October, but already, too, there was evidence that Vargas had been right to stress the danger of sharp conservative reaction in the name of democracy. His recent anti-trust legislation, for example, issued in June and coming into force on 1 August, had aimed to curb monopolies and the penetration into Brazil's economy of foreign capitalist interests, which, Vargas had argued, too easily worked against the real interests of the Brazilian people. Although in line with his other stands on economic nationalism, this legislation, largely the work of Agamemnon Magalhães, reflected an early awareness of the ease with which in the post-war period, foreign, especially United States, interests could operate in Brazil. It was strongly opposed by United States business interests and by the UDN, who claimed to represent free enterprise capitalism as against the illegitimate state control exercised by Vargas.[1] Those who saw Vargas, therefore, as the spokesman for Brazilian nationalism and of opposition to the social interests most strongly expressed in the UDN were merely confirmed in their support when one of the first acts of the Linhares government was to repeal the anti-trust legislation, while also starting a sharp, though brief, attack on left-wing groups just as they were emerging in the new ostensibly democratic system.

This was for the *Queremistas* and those who had heeded Vargas's warnings with regard to 'powerful reactionary forces, some hidden, others visible', only one straw in the wind: but it was enough, together with other evidence, to make them hesitate to give unreserved support to the official PSD presidential candidate, General Dutra, towards whom Vargas himself had been so conspicuously cool. The position, therefore, which Vargas would adopt in his seclusion in Rio Grande do Sul became an increasingly important factor as the election approached.

One obvious reason for this was that two of the major parties, the PSD and the PTB, had been created by Vargas, still reflecting his patronage through a wide net of political clientele rather than any clearly expressed demands from below. In this respect the new political institutions were able to transmit throughout the country, and translate into electoral behaviour, the widespread fear that the removal of Getúlio might mark a move towards reaction and a concession to foreign interests working through a narrow group of Brazilian associates. Increasingly, therefore, the country watched for a sign from Vargas. For his part Getúlio made very clear his hesitancy and doubts about Dutra, who might well have been dropped as PSD candidate but for the continuing support of his military colleague, Góes Monteiro.[2] It was only on 28 November, four days before the elections, that Vargas, now convinced that continued silence might lead to a victory for Gomes and the UDN, at last made a statement supporting Dutra, so putting the whole weight of the PTB as well as PSD organization behind him.[3]

It would be wrong, on the other hand, to conclude, as sometimes has been done, that the success of Dutra, beating Eduardo Gomes by 3,251,507 (56 per cent) votes to 2,039,341 (34·7 per cent), was simply due to Vargas's support, or that the influence of Vargas on the electorate sprang solely from the patronage he had been able to command as president. Already by 1945, as previously argued, the social-class contours of Brazilian politics were emerging, not least in the confrontation between the UDN and those political groups and parties who, in however limited a degree, represented the demand for change and a more substantial share of power and resources to those who previously had been excluded. The demand for change, as well as a recognition of the social content of Vargas's legislation in recent years, was directly reflected in the Congressional vote in 1945 as nearly 6 million Brazilians cast their vote, as compared with well under 2 million male voters in the crucial presidential election of 1930. The UDN polled 26·3 per cent of the total vote (1,575,375) as compared to a combined total for the PSD and PTB, of 3,135,440 (53·4 per cent of the total). Other parties took 20·3 per cent of the total, 1,213,797 votes. The choice between Dutra and Gomes for president was not such as to reveal the strength of feeling over the need for reform, though even the presidential election gave some clues in providing nearly 10 per cent of the total vote (569,818) for Yeddo Fiuza, a former mayor of Petrópolis, not himself a Communist, but who stood as the candidate of the Communist Party and was able to win such a high degree of electoral support.[4] But the Congressional elections gave much more evidence of a widespread sympathy for policies more nationalist and reformist than those represented by the UDN.

After ten years of repression and clandestine life the PCB (Brazilian Communist Party) provided in some respects the biggest of the electoral surprises, again reflecting the support within the country for policies which promised reform. As well as the 10 per cent vote for Fiuza in the presidential elections there was a 9 per cent Communist vote in the Congressional elections, returning one senator and fourteen congressmen (out of the total of 286 seats in the lower house). Such results scarcely pointed towards a pro-Communist landslide, but were sufficiently impressive in terms of the early chequered history and weak organization of the party and, above all, the repression suffered by it over the last decade. The vote partly reflected a more sympathetic attitude towards the Soviet Union as an ally during the war. It depended greatly on the personal prestige of Luís Carlos Prestes,[5] and of some of the other leading PCB candidates, such as, for example, the novelist Jorge Amado and the forceful Carlos Marighela, both of whom were elected.[6] The Communist vote, while influenced by personalities, also revealed genuine awareness of class divisions and substantial social issues on the part of many of the urban electorate who voted for the Communist candidates. It was, however, a vote for reform rather than for revolution, since the Communist Party leaders had already made clear their commitment to work through a democratically elected assembly, while also being willing to accept, in the short term, the continuation of Vargas as president. They were more willing to side with him and his growing appeal to urban labour than to trust his bitter opponents in the UDN. The party's analysis has been severely criticized in later years, as opportunist or shallow or fatally compromising, but it also seems to have reflected a genuine optimism on the part of the PCB that the main fascist threat was over and that the party would be allowed to work within the liberal democratic system, especially working through the trade unions, as the most prominent force of the organized working class. But such hopes were also mingled with a deep suspicion of General Dutra and other army leaders, again reinforcing the move towards Vargas and the *Queremistas*.

The controversy over the PCB's analysis and role is a large one, still growing in Brazil in relation to interpretations of the period 1945 to 1964, and made more poignant and relevant by experience in other societies, most notably in Chile from 1970 to 1973. PCB strategy was also sharply criticized at the time both inside and outside the party. Within the party much of the criticism turned on the personal role of Prestes,[7] while critics to the left of the PCB, especially the Trotskyists, were most concerned about the Communists' too exclusive identification with the trade union movement, their failure to perceive a more genuinely revolutionary role for the working class, and their willingness to compromise with Vargas and the whole process of 'bourgeois democracy'.[8] The political experience of the Brazilian left over the next few years was to reinforce rather than discredit such criticism, as Eurico Dutra now took office and began the process of reaction and conservatism which many feared would follow the first burst of democratic euphoria.

Constitution and Reaction

One of the senators returned in 1945 was Vargas. He had eventually agreed to presenting himself as candidate and now showed the strength of his personal following, notably among the industrial workers of São Paulo, who, in marked contrast to São Paulo's middle-class politicians and wealthy newspaper-owners, had continued to support Vargas ever since 1930. Getúlio was elected as senator from São Paulo and the Federal District and as congressman from the Federal District and six states.

Even before Vargas returned to Rio de Janeiro to take his senate seat, rather belatedly, in June 1946, there were disturbing signs of the move towards reaction which he and many others in Brazil had feared from President Dutra. The first signs of such a move came between March to May 1946, and fairly predictably, centred around the PCB; but the issues involved evidently went deeper and further than the hostility and suspicion of Dutra and other army and civilian political leaders for the party which had called for revolution in 1935. They were grounded in the party's increasingly successful activity to organize industrial workers, especially as represented by a growing number of strikes and industrial disputes. The Communist challenge represented, therefore, a major issue not just for the PCB, but for all parties and groups linked to the working-class movement and likely to find themselves in dispute with the government and employers.

It is important in this respect to stress again the intensity of popular and working-class activity in the immediate post-war period, since 1945 to 1946 was, in fact, to produce a wave of strikes and industrial action unequalled in scope and intensity until the early 1960s, in the period of acute confrontation under Quadros and Goulart immediately before the *coup* of 1964. Such activity should especially be stressed in the light of interpretations of the Brazilian working class which ascribe to it a lack of capacity for organizing and expressing demands, interpretations usually associated with the idea of the relative 'backwardness' of Brazilian workers or their malleability resulting from rural, and later urban, patronage, both social and political.[9]

The reaction to this activity was eventually to affect all parties and groups concerned, but in 1946 the most obvious target was the PCB, which was, indeed, most involved in industrial and working-class organization, but which was also the most vulnerable as the short post-war honeymoon period in international relations gave way to the start of the Cold War and the long period of mutual suspicion and antagonism. Despite the safeguards supposedly contained in the new democratic system, Communists were arrested, the party offices occupied, and in May 1946 all known Communists were removed from all government posts. It was arguable that such treatment of the PCB was exceptional, and that similar reaction would not necessarily affect parties which did not have the PCB's background of revolutionary involvement and its now highly suspect international connections. But this was at best a slender hope.

Similar tensions were seen in the new constitution of 18 September 1946. This gave the vote to Brazilians over eighteen, but with some exceptions, most notably in the case of illiterates and enlisted men in the armed forces. These exceptions were, however, enough still to exclude from the franchise over half of Brazil's population, and were to be a source of trouble in the future. More seriously still, the new constitution took over largely intact the whole body of corporatist-inspired social and labour legislation from the *Estado Novo*, confirming the federal government's much-extended power in these areas, but also establishing what were, in effect, legal and institutional contradictions of a system which now claimed to aim at wider, more genuine representation for the mass of Brazil's people. The previous legislation had sought to make the trade union movement merely another arm of the state apparatus. The new constitution still seemed to envisage a controlled, ultimately pliable, trade union movement rather than an organization of and for the working class which could offer effective challenge, when necessary, to employers and the government, and which could substantially modify the previous balance of political power and social privilege. Here again, as in the issue of the limited electorate, was to be one of the main points of persistent tension over the next two decades. Were the working-class movement and popular political forces to be, at the end of the day, little more than tools, part of a wider mechanism of control, in the hands of those who held economic and political power, or would they be allowed some genuine autonomy in a democratic process which might, albeit gradually and without violence, substantially change Brazilian society?

All these questions became sharper in 1947, following state elections in January and supplementary elections for Congress. The PCB now had two new federal deputies and 46 state deputies in 15 state legislatures, being especially strong in the Federal District and in São Paulo, where the PCB vote was larger than that for the UDN. This again represented about 10 per cent of the vote, even though the number of parties had now reached fourteen. Party membership was estimated at about 200,000, the great majority of them trade unionists, being especially influential among dock unions, metalworkers, printing and textile workers, with the party exerting most of the influence in the Confederation of Brazilian Workers (Confederação dos Trabalhadores do Brasil, CTB), as it developed from September 1946.

By early 1947 the PCB was obviously becoming a major political force and a serious challenger to the UDN and those in the PSD who were willing to work closely with UDN politicians. The party had divided the working-class vote in São Paulo with the PTB, and shown its electoral skills by bargaining with the former *interventor*, Adhemar de Barros, in helping him to be elected as governor. Dutra and his advisers became thoroughly alarmed at such success, so unpalatable not only to Dutra but to other vocal anti-Communists, such as the Minister of War, General Canrobert Pereira da Costa, and to the essentially conservative cabinet, which even included members from the UDN. This coalition between the PSD and UDN already had been condemned by Vargas, who strongly criticized the new government for its conservatism and its increasing subservience to foreign governments, and for its ever more observable connections with foreign financial interests. Such criticism did not, however, deter Dutra and his colleagues from moving against the PCB, using a clause in the 1946 constitution which allowed the exclusion from politics of 'anti-democratic' parties. The whole emphasis of the PCB was, of course, that it *was* a democratic party, committed to working through the electoral system and Congress, and it was indeed largely its success in electoral politics which was now moving its opponents to suppress it in the name of democracy. In May 1947 the PCB was declared illegal and in October the Senate voted to remove all Communists from elected office, a process fully approved by the army leaders who had remained resolutely anti-Communist and by other interests outside Brazil, especially in the United States, now moving quickly into Cold War confrontation. The suppression of the PCB was accompanied by further moves against working-class groupings, most notably the Confederation of Brazilian Workers, and, in all, the government 'intervened' in 143 out of a total of 944 unions to remove what it described as 'extremist' elements.[10]

The significance of this reaction of the Dutra government on the shaping of party politics and the future of Brazilian democracy almost certainly has been underestimated. Previous attempts at popular organization, as in the period of and immediately after the First World War, had been repressed, when they seemed to offer a serious challenge. The 1930s had seen the further limitation of the expression of popular demands. The opening of the political system in 1945 had seemed, on the other hand, to promise new opportunities, working through an electoral party system and by means of legal industrial activity to improve wages and conditions, especially through a trade union movement which really had some teeth. The swift reaction against the PCB, and the evident threat of further moves against any other movement described as 'extremist', both disappointed those who had hoped for a more open political system capable of producing social and economic reforms, and confirmed the analysis of others, who had always regarded with judicious scepticism the claim of Dutra and others to be offering democratic government to Brazil. In terms of future political practice this reaction was especially important, since it sharply underlined the difficulty of developing explicitly class-based policies and opposition movements within the existing system. The removal of the PCB, and of other groups who had gone beyond the permitted limits of opposition and political demand, pointed to, and now further encouraged, a style of politics which blurred and confused such demands, movements and parties which could at most be multi-class in their membership and programme, which too easily turned to demagoguery rather than hard-edged social analysis and which too readily confused emotional nationalism with a serious, substantial programme of social change for the majority of Brazil's people. The removal, in other words, of the PCB and other more explicitly class-based groupings from electoral politics slowed down and damaged the electoral system, weakening its credibility and lessening its capacity for accommodating and channelling wider social and economic demands than the previous political systems of Brazil had tolerated. Together with other processes working simultaneously in the post-war period the reaction pushed Brazil further towards what later was to be described as 'populist' politics. This loss of an independent working-class movement was to have far-reaching consequences for Brazil.

Meanwhile the Dutra government, strongly encouraged by the United States, continued for its first two years with policies of economic liberalism and free trade, allowing the free entry of consumer goods and other imports, which soon began to drain the foreign reserves of US$800 million with which the new government had started in 1945. There was strong criticism of policies which seemed so blatantly to favour those social groups who could afford imported consumer goods, but the government was at first determined to avoid as far as possible state intervention and state controls such as had been developed in the *Estado Novo*. A serious deterioation in its exchange reserves by mid-1947 forced it to think again, imposing exchange controls and a system of import licences, which substantially slowed down the import of consumer goods in favour of more urgently needed capital equipment. The change also provided new stimulus to Brazilian industry, quickening the process of import substitution to satisfy home demand, a move further encouraged by a high rate of exchange for the cruzeiro, which helped to encourage production for the domestic market rather than for export. The result of such measures, however reluctantly they had been adopted, was an annual growth-rate for 1945 to 1951 of about 6 per cent, an early sign of the dynamism of the Brazilian economy. Another more positive aspect of the Dutra government was an effort to come to grips with regional development, especially in the São Francisco valley, Amazonas, and the north-east.

The whole thrust of the Dutra administration, however, was unmistakably conservative, seeking to satisfy the wealthier sections of society not only by the import of luxury consumer goods, which squandered precious foreign currency, but also by allowing others in society to bear most of the brunt of the post-war inflation by refusing to increase wages. While, therefore, the growth-rate increased, the real minimum wage steadily declined. falling from a base of 100 in 1944 to 84·2 in 1945, 74·1 in 1946, 60·7 in 1947, 58 in 1948, 54·4 in 1949, and 50·9 in 1950.[11] Resources, it seemed, rather than being transferred from the richer to the poorer groups in Brazilian society, were going the other way under a government whose ideological commitment to free enterprise capitalism, under the strong influence of the United States, made it a ready target for reformist and nationalist critics, who now began to be even more vocal as the 1950 elections approached.

Vargas and Brazilian Populism

The elections of 1950 brought the first real excitement to electoral politics since the presidential election of 1930, but now the electorate was far bigger and the experience, in particular, of the last five years had made the issues much sharper and the debate more intense. The elections were also made much more real for most of the voters, as the candidates now had to tour the country, flying great distances to places previously remote from the centres of national political activity, wooing the electorate in a way never before required. Above all, this was a new experience for Getúlio Vargas, presenting himself as a popular candidate for the office he had held for fifteen years, arguing and debating in an exhausting electoral campaign to urge his case against that of the UDN candidate, Eduardo Gomes, and the official PSD choice, a conservative *mineiro* politician, Cristiano Machado.[12]

Vargas had agreed to run for presidency, after an initial show of reluctance, backed by the PTB and by those elements in the PSD who were unhappy about the recent alignments of their party with the UDN. The electoral campaign which he now undertook marked the full, clear emergence of what since then has become known as Brazilian 'populism'.

Of all the neologisms to appear in recent political writing, especially on Latin America, 'populism' is one of the most confusing and least precise, despite the almost neo-scholastic debate it has engendered and the many, laborious, attempts at refinement. The term as applied to Latin America was from the first a rich source of semantic confusion, since its usage was markedly different from that found elsewhere, especially in writing on Russian politics, where 'populism' was already established as a shorthand term to describe the romantic *narodniki* movements of the nineteenth century.[13] Despite this confusion, however, the term has persisted, mainly because otherwise some other word would have to be used to describe what currently is understood, however vaguely, by 'populism'.

Originally in the Latin American context the term 'populism' was used by Argentine social scientists in their efforts to analyse Peronism in the 1940s and 1950s, then applied elsewhere in Latin America in an attempt to provide a more comprehensive explanation of the pattern of politics in the whole area.[14] Without entering the now tangled debate on the meaning and use of the term it is enough to notice that it generally refers to political movements, political regimes, or even political systems which are characterized by a mass appeal which is multi-class rather than confined to one class or group interest, which is often associated with some emotive call, for example, to nationalism, and which often, though not always, is linked to a particular political leader, such as Perón. The attempts to define 'populism' more precisely have invariably come to grief, largely because it has been used to cover a wide variety of phenomena, so ending up as a cluster or loose bundle of associated characteristics rather than as a rigorous, relatively scientific definition. The term has also suffered in being applied to movements as well as regimes, to political style as well as political content, and in being used in many contexts as a pejorative term, connoting political manipulation from above, rather than as a more objective category to measure political behaviour. Partly, too, it has suffered from being used *negatively*, namely, as describing a movement or regime which was not based on class interest or sharpened class-consciousness, but on a diffuse amalgam of interests ultimately contradictory and incapable of sustaining what was perceived as more 'genuine', namely class-based, political activity.

Yet in relation to Brazil, as to Argentina and elsewhere, the term is useful, so has meaning, since it allows easy reference to phenomena with which any analysis must come to grips. Even in relation to Brazil there are two related, but still sufficiently distinct uses of the term. One, the less common, is similar to the usage of 'populism' in relation to nineteenth-century Russia, referring broadly to the attempts of intellectuals, mostly from the cities, to work with the peasantry and to seek political solutions in large measure derived from peasant traditions and institutions. Such movements, strongly marked in many societies by an anarchist intellectual heritage which tended towards a romantic 'noble savage' view of the peasantry, are paralleled in Latin America, notably in some of the attempts of students and intellectuals to bridge the gap between themselves and the peasantry, as in certain instances in Cuba, Peru under Belaúnde Terry, Bolivia, and in Chile under *Unidad Popular*. There are also elements of this form of 'populist' activity in the work of radical Catholic groups, particularly in the north-east of Brazil, especially in the early 1960s.[15] Such activity mainly involves *rural* communities, but is not exclusively confined to them, since attempts at *conscientização*, the changing of social and political consciousness, have been made also in the cities.

The other use of 'populism', which is much more common in relation to Argentina and Brazil, mainly refers to *urban* rather than rural politics, principally because it relates to the politics of a mass electorate, which historically has developed in the cities rather than the countryside. Again, however, it is in no sense exclusively urban, developing in a rural context as soon as the rural vote becomes important, as in the case of the politics of Francisco Julião in the north-east, or of Christian Democrat politicians in rural Chile under Frei, or again, to some degree, in Belaúnde Terry's campaigns among the Peruvian peasantry, though *Cooperación Popular* fits more closely into the first usage of populism as already described. One of the most frequent contexts in which populism is used in relation to urban electoral politics is in reference to the continuous success of Adhemar de Barros in São Paulo, who, after having been *interventor* in the 1930s, was elected governor in 1947, with the help of the PCB, then managed to retain his hold, building up a political machine in the form of his own political party, the PSP (Partido Social Progressista), supported by widespread patronage and a constant readiness to oil the political wheels whenever it should be necessary. Both as governor and as mayor of São Paulo, Adhemar de Barros was generally regarded as a corrupt politician, but he built up a remarkable political machine, particularly interesting in that it covered not just the city, but much of the state of São Paulo.[16] But it was not just the corruption of machine politics, delivering material benefits to its clients, which won votes for de Barros. He could appeal successfully to many of the poor and 'marginal' people of São Paulo, who, even if they regarded him as a crook, believed he was effective and responded to his 'populist' rhetoric and lavish promises.[17] Eventually the PSP was to extend well beyond São Paulo, winning in the Congressional elections of 1958 7·4 per cent of the national vote, electing 25 deputies, and in 1962, 4·7 per cent, electing 23 deputies.

As it is applied to Vargas and his associates the term 'populist' lays less emphasis on 'machine' politics, though the PSD and PTB represented a formidable combination of patronage and electoral control, and has far less connotation, as compared with the 'populism' of Adhemar de Barros, of direct systematic corruption for personal gain. It draws attention, rather, to a particular political style, in terms of the appeal to the mass urban electorate, especially through *trabalhismo*, and to the element, however conscious or otherwise on the part of Vargas and his associates, of the *manipulation* of a *multi-class alliance*, which further hindered the emergence of a more authentic, autonomous working-class political movement.[18]

The debate over the nature and significance of populism is a tangled one, raising such highly controversial issues as whether a more independent strategy on the part of the PCB would really have allowed the development of a more challenging popular political movement, and whether, despite the elements of class alliance so often emphasized in subsequent analyses, the populist politics of Vargas and his successors did not, after all, represent a genuine challenge to that pattern of political control required by their enemies, gathered in, or associated with, the UDN. Certain features of Vargista populism are, however, beyond dispute.

The first is that it was closely associated with the rapid expansion of the electorate and the adoption of a liberal democratic electoral system after 1945. There were, as we have noted, signs of a turn towards a direct appeal to the people, based on the reformist content of the social and labour legislation, well before 1945, but only when the need to begin to court a future electorate already had been perceived. There were even elements of 'populist' politics much earlier, notably in the presidential election of 1930; but there was no sign of it in the intervening years, especially in the first years of the *Estado Novo,* when electoral appeal was unnecessary. Secondly, it was a political style geared to an increasingly urban wage-earning electorate, if not necessarily to an industrial electorate in a narrow sense;[19] and, thirdly, as primarily a form of electoral politics, it required as comprehensive an appeal as possible, to win voters of different social groups, so precluding any narrow, explicitly class-based programme, a factor which further encouraged the broad appeals to nationalism. Finally, whatever may have been the objective class content and purpose of Vargista populism as developed in the post-war years, there is no doubt that, right from the start, it was *perceived* as presenting a major social and political threat by powerful conservative forces both inside and outside Brazil. Rightly or wrongly it was perceived as being radical. This last point is also relevant for evaluating the role of the Brazilian Communist Party and the whole shaping of a multi-class alliance working for gradual change. An attempt at direct confrontation in 1935 had proved a disaster. Even the limited successes in mobilizing voters' and workers' protest from 1945 to 1947 had produced a predictable reaction and the repression of the party. A brief revival of a more aggressive strategy in the next two years had found little support. The commitment, therefore, to a more gradualist policy from 1950 onwards did not merely reflect the PCB's hope for collaboration with the 'national bourgeoisie' in moving towards a 'bourgeois revolution'. It was also a response to its own recent experience, an awareness that in the political context of the late 1940s and 1950s a 'populist' strategy was the most that would be *allowed* by the leaders of the armed forces and those social groups most strongly represented in the political system.

The elections of 1950 showed all these features already well developed. Vargas by now had aligned himself with the PTB, the party he had recommended to the workers in 1945, especially using it to build an urban electoral base, without at the same time breaking with his friends in the PSD, who could help to deliver the vote in rural areas. Always a realist in politics, he took care to ensure that the senior officers in the armed forces would allow his candidacy to proceed, sounding Góes Monteiro on their probable reaction, and agreeing to tone down to some degree his opposition to General Dutra's government.[20] Once reassured over the army leaders' attitude, Getúlio accepted the presidential nomination of the PTB and of Adhemar de Barros's PSP, while also managing to defuse some of the PSD support for its official candidate, Cristiano Machado, through his influence with former *interventores* in many states.

In a vigorous, though cautious, campaign Vargas remembered the warning of Góes Monteiro not to attack General Dutra personally, but he severely castigated the policies of the Dutra government, especially its economic policy, while defending his own previous record, above all in relation to social and labour legislation and in the development of Brazil's industry and infrastructure.[21] In direct contrast to the UDN candidate, Eduardo Gomes, he identified himself with the new, expanding, industrial and urban Brazil and with the mass of the Brazilian people, especially its working population, as contrasted to the social privilege and subservience to foreign economic interests which he alleged were represented by the UDN. One of his earliest speeches in the campaign was typical of most that were to follow. His time in São Borja, he emphasized, had given him time to reflect, moved by the confidence in him expressed by so many Brazilians, often his former opponents,[22] so that now he was willing to take on again the responsibilities urged on him by political forces and the 'popular masses'.[23] Criticizing recent government policy, and at the same time offering conciliation rather than opposition, he especially noted the impact of recent economic strategy on the workers of Brazil, promising to implement the social and labour legislation of the 1946 constitution.[24] At the same time, however, he stressed that he was no wild iconoclast; one must not confuse conservatism with reaction. It was possible to be conservative, yet anti-reactionary: the polity of tomorrow must be the work of those who can conserve what is good, and transform that good, if not into the best, at least into the better. What everyone wants, in the last analysis, is a higher standard of living for the Brazilian people ('povo brasileiro'), which can only follow the courageous and harmonious solution of the nation's economic problems, central to which is the development of industry, especially basic industries.[25] But there must also be attention to agriculture, partly to expand the internal market,[26] and all economic and social strategy must be supported by a foreign policy concerned, above all, with the good of Brazil and its people.[27]

These, in varying degrees, were to be the themes of the whole campaign: an emphasis on his own record, as contrasted with that of Dutra and the policies offered by his UDN opponents; special appeal to industrial workers and industrial interests, but without alienating those involved in agriculture; and the promise of a flexible, independent policy in relation to other nations. The emphasis was on reform and change, without going to excess, pointing to whatever examples might serve—the cautious, limited nationalization in Great Britain, for example,[28] and the emphasis on man's dignity and equality contained in the encyclicals of recent popes.[29]

The whole campaign was cast in the same mould, vigorous enough to attract the votes of those who wanted change, but always judicious and attentive to the anxieties of those who, at best, wanted to make haste slowly.[30] As he journeyed through Brazil, he carefully modified his appeal as occasion demanded. In São Paulo, the land of the *bandeirante*, he reflected how all Brazilians in some measure were *paulistas*, and recalled with satisfaction the warmth of his reception in São Paulo in 1930 and 1938 (though passing silently over 1932), and his election as senator for São Paulo in 1945.[31] He had due praise for his political ally, Adhemar de Barros, but recalled, too, the benefits which his own government had brought to São Paulo's industry and the support which, he emphasized, had always been given to him by the *paulista* working class.

In Santos his stress was on the importance of coffee to Brazil's economy.[32] In a brief stop in Pirapora, Minas Gerais, he recalled the contribution of the *mineiros* to the revolution of 1930 and the winning of the secret vote,[33] while in the Federal District, again in an important centre of the urban, industrial vote, he emphasized particularly the benefits his government had brought to the working class, claiming that he had governed with the people and the workers ('com o povo e com os trabalhadores'). Now, however, in Rio de Janeiro he went beyond the usual diffuse language of populism, with its references to the undifferentiated mass of the people ('o povo'), to use the sharper, more evocative language of class confrontation. In his time, he said, Labour Day had become a day of celebration, of large open-air gatherings, expressing unity and enthusiasm: '. . . It was the time when the government took stock of the measures taken on behalf of the proletariat [das medidas tomadas em favor do proletariado] and announced new labour laws . . .'[34] Recalling the achievements of his previous government, including Volta Redonda, the nascent motor industry, and attention to the country's road network, he especially noted the continuous improvements in the state of the navy, the way in which 'the army became one of the great forces of the Continent, provided with modern equipment and ready to undertake the most difficult missions', and how the air force was developed to take its place, together with the other services, in accepting the challenge of the Axis powers.[35] But, above all, it was on his relations with the working class, and his current appeal through the PTB, that Vargas laid most emphasis. During his previous time in office the people was the government and the government was the people ('o Govêrno era o povo e o povo era o Govêrno'.)[36] Now the PTB is the political arm of the people ('a arma política do povo'), to carry out the people's wishes and protect the people's rights.[37] The people, Vargas repeated, had suffered too much from the financial policies of the present government, hit by soaring inflation as foreign reserves were squandered. He had not intended again to seek public office, but the people had called him back: 'If I should be elected on 3 October, as I take office the people will climb the steps of the Catete with me, and will stay with me in government.'[38]

As he toured Brazil, Vargas repeated these same points, standing on his record, criticizing the current government's policies, and promising renewed attention to social reform and wider opportunities and a share in national wealth to the mass of the people, without, at the same time, appearing too extreme or irresponsible in his demands. This last is a point to be underlined. Vargas was now in his final electoral campaign, looking back at the age of sixty-seven and vindicating his whole political career, while also engaging vigorously in the new electoral campaign. He now, sadly, had only four more years to live before his tragic death in August 1954. Reading, therefore, through these campaign speeches, one wonders where is the populist demagogue, rich in easy promises, ready to make highly emotive appeals directly to the people, as so often Vargas is portrayed by his critics? The style, certainly, is highly coloured, the language often emotional, the appeal varied as his changing audience required: but such is the technique of electoral campaigning in most societies. At no point does Vargas touch the froth and frenzy of campaigns in many other societies thought to be so much more 'developed' and 'modern' in their politics: nor is his rhetoric half as colourful as much that is considered perfectly proper elsewhere.

Part of the answer seems to be that the subsequent image of Vargas the populist leader was largely created by his enemies, eager to portray him as an irresponsible demagogue, while it was also embellished by confusing the political style of Vargas with that of some of his successors and associates. When under severe pressure in his last years, he responded, understandably, with emotion and passion, as seen above all in his final message to the Brazilian people. But in the campaign of 1950, it is worth emphasizing, he still remains closer to Vargas the candidate of the Liberal Alliance in 1930, the mature, responsible ex-Minister of Finance, than to that archetype of rabble-rousing demagoguery so often sneered at by his enemies.

It was not, however, simply Vargas's speeches and campaigning which brought him victory in 1950. His opponents were divided, split between their support for Eduardo Gomes and Cristiano Machado, and further weakened by the covert, and often not so covert, allegiance to Vargas of many of the PSD organizers throughout the country. He was further helped by the relatively colourless campaign of the UDN candidate and by a general disenchantment with the Dutra government. On 3 October, out of a total population of just under 52 million, and out of a registered electorate now numbering 11,455,149 (namely 22 per cent of the population), just over 8¼ million Brazilians cast their vote (8,254,989), a turnout of 72·1 per cent. Of these, 1,697,193 (21·48 per cent) voted for Cristiano Machado, 2,342,384 (29·65 per cent) for Eduardo Gomes, and 3,849,040 (48·73 per cent) for Getúlio Vargas.[39] Vargas's proportion of the vote was less than that won by Dutra in 1945 (55·3 per cent), but higher than that achieved by the victors in the two other presidential elections which were to be held in Brazil between 1950 and the *coup* of 1964.[40] Faced with such a resounding electoral defeat, the opponents of Vargas, especially in the UDN, still tried to prevent his taking office, by arguing that the constitution of 1946 required an absolute majority. It was scarcely a creditable or dignified objection, and difficult to square with their democratic protestations of only a few years earlier; but it was another straw in the wind, a further hint that there were powerful interests in Brazilian politics which would again be willing to change the rules of the game, or even to bring the game to a close, if the score seemed to be going against them. In January 1951, the Superior Electoral Tribunal quashed the objection, and on 31 January 1951 Getúlio Vargas was again president of Brazil.

The People's President

Vargas was well aware of the extent and intensity of the opposition being organized against him. His preference for moderation and conciliation was, therefore, further strengthened as he came to office in 1951 by the knowledge that he must belie the charges of irresponsibility in social and economic policy and of opportunism and personal ambition in his political strategy. He also knew how serious were the problems facing him, not only the economic and financial difficulties bequeathed by the Dutra government, but, more intractable still, the mounting social tensions, exacerbated by Dutra's refusal to raise wages and his repressive attitude towards popular political organization. Vargas had no illusions as to the size of the job facing him, as he clearly warned his enthusiastic supporters right at the start of his new presidency: 'I am not coming to sow illusions: nor should you expect of me prodigies and miracles'.[41] He was no magician, he said. Nor would he offer a programme which was unrealistic and deceptive:

> But you do have a right to a better life, and to a gradually increasing, more equitable share in the product of your labour, in the wealth of the community, in the fruits and benefits of progress, and in the comforts and amenities of life . . .[42]

But such advances, he emphasized, should be made available to *all* Brazilians. All should have greater equality of opportunity in such crucial areas as education, earnings, and economic security, protected from speculators growing fat on illegal profits and those who traded on the misery and exploitation of their fellow citizens. His appeal, therefore, was for greater unity, behind a government which was not the tool of 'parties, groups, classes, or interests', but which worked for all classes, for all the people.

This same need to emphasize unity and collaboration rather than factionalism and party interest was also reflected in the membership of Vargas's new cabinet. Far from being composed of the more extreme spokesmen for social change, still less for revolution, it was a careful balance of different interests, and an acknowledgement of the heterogeneous electoral support which had returned Vargas to office. The help given by Adhemar de Barros's PSP was rewarded by the Ministry of Transport; the Ministry of Finance went to the PSD, in the person of Horácio Lafer, a *paulista* industrialist; while the PTB, significantly enough, received only one ministry, albeit a key one, the Ministry of Labour, which was given to one of Getúlio's most energetic supporters, Danton Coelho. Even the UDN was not excluded, as Vargas acknowledged help given to him in Pernambuco by João Cleofas, the state UDN leader, who had sided with Vargas when the PSD in that state had agreed to support Machado. Cleofas was now made Minister of Agriculture, never an important ministry, but enough to show Vargas's readiness to collaborate across party lines rather than sharpen and intensify political differences.

Even in 1951 Vargas knew he was walking a political tightrope: hence these attempts at conciliation and a general political strategy which at every point was comprehensive rather than exclusive, as seen again in his military appointments. His new Minister of War was General Estillac Leal, a former *tenente* who had been on the march with the Prestes Column, and who now was one of the military spokesmen for a more nationalist economic policy. The Ministry of the Air Force went to Colonel Nero Moura, who had served with distinction in Italy, and who had expressed his dissatisfaction over the summary removal of Vargas in 1945. No one knew better than Getúlio Vargas the absolute need to keep the armed forces on his side, loyal to the elected president. In fifteen years of government he had seen them intervene decisively in every political crisis, and he now evidently hoped that he could associate them with his new government and his limited, deliberately circumspect proposals for change. Unfortunately, events were to prove this a forlorn hope, as the officer class of the Brazilian armed forces, when faced with the choice between loyalty to the elected, constitutional president and acquiescence in a process of limited social change, chose to abandon their constitutional role, first to depose Vargas, then his political successor, João Goulart. By 1964 their record was such that from the end of the term of President Artur Bernardes in 1926 to the removal of Goulart in 1964 only two elected presidents left office peacefully, in accordance with the constitution, at the end of a full term—Dutra in 1950 and Kubitschek in 1961. At every other point, with the exception of the resignation of Quadros, the armed forces had intervened decisively in one way or another. Vargas's hopes of governing with the armed forces, while responding adequately to demands for change, unfortunately ran counter to the ideology of the officer corps, especially as it now was reinforced by intense Cold War propaganda under the growing influence of United States colleagues as expressed in the Escola Superior de Guerra, the National War College,[43] founded in 1949.

The role of the armed forces and the importance, in particular, of the ESG (Escola Superior de Guerra) are discussed in more detail later. It is worth noting, however, one feature of military politics evident by the early 1950s. This was that already, at the very start of his term in office, Vargas was being criticized, even openly opposed, by an ever more confident and coherent 'interventionist' group among senior military officers, especially in the army. The difference in the degree of confidence and of explicit ideology between the armed forces' leaders in Brazil in 1964 and in, for example, 1889 has been noticed already; but even by the early 1950s there was a distinctive group of army and air force officers whose concept of the political role of the armed forces was changing significantly. The change partly stemmed from the recent political tradition of the Brazilian officer corps, but mostly from the impact of the ESG, founded in 1949.[44] Brazilian officers already had a strong tradition of concerned, thoughtful involvement in national politics, as seen in the protests of the *tenentes* in the 1920s, in the demands for a more aggressive economic nationalism in the 1930s, and in the general concern over the shaping of Brazilian politics, both national and international, as expressed by army spokesmen such as Góes Monteiro, always closely involved with civilian as well as military politics. But the founding of the ESG introduced a new dimension to such military involvement. Building on contacts with the United States armed forces in Italy, it provided courses both for civilian as well as military personnel and rapidly elaborated a coherent ideology of national development and national security to guide future choices on economic and political issues. The nature and content of that ideology are discussed elsewhere, but, in evaluating the position of Vargas in his final years, it is at least important to remember the existence, even in the early 1950s, of this group of officers, typified by men, such as the ex-*tenentes* Cordeiro de Farias and Juarez Távora, who saw Brazil firmly aligned with the Western bloc, whose earlier anti-communism had been intensified by more recent Cold War propaganda, and whose earlier, more 'liberal' view of the army's role, already eroded during the *Estado Novo*, was now giving way to a readiness to accept direct intervention and control by the armed forces, should this seem to be in the 'national interest'.

The whole question of the meaning of this 'national interest', especially of how the armed forces' leaders and the politicians associated with the UDN understood it, was made still more intense by the economic and social issues facing Vargas as he took office. Two questions, in particular, caused him concern, both fundamental to the whole political economy of Brazil and both to prove a source of persistent tension and disagreement long after the death of Vargas. The first was the role of international capital and foreign interests in Brazil's economy. The second was the direction and pace of redistribution of wealth and opportunity, especially in an economy already hit by rapid inflation. Both these questions, raising the crucial issues of who gets what, and how, and why, were scarcely new in Brazil. Nor were they in any sense exclusive to Brazil or Latin America. They were, however, to come to the forefront of Brazilian political debate, making that country's experience, and the reflection on that experience, all the more valuable in later years, when problems once elsewhere considered, rather smugly, to be peculiarly 'Latin American' suddenly began to impinge more sharply on other societies. These, too, now found themselves similarly hit by inflation, similarly open to demands for wage increases and wider distribution, and, a happy irony, similarly vulnerable to exploitation by rapid international deals against their currency, or by the arbitrary, seemingly uncontrollable, behaviour of large international corporations.[45]

Vargas's criticism of the open-door policies of the Dutra regime and its ready response to the demands of foreign business and financial interests, especially from the United States, had already involved him in the swelling debate on the need for tighter, more 'nationalist' controls. Again this discussion, later to be defined more clearly in the controversy over 'dependent' capitalism, was already an old one in Brazil. It had been seen in the *tenentes*' attacks on the vulnerability of the coffee economy in the 1920s and in the long discussions leading to the establishment of a national steel industry in the late 1930s and early 1940s. This latter debate had shown that on the issue of economic nationalism Vargas could expect much more support from the armed forces than he might receive, for example, on the question of redistribution of wealth; but, as he now became more embroiled in the debate over the role of foreign capital, and especially as he faced the issue of a national petroleum industry, he became more fully aware of the strength of the opposition to his demands for tighter control and state intervention.

In all his early statements on the role of foreign capital Vargas was again careful to adopt a moderate tone, stressing that it had its place as long as it behaved responsibly. He soon found, however, for a variety of reasons, that profit remittances were unacceptably high, and that further controls were necessary. The issue was a complex one, not simply dictated by doctrinaire nationalism, since even the Dutra government, faced by 1947 with a deteriorating balance of payments, had had to impose limits of 8 per cent profit remittance of registered capital.[46] In the next few years, as inflation grew worse, the official exchange rate was kept at the overvalued level of 18·5 cruzeiros to the dollar, as compared to a black-market rate of scarcely half that value. One result of such overvaluation was that: 'foreign investors were in effect subsidised when remitting profits (dollars were artificially cheap) and penalised when making new investments (cruzeiros were artificially expensive)',[47] so that: '. . . In the seven years between 1947 and 1953, the inflow of venture capital averaged only 15 million dollars per year, while profit remittances averaged 47 million dollars . . .'[48] The full significance of such figures can be disputed:[49] nor were they fully known by Vargas and his associates at the time. There was, however, a strong, growing conviction that profits going abroad were excessive, and that something should be done to prevent wealth produced in Brazil being drained off abroad. Vargas was not looking for confrontation. He had already co-operated with foreign advisers in examining the state of Brazil's economy, notably in relation to the American Technical

Mission of 1943 (the Cooke Mission), the SALTE Plan of 1948, the Programme of the Mixed Brazil–United States Commission (the Abbink Mission) of 1949, and, currently, the Joint Brazil–United States Economic Development Commission, which began work in July 1951 and finally published its report in 1954.[50] Vargas welcomed, for example, the creation of the BNDE (Banco Nacional do Desenvolvimento Econômico: National Development Bank), set up in 1952, seeing the advantages of closer ties with foreign investment and financial institutions, but, without having a fully clear and detailed grasp of the flow of foreign capital up to 1951, he was aware that something had to be done to halt what seemed to be a negative trend for Brazil.

When all the qualifications have been made, the most recent figures support his fears—a *total* loss, calculating both risk and loan capital, in 1948 of 165 million dollars, in 1949 of 44 million, and in 1950 a loss of 107 million.[51] Having set up a committee to examine the question of profit remittances in relation to the whole economy, especially the balance of payments problems, Vargas made a strong attack on excess profits in a speech of 31 December 1951. Noting Dutra's law of 27 February 1946, which limited repatriation of capital to 20 per cent annually and remission of profits to 8 per cent, he explained how that law had been sabotaged by another ruling in 1946, redefining 'capital' and allowing the removal from Brazil of 'the fruits of the labour of millions of Brazilians', a total sum almost equivalent to all the money circulating in the country.[52] He then delivered a blistering attack on all the subterfuges used to get around the profit remittance law, noting that as a result Brazil now must '. . . pay what we do not owe, restore what we have not received, and what is our own . . .'[53] Foreign investment and foreign capital, he said, should certainly be encouraged, and should have a fair return; but no one could allow such greedy pillaging of the nation's patrimony.[54] The interests of the Brazilian people, of Brazilian workers, would now, he promised, be defended.[55] The immediate result of this concern was a decree of January 1952, imposing a limit of 10 per cent on profit remittances, but still with the proviso that SUMOC should apply that limit only when the balance of payments situation required it. In practice, as exports expanded, this was not thought necessary, and in 1953 capital was allowed to move freely in and out of Brazil at the free rate of exchange, the facilities to foreign investors being further extended in 1955 and 1967.[56]

The distinction between Vargas's vigorous rhetoric and subsequent action again indicates his persistent preference for moderation. His critics made much of his alleged move to the left and his adoption of a more radically nationalist tone; but such criticism was either wrong-headed or aimed to present Vargas as an extreme nationalist demagogue. Essentially Vargas had not changed his position. His determination in 1951 to curb excessive profit remittances and protect Brazilian interests was entirely consistent with his earlier anti-trust legislation and his efforts to exert more control over the national economy during the *Estado Novo*, most notably in establishing the national steel industry. The difference was, rather, in the much greater challenge he now faced, as foreign businessmen and investors quickly realized the opportunities offered by Brazil, already impressed in the early post-war years by its evident capacity to develop rapidly as an industrial nation, as well as providing potential markets and a source of raw materials. The Dutra years had shown how vulnerable the Brazilian economy could be to foreign penetration, even foreign exploitation. In pointing to these dangers, however unpalatable that might be to foreigners eager for the profits of an open-door, 'free trade' system, Vargas was merely echoing the fears of many Brazilians, of all classes, including some of the most thoughtful officers in the armed forces. He was simply underlining, clearly and forcefully, some of the main issues in the swelling debate throughout the whole of the 'Third World' on the possibility of an autonomous development, especially through industrialization, which would bring, in this case, to the people of Brazil that greater share of wealth and opportunity Vargas had promised. He constantly stressed that such advances could not be made overnight. He accepted that collaboration with more developed economies would be needed, so would be welcomed: but already, too, he realized that foreign interest was not primarily or essentially altruistic. He was keenly aware that certain forms of 'modernization' or 'development' could be bought at too great a cost, the sell-out, as he put it, of Brazil's patrimony, handing over the wealth produced by the work of Brazil's people to those already rich in other countries, transferring its industries increasingly to foreign ownership, and leaving the nation deeper in debt internationally. It was sound commonsense and concern for his country, rather than demagogic doctrinaire nationalism, which made him fear such a future, as he again made clear as he faced up to another highly charged political and economic issue, the ownership and control of the Brazilian oil industry.

Vargas and the Politics of Oil

One of the most interesting features oft he politics of oil in Brazil is that right from the start it had involved the active participation of the armed forces, with soldiers taking the lead in developing overall policy. The *Estado Novo* had seen the introduction of two important laws, Decree Law 395 of 29 April 1938 and Decree Law 538 of 7 July 1938, which established the National Petroleum Council (CNP). This Council was largely the work of General Júlio Caetano Horta Barbosa, who remained as director of the CNP until 1943,[57] and who was much influenced by the writing and achievement of General Enrique Mosconi, the Argentine army officer who had built up Yacimientos Petrolíferos Fiscales (YPF) to try to establish Argentine control of its oil industry. Horta Barbosa was particularly concerned over the security aspects of Brazil's heavy dependence on foreign oil sources, revealing that long connection in military thinking between 'security' and 'development' which was to be more sharply defined in later years, and was especially impressed by Italy's invasion of Ethiopia in 1936, which in large part he interpreted as a search for oil. He was alarmed at the backwardness of Brazil's oil industry at a period (1931–40) in which Brazil's oil needs were growing at an annual average of 6·4 per cent, and dismayed at the grip being imposed on Brazil by a small group of international companies:

> . . . In marketing, Brazil was tied to an oligopoly of five foreign companies led by Standard Oil of New Jersey and Anglo-Mexican, the Royal Dutch Shell affiliate. Almost all the gasoline, fuel oil, diesel oil, and lubricants were imported from American and British refineries on the Gulf of Mexico or in the Dutch Antilles . . .[58]

These international corporations already had concessions to explore for oil in Brazil, but showed virtually no interest in doing so,[59] while Brazil itself largely lacked the resources to undertake such work. The oil companies could make large profits, were cushioned by a government which was grateful for oil taxes, but not yet sufficiently concerned over the costs of oil imports. These companies were also able to maximize their profits without undertaking the expense of looking for oil in Brazil itself.[60] They were, however, alarmed at growing Brazilian interest in developing refineries, following the examples of France, Argentina, and Uruguay, so acted to establish a foothold in refining before foreign companies might be excluded. Between 1936 and 1938 Standard, Texaco, the Atlantic Refining Company, and Anglo-Mexican all proposed to establish big refineries in Brazil, breaking with their usual practice of refining near the source. By this time, however, it was too late, as Horta Barbosa took the initiative, spurred on by growing demands from Brazilian entrepreneurs and nationalist spokesmen, and by further evidence that oil might be produced as well as refined in Brazil.

The debate, both on economic and political grounds, was a complex one, now to be conducted against the uproar over closer national control of oil in Mexico and the fierce reaction of enraged international oil interests. Greater state intervention in oil was, however, fully in accord with the whole thrust of the *Estado Novo* and its expression of the demands of a more nationalist bourgeoisie looking for a stronger state apparatus. Vargas was sympathetic to proposals from Horta Barbosa, who essentially wanted to start with refining, then move back to production, which would be made easier with the profits from refining. The early proposals, made in January 1938, were very modest, welcoming foreign capital and envisaging distribution still under foreign control, the emphasis being on national takeover of production and refining and sufficient protection from reprisals by foreign companies. Vargas received a bill along these lines in March 1938, putting it to the CFCE (Foreign Trades Council) in April. He then signed Decree Law 195, which appeared on 1 May, to the surprise and indignation of the international oil companies, now further alarmed by an oil agreement between Brazil and Bolivia in return for help to build a railway from São Paulo to Santa Cruz.[61]

Despite this legislation, the international oil companies renewed their efforts over the next few years to win a stronger foothold in the Brazilian oil industry, being held back mainly because of commitment within the armed forces to the concept of Brazilian control of such a vital branch of the economy. There were, however, vocal critics who argued that such commitment hindered faster development, because of the lack of capital and technological skills, and that a greater measure of foreign involvement was the necessary price to pay. The debate grew fiercer and polarized opinion both on the degree of national control and the necessity of state rather than private ownership, especially as the war ended and the pressure for more 'liberal' economic policies grew stronger. Demand for oil and petrol was also rising quickly in the post-war period, at about 16 per cent yearly, and the new head of the CNP, Colonel João Carlos Barreto, was more inclined to give in to pressure from companies such as Standard Oil and to Brazilian private interests. The latter were in 1945 allowed to bid for concessions to build refineries, working with foreign backing, but the international companies were by now more interested in developments elsewhere, notably in Canada and the Middle East. They were, consequently, much cooler over Brazilian developments, so further fuelling the charge that their overriding interests were in maximizing profits rather than in developing Brazil, and that their ability to shift interest and resources showed the need for more autonomous Brazilian control. Efforts at creating a mixed corporation also failed to attract even Brazilian capital, so that Brazil's first refinery at Mataripe in Bahia in 1948 was fully government-owned.

The Dutra government looked much more favourably on foreign intervention, producing a new Petroleum Statute, in 1947, which sought to keep Brazilian control of the industry and speed up its development, while allowing concessions to foreign companies. Such proposals were, however, insufficient for the international companies:

> Laws similar to Venezuela's were apparently what the majors (major oil companies) had in mind. . . . The least they were prepared to accept was 51 per cent control of the refining and transport sectors, the right to dispose freely of their crude oil in international markets, and the authority to decide when and where to bring oilfields into production . . .[62]

There was much support for those who criticized what was, they argued, too narrow a concept of national control in earlier policy, with even the PCB hoping for Soviet aid to develop Brazil's oil industry; but, as the debate grew, so opinion hardened in relation to Brazil's treatment by foreign interests, especially by the United States, full of promise in the wartime crisis, but neglectful, and preoccupied elsewhere, once the war was over. The question of Brazilian oil became a touchstone of nationalist sentiment and a sensitive issue in the debate on the international capitalist exploitation of Brazilian wealth. By the late 1940s it was perhaps the most highly charged, most emotive political issue yet to emerge in twentieth-century Brazil.[63] The new Petroleum Statute was vigorously defended by the ex-*tenente* General Juarez Távora, arguing for limited foreign intervention, while the stricter nationalist position was again urged by Horta Barbosa, emphatic on the need, above all, for Brazil to control refining.

Vargas himself had always adopted a characteristically moderate but astute position. The CNP had fitted the general pattern of enlarged state control in the *Estado Novo*, but his support had never been rigid or doctrinaire and he saw the need for capital and technology which Brazil could not easily provide. He also saw, however, especially during the Dutra government, the growing influence of international corporations and the political power they could muster. He was impressed by the intense popular support for the CEDP (Centre for the Study and Defence of Petroleum), founded in 1948, which finally prevented the Petroleum Statute from getting through Congress, and he followed closely the further developments under Dutra, as oil development was now made part of an overall plan to co-ordinate public spending in the so-called SALTE programme.[64] These proposals ran into difficulties because of rising demands and costs, but produced important results in plans for refinery and associated developments at Cubatão near Santos. They still failed, however, to satisfy those who demanded fuller state control, and Vargas now found himself pushed further towards this solution as the 1950 election approached and the oil question, together with that of excessive foreign profits, became a focus of intense popular debate.[65]

The proposals made by Vargas for the national oil industry in 1951 were characteristically moderate. The bill which he sent to Congress in December aimed to create a mixed corporation, with majority ownership by the state. This new corporation, to be called Petrobrás (Brazilian Petroleum Corporation), would control the production of oil and of future refineries, while existing refineries could remain in private ownership, as could distribution. It is a bill which is worth studying in detail, since, despite Vargas's strictures in the same month on the illegitimate role of foreign capital, he still showed his readiness to welcome responsible foreign help in this most sensitive branch of the economy. His primary aim was not simply to win political advantage but, rather, to propose a viable, financially realistic solution for Brazil's current and future oil needs, which now were growing at over 10 per cent a year and making heavy demands on foreign exchange. He seemed to expect that the bill would pass through Congress relatively easily, but it immediately provoked an impassioned national debate.[66] It was a controversy which in many respects Vargas did not want, and which embarrassed him in his wider plans for development. His whole approach to such questions as energy and transportation was pragmatic and eclectic rather than doctrinaire, and his plans for the oil industry were only part of a wider strategy, which included road and railway expansion, the motor-car industry, a National Coal Plan, and the development of Brazil's electrical energy. In the case both of oil and electricity he eventually was to favour more exclusive state control, but largely as a result of pressure both from within and outside Congress. The popular campaign for more direct state control of Brazilian oil was largely stimulated by the Communist Party, anxious to curb excessive United States influence in Brazil's economy and, consequently, in national politics, but the demand was echoed by other very different groups. Many Brazilian industrialists and financiers were unwilling to see the rich profits of oil going abroad, so that the Communists' anti-imperialism was, in effect, supported by indigenous bourgeoisie who throughout the *Estado Novo* had called, whenever necessary, for state intervention to protect their interests. So in 1953 even the UDN, the party most bitterly opposed to Vargas, and usually most ready to collaborate with foreign capitalism, proposed changes in Vargas's bill to extend national ownership not only to future but to existing refineries. Oil was, many now argued, a special case demanding public ownership. Fuel imports were rising 20 per cent a year in an economy whose industrial expansion would be increasingly dependent on oil. Brazil's vulnerability in its dependence on foreign supplies had been seen during the Korean War and in recent disagreements between Great Britain and Iran. Generals as well as politicians, bankers as well as Communists, all now argued the urgent need to establish maximum control of oil supplies, in production, refining, and distribution, as a necessary condition of national industrial development.

The merits of such arguments may be disputed, and the debate in recent years has intensified and become more acute. In terms, however, of an evaluation of Vargas and his policies and of the persistent pressures shaping contemporary Brazilian politics, it must be stressed that the bill which became law in October 1953, establishing Petrobrás and the state control of Brazilian oil, was not the result of doctrinaire commitment by Vargas; still less was it merely an opportunity for indulging in irresponsible, vote-catching demagoguery, or even a weak submission to left-wing, mainly Communist, demands. It was the result of a long period of mature debate, careful advice, increasing anxiety over the priorities of international oil companies,[67] and a genuine attempt to solve Brazil's energy needs in relation to current and projected growth as an industrial nation. The first president of Petrobrás, significantly, was Juracy Magalhães, the former *tenente*, now a notably conservative UDN leader. A study of Petrobrás and its politics, in other words, again fails to support the myth of Vargas the dangerous 'populist', revealing, instead, a moderate, responsible, flexible politician, able to reconcile widely divergent interests, both military and civilian, foreign and domestic, while still maintaining the confidence of the mass of Brazil's working people.

Vargas and the Working Class

The relation between Vargas and the working class, and the threat it seemed to pose for more privileged social groups, was the second major theme of his last years in power, and the source of his most bitter opposition. When Vargas took office, the minimum wage had not been adjusted since 1943 and its real purchasing power had been almost halved between 1945 and 1951, a downward trend clearly visible in the figures for real minimum wages in Guanabara and São Paulo:

Real Minimum Wages: Guanabara and São Paulo 1944–54[68]

Year	*Indices* *Base 1944=100*		*Annual Variation*	
	Guanabara	*São Paulo*	*Guanabara*	*São Paulo*
1944	100	100		
1945	84·2	80·3	−15·8	−19·7
1946	74·1	70·9	−12·0	−11·7
1947	60·7	53·8	−18·1	−24·1
1948	58·0	49·6	− 4·4	−17·8
1949	55·4	50·4	− 4·5	+1·6
1950	50·9	47·9	− 8·1	− 5·0
1951	53·6	53·0	+ 5·3	+ 10·6
1952	122·3	124·8	+128·2	+135·5
1953	107·1	101·7	− 12·4	− 18·5
1954	144·6	138·3	+ 35·0	+ 36·0

Vargas already had attacked in his presidential campaign the suffering imposed on the working class and the poor, and the very many Brazilians who did not receive wages at all. The trend, he had argued, was to transfer resources, not from the wealthy to those who were worse off, but in the other direction. While urging moderation, he had promised change, and in December 1951 decreed a new minimum wage, which still, however, barely kept up with recent rises in the cost of living. At the same time he made easier the expression of workers' demands and the use of the right to strike, which had been so effectively curbed by Dutra's Decree Law 9.070 of 15 January 1946, which had required that strike attempts should be submitted to the Ministry of Labour.[69] He also removed the 'ideology test' (*atestado de ideologia*) imposed by Dutra. One result was a series of union elections less controlled and intimidated by the state apparatus, providing a more autonomous vehicle for the demands of an industrial working class which between 1940 and 1953 had almost doubled in size, from about three quarters of a million to about 1½ million.[70] This greater freedom of action, combined with open debate on the whole structure of the economy and society, together with a steadily worsening economic situation for the working class, brought the whole issue of rewards and distribution to the front of popular political debate. The PCB, by now well established in the trade union movement, focused the issues more clearly, but simply helped to express demands and tensions which already were widely felt.

One of the most important single expressions of these renewed pressures in national politics was the extensive strike in São Paulo in

March and April 1953, a strike which affected 300,000 workers and which contributed to important government changes in June and July. The strike came closely after the election of Jânio Quadros as mayor of São Paulo, in what was, in effect, a serious electoral setback for Vargas whose candidate had been rejected, and followed a steady rise in strikes during the previous year, which, in all, had affected over one million workers.[71] The strike in São Paulo, however, was larger, better organized, more violent, and more important in sharpening social and economic issues than any of the previous few years.[72] It lasted for twenty-nine days, involving workers from a wide variety of industries, spearheaded by the textile workers, 8,000 of whom met in São Paulo on 10 March to demand wage rises to counter the rising cost of living. The initial demands were for a rise of 60 per cent, and were supported by the steelworkers who on 26 March also agreed to strike. On the first day of the strike, 27 March, the press estimated that 30,000 textile workers, out of about 120,000, and 30,000 steelworkers, out of 96,000, were already on strike.[73] Almost at once there were clashes between pickets and the police, which then involved the DOPS (Departmento de Ordem Política e Social) of the state of São Paulo, who, in turn, asked help from the Força Pública of São Paulo. An appeal was also made to the garrison of the federal army in the city.

The strike soon showed that existing machinery was inadequate, since the dispute was taken to the Labour Court, under Dutra's Decree 9.070, but this process was at once rejected by the strikers. On 28 March the strike reached Osaco, then spread further throughout the state, by now involving 31 metallurgical firms and 50 textile firms. The employers resolutely refused to meet workers' demands, talking at most of wage increases of 20–30 per cent, though the state governor, Lucas Nogueira Garcez, showed some sympathy with the workers, and Jânio Quadros, the new mayor, spoke of the need for a wage rise of 100 per cent. On 31 March, after joiners, cabinetmakers, and associated groups had also come out, there was a fierce clash in the Praça da Sé, with bloody fighting lasting several hours.

The details of the strike are not important here, except to indicate its intensity and significance, as it spread to workers in the paper and edible fats, beer and paint industries, to glass workers, telephone workers, the building industry, the gas industry, and producers of shoes, tinned foods, and sweets. It also began to win support from some professional groups, including doctors, offering their services free to strikers and their families, and lawyers, both of which groups had themselves protested recently over salaries. But equally important, and to be underlined, was the *reaction* to the strike, a massive reaction of alarm and indignation on the part of employers and owners and the conservative press, especially against Vargas, who was accused by the *Estado de São Paulo* and similar papers of deliberately fomenting trouble, so that he might stage a *coup* to continue in office. There was not a shred of evidence to support such charges. Indeed, Vargas was himself alarmed, embarrassed, and unsure of his ground. He was under attack from many of the strikers for having failed to live up to his promises, from the UDN for instigating the strike, and from mainly PSD spokesmen for the Ministry of Labour for having been too liberal towards the unions and having removed, in particular, the *atestado de ideologia,* the ideological test for candidates in union elections. Finally, as the strike still spread, Vargas said he would at once review the minimum wage, only to be attacked by his own PSD Minister of Labour, Segadas Viana, for what was, he said, a move towards *continuismo.* Towards the end of April the strike was over, officially with a wage increase of 32 per cent, though some workers, such as the printers, won about 70 per cent and others less than decided by the Labour Court. Its repercussions were, however, to be far-reaching in national as well as labour politics.

One very interesting result of the 1953 strike was the start of a system of an alternative, or parallel, union structure, providing a potentially more effective vehicle for workers' demands than the official, state-controlled union system, still so heavily controlled by *pelegos,* men who more often represented the government or the owners than their own rank-and-file. This parallel structure partly stemmed from the Intersindical Strike Committee set up in 1953:

> The Intersindical Strike Committee was later superseded by the Pacto de Unidade Intersindical (P.U.I.). Years later this was to result in the Pacto de Unidade e Ação (P.U.A.) which was one of the pillars of the Comando Geral de Trabalhadores (C.G.T.) during the years of the Goulart government.[74]

It was these groups which in later years helped the radicalization of the trade union movement and produced more effective challenge to the established political and social order, which, in turn, contributed to the reaction of the *coup* of 1964.[75] More immediately important, however, were the effects of the strike on Vargas's government and on the political forces aligned against him.

The changes Vargas made in his cabinet in mid-1953 were not simply a response to the São Paulo strike or to working-class agitation more generally. This was especially seen in the appointment of his old friend Oswaldo Aranha as Minister of Finance, a post he had held in the early 1930s. Aranha was appointed to help with measures of stabilization and to solve the alarming balance of payments deficit which by June 1953 was over one billion (American) dollars. Brazil had been importing too much during the Korean War,[76] industrial production was falling, and inflation was around 20 per cent. Aranha's brief was to cut public spending, limit credit, and provide stringent exchange controls, including a multiple exchange rate to help Brazilian exports,[77] limit non-essential imports, yet maintain the necessary supplies for industrialization. All this was included in the 'Aranha Plan' of October 1953, a moderate, distinctly orthodox strategy to stabilize the economy, which should recommend itself to foreign bankers and the United States government, especially since Aranha was so widely respected as an able, responsible statesman. Unfortunately, various factors undermined these efforts. United States interests were angry over the Petrobrás campaign, and the new Eisenhower government, with George Humphrey at the Treasury and John Foster Dulles as Secretary of State, was markedly unsympathetic to governments which seemed at all left-wing or challenged United States business interests. The climate had changed. The Joint Brazilian–United States Economic Commission was ending. Little help was forthcoming to aid Aranha, and consequently Vargas, to solve the financial and economic, and, by implication, social and political, problems facing a developing country struggling in the early stages of industrialization.

The appointment of Aranha and the effort at stabilization again underlined the essential moderation of Vargas's policies and his willingness to work with foreign bankers and investors where possible. Such willingness drew heavy fire from the PCB and more extreme nationalist groups right across the political spectrum, but Vargas remained pragmatic and, above all, realistic in political strategy. His other major appointment in 1953 brought, however, much sharper and more dangerous attacks, from right-wing politicians and, more seriously still, from influential members of the armed forces. By 1953 inflation seemed to be biting deeply into middle-class living standards and expectations. The adjustments following the minimum wage legislation of December 1951 had temporarily lifted the real income of unskilled workers, but most of this gain was swallowed up within a year by rising living costs, and by the greater flexibility of response of other social groups.[78] Middle-class wage-earners were, however, similarly affected, and determined to keep up in the inflationary race:

> The standard of living of civil servants and the military had been so seriously affected . . . by the acceleration of inflation that Congress passed a law in December 1952, providing for a general

> increase in pay ranging from 7 to 10 per cent for the highest categories, 15 to 30 per cent for those immediately below, and 40 to 70 per cent for the vast majority in the middle and lowest categories.[79]

The rapid rise of inflation was already inducing panic and heightening social tensions, and producing, in particular, a notable middle-class resentment against groups lower in the social scale who appeared to command, by means of their unions, greater bargaining power.

Some evidence of this had already been seen in the growing reaction within the officer corps of the armed forces to any moves which appeared to favour more militant trade union organization and which, in particular, seemed to reflect a renewed tolerance of Communist activity.[80] There had been a substantial body of opposition among military officers to Vargas being allowed to take office, which now was strengthened as the Cold War intensified and as the government seemed to be favouring, even cultivating, the trade unions and the urban working class. Growing middle-class resentment was directly reflected in debate within the army, further stimulated by pressure from the United States, who even wanted a Brazilian force to be sent to Korea,[81] so heightening the disagreements within the Brazilian officer corps. Men later to play a prominent role in the *coup* of 1964, such as General Cordeiro de Farias, one of the forces behind the ESG, now took a leading role in the Cold War debate, bringing together a confused but powerful opposition to Vargas's more nationalist stance on the oil question and on profit remittances, his greater leniency towards the trade union movement, and his tentative measures of redistribution. Much of the opposition initially focused on General Estillac Leal, president of the Clube Militar and Minister of War in 1951, growing so intense that in March 1952 he had to resign his ministry. One powerful right-wing, pro-United States, and anti-Vargas pressure-group was the 'Democratic Crusade', whose honorary president was Eduardo Gomes and which was closely linked to the UDN. Its growth was made easier by the fact that during the Dutra period key posts had gone to officers more sympathetic, in broad terms, to the UDN and the interests associated with it. These officers still held positions of strength under Estillac Leal and heavily outweighed those more sympathetic to a more 'nationalist' economic policy and, even more so, those in favour of Vargas's reformist measures. The strength of right-wing opinion in the officer corps was seen, above all, in a crucial test in the first few months of 1952 in elections in the Clube Militar, always a good guide to the current climate of military politics. General Estillac Leal and General Horta Barbosa, the man who had done so much to shape Brazil's oil industry in the late 1930s, were resoundingly defeated by officers who favoured other policies, less 'nationalist' in relation to oil and the role of foreign business interests. Those who won were also markedly hostile to Vargas's policies towards the trade unions and the working class, so that the results were a major setback for Vargas. To be at all successful he had to be able to carry military opinion with him. These elections showed that he was failing, and that a growing number of officers was coming to share the opinions of the UDN opponents of Vargas.

In this growing atmosphere of suspicion, insecurity, and hostility Vargas's appointment of João Goulart to the Ministry of Labour in 1953 played into his enemies' hands. He needed, as the São Paulo strike had shown, to pay more attention to working-class demands, and he also needed, as seen by the criticism of him coming from the PSD-dominated Ministry of Labour, to protect himself from the more right-wing faction within his own camp. It is also arguable that nothing he could do would have pleased his bitterly hostile critics in the UDN, and that, unless he could genuinely democratize the armed forces, he must inevitably clash with them over his proposed reforms.[82] However plausible these arguments, the fact remained that the appointment of Goulart made confrontation inevitable, heightening fears that the government was endangering middle-class interests partly by a series of inflationary gestures to win popular support,[83] and partly, and more seriously, by policies corrosive of the existing social order.

João Goulart, a rich *gaúcho* landowner, aged thirty-five, was a neighbour and close political associate of Vargas in Rio Grande do Sul, well placed to establish PTB control of the Ministry of Labour. Such control was more evidently necessary after the repeal of the ideological test in union elections in September 1952, which had allowed the renewed growth of PCB influence, and Vargas was, in any case, already looking towards the next round of elections in 1954. These would replace all federal deputies, two-thirds of the Senate, and most governors, so that Vargas was anxious to establish a wider electoral base. The appointment of Goulart was therefore a sensible piece of electoral politics, a way of curbing the PSD in the Ministry of Labour, a response to the dissatisfaction expressed in the São Paulo strike, and a genuine effort to produce the wage increases Vargas believed to be overdue.

The appointment brought an uproar of protest, with attacks in most of the press, the general line being that Goulart intended to form a 'trade union republic',[84] similar to that which allegedly was being established by Perón in Argentina. Such a move, it was argued, would rapidly undercut Brazil's new 'democracy', allowing a direct appeal to the organized trade union movement. It was also intended, so the argument went, to align this new 'sindicalized' Brazil with Argentina and Chile in a bloc hostile to the United States. Goulart was in many respects a most unlikely candidate for such a demonic role. He was a rich landowner of little proven ability, either political or rhetorical. He had scant acquaintance with urban industrial society and no recorded intentions or ambitions to lead a social upheaval based on trade union power. He was immediately, however, made the victim of an intense, vituperative, scaremongering campaign by the right-wing press, and of alarmist rumours among military officers and throughout what broadly could be described as middle-class political circles.[85]

Most informed opinion agreed that adjustments in the minimum wage and wage levels generally were overdue, though often the proposals were only that these should keep pace with inflation, so keeping relative differences in earnings as before. Goulart on taking office claimed, with obvious sincerity, that he was a firm supporter of democracy, and he looked hard and carefully at the whole question of wage levels, especially as working-class agitation continued, spurred by growing difficulties in keeping up with price increases. He was, however, right from the start, subject to harassment by a press and communications network largely controlled by the enemies of Vargas, and eager to attack the president through his new Minister of Labour. The most severe attacks came from a facile journalist and ambitious politician, Carlos Lacerda, who in his own paper, *Tribuna da Imprensa*, issued ceaseless attacks on Vargas and Goulart, the main burden of which was in effect that, if a free electoral system could elect a president such as Vargas, there must be something wrong with free elections, an argument carried to its logical conclusion in 1964 and subsequent years. Such paradoxical views in one who claimed to be struggling to uphold democracy were also matched by his vivid political rhetoric, used to condemn politicians who irresponsibly used vivid political rhetoric. Similar demagoguery aimed at the middle class was indulged in by the Chateaubriand newspaper group, *Diários Associados*, and *O Globo*, which were solidly anti-Vargas. The *Estado de São Paulo* was generally more responsible in its attacks, though no less hostile, having been aligned against Vargas since his assumption of power in 1930, a hostility fed in 1932 and during the subsequent exile of its owner.[86] Partly to counter this hostile domination of the media, Vargas approved a loan from the Bank of Brazil to Samuel Wainer, to help to found a paper sympathetic to the government. This appeared as *Última Hora*, but, unfortunately, it really did appear at the eleventh hour as far as Vargas was concerned. It never reached the level of prestige and professional competence of much of the right-wing press. Being aimed, too, at a wider, more popular audience it never won important ground among middle-class readership. It did, however, spark off fierce charges of 'corruption' and misuse of public money, which further quickened, or at least supported, anti-Vargas feeling. By the end of 1953 the opposition to Vargas and Goulart had won more support among self-styled 'moderate' opinion, both civilian and military, which was now moving steadily away from the president on the key issues of inflation and the nature and pace of social and political change.

One important indication of this shift of opinion came in February 1954, in a long memorandum to the Minister of War, signed by over eighty army officers, all of the rank of lieutenant-colonel or colonel. Published on 20 February, this memorandum was an ominous sign of discontent, insecurity, and a greater readiness for political involvement on the part of men worried over their social and professional status and influenced by the rising climate of middle-class political agitation. In most respects it echoed the language of such documents in most societies faced by social change and worried over inflation. It listed areas in which the army had been neglected, but also referred to a 'crisis of authority', the threat from communism and the danger of 'subversion', and the benefits to be won by other groups in society at the expense of the officers of the armed forces. Coming from any other social group the memorandum would have been an interesting, useful indication of corporate opinion and anxieties. Coming from middle-ranking officers in 1954 it was a further sign of how far Vargas had failed to satisfy the demands of the officer corps, and of how balefully the proposals for revised working-class wages would be regarded.[87]

Two days after the memo was published Goulart made known, on 22 February, his long-awaited proposals for an increase of 100 per cent in the minimum wage, bringing it in the Federal District to 2,400 cruzeiros monthly, equal to the basic pay of an army second lieutenant. Knowing that these proposals would be a political embarrassment, Goulart also offered his resignation, which was accepted, scarcely the action, on the part both of Goulart and Vargas, of irresponsible politicians out for confrontation. At the same time Vargas also replaced General Espírito Santo Cardoso as Minister of War with a well-known anti-communist, but former defender of Vargas, General Zenóbio da Costa. These ministerial changes again underlined the severity of the political crisis and the strength of the opposition. Goulart's proposals were, arguably, excessive in terms of their predictable inflationary impact,[88] but it was their political significance more than any other which had caused Vargas to give ground so abruptly, revealing a weakness still further underlined as his enemies now proposed to impeach him, first for negotiating with Perón for an anti-United States pact, then, when that charge was shown to be absurd, for corruption.

Despite these attacks Vargas was convinced that massive wage increases were needed to prevent a serious decline in the living standards of Brazil's working population, and in order to modify to some degree the severely inequitable distribution of wealth and remuneration. On 1 May 1954, Labour Day, Vargas announced that the increase in the minimum wage would be 100 per cent, as Goulart had recommended, a rise he defended in relation to the cost of living increases in recent years,[89] but which produced a massive wave of criticism, as being irresponsibly inflationary, designed merely to catch working-class votes, and further evidence of the neglect by Vargas of the middle class.

Too much can probably be made of the importance of this decision. The opposition to Vargas was, in any case, implacably hostile and determined to destroy him. Had the wage increase been 40 per cent or 60 per cent, opposition would have been scarcely less intense. Much more important was the steady continuing assault in the press and the media, and the deliberate attempt to swing middle-class opinion, including that of the officer corps, against Vargas, using, as Lacerda and others already had shown, any means available, however false or otherwise the charge. The attacks on Vargas were, on the other hand, made easier by this decree and by the worsening economic situation, for which, however, Vargas was by no means solely responsible.

Faced with the election in October, Vargas was suddenly hit by much the most serious blow so far. A group of his supporters decided to take direct action to remove his most bitter critic, Carlos Lacerda, who already was guarded by air force officers, among whom he had a considerable following. Early in the morning of 5 August a gunman fired on Lacerda as he returned to his home in Rua Toneleros, Copacabana, slightly wounding him, but killing an air force officer with him. The attack was then traced to Vargas's palace guard, though the president himself had no knowledge of it.

The reaction was immediate, with Lacerda making all possible political capital out of the incident to renew his earlier charges of corruption, both in the press and on the radio. The murder, it was argued, showed the serious decline in moral standards in government, and the association of Vargas with corruption, violence, and intimidation. Vargas responded calmly and with dignity, agreeing to dissolve the presidential guard and to hold full inquiries; but by now the hunt was in full cry. Generals associated with the UDN demanded that the president should resign, a course they had wanted ever since his election, and which was being loudly called for in the anti-Vargas press. Military opinion was clearly divided, but moving towards agreement that the president should go. Eduardo Gomes and other air force officers publicly demanded his resignation on 22 August, being joined by senior army commanders, including the former commander of the FEB, Marshal Mascarenhas de Moraes. The next day a further manifesto associated with this demand not only senior officers long hostile to Vargas, but others who had previously clung to their belief in the 'constitutionalist' role of the armed forces. Centre opinion in the officer class of all the services had now gone against the president, who already had told his vice president, Café Filho, that he would never leave office alive. Vargas was prepared, even at this stage, to agree to a temporary leave of absence till the question of responsibility for the murder of the air force officer was cleared up. The discussions went on all through the night in the Catete Palace and in the city, but at last Getúlio's brother, Benjamim, had to tell the president that the generals, afraid of Vargas's return to office, were determined that the 'leave of absence', already announced to the nation at 4.45 a.m., must be permanent. Vargas heard the news shortly after 8 a.m., withdrew quietly to his bedroom, and shot himself.[90]

The death of Vargas was all of a piece with his life and career, a long life of hard work, dedicated to the service, as he understood it, of the Brazilian people, in a career now ending with an act of political defiance which confused and confounded his opponents. Vargas was by far the most able politician of modern Brazil, a superb consensus politician, able to reconcile widely divergent interests over a long, difficult period, but who yet was not afraid of confrontation when this seemed necessary, and for whom some compromises were not acceptable. He died anything but a wealthy man, despite his long years in power. Hounded by his enemies, tired and depressed, he was still vigorous enough to leave behind a scathing indictment of those who had worked ceaselessly to pull him down:

> . . . The underground campaign of international groups joined that of the national groups which were working against the policy of full employment. The excess profits law was held up by Congress. Hatreds were unleashed against the just revision of minimum wages. [He] wished to bring national freedom in the use of our resources by means of Petrobrás; this had hardly begun to operate when the wave of agitation swelled. Electrobrás was obstructed

to the point of despair. They do not want the worker to be free. They do not want the people to be independent . . .

Yet even in this last message the language was studied and the passion controlled, still the expression of the quiet, dignified administrator rather than the wild demagogue painted by his enemies. Vargas was still ready to be judged on his record, as the man who, more than any other single politician, had helped to unify Brazil and create the Brazilian state, who had strengthened the foundations of Brazil's modern industrial economy, but who had also kept firm to his promise to improve the conditions and opportunities of those who previously had had little share in the nation's wealth and no part in its political life. Subsequent, as well as contemporary, critics found much to object to in Vargas's career. Those further to the left could argue, with justification, that his policies in relation to the working class were essentially corporatist and elitist, more redolent of control from above than of autonomous mobilization from below. He helped, therefore, so it is argued, to build a trade union organization which was itself part of the state apparatus, an instrument to manipulate the working class rather than to provide effective organization on its behalf, a means to split rather than unite the working-class movement. Such criticism was well founded. Vargas was, however reformist, a man of the centre. He never was or called himself a socialist, still less a revolutionary socialist. He was, even by 1930, a politician set in his ways, a moderate, shrewd, political realist, always aware of what he could achieve in any particular context. He was, in the terms of the more radical left, elitist, even paternalistic, in his concept of working-class organization, strongly influenced by corporatism, eschewing the language of class confrontation, seeking to work with widely divergent interests. But in his elitism and his political flexibility he had much in common with many of his critics, including, for example, the PCB, which was scarcely less elitist in its approach, and scarcely less willing to compromise, however judiciously, for political ends.

There was also, it should be remembered, even in the PCB's own analysis, reason to acknowledge the achievement of Vargas in helping to shape an industrial society linked to a much stronger state, reflecting the influence of the national industrial bourgeoisie, as a prerequisite of a 'bourgeois revolution'. Whatever qualifications must be made, Vargas was sincerely committed to the improvement of the condition of the Brazilian working class, both in terms of wages, and of opportunities. His vision was limited, with relatively little concern, for example, for the great mass of Brazil's rural population. But his efforts to work for the common people of Brazil, in the terms in which he understood that task, were genuine and consistent. They also resulted, even before his death, and certainly in the decade after it, in a shift in political power sufficient to challenge those who previously had controlled Brazilian politics, and sufficient to provoke them into vigorous reaction.

In judging Vargas, this last point must always be kept in mind, the strength of the social and political forces which opposed him. Right from the start, in 1930, he was faced with bitter, entrenched opposition, and always he had to survive a delicate balancing act between conflicting political interests, civilian and military, foreign as well as domestic. The intensity of the reaction to his proposals for greater national control of the economy and a wider distribution of wealth was a measure of the opposition aligned against him. A lesser politician would never even have started on the task, whereas Vargas survived for almost two and a half decades, in large part because of his moderation and keen sensitivity as to what could and could not be done. Had he been even a fraction as immoderate, irresponsible, or wildly 'populist' as his critics portrayed him, he could not have come through the changes and challenges of his many years in office, which he survived with a phlegmatic calm infuriating to his enemies.

His critics on the right, especially in the UDN and among officers of the armed forces hostile to him, regularly accused Vargas of endangering democracy; but it was they, not Vargas, who in 1945, 1954, and subsequently in 1964 called in the armed forces, to whom for so long they had directed their propaganda. It was they, not Vargas or his successors, who did damage to democratic representative government in Brazil, supported by groups outside the country, who also protested their support for Brazilian democracy, only until such times as their interests appeared to be threatened. It is possible to criticize and sneer at Vargas, and his achievements, but few countries have been served by any politician so long and so well.

The Continuing Crisis

The real nature of the opposition to Vargas was seen in the political crisis which continued even after his death, especially in the efforts of his opponents to prevent the succession of other men who might follow the lines he had laid down. The particular political crisis which killed Vargas ended, in this sense, only with the succession of Kubitschek, after Lacerda and others again had called on the armed forces' leaders to intervene, but this time without success, provoking instead a military *coup* on behalf of the constitutionally elected candidates. The history of these months is highly complex, but crucial to an understanding of political forces which eventually were to lead to a very different *coup* in 1964.[91]

The immediate effect of Vargas's suicide was an intensely emotional popular reaction in sympathy with Getúlio and against those who had hounded him, so that Lacerda, for example, first had to go into hiding, then leave the country till the hue and cry died down. In other respects, however, the direct political impact of the president's tragic death was less than might have been expected. The presidency was taken over by a member of the PSP, the party of Adhemar de Barros, vice president Café Filho, a north-easterner from Rio Grande do Norte, who had opposed Vargas during the *Estado Novo*, but who had been accepted as vice-presidential candidate as part of the electoral agreement with Adhemar de Barros.[92] The new president had some difficulty in finding pro-Vargas politicians to serve with him, but the right-wing emphasis in his government was mainly a reflection of his own political position by 1954. His Minister of Finance, for example, was Eugênio Gudin, a noted conservative economist, the Minister of Labour was Colonel Napoleão Alencastro Guimarães, who was a stern critic of Goulart and determined to curb Communist influence in the unions. The Minister of the Air Force was the former UDN presidential candidate, Eduardo Gomes; the head of the Military Household was General Juarez Távora, a former *tenente* and supporter of Vargas, but prominent in the moves against him in 1954. The Ministry of the Navy went to another officer prominent in the Escola Superior de Guerra, while soon, too, the Ministry of the Army was taken from General Zenóbio da Costa, who had tried hard to prevent Vargas's removal, and given to General Henrique Teixeira Lott, who was to play a key role in military politics over the next few months. Other UDN members were given important posts, so that the opponents of Vargas could feel well satisfied.

Despite their success, however, the UDN leaders were afraid to face the elections due to be held in October. Their attitude, to become even more common in the following months and years, was to support free elections when they could feel confident of victory; but not otherwise. When, however, the elections were held, these anti-democratic proposals on the right were seen to be unnecessary. Lacerda was elected as federal deputy in the federal district and Goulart, the most prominent political heir of Vargas, could not even win election to the Senate in his own, and Vargas's, home state of Rio Grande do Sul. The general pattern of the elections did not suggest that the death of Vargas had had a lasting impact on voting behaviour. The PSD now won 22 per cent of the Congressional vote, as compared with 22·2 per cent in 1950 and 42·3 per cent in 1945.[93] The UDN had 13·6 as against 14·0 and 26·3 in 1950 and 1945, and the PTB won in 1954 14·9 per cent of the votes, as against 13·6 per cent in 1950 and 10·1 in 1945. The general character of Congress was not, therefore, greatly changed. It remained substantially conservative, partly because of the over-representation of smaller and more backward states, resulting from the laws regulating the number of deputies to be returned from each state.

Despite the smooth progress and unexceptional results of the Congressional elections, the anti-Vargas, conservative interests in both the UDN and among senior military officers were still unhappy about allowing a free presidential election on 3 October 1955. Moves already were being made to find the most effective candidates and there was growing alarm at the possibility of the PSD choosing Juscelino Kubitschek de Oliveira, who in 1950 had won the state governorship of Minas Gerais. He was officially chosen by the PSD in February 1955, but, even before this choice, some of the most prominent military leaders had expressed their unease, urging Café Filho in a secret memorandum to avoid the upheavals of an election and find a candidate of 'national unity', that mythical political animal so beloved of right-wing politicians the world over.[94] The memorandum was leaked to the press, so that Café Filho, after consulting the officers who had signed it, made the document public.[95] Kubitschek was now able to capitalize on the indignant reaction to this military involvement in the democratic process, and won the PSD nomination. Many armed forces officers, however, never forgave him, as Café Filho notes in his memoirs, commenting that, while the officers who seized power in 1964 were different, the spirit behind this memorandum of 1955 and the *coup* of 1964 was the same, as Kubitschek found in June 1964 when he was deprived of his political rights for ten years.[96]

The opposition to Kubitschek mostly sprang from his ties with the PSD, founded by Vargas, so that he was tarred with the same brush, even though he was in no obvious sense a radical, or even a notably reformist, politician. More seriously still, however, in their eyes was his choice of vice-presidential candidate—the former Minister of Labour and close associate of Vargas, João Goulart, a choice which brought together the PSD and the PTB in a formidable electoral combination. The opponents of Kubitschek and Goulart found difficulty in choosing a candidate to run against them, but eventually, after several false starts, agreed on General Juarez Távora, who was already a candidate of the small Christian Democrat Party, PDC. This candidature was also supported by the recently elected governor of the state of São Paulo, Jânio Quadros, who also had been associated with the PDC. Aged thirty-seven, Quadros had won a remarkable electoral victory the previous October and now concluded a series of political deals with the opponents of Kubitschek, agreeing to support Távora. Quadros's main political opponent in São Paulo, Adhemar de Barros, also decided to stand as presidential candidate in what soon became a highly controversial campaign.

One of the principal features of the run-up to the election was the strenuous effort to discredit Kubitschek, especially by Carlos Lacerda, who both in the press and in Congress also urged that the coming election would be corrupt, invalid, and against the best interests of the nation, so should not be held. He argued that an emergency government should be installed, which could reform the electoral system. In effect, what he wanted was a more tightly controlled system, so designed as to favour candidates of the right, especially the UDN. Not all UDN spokesmen were as overtly subversive of the constitutional process,[97] but Lacerda found a sympathetic hearing from many who already were alarmed at what they believed was the spread of Communist influence, which they generally associated with popular movements, especially in connection with the trade unions.[98] They were aware of 'the menacing reorganization of those forces defeated in 1954'[99] and the party was soon divided between those who favoured a military *coup* and those who did not:

> . . . In such a confused period as 1955 it is difficult to say who was sincere and who was not, who was for the legal democratic process and who against it. Within the UDN there was, it is true, a strong group favouring a *coup* [*uma forte corrente golpista*]. Its incontestable leader was Carlos Lacerda. In Congress and in the *Tribuna da Imprensa* this deputy-journalist began openly to defend the setting-up of an 'estado de exceção' which ought to last two years. In essence this would be a dictatorship for a fixed period. My position as leader was terribly difficult, with this colleague at my side, a vigorous speaker and writer, already at that time the focus of a growing personal fanaticism and trust on the part of younger members of the armed forces [*nos meios militares jovens*]. His attacks and his proposals, almost always crazy but brilliant, had a much bigger impact than my explanations . . .[100]

Among those who opposed the Vargas tradition (*getulismo*) there was a general unease over their ability to win enough votes from an electorate which now numbered 15¼ million, an electorate growing by about 20 per cent every four years and increasingly reflecting the tensions and demands of a mostly urban working population, as the last few years had shown.[101] This lack of confidence was partly reflected in their demands for changes in the electoral system, mostly involving a different form of ballot paper, shifting to a *cédula oficial*, an officially printed ballot paper, instead of the current practice whereby different kinds of ballot papers (*cédula avulsa*) were distributed for the individual candidates for office. The eventual compromise was a switch to a *cédula única*, namely a ballot bearing the names of all the candidates for a particular office, but which could be printed by the parties as well as by the government. The burden of the UDN's argument for such change was that it would lessen the chances of electoral intimidation and corruption. There was much to this argument, but the more significant feature of the whole discussion was the way in which Lacerda and others used it to discredit the current system which they believed was not working in their favour.

A much more serious sign of this lack of confidence in their ability to win the presidential election was the intrigues of right-wing politicians with senior army officers sympathetic to them, manoeuvres which were to produce a serious political crisis later in the year and which pointed directly to the eventual *coup* of 1964. On 5 August, for example, the president of the Clube Militar and Chief of Staff of the Armed Forces, General Canrobert Pereira da Costa, spoke at a meeting in the Air Force Club to mark the first anniversary of the death of Major Vaz, the air force officer killed in the attack on Lacerda in 1954. The meeting was, in any case, tendentious in the strained political climate of 1955, but Canrobert plunged directly into current controversies, by warning against the threats now being posed to the 'military classes', of the bitterness which disturbed the country, and of 'the democratic falsehood in which we insist on living'.[102] The speech produced a predictable uproar, with demands for Canrobert's resignation, but the general, who was already ill and was to die at the end of October, was defended by the Minister of War, General Lott, who also expressed his own alarm at the agreements being made between Kubitschek and the PCB.

Kubitschek firmly denied such agreements, and went on with his campaign, stressing the need for even faster development of Brazilian industry and making a strong appeal to middle-class voters, whose support he realized was crucial.[103] His opponents kept after him, again insisting, without much conviction, that the winning candidate must have an absolute majority. They also accused Goulart of being in close touch with Perón in Argentina and of having secretly brought arms into Rio Grande do Sul, the aim allegedly being to arm the workers. On the basis of a letter said to have been written by a Peronist congressman an investigation was started by military officers, but the main purpose, and function, of the charge, raised by Lacerda in *Tribuna da Imprensa,* was simply further to discredit Kubitschek and Goulart and further provoke military officers inclined towards direct intervention, most of whom were now to be found in such political organizations as the Brazilian Anti-Communist Crusade, headed by Admiral Carlos Pena Bôto.

The election on 3 October brought the victory for Kubitschek and Goulart which Lacerda and those favouring a *coup* had so much feared. The margin of victory, on the other hand, was smaller than might have been expected, with Adhemar de Barros taking votes from both principal candidates. Of a total valid vote of 8,642,877, Kubitschek won 3,077,411 (35·63 per cent), Juarez Távora 2,610,462 (30·26 per cent), Adhemar de Barros 2,222,725 (25·77 per cent), and the former Integralist leader, Plínio Salgado, 714,379 (8·28 per cent). It was scarcely a resounding victory, giving Kubitschek a smaller proportion of the national vote than any other presidential post-war candidate, a pattern seen even more clearly in breaking down the percentage won in the four key states of Guanabara, Minas Gerais, Rio Grande do Sul, and São Paulo, where Kubitschek won only 31·79 per cent of the votes, as compared with Dutra's 56 per cent in 1945, Vargas's 51·81 per cent in 1950, and Quadros's 49·21 per cent in 1960.[104] The narrowness of the victory brought renewed demands for a ruling that an absolute majority should be required, but, more seriously, the electoral success of Kubitschek and Goulart gave further impetus to manoeuvres to halt the constitutional process by some form of military *coup*, efforts which were to lead to the most serious civil–military crisis experienced by Brazil until the *coup* of 1964, which the events of late 1955 so clearly foreshadowed.

The arguments for such measures mostly centred on the alleged illegality and corruption of the recent election, the help supposedly given by members and supporters of the illegal PCB, and, above all, the reiterated determination that those associated, however loosely, with Getúlio Vargas and his policies should not return to power. The UDN leadership did not support demands for a *coup*, and, more importantly, the Minister of War, General Lott, had made clear that he would oppose any such effort, even though he had himself voted for Juarez Távora and had strong reservations about Goulart.[105] The plans for a *coup* were, however, already well in hand, having been laid as early as June or July,[106] and Lacerda and his supporters now intensified their attacks both in Congress and through the media.

At the end of October, General Canrobert Pereira da Costa died. He had been one of the strongest opponents of the 'Nationalist Crusade' of Generals Horta Barbosa and Estillac Leal during

Vargas's last government and had supported General Etchegoyen's candidacy for president of the Clube Militar in the key elections of 1952. He had succeeded Etchegoyen as president and, as one of the leading Cold War warriors among senior officers, had been a vigorous critic of the candidacy of Kubitschek and Goulart, notably in his controversial speech of 5 August, marking the anniversary of the death of Major Vaz. At his well-attended funeral on 1 November after Lott and others had spoken, a member of the 'Sorbonne Group' in the ESG, Colonel Jurandir Mamede, made a speech on behalf of the Clube Militar. Mamede, like Canrobert, was one of the leaders of the 'Democratic Crusade' which had won the contest in the Clube Militar in 1952, and he now used the funeral as an opportunity to make a highly controversial political statement.[107] He praised Canrobert as one who had done everything possible to unite the armed forces and had always defended the interests of the 'military class'. Above all, Mamede spoke of the gratitude owed to Canrobert for his courageous warning of last August, when, though ill, he had drawn attention to the dangers facing the country. Mamede referred to the commitment of the armed forces to morality, reason, and national unity, then warned of the continuing dangers from those who would abrogate to themselves the right to oppress the nation.

He rejected the hypocritical scandalized reaction to Canrobert's warnings about 'corrupt and immoral pseudo-legality' on the part of those with most interest in the 'democratic lie'—'which they know and exploit so well, and in which they seek easy justification for their appetites for power and domination'. He criticized a system which could give such enormous executive power to a minority-elected president, and hoped that Canrobert's example would be an inspiration to all who followed him.

Lott was surprised and angry over the speech, and determined to take action against Mamede; but he faced strong opposition from the Clube Militar, and did not have direct jurisdiction over Mamede, who, as a member of staff of the ESG, came under the Estado Maior das Forças Armadas, the General Staff of the Armed Forces, which was directly answerable to the president. But it was at this point that the crisis deepened, as Café Filho suffered a mild heart attack,[108] and on 8 November had to delegate presidential powers to the man next in line in accordance with the constitution, the president of the Chamber of Deputies, Carlos Luz.

Luz had been one of the first to congratulate Mamede after his speech on 1 November.[109] He now refused to take action against him, and on 10 November Lott resigned as Minister of War, replaced by General Fiuza de Castro, who had been another prominent enemy of Vargas in 1954. Lacerda was now once again in full cry, referring in *Tribuna da Imprensa* to this 'hour of decision' for the armed forces, and insisting on 9 November, as Luz took office, that he was not taking over to prepare the way for Kubitschek and Goulart: '. . . These men cannot, should not, and will not take power . . .'. It *was necessary*, he said, *to speak the truth,* namely, *that the new government had been born, and would continue only with the agreement of those military leaders who had been responsible for the events of 24 August* (the removal and death of Vargas).[110]

The lines were now being drawn between those determined, at all costs, to stop the inauguration of the newly elected president and vice-president, and those, civilians and armed forces officers, committed to the constitutional process. Some of these officers had now come together to counteract the *golpista* faction in a group called Movimento Militar Constitucionalista, MMC (Constitutionalist Military Movement), which could count on the support of, for example, Vargas's ex-Minister of War, General Zenóbio da Costa, and General Odílio Denys, commander of the army's Eastern Military Zone, including Rio de Janeiro.[111] Lott was cautious in his response to pressure from such groups as he left office, though understandably upset over the circumstances of his replacement.[112]

This last point needs to be emphasized in relation to the whole pattern of civilian–military politics both in 1955 and up to 1964. Many officers refused to identify themselves with Lacerda and the more extreme, frenetic Cold War members of the officer corps, but at the same time were uneasy over any drift to the left under the cover of the 'constitutionalist' cause. They were unwilling, in other words, to accept Mamede's recommendations, which logically implied a right-wing *coup*, but they felt that there was something in this charge that other groups to which they were also opposed might win ground through support for Kubitschek and Goulart. It was a familiar crisis for 'centre' opinion among officers trained in a broadly liberal tradition, which in, for example, the case of Chile was to be played out between late 1970 and late 1973. In Brazil the process of decision, which ultimately ended in a victory for the right wing, took longer to emerge; but November 1955 was a crucial point in that development.

After several meetings of officers in key commands, the most important being in the house of General Denys on the night of 10–11 November,[113] Denys and his colleagues decided they must wait no longer, largely because of the damage they believed was being done to 'discipline and authority'.[114] In the early hours of 11 November Lott finally agreed to head a pre-emptive *coup*. Troops were quickly mobilized to take over key positions and seize, for example, Lacerda's

Tribuna da Imprensa, that newspaper which had called so loudly for a military *coup*, and now was taken over by one.

The immediate aim of the *coup* was to remove Carlos Luz, put an end to the political uncertainty over the succession, and calm the agitation in the officer corps of the armed forces. The acting president and those associated with Lacerda in his efforts to produce a different sort of *coup* then embarked, literally, on a bizarre episode. A group which included Lacerda and Mamede sailed out of Rio de Janeiro in a cruiser, the *Tamandaré*, commanded by Admiral Pena Bôto, head of the Brazilian Anti-Communist Crusade. It was perhaps the shortest-lived government-in-exile in history, which did not even leave territorial waters, the general, confused idea being to sail for Santos, in the hope that the state governor, Quadros, and others, including the military commander, would side with Luz and his colleagues on the cruiser.

While the *Tamandaré* sailed slowly down the coast, Congress was called into special session on 11 November, voting by 185 to 72 in the Chamber for the removal of Carlos Luz, which then was approved by the Senate, so making Nereu Ramos, the Speaker of the Senate and next in line, the acting president of Brazil till Café Filho should again be well enough to take over.[115] The UDN, who voted against the setting-aside of Carlos Luz, fiercely attacked the intervention of Lott and his military supporters, noting with evident frustration and chagrin that they who had been accused of plotting a *coup* had now been made the victim of a *coup*.

It was, indeed, a happy irony, and not to be repeated again. But the decisive action had been taken and the succession of Kubitschek and Goulart assured. The excitement was not yet over, however, since, though Luz was removed without difficulty, Café Filho was still president. On 21 November, ten days after the *coup*, and now out of hospital, Café Filho announced that he intended to take over control. There were still doubts about his health, but he was determined to leave office only if deposed. The generals were equally determined that there should be an end to uncertainty and further political wrangling. Troops surrounded Congress and Café Filho's home, repeating the pattern of 11 November. On 22 November, in a noisy, emotional session, Congress accepted the realities of power, and agreed to the deposition of Café Filho. Nereu Ramos was to continue as acting president till Kubitschek was due to take over, with a 'state of siege' declared for thirty days, which then was renewed till Café Filho's term was ended.

The crisis of November 1955 is worth looking at in some detail, partly because it was the culmination of a political struggle which had started with the re-election of Vargas in 1950 and continued after his death, and because it was a significant watershed in terms of subsequent relations between those contending interests which cut across civilian and military politics. The bitter opposition to Kubitschek and Goulart was not principally, or even largely, against Kubitschek, but against Goulart, and, again, not for what was known of him personally or directly, but for what he represented as the most conspicuous heir of Vargas and, by implication, of the policies most recently associated with the dead president. In this sense the struggle was, essentially and fundamentally, a class confrontation, about maintaining or challenging interests in society and the economy. The issues were never expressed very precisely on either side, but, in however diffused a manner, Vargas and *getulismo* by 1955 had come to represent a general commitment to wider distribution of resources and opportunities and a tighter control of Brazil's economy and wealth in relation to vested interests based outside the country.[116] Such aims, for many reasons, but notably through ideology and propaganda associated with the Cold War, had come to be identified by many Brazilians, civilian and military, with the 'subversion' which they believed to be contained in forces on the left wing of politics, most obviously the PCB, but, commonly enough, any movement requiring reform or change, especially if linked to organized labour.

At a more explicit level the confrontation was not immediately about social class interests. Men like Generals Lott, Denys, and Mascarenhas de Moraes were immovable in their hostility to the PCB and deeply suspicious, in particular, of João Goulart. They were, however, sensitive about the 'unity' of the officer corps and the 'discipline' and 'authority' required by the armed forces—hence their reaction to Carlos Luz's treatment of Lott—and, equally, they were anxious to preserve the reputation of the armed forces for respecting Brazil's liberal democratic system. This, paradoxically, led them to stage a *coup* which cut across all constitutional legality, both in removing Luz and, still more, in putting pressure on Congress to depose Café Filho.

The confrontation of 1955 left deep marks on Brazilian politics. It again showed, as recently in 1945 and 1954, that decisive power rested with the soldiers and, again, as in 1954 in the removal of Vargas, it showed that respect for 'democracy', on both sides in the conflict, very much depended on each group's understanding of what 'Brazilian democracy' really meant. On 31 January 1956, in relative calm after the intense excitement of the last few months, Kubitschek and Goulart at last took office. Lott still remained as Minister of War and other senior commanders, including Odílio Denys in the Eastern Military Zone, kept their posts. Despite, however, the calm and orderly constitutional procedure, no one now had any illusions as to where real power lay, or how easily the conflict might be renewed.

Notes

1 See Mello Franco, op. cit., 288–307.

2 Coutinho, op. cit., 425–6.

3 Dutra himself is said to have acknowledged in later years that, without Vargas's statement on his behalf, he would not have won in 1945. Dulles, op. cit., 281.

4 In the four key political states of the Federal District, São Paulo, Minas Gerais, and Rio Grande do Sul, the vote for Fiuza was 12 per cent.

5 Prestes was elected as senator for the Federal District and deputy for São Paulo, Estado do Rio, Pernambuco, the Federal District, and Rio Grande do Sul. He chose to sit as senator, so allowing 'alternates' from his party to sit in the other seats he had won, in accordance with the system of proportional representation.

6 Apart from Prestes three other members of the Central Committee were elected: Maurício Grabois and Agostinho Dias de Oliveira for Pernambuco and João Amazonas for the Federal District. Among the others elected was the historian Caio Prado Júnior in São Paulo.

7 See, for example, Leoncio Basbaum, *História Sincera da República*, III (São Paulo, 1962), 148. On the different elements in the party at this time see Osvaldo Peralva, *O Retrato* (Belo Horizonte, 1960).

8 There is much interesting debate in the Trotskyist journal founded in 1945, *Vanguardia Socialista*.

9 See especially on this Flynn, 'Class and Politics in Brazil' and 'Class, Clientelism and Coercion', where the central theme is that the alleged 'backwardness' of the Brazilian working class is greatly exaggerated, as is the impact of clientelist politics. Such interpretations may help to justify military intervention, but are less helpful in understanding popular political behaviour than those which draw attention to the recurring pattern of repression and state control whenever effective challenge is offered.

10 See Jover Telles, op. cit., 40–1.

11 See Alberto Mello y Souza, 'Efeitos econômicos do salário mínimo' in *APEC A Economia Brasileira e suas Perspectivas* (Rio de Janeiro, 1971), quoted Francisco de Oliveira, 'A Economia Brasileira: Crítica á razão dualista' *Estudos CEBRAP*, No. 2 (São Paulo, 1972).

12 Morazé, op. cit., 160–1 contains an interesting diagram of the campaign journeys of the three candidates in 1950, of which much the most thorough and effective was that of Vargas, covering the whole country from Rio Grande do Sul and back between 9 and 21 August.

13 For some discussion of this see I. Venturi, *Roots of Revolution* (London, 1960) and G. Ionescu and E. Gellner (eds.), *Populism: Its Meaning and Characteristics* (London, 1969).

14 See, for example, Torcuato di Tella, 'Populism and Reform in Latin America', in C. Veliz (ed.), *Obstacles to Change in Latin America* (London, 1965).

15 See the discussion of this in E. de Kadt, *Catholic Radicals in Brazil* (London, 1970), especially 94–8.
16 There seem to be few cases where the city political machine has been extended well beyond the city in this way. Adhemar's career is worth more careful study than it has yet received.
17 An interesting, small example of such support can be found in Carolina Maria de Jesus, a São Paulo *favelada*, whose diary makes clear her support for Adhemar. See *Child of the Dark* (New York, 1962).
18 See, in particular, Francisco Weffort, 'Estado y masa en el Brasil', *Revista Latinoamericana de Sociologia*, I (March, 1965), 53–71; 'Política de Massas' in O. Ianni *et al*, *Política e Revolução Social no Brasil* (Rio de Janeiro, 1965), 161–98; and *Partidos, Sindicatos e Democracia: Algumas Questões para a História do Periodo 1945–64*, CEBRAP (São Paulo, 1974) (mimeo). See, too, Octávio Ianni, *Crisis in Brazil* (New York, 1970).
19 Figures of the numbers of *industrial* workers and their relation to populism can be misleading, since they sometimes leave out such vitally important political groups as transport workers, especially railway workers, and dockers, whose unions were among the most active even in the late 19th century (above, p. 76). though they were not employed in 'industrial establishments'.
20 Góes Monteiro later described how in October 1949, for the first time, there was no celebration to mark the anniversary of Vargas's removal in 1945. He also claimed that he was asked to run as candidate for the vice-presidency, which he refused on grounds of ill health and because he had no such ambitions. Coutinho, op. cit., 495–6.
21 See particularly his campaign speeches in *A Campanha Presidencial* (Rio de Janeiro, 1951).
22 ibid., 19, 16 June 1950.
23 ibid., 23.
24 ibid., 26.
25 ibid., 28.
26 ibid., 29.
27 ibid., 31.
28 ibid., 27–8.
29 ibid., 26.
30 The volume of speeches *A Campanha Presidencial* covers the campaign from this first speech of 7 June, released in São Borja for the conference of the PTB in Rio de Janeiro, through the journey through Brazil in August, and up to the end of September. It is a splendid source for understanding Vargas's political style and the conciliatory, yet exhilarating, appeal of his low-keyed 'populist' rhetoric.
31 ibid., 55–74. Speech 10 August 1950.
32 ibid., 83–6.
33 ibid., 105–7, 19 August 1950.
34 ibid., 92, 12 August 1950.
35 ibid., 93.
36 ibid., 92.
37 ibid., 96.
38 Interestingly, by comparison with the earlier reference to the 'proletariat', Vargas now says how lack of sound policy has hit the 'classes produtoras', and how the poor ('os pobres') have suffered while exploiters and parasites have flourished. Except on rare occasions his language is always that of populism, 'productive classes' rather than 'working class', 'povo' rather than more specific reference to a particular class.
39 The fourth candidate, João Mangabeira, received 9,466 votes (0·11 per cent).
40 In 1955 Kubitschek was to win 35·63 per cent of the national vote and in 1960 Quadros won 48·26 per cent.
41 Vargas, *O Govêrno Trabalhista do Brasil*, 2 vols. (Rio de Janeiro, 1952), I, 28. Speech of 31 January 1951.
42 ibid.

43 See below, pp. 318–25.

44 Although it is discussed elsewhere, it is worth noting again here the useful material on the ESG and its influence in R. M. Schneider, *The Political System of Brazil* (New York, 1971) and in A. Stepan, *The Military in Politics: Changing Patterns in Brazil* (Princeton, 1971).

45 The point scarcely needs emphasizing, but the Latin American countries could fairly experience a certain *Schadenfreude* in seeing other countries in the 'developed' world struggling with problems often assumed to stem from 'Third World underdevelopment', or simple mismanagement. More substantially, however, it is precisely the valuable Latin American *reflection* on its own experience which makes a study of Latin American society so useful for other countries, now also faced with rapid inflation, more acute political tension and 'instability', even, *mirabile dictu*, with talk of a 'middle-class' reaction which could lead to military intervention. On this Latin American contribution see P. Flynn, 'Latin America: the ideology of political analysis', *Bulletin of the Society for Latin American Studies*, No. 20 (May 1974), 13–22.

46 SUMOC Instruction 25, 3 June 1974. SUMOC (Superintendência da Moeda e do Crédito) was founded in February 1945, to share certain central bank functions with the Banco do Brasil, its main job being to control the total supply of credit. See the note on SUMOC in the meticulous study of Brazilian inflation in R. Kahil, *Inflation and Economic Development in Brazil: 1946–1963* (Oxford, 1973), 254–5.

47 E. Baklanoff, 'Foreign Investment in Industrialization in Brazil', in E. Baklanoff (ed.), *New Perspectives of Brazil* (Nashville, 1966). 101–36, 128–9.

48 ibid.

49 Baklanoff (p. 129) argues, for example, that, when restrictions on profit remittances were removed (1954–61), new venture capital (excluding re-invested profits) averaged $91 million annually, while profit remittances fell to an average of $33 million.

Kahil, op. cit., 213 produces a table of the 'Movement of Foreign Capital and its Earnings, 1947–63'. He notes that: '. . . from 1947 to 1953 the transfer abroad of profits and dividends belonging to non-residents exceeded almost every year the net inflow of risk capital so that there was a net outflow averaging 33 million dollars per annum. Because of the inflow of loan capital the total balance was positive, however, for the period as a whole.

The situation improved considerably from 1954 to 1961, when the average inflow of foreign risk capital increased sixfold to 91 million dollars, at the same time as profit remittance declined by roughly a third to 32 million dollars on average, thus leaving a positive balance of 60 million dollars annually. Furthermore, as the inflow of loan capital also increased substantially over the period, especially in the last year, the total positive balance almost trebled to 164 million dollars annually . . .' ibid., 212–14. The main reason for the change from 1954 on seems to have been that investors now found it less advantageous to remit profits abroad and far more advantageous to reinvest them in Brazil.

50 Further plans were the *Programa das Metas* and the 1963–65 *Plano Trienal*. See below, pp. 242–7.

51 Kahil, op. cit., 213. One should also bear in mind that these figures certainly understate the real levels of profit, since much of what was really profit could be hidden under some other name, a common practice of international companies working in Latin America, and elsewhere.

52 Vargas, *O Govêrno Trabalhista do Brasil*, II, 68–9.

53 ibid., 71.
54 ibid., 72.
55 ibid., 78–9.
56 Kahil, op. cit., 214. Especially important was the establishment of virtually a multiple exchange-rate by SUMOC Instruction # 48 (February 1953) and Instruction # 70 (October 1953). The result was to make Brazilian exports more competitive and allow more selective control of imports.
57 On the career of Horta Barbosa, and on the early history of oil politics in Brazil see especially J. D. Wirth, *The Politics of Brazilian Development 1930–1954* (Stanford, 1970), 133–224.
58 ibid., 136–7.
59 An American-owned subsidiary of Jersey Standard, the Cia-Geral de Petróleo Pan-Brasileira, was started in 1930. It did virtually nothing, though holding at one point as many as 96 leases. In 1934 the Mining Code, under the inspiration of *tenente* nationalism, made all sub-soil wealth the property of the nation. In 1941 Pan-Brasileira ended when foreign-owned subsidiaries for exploring for oil were made illegal. Wirth, op. cit., 247.
60 Wirth refers to a letter from Oswaldo Aranha to Vargas, 12 February 1935, which explains how the oil companies protected their dollar earnings: '. . . by invoicing gasoline exports at double the real cost to themselves and then demanding full exchange cover for the padded invoices. . . .' (247).
61 These early links between Brazilian and Bolivian oil developments are especially interesting in relation to more recent negotiations in 1973–74, as the politics of oil has again become a major issue.
62 ibid., 166.
63 Wirth, ibid., 168 rightly speaks of the oil question as 'a public passion unequaled since the abolitionist campaign over sixty years before'.
64 The SALTE plan, drawn up by DASP (above, p. 104), was proposed in 1948, its name coming from its four main concerns—Saude, Alimentação, Transportação, Energia (Health, Food, Transport, and Energy). It was an early attempt to co-ordinate public spending over five years, but lasted scarcely more than a year.
65 See Vargas's speech in Salvador (Bahia) during his 1950 campaign—30 August 1950. Vargas, *A Campanha Presidencial*, 256.
66 For Vargas's speeches in this debate, and for an account of how the issues were developed, see Getúlio Vargas, *A política nacionalista do petróleo no Brasil* (Rio de Janeiro, 1964). Also the very useful chapter in Wirth, op. cit., 184–216.
67 Wirth notes, for example, how Vargas and his leading adviser, Almeida, became convinced that the oil companies did not share their objective of a crash programme to solve Brazil's oil needs: 'Glutted with crude oil, the companies did not see their interest in prospecting vigorously: they wanted reserves at little cost . . .', ibid., 189. The companies also told the Brazilians that they 'considered their investments globally rather than in terms of a specific area . . .', ibid., 255.
68 Source: Francisco de Oliveira, op. cit.
69 Article I said that disputes between employer and employee should be submitted to the arbitration of the Labour Court. Article 9 allowed one party to withdraw his labour or close down the place of work if the other party did not accept the court's judgement.
70 Figures from Jover Telles, op. cit.
71 ibid. Telles also produces (p. 58) a table which tries to evaluate the main grievances behind strikes which took place in 1951–52. 36·3 per cent (96) were for wage increases, another 14·4 per cent (38) were for payment of

late wages. 10·2 per cent (27) are described as occurring out of 'class solidarity' and only 4·9 per cent (13) arose out of demands for better working conditions.

72 There is a most useful account of it in J. A. Moíses, *The Political Participation of the Working Class in Brazil*, unpublished dissertation (University of Essex, 1972).

73 ibid., quoted *Folha da Manhã* of 27 March 1953.

74 ibid., 66.

75 Weffort, in *Partidos, Sindicatos e Democracia*, discusses briefly these 'parallel unions' (35–6 and 117–18). Their history is still obscure, but he sees them as a means for directing and mobilizing the workers by the PCB rather than as offering more effective representation.

76 The volume of imports, after rising in 1949 by 20 per cent over its average 1945–48 level, exceeded it by over 50 per cent in 1950, and was more than double this level in 1951 and 1952. Kahil, op. cit., 267.

77 Kahil notes how exports especially sank in 1951 and 1952, when Brazil's major export commodities were priced out of world markets 'owing to the maintenance of a fixed foreign exchange rate, despite the continuous rise of internal prices . . .', ibid., 266.

78 ibid., 285–6.

79 ibid., 286–7.

80 Nelson Werneck Sodré, *História militar do Brasil* (Rio de Janeiro, 1965), 304ff.

81 Skidmore, op. cit., 106. The whole question of the nature of United States pressure, first against Vargas, then his successors up to 1964, is discussed below. There is no question, however, that, even in this period, influences were being exerted essentially similar to those used in Latin America over the next two decades, and even defended by President Ford when in 1974 he was forced to comment on United States influence in Chile under Allende.

82 This point is argued in detail later. It may at least be noted, however, that by 1953 the armed forces, or at least the officer corps, had been heavily indoctrinated with Cold War propaganda and a massive ideological assault, largely through the ESG which was fundamentally inimical to Vargas's reformist commitments.

83 It should perhaps again be noted at this point that most opposition to deflationary policies came in this period from those who benefited most from the inflationary spiral. See Kahil, op. cit., 333: '. . . attempts at stabilisation . . . were vigorously denounced in the press and invariably aroused storms of protest, particularly on the part of the bankers . . .'.

84 The concept was frequently used by, among others, Góes Monteiro, but was common coin among military officers and the UDN.

85 This deliberately alarmist scaremongery has since been repeated on various occasions, notably in Brazil before 1964 and in Chile under Allende. On this second occasion, as is now known, roughly £8 million (or about £40 million on the black market rate of exchange) was spent by the CIA to whip up middle-class fears, and subsequent political reaction.

86 Vargas could never hope for a fair hearing from his heavily right-wing press, a problem faced by reformist politicians in so many societies. See, for example, Skidmore, op. cit., 125: '. . .Vargas, upon returning to the presidency in 1951, found the weight of press opinion heavily against him. He could never hope for sympathy or even objective coverage from the anti-getulista press. . . .'

87 This is not to suggest that, even if Vargas had given much more to the armed forces in terms of salaries, equipment, and marks of prestige, he would have

avoided a political clash. Allende in Chile during 1970–73 did all he could to assuage military opinion and associate the armed forces with his regime, only to be removed in the end by a military *coup*. In any case, Vargas had always taken care to look after the armed forces as best he could.

88 On these proposals see Kahil, op. cit., 294–300. Kahil notes that by early 1954 the median wage of industrial workers had fallen in terms of food by nearly 25 per cent from its 1946 level. The price of clothing, which had increased moderately from 1950 to mid-1952, had risen more sharply later, especially in 1953: '. . . It was thus to be expected that the government should attempt to redress the balance early in 1954, by raising the minimum wage. What can less easily be justified is its decision to increase the wages of the mass of urban unskilled workers and lower employees throughout Brazil at rates—varying according to the region between 70 percent and more than 100 percent—which were completely out of proportion with the rise in the price of food and other items in the cost of living. Thus, the minimum wage for the city of Rio de Janeiro was fixed at double the level decreed in December 1951—which was itself too high as already noted—though the price of food had increased in the meantime by only 60 percent, and the cost of living by little more than 50 percent' (295). Kahil also points out, however, that the acceleration of inflation was not merely due to the minimum wage decree. In general he is more concerned with the relative loss in earnings of *skilled* as compared to unskilled labour (299) and the growing illusion that *real* increases in earnings could come simply from political agitation (300).

89 On this whole debate see Afonso César, *Política, Cifrão e Sangue: Documentário do 24 de Agosto* (Rio de Janeiro, n.d.).

90 One of the clearest accounts of the death of Vargas is in R. Bourne, *Getúlio Vargas of Brazil, 1883–1954* (London, 1974), 185–97.

91 The two clearest accounts in English are in Skidmore, op. cit., 143–58 and J. W. F. Dulles, *Unrest in Brazil. Political–Military Crises 1955–1964* (Austin, 1970), 3–61.

92 See, in particular, his two volumes of autobiography: João Café Filho, *Do Sindicato ao Catete*, 2 vols. (Rio de Janeiro, 1966), which also has an introduction by the Minister of Agriculture in his government, Munhoz da Rocha, a man who also provided one of the most useful accounts of the crises of this period: Bento Munhoz da Rocha, *Radiografia de Novembro*, 2nd ed. (Rio de Janeiro, 1961).

93 See the table in R. Schneider *et al*, *Brazil Election Factbook*, No. 2 (Washington D.C., September 1965), 60, a most valuable summary and guide. The total votes showed less variation in the three elections:

	PSD	*UDN*	*PTB*	*Total Valid Vote*
1945	2,531,944	1,575,375	603,500	5,990,456
1950	2,068,405	1,301,459	1,262,000	9,309,213
1954	2,136,220	1,318,101	1,447,784	9,704,469

94 See Joffre Gomes da Costa, *Marechal Henrique Lott* (Rio de Janeiro, 1960), 231–2.

95 They included Marshal Mascarenhas de Moraes, former commander of the FEB, Generals Teixeira Lott, Juarez Távora, Canrobert Pereira da Costa (as army Chief of Staff), Brigadier Eduardo Gomes, and the other military ministers. See Café Filho, op. cit., II, 498.

96 ibid.

97 In his memoirs, for example, Afonso Arinos de Melo Franco, one of the

most prominent party spokesmen, defends the UDN against the charge that they were anti-constitutional and eager for a military *coup*. See Afonso Arinos de Melo Franco, *A Escalada* (Rio de Janeiro, 1965), 339–40. The context refers to the period immediately before the death of Vargas, but the defence is general. See, too, his justification for wanting a government of national unity (359–60).

98 Melo Franco notes, for example, the difficult position of Café Filho: '. . . Without being a *Getulista* he had been elected with Getúlio, and his rise in public life had not proceeded along those conservative lines which could reassure the military. The fall of Vargas had been due to them and they did not seem ready to withdraw. Their situation at the time was not the same as now (1965), but already they were moving in that direction. Today they think they can impose political solutions. At that time they wanted to avoid those of which they disapproved . . .' ibid., 365–6.

99 ibid., 366.

100 ibid., 366–7.

101 The Brazilian electorate grew rapidly after 1945. In that year out of 7·5 million registered voters, 6·2 million went to the polls. In the 1962 Congressional elections there were 18·5 registered voters, of whom 14·8 million voted. See Schneider *et al*, op. cit., 19. Schneider also notes that, although the increase in the number of voters was about 20 per cent every four years, there was a rate of increase of less than 50 per cent in the ratio of voters to total population from 1945 to 1962. Many Brazilians, of course, were disenfranchised because of the literacy qualification required, and because over half the population was under eighteen.

102 *Correio da Manhã* (6 August 1955), quoted Dulles, op. cit., 19–20.

103 There is no satisfactory account of Kubitschek's career. His early life is described in Francisco de Assis Barbosa, *Juscelino Kubitschek. Uma Revisão na Política Brasileira*, vol. I (Rio de Janeiro, 1960). The campaign of 1955 and some of the details of his programme are to be found in a laudatory account: José Moraes, *Juscelino O Homen, A Candidatura, A Campanha* (Belo Horizonte, n.d.). Moraes tells us that in his 'odyssey' of ten months' campaigning, Kubitschek flew for 661 hours and 31 minutes[!], travelling, in all, 173,300 kilometres ('more than four times round the world, all in Brazil'). He visited 372 towns and cities and made 412 different speeches, a record for Brazilian politics. Despite its adulatory character the study contains useful information on the campaign as a whole. See, too, Maria Victoria de Mesquita Benevides, *O Govêrno Kubitschek. Desenvolvimento Econômico e Estabilidade Política* (Rio de Janeiro, 1976).

104 Schneider *et al*, op. cit., 56–7.

105 See Munhoz da Rocha, op. cit., 25–47 and José Viriato de Castro, *Espada X Vassoura. Marechal Lott* (São Paulo, 1959), especially 21–8. Also Dulles, op. cit., 26–8

106 Viriato de Castro, op. cit., 21.

107 The speech is printed in full, ibid., 23–6.

108 Munhoz da Rocha, op. cit., 59–68.

109 Dulles, op. cit., 32.

110 *Tribuna da Imprensa* (9 November 1955)—my italics.

111 For useful information on these movements against the *golpista* element see Gomes da Costa, op. cit., passim.

112 He was kept waiting in an anteroom by Carlos Luz, a fact made known by radio and television, then had his resignation accepted immediately when Luz refused to discipline Mamede, a process Lott described as a 'fourth class burial'. The manner and speed of the replacement, with the retired

General Fiuza at once put into office, had all the marks of a carefully arranged manoeuvre, annoying and alarming military leaders unhappy about such civilian–military collusion. See on this the memoirs of General J. Justino Alves Bastos, *Encontro com o Tempo* (Rio de Janeiro, 1965), 296–8.

113 A list of those present can be found ibid., 297. They included those in key commands in Rio de Janeiro and General Olímpio Falconieri da Cunha, commander of the Central Military Zone, which included São Paulo, whose support was also critical. The meeting was addressed by General Manuel Azambuja Brilhante, commandant of the 1st Infantry Division.

114 The phrase is used in the memoirs of another senior commander, the former head of the FEB in Italy, Marshal Mascarenhas de Moraes. Like Lott, Mascarenhas de Moraes had signed the memorial presented to Vargas in 1954, but was alarmed over the political crisis and the damage it might do to the armed forces as much as to the democratic system. See J. B. Mascarenhas de Moraes, *Memórias*, 2 vols. (Rio de Janeiro, 1969), II, 597–9.

115 The debate is given in full in José Loureiro Júnior, *O Golpe de Novembro e Outros Discursos* (Rio de Janeiro, 1957).

116 Some commentators saw the defeat of Lacerda and the *golpistas* around him as a definitive victory for nationalism as against the *entreguistas*, those who would sell out Brazil to the foreigner. See, for example, Plínio de Abreu Ramos, *Brasil, 11 de Novembro* (São Paulo, 1960). Also the comments of Nelson Werneck Sodré, both in his preface to the work of Abreu Ramos and his own *Introdução à Revolução Brasileira*, which is quoted by Abreu Ramos, ibid., 126–7.

1956–61

7 Confrontation and Crisis

The Years of Confidence

In striking contrast to the years of crisis and confrontation which both immediately preceded and followed, the presidency of Juscelino Kubitschek stands out sharply as a short, but welcome, period of national confidence, exuberance, and substantial success. The success, admittedly, was limited, the confidence sometimes rang hollow, and the enthusiasm was more justified in the case of some social groups than of others. There was, too, always at least the threat of political crisis and an uneasy awareness of how quickly earlier confrontation might be renewed, since, both in office and in subsequent years, Kubitschek drew heavy criticism. Yet he remained, long after his presidency and well after his removal from politics, probably the most formidable politician in Brazil, and the one most likely, if presidential elections were again allowed, to appeal to a mass popular vote, being, at least in this respect, that political heir of Vargas so feared by those who had succeeded in eliminating Getúlio, but failed to keep out Kubitschek.

Kubitschek, like Vargas, knew how to build on earlier experience, to translate to the national level the techniques and appeal of earlier achievements in state politics. As Vargas had drawn on his formation in Rio Grande do Sul, so Kubitschek learned from his career in Minas Gerais, again a hard forcing-ground for ambitious young politicians, easing his way among the political party rivalries of what till recently had been Brazil's most populous state, and still one of its politically most powerful.[1] State politics had remained bitter in Minas Gerais throughout the last two decades, feeding on, for example, the hostility to Vargas of the Melo Franco family and other state political leaders after their disappointments in 1933.[2] Kubitschek was firmly identified as being in the Vargas camp, in that he was a protégé of Benedicto Valladares, the relatively obscure *mineiro* politician chosen as *interventor* by Vargas,[3] an influence which had helped Kubitschek to become mayor of Belo Horizonte in 1940 and governor in 1950.

As a *mineiro*, coming from the only landlocked state of Brazil important in terms of wealth and population, Kubitschek had other experience useful to him as president. He could be expected, for example, to have more sympathy with plans to develop Brazil's interior, including the long-repeated aim to build a new national capital deep inland, particularly since Belo Horizonte, and the capital, Goiânia, of its neighbouring state, Goiás, were both planned cities. He had, too, already shown his energy and determination in pushing through policies for infrastructural development, especially in the key fields of energy and transport, again so crucial to a large interior state. His election campaign had reiterated the need to modernize and develop Brazil's whole industrial economy, so continuing that commitment already given by Vargas, and now expressed through that Vargista party, the PSD, of which Kubitschek's patron, Valladares, was one of the most prominent founder-members and spokesmen. Born in 1902, Kubitschek, when he took office as president, was nearly fifty-four, almost seven years older than Vargas when he came to power in 1930. He was, in other words, again like Vargas, a tried, mature politician, trained first in medicine, but mostly formed in the tough political tradition of his native state, already a man of wide experience and solid achievements, closely associated with the business interests and ambitions of Minas Gerais, more anxious to conciliate than to look for conflict, and fully aware of the size of the problems he now faced.

If, like Vargas, Kubitschek fully appreciated the need for a cool political head and a readiness for compromise, he differed sharply in his political style, even when pursuing policies essentially the same as those laid down by Getúlio. He now brought to national politics an exhilarating, much-needed panache and a seemingly unshakeable confidence. His infectious ebullience made others believe that his promises could be fulfilled, swiftly turning a crisis of national confidence into a widespread acceptance that Brazilian development could, and must, be achieved by a concentrated effort of will, which would break through, once and for all, the bottlenecks and obstacles of recent years. The most obvious example of such achievement was, of course, the construction of Brasília. The lasting symbol of Kubitschek's determination to build quickly and imaginatively for the future, this city of startling beauty was to be a focus for economic and social change in the heart of Brazil's previously neglected interior. It was a statement of confidence in the nation's future, of a determination to possess the whole country and end those long years during which Brazilians had clung to their coastline, looking outwards to other countries instead of inwards to Brazil. The cost of Brasília was high, using resources which many believed should have been spent elsewhere, on improving, for example, cities already overcrowded and severely under strain. But Brasília was much more than just a piece of urban planning or regional development. It expressed a fundamental ideology which guided Kubitschek's entire presidency, to build rapidly and push forward dramatically without too carefully weighing the costs, to impose new forms on Brazil, quickly and forcefully. In contrast to Rio de Janeiro, where the grandeur and exuberant beauty of its natural setting so completely eclipsed the city inserted in it, Brasília was entirely fashioned by man, its impact coming not from its natural context, a flat red plain, but from its sculptural qualities of line and space, from forms conceived and imposed by man rather than dictated, as in Rio de Janeiro, entirely by nature. In his economic policies Kubitschek promised fifty years' progress in five, determined to catapult Brazil forward along the road to development, swiftly enlarging the nation's infrastructure, giving urgent stimulus to its industries and every incentive to investment, both domestic and foreign.[4]

Political Tensions

The Armed Forces

Kubitschek's plans for the economy are discussed elsewhere, weighing their success against their costs, especially in terms of their impact on inflation and their relation to the rapidly growing demands for a more equitable pattern of distribution of national wealth and resources. In terms, however, of the shaping of Brazilian politics and of the relation between the Kubitschek years and those which followed, it is important not to allow the controversy over economic strategy, or the excitement of Brasília, to distract attention from the continuing political crisis, all part of that persisting tension which eventually led to the *coup* of April 1964.

In the political sphere, in sharp contrast to the economic, Kubitschek was content to make haste slowly, aware of the opposition aligned against him. As he took office, the state of siege was continued for a month, reflecting the government's apprehension over groups, especially in the armed forces, who opposed the return, as they believed, of political enemies removed in August 1954. Such opposition had little immediate chance of winning wide support, but its continuing existence was revealed in a matter of weeks, with a revolt of air force officers on a distant aerodrome in Amazonas.

The revolt of air force officers in Jacareacanga in February 1956 was a reversal of the famous dictum that history repeats itself, the first time as tragedy, the second time as farce. In the case both of the Jacareacanga revolt and that of Aragarças in December 1959,[5] the farce came first. The first revolt was led by a young air force engineer, Major Haroldo Veloso, whose previous service mostly had been spent in building airstrips in the interior. On 11 February 1956 he and another officer flew in a small Beechcraft aeroplane to Jacareacanga, deep in the interior, heading for Santarém at the junction of the Amazon and the Tapajós rivers. It was a most improbable area to choose as the springboard for revolution. Indeed, one sign of its remoteness and political insignificance was that within a few days a handful of rebellious officers was able to take control of the airbase at Cachimbo, a string of towns along the Tapajós, and Santarém. Their general, confused aim was to give a lead to colleagues on the coast, hoping to spark off a wider revolt, and there was, in fact, some limited support in several air force bases. The movement dragged on till the end of the month, largely because of the remoteness of the area in which the revolt was centred, as a small force of marines was sent up the Amazon to Belém. The ripples of the disturbance reached Rio de Janeiro, but the movement was obviously a local one, easily contained, lacking support among senior officers, and posing no real threat to the new Kubitschek government.[6]

The revolt in Jacareacanga did show, however, the persistence of hostility to Kubitschek within the armed forces, especially among air force officers, who saw his success as the return of those who, through Gregório Fortunato, had killed Major Vaz in the attack on Lacerda, a politician who still had great support among air force officers. More generally, the revolt led by Major Veloso reflected a widespread belief among many serving officers that they knew the Brazilian interior and the problems of its people far better than city-bound politicians deep in political intrigue. It represented, therefore, a diffuse but important set of social and political perceptions, analogous to those of the *tenentes* in the 1920s, a reaction of men who had direct experience of the harsh conditions of work in the interior against what they easily perceived as the softness, hypocrisy, and corruption of political life in the coastal cities. It was an attitude which had been evident, for example, in men like Juarez Távora as a young *tenente*, deeply suspicious of all politicians and contemptuous of their claims to offer solutions for the nation's problems.

Throughout the government of Kubitschek this discontent rumbled on, with, for example, some of his opponents in the navy vehemently objecting to a naval salute to the president in early 1957, while his old enemy, Admiral Pena Bôto, even plotted to seize Kubitschek on board the cruiser *Barroso*. This was to make up for the humiliation to the navy during the *Tamandaré* incident, involving the former captain of the *Tamandaré* in the new plot. There was, once again, a comic opera quality about the whole affair,[7] since it was difficult to reach inter-service agreement on virtually anything at the time, and Admiral Pena Bôto and his friends had no chance of army or air force support. But, again, it was a straw in the wind, a sign of how readily some senior officers saw themselves as above the law, presuming to take matters into their own hands. Kubitschek, on the other hand, persisted in taking a soft line with military personnel who involved themselves directly in national politics, so, in effect, encouraging behaviour which no elected civilian government could normally be expected to tolerate. Both publicly and in the semi-privacy of military clubs, senior officers criticized and defied both the president and his Minister of War, exhibiting, for instance throughout the whole of 1958, a defiance of authority which in a more disciplined military establishment would have brought swift reaction. Kubitschek paid lip-service to the idea of disciplining officers who became involved in politics, as in November 1956, when the government ruled that military personnel should not make political pronouncements. But he never gave the ruling any teeth, failing to take firm action against officers who immediately acted against it.

Military opposition again came to a head in December 1959, following attempts to reach inter-service agreement on the need to remove Kubitschek and 'purify' national life. The movement again involved the now Lieutenant-Colonel Haroldo Veloso, pardoned after his earlier rebellion, together with another air force officer of the same rank, João Paulo Moreira Burnier,[8] who were especially alarmed at the decision of Jânio Quadros on 25 November to withdraw from the presidential election of 1960, a decision which eventually he changed, but which seemed to open the way to the successful candidacy of the Minister of War, General Lott. The rebels launched a manifesto condemning corruption in national politics, confident of the support of 324 conspirators[9] and hopeful of the backing of prominent UDN politicians such as Lacerda, Magalhães Pinto, and Otávio Mangabeira, the last of whom was the only prominent politician to side with the rebels. Essentially the plan was the same as in 1956, to seize towns in the interior and provoke revolt elsewhere. Early on 3 December 1959 the leaders flew into the interior, aiming to set up a base at Aragarças, a small town on the borders of Matto Grosso and Goiás, directly to the west of Brasília,[10] again a most implausible base for national insurrection. A passenger plane was seized on a domestic flight from Rio de Janeiro to Belém and diverted to Aragarças, where the plotters, again hoping to link up with other far-flung centres such as Jacareacanga and Santarém, were already in a state of confusion.

The wider political impact of this second military revolt was greater than in 1956, with prominent UDN politicians, such as Lacerda and Afonso Arinos de Melo Franco, careful not to identify themselves with the revolt, but equally anxious to make out of it as much political capital as possible. There was praise in Congress for the idealism of the rebels and sympathy on the UDN benches for their motives, even though the rebellion was soon over, with the leaders taking flight on 4 December. Lacerda and others tried to argue that the plot was a fabrication, perhaps to justify the cancellation of the coming presidential election. Excitement then mounted further when Quadros said he would stand after all, a decision hailed by the conspirators, now abroad, as justification for their revolt.

The two revolts, in Jacareacanga in 1956 and Aragarças in 1959, could only have been planned by air force officers, used to ready acceptance of journeys over vast distances and impassable terrain. Both, in any case, were acts of defiance rather than serious attempts at armed revolution to overthrow a government. Neither was well planned, lacking sufficient support, both military and political. The revolts were, however, symptomatic of a persistent tension between many military officers, broadly aligned with the UDN, and an elected government perceived by them as following the tradition and guidelines of Vargas. In 1956 and 1959 the supreme military command, as represented by General Lott, was loyal to the elected president. Kubitschek was assiduous in his wooing of the armed forces and able to carry along with him enough military opinion in support of his policies of rapid national development. He was always equally careful not to spread alarm over the wider role to be allowed to other social groups. In a period, on the other hand, of relative calm and agreement in civil-military relations the revolts and constant rumblings of military dissidents were a clue to later eruptions as social and political tensions increased.

Industrialization and the Working Class

The most evident reason for Kubitschek's survival, and his ability to hold together the leadership of the armed forces, was his relationship with the Brazilian bourgeoisie, or, at least, with those important elements in the bourgeoisie involved in that process of rapid import-substitution industrialization which was central to the whole Kubitschek regime. Politically this allegiance was expressed through Kubitschek's support in the PSD. It was on this element of the PTB–PSD Vargista bloc that he drew most heavily, in contrast to

Vargas himself and in marked contrast to Goulart. This basis of PSD support made his whole political programme much more viable than that of Goulart, who had to rely on a more direct appeal to the urban working class, so further provoking middle-class alarm. Kubitschek, despite the image so sedulously cultivated by his opponents, was essentially a politician of and for the middle class, riding high on the new wave of import-substitution industrialization and his overall programme to expand Brazil's industrial base. One cost of this success was, on the other hand, a lessening grip on working-class support, resulting in a shift in working-class politics, where Kubitschek's nationalist development ideology was less appealing than it was in middle-class political circles.

The relation of industrialization under Kubitschek to the shaping of Brazilian politics is obscure and not widely studied.[11] Industry grew relatively slowly in 1956 and 1957, but in 1958 it expanded by 16·2 per cent, in 1959 by 11·9 per cent, and in 1960 by 9·6 per cent. Between 1954 and 1958 the average annual growth of industry was almost 10 per cent and, despite the sharp fall in 1963, to 0·2 per cent, the average expansion of industry from 1959 to 1963 was around 8 per cent.[12] GDP increased by 3·2 per cent in 1956, 8·1 in 1957, 7·7 in 1958, 5·6 in 1959, 9·7 in 1960, and 10·3 in 1961. Growth was especially rapid in such key areas as heavy goods and state-owned industry, reflecting the high priority assigned to infrastructural development by the Kubitschek government:

> . . . From 1953 to 1962, the production of cement more than doubled, together with electric power supply and installed capacity, while the production of steel trebled and that of chemicals increased almost eight-fold, and that of electric material more than six-fold . . .[13]

It has been argued that one result of the government raising minimum wages in this same period was a continuous decline in the real wages of skilled workers as compared to unskilled workers, a somewhat paradoxical pattern at a time of rapid industrial expansion, but which resulted, for example, within industry in Guanabara in a fall of the ratio of the highest to the lowest wage from 1–11 up to March 1954 to 1–6 the following June, at which level it remained for at least three years, till March 1957.[14]

At the same time, however, as skilled wages were declining in relation to unskilled, the real minimum wage was also falling in absolute terms. In Guanabara, for example, taking a base of 100 in 1944, it moved from 142·9 in 1955 to 159·8 in 1957, then to 106·3 in 1959. In São Paulo the fall was from 139·3 in 1955 to 153·8 in

1957 and 101·7 in 1959. The tables for movements in real minimum wages and for rises in prices are worth setting out in full, both in the context of this discussion of the Kubitschek period and of later years.[15]

Real Minimum Wages: Guanabara and São Paulo
Table I

Years	*Indices (Base—1944=100)*		*Annual Variation*	
	Guanabara	*São Paulo*	*Guanabara*	*São Paulo*
1955	142·9	139·3	– 1·2	0·7
1956	150·9	147·0	5·6	5·5
1957	159·8	153·8	5·9	4·6
1958	140·2	133·3	–12·3	–13·3
1959	106·3	101·7	–14·2	–23·7
1960	140·2	130·8	13·2	28·6
1961	161·6	146·2	15·3	11·8
1962	137·5	123·9	–15·0	–15·3
1963	128·6	114·5	– 6·5	– 7·6
1964	124·9	116·3	– 2·1	1·6
1965	119·6	112·8	– 5·0	– 3·0
1966	107·1	97·4	–10·7	–13·7
1967	104·5	95·7	– 2·4	– 1·7
1968	103·6	94·0	– 0·9	– 1·8

General Price Index
Table II

Years	*Percentage Annual Increase*
1955	12·4%
1956	24·4%
1957	7·0%
1958	24·3%
1959	39·5%
1960	30·7%
1961	47·7%
1962	51·3%
1963	81·3%
1964	91·9%
1965	34·5%

If, then, one asks who was benefiting from the sudden surge of industrialization and the rapid jump forward under Kubitschek, the broad answer seems to be foreign investors[16] and Brazilians from what may roughly be described as the 'middle class' upwards, but, in particular, those groups who on subsequent analysis also appear to have done best out of inflation up to 1963, namely, 'financial intermediaries (mostly bankers) and employers in the services sector . . . big industrialists, merchants and contractors, together with big landlords . . .'[17]

'Middle class' in this context is, however, too wide and vague a term, since many middle-class groups were also suffering from the inflation which accompanied a 'government which . . . appeared not to be particularly inhibited by financial considerations . . .'[18] The relative decline in earnings affecting skilled workers also seems to have hit many of the 'middle class', since one result of the inflation of the late 1950s and early 1960s was in 'permanently reducing the real incomes of the upper classes of workers, employers, and civil servants, and presumably also of public-utility companies (mostly foreign-owned) and of medium enterprises using labour-intensive methods of production or specialising in popular consumer goods . . .'[19] It would seem therefore that, while wage-earners generally were losing ground—as were, obviously, the mass of the population not earning regular wages, those in the 'informal' sector or in the large 'marginal' population—so, too, were many of the lower-middle class. Those who gained most were, in general, the larger financial and industrial interests, and the agrarian bourgeoisie linked to the production and export of coffee. It was, however, precisely to those elements that Kubitschek could appeal through the PSD, and from which he drew his continuing support for an overall policy of rapid capitalist development for Brazil, firmly geared to industrialization, but never neglectful of the coffee economy, a strategy which also depended heavily on foreign confidence and foreign finance, but which, in this respect, ran into trouble as inflation got out of hand.[20]

Leaving aside for the moment Kubitschek's relations with foreign financiers, it is important to notice during his term of office other internal political developments which were to be of mounting significance in future years. The period was, as already emphasized, a relatively tranquil one and, despite the apparent decline in real wages just noted, there were many not only in the middle class, but among working people, too, who enthusiastically supported Juscelino. One undoubted feature of such support, to be discussed more fully later, was the highly successful ideology propagated by his regime, primarily stemming from a pervasive, infectious nationalism.

Although stronger in its appeal to middle-class groups, the nationalist ideology was powerful throughout the whole of society as people of all classes were caught up in the general sense of enthusiasm associated with confidently asserted government policies and a series of specific achievements ranging from the building of Brasília to the renewed, enormously popular, success in the World Cup. Brazil really did seem to many to be moving forward vigorously and surely, at last achieving the heady promises always offered but previously so elusive.

The impact on working-class politics of what sometimes has been described as 'developmental nationalism' still has not been sufficiently studied, but one feature of the Kubitschek years seems to have been, to a striking degree, the reinforcement of corporatism as the most dominant theme in the ideological state apparatus by an aggressive nationalism through which the government associated with its economic policies social groups whose real interests by no means had been shown to be identified with those policies. It was a period, for example, in which corporatist-inspired legislation and a basically corporatist pattern of relations between the government and the trade union movement no longer seemed to be resented, as previously by that movement, but almost, it seemed, accepted as the 'normal' framework within which working-class and trade union politics should develop.[21] Such ideological factors were especially linked to the growth of ISEB (Institute of Advanced Brazilian Studies), which provided, as discussed later, the main ideological rationale of the Kubitschek government. Through the PSD–PTB coalition the trade unions were now to some extent identified with the regime as headed by Kubitschek and with control of at least part of the state apparatus, if not yet to the degree to which this was to be reached under Goulart. The result, however, by means of the dominant nationalist ideology developed by Kubitschek and his supporters, was, paradoxically, to provide even tighter control of the official trade union movement, already so caught up in earlier corporatist legacies. Nationalism now became an important mobilizing ideology for *all classes*, even if more strongly for the bourgeoisie than for the working class of Brazil. It caught up many in support of Kubitschek who otherwise might have been expected to resist policies which objectively were not directly in their interests.

Such success, however, contained serious contradictions, resulting eventually in a major crisis for the whole Vargista system of multi-class 'populist' politics. That system had always contained severe tensions, seeking both to hold together a multi-class coalition, yet also to offer a measure of redistribution and reform and a greater degree of political participation to previously excluded social groups, who inevitably would tend to challenge the very system through which their opportunities had been provided. The years of Kubitschek's government saw these tensions increase, notably in terms of the renewed activities of the PCB and the emergence of other forms of working-class organization, which paralleled the official state-directed system and immediately presented a challenge to that alliance so successfully headed by Kubitschek.

A frequent criticism of populist political systems is that, being essentially *multi-class* in composition and appeal, they are incapable of producing more autonomous political movements on behalf of the working class, or of sustaining effective challenges to the social and economic system of which populist politics are an expression. There are, undoubtedly, grounds for such charges, but they can be and, certainly in the case of Brazil, have been exaggerated. The suppression of the PCB under Dutra, as already argued, imposed severe limits on the capacity of the party system to express explicitly class-based demands or antagonisms, while the system of *peleguismo* further curtailed the opposition to government or employers which might have come from the trade unions. The *pelego*, essentially, was a figure in the trade union movement who, while ostensibly a labour leader and as such a spokesman for the workers organized in that union, was much more effectively an agent of the federal government within the corporatist-based trade union system imposed on the country by Vargas. The term *pelego* originally means a sheepskin which is placed, wool side up, between a horseman and his saddle, or, more commonly, between the saddle and the horse, in order to make the ride more comfortable. The quite simple, but forceful, analogy, therefore, in terms of the trade union movement was that the *pelego* was a man who made it easier and more comfortable for the government and employers to ride on the back of the labour movement. Essentially, he reduced friction. It is a vivid, and very Brazilian, metaphor, perhaps not found as forcefully in any other society, a significant reflection of the perception on the part of the working class of how the corporatist labour legislation worked in practice.

The social and political phenomenon of *peleguismo* is crucial to an understanding of working-class politics in the post-war period. The influence of the *pelego* was part of that wider system of political patron-clientage already discussed in some detail, stemming, in large part, from the corporatist *impôsto sindical*, or trade union tax, equivalent to one day's pay per year, deducted from every worker whether union member or not, and distributed to the officially recognized unions through the Ministry of Labour. Such funds were, in theory, to be spent in certain defined ways, mostly social, educational, and medical, as laid down in the labour code.[22] They were not to be spent as strike funds or for similar political purposes, reflecting again the social welfare, corporatist, and integrative features of Brazil's trade union system. In practice, these funds were often used by union leaders, the *pelegos*, either for their own ends, or, in effect, to extend their patronage and control. More importantly, however, they themselves, while acting as patrons towards their members, were first and foremost clients of the Ministry of Labour and the state, acting on behalf of their own patron.[23] The *pelego*'s behaviour was, it has been argued, 'characteristically anti-worker', being at best paternalistic in his attitude, regularly preaching conformity, restraining attempts at revolt, and containing the class struggle.[24]

It has been argued that '. . . During the 1950s there was little danger that ultimate control of the labour movement would slip from the hands of the political establishment'.[25] This seems indisputable, the chance of such a shift coming, rather, in the 1960s. But, at the same time, there is some evidence that even during the Kubitschek years the populist alliance was under strain, with more challenging political forces emerging, even though the tensions became more severe and more evident only in later years. The period from 1952 to 1962 has even been described as 'a golden era for the modern Brazilian trade union movement, both on the level of purely trade union activity and that of politics',[26] a period during which trade union activity recovered from the stagnation, even the retrogression, of previous years, to reach again the level of activity seen around 1945–46. Unions increased substantially in numbers and spread throughout most of the country, including the interior. The number and intensity of strikes, and other commonly accepted indicators of union activity, were not comparable to the years before the suppression of the PCB, but the number of disputes and strikes was certainly growing. Their extent is difficult to chart with accuracy. One estimate of industrial disputes, using limited, official statistics, calculates a rise from under 400 in 1953–54, to over 500 in 1959, about 700 both in 1962 and 1963, and over 1,000 in 1964.[27] Such estimates are certainly too low, since they do not take into account unofficial or partial stoppages. A better indication of the range of strike activity is given in the work of Jover Telles,[28] who cites, for example, the *Estado de São Paulo* (10 January 1961), reporting that in 1959 in the state of São Paulo alone there were 954 strikes. These affected 901 firms in the city, 53 in the interior, involved in São Paulo alone 354,215 workers and cost 3,259,069 man hours.[29]

More significantly, there are signs that throughout these years the grip of the *pelego* was beginning to be broken, as new forms of organization appeared and as, in particular, the PCB extended its influence throughout the trade union movement. There had been early attempts to form parallel union organizations less dependent on the corporatist system. In September 1946, for example, at the Trade Union Congress of Brazilian Workers (Congresso Sindical dos Trabalhadores do Brasil) in Rio de Janeiro, the then Communist deputy João Amazonas headed a movement which resulted in the creation of the CTB (Confederation of the Workers of Brazil), linked to workers' groups throughout the country, which were, however, ended when the PCB was again declared illegal. During the important strike in São Paulo in 1953, already discussed, a further effort at inter-union organization resulted in the Pact of Unity between Trade Unions (Pacto de Unidade Intersindical (PUI)), which remained active, especially in the city of São Paulo, over the next five years, linking over one hundred unions.[30] Other organizations also were formed, sometimes by those who opposed Communist union activity, as in the Democratic Trade Union Movement (Movimento Sindical Democrático) and the Movement for Trade Union Renewal (Movimento de Renovacão Sindical). The most important groups were, however, those most influenced by the PCB, notably the PUI in São Paulo, the similar organization in Guanabara, CPOS (Permanent Committee for Trade Union Organizations), also started in 1958, and the PUA (Pact for Unity and Action; Pacto de Unidade e Ação), founded in 1960, all of which in 1962 gave way to the Comando Geral dos Trabalhadores, (the General Workers' 'Comando').[31]

The emergence of these 'parallel' and 'horizontal' groups was especially important, pointing to a break in the whole structure of government-controlled unions in the corporatist pattern developed since the 1930s. The Kubitschek government was aware of the challenge, though not yet perhaps sufficiently concerned to react sharply to it.[32] It replied to growing working-class pressure by concessions, especially in wages, as in the increase of the minimum wage of July 1956 (increases ranging from 60 per cent of the May 1954 levels in Rio de Janeiro and São Paulo, to 100 per cent in other cities). These rises were associated with others in the salaries of civil servants and the military, and helped to increase federal expenditure by almost 70 per cent in 1956.[33] Similarly, on 28 December 1958, at the end of a year of intensified working-class activity, Kubitschek announced an increase of 58 per cent in the minimum wage, as of 1 January 1959, and a rise of 30 per cent in the salaries of civil servants and the military.[34] One result of this, it has been argued, was a rapid increase in the price of food, about 30 per cent in the five months January to May.[35] Such direct causation may be queried, but the evidence, taken as a whole, is enough to suggest that inflationary pressures building up in the Kubitschek period were now combining with an increasing militancy on the part of the labour movement to make substantial demands on the government, pointing the way to much more acute pressures over the next few years, notably under João Goulart.[36]

In terms of his relations with the organized working class, Kubitschek was both skilful and lucky, with luck playing the more conspicuous part. His identification with the Vargista PSD–PTB coalition, though much weighted towards the PSD, won him initial sympathy and support, especially after the intense campaign to exclude him on the part of right-wing opponents. His exuberant style and the rapid industrial growth associated with his policies further defused popular opposition, especially since it took some time for inflationary pressures to work through the system and for those most affected to realize that the current economic strategy was not really bringing substantial benefits to them. Such realization was further hindered by the infectious ideology of nationalist development so assiduously cultivated by Kubitschek and his supporters, allowing a growing nationalist fervour to mask, at least for a time, the real impact of government policies on wages and salaries.

It seems fair to say that this comparatively amicable relationship could not have lasted much longer. Already, as Kubitschek's term of office drew to a close, there were new movements which offered more effective challenge to the whole corporatist structure of labour relations and to the populist political system more generally. As Kubitschek's presidency proceeded, the pressure of rising prices combined with these new trends to make much heavier demands on the government, which Kubitschek, like his successors, would have found difficult to handle. The nature of those pressures is discussed later. One interpretation stresses in particular the capital accumulation process being followed in Brazil and the increasing difficulty, within the existing economic and political system, of extracting the surplus necessary to sustain that process.[37] Kubitschek survived, to hand over office peacefully to his successor, but the pressures were already apparent and already, it may be noted, important in his handling of a much more immediate issue, the problem of stabilization and the complex relations between Kubitschek and those foreign financiers and bankers whose confidence he so urgently needed to maintain.

The International Context

One of the paradoxes of Kubitschek's presidency, and further evidence of his political skill, is that while in practice he encouraged and collaborated with foreign, especially North American, investment and business interests, he at the same time supported those groups within Brazil most active in elaborating a coherent, critical theory of nationalist development. His economic policies depended on continuing support from foreign interests, yet he was willing to give federal financial support for the Institute of Advanced Brazilian Studies (ISEB), the most influential source of nationalist ideology in the late 1950s, whose staff and students were among the most vocal defenders of a tougher, more nationalist development strategy for Brazil.[38] They played an active part in government and administration, providing a corps of *técnicos*, or specialist economic and social advisers, whose thinking on the degree of nationalist control needed in shaping Brazil's economy often differed sharply from policies the Kubitschek regime was required to follow.

It is wrong to attribute too great a coherence to these theorists of nationalist development, since there was often sharp disagreement over the nature and degree of foreign involvement required. As long, too, as Kubitschek's relations with foreign governments and agencies, particularly in the United States, ran smoothly, the more extreme nationalist critique was kept muted. It was Kubitschek who proposed an ambitious collaborative programme of economic development as a necessary basis for social reform, a plan which he put to President Eisenhower under the title of Operation Pan-America, and which, though coldly received by Eisenhower at the time, was in its essential form subsequently revived under President Kennedy as the Alliance for Progress.

In all his early dealings with foreign agencies and bankers Kubitschek showed a readiness to collaborate by seeking a stabilization programme compatible with the commitment to public spending contained in his Target Programme. He willingly accepted, for example, an elaborate strategy drawn up by the director of the BNDE (National Economic Development Bank), Roberto Campos, and the Minister of Finance, Lucas Lopes, who previously had also directed the BNDE. This implied close collaboration with the International Monetary Fund and other institutions whose cautious banking instincts were already alerted to the inflationary threat contained in Kubitschek's plans for rapid industrial development. Kubitschek at first seems to have seen no major difficulty in reconciling rapid growth and a tolerable degree of inflation, and certainly offered no intransigent ideological opposition to the idea of working closely with foreign financiers: quite the contrary. His aim was to satisfy the demands of the Brazilian industrial and financial bourgeoisie, from whom through the PSD he drew much of his support, without at the same time alarming or antagonizing those groups abroad whose continued confidence and financial help he also needed. While encouraging the industrialists, he was, however, also anxious to protect the other major fraction of the bourgeoisie, the coffee-growers and exporters, mainly by buying up surplus stocks of coffee to maintain world prices.[39] It was a difficult balance to keep, not least when growing wage demands, as noted already, also threatened the stabilization programme, sharpened the choice for the regime between an even fuller commitment to bourgeois interests or a greater measure of distribution, and, above all, endangered that happy initial relationship with foreign financiers which was an essential factor in Kubitschek's whole development strategy.

Unfortunately, as Kubitschek's term in office proceeded, the dilemma became even more acute. Wage- and salary-earners grew louder in their claim for more money to keep up with inflation; industrialists demanded continued, even wider, credits to finance their growth; foreign bankers grew steadily more alarmed at the rising inflation, and at a swelling chorus of nationalist criticism which accused interests outside Brazil of being more anxious over their investment and rate of profit than the needs of Brazilian industry and national development more generally. Kubitschek was caught between the conflicting interests not only of the working class and, broadly speaking, the bourgeoisie, but, which was even more of a problem, between different elements or fractions of the bourgeoisie. This again was not just the coffee interests versus the industrialists, but different groups of industrialists—those more exclusively based in Brazil and others more directly dependent on foreign finance and investment, those representing small and medium-sized industry and those representative of large industries, while, of course, he had also to choose between more vigorous support for state-owned enterprises and others. At the same time, other groups, too, were contending for influence and control, elements within the armed forces, as seen already, and the growing, ever more influential body of civil servants and administrators. Public employees were growing rapidly in numbers as a distinctive branch of the state apparatus, and their claims for resources, and mounting anxiety over their relative placing in an inflationary economy, now became one of the major factors of national politics.[40]

As pressure grew, something had to give, if not immediately, at least in the years ahead. In the short run those who gained most were the state-owned sector of industry and those most representative of and financed by foreign capital.[41] But one notable feature of the politics of the Kubitschek period, was in fact the failure of any single group to establish complete hegemony in terms of controlling the state apparatus. The industrial bourgeoisie can be seen to have grown strongly in influence in relation to the coffee interests, but, similarly, the state bureaucracy also emerged more powerfully, so that it is difficult to argue that any one group established by the end of Kubitschek's term, or even by 1964, a distinctive or commanding hegemony, a feature of Brazilian politics which was to prove important in the eventual take-over by the leaders of the armed forces and their civilian supporters.

One group, however, which drew increasing attention in this changing pattern of class and group interest was the foreign bankers and financiers whose involvement in Brazilian industry and society had increased so markedly in recent years. In particular, the IMF became both a target for nationalist criticism and, arguably, a scapegoat for charges which more readily might have been laid elsewhere, especially since some of those nationalist critics, vehement in their condemnation of the IMF, were conspicuously silent over the more general penetration of foreign capital and the emerging monopolistic pattern of control.[42]

One frequent criticism of the IMF in its dealings with the Kubitschek government is that it was seeking to apply to Brazil, a country fully committed to rapid industrial expansion, criteria of financial orthodoxy derived from, and only fully applicable to, more developed economies. Apart, however, from the economic issues involved, probably the most important factor on all sides was political. The IMF had an overall policy on the need for stabilization, as it showed in its dealings with Argentina and Chile, while already there was growing apprehension in United States government and business circles over the strength of a more radical nationalist critique, especially as associated with the Brazilian Communist Party. In Brazil it was not, however, just the PCB which voiced increasing disquiet over the allegedly constricting, unsympathetic role of the IMF and the evident dependence of Brazilian policy-makers on the continuing goodwill and support of foreign bankers. Such criticism ranged across the political spectrum, making the question of foreign involvement in, and control of, Brazil's economy the most fiercely debated issue in national politics.

This rising tide of criticism came, in many respects, as a welcome relief to Kubitschek, distracting attention from a more fundamental critique of his policies, such as their depressing effect on wages and the failure to direct resources towards the less privileged members of Brazilian society. Nationalist resentment, however well-founded in some of its charges, obscured and confused more radical and far-reaching debate, including an analysis of how inflation was used by Kubitschek as a means of *political* control. It was, however, only by inflation that Kubitschek, like Goulart, was able to hold together his political support and maintain his politics of conciliation. The broad populist coalition on which he depended could only be preserved by concessions on all sides, to the organized working class, to the various fractions of the bourgeoisie, to the swelling ranks of public employees, and to the armed forces. As long as no one group achieved a monopoly of state power, Kubitschek and his successors had to maintain support not by genuine, but by apparent, concessions and increases, namely, by feeding inflation.[43] A severely realistic stabilization policy was, therefore, *politically* as well as economically unacceptable, especially as his presidency drew to a close and the 1960 presidential election came nearer. Kubitschek already had his eye on re-election in five years' time: the nationalist clamour, therefore, merely served to reinforce the logic of electoral politics.

The controversy over foreign constraints on Brazil's development came to a head in June 1959, when Kubitschek dramatically broke off negotiations with the IMF, a move widely acclaimed throughout Brazil, not only on the left, but also by those representatives of the industrial bourgeoisie who most had benefited from recent expansion.[44] The defiance of the IMF also found much sympathy abroad, notably in Europe, where many shared Kubitschek's belief that Brazil had not been treated imaginatively or generously enough. As Kubitschek prepared to leave office, therefore, he regained much of his initial support on the left for his stand against the *entreguistas*, those who were willing to hand over Brazil to the foreigners, while he could also appear as an imaginative, forceful, and courageous politician who, in the interests of national development, had defied attempts to place illegitimate constraints on Brazil's rapid progress towards being a modern, industrialized nation. He also had the distinction of being the first elected civilian president since his *mineiro* predecessor, Artur Bernardes, in 1926 to hand over office peacefully to his successor at the end of a full term.[45] He was also to be the last until the *coup* of 1964, when military presidents were to take charge.

The Mounting Crisis: Quadros to Goulart: 1960–61

The break with the IMF, despite the excitement and noise it occasioned, was in retrospect more of a dramatic gesture than an act of lasting political significance, just as the popularity and support it won for Kubitschek were also to prove shallow and short-lived. The real test of political effectiveness was whether Kubitschek could successfully pass on executive power to a member of that party, the PSD, from which he had drawn most support, and in this respect he failed. In the long political history of Brazil the presidential election of 1960 was in fact conspicuous as the first in which the government of the day was unable to return its own candidate, a clear sign that, with an electorate of over 11½ million, the degree of political control over the electorate was now markedly less than in previous years.

The idiosyncratic, even bizarre, political style of Jânio Quadros, and the abrupt dramatic manner in which eventually he left office, should not be allowed to obscure his real political skills and the importance of his election to the presidency. His electoral success was complete and convincing: Quadros won 48·26 per cent of the total vote (5,636,623) as against 32·93 per cent (3,846,825) for Marshal Lott, the candidate for the PSD and PTB, who as Minister of War had guaranteed the constitutional succession for Kubitschek, and compared with 18·79 per cent (2,195,709) for the São Paulo political boss, Adhemar de Barros.[46] In part this victory reflected the rather dull, if earnest, character and electoral campaign of Marshal Lott, who, despite his prominence in recent years, was relatively unknown to the electors and completely lacking the verve of Jânio Quadros. Lott was not a politician and had no experience of popular elections: Quadros, on the other hand, had the reputation of always winning elections, no matter how much of an outsider he seemed to be.

Quadros still remains a fiercely controversial figure, a man whose motives and impulses seem to have been obscure and confused even to himself, who never seems to have disentangled the rhetoric and the reality of politics, the histrionic gesture from the effective political act. Even a highly laudatory, often fulsome, study of him, prepared for the election of 1960, notes, apparently in all seriousness, that Quadros seems to have been influenced by five historical figures, Jesus Christ, Shakespeare, Lincoln, Lenin, and Chaplin, then adds, somewhat dolefully, that it was, unfortunately, not always clear which of these models he was imitating at any given time.[47] Such remarks, however, should not be allowed to distract from Quadros's very significant success, not only in 1960, but earlier in his career. His election is indicative of certain elements in Brazil's electoral politics and, more significantly, of growing tensions between important social forces and the political parties and political institutions more generally, evidence of a greater intensification of what already has been described as a 'crisis of hegemony'.

The immediate significance of Quadros's success was that it was won against all the odds, with only limited support from an official party apparatus, largely, indeed, in defiance of the political machines, stemming mostly from Quadros's own reputation as an individualist, even a political eccentric, who, fired with a powerful, if unpredictable, reforming enthusiasm, cut across party lines to appeal directly to the people. In a political system in which parties only recently had been created, still lacking sharp definition, it was not too surprising to find in Quadros a man who sat lightly to party labels. His early association was with the small PDC (Christian Democratic Party). Born in Matto Grosso in 1917, the son of a doctor, he moved to São Paulo in 1930, was elected *vereador* (city councillor) in 1948 and state deputy in 1950. In March 1953 he won election as mayor of São Paulo, then, a year later, having parted company with the PDC, he was elected governor of the state, a great electoral achievement won against the formidable populist machine-politician Adhemar de Barros. In 1958 Quadros became federal deputy for Paraná, and in 1960 president of Brazil. Throughout this whole time his party affiliations varied, often rather sharply, as when in 1958 he was elected as PTB deputy for Paraná, with more votes than any other Paraná deputy, while at the same time he opposed the PTB in the election for governor of São Paulo, to succeed him in that office, giving his support to Carlos Alberto Carvalho Pinto, state secretary of finance, who was the joint candidate of several parties, including the PDC and, notably, the UDN.[48] (Carvalho Pinto was also the candidate of several small parties, the PTN, PR, PL, and PSB.)

This lack of any clear party label is less significant than Quadros's evident ability successfully to defy the massive, entrenched power of local patronage and the intricate ties of political clientage, as was shown, in particular, by his election as mayor of São Paulo in 1953 and, above all, as governor of the state in 1954. He had no personal wealth or powerful connections, yet his reiterated appeal to honesty and hard work, his insistence on the need for administrative reform and efficiency, and his direct, emotional, yet reasoned, appeal to the electorate was, very obviously, a combination which worked: Quadros could win elections.

At the same time, one should not exaggerate the image of Quadros as the individualist, eccentric politician winning votes on the strength of his personal appeal as against the big battalions of the major parties. In 1960 he was chosen, albeit after much hesitation, as the official candidate of the UDN, and, as such, represented important social and economic interests. Quadros largely owed his nomination to Carlos Lacerda, who shrewdly understood that here was a candidate with whom the UDN could win. Lacerda himself was essentially a political pragmatist, refusing to be tied to rigid party loyalties, anxious, above all, to find a candidate who could win and who might at the next election help Lacerda to reach the presidential office he coveted. In early 1959 Quadros was chosen as official candidate by several small parties; Lacerda then pressed his case with the

UDN and in November 1959 Quadros became the UDN candidate, as against the party's president, Juracy Magalhães.

Jânio's electoral symbol was a broom, with which he would, allegedly, sweep away political and administrative corruption: but it was also a sign of how he would brush aside all opposition. It has been suggested that from about 1930 onwards Brazil experienced what is sometimes called a 'crisis of hegemony', a situation in which no single socio-economic group could impose definitive control of national policy through the state apparatus. Before 1930 such control was much more clearly defined, resting with the coffee interests centred in São Paulo. Under the *Estado Novo* a relatively stronger hegemonic pattern was also apparent, as the industrializing bourgeoisie, again mainly centred in São Paulo, managed to win at least temporary command of the now more fully centralized and greatly strengthened state apparatus, backed by the leaders of the armed forces, and ably supported by Getúlio Vargas in a system where the new corporatist and nationalist ideology reinforced the demands of Brazil's industrial interests.

This industrial bourgeoisie was not simply a 'national' bourgeoisie in any clear or unambiguous sense. Right from the start it was closely tied, as had been the coffee oligarchy, to whom these new men were often linked by family and financial connection, to other groups operating from outside Brazil. But in the late 1930s and early 1940s the *local* bourgeoisie was on most counts stronger than it would be in subsequent years. From 1945 to 1960 foreign influence grew stronger and more pervasive in Brazilian society and the economy. The swelling nationalism, so evident under Kubitschek, was in large measure the result of a growing awareness of how far such foreign involvement had increased in the post-war years.

But, at the same time, as many political sociologists have stressed, Brazil's political institutions, especially the parties and Congress, failed to represent adequately some of the most powerful forces in the country's economy. The UDN, for example, however much it might express the demands of the large landowners and of financial and business interests, both Brazilian and foreign, could never guarantee control of that electoral system which UDN leaders had so loudly called for in 1945. The UDN, paradoxically, was always a minority party electorally, above all in elections for the presidency in a system where executive power was so important, hence the repeated, almost desperate, attempts of Lacerda and his associates to subvert the electoral process when it seemed to be going against them.

Taking a long view of the political development of a nation, it is possible to speak, as here, of a 'crisis of hegemony' lasting for years or even decades.[49] But by 1960 in Brazil it was also possible to discern a more immediate crisis. The concept of 'hegemony', however controversial and hotly debated in contemporary social theory, must always imply control, in one form or other, of the social process. It must, when applied to a particular society at a certain stage of development, refer to some mechanism or process of control. In post-war Brazil such processes were formally associated with the electoral system as expressed through party politics and the control of Congress. But by 1960 it was increasingly clear that some of the most powerful forces in Brazil's political economy were either not directly and adequately represented through the existing political institutions, or did not exercise sufficient weight as compared with an earlier period. There was, in consequence, a general tendency to short-circuit the formal system, to try to act directly on the levers of power, notably on the executive, and, in moments of crisis, even to try to change the rules of the game, to alter the whole structure of national politics. All schools of political analysis, whether mainly functionalist or primarily neo-Marxist, agree on this relative weakness of Brazil's political institutions, and the associated political crisis which was intensifying by the late 1950s and early 1960s, at the same time as inflation and its accompanying tensions were promoting even greater disquiet and uncertainty.[50] In terms of class interest, for example, the industrial working class, let alone the rural workers and the mass of the Brazilian poor, were very weakly represented in the political system: yet so, too, were powerful economic forces linked to industry and finance, especially the increasingly important international and foreign interests operating in Brazil. Their pressure on the system had to be expressed indirectly or informally, so further weakening, in important respects, the formal institutions of party and Congress.[51]

It is possible, and certainly misleading, to exaggerate the importance, in itself, of this relative lack of representation in the Brazilian system. The main crisis was not over *institutions*, but over *control* of those institutions and the political process more generally, the question of hegemony. But this issue, as already argued, involved control of Brazil's formal political institutions, which by 1960, and certainly with the resignation of Quadros in August 1961, was the acute problem of national politics.

Whatever the complexities of his character and the obscurity surrounding his resignation, it is clear that in 1960 Quadros was the great electoral hope of the more conservative forces in Brazil, and of all those who since at least the early 1940s had firmly opposed the Vargista tradition, first under Vargas himself, then in modified form with Kubitschek, and as currently represented in 1960 by João Goulart. Quadros had proven electoral abilities, having shown that he could appeal with success to a mass electorate. He also had an impressive administrative record in São Paulo, where he had presided over the industrial boom under Kubitschek and impressed the business and financial community by his confident, if idiosyncratic, handling of state government. The publication of his *bilhetinos*, notes of instruction to those working with him, helped to strengthen this image of a crisp, effective administrator, who could be expected to bring to national government the drive, reforming zeal, and a certain sense of humour, expressed in his earlier career, and to do for Brazil what already he had done for São Paulo.[52] While, however, his administrative record commended him to UDN leaders, the more important factor was his previous association with São Paulo industrialists and the economic policies favoured by them.

The more bizarre features of Quadros's administration, including some of his *bilhetinos*, have been deliberately reinforced by his political opponents to make him something of a comic figure, but such emphasis distracts attention, not only from his real abilities, but also from his distinctly coherent social, economic, and political programme. In all his policies, despite his almost exaggerated populist style and his successful appeal to the mass electorate, Quadros followed essentially anti-popular policies, firmly supporting financial and industrial interests, even in his highly controversial foreign policy. One early feature of his economic policy was a determined attempt to curb inflation. In part this was done by cutting the inflationary subsidies on such essential imports as wheat and petroleum, which, while it helped to reduce the government's budgetary deficit,[53] also put up the price of food and transport, including bus fares. The government simplified the multiple-exchange-rate system (SUMOC Instruction 204 (13 March 1961) and Instruction 208), so, in effect, devaluing the cruzeiro by 100 per cent.[54] This gave increased incentive to Brazilian exports, a feature of Quadros's policy which was also to be so evident in his new pattern of foreign relations. At the same time he introduced a credit and wage squeeze, all of which showed results in terms of renewed confidence on the part of foreign creditors, who announced substantial new credits as well as extension of earlier short-term agreements. In part this renewed support from abroad reflected growing unease over the security of the hemisphere following the success of the Cuban revolution. Kennedy had now launched the Alliance for Progress, in marked contrast to his predecessor's cool reception of Kubitschek's similar proposals, and there was a general conviction that everything possible should be done to help Quadros, the outstandingly successful candidate of the middle classes.

One further consistent feature of this image of Quadros as a man to back was, however, a distinctly tougher line taken by him against the Brazilian working class and, in particular, the trade unions. The Quadros government was mainly composed of UDN politicians and members of smaller political parties, being characterized in particular by the strong presence of anti-Vargas figures, such as the new Foreign Minister, the *mineiro* Afonso Arinos de Melo Franco, a leading member of the UDN. The Finance Minister, Clemente Mariani, was also from the UDN, as was the holder of the newly created Ministry of Mines and Energy.[55] The PSD and PTB, by contrast, were scarcely represented at all, despite Quadros's earlier election as a PTB deputy. The Ministry of Labour went to the PTB, but to a group within it which opposed João Goulart,[56] who had been elected as vice president of Brazil at the same time as Quadros. Among key military posts, which in the longer term were to prove more important than the civilian, the Ministry of the Army remained with General Odílio Denys, who, though he had sided with Lott in 1955, was very conservative, believing that his earlier action had prevented the success of officers more sympathetic to reformist politics. Denys was later fiercely to oppose the accession to presidential office of João Goulart, when he would also be supported by the ministers of the Navy and Air Force appointed by Quadros, Sílvio Heck and Gabriel Grün Moss. Both these officers had been strong opponents of Kubitschek, and quickly appointed equally conservative officers to key posts under their command, a pattern of appointments which was to be crucial in the next few years, when Denys, for example, became one of the leading initiators of the 1964 *coup*.

Throughout his electoral campaign Quadros had presented himself as a man of the people and a friend of the working class.[57] His early stabilization measures, however, while they benefited exporters and stimulated foreign confidence, fell heavily on wage-earners, faced with rising food and other costs, and now held back by a wage-freeze. In his previous dealings with strikers and the trade unions Quadros had generally been ready to express his support, often taking up an extreme stance on their behalf, as during the São Paulo strike of 1953, shortly after Quadros's election as mayor of São Paulo. Once in office as president, however, he was less able to indulge in such ready expressions of sympathy, and began to take up a much harder line in relation to wage-earners and the trade unions. One reason for this was the rapid growth not just in the number and intensity of strikes, but, more significantly, in first the number of strikes for *political* as distinct from narrowly economic reasons and secondly, the distinctive shift in strike action from the private to the *public* sector, a move which alarmed Quadros. Before 1960 there were relatively few strikes in the public sector. The important strikes of

1953 and 1957, for example, in São Paulo were mainly in the private sector of industry. After 1959, by contrast, 55 per cent of strikes recorded were in the public sector, with workers in that sector taking the lead, in particular, in essentially political strike action.[58]

The reasons for this change are still not entirely clear, but in large measure they seem to have been linked to a change in policy on the part of the PCB, which was now so dominant within the trade union movement, especially in the public sector. The change also accompanied the dissolution in 1959 of the PUI (Pacto de Unidade Intersindical) and the formation of the Frente de Unidade Intersindical de Ferroviários, Marítimos e Portuários, the first name of what was to become the PUA (Pacto de Unidade e Ação). This change, already mentioned above, mainly represented a swing towards workers in the public sector, since the PUI had mostly contained those from the private sector, in contrast to the PUA, which now drew completely on public-sector workers, such as merchant seamen, dockers, and railway workers, who, again, formed the base of the CGT (Comando Geral dos Trabalhadores), founded in 1962.[59] It was the public-sector workers who now won much the biggest increases. (The employees of Companhias Loide e Costeira, for example, seem to have earned in 1961 an average wage per month five times that of the average industrial wage in Guanabara. The railwaymen, too, had higher wages. Most railways were now state-owned, so that, for example, the Rede Ferroviária Federal alone employed in 1958 153,000 workers and administrators, almost all as public servants.) This partly again reflected their greater cohesion and organization than workers in the private sector, especially in the more traditional industries producing consumer goods, who, within the private sector, were losing ground to employees of large foreign-based companies, which frequently gave higher wages to anticipate and prevent industrial action.[60] The public-sector workers, were, however, not merely better organized, and perhaps more politicized, but also determined within an inflationary economy to hold onto their stronger position. Like most trade unionists, their primary concern was economic rather than political, and by the early 1960s they were exerting all the pressure available to them.

Quadros regarded with dismay this rapid upsurge of political action within the public sector, in large part because of its evident links with the PCB, a party he always opposed. One of the most far-reaching reforms he envisaged was, therefore, to curb the power of the unions, largely through the abolition of the *impôsto sindical*, or trade union tax, which would be replaced by voluntary contributions.[61] This seemed at one level to aim at liberalizing the trade union movement by weakening its corporatist links with the state, but, since at the factory or work-place level there was generally no union representative (*delegado sindical*), it would, in practice, have greatly weakened union finances if members had to 'contract-in'. One interpretation of this proposal is that Quadros was consistently aiming to block the further expansion of trade union activity within the public sector, in order to prevent the unions from acting as part of the state apparatus by themselves taking over even greater state power, not now being used and manipulated, as in the past, by the corporatist state machinery, but inverting that process and using state power in the interests of the unions.[62] In this respect Quadros differed sharply from his successor, Goulart, who supported, and sought to use, union activity in the public sector, seeing it not as a challenge to his overall social policies, as had Quadros, but rather as a useful political tool. Quadros's attitude, however, directly reflected that of many on the right, both civilian and military, who increasingly feared a *república sindicalista* (the phrase was used, it will be remembered, by Góes Monteiro in his memoirs, when discussing Vargas in 1945 and the way in which Goulart allegedly later followed similar policies to bring about a 'trade union state' or *república sindicalista*) in which the organized working class, through a trade union system tightly enmeshed in the state apparatus, would win a substantial share of state power, first, to win economic advantages, then a step towards more far-reaching political and social reconstruction. Quadros's concern, therefore, over enlarged union activity, especially the political strikes in the public sector, was again an expression of his alignment with those political groups, both civilian and military, whose 'outcry against the threat of the development of a *república sindicalista* . . . was nothing else than a reaction against increasing popular mobilization both inside and outside the trade union movement'.[63]

Quadros's policies and attitude towards the labour movement were, in part, an indication of his overall support for the more modern sector of Brazilian industry, and of his association with the industrial interests of São Paulo. So, too, paradoxically, was his new line in foreign policy, an area in which he drew fierce criticism from many conservative politicians for what they regard as arbitrary and dangerously irresponsible behaviour. A 'radical' foreign policy of non-alignment was not, however, merely a flamboyant act of defiance, even though the granting of Brazil's highest honour to Ché Guevara in August 1961 was, in the circumstances, both flamboyant and defiant. Quadros's foreign policy is better understood as serving two distinct but related functions, both consistent with his domestic politics.

The refusal to be tied exclusively to the 'Western' bloc, meaning, in practice, to follow closely the lead of the United States, served in the first place to pacify those nationalist groups who had so loudly applauded Kubitschek's break with the IMF and were still loud in their criticism of Brazil's dependence. Much of the so-called 'radical nationalism' was essentially anti-Yankee, often with little radical content in terms of domestic politics. Quadros was, therefore, able to maintain support among nationalists, and on the left more generally, by his refusal to follow the United States in its policies for Latin America, especially Cuba, and towards countries of the socialist bloc, even while at home he was developing strategies which the left should have criticized vigorously. In this respect the foreign policy of non-alignment provided an ideological front for Quadros similar to that which his association with the ISEB and his ultimate break with the IMF had provided for Kubitschek.

But the presentation of Brazil as an ally and potential leader of the 'Third World' was more than just a clever political tactic. The appeal to the 'uncommitted nations', especially in Africa and Asia, but also to the socialist countries, was part of Quadros's concern for Brazil's rapidly expanding industrial economy. It reflected his awareness that the modern industrialized Brazil he envisaged would need new markets for its exports, in a world of fierce trading competition in which flexibility, flair, and pragmatism would be more important than ideological rigidity and a narrow commitment to the 'Western bloc' as defined in Washington. Many Brazilian industrialists, businessmen, diplomatists, and even some leaders of the UDN, supported Quadros in his foreign policy, aware of the many advantages of non-alignment abroad combined with solidly conservative policies at home. There were also many critics, especially over the decision to re-establish diplomatic relations with the Soviet Union, but it is interesting, in this respect, to note how far Quadros's policies foreshadowed, in many essential features, those followed by the military regime after 1964. Then, while totally committed to capitalist development in close alliance with the United States, the commercial, especially the exporting, policies of Brazil were again to recognize no ideological frontiers. The more dramatic, tendentious gestures of the Quadros period were not repeated, since in any case there was no similar body of strongly vocal nationalist opinion to satisfy, but the flexibility and pragmatism of commercial policy were to be remarkably similar in an economy vitally dependent on industrial, and other, exports.

The greatest weakness of Jânio Quadros was that feature of his politics which had been his greatest electoral strength, the fact that he sought to be independent of party labels and party organization. His earlier electoral successes had been won against the entrenched political machines, by appealing in a populist manner directly to the electorate. Such an appeal was possible in the heightened atmosphere of an election, but it was scarcely a basis for carrying through policies which required sufficient support in Congress, both in the Chamber and in the Senate. It was also in this sense that Jânio found, in contrast to Getúlio Vargas and to Kubitschek, that the techniques and tactics which had made him such a successful city, and even a state, politician were inadequate, or even a positive hindrance, at the level of federal government and national politics. The point has been made earlier, but bears repeating, especially since Quadros not only failed to master sufficient Congressional support, but actually alienated opinion in Congress, producing uncertainty, resentment, and hostility among members of all parties during his few months in office.

Jânio Quadros's main party support had to come from the UDN, the party which had adopted him in 1960; but the UDN was seriously split on many issues, including that of support for Quadros. By the middle of 1961 the president still had substantial UDN backing, but there was mounting criticism, including from such influential quarters as the *Estado de São Paulo*, over the approaches to the Soviet Union and the more 'leftist' features of Quadros's political style. On the other side of the political spectrum, the PTB and the Communists now expressed sympathy for Quadros's behaviour over foreign policy, but were increasingly uneasy and critical of the direction of his domestic policies, especially as tension grew between the president and Goulart, and '. . . it became apparent that Quadros intended to discredit Goulart as the PTB leader and isolate him in the vice presidency by keeping him busy with the duties of office'.[64] A struggle was emerging for control of the PTB between those who supported Quadros, such as the Minister of Labour, Castro Neves, and union leaders, such as Dante Pelacani,[65] and those who backed Goulart, who by now was thinking of forming an anti-Quadros coalition, an 'alliance of popular forces', to include elements of the PTB, the PSD, and the PSP.[66] The PSD was similarly caught in a tension between those who supported Quadros and others who distrusted him, while the whole party was confused and disorientated at finding itself out of office, unaccustomed to the role of opposition and even unsure whether it should press opposition against so popular a president. Some PSD leaders, such as Benedicto Valladares, who had previously given important backing to Kubitschek, now supported Quadros, thinking of a working alliance with the UDN, but others in the PSD rejected any such move to the right, which was also viewed with suspicion by many in the UDN.

In all this political uncertainty, during which time Quadros could possibly have redrawn the lines of party politics, the president showed instead a persistent neglect, even contempt, of Congress and parties, apparently believing that his own election in 1960 superseded that of deputies elected in 1958.[67] Members of Congress found that access to the president was difficult, and there was a growing belief that Quadros wanted to short-circuit Congress, if possible by direct appeal to the people to carry through his programme.[68]

> He [Quadros] did not trust parties and had no intention of working with them to broaden the government's influence in the Congress. His plan was to demoralize all the parties, divide them, and blame the Congress for the difficulties of his administration—in short to make a popular scapegoat out of the Congress. He almost succeeded.

Such strained relations further heightened the tensions already present in the Brazilian system between the executive, usually a president elected on a 'populist' vote, and a legislature which normally was more conservative and certainly in less of a hurry than Quadros in 1961.

Another associated source of friction concerned Quadros's method of government, largely a continuation of his technique in São Paulo, including the use of his *bilhetinos*. Sometimes his virtual edicts were as improbable as they were startling, as when he banned the use of bikinis in beauty contests, a proclamation, one would imagine, almost deliberately designed to provoke amazement and indignation in a society in which the bikini was so regularly seen to the greatest possible advantage. But this and similar edicts merely reinforced the image of Quadros as an arbitrary, quirky, and rather dangerous eccentric, whose disregard of due procedure was often imaginative, sometimes amusing, but always slightly alarming. His critics found it easy to reinforce the growing perception of the president as a slightly unbalanced, if able, administrator, unwilling to accept the limits on executive power laid down in the constitution and sanctioned by political practice. Some of the indignation was relatively trivial, as in the case of civil servants made to work regular hours and deprived of their accustomed pluralism, whereby some had two or even three jobs to stave off the effects of inflation. Other fears ran deeper, as of those who saw the president aiming at greatly enlarged power for the federal executive, accountable only to himself. Quadros by mid-1961 was in an exposed political position, rapidly alienating support on all sides, just when he most needed a sound institutional base in party and in Congress.

In August 1961 the crisis came to a head with the decoration in

Brasília of Ché Guevara. Such an award was flamboyant, apparently hasty and ill-considered, but, more importantly, it was intensely provocative to right-wing opinion, above all in the armed forces, whose continued support Quadros, like every Brazilian politician, so urgently needed to maintain. As a populist gesture, and an assertion of political independence, it was effective: but this, for Quadros, was not the time for populist defiance of those very groups on the right whose interests, in practice, he had defended, and whose backing he still must have.

Even at this point there was no reason to suppose that Quadros could not easily weather the storm. Unlike the case of Vargas in 1945 or 1954, no major political group, still less a powerful civil–military coalition, was baying for his blood and demanding he should go. There was alarm and some despondency among politicians of all those groups who had backed Quadros only a few months earlier; but there was no powerful, irrepressible movement to get rid of Jânio. Rather the contrary, since no one wished to precipitate a political crisis. And Quadros, more than anyone, knew this. He believed he was indispensable and that he could cast down the gauntlet to all his critics, threatening to pull down the structure, by resigning, so that he would immediately be recalled with the wider powers he wanted, having shaken off his critics in his appeal to the people, or, rather, to the leaders of the armed forces.

The details of Quadros's quarrel with Lacerda are not in themselves important.[69] The main point is that neither this quarrel, the decoration of Guevara, nor the subsequent attacks by Lacerda, in any sense required Quadros to resign. His aim, however, seems to have been to precipitate a crisis by forcing the politicians and, in particular, the leaders of the armed forces, to choose between accepting Goulart, whom they so deeply mistrusted, or recalling himself with the full powers he wanted. In effect, what he was seeking was a *coup d'état* in his favour.

It was scarcely coincidence that Quadros decided to resign on 24 August 1961, the anniversary of Vargas's suicide in 1954, even though he only announced his resignation the following day. The resignation of Quadros compared to the death of Vargas was in a sense a measure of the difference in stature of the two men. Quadros wanted the drama and the popular reaction attendant on Vargas's tragic act, but not its irrevocable finality. His letter of resignation was evocative of Vargas's death note:

> I have been beaten by reaction, and, so, I leave the government. In these seven months I have done my duty. I have done it day and night, working tirelessly . . . I wanted a Brazil for the Brazi-

> lians, opposing, in this dream, the corruption, lies, and cowardice which subordinated the general interest to the appetites and ambitions both of groups and individuals, including those outside Brazil. I feel myself crushed. Terrible forces have been brought to bear against me . . .[70]

Behind this rhetoric lay a clear awareness that he was provoking a political crisis, posing a serious dilemma for Congress and, above all, the military leaders of Brazil. His hope seems to have been that, faced with such an institutional crisis, the military would either recall him, or someone else, within a modified institutional framework giving greatly increased power to the president.[71] Again, in this respect, he foreshadowed the solution adopted after 1964, when a much-strengthened executive would be able to impose policies untrammelled by the deliberations of Congress.

There seems little doubt that Quadros believed he would be recalled, if not immediately, at least within a year or so.[72] In retrospect it was not an unreasonable gamble. Despite his populist language and the rhetoric of his resignation letter, his hopes were not pinned on a mass reaction in the streets; he was not appealing directly to the people, believing, as it were, his own political rhetoric. His aim, much more precise and realistic, was at the real arbiters, as he knew, of Brazilian politics, the leaders of the armed forces. His subsequent failure was not primarily that the political parties failed to back him, or that there was no mass turnout demanding his return, but rather that by August 1961 he had lost the confidence of too many senior military officers. As in 1955, when Lott guaranteed the accession of Kubitschek, the officer corps had doubts over its duty, on the one hand, to preserve constitutional form, and turn to Goulart, or to abandon the constitution, and impose another solution. Eventually, to avoid a serious institutional crisis, the military leaders sought a compromise solution, which, in their terms, failed. But Quadros was allowed to go, having appeared to many senior officers as too wayward, unpredictable, and histrionic and, above all, not really sound on matters of national security, especially in his attitude to the Soviet Union, the socialist bloc, and even, in the case of Cuba, to a perceived political threat within Latin America itself. Quadros's appeal in his resignation, though ostensibly to 'populism' and the left, was in fact to conservatism and the right. In this it was all of a piece with his earlier populist style and his essentially conservative politics. Unfortunately for him, by August 1961 this formula was no longer effective.

Notes

1 For a glimpse of the ferocity and rancour of *mineiro* politics in previous decades see the section on the *caso mineiro* in Flynn, 'The Revolutionary Legion . . .', together with the other references provided there.
2 See above (pp. 67–8) on the Minas Gerais political crisis of 1933.
3 See above (pp. 67–8) for references on this. For Valladares's later career see *Tempos idos e vividos*.
4 See *Programa de Metas* (Rio de Janeiro, 1958).
5 See above, pp. 194–5.
6 There is a fairly detailed account of the whole affair in Carneiro, *História das Revoluções Brasileiras*, 2 vols. (Rio de Janeiro, 1965), II, 504–17 and a short description, and a helpful map, in Dulles, *Unrest in Brazil*, 65–73.
7 ibid., 79–81.
8 Carneiro, op. cit., II, 519–31.
9 ibid., 521.
10 It is now being linked by the projected road BR–070 from Brasília to Cuiabá, but in 1959, 300 miles west of Brasília, it was only within easy reach of the rest of Brazil by air.
11 In particular see on import substitution industrialization in the 1950s: W. Baer, *Industrialization and Economic Development in Brazil* (Homewood, 1965); J. Bergsman, *Brazil's Industrialization and Trade Policies* (New York, 1970); J. Bergsman and A. Candal, 'Industrialization: Past Success and Future Problems' in H. S. Ellis (ed.), *The Economy of Brazil* (Berkeley and Los Angeles, 1969); and Kahil, op. cit., 289–323.
12 Kahil, op. cit., 289; and the table on 'Brazil: Real Growth Rates by Sectors of the Economy' in W. Baer and I. Kerstenetzky, 'The Brazilian Economy' in R. Roett (ed.), *Brazil in the Sixties* (Nashville, 1972), 107.
13 Kahil, op. cit., 290.
14 ibid., 299. In March 1957 the series of data on which this calculation was based was discontinued. See, however, the tables on real wages of selected categories of workers, 1940–62; ibid., 67, 72, 73. These show, for example, that, taking an index for 1953, a mason in São Paulo dropped from 79 in 1940 to 71 in 1962, a carpenter from 74 to 65, and a mechanic from 146 to 80. Most of this decline was between 1950 and 1962, the levels for these categories in 1950 being 161, 137, and 137. An unskilled worker, by comparison, moved from 80 in 1940 to 134 in 1962.
15 The figures for minimum wages are to be found in Francisco de Oliveira, op. cit. Both this table and that for price increases can be found in André Fernandes, 'Le passage à un nouveau mode d'accumulation au Brésil: les racines de la crise de 1964', in *Critiques de l'Economie Politique*, 16–17 (Avril–Septembre 1974), 144–5. The whole issue on *Amérique Latine. Accumulation et Surexploitation* is much to be commended as a piece of thoughtful, well-informed analysis.
16 Kahil, op. cit., 213, Table V.9 'Movement of Foreign Capital and its Earnings, 1947–63'. Even his conservative estimate shows for the Kubitschek years a total balance rising from US$31 million in 1955 to 115 million in 1956, 165 in 1957, 199 in 1958, and 306 in 1959.
17 ibid., 332.
18 ibid., 303.
19 ibid., 333.
20 See below, pp. 242–50.

21 This point is well made in F. Weffort, *Partidos, Sindicatos e Democracia*, 60–1.

22 See *Consolidação das Leis do Trabalho*, Article 592, as quoted in K. P. Erickson, 'Corporatism and Labour in Development' in H. J. Rosenbaum and W. G. Tyler (eds.), *Contemporary Brazil: Issues in Economic and Political Development* (New York, 1972), 143.

23 See on this the very suggestive comments in José Albertino Rodrigues, *Sindicato e Desenvolvimento no Brasil* (São Paulo, 1968), 151–4.

24 ibid., 152–3.

25 Erickson, op. cit., 151.

26 Albertino Rodrigues, op. cit., 132.

27 Kahil, op. cit., 300.

28 Jover Telles, *O movimento sindical no Brasil* (Vitória, 1962). See especially 78–122.

29 op. cit., 89.

30 Albertino Rodrigues, op. cit., 163. On all this activity see Telles, op. cit., 78–122.

31 For an account in English of the role of the Communist Party within Brazil, including the trade union movement, see Chilcote, op. cit. He notes the PCB control of the PUA, which mostly represented dockers and railway workers (153). Also see the comments in J. W. F. Dulles, 'The Brazilian Left: Efforts at Recovery, 1964–70', in D. L. Herman (ed.), *The Communist Tide in Latin America* (Austin, 1973), especially 144–5 on the 'horizontal' unions. The best account, however, is still probably that of Jover Telles.

32 This seems a more satisfactory understanding of the relation between the government and these new union organizations than that suggested by, for example, Chilcote, op. cit., 153: 'The apparent success of Communists in penetrating the labour movement in the late fifties and early sixties was due in large measure to the government's temporary loss of control over union activities'. The penetration was real rather than apparent and the loss of control, as a direct result of Communist and other left-wing groups' success, was probably permanent, unless the system were to be changed through violent repression, as happened after 1964. The point is important, since essentially it turns on whether one sees popular politics increasing its challenge before 1964, growing stronger, or merely leading to sterile confrontation.

33 Kahil, op. cit., 303.

34 ibid., 311.

35 ibid., 312.

36 A crucial turning-point, it has been suggested, for the development of labour power before 1964 was the passing by Congress of the social security law of 1960. See below, pp. 242–4, and Erickson, op. cit., 150–1.

37 See below, pp. 246–7.

38 A useful source for understanding the shaping of nationalist ideology in the ISEB is *Cadernos do Povo Brasileiro*, a series of pamphlets reflecting the more radical phase of nationalist thinking.

39 On coffee policy in this period see Kahil, op. cit., 311–12. The dollar price of coffee had remained steady in 1955–57, but fell by about 10 per cent in 1958 and another 20 per cent in 1959. The coffee exchange rate had been overvalued, but the government now doubled the amount of *cruzeiros* the coffee sector was to receive per dollar.

40 In particular, one should notice during these years the increasingly important role in decision-making of the so-called 'Executive Groups', a major development under Kubitschek.

41 Kahil, op. cit., 213.

42 It may be noted in passing that this seems to have been a general feature of ECLA critics, not just in Brazil. Their main theme seems to have been for a greater Latin American share in decision-making rather than a radical scrutiny of the role of foreign capital.

43 See on this the interesting comments of Paulo Singer, *O Milagre Brasileiro*, Caderno CEBRAP (São Paulo, 1972), 49.

Speaking of the Kubitschek period he notes: 'the only viable solution which reconciled the needs of accelerated accumulation with the demands of the electorate, at least in appearance, was inflation'. See, too, on this the very thoughtful analysis in Regis de Castro Andrade, 'Movimento Trabalhista e Sindicatos sob o Nacional-Populismo no Brasil', mimeo–CEBRAP (June 1974), especially 7–10.

44 Skidmore, op. cit., 386 quotes the personal expression of support sent to Kubitschek on 30 June 1959 by Oscar Augusto de Camargo, president of the Federation of Industries of the State of São Paulo. Many Brazilian industrialists were as loud in their support of the defiance of the IMF as were the spokesmen for the Brazilian left.

45 President Dutra was technically a civilian, but not a civilian politician in the usual sense of the term.

46 Schneider *et al*, *Brazil Election Factbook* (Washington, 1965), 56.

47 Viriato de Castro, *O Fenômeno Jânio Quadros*, 3rd ed. (São Paulo, 1959). The cover also presents a sharp contrast between Jânio in his different roles, showing him, on the one hand, smooth, well-groomed, if slightly fierce, a man to move in business and government circles, and, on the other hand, as *vereador* (councillor) in 1948, looking, wild, haggard, and unshaven, the ascetic, tireless man of the people. Despite its partisan character, the book contains useful information on Quadros's earlier career.

48 Dulles, *Unrest in Brazil*, 104. Also Viriato de Castro, op. cit., 216–23. Carvalho Pinto was also the candidate of several small parties, the PTN, PR, PL, and PSB. See, too, Quadros's speech as he handed over to Carvalho Pinto, 31 January 1959. Viriato de Castro, op. cit., 224–6.

49 See especially the discussion in Antonio Gramsci, *Selections from the Prison Notebooks*, ed. Q. Hoare and G. Nowell Smith (London, 1971), 55–61, 180–5. Also, for example, Juan Carlos Portantiero, 'Clases dominantes y crisis política en la Argentina actual', in *Pasado y Presente* (abril/junio 1973), 31–64, especially 33–40.

50 The broadly functionalist school of analysis which discusses this problem is represented, for example, by S. P. Huntington, *Political Order in Changing Societies* (New Haven, 1968); R. M. Schneider, *The Political System of Brazil* (New York, 1971); P. C. Schmitter, *Interest, Conflict and Political Change in Brazil* (Stanford, 1971). For a more detailed discussion of this question see: P. Flynn, 'Class, Clientelism and Coercion: some mechanisms of social control', *Journal of Commonwealth and Comparative Politics*, XII, No. 2 (July 1974); and 'Brazil: Authoritarianism and Class Control', *Journal of Latin American Studies*, Vol. VI, Part 2, 315–33.

51 See, too, on this process the reflections in H. Jaguaribe, *Economic and Political Development. A Theoretical Approach and a Brazilian Case Study* (Cambridge, Mass., 1968). Also N. H. Leff, *Economic Policy-Making in Brazil, 1947–1964* (New York, 1968), especially on the way industrialists exerted pressure on the system.

52 Some examples of these *bilhetinos* can be found in Viriato de Castro, op. cit., 227–32. One note, for example, to Carvalho Pinto, expressing concern over a proposed financial transaction, read:

'Professor:
! ! !
$ $ $
? !
(a) J. Quadros
Another was to appoint as a palace messenger a youngster, who had found 20,000 *cruzeiros* in the Praça da Sé and returned it to the police. The *bilhetino* to the head of the Civil Household ran: 'Whoever, in this day and age, returns money which doesn't belong to him, ought to have government protection'.

53 By the start of the 1960s, Brazil's foreign debt was already more than $2 billion. See Baer and Kerstenetzky, op. cit., 104–45. Skidmore, op. cit., 194 says the retail price of bread was doubled.

54 SUMOC Instruction 204, 13 March 1961, and Instruction 208. See Kahil, op. cit., 316: 'An important reform of the exchange system was introduced on 13 March by SUMOC Directive 204. The exaggeratedly low exchange rates applicable to the imports of wheat, petroleum, newsprint, and equipment were raised from 100 to 200 cruzeiros per dollar; foreign exchange auctions were abolished and most imports transferred to the free market, where exporters were authorised to negotiate a greater proportion of export proceeds; and importers were required to deposit with Banco do Brasil the full value of imports transacted. As is obvious, Directive 204 was bound to induce a sharp rise in the prices of the previously favoured imports'.

55 Dulles, *Unrest in Brazil*, 113.

56 ibid.

57 See on the campaign as a whole V. Reisky de Dubnic, *Political Trends in Brazil* (Washington DC, 1968), 102–24, and on Quadros's reiterated support for labour and social reform, 110–11. Reisky de Dubnic stresses very well Quadros's attempt to appeal over and beyond the political parties, but seems very wide of the mark in arguing that (106) 'An analysis of Quadros' behaviour as President reveals that he was influenced neither by the left nor the right'. In these terms both his appointments and his policies put Quadros unambiguously on the right.

58 See on this the important material in Castro Andrade, op. cit., 10–14.

59 ibid., 10–11; Weffort, *Partidos, Sindicatos e Democracia*, 74.

60 See wages data (stevedores, seamen, railway workers) in Castro Andrade, op. cit., 11.

61 See his *Mensagem ao Congresso Nacional* (Brasília, 1961).

62 Castro Andrade, op. cit.; and Weffort, op. cit., passim.

63 Weffort, op. cit., 77.

64 Reisky de Dubnic, op. cit., 54.

65 ibid., 55.

66 ibid., 55–6 quoting *Jornal do Brasil* (1 June 1961).

67 Dulles, *Unrest in Brazil*, 116.

68 Reisky de Dubnic, op. cit., 47.

69 The details of the quarrel and the circumstances surrounding Lacerda's visit to Quadros in Brasília on 18–19 August are given in Dulles, *Unrest in Brazil*, 127–33. In essence, the row was over the fact that Lacerda felt slighted during his visit to Quadros.

70 See the text in Jânio Quadros and Afonso Arinos de Melo Franco, 'O Porquê da Renúncia', *Realidade*, Ano II, Numero 20 (Novembro 1967), 31–2. This issue of *Realidade* presents an interesting, if partial, account of the resignation, written by Quadros six years afterwards.

71 ibid., 34.

72 Carlos Castello Branco, press secretary to Quadros as president (and no relation to the military president 1964–67), tells how, on the day after his resignation, Quadros rejected the idea of strikes in his support in Rio de Janeiro, the state of Rio de Janeiro, and Santos, and said he believed he would be recalled by popular demand: 'Brazil at present needs three things —authority, the capacity for work, and courage and speed in decisions. Apart from myself there is no one, absolutely no one, who has these three necessary qualities . . .', ibid., 40.

1961–64

8 From Crisis to *Coup*: João Goulart

The Succession Crisis: August–September 1961

The abrupt resignation of Quadros brought exactly the political crisis he had expected, but not the result he had wished. His aim was to produce a response similar to that which eventually occurred in 1964, namely a swift intervention by the armed forces, but resulting, on this occasion, in his own recall as president with much more extensive executive powers, in a system whose stability and maintenance would be guaranteed by the army. His plan backfired, not only because of the considerable mistrust of Quadros among important military leaders, but, ironically, because their concern over the possible accession of Goulart was so great as to concentrate attention on him rather than on Quadros. The ex-president, to his evident surprise, was allowed to withdraw quickly and quietly, eventually sailing to Europe with his family, after the president of the Chamber of Deputies, Ranieri Mazzilli, was accepted as acting president in the absence abroad of Vice-President Goulart.

The immediate crisis, though less dramatic and emotional than that produced in 1954 by the suicide of Vargas, was in many respects more serious. The middle classes had voted overwhelmingly for Quadros, and now, only a few months later, faced the choice of either military involvement and a break with the constitution, or the acceptance as president of João Goulart, a vice president diametrically opposed to all they had sought when voting for Quadros. The vice president was deeply suspect to many of the UDN and their military supporters, because of his association with Vargas, his close contacts with the labour movement, and his alleged commitment to far-reaching policies of social change. The sudden resignation of Quadros had reopened the whole question of political power within the liberal democratic system, once more underlining the fragile control exercised within that system by the social groups who most supported the UDN, a party which now again saw itself deprived of executive power and threatened by those social forces it believed lay behind Goulart and his wing of the PTB.

Some UDN leaders insisted that due constitutional process should be observed and Goulart should take office: others were horrified that a sudden political mischance should again give power to those Vargista opponents they had sought to defeat, both by electoral and other means, for the last three decades.[1] There was among many of the UDN, and the right more generally, a growing conviction, similar to that expressed by many in Chile after Allende's victory in 1970, that if João Goulart could come to power through due constitutional process, there must be something sadly wrong with the constitutional process. But the party was split and indecisive on the constitutional issue, with many of its members, though unhappy about Goulart, refusing to accept a military intervention to set aside the constitution.

In the days immediately after the *coup* the military ministers of Quadros, General Odílio Denys, Brigadier Grün Moss, and Admiral Sílvio Heck, made clear their personal opposition to accepting Goulart, a view which had much support among military officers, and which was echoed by the two most prominent conservative newspapers, the *Estado de São Paulo*, owned by Vargas's irreconcilable opponent Júlio de Mesquita Filho, and the *Tribuna da Imprensa*, the paper of Carlos Lacerda. But the armed forces were also sharply split on the question of maintaining or breaking with the constitution, with the foremost spokesman for legality again being Marshal Lott, who now was imprisoned, together with other legalist officers.

As the debate intensified, in the last days of August and the beginning of September 1961, it became clear that the country was severely and seriously divided, with part of the UDN supporting the military ministers, while others, especially in Congress, agreed with Marshal Lott, and others, again, especially the PTB and the mass of trade unionists, as well as such groups as the National Union of Students, positively welcomed the idea of Goulart as president.[2] Above all, the Goulart succession was strongly urged in his own state of Rio Grande do Sul by the state governor, who was also Goulart's brother-in-law, Leonel de Moura Brizola.

Over the weekend of 26 to 27 August excitement and rumour increased, as Marshal Lott was taken to the fort of Lage and several São Paulo newspapers published a statement by Lott. This explained how he had appealed by telephone to General Denys to honour the constitutional provision, allowing Goulart to take office; he now called on 'all the vital forces in the country to demand respect for the constitution and the full preservation of Brazil's democratic regime'.[3] Lott's appeal, and the fact of his arrest, brought an immediate response from Congress, with a message of solidarity from the Chamber of Deputies, placing special emphasis on the fact that the military ministers, Denys, Moss, and Heck, did not represent the democratic traditions of the armed forces.[4] UDN deputies joined in the protest against the attempt by the military ministers to impose their views on Brazil,[5] and, when acting president Mazzilli reported to Congress that the military ministers had urged that the return of Goulart would be 'absolutely wrong, on grounds of national security',[6] Congress appointed a committee of six senators and six deputies to examine the question. On 29 August the committee refused to accept the immediate exclusion of Goulart, proposing instead the idea of a constitutional modification which would limit the powers of the president under a 'parliamentary' system, a change which already had been under discussion for some years.[7]

The Congressional resistance to the military ministers' demand to exclude Goulart was accompanied by alarming reports that Leonel Brizola was preparing Rio Grande do Sul for armed resistance in support of 'legalist' officers. Some of these reports were soon found to be exaggerated, but it was perfectly evident that both the civilian politicians and the armed forces were still seriously divided and that there was not sufficient support for what would be, in effect, a *coup* to exclude João Goulart. Once such soundings had been taken, a compromise solution had to be found. The excitement continued for several more days, with a fevered exchange of telegrams and telephone calls as Goulart travelled, without undue haste, via Hong Kong and Paris towards Brazil, issuing reassurances concerning his commitment to democracy, and receiving contradictory, confusing advice from friends and supporters. There was much talk of resistance, even civil war, as the commander of the Third Army,[8] in Rio Grande do Sul, General Machado Lopes, made clear his support for Goulart's succession, while the military ministers issued a further statement, explaining more fully their opposition to Goulart. General Machado Lopes was ordered to be replaced by General Cordeiro de Farias, the Chief of General Staff under Quadros, who, after being a prominent *tenente* in the 1920s, had been involved in removing Vargas in 1945, had founded the Escola Superior de Guerra in 1949, and became one of the most able officers associated with the so-called 'Sorbonne Group'. He had also served as *interventor* in Rio Grande do Sul from 1938 to 1943, so was familiar with the state and its politicians. He was now told, however, by General Machado Lopes, that he would be arrested if he arrived in Pôrto Alegre, which was rapidly being put on a war footing in order to reject the solution of the military ministers.

There was mounting evidence that other military units, air force as well as army, were prepared to defend the 'constitutionalist' position, especially those stationed in the south. This lack of military solidarity, combined with the increasing criticism of civilian politicians, showed clearly that the military ministers had misjudged the situation, had overestimated their political base, and had acted prematurely. As Goulart arrived in Montevideo on 31 August, a compromise was hurriedly being sought, both by Congress in Brasília and by the military ministers in Rio de Janeiro. Already names were being proposed for the post of prime minister in the new 'parliamentary' system, but there was still doubt about the attitude of Goulart and, more problematic still, of Brizola. Some PTB deputies believed Goulart could hold out for full presidential powers, but others, especially the national leadership of the PSD, thought he should accept a compromise solution. There still seemed a chance that, like Vargas in 1930, Goulart might lead a movement on Rio de Janeiro from Rio Grande do Sul, and many PTB deputies wanted at least the assurance that any constitutional amendment would provide for a plebiscite on the question of the new system of government. Eventually, however, Congress on 2 September voted firmly in favour of the constitutional amendment, with 236 deputies for and 55 against; 48 senators for, 6 against. This provided the two-thirds vote in Congress in favour of amending the constitution, as required by the constitution of 1946. Goulart had arrived in Pôrto Alegre the day before, amidst great excitement, and, at last, on 5 September 1961, he arrived in Brasília to be inaugurated on 7 September, the anniversary of Brazilian independence. After careful discussion the delicate and difficult job of prime minister was given to a leading *mineiro* politician, Tancredo Neves, who had served as Minister of Justice in Vargas's last term of office and already had negotiated with Goulart in Montevideo. He was an important leader of the PSD, which, as the largest party, should provide the prime minister, but, at the same time, he was acceptable to the Goulart wing of the PTB. The immediate crisis was over, and João Goulart, at the age of forty-three, was president of Brazil, albeit with reduced presidential powers.

The crisis of August–September 1961 is well worth more careful consideration than is often given to it. Like the earlier crises already examined, it again illustrated the major tensions in the political system, especially the persisting, even growing, unease and suspicion with which many senior military officers and their civilian allies viewed the Vargista political alliance, as most clearly represented by Goulart. Above all, it again reflected that general 'crisis of hegemony' already discussed, which now was brought out so sharply and made so much more immediate by the resignation of Quadros. The powerful economic interests, both domestic and foreign, associated with the ESG in its concern for 'internal security' and a particular form of capitalist development for Brazil, had suffered a severe setback in the loss of Quadros and the failure of the military ministers. The UDN and the social forces it most strongly represented were now again in a much weaker position within the formal political system, with executive power once more in the hands of the PTB/PSD. Powerful business and financial groups, especially in the United States, were seriously alarmed at the emerging pattern of Brazilian politics, at the repeated failure of the right to maintain control, and the threat they thought was contained in the new presidency of Goulart. The crisis of 1961 had now shown clearly to many who shared this concern that the political system they required would only be achieved by a direct seizure of power in alliance with the armed forces.

As Goulart took office, the contrast was becoming even more sharply defined between those who, broadly speaking, wanted a tighter, more 'nationalist' control of the economy and who, again in the most diffuse and general sense, were committed to social reform and some measure of reconstruction and redistribution, and those who were, essentially, afraid of such measures, and committed, above all, to a strategy which supported the existing social formations in Brazil as part of an overall pattern of capitalist development, closely linked to the economy and polity of the United States. By late 1961 the first group, rightly or wrongly, was identified with Goulart; the second, with more evident justification, with those who opposed him.

João Goulart: The Key Issues

In all the confusion and excitement of national politics between September 1961 and April 1964 one fact stands out clearly, and demands explanation, both in terms of the particular development of Brazilian politics and the wider, comparative debate concerning civil–military relations in contemporary capitalist society. In September 1961 the majority of civilian politicians (including most leaders of the UDN) and a sufficient majority of senior army officers were unwilling to support a *coup* to exclude João Goulart. By April 1964 that reluctance had vanished, replaced by a general determination that Goulart must go. The key issue, therefore, is why had this change occurred, and what did it imply in terms of major shifts in Brazilian politics in the intervening two and a half years? It is the same question which, *mutatis mutandis*, is asked of Chile between September 1970 and September 1973, as well as of other societies in which military *coups* have significantly changed the whole political economy. Why would the armed forces intervene on the one occasion and not on the other? Was it that the issues had changed significantly, or, rather, that the military leaders merely perceived them more clearly by 1964? How important were such specific and immediate factors as the rapidly rising inflation and an overall crisis in the economy, or, again, the social dislocation and threat of political 'subversion' which many critics of Goulart so feared by early 1964? What did Goulart really stand for, and were, in particular, he and the 'populist' alliance he headed in any sense 'radical', let alone 'revolutionary'?

If Goulart and his supporters were not, by most contemporary criteria, notably radical, but at most reformist, still committed to the overall pattern of Brazil's recent capitalist development through import substitution and the social structure reinforced by that process, why did the *coup* occur? Was it merely over-reaction on the part of the military leaders? This question can only be fully answered by examining the policies adopted *after* the *coup*, to see how far the new government imposed significantly different policies favouring other social and economic interests, especially foreign, or trans-national, interests. Such reflection also raises the tangled issue of how far Goulart was pulled down through foreign, especially United States, involvement in Brazilian politics, both immediately in 1964 and, in the longer term, through its influence on such institutions as the Escola Superior de Guerra and its close links with senior military officers. Were, again, the military leaders of the *coup* largely used by such economic interests, and, too, by those old opponents of Vargas, men like Carlos Lacerda, who on so many occasions since 1945 had tried to set aside the constitutional process?

Many elements came together by 1964 to end the Goulart government, with the *golpistas* being by no means a homogeneous group of easily identifiable, still less identical, interests. The struggle for power was not to end in April 1964, but merely to enter a new phase. But 1964 was a major watershed, and the struggle which was fought out from September 1961 was to be crucial for Brazil's immediate future. In this respect there is one absolutely vital question to be faced, though tackled more fully in a separate chapter. Was the intervention of the armed forces in 1964 to some degree arbitrary, in the sense that it might have gone the other way, favouring Goulart and what he was perceived to stand for, just as, in the case of Chile, it may be asked whether the armed forces might, even by September 1973, have sided with the elected government? Or, must one accept that in modern capitalist society the armed forces, as an essential part of the state apparatus, will always, when they perceive, rightly or wrongly, that the capitalist system is in danger, react vigorously to protect it, acting on behalf of the dominant social groups against those who are offering a serious challenge? Will the officer corps, exercising effective control over those under it, always show a deeper loyalty to capitalism than to liberal democracy? Is this, indeed, the norm to be expected, flowing from the very nature of capitalist society and the relation to it of the armed forces? These are large, important questions, not easily solved, but real and vital, not just for academic political analysis but for effective political strategy. It is this which makes the experience of Brazil under Goulart so fascinating.

Goulart and the Attempt at 'Conciliation'; September 1961–January 1963

Reflecting on Goulart and, more importantly, what he represented within the politics of Brazil, he at once appears as a remarkably improbable leader of a far-reaching radical or revolutionary movement. Not only was he a wealthy landowner, part of that group who traditionally had most to lose in Brazil, but, as the direct political heir of Vargas, he was already deeply involved, mostly through his time in the Ministry of Labour, with the whole pattern of manipulative populist politics directed by the federal government through the *peleguismo* system. He was a quiet, undistinguished figure, utterly lacking the excitement of Kubitschek or the colour of Quadros, a politician whose dismal electoral record was a fair reflection of his general mediocrity and lack of charismatic appeal.[9] His one advantage was that he was a political figure of national rather than regional standing, with his main political base, unlike many Brazilian politicians, less in state and regional politics, but firmly set in the much wider structure of the trade unions and their interrelation with the Ministry of Labour and the federal government, as well as the PTB, of which Goulart was by 1961 undoubtedly the most prominent, if not the most able, leader.

At the same time, however, Goulart's close personal links with Vargas, and the position he held in relation to organized labour, made him, in many eyes, the obvious candidate to head that *república sindicalista*, or 'trade union state', which many on the right had feared was emerging ever since the early 1940s. Although in so many respects an implausible candidate, Goulart was quickly cast in the role of demoniac leader of the left, very much made to feel as he took office in September 1961 that he was there on sufferance and, in many respects, on approval, an attitude he strongly resented.

The more interesting question with regard to Goulart is less what he was himself, but, rather, what social forces he represented, or to which he gave enlarged opportunity, or, even, by which at times he was carried along. Such questions are discussed later. In the first period of his presidency, however, the most prominent consideration for Goulart himself seems to have been to regain full presidential powers, which was partly linked to his overall strategy of attempted conciliation. But this was only in part a tactic to establish himself both nationally and internationally as a moderate, credible, and reliable politician, fit to be president: the more obvious explanation of Goulart's first phase in office (September 1961 to January 1963) is that he was, in fact, such a politician. Despite the abuse later poured on him by his enemies, he was not by temperament, ideology, or still less by virtue of his own social and economic position, a man of the far left. As vice president under Kubitschek he had worked closely with all groupings within the trade union movement, including, of necessity, the Communists, as their influence in the unions increased; but, equally, he had worked with those who opposed the growth of Communist influence, and his party political base remained firmly in the PTB, identified with its populist role of controlling the vote of the urban working class. At the same time his own agrarian wealth and personal connections linked him directly and easily to the agrarian base of the PSD and, indeed, to part of the UDN. In so far, therefore, as Vargista populism represented a manipulative multi-class alliance directed from above, João Goulart was its archetypal representative. He was certainly no tribune of the people, or political activist committed to workers' control at factory or plant level, still less to a radical restructuring of rural society. In so far as he became a more radicalized figure in the latter part of his presidency, as distinct from how he may always have evoked that image among a right-wing minority, he was made more radical both by the attacks of his opponents and by the pressure of events.

It may even be doubted whether, when Goulart was suddenly thrust into office in 1961, he had any clearly defined idea of what he wanted, still less an explicit set of policies. His government was a moderate one, with four ministries going to the PSD and two major posts to members of the UDN, a significant concession in a system in which the president's power was now more carefully limited by the constitutional need to work in close conjunction with his ministers. He spoke of the need for basic reforms,[10] but insisted on his commitment to democracy and resistance to communism, and did all he could to identify his government with the attack on inflation already launched under Quadros. There was a rise in the minimum wage in October 1961, soon after Goulart took office, but this was already in the pipeline and, in any case, was, at 40 per cent, roughly in step with the rise in the cost of living in Rio de Janeiro (38 per cent) and São Paulo (42 per cent).[11] At the same time 'a serious effort to contain Federal expenditure was made in the first months of 1962 and, to a lesser extent, of 1963'.[12] Various immediate factors contributed to the rising inflation of late 1961, including Directive 204, mentioned above, while:

> . . . Another important factor, also psychological, was the political and military crisis at the end of August, which led to panic cash withdrawals from banks, intensified speculation against the cruzeiro, and induced additional federal expenditure on troop movements . . .[13]

At the same time industrial expansion continued, especially in the chemicals (21 per cent) and drinks (16 per cent) industries, with the average rate of expansion of the manufacturing sector being about 11 per cent, rather higher than in 1960. Goulart was anxious to make clear his commitment to stabilization and his general willingness to collaborate within all reasonable limits with the IMF and other financial agencies, a point he especially stressed during a visit to Washington in April 1962, when he also agreed to United States control of the use of substantial new development funds allocated to the north-east. His whole tone, whether in discussions with President Kennedy or in formal speeches to the United States Congress, was moderate, judicious, and reassuring. He discussed such sensitive issues as the appropriation of United States holdings in Brazil, but in a sober, rational manner, considering the most reasonable methods of compensation, so as not to stampede an over-intense reaction.[14] After six months in office he was moving well towards establishing that credibility and regaining those wider powers he believed he needed.

One difficulty in assessing this general appearance of moderation and sweet reasonableness in Goulart's early months, a problem both for contemporaries and for subsequent political analysts, is to know how far Goulart was himself involved with, and condoned, more extreme statements and measures on the part of some of his closest colleagues and supporters. The situation was similar to that under Kubitschek, when the president's moderate stance was paralleled by the more extreme nationalist demands stemming from the ISEB, or under Quadros, when conservative policies within Brazil were accompanied by a more flamboyant, though still essentially conservative, foreign policy. At the very least, Goulart was able to be associated with gestures towards more 'radical' nationalist opinion by means of his PTB Minister of Foreign Affairs, San Tiago Dantas, and through his brother-in-law, Leonel Brizola. Dantas at the Punta del Este meeting of Foreign Ministers in January 1962 maintained Brazil's 'independent' foreign policy, especially in relation to Cuba. This was an important stand against United States demands, but sharply criticized at the time, and later, by those who saw such demands as fully legitimate, or who at least believed that the Goulart government, as a relatively weak one in a situation of dependence on the United States, should have moved more cautiously.[15] Such criticism has some merits in terms of *Realpolitik*, but too readily assumes or allows some kind of 'natural' hegemony of the United States in Brazil and Latin America more generally. San Tiago Dantas and, by association, Goulart were, on the other hand, expressing a general, and growing, resentment at the easy assumption of such a dominant role, both economic and political, on the part of the United States. The refusal immediately to exclude Cuba from the community of American nations was, therefore, in part merely an acknowledgement of the importance of Cuba's defiance of a nation which by the 1960s so readily assumed that it should have its way throughout the whole hemisphere, and beyond. Nor, as already argued in terms of Quadros, was such a stance exclusively, even essentially, 'radical', since the 'independent foreign policy' was favoured by many in Brazil's business and diplomatic community as a necessary move in the search for wider markets, pointing, at least in the commercial sphere, to that pragmatism in terms of export markets which was to emerge so clearly after 1964.

The further relation between Goulart's presidency, the crisis of import substitution industrialization, and the search for alternative strategies is discussed later. The defiance of the United States at Punta del Este was, however, also supported, it should be noted, by the Brazilian Congress, which refused to back criticism, mostly stemming from the UDN, of the stand taken by San Tiago Dantas, who also found support throughout the country, from trade unions, from students, from the mass of the PTB, and many outside it. It must not, in other words, be assumed that the 'independent foreign policy' and its implied challenge to the control exercised in Latin America by the United States was, by virtue of that challenge, notably radical. Many in the United States made this easy identification, as did their close associates in Brazil, but the more 'nationalist' stance in foreign policy was well within the tradition of Vargista nationalism and the search for a more 'independent' position, and commanded much support from groups who, anything but radical, welcomed the chance of wider markets and less rigid financial and economic ties to the United States.

But the early 1960s, especially in the wake of the Cuban revolution, was a time when any challenge to United States control in Latin

America was readily identified, and strongly opposed, as 'radical', even 'Marxist', a term carelessly and loosely adopted on all sides. So Goulart, even in his early phase of conciliation of and reassurance towards the United States, the foreign financial agents, and his critics within Brazil, became involved in other emotionally charged debates, notably that of the expropriation of United States interests. The immediate occasion was the takeover by Brizola in Rio Grande do Sul of a subsidiary of ITT (International Telephone and Telegraph), a giant corporation capable of exercising great political influence both in the United States and in Latin America. Brizola's move in January 1962 was again part of the general concern in Brazil over the role of such transnational corporations, but Goulart swiftly agreed to measures aimed at reconciliation, especially since he was about to visit Washington. The incident served as a reminder that strong nationalist currents existed in Brazil, but also furthered the suggestion that Goulart could act as a judicious broker in such matters. He was, therefore, on the one hand, able to rely on the veiled threat of more extreme nationalist and radical demands, while also appearing as the man who could best control and channel such political currents.

The conciliatory politics of Goulart's first year or more in office greatly helped to prepare the way for a return to full presidential powers, which, in any case, was also wanted by other prominent politicians, such as Kubitschek, who had presidential ambitions for 1965. The question was kept alive throughout 1962, regularly coming to the front of political debate, as, for example, in June, when Tancredo Neves resigned as prime minister, and Goulart named to succeed him San Tiago Dantas, the PTB Foreign Minister who already had provoked such controversy.[16] This nomination predictably brought strong protest, not least from the PSD, and on 28 June was rejected by the Chamber of Deputies by 174 votes to 110.

It is still difficult to know how far Goulart was deliberately seeking to provoke a crisis on this occasion, to underline the difficulty of his position as a president so weakened by the new constitutional provisions as to be unable to control Congress. But the issues were sharpened still further by what looked like a direct confrontation not only between the executive and legislature, but more seriously, as it seemed to many, between the elected Congress and increasingly powerful forces outside Congress to which a populist president could appeal. These were, above all, organized labour, ever more under the influence of the Communist Party and other left-wing groups, especially as represented in the CNTI, the National Confederation of Workers in Industry, which soon was to form part of a still larger, militant organization, the CGG (Comando

Geral de Greve, or General Strike Commando), later to become the CGT, General Commando of Workers (Comando Geral dos Trabalhadores). The union organizations now being formed were more militant, more political, and more disciplined than ever before, with much closer control being exercised by the PCB. In the biennial elections within the CNTI in December 1961 the Communists and the left had made important gains, winning control of a confederation made up of more than fifty federations of industrial workers, so giving the left control of the official trade union apparatus, especially as they now found support in the other most important confederations, CONTEC and CNTTMFA, while also having powerful elements within the other confederations, as, for example, among the federation of railway workers within the CNTTT. (The CNTI was the largest of five confederations of workers' unions, the second biggest being the CNTC, the National Confederation of Workers in Commerce. These two were also the oldest, both founded in 1946. The other three confederations were the CNTTT (National Confederation of Workers in Land Transport), the CONTEC (National Confederation of Workers in Credit Establishments), and CNTTMFA (National Confederation of Workers in Sea, River, and Air Transport.)

This leftward, or more specifically pro-Communist, shift within the trade unions was extremely important, indicating that feature of politics in this period already noted, namely, that the official apparatus of the trade union system was now moving from its earlier explicitly corporatist pattern, in which it was tightly controlled by the state as an effective mechanism of social control, into a new alignment in which the unions, taking advantage of their integrated role within the state apparatus, could themselves exercise wider, more direct influence on behalf of their members.[17] Goulart, as head of the executive and answerable to Congress, might have limited constitutional power; but as the foremost spokesman for organized labour he clearly had potentially massive support on which he could call. The nature of this *pacto populista* is discussed later. For the moment it is enough to emphasize how in the crisis, however deliberately engineered, of June–July 1962 Goulart seemed to many of his critics to be pointing towards exactly that extra-constitutional *república sindicalista* they had so long feared, an anxiety in no way allayed by the evident fact that forces on the right had equally powerful, or, as it turned out, much more powerful backing through their own pressure-groups. Such pressure, as seen for example in the attacks on San Tiago Dantas, was, however, regarded as normal, as somehow natural and legitimate, by the groups who traditionally had exercised political power in Brazil.

The lines were now drawn up, with Congress refusing to accept San Tiago Dantas, but with the CNTI already threatening a general strike in order to impose a solution favourable to Goulart. The president now nominated as his prime minister the president of the Senate, a PSD leader, Auro de Moura Andrade, whom Congress quickly approved by 222–51; but the machinery for strike action and direct political opposition was already in operation, coming to a head on 4 July with a call for a general strike, 'the biggest political strike in the history of the working-class movement in Brazil'.[18] The crisis now deepened as the strike worsened and there were outbreaks of violence and some looting. Goulart still seemed to be seeking some form of conciliation, but Moura Andrade resigned almost at once and the country was left without a ministry, again underlining, as it seemed to many, the difficulties under the 'parliamentary' system of providing sufficiently resolute and effective government.[19] The president was now negotiating directly with the labour leaders, providing further evidence of the more powerful, autonomous role being played by the unions and organized labour in a '. . . political strike of national proportions . . . a powerful sign of the strength of the workers, which influenced the shape of politics and revealed the heightened level of political consciousness and organization of the working class . . .'[20]

Whether or not this was, indeed, the most important strike in the history of the Brazilian labour movement is obviously open to question, as is the degree of political consciousness it demonstrated. More important is that at the time the strike and the crisis which underlined it were widely perceived, both on the left and on the right, as a very serious test of strength, with each side drawing its own conclusions as to the lessons it contained. But it was a crisis which could not be prolonged, since a government of some sort had to be made quickly, especially with Congressional elections fixed for 7 October 1962. The result of intense lobbying and heated discussion was the nomination for the premiership of a politician who was, like Moura Andrade, a member of the PSD, but who, if anything, was more to the left than San Tiago Dantas, the nominee already rejected by Congress. The new choice was Francisco Brochado da Rocha, a *gaúcho* who had been Secretary of Justice and the Interior for Rio Grande do Sul under Brizola, and, as such, had been deeply involved in February 1962 in the expropriation of the ITT subsidiary. It was a remarkable nomination, suggesting that Goulart, despite his claims to be politically shackled by Congress, was aware that ultimately he could get his way. The alternative was to prolong the constitutional crisis and immediately intensify a serious struggle for power, a confrontation for which neither side was yet prepared.

On 10 July Congress agreed to accept Brochado da Rocha, giving that round decisively to Goulart, or, as many on the right concluded, to those extra-parliamentary forces which on this occasion had supported him. The key issue, however, was how far these forces might back him in future, and how far, by comparison, those groups who opposed Goulart could marshal their own, perhaps more effective, extra-Congressional support, a question which was to be resolved over the next two years.

Despite all the excitement over this choice of prime minister, the post did not, in fact, carry very extensive powers, since effective control still lay with the president, and, as a relatively unknown, inexperienced politician at the level of national politics, Brochado da Rocha was even more dependent on the federal president. Most attention during his ministry, lasting until early September 1962, remained centred on Goulart, and on the question of a presidential versus a 'parliamentary' form of government. Increasingly, opinion was moving in favour of a return to fuller executive powers, since the left generally believed that the parliamentary system was a device to shackle a reformist president, while many on the right, including some of Goulart's fiercest opponents, now thought that only full executive power would reveal the president in his true colours, and that under the current system he could always avoid responsibility both for his actions and for those of his supporters, as well as, at times, for inaction. Most important of all, a substantial number of senior military officers also favoured a return to full constitutional powers for the executive, including officers in the crucial commands in Rio de Janeiro (General Osvino Ferreira Alves), São Paulo (General Pery Constant Bevilaqua), and in Pôrto Alegre (General Jair Dantas Ribeiro).[21] The military ministers appointed by Goulart also spoke out for a plebiscite on the issue of executive power, urging that it be held much earlier than 1965, the date which in the constitutional amendment of September 1961 had been decided as the time to re-examine Brazil's form of government. The new prime minister asked for the plebiscite in December 1962, while Goulart argued that the issue should be put to the nation at the time of the Congressional elections in October. Once again there were rumblings in Rio Grande do Sul, with threatening noises from General Dantas Ribeiro, obviously backed by Brizola, with further threats of a general strike from the CGG (Comando Geral de Greve). The new prime minister was also asking for special powers for the Council of Ministers, presenting Congress with a wide-ranging programme which included, at least on paper, substantial initiatives for agrarian reform, nationalization, anti-trust laws, and more extensive state controls.

Once again tension was building up between Congress and the president, both deeply involved in bargaining, rapid compromise and a repeated show of strength, with the new call for a general strike and renewed charges and counter-charges from Lacerda and his supporters against the president and all who were associated with him.[22] Both Congressional and military opinion was divided, but with many willing to bring forward the plebiscite while unwilling to accept the prime minister's request for special powers and reforms. The suggestion of agrarian reform, in particular, greatly alarmed many in Congress, especially among the PSD who otherwise sided with Goulart and his PSD prime minister. Excitement was intense when on 13 September 1962 Congress refused to agree to Brochado da Rocha's plea for special powers, and the prime minister and his cabinet resigned, again leaving Brazil without a government.

To a large extent this whole constitutional crisis was a sham and a diversionary tactic on both sides. The central issue was not about constitutional form, but rather a struggle for political power and, ultimately, about divergent social and economic policies. The parliamentary system could have been made to work, but by now had become a convenient issue, even an excuse, for both sides to seize. To Goulart and many of his supporters the parliamentary system was a humiliating restriction imposed by their foes, to be clearly shown up as an obstacle to stable, efficient government. To many in the PSD, and elsewhere, it was, too, a convenient issue to distract from more alarming demands for reform, especially agrarian reform, while again to others, especially the military leaders, the debate was an evident nuisance, preventing for whatever reason the smooth process of government. Many felt it was convenient to give way on the plebiscite, while refusing wider powers to Goulart's Council of Ministers, and it might even be wise to give Goulart enough rope to hang himself. On 16 September Congress agreed to a 'popular referendum' on the parliamentary system, to be held on 6 January 1963.

The fundamental issue, behind all this surface excitement and confusion, was that which had dominated Brazilian politics since at least 1930 and even more clearly since 1945, namely, who was to control the Brazilian state, and in whose interests, and how was such state power to be won or maintained. The crises of 1962 were, therefore, only further symptoms of this long social and political struggle, most clearly seen in the repeated crises and confrontations already described, and now to become more intense up till the *coup* of April 1964. By contrast, the Congressional elections of October 1962, and the elections for governor in eleven states and of 45 federal senators, were both calm and relatively insignificant. Out of a total valid vote of just over 14¼ million in the Congressional elections the PSD had the largest share (15·6 per cent), the UDN had 11·2 per cent, the PTB 12·1 per cent, and the other smaller parties 5·1 per cent between them. There was also just over 15 per cent blank votes. As in previous post-war elections, there was a marked tendency for those already holding office to be re-elected and a stable division of the national vote between the major parties, with smaller parties and groups having to seek coalitions both among themselves and with the three large parties, so that, in all, 41·0 per cent of the total Congressional vote went to coalition candidates. The result was an even greater blurring of party divisions than in previous elections, with more attention to immediate, local questions and to the personalities of the particular candidates, rather than to general, national issues or differences of ideology. Money, too, played an increasingly important role in the 1962 elections, as the services and favour formerly offered to supporters by the candidates were now more and more commuted into money payments.[23] It was estimated, for example, that in São Paulo a member of Congress seeking re-election would now spend about 20 million cruzeiros (US$50,000), while a man standing for the first time might spend more than twice as much (about US$120,000). Even in preponderantly rural areas costs were heavy, perhaps as much as US$100,000 for a Congressional campaign in Ceará.[24] But these were all developments within the pattern set since at least 1945, reinforcing a general impression of a political party system slow to change and still heavily weighted to the right, especially with the disproportionate influence of smaller, poorer states in which landlord influence could still so easily return to Congress men firmly set against any substantial reform.[25] The exclusion of the Communist Party from electoral politics had removed one potentially important source of political dynamism and challenge, pushing the parties further towards a pattern of confused multi-class populist alliances, and further reinforcing the PSD and PTB share of the vote. The overall impression, even as late as the 1962 elections, was therefore one of 'plus ça change . . .', with the same faces in Congress as for many years past, the same names and families still very much in evidence, and little sign of the emergence of a flexible party system, open and able to respond to those demands for change, reform, and at least some measure of distribution which by the early 1960s were being heard in Brazil.[26] The main sources of political power, and in consequence the principal focus of political interest, were increasingly outside the formal political system of parties and Congress. This is in no sense to argue that parliamentary democracy was not viable in Brazil in the early 1960s, but rather that those who since 1945 had dominated Brazilian politics had, it seemed, failed, or better refused, to allow the liberal democratic system to contain, and possibly solve, some of the most serious political and social struggles of the last two decades or more, which now increasingly were being resolved *outside* the party and Congressional system. The debate concerning a 'parliamentary' versus 'presidential' system was therefore really of secondary importance, as were the results of Congressional elections held within a too rigid political framework, which by 1962 had removed from formal politics so much of that radical debate most relevant for Brazil's response to social and political pressures. On 6 January 1963 the electorate voted overwhelmingly to give full presidential powers to Goulart, but the real struggle for power still lay ahead.

Goulart and the Struggle for Control: January 1963–March 1964

The Plano Trienal: Stability, Growth, and Reform?

The period of about fourteen months in which Goulart exercised full presidential power, ending with the *coup* of April 1964, is still the focus of sharp political controversy, with at the same time many important issues still relatively obscure. In the light, however, of much of the bitter, sweeping criticism of Goulart which came after the *coup* it is important to note the really positive efforts he made in the first six months of 1963 to solve some of the intractable problems then facing Brazil, problems which, moreover, in later years have been tackled, often with no greater success, by politicians of widely differing convictions in many other societies. The first issue was that of inflation, already running at over 50 per cent at the start of 1963, which now was to be attacked in a comprehensive three-year plan, largely drawn up by Celso Furtado.[27] This *Plano Trienal* was published just before the plebiscite and, as its name indicated, was an ambitious, imaginative attempt to treat both economic and social problems together, seeing them as integrally connected. In this respect it differed significantly from some earlier plans, such as, for instance, the Roberto Campos and Lucas Lopes plan of 1958–59, which had tended to present financial and economic issues to some degree in isolation from social and political factors. But the need to stress the intertwining of the social, political, and economic dimensions of planning had been further brought home to Furtado by his experience in the north-east, so that the *Plano Trienal*, now strongly backed by Goulart and his Minister of Finance, San Tiago Dantas, was, though hurriedly produced, the result both of mature academic reflection and sobering practical experience. Its economic analysis of the source of recent inflation emphasized the external sector, noting in particular Brazil's declining import capacity in the late 1950s and early 1960s, while now seeing Brazil as being in an increasingly disadvantageous position as compared with developed industrial societies and with other developing countries, especially the newly independent European colonies. As an exporter of primary products, the argument ran, Brazil was faced by declining prices for its own exports and with rising costs of imported manufactured goods: hence the need for a much quicker industrialization, so that Brazil, too, might share in the growing international market for manufactured goods.[28] This argument was also linked to the insistence that, while inflation must be cut back, it should not be at the expense of growth, the aim being to contain inflation at an acceptable rate of about 10 per cent while keeping a growth-rate of around 7 per cent. This target was in itself difficult, but, as expressed in what became known as the Dantas–Furtado programme, it was also combined with a commitment, inescapable for a president like Goulart who relied on reformist, populist electoral support, to a wider strategy of distribution and social reform.

The strategy now being outlined, which it was hoped would recommend itself to foreign investors and observers, especially in the United States, has been described as 'the most ambitious program of any postwar Brazilian regime'.[29] The description is justified in so far as a government, already faced with such high rates of inflation, was seeking to provide, and in a short time, realistic measures of inflation together with high rates of growth, combined with the satisfaction within a democratic system of rising popular demands for the more equitable distribution of wealth and much greater attention to basic structural reforms throughout Brazilian society. And all this had to be done, in effect, without alienating still further groups within the armed forces and among more conservative politicians, who already were hostile to, or suspicious of, Goulart, and without producing a serious loss of confidence on the part of foreign bankers and investors, who already had been made anxious over the rise of inflation since the Kubitschek administration and over the increasing signs of political and social 'instability'. The task, it seemed to many, both then and since, was an impossible one. Something, arguably, had to go, as eventually it did after 1964. The choice then made was for 'stability' and growth, but, at least in the short term, at the expense of democratic politics, distribution, and social reform.

The *Pacto Populista*: the Social Compact

That the reconciliation of these conflicting demands was doomed to failure is perhaps arguable with hindsight. If, however, the failure to reconcile stability, growth, distribution, and reform within a democratic system in Brazil before 1964 was to some degree inevitable, the outlook must be equally bleak for other societies which, albeit later and at a different stage of industrial development, find themselves faced with similar demands to curb inflation, stimulate growth, and maintain a satisfactory measure of reform, all within a democratic framework. It is a question, therefore, which needs more careful examination. At least it should be noted that within the Brazilian context perhaps only Goulart, or certainly a politician with a similar basis of support both electorally and among the unions, could have made the Dantas–Furtado programme work. And again, in fairness to Goulart, it is important to acknowledge how well, in many respects, he set about the task.

Goulart set out some of his plans for social and economic development in his *Mensagem*, his annual address, to Congress in March 1963,[30] where he stressed the need to provide 'a high rate of development, but at the same time, reducing its social cost and working for a more just distribution of the growing wealth of the country', arguing that, in order to tackle the causes of inflation the government must face up to the structural reforms required for development.[31] Among these necessary reforms, he argued, were changes in the tax system, in banking, in government administration, in housing policies, and, above all, in the structure of Brazilian agriculture which currently is 'an enormous obstacle to our economic and social progress'.

> I consider that it is the duty of my government, inspired by the Christian and democratic spirit of the Brazilian people, to introduce a just agrarian reform, and I am certain that in carrying out this commitment we have made with the people I shall not lack the patriotic co-operation of the National Congress . . .[32]

The whole tone of the *Mensagem* was sober and the aims proposed were moderate, though Goulart stressed that the Brazilian people wanted progress and reforms, and that he himself was loyal to the ideas of economic emancipation and social justice bequeathed by Getúlio Vargas and expressed in his farewell letter. The people, he said, had now given him a mandate in the recent plebiscite and had shown their solid determination to carry through 'those structural reforms which I have always held to be a necessary condition for the social stability and progress of the country'.[33]

This, again, was the argument recurring throughout both the *Mensagem* and Goulart's other speeches and statements of this period: that structural reforms, above all agrarian reform, were necessary for development, to increase productivity and employment, to expand the internal market, and to quicken the rate of growth by removing some of the major obstacles to development. These were arguments taken straight from the *Plano Trienal*, in line with the best developmental theory of the day, and revealing a firm commitment to planning, the defence of which takes up eight pages of the *Mensagem*. What Goulart and his government were offering was, in other words, a reformist package to make the existing system work more smoothly and effectively, rather than a radical alternative or subversive, 'revolutionary' programme.

In view of the subsequent collapse of Goulart's attempt at stabilization it may seem strange to suggest that only he, or a politician with a similar electoral and trade union base, could have made the Dantas–Furtado programme work. The point, however, is that a necessary though, as will be seen, not a sufficient condition for such success was the broad support of the trade union movement in attempting to keep wage demands within certain bounds. This is not to suggest that such wage demands were the main, or even a primary, source of the inflation of the early 1960s, since other obviously important factors in achieving stabilization included the control of public spending, the control of prices, tax reforms, and, in the short run, both improvements in Brazil's terms of trade and, above all, a readiness on the part of foreign creditors to express their confidence in Brazil's efforts to curb inflation, by giving positive help to Goulart's government. Central to all this, however, granted the highly dependent nature of the Brazilian economy, was the need to reassure foreign creditors and investors that the government could maintain overall political 'stability' and in particular could contain rising wage demands, an issue which, rightly or wrongly, had become by 1963 a touchstone of the seriousness of intent of the government. This again, as will be seen, was far from being the whole story, since even more fundamental to the response and attitude both of foreign financiers and their allies in Brazil, both civilian and military, was to be their reading of the wider political situation, namely, how far they believed Brazil was likely to produce major social and economic changes by 1963 and 1964, breaking substantially with its previous pattern of social, political, and economic relations, both internal and external. In this respect, although the issues of inflation, of workers' demands, possible strike action, and the relation, broadly speaking, between capital and labour were to be the main, immediate focus of tension and contradiction from January 1963 to April 1964, the central, fundamental issue, not always explicitly stated, was how far Brazil might move decisively to the left, starting at least along the path towards a socialist society, and thereby seriously challenging many vested interests, both domestic and foreign.

The debate on how far Brazil was indeed capable of moving towards a radical social reorganization by 1963 or 1964 still continues, renewed and reinvigorated by events over a decade later in Chile and even more so in Portugal, with at the same time direct relevance for other industrial societies, such as the United Kingdom and Italy, where the Brazilian debate on inflation in the early 1960s is echoed so clearly. The contours of this wider discussion are set out later. For the moment it is again worth stressing that any attempt at a successful stabilization policy by 1963 in Brazil required the working consent of the trade union movement, both on the shop floor and through its main representatives in Congress. And within the Brazilian system João Goulart, as the heir of Vargas and the man who over the last decade and a half had worked most closely with organized labour, was the politician of national stature most likely to carry weight both with union leaders and with those members of Congress who sought to speak for the working class. Much, therefore, depended on the nature and strength of Goulart's base in the unions and Congress, what in later years has been described as the *pacto populista*, which by 1963 was in fact being modified, mainly through changes within the broad left wing of Brazilian politics.

In discussing the crisis of June–July 1962 emphasis was laid on the growing extra-Congressional influence which Goulart could exercise, with the CNTI on that occasion threatening a general strike to influence ministerial appointments. The strength, too, of political forces outside Congress, and the continuing exclusion, or at least under-representation, of important groups, such as the industrial working class and the representatives of a more international financial and industrial bourgeoisie, were also stressed when discussing the results of the 1962 elections. The general trend, in other words, was for important political forces to work outside the formal political institutions, a tendency which, on left and right, threatened to weaken, even destroy, the liberal democratic system, a process which became intense in 1963, reaching a crisis in late March 1964. Interpretations differ sharply as to how far such a breakdown was always probable, perhaps virtually inevitable, as social and political tensions grew and as in particular the pressure of demand from the working class and others previously excluded from, or tightly controlled within, the political system began to be felt. It does, however, seem fair to say that if inflation were to be contained within the existing system, such policies required the consent not only of sufficient members of Congress, of trade union leaders, and arguably the majority of trade union members, but also of a substantial section of the bourgeoisie—of the financial and business community and of the leaders of Brazilian industry, whose collaboration and goodwill were every bit as necessary for the success of Goulart's policies as were those of the trade unions.

In terms of this last point it is worth remembering the growing evidence that among the most vigorous opponents of stabilization measures were those financial intermediaries, big industrialists, and others who most benefited from inflation, so that 'intermittent attempts at stabilisation . . . were vigorously denounced in the press and invariably aroused storms of protest, particularly on the part of bankers'.[34] Nevertheless, Goulart's whole policy, to achieve both financial stabilization and political stability in the first seven or eight months of 1963, depended on the strength of his 'populist pact'. This was a political understanding within Congress, between Goulart, the PTB, most of the PSD, and even some of the UDN, and, outside Congress, between Goulart, the trade union leaders, and the leadership of the PCB, the Brazilian Communist Party, which now was so influential within the trade union movement, especially in the public sector. Essentially, in social and economic terms, this represented and was understood to be a pact or working agreement between the working class and what was commonly referred to as the 'national bourgeoisie'. It was at best a delicate, fragile alliance, seeking to reconcile severely divergent groups: but it was an alliance which had to be maintained if the existing system were to survive.[35]

There was, of course, a coherent analysis, stemming from groups further to the left than Goulart, his 'populist alliance', and the PCB, which argued that the existing political system could not, and should not, survive, since it essentially shored up an indefensible pattern of class relations and group interests, both inside Brazil and internationally. The more immediate issue is what conditions were required for the *Plano Trienal* to have any chance of success, and for Goulart to have any real chance of survival. Basically, and without oversimplifying too severely, he had to be able to satisfy, or at least contain, his own supporters both inside and outside Congress, and those much further to the left. At the same time he must not alienate, or at least too greatly alarm, those elements in the PSD, the UDN, in the officer corps of the armed forces, and above all among Brazil's creditors and foreign investors abroad, especially in the United States, who were not yet, by early 1963, implacably hostile to Goulart and all which they believed he represented. Many civilian politicians, soldiers, and some interests abroad were already his enemies, hostile to Goulart, to the Vargas tradition of *trabalhismo*, and to the promise, or threat, of social change and reform it contained. But others were not: they might have strong reservations about Goulart, but stronger still was their commitment to Brazil's democratic constitution and party system. Many, therefore, even in the UDN leadership, hoped Goulart would survive till the next presidential election.

A Question of Confidence

A crucial issue was that of confidence, both domestic and foreign, and it is in this respect that the immediate reaction of foreign creditors and investors to the *Plano Trienal* was so vital to the shaping of political opinion in Brazil during 1963, and therefore to the survival of Goulart and eventually of party politics within a democratic framework. If the stabilization programme were to have any chance of success, it needed effective but sensitive support from Brazil's foreign creditors, especially in the United States. Unfortunately, there was growing unease over both Goulart's real commitment to the stabilization programme and his ability to carry it through. The general attitude in the United States embassy since Goulart's inauguration had been 'to give him the benefit of the doubt, to be friendly or at least proper',[36] but there was increasing alarm over the rapid growth of nationalist demands, especially on such issues as profit remittances, over the vociferous groups to the left of Goulart, both inside and outside Congress, and over a perceived leftward swing in Brazilian politics, judged by many to be inimical to United States interests:

> . . . even as Dantas was negotiating the loan agreement with the Kennedy administration in March 1963, Gordon was testifying before the House Foreign Affairs Committee on Communist infiltration of the labour movement, student organizations, and the government itself in Brazil. Assistant Secretary of State Thomas Mann later testified that he was aware in January 1963 'that the erosion towards communism in Brazil was very rapid' . . .[37]

Observers abroad were already aware, too, of the mounting resistance to stabilization measures within Brazil, as opposition to them came from both left and right. The removal, for example, of subsidies on oil and wheat imports and the introduction of more realistic exchange rates implied a substantial jump in food and transport costs, perhaps as much as 40 per cent on transport and 177 per cent on bread and wheat.[38] Such increases, though apparent evidence of the government's serious intent, brought protest from the left, especially from the PCB and trade union leaders, but, equally, annoyed many financiers and businessmen. They complained of the severely restricted bank loans to the private sector, and were further concerned that the stabilization measures of January–April 1963 '. . . were applied immediately after minimum wages had been increased by 60 per cent, that is, when labour costs were sharply rising . . .'.[39] Goulart's plans for stabilization were, it seemed, acceptable neither to right nor left, a tension increasingly evident to foreign creditors and investors. Foreign observers, therefore, were not really convinced by the stabilization programme of 1963, and the resulting lack of confidence was to make more intense an economic decline which already was becoming apparent.

The stabilization programme was rightly perceived at the time as an acid test of Goulart's ability to work within the existing political framework, including that wider international context in which continuing support from abroad was a necessary condition for the successful containment of inflation. Much, therefore, depended on the result of San Tiago Dantas's visit to Washington in March 1963, when reactions to the stabilization plans would be made clearer, and expressed in United States government policy. The negotiations were closely followed in the press of both countries, as Dantas talked with President Kennedy and his advisers, who, eager to make the Alliance for Progress work, and aware of the crucial role of Brazil in such schemes,[40] nevertheless were alarmed at the reported leftwards drift of Brazilian politics, as described by Lincoln Gordon at the time and even noted by Dantas as a reason for more vigorous support for the proposals he now laid before Washington. In the end financial caution and political suspicion prevailed, with an agreement of a total package of 398·5 million dollars for Brazil, but only 84 million of which would be made immediately available. Further help and renegotiation would depend on the vigour and success with which the Goulart government carried out its plans, a process which would be further examined by an IMF mission to Brazil in May 1963, which, in particular, would want to see how far the Brazilian government really could keep down wage and salary increases, one of the central features of its stabilization programme.

There is reason to doubt whether, even if wider, more generous support had been forthcoming, Goulart's stabilization programme would have worked, whether he did, indeed, have the political muscle to carry through his policies against strong opposition from both left and right, when illusory wage gains through inflation were becoming a necessary *political* condition for his success, or survival, as a populist president. What is clear, however, is that the relative failure of the Dantas mission to Washington, and in particular the way in which it was presented to and interpreted by the Brazilian public as further evidence of a continuing, debilitating dependence on foreign bankers and foreign governments, both further excited nationalist opinion and, in effect, ended Goulart's attempt at reconciling stabilization, growth, and reform. The refusal of swift, adequate support ended any chance he had of holding together his 'populist pact' with an effective appeal to organized labour and Congressional support in an alliance of the working class and the more nationalist bourgeoisie. In one form or another the political lines had to be redrawn, a process which accelerated from mid-1963, as Goulart now accepted the need for 'basic reforms'.

Political Tension and Cabinet Change: June 1963

The most important test for the Dantas–Furtado programme within Brazil would come, as everyone knew, over wages and salaries. There were strains over the supply of credit, over federal expenditure, and over exchange policy, but the most sensitive issue was wages, with, unfortunately, some of the most powerful political groups coming next in the wage queue—civil servants, and the armed forces. These were concerned not only with relativities, but with absolute levels of income, refusing to accept the limit of about 40 per cent which Dantas had indicated during his visit to Washington in March. The government in April asked for rises up to 55 or 56 per cent, but eventually had to agree to 70 per cent in July. Such rises knocked a hole through the whole stabilization programme, further convinced foreign creditors and investors that Goulart could not control the rising inflation, and led trade union leaders and workers to argue that they too had to keep up the wages race.

But by May–June 1963 it was already becoming clear that the overriding, most fundamental issue was not about inflation, about the control of wages, government spending, credit or exchange policies. Behind and beyond these debates, becoming ever sharper and clearer, was the question of *political power*, about the shaping and control of the Brazilian state, and in whose interests, and by whom, state power would be exercised, an issue which by mid-1963 was being mainly expressed, though also in large measure confused, in the nationalist critique of the Goulart government.

The charting of Brazilian politics in the last months of Goulart's presidency is a delicate, controversial exercise, still provoking fierce debate. It is made difficult not only by this strength of feeling and by the importance of the issues involved, but by the uncertain nature of the evidence, the general confusion of events, and, perhaps most of all, by the speed of those events in only a few short months, making difficult any longer-term prediction as to how politics would have moved had not the *coup* of April 1964 abruptly changed the political economy of Brazil. Even the role of Goulart is difficult to assess with confidence, as, abandoning his stabilization programme, he sought to reconcile sharply different political pressures, now seeming to try to control and curb nationalist critics, then trying to use them, but offering no clear solutions in a series of political responses largely compounded, it seemed, of improvisation and opportunism.

One such response came in June 1963, when Goulart dismissed the whole of his cabinet, a well-balanced mixture of able men. It included Celso Furtado, now again minister without portfolio; Almino Afonso, Minister of Labour and an energetic leader of the PTB's *Grupo Compacto*, a coherent pressure-group to the left of the party; Elieser Batista, Minister of Mines; and Hélio Almeida, Minister of Transport; as well as San Tiago Dantas, who as Minister of Finance was by now the most prominent member of the government. This sweeping change came in the wake of rising criticism of Goulart from both left and right. His nationalist critics, as represented on the one hand by Brizola, on the other by Lacerda, attacked the efforts of San Tiago Dantas to reassure United States and other interests over their holdings in Brazil. Dantas wanted to reach agreements which would not alienate foreign investors and creditors, especially in his handling of one of the biggest foreign-owned public utilities in Brazil, the American and Foreign Power Company (AMFORP). Goulart had discussed this question in Washington in April 1962 and Dantas, on taking office, had given clear assurances as to his own attitude, which was made good in the agreement announced in April 1963, giving a generous price for the holding, 75 per cent of which would be reinvested in non-utility holdings in Brazil, the rest to be paid in dollars. It was a settlement evidently aimed at assuaging foreign fears and further underlining the moderate stance of the Goulart government; but the news broke just after Dantas returned disappointed from Washington, fanning nationalist indignation and producing fierce protest from Brizola and the nationalists on the left, as well as from Lacerda and his associates, who, though later they were to work so closely with foreign interests, now seemed afraid that Goulart's and Dantas's moderate policies might consolidate the power of their old opponents, particularly in terms of the next presidential elections. Goulart would not be eligible to stand in the election of 1965, but already the leading contenders were taking up stances with an eye on the presidential campaign. Nationalism was too good a cry for Lacerda to leave to his opponents, so now he berated Goulart for paying through the nose for obsolete equipment. Goulart therefore found himself under attack from what is often described as the 'negative left' and from what, with equal justice, may be referred to as the 'negative right'.[41] This group to the right of the UDN:

> wanted at all costs to discredit Goulart's entire programme, above all, the reforms . . . These long-term enemies of the 'Vargas system' could not bear the thought that anything could be achieved under Goulart's aegis. His failure was their surest guarantee of greater electoral strength in 1965. They were, therefore, hardly a 'loyal opposition'; on the contrary, they turned to the Cassandras who warned that the President's *real* motive was to subvert the constitutional order . . .[42]

The charges that Goulart was really seeking to subvert the existing order hardly squared with his efforts, so loudly described as excessive, to reassure foreign creditors and financiers. From the left his government was seen as compromised, timid, and subservient to foreign interests: from the right it was portrayed as dangerously radical, 'anti-democratic', but equally subservient to foreign interests. In particular, there was a determined effort from the right to identify Goulart with the much sharper nationalist demands of his brother-in-law, Brizola, and with the more radical wing of the PTB, whose ideas were now being set out in a programme drawn up by the new Congressional leader of the PTB, Luís Fernando Bocaiuva Cunha. This envisaged much wider nationalization of industry and financial institutions, worker participation in industry, stricter laws on profit remittances, voting rights for illiterates, the wider use of popular referenda to gauge national opinion on sensitive issues, rural trade unions, and an effective agrarian reform, with extensive credit for those to whom land would be redistributed, but with compensation in government bonds to expropriated owners. This was no more than a proposed programme of action, not yet set out in detail, not wildly radical, and above all not endorsed by Goulart, who, rather, seemed embarrassed by the more extreme statements of Brizola and the nationalist left wing of the PTB. Brizola, after having been elected in October 1962 as federal deputy for Guanabara, with more votes than any Congressional candidate had ever previously received, was now riding high as the foremost spokesman of the more radical nationalists, though, as brother-in-law of Goulart, he was not eligible to be a candidate for the presidency in 1965. But the president was careful not to identify himself with Brizola's position. Nor could he, indeed, since much of the impassioned nationalist criticism was directed against himself and his ministers. If anything, he moved in the opposite direction, even supporting attempts to build up a parallel organization to the Communist-led CGT, the new *União*

Sindical dos Trabalhadores (UST), which was proposed by its principal organizer, Goulart's labour adviser Gilberto Crockatt de Sá, as a left-wing, but non-Communist alternative to the CGT. Many people, however, were all too ready to identify Goulart and his government with more extreme left-wing and nationalist demands, and there was, as commonly in such circumstances, the danger that the repeated charges of his enemies would stick and even become self-fulfilling prophecies.

Despite the intense pressure, Goulart, firmly in the Vargas tradition, but without Vargas's skill in circumstances as difficult as any Vargas had faced, was trying to conciliate widely different groups and maintain a system of consensus politics, as again he showed when a row flared up between his Minister of War, General Amaury Kruel, and the commander of the First Army (Rio de Janeiro), General Osvino Ferreira Alves. General Alves was one of the many officers who sympathized with both nationalist and reformist demands, standing in this respect broadly in the *tenentista* tradition of concern for social change and firmer economic nationalism, a position also comparable to that of the reformist military officers who were to take power in Peru after 1968. As a prominent officer within this group Osvino Alves was highly regarded by the CGT and by other foci of nationalist/reformist opinion, such as the UNE, the National Union of Students. In both March and April 1963 Alves clashed with General Kruel. The first time it was over Alves offering military protection to a large protest meeting which objected to Lacerda's banning of a meeting in support of Cuba. In May, after a meeting of hundreds of army sergeants in Rio de Janeiro, Kruel transferred one of their spokesmen to Matto Grosso and imposed a short term in gaol, so provoking an uproar from Brizola and his group, with whom the sergeants had sided. Alves, too, was known to be sympathetic to the sergeants' demands for wider political rights, including that of holding legislative positions. Again, these demands were not unreasonable, but Kruel, like many officers, was concerned about the potential threat to military discipline and command contained in this unprecedented political activity of other ranks. The army had always been involved in politics in Brazil, but in terms of direct, active initiative only at the level of the officer corps. Now the pattern seemed to be changing and the War Minister, already concerned at what he perceived as a growing 'Communist' threat, reacted sharply to the political involvement of the other ranks. His concern, though understandable, was in marked contrast to the lack of reaction to, for example, the political involvement and intrigue of senior military officers during the presidency of Kubitschek; but it sharply underlined the strength of feeling among many military officers at the apparent tendency to 'politicize' other ranks, and even to call in question established patterns of military command. This again was to become a serious issue in 1964, just as a decade later in Chile, appeals to 'democratize' the armed forces, especially the navy, were to be an important immediate factor in precipitating a *coup*.

Goulart once more handled the affair calmly, but he was only papering over the cracks. By May 1963 it was clear that his stabilization programme was collapsing, with the cost of living in Guanabara in the first three months jumping 25 per cent, as compared with the official target to keep inflation inside 25 per cent for the whole year. The IMF mission was clearly not impressed by the stabilization efforts of the Goulart government, arriving in mid-May just before the cabinet agreed to the 70 per cent rise for civil servants and the armed forces, finding, too, an atmosphere of heightened political excitement and uncertainty. The tensions within the government were also becoming increasingly apparent, between, for example, Dantas, still struggling to hold together his stabilization programme, and others, like the able Minister of Labour, Almino Afonso, who believed that arbitrary wage increases agreed on during Dantas's Washington visit could not be maintained. Afonso was also one of those government members committed to a more thoroughgoing programme of reform, so was unhappy about the government's uncomfortable attempt at fence-sitting, especially in relation to the CGT and the labour movement generally.

This last issue, namely the clearer political definition of the government's position, became even more cogent during May on the crucial question of agrarian reform, which also underlined Goulart's more general problem of commanding sufficient Congressional support to carry through any substantial programme of reforms. In March 1963 an agrarian reform bill had been laid before Congress, proposing compensation in government bonds. This required a constitutional amendment, which needed the support of two-thirds of Congress. It was evident that Goulart could not muster such support, above all over agrarian reform, an issue on which the landed interest in the PSD, and many in the PTB, sided with the most conservative landowners among the UDN. The Vargista coalition had depended on a working alliance between an urban electorate largely represented through the PTB and the rural interest expressed through the PSD. To open up the question of landownership was political dynamite, however urgently needed the reforms might be. Vargas had never attempted it. Goulart, by contrast, already having touched one of the most delicate political nerves by being associated with what some military leaders saw as a challenge to military hierarchy and command, was now responsible for introducing what many, both inside and outside Congress, saw as an outrageous assault on what was still the single most important source of wealth and status, the ownership and control of land and rural property. These interests were very strongly represented and expressed in Congress, heavily weighted in favour of the landowning interests from rural states and districts which were over-represented in Congress. In May 1963 a committee of deputies rejected the agrarian reform bill. Goulart was again faced with a political impasse, and further evidence, so Brizola and his supporters argued, that to hope to achieve significant reform through the existing political institutions, especially a suspicious, hostile Congress, was pure self-delusion.

Bitterly criticized, from both left and right, both at home and abroad, with his stabilization programme collapsing, his government uncertain and divided, unable to command sufficient Congressional support, and in danger of losing his base in the trade unions, Goulart had to seek a new direction. If even the appearance of consensus and conciliation were to be maintained, he could not strengthen one element in his cabinet at the expense of another: hence his decision to make a clean sweep, dismissing the whole cabinet in June 1963. But Goulart's choice of new colleagues is again worth noting as evidence of his refusal, or inability, even at this stage, to opt decisively or overtly for any one faction, and certainly not for the more extreme radical/nationalist camp or for extra constitutional solutions to the problems facing him. The Ministry of Finance, for example, the hardest and most sensitive cabinet post, went not to Leonel Brizola, who reportedly had wanted it,[43] but to the former governor of São Paulo, Carlos Alberto Carvalho Pinto, who previously had served as Secretary of Finance of the state of São Paulo, under the state governorship of Quadros. Carvalho Pinto was a well-respected, cautious financier, now a prominent member of the Christian Democrat Party, whose appointment should in no way alarm the business and financial community. The Army Ministry, on the dismissal of General Kruel, went not to General Osvino Alves, whose appointment would have indicated a firm step towards the nationalist/reformist camp, but to General Jair Dantas Ribeiro, commander of the Third Army (Rio Grande do Sul). He had been associated with Goulart and Brizola in their native state, and in September 1962 had urged the need of a plebiscite on the question of the parliamentary or presidential system, but his appointment simply suggested that Goulart wanted a well-disposed, reliable minister, rather than that he was seeking to promote extremists. Similarly, to another key post, the Ministry of Labour, he appointed as successor to Almino Afonso not another prominent spokesman for the left of the PTB, but Senator Amauri Silva, able, reliable, sympathetic to the CGT and its demands, but still a relatively obscure politician at the time of his appointment.[44] Goulart, it seemed, was still seeking to maintain a working consensus within the existing system.

Political Perception and Political Reality

But was consensus still possible, and could the existing system accommodate and survive the demands and pressures now being felt? How far, too, by June 1963 was Goulart still sufficiently in control of events, and how far did his government adequately represent the demands for change being expressed by social groups and interests previously unrepresented, or under-represented, in national politics? By April 1964 it is arguable that political *perceptions*, what people thought or alleged was going on in Brazil, were more important than the changes which really were taking place: but it is necessary to assess as far as possible what new forces and demands were now being felt, and how they were likely to change Brazilian society. Such assessment is especially necessary in so far as the fear of 'subversion', of far-reaching political change, became by April 1964 one of the most urgent rallying cries of those who supported the military *coup*.

This last point, the *political* dimension of the movement against Goulart, is crucial to an understanding of the process which led to his removal, not least in so far as the mounting financial and economic crisis was in large measure, though by no means solely, political in origin. It is true that by 1963 the first vigorous phase of import substitution industrialization was coming to an end, but the issue of inflation and, in particular, the question of foreign confidence and support, were always inextricably linked to Brazil's internal politics and to the reading of that political process by foreign creditors and financiers and by foreign governments. This reaction, in turn, influenced the attitudes of interested groups within Brazil, both civilian and military. It is not, therefore, even possible to separate for purposes of analysis the economic and political factors in the build-up to the *coup* of April 1964, especially when discussing inflation. Too often the reasons for the *coup*, and the subsequent changes in Brazil's political economy, are presented in narrowly exclusive economic terms, as if the intervention of the armed forces were merely a reaction to the inflationary spiral. In this respect it is worth remembering the conclusion of the most complete analysis of inflation in Brazil:

> . . . no compelling force stemming from structural weaknesses in the economy ever played a significant role in the persistence or

> aggravation of inflationary pressures . . . There is reason to think that the factors ultimately responsible for the inflationary process were chiefly political not economic. . . . Thus, however reluctant I may have been so far to move out of the strictly delimited field of economics, I am now irresistibly led by my search for the primary causes of inflation to make some incursion into the closely related field of political economy . . .[45]

Apart from having to struggle with sharply rising inflation, with the cost of living rising by over 30 per cent from January to June 1963, Goulart also had to contend with a very severe drop in total investment, and the collapse of the industrial growth-rate from an average of 9 per cent from 1945 to 1957, and 11 per cent from 1958 to 1961, to under 8 per cent in 1962 and virtually nil in 1963. At the same time the overall balance of payments on current and capital accounts moved from a surplus of 65 million dollars in 1961 to a deficit of 622 million dollars over the next two years. As a result Brazil, finding it difficult to obtain long-term credit abroad, had to sacrifice 136 million dollars' worth of gold reserves and take on trade debts of up to 177 million dollars.[46] These figures represent a devastating economic collapse and were certainly an important element in convincing many who on earlier occasions had refused to support a *coup* that in March–April 1964 drastic action was necessary. But such a collapse, quite obviously, could not all be attributed to Goulart and his government, since here again the political factor was paramount, especially in so far as current interpretations of the political situation produced a disastrous lack of confidence, which gave Goulart's government no chance of survival. Hence the need for more careful assessment of the political struggle in the months before the *coup*.

Reflecting on the relation between political perceptions and reality, it is clear that the gap between them could be as wide, often wider, on the left as on the right, since all contending political groups built strategies related to how they believed Brazilian politics were being shaped in the early 1960s. On the left, in particular, there was always the danger of wishful thinking, of exaggerating the strength of popular support for left-wing movements and the readiness of the country for far-reaching social change. There was a tendency, too, for certain groups on the left too readily to believe their own rhetoric and propaganda, resulting in claims of support and proposals for action which not only were self-deluding, but which, more seriously, provoked and alarmed their enemies both inside Brazil and abroad. Exaggerated, noisy claims merely played into the hands of those who were only too ready to raise the alarm over Brazil's allegedly rapid move to the left, allowing them more easily to appeal for armed intervention to preserve political and social stability. Compounding such confusion still further, some of the leading participants on the left, anxious after the event to portray themselves to an international left-wing audience as fully committed to clear-sighted radicalism in the period before the *coup*, have further exaggerated in post-1964 memoirs and analyses their degree of radicalism and, even, the extent to which Brazil by 1963 was ready for a revolutionary socialist solution. This is particularly true of some accounts of developments in the north-east, especially in relation to the Peasant Leagues, and also to certain evaluations of the urban labour movement, of the trade unions, of student politics, of groups within the Catholic Church, within the armed forces, both officers and men, and even within the Goulart government. It is important, therefore, to look more carefully at all these groups, to see to what extent the working class and its allies in Brazil were by 1963 or 1964 offering, or capable of offering, that revolutionary, socialist challenge to the existing order which many who called for the *coup* claimed was imminent, and which in later years has been offered as adequate justification for military intervention and continuing authoritarian control.

The North-East

A principal focus of attention by the early 1960s was the north-east, frequently portrayed as an area whose extreme poverty and misery could easily spark off radical political demands and movements which might then spread throughout Brazil. There was much excitement about the growth of 'Peasant Leagues' in a region whose population, with its high indices of infant mortality, disease, illiteracy, and unemployment, had always been kept under the political control of landowners. Here in the past political participation had meant, at most, to provide further support for the *status quo* through the notorious *voto do cabresto*, the 'herd vote', by which the manipulated electoral system reinforced the fabric, first, of local and regional politics, then, by extension, of the national system. Now, it seemed, the whole pattern of social and political control in rural areas was under attack as the peasants in many districts began to be organized while, at the same time, the growing body of wage-earners in the rural labour force was allowed to form rural trade unions by an extension of the rural sector of the trade union system already established among urban, industrial workers.

While these developments undoubtedly provoked much excitement, and, in some quarters, alarm amounting almost to panic, or at least simulated panic, it is still not clear how significant were either the Peasant Leagues or the rural trade unions as expressions of substantially greater political consciousness, demand, and powers of organization among the rural poor and working class. The evidence, on balance, suggests that, while these movements have to be taken seriously, and while eventually they might have produced a major change in the relation of social and political power in the rural north-east, their effectiveness by 1964 was still very limited and perhaps even diminishing. There is reason to believe that as spontaneous expressions of demand they were always weak and that by 1964 both the Leagues and the rural trade unions were coming increasingly under control from the centre, being incorporated into the more general system of 'populist' manipulation. Claims or allegations that they were poised to become the motor of revolutionary change either in the north-east or in Brazil as a whole are certainly much exaggerated, however suasive they may have been in late 1963 and early 1964.

Looking first briefly at the Leagues,[47] it is important to remember that they varied considerably both over time and from place to place, even in the north-east. In part they began as a response to a changing use of land and organization of estates, which threatened the already limited security of tenure enjoyed by the peasants, as in the case of some of the earliest leagues to be formed on the *fazenda* Galileia in Pernambuco[48] and in Sapé in Paraíba.[49] This often was associated with a swing towards cattle-farming, as in the case of Galileia, or in a change of ownership, as in the case of Sapé, where the founder of the League, João Pedro Texeira, was eventually shot dead in 1962. Among the stratified peasantry the leaders of the Leagues, as in both these early cases, were often men who had been on their land for a considerable time and held posts of responsibility on the estate, but who now were faced with the loss of their land, as happened to Zé de Galileia, the leader of the first League to be started on the Engenho Galileia of Vitória de Santo Antão in 1955.

The general background to this early development was of a region which most starkly reflected the distribution of land into very large estates belonging to a few owners and tiny holdings, often not viable, with the majority of the rural population being landless agricultural workers, dependent on the landowner. For Brazil as a whole in this period the Institute of Agrarian Reform calculated that 76 per cent of properties belonged to small landholders (*minifundiários*), occupying under 14 per cent of land registered as private property (a total of about 40 million hectares), while only 150 large landowners had private ownership of about 32 million hectares, each owning more than 100,000 hectares.[50] The dominance of this *latifúndio* system was especially marked in the north-east, where other climatic and social conditions often made the life of the rural poor even harsher and more uncertain. In the 1950s a boom in the sugar industry, resulting in the more intensive cultivation of cane, forced many subsistence farmers from their plots in the *zona da mata*, the coastal belt, a process also quickened by the growth of cattle-farming and by other changes in the system of producing and marketing foodstuffs, essentially consisting of a more rationalized system to produce food for urban markets.[51] The peasant found himself subjected to still further strains and demands both as agrarian producer and as a consumer of manufactured goods, with his real income declining. The little security of tenure and the system of provision and support through his *patrão* which formerly he had known were now being threatened.

Even within the north-east, itself a very large area, conditions varied sharply from one region to another, while, in terms of the organization and development of Brazil's rural population as a whole, the north-east provided no easy guide or paradigm. What, therefore, may be said of peasant associations in the north-east may not hold good for others in, for example, Bahia, Minas Gerais, or Santa Catarina. Within the north-east, however, one of the most important distinctions is between developments in the three main geographical zones, the *zona da mata*, the coastal, mainly sugar zone, the *agreste*, an intermediate zone of mixed cultivation, and the much drier *sertão*. Very few Leagues were established in the *sertão*, relatively few in the *agreste*, and by far the most in the *zona da mata*, the most heavily populated of the three zones.[52]

The nature, aims, and significance of the Leagues varied over the period of almost a decade from the start of the Galileia League till the *coup* of 1964. The early organization was distinctly *ad hoc*, working under names such as The Farmers' and Cattle-Breeders' Association of Pernambuco, seeking to provide seeds, fertilizers, and tools within the context of an agricultural co-operative, and noting other immediate requirements, including that of a decent burial for peasants' children. The aims were scarcely radical, far-reaching, or overtly political, not even demanding implementation of laws already passed, such as that requiring a minimum rural wage, which remained ignored.[53] At the beginning some landowners seemed well disposed towards the Leagues, but, becoming alarmed at the potential threat they contained, quickly reacted with evictions and the use of violence. The Leagues' aims then widened over time as it became evident that the peasants had little chance of redress through a legal system largely designed to protect the interests of the landlords. Their attempts to work through the law explains, on the other hand, their approach to lawyers such as Francisco Julião, already experienced in rural litigation and already set on a political career.

There are important distinctions to be made between those Leagues which largely worked under the guidance of Julião, those which were organized by priests and Catholic activists, and those whose leading members belonged to the Communist Party or other political groups. One reason for the persistent image of the Leagues organized by Julião as important sources of revolutionary challenge is that after the *coup* of 1964 Julião presented himself as much more radical than previously he had done.[54] The same image, however, was built up before the *coup* by exaggerated reports in both the Brazilian and foreign press, stressing the 'Marxist' and revolutionary content of the Leagues.[55] This image is not supported by the stated aims of the Leagues or by a cooler assessment of their leadership, including Julião. One general aim, common to all Leagues, was the diffuse one of awakening in the peasantry a sharper social and political consciousness, making the peasant think and act for himself, making his life more 'human'.[56] This general aim, it is true, had far-reaching implications:

> The goal implied profound changes, it was a challenge to the whole sugar society of Pernambuco. An 'awakened' peasantry would have weakened the control of the landed elite in the economic and political sectors as well as in the judicial system. It would have meant raising the status of peasants in all sectors of society—giving them dignity, not just better wages . . .[57]

An 'awakened' peasantry would, inevitably, make far greater demands on north-eastern society, changing long-established patterns of social relations between the peasant and landlord; but these relations, in any case, were being changed by precisely those forces within the economy of the north-east, especially in the *zona da mata*, which had first produced the Peasant Leagues. In particular, the organization of the peasantry might threaten the control and social position of the *senhor de engenho*, the plantation-owner and sugar-producer. Changing relations between the *senhor de engenho* and the *usineiros* (the mill-owners) meant that in effect the *senhores de engenho* were becoming no more than middlemen in a system in which the *usina* could, if necessary, deal directly with, for example, a peasant co-operative, cutting out the *senhor de engenho* altogether. Any attempt, therefore, to 'awaken' the peasantry was certain to produce sharp reaction.

More specific aims appeared over the years, though not all were shared by the different kinds of Leagues, even within the north-east.

One formulation of aims by Julião, in 'The Ten Commandments of the Peasant Leagues for the Liberation of the Peasant from the Oppression of the Latifundia', demanded comprehensive agrarian reform, including progressive land tax and compensation in bonds for land expropriated,[58] and there was general agreement among all the Leagues on the need of some kind of land reform. This was clearly stated after the First National Congress of Farmers and Agricultural Workers in Belo Horizonte in 1961, but still only in vague terms, attacking the monopolistic control of land and the need of access to land by those who wanted to work it: 'No group seems to have had a clear blueprint for a functioning agrarian reform program . . .'[59] There were, however, some specific points of agreement. These included the abolition of *cambão* (the provision by the peasant of a day's free labour every week to the landowner)[60] and the right to rent land at a just price, with some security of tenure. Other aims related more closely to the paid rural workers and rural trade unions, for example, the recognition of such unions by the Ministry of Labour, an increase in minimum wage, the provision of social security for rural workers, and the election through the rural *sindicato* of a delegate from every *engenho*. Other demands were wider still, notably the enfranchisement of illiterates.

None of these demands could be regarded as extremely radical, except perhaps within a long-established tradition of repression and control, in a world where *any* attempt at self-help and improvement of conditions on the part of the peasantry was regarded as outrageous. Nor were most of the demands, as expressed, for example, at Belo Horizonte, generated by the Leagues of the north-east. The conference of 1961 showed, rather, how relatively little weight those Leagues had at the national level, to what a large extent Julião, in particular, was primarily a north-eastern regional politician of limited appeal, and to what degree already the demands of rural workers and peasants were being absorbed into national 'populist' politics.

The local, north-eastern character of Julião's appeal is especially worth stressing, even if one accepts that its wider aim was to seek a springboard into national politics.[61] Julião was himself a *latifundista*, a lawyer specializing in agrarian litigation, and already a state deputy when he became associated with the Leagues. His rhetoric was entirely of the north-east, as seen in the title of his 'Ten Commandments' and his persistent appeal to such 'revolutionary' exemplars as Jesus Christ and St Francis of Assisi. Despite his visits to Cuba and China he had virtually no knowledge of Marxism: he had read Mao Tse-Tung, but only, it seems, his poetry. His main relationship with the Communist Party was one of mutual suspicion and distrust, in competition rather than alliance for local political leadership, with Julião insisting from the start on priority for peasant associations, while the PCB stressed the need of organization and legal standing within a union system, appealing mainly to paid workers.[62]

At the grass-roots level, too, the Leagues were much less formidable than often they are portrayed. Most of the leadership, whether in the Julião Leagues, or those organized by the Church or by the Communist Party, came from outside, with relatively little participation, still less leadership, on the part of the peasantry. The Leagues organized by the Catholic clergy were often conceived as a force to counter a 'Marxist' movement in the countryside, with the more positive content stemming from vague, generalized social encyclicals, such as *Mater et Magistra.* The social content of church involvement was, for the most part, still couched within its traditional concepts of conciliation, limited reformism, and rejection of any essential notion of social or class confrontation, still working, therefore, within the traditional social and ideological framework of the north-east. There were some marked exceptions to this rule among clergy who challenged the current role of the Church, especially its links with the *latifúndio* system, but such forces were not yet strong, and certainly not dominant, by 1964.[63]

An obvious difficulty in assessing the *potential* of the Leagues as vehicles for far-reaching change, including the mobilization, active participation, and even leadership of the peasantry, is the very short time they existed and within which they could organize and develop, less than a decade in all, in a region and social milieu in which organization was notoriously difficult. It is arguable that the landowners, in their quick, predominantly hostile, often violent, reaction, were right to perceive a radical threat in *any* attempt to mobilize the peasantry, for almost any reason, arguing that once this took place, the north-east would never be the same again.[64] It is certainly true that already by the time of the *coup* of 1964, which ended any chance of effective action and participation by the peasantry, there was evidence that the peasants were throwing up their own leaders, so that the provision of leaders from outside the peasantry might only have been the first phase of a more autonomous peasant movement. A further sign of the increasing political importance of the peasantry was precisely that urban politicians and lawyers should have thought it necessary or opportune by the mid-1950s to cultivate peasant support as part of their political base.

But how the Leagues might have developed, although such prognosis was a powerful motive of political action at the time, remains a matter for conjecture. Most of the available evidence, in any case, runs in the other direction, suggesting that already by the eve of the suppression of the Leagues their principal leader, Julião, was more interested in a career in federal politics, now having been elected as federal deputy, that leadership more generally was still weak and uncertain, the movement ill-defined, and increasingly being drawn into the wider pattern of national politics, more open to manipulation from the centre. The peasant political movement in the north-east was perhaps more united than before, with the Federation of Rural Workers, sponsored by the Church, joining with the more militant Catholic group Ação Popular, and both coming closer to organizers from within the Communist Party and the Goulart government. Some agreement was reached in October 1963 at a meeting in Rio de Janeiro which founded a national confederation of agricultural workers (CONTAG).[65] But such developments further absorbed the Leagues into a system directed from the centre, with particular losses to the church-directed Leagues:[66]

> The Goulart government commanded both the monetary and the legal resources to inhibit independent action within the rural labour movement and to force unions into a national confederation fully controlled by the government.[67]

This link with the centre was, however, in many respects a great advantage for the Leagues, providing important access to federal support and to the sources of state power. The relative loss of local control was, in this sense, a small price to pay for central government help based on a wider, stronger political organization, which now passed on to the peasants some of the gains being won first for the urban, then for the rural paid workers. Again, while more benefits went to the paid workers organized in the rural trade unions, and while peasant organizations were rarely consulted in the formulation of new legislation or agreements, 'the existence of peasant organizations made it easier for the government to enforce its program against the opposition of large landholders'.[68]

Much the most important point, however, in assessing the significance, especially the 'revolutionary' content or threat, of the Peasant Leagues as one factor leading to the 1964 *coup*, is that by the time of the *coup* they already were being incorporated into the wider national system of politics. They are to be judged, therefore, not in isolation as the spearhead of revolution, starting in the north-east, then spreading through Brazil, but as only one element in the overall pattern of reformist, 'populist' politics in the period leading to the *coup*.

This feature of the development of the Leagues is reflected in their most dramatic success in the last months of 1963, working in alliance with the rural unions. In October 1963 the Federation of Rural Workers, largely stimulated by Catholic leaders, most notably Padre Antônio Melo from Cabo, Pernambuco, began a move to increase the minimum wage of rural workers, by 80 per cent. The move came against a background of concessions to rural workers from the Goulart government, especially the Rural Labour Law, finally passed in March 1963, after having been first presented to Congress in 1951. The statute gave powerful stimulus to the rural unions, providing for their payment of the *impôsto sindical*, for job security, holiday rights, and wider educational opportunities for workers' children, being followed in November 1963 by a decree extending social security to rural workers. There would obviously, as in the case of urban workers, often be a wide gap between legislation and social practice, but the new laws were further proof of the Goulart government's concern to work with rural labour, heightening expectations throughout rural Brazil. The statute also imposed severe limits on rural workers, requiring conformity to strict bureaucratic controls and explicitly forbidding the use of funds for political purposes, including strikes.[69] To a large degree, therefore, it represented an attempt on the part of the Goulart government to maintain or assert control of rural unions and peasant groups, a phenomenon regularly found in populist regimes throughout Latin America, and beyond.[70] At the same time it was further proof of the need of the government, and of politicians generally, to look for support among rural workers, especially among the paid rural labour in the more developed areas of the centre-south, since, as the Belo Horizonte conference had shown, the main weight of rural political demand, despite all the excitement about the north-eastern Peasant Leagues, lay in the south and centre-south of Brazil.

Within this increasingly favourable legal and political context the Federation of Rural Workers began its demands in October 1963, working with Ação Popular and calling on the Leagues and the Communist unions to help. Negotiations with the *senhores de engenho* and the *usineiros* soon broke down and on 18 November there began a general strike of paid workers in the sugar industry, ending after three days with the employers' promise to raise the minimum wage by 80 per cent and to make other concessions,[71] affecting about 200,000 rural workers. Many employers subsequently ignored this agreement,[72] but the strike was perhaps the most telling evidence so far of the growing effectiveness of north-eastern rural labour, especially the rural unions working in conjunction with the Leagues and other groups. Again, however, it showed the Leagues working not as a revolutionary or violent force in the north-east, but, increasingly, as part of a broader movement, linked through the rural unions to the wider political demands expressed by urban labour in association with the Goulart government. To the extent that the Leagues were being absorbed in *trabalhista* politics at the national level they were both strengthened by their access to state power and patronage, and, arguably, depending on one's interpretation of Goulart's 'populism', weakened in their autonomy and made more open to manipulation from the centre. Whatever their potential for challenge in the long term, however, they certainly did not present the wild, extreme challenge to law, order, and due authority ascribed to them both by conservative interests in the early 1960s and in much subsequent justification of the *coup* of 1964.

The End of Consensus: June 1963–March 1964

By the middle of 1963 there seemed to be few people in Brazilian politics who were able to make a cool, reasoned assessment of the relative weight of the contending social forces and political groupings. Rumour fed on rumour in an atmosphere of rising excitement and uncertainty with growing evidence, right across the political spectrum of a lessening confidence in the government, or even in Goulart's ability to hold the system together. From June onwards there appeared an increasing polarization of politics, with political rhetoric replacing hard analysis, leading to, and feeding on, a series of sharp, much dramatized political crises, all of which further eroded Goulart's credibility and control. The new cabinet was hurriedly put together, reinforcing the impression of uneasy adjustment to immediate pressures, while, more seriously, the government's economic policy was now seen to be in ruins, shattered by the high salary increases the president was forced to make, significantly enough, to the armed forces and the civil service. There was a growing sense of a government drifting uncertainly, while, worst of all, Goulart was now virtually forced into a series of moves which weakened his own political base, strengthened his enemies, and made ever slimmer his chances of serving his full presidential term.

One case of this was his relations with the PSD over the question of agrarian reform. This element in the traditional Vargista alliance continued firmly opposed to any far-reaching change in relation to rural property-holding or to any tampering with the social and economic basis of their own local prestige and political influence. There was resistance, in particular, to proposals in the government's programme to pay for expropriated property in government bonds, and to the compulsory renting of land which was not being used productively. This was an issue on which some agreement could perhaps have been found, as PSD leaders hinted in July 1963, suggesting amendments to the proposals made to Congress. But, as they stood, these amendments were much too conservative, protecting, for example, properties of under 10,000 hectares, only making clearer how deeply rooted was the unwillingness of Brazilian landowners really to take seriously the ever louder demand for some measure of genuine land reform. Goulart, aware of the strength of such demands, turned down the PSD amendments, evidently in the hope of winning larger concessions by relying on less intransigent representatives of the PSD, men such as the governor of Minas Gerais, Magalhães Pinto, who saw, at least, the electoral value of supporting a more serious agrarian reform programme. But in a markedly conservative Congress the weight of opinion against such reform was too great, so that when PSD members joined with representatives of the UDN in voting on the project in October, the government's programme was soundly defeated by 176 votes to 121.

The agrarian reform programme, like most of the issues concerning basic reforms currently under discussion, should normally have been renewed, returned to Congress, and become part of the debate already growing in relation to the presidential election of October 1965. It was an issue on which a reformist government might expect initial defeats, but hope to come back more strongly in future. But in Brazil by late 1963 such rational procedures were becoming ever more difficult. The right, especially those close to Lacerda, portrayed the demand for agrarian reform as the thin end of the wedge, the start of an attack on all private property. For many on the left the failure of Congress to pass the reforms, including the constitutional amendment needed to allow compensation in bonds, was evidence of the acute difficulty, even impossibility, of achieving adequate changes through the existing political system. There was talk of appealing, as on the parliamentary issue, to a plebiscite, with moves to mobilize popular opinion through a widely-based Frente de Mobilização Popular (Front for Popular Mobilization). This Front never got much beyond the stage of political rhetoric, but provided welcome backing for those enemies of Goulart, and of the whole Vargista tradition, who again could point to the alleged growth of popular, 'subversive' extra-Congressional forces, a rallying cry which was finding growing support in both military and civilian circles.

In terms of his own political base Goulart was now caught in the contradiction which had been evident right from the start in the 'populist pact', namely, the sharp difference of basic interest between the landowning, heavily agrarian block of the PSD, still deeply locked in the net of rural clientelism, and the more urban, popular, and more reformist character of the PTB. This contradiction, at the heart of every multi-class populist alliance, whether in Brazil or elsewhere, could be seen as the tension between the mobilizing elements of populism, with a necessary measure of reformism, and its controlling, co-opting elements, those features of populism which allowed it to work as an effective mechanism of social control. Unfortunately, in so far as Goulart's populist movement could become a genuine vehicle of popular demand and class challenge, or even to the extent to which, albeit unwillingly, it was pushed along and outstripped by popular pressures, the tensions between the PSD and PTB, as well as between different strands *within* the PTB, would inevitably become more severe. These were contradictions which had never appeared in a serious way during Vargas's lifetime, but by 1963 they were acute, too strong for Goulart to contain, or even to be reconciled within that political system which largely was Vargas's creation and of which Goulart was now the confused, harassed head.

From the start of his presidency Goulart had, in particular, played a strange game with the trade unions, the core of his political base. While accepting Communist support, he had always been apprehensive of their growing control within the trade union movement and the challenge they offered to his own PTB. As head of the state apparatus he was, too, the target against which strikes, especially in the public sector, were directed, and yet the nominal leader of the forces directing those strikes, a position which became even more anomalous as the unions found themselves after 1961 part of the highest directing mechanism of the state apparatus. Stranger still was the phenomenon, still too little investigated, of the Goulart government, through this close relationship with the state, needing some measure of hostile strike action to foster its own policies. This, again, is a pattern found elsewhere, but in Brazil of the 1960s, as subsequently in other societies, it served further to quicken fears of a *república sindicalista*, one in which organized labour might wield excessive political power.

The situation both within Goulart's coalition and outside was at best a delicate one, but, as with the PSD on the issue of agrarian reform, the president by mid-1963 now found himself squeezed by opposing forces, with events running ahead of him. An enigmatic, still shadowy figure in Goulart's dealings with the unions was his adviser on union affairs, Gilberto Crockatt de Sá, whose main job in recent years had been to build up a countervailing force against the influence of the Brazilian Communist Party, mainly centred in the União Sindical dos Trabalhadores (UST). Crockatt de Sá claimed, unconvincingly, that this was 'an absolutely spontaneous movement',[73] but it seems to have been organized deliberately, with

Goulart's approval, as a 'neutral' force within the unions. By August 1963 Goulart no longer felt it wise to divide the union movement, appealing instead for workers' unity to help push through the basic reforms whose importance he now stressed. De Sá, however, remained resolutely anti-CGT, as he showed in the brief 'general strike' in São Paulo in October 1963, raising further doubts on the left of the labour movement over Goulart's own position. Such doubts were now increasingly being expressed by Leonel Brizola, who was applying strong pressure for Goulart to move further and faster to the left.

These strains came to a head in October 1963. In a deteriorating political situation Goulart was at odds with the governors of São Paulo, Adhemar de Barros, and of Guanabara, Carlos Lacerda. Both were charging the president with being the tool of the labour movement and of 'Communists', and publicly criticizing the government in such a way as to encourage plots to remove Goulart from office. There were rumours of plans on both sides to seize or kidnap the president and, conversely, to arrest Lacerda and Adhemar de Barros. Goulart was advised, from various quarters, that to secure public order, to defuse criticism of his dependence on more extreme labour groups, and to gather enough strength to push through his policies he needed special powers, and that he should call on Congress to declare a 'state of siege', initially for thirty days. But such powers could, obviously, be used for many purposes, to strengthen the reformists against opponents such as Lacerda and de Barros, or to curb the unions and the growth of popular demands, and neither side sufficiently trusted Goulart. Many in the PSD were already alarmed over the talk of special powers to put through agrarian reform, while the PTB, mistrustful of the support for the 'state of siege' from Goulart's military leaders, were afraid that these special powers might be used to stifle rather than promote social and economic reforms. Miguel Arraes in Pernambuco was especially apprehensive that he too might be removed. The CGT, despite Goulart's pleading, threatened a general strike; the head of the PTB in Congress, Bocaiuva Cunha, first supported, then opposed the request, and Leonel Brizola, again after initial support, also turned against the idea. On 7 October, only three days after asking Congress for the state of siege, Goulart had to withdraw his request.[74]

The failure to win Congressional support for the 'state of siege' showed how difficult was Goulart's position. Unable to hold together his stabilization programme on a quasi-voluntary basis, he had had to give in to the crippling wage demands of the civil service and the armed forces. Unable to win sufficient PSD support, he had failed to put through even his early tentative plans for agrarian reform.

Now it was becoming clear that even the PTB and his supporters further to the left, though unable to carry enough weight in Congress, were also unwilling to trust Goulart with special powers to strengthen the executive. A situation was being reached, it seemed, in which the growing demand for reform was being blocked within the formal political system, while at the same time there seemed little or no chance, at least constitutionally, of short-circuiting that system. April 1964 was to see an end to that deadlock, but in a very different way from that envisaged by Goulart and his supporters.

It would be wrong, however, to see the central issues of Brazilian politics by late 1963 mainly in terms of political institutions or the capacity of the political system to contain divergent or contrary demands, or, still less, in terms of Goulart's personality and his relations with both his supporters and his enemies. The party structure and political system were not the product of chance or historical accident, but of a long political process determined by conflicting social forces. If the parties and Congress still remained weak vehicles for the expression of group or class interests, this was simply part of the whole pattern of 'populist' politics, imposed from above to be as much an instrument of social control as of popular mobilization. If the political system was inadequate to reconcile conflicting demands, this was in large part because of deliberate decisions over the past two decades or more by those who controlled that system, by, for example, excluding the Communist Party from party politics and by refusing the fuller participation of other sources of social challenge. The political system, in other words, whatever its weaknesses, was not God-given, but the creation of those who had shaped and controlled it in recent decades, an important point to remember in relation to explanations of the *coup* of 1964 which see it as an almost inevitable response to the structural weaknesses of Brazil's post-war political system.

The contending class interests became even clearer as the political crisis deepened between late 1963 and late March 1964. In particular, it now can be seen that those around Brizola, the left of the PTB and their allies, were to a large degree justified in their fear of granting special emergency powers to the president. Not only were the reasons for his request ambiguous, stemming mainly from his military advisers, but, as seen from the left of the political spectrum, it came at a time when civilian and military reaction to change was building up rapidly. There were many centres of this reaction, some of which could be traced back many years among opponents of Goulart and the whole Vargista tradition. Often there was little communication between these various elements,[75] but, as so often in Brazilian politics, the most important centre was in São Paulo.

Civilian leadership, as in the 1932 resistance to Vargas, was gathered round the *Estado de São Paulo* and the Mesquita family, implacable opponents of all which they believed Vargista politics to represent, pulling together business, industrial, and financial interests, as expressed, for example, in IPÊS (Instituto de Pesquisas e Estudos Sociais; Institute of Social Studies and Research). Founded in 1961, this was mainly an organization of *paulista* businessmen to oppose Goulart and his alleged 'leftist' programme, collaborating with all anti-Goulart groups, such as the Instituto Brasileiro de Ação Democrática (IBAD), organized in the 1962 elections,[76] and increasingly with military opponents of the regime. These, too, were scattered throughout the country, but were allowed an extraordinary free rein, as, most conspicuously, in the case of General Olímpio Mourão Filho. Nearly three decades earlier, as a young captain deeply committed to the *Integralista* movement, Mourão Filho had furnished the Cohen Plan, the supposed 'Communist plot', used to justify the introduction of the *Estado Novo*. As head of the 3rd Infantry Division in Santa Maria, Rio Grande do Sul, he had openly advocated Goulart's removal, which he did even more rigorously as commander of the 2nd Military Region in São Paulo after February 1963. Between then and August 1963, when he was transferred to command the 4th Military Region in Juiz de Fora, Minas Gerais, Mourão worked intensively to co-ordinate both military and civilian opposition in São Paulo. He was at first widely regarded as a rather unbalanced right-wing extremist, but his movement grew steadily stronger, not even pretending to secrecy.

Although this gathering of anti-government forces was important and understandably alarming for those on the left, it was in itself less serious than the steady shift of support from the broad centre of Brazilian politics, both military and civilian, a movement which gathered speed from late 1963 onwards. In military circles this move away from Goulart gained important stimulus from the sudden revolt in September 1963 of a group of sergeants and non-commissioned officers in Brasília. In itself the revolt was insignificant, occasioned by the refusal of the Supreme Court to allow non-commissioned officers, if elected, to sit in Congress. The revolt broke out early on 12 September and was over in a few hours. There seems evidence that it was sparked off by anti-Communist agents who had infiltrated the leadership of the movement of NCOs[77] and it seems that most of the few hundred men involved had no clear idea of what they were doing.[78] It was a limited protest action on a specific issue, rather than a serious, co-ordinated attempt to take power and introduce a left-wing regime. But it was eagerly seized on by the right as further evidence of a growing subversive conspiracy between groups in the armed forces and the trade unions as represented especially by the CGT.

That such views exaggerated the strength of the unofficial CGT was seen in October 1963 during the abortive 'general strike' in São Paulo. Many workers ignored the CGT's strike call and after only four days the stoppage was over, serving mainly to show the increasing readiness of the army and Força Pública to intervene against the workers, arresting hundreds of them as the strike was declared illegal. The principal achievement of the strike was, ironically, to push more military officers towards favouring intervention against Goulart, especially when he sided with the strikers and replaced the commander of the Second Army, General Pery Constant Bevilaqua, with General Amaury Kruel. There was now growing concern on the left over the hardening of military opposition, an anxiety which the president himself seemed to share as he made other changes in senior military posts to ensure continued loyalty to the constitutional government.

Pressure was building up on Goulart from all sides and in the closing months of 1963 he entered a tangled series of negotiations which on present evidence seemed mainly designed to hold the political system together by preventing in particular an open breach between labour leaders and senior military officers. This hope already lay behind his support, however wavering, for efforts by Crockatt de Sá and others to develop a viable, non-Communist, or even anti-Communist, union movement, mainly through the UST. These moves were still under way, with a renewed campaign against the CGT and with an all-out effort by those who were behind the UST to win high office in the elections of the CNTI, the official national confederation of industrial workers, with its membership of about one million. The intrigue and counter-intrigue became intense and, while many of the details still remain obscure, the efforts, of which already there is evidence, to buy off important labour leaders and directly influence the CNTI elections are an indication of how many diverse groups, not all located in Brazil, were now fishing in the troubled waters. But some leading trade unionists refused to be bought, and publicly denounced the inducements to make them side with the UST. They vigorously attacked Goulart's temporizing and what they saw as his betrayal of the labour movement and the rising demand for basic reforms. In January 1964 the CNTI elections confirmed the position of more left-wing trade union leaders. Most of them were associated with 'radical nationalism', with the PCB rather than with groups further to the left, but this in itself was evidence that the efforts behind the UST had not been successful, and was certainly enough to provoke further alarm among military officers already subjected to a barrage of propaganda from the right.

The gap between such alarmed reaction and the nature and significance of this 'radical nationalist' leadership in the CNTI must be stressed, not only because of its importance in 1964, but because confusion about it has persisted in later years. The CNTI leadership, as confirmed in the elections of January 1964, did *not* represent, in any strict sense, a victory for the Communist Party, and certainly not for revolutionary communism as presented by those who used the election results as further evidence of the spread of subversion in Brazilian labour politics. The leadership reflected, rather, a broad front or agreement within the labour movement, principally concerned with issues of wages, jobs, and working conditions. When the Communist trade unionists were successful in winning office, this was not only because they worked hard to do so, but because the aims they proposed found widespread sympathy among the mass of workers. The PCB programme was principally concerned with short-term improvements, with wages and welfare legislation, fitting easily into the demands of other political groups and organizations of industrial workers. The main charge against the party from the left, both in 1964 and later, was indeed that the PCB had abandoned any genuinely revolutionary strategy it might have had, a charge which could readily be substantiated within the logic of revolutionary thinking.

It is, moreover, dangerously misleading to harp on the PCB links or associations of this CNTI leadership, often in language evocative of revolutionary purpose, even when at the same time due note is taken of the lack of revolutionary content in CNTI and even PCB strategy and demands. One study, for example, discussing the CNTI elections says that

> Elected in early 1964 were pro-Communist Clodsmidt Riani (President), former Communist Dante Pelacani . . . (Secretary General), São Paulo Communist leader Luís de Tenório Lima . . . (Secretary for Organization), and Communist sympathizer deputy Benedito Cerqueira . . . (Secretary for Social Security).[79]

In other words, only one of these four men was an active PCB member, the others having to be described as 'pro', 'former', or 'sympathizer', but with the obvious danger that these others, both in 1964 and in later accounts, become 'guilty by association'. This danger is then increased by the repeated use of evocative language, noting Communists 'penetrating' the labour movement, with 'its cadres . . . entrenched in the labour movement',[80] even when describing the PCB objective as:

> a coalition of workers of Communist, PTB, socialist, Catholic orientation to work toward containing the high cost of living, toward a readjustment of salaries, toward social welfare legislation and labour reorganization.[81]

Communists were certainly active and influential in the organized labour movement, and there were 'pro-Communist leaders' and 'pro-Communist segments'.[82] But how 'pro-communist' is 'pro-Communist', and, in terms of the PCB in 1964, how revolutionary is 'Communist'? The evidence available strongly suggests that, as in many other Western industrialized societies, the PCB had abandoned the idea of direct revolutionary action in favour of a strategy of seeking more gradual change in alliance with organized labour. Excluded since 1947 from the official party system, Brazilian Communists could only exert influence indirectly through the labour movement, but then only by offering a programme acceptable to the broad mass of trade unionists who, while wanting improvements in wages and conditions of work, were not Communists or even sympathetic to many of the wider aims associated with the Communist Party.

If, however, there was no immediate danger of the revolutionary subversion against which right-wing propagandists solemnly warned, there was emerging by January 1964 a serious crisis within Brazil's political system, not structural, in the sense that the political institutions could not work, but rather socio-political, in that too many people either believed the system could no longer work adequately, or were unwilling to make it work. Goulart now found himself increasingly isolated, with no firm Congressional base, but without special powers to circumvent Congress. He was aware that conspiracy against himself and his government was spreading, but realized that he was also steadily losing ground among the more 'nationalist' military officers and those who previously had held to a 'constitutionalist' or 'legalist' position.

With virtually all groups in national politics trying to short-circuit the formal political system, Goulart followed suit, deciding on a direct appeal to the mass of the Brazilian people for support in pushing through a programme of 'basic reforms' which he now began to outline more clearly, and which he also hoped in part to implement by the fullest use of the powers which the executive already possessed. From now on he was, in effect, giving up as lost all attempts at conciliation, relying instead on the more radical, or apparently radical, elements in his broad multi-class coalition. It was not a path he had wished to follow, being forced along it as all other routes were closed; but in doing so he played right into the hands of his enemies. In this sense, the political system may be said to have broken down at the start of 1964 rather than in March or April, not so much as a result of Goulart's malice or inability, as of the pressure generated by those who opposed both him personally and the social forces and demands which they understood him to represent. Over the next few weeks the situation deteriorated rapidly, so that in the end many people accepted, if they did not support, the *coup*, mainly in the hope that a viable political system might again be restored. The reason, and blame, for the breakdown rested, however, less with Goulart than with those groups, both in Brazil and abroad, who did not scruple to sabotage the political system when their interests appeared to be in danger. The weeks from early January to the end of March merely allowed them to win extra support from both civilians and military officers whose backing of the *coup* was no more than a reluctant grasp at what seemed a last straw.

The measures which Goulart proposed to push through were not in themselves very radical, but they touched issues which were both socially and politically sensitive. One was the bill on the remittance abroad of profits made in Brazil, a question which had been left in abeyance since September 1962. The bill determined that remittances could not be calculated to include reinvested profits which now were defined as 'national capital'. Goulart's signing of it in January 1964 was a political gesture of defiance, offering, as many believed, too little too late, at a time when foreign investment already had virtually dried up. There was a similar symbolic content in the decree now prepared to allow expropriation of land within ten kilometres of certain federal development projects, alongside roads, railways, and dams and irrigation projects. These new proposals, hurriedly prepared in collaboration with SUPRA (Superintendency for Agrarian Policy), could be of very limited application, and still avoided the basic issues of more far-reaching agrarian reform and compensation. Their importance was immediately political, part of Goulart's more defiant stance, fitting, like his attacks on certain rulings on concessions in the mining industry and on the workings of private oil refineries, into the wider political pattern of a more dramatic, direct appeal to the people, over the heads of Congress and politicians.

What Goulart can have hoped to gain by this new political tactic is still not clear, and perhaps its most striking quality is that of bewildered desperation, growing stronger in the first three months of 1964. He seems always to have been determined not to encourage or sanction political violence as a means to achieve his ends, yet, paradoxically, his increasingly emotional appeals and heated rhetoric gave exactly the opposite impression. So too did the appeals of Brizola for the organization of 'nationalist commandos', or Groups of Eleven Comrades (Grupos de Onze Companheiros).[83] These were to be, essentially, cells which would prepare to resist reaction and apply pressure for reforms, a call which was echoed in Brizola's new weekly, *O Panfleto*. Here again was political rhetoric rather than effective organization, since the Groups never became, or seemed likely to become, the vehicle for mass organization as apparently conceived by Brizola; but they gave further credibility to those who warned of the rapid shift towards subversion and disorder.

Prominent among those who both gave such warnings and, it seemed, were most ready to act on them were the principal representatives of the United States government and business interests in Brazil, who had always viewed Goulart with scarcely disguised hostility.[84] By early 1964 most foreign business and financial groups had already voted with their feet, leaving a country in whose government they had no real confidence, so further lessening Goulart's chances of survival. This was the usual flight of capital and business in such circumstances, needing no conspiracy theory to explain it. But in the relations between the representatives, both direct and indirect, of the United States and the Goulart government there was more than mutual suspicion and mistrust. The new United States ambassador, who arrived in Brazil just after Goulart was inaugurated, was Lincoln Gordon, a man already familiar with Brazil, a former Harvard professor, who had written on the Brazilian economy and whose experience as an aid administrator and links with the Kennedy team made him an influential representative of his country. Till mid-1963, while Goulart was genuinely seeking to be conciliatory, relations with Goulart, and through him with the United States government, remained at best cool, but with some apparent chance of improvement. There was talk of Kennedy visiting Brazil and an understanding that more aid would be given if the Brazilian government could begin to solve its economic problems. But already the suspicion towards Goulart in the United States was hardening into hostility. In March 1963 Gordon, before the House Foreign Affairs Committee, testified to the growth of Communist infiltration in the labour movement, student organizations, and even the government,[85] and the belief now grew stronger that the country was moving fast towards the left, into a position inimical to United States interests. There was growing fear that the Alliance for Progress, widely seen as a substitute for more far-reaching radical movements, would falter in Brazil, and, in the climate of fear and antagonism following Castro's victory in Cuba and the confrontation of the missile crisis, United States policies hardened still further.

Sugar Mill, Pernambuco:
Rugendas 1827
Rugendas was one of a series of foreign artists whose detailed work provides a rich source for nineteenth-century social history, especially slavery

The Emperor Pedro II (1825–91)

(Top left) Coffee pickers, São Paulo, about 1910. Many workers on these plantations were Italian immigrants. Their labour was also vital to the rapid development of São Paulo's industry and commerce

(Left) Wealth from Amazonian rubber built the magnificent opera house in Manaus, but did little for these three generations of rubber collectors, pictured with their total possessions

(Above) *Coronelismo*, the system of 'boss' politics, used social and economic patronage, backed by coercion, to maintain and reinforce political control. In modified form the process still continues

Rui Barbosa (1849–1923), firm opponent of military involvement in politics

Luís Carlos Prestes. Having seized the imagination of Brazilians in the 1920s, Prestes, as the leader of Brazilian communism, was forced to spend most of his life abroad

Getúlio Vargas (*right*), Góes Monteiro (*left*), and Gustavo Capanema. It was mainly under Góes Monteiro that the federal army in the 1930s became the most powerful element in the state apparatus

Vargas and Oswaldo Aranha.
Aranha, the principal organizer of the 1930 revolution, was an outstanding cabinet minister and one of Brazil's most imaginative and internationally respected statesmen

Kubitschek (*right*), Jânio Quadros, and João Goulart at the inauguration of Quadros, with the military in the wings

AO PRESIDENTE JUSCELINO KUBITSCHEK DE
OLIVEIRA, QUE DESBRAVOU O SERTÃO E ERGUEU
BRASÍLIA COM AUDÁCIA, ENERGIA E CONFIANÇA, A
HOMENAGEM DOS PIONEIROS QUE O AJUDARAM
NA GRANDE AVENTURA.

(Top left) The bust of Kubitschek de Oliveira in Brasília. The inscription reads: 'To President Juscelino Kubitschek de Oliveira, who tamed the sertão and raised up Brasília with boldness, energy, and confidence. A tribute from the pioneers who helped him in this great adventure'

(Left) The homes of some of the 'pioneers', with Brasília in the distance

The Itamaraty, or Ministry of Foreign Affairs, Brasília

(Left) Quadros, Costa e Silva (*right*), and Carvalho Pinto (*left*)

(Bottom left) Quadros and Ché Guevara, August 1961

A peasant leader in Galileia, Pernambuco, José Francisco de Sousa. On the wall of his home, with, significantly, an oleograph of the Sacred Heart and a report of the Peasant League, is a picture of Francisco Julião

João and Maria Teresa Goulart at the mass rally of 13 March 1964

Castello Branco, a speech or
taking office, April 1964

Roberto de Oliveira Campo
The principal architect of
economic planning after 19
his far-reaching Ten-Year P
was abandoned by the Cost
Silva government

Antônio Delfim Neto, Minister of Finance under Costa e Silva and Médici. Praised, and criticized, for promoting the 'Brazilian model', he left office just as the strains were becoming most apparent

General Geisel takes over the presidency from General Médici, March 1974

Football in the Minerão, Belo Horizonte. The passion for football and World Cup success were particularly used by the Médici regime in an attempt to win popular support

Carnival: the parade of the 'Samba School'. Sambas sing not only of sun, sand, and sex, but of poverty and protest; so often have been censored

São Paulo. The heart of Brazil's vigorous industrial development and the centre of the conspicuous consumption integral to the 'Brazilian miracle'

The Ilha Solteira works in the Urubupunga complex, R. Paraná, part of Brazil's great advance in harnessing its vast hydro-electric potential

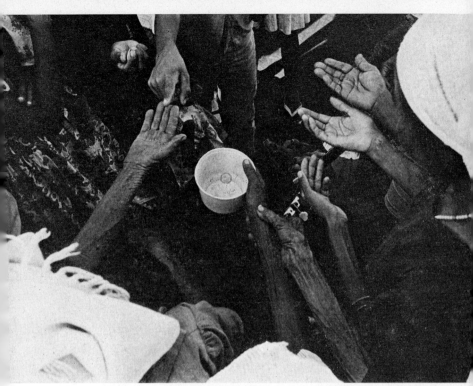

(Top left) Construction of nuclear power station, Angra dos Reis. Brazil is fast developing its nuclear energy capacity, especially urged by the need to find energy resources other than oil

(Left) 'Looking in'
Endemic hunger in the north-east forces many to beg, especially children, the old, and the sick

(Above) 'Hands'
The outstretched hands of the poor, a picture from north-east Brazil

Dom Helder Câmara, Archbishop of Recife and Olinda. One of the most vigorous defenders of the poor, he symbolizes the persistent tension between the Church and the regime

'Esperando, esperando . . .' Children in Ceará. What does their future hold?

Often these were based on the belief that North American advisers knew better than the Brazilians themselves the direction their politics were taking, as an AID director for the north-east put it: '. . . we were in a very serious political situation; we thought that the Communists were going to run all over the place. That was uppermost in our minds . . . Furtado said that SUDENE only needed capital. They did not see their problems as clearly as we felt we did'.[86] The United States now began to look for 'islands of sanity' within the Brazilian political system, co-operating more closely with individuals and groups who might oppose or halt Goulart's move towards the left in collaboration with 'Communists'.[87] The United States embassy was well informed of the growth of the movement against Goulart, and made no secret of where its own sympathies lay.

The more difficult question is how far agents of the United States, official or otherwise, actually provoked and assisted the removal of Goulart. There is no doubt that those planning the *coup* were encouraged by knowing that such a move would have the approval of the United States embassy and would find swift recognition and financial and other support. There was especially close liaison between the senior military officers preparing to overthrow Goulart and Colonel Vernon Walters, the United States military attaché, who was an old friend of General Castello Branco, having served with him in Italy; but Walters was only part of a larger team who were all kept informed of the development of the anti-Goulart movement. The consul-general in São Paulo, Niles Bond, was close to the São Paulo governor, Adhemar de Barros, and to other plotters in São Paulo: 'United States officials were in some cases, such as that of Bond, present in the command posts of the Revolution'.[88] Information was not, in fact, difficult to come by, since even the Goulart government knew much about the plotting,[89] but United States officials were exceptionally well informed, even discussing with leaders of the military movement the possibility of giving arms and direct help, if necessary.[90] Once the *coup* had occurred, the United States not only moved with almost embarrassing speed to recognize and welcome the new regime, but, again, mainly it seems, through Colonel Vernon Walters, was influential in the choice of Castello Branco as the new president. Castello Branco's case was vigorously and swiftly urged by Carlos Lacerda, who swung the other important state governors behind this choice, but who also kept in close touch with the United States embassy all through the critical discussions:[91]

> Lacerda had moved so quickly in articulating the choice of Castello that rival movements never really got off the ground . . .

Castello, a close friend of United States Military Attaché Vernon Walters, was clearly the candidate most preferred by the United States Embassy, and Borges claims that Lacerda received at least two calls from Ambassador Gordon during the governors' meeting.[92]

Ambassador Gordon and his staff later claimed that, despite these very close ties with the opponents of Goulart both before and immediately after the *coup*, the movement itself was entirely Brazilian, explicable simply in terms of internal political forces whose workings were discernible in the whole post-war period,[93] and that, in particular, when he emphasized that 'Neither the American Embassy nor I personally played any part in the process whatsoever', he included the CIA in that statement:

> Yes. In the Brazilian situation, whatever may have been the case in other countries at other times, there was no lack of coordination and there is none, among the C.I.A. personnel, the military attachés, the political officers of the Embassy, the AID mission, the USIS mission, and the Ambassador. This was and is all one team.[94]

These claims have a fine ring to them, but need, at the very least, severe qualification. Apart from evidence of close collaboration with and support for the plot against Goulart, it has to be remembered that virtually all the arms and equipment which the senior Brazilian officer rightly said was enough to overthrow Goulart and counter possible resistance came from the United States, supplied as part of a deliberate policy to build up the armed forces of Latin America to counter precisely the sort of move towards 'subversion' which allegedly was taking place in Brazil. There was no need for the United States to supply arms in 1964: they had been supplied steadily over many years. Nor, similarly, was there great need for any direct, immediate participation in or direction of the *coup* from the United States embassy, since throughout the post-war period the United States policy had been to develop and strengthen 'anti-Communist' and 'pro-American' ideology among Brazilian military officers and personnel, an aim most effectively achieved in the Escola Superior de Guerra. The tight intertwining of the Brazilian and United States military establishments since 1945 assured exactly the type of reaction which occurred in 1964, again reducing the need for cruder, direct interference.

There still are reasons, however, to suspect that more immediate, direct involvement by the United States did occur, even if there is not yet available the clear, unambiguous evidence to be found in other societies, in analogous situations, throughout the 1960s and early 1970s. The Brazilian case remains obscure, not yet illuminated by revelations of former CIA agents, even those who have written about Latin America, since this evidence has come mainly from Spanish America.[95] It is known that at the time of the *coup* the United States had contingency plans linked to Operation Brother Sam, mobilizing a naval carrier task group off the Brazilian coast close to Santos.[96] The purpose of this naval force was 'to establish a U.S. presence in this area when so directed and carry out such additional tasks as may be assigned'.[97] The force was made up of petrol tankers, reflecting the Brazilian military's preoccupation about oil and petrol supplies in an emergency,[98] but there was also a strong force of helicopters, and there were instructions to 'sail necessary replenishment forces as required'.[99] Preparations were also made to supply arms and ammunition from the Ramney Air Force base in Puerto Rico, from Fort Dix and McGuire Air Force Base:

> C.S.A. (Army Chief of Staff) will prepare and ship 100 S/T small arms/ammunition MARKED BROTHER SAM in support of USCINSCO OPLAN 2–61 to arrive MCGUIRE AFB NLT 011200 EST for onward movement as directed by JCS. Procedure of SM–1090–62 apply.[100]

It was, however, made clear that

> The 110 tons of arms and ammunition will be kept in McGuire Base until Ambassador Gordon shall decide whether the Brazilian military forces or the police forces of the State will need the anticipated American help.

The task force with its aircraft-carriers should continue towards the South Atlantic till the ambassador should declare that a visit to Brazilian ports or other American demonstrations of naval strength were definitely not required. Only that part of the political movement should be maintained which the ambassador thought essential to the current situation.[101] In the end Ambassador Gordon decided that these contingency plans need not be put into operation, but that all was going smoothly.[102]

The persistent United States version of its role in the movement against Goulart is that there was no deliberate 'destabilization' such as occurred elsewhere, most conspicuously in Chile.[103] It is clear that substantial sums of money were spent on helping Goulart's opponents both in 1962 and later, some of it coming through United States–Brazilian firms and some, in the case of CIA money, coming through phantom companies, used simply to channel CIA funds.[104] The United States government and embassy also made clear where their sympathies lay, with Ambassador Gordon convinced that Goulart had as his models by early 1964 Vargas and Perón.[105] The distinction between direct involvement in and heavy responsibility for the *coup* is, in any case, a fine one. By 1964 the cruder forms of 'destabilization' used elsewhere were not, as events showed, really necessary in Brazil. The United States, particularly through the close personal and ideological ties between its military officers and those of Brazil, and the close intertwining of business and financial interests, had long made preparation for handling the kind of threat perceived to be offered by Goulart. The naval and military presence held in readiness at the time of the *coup* was not needed: the much longer strategy and preparations proved to be adequate.

The Military *Coup*

As the first weeks of 1964 went by, it became increasingly clear that the opposition to Goulart was being better orchestrated and becoming more effective. The sergeants' revolt in Brasília had already shown the presence of agents provocateurs, who in various forms were also active in disorders and harassment of politicians associated with Goulart at public meetings in São Paulo and Minas Gerais. There were protests and even physical assaults at meetings held by, for example, Miguel Arraes, Almino Afonso, João Pinheiro Neto, and Brizola, with growing resistance from women's organizations such as the União Cívica Feminina in São Paulo and from similar groups in Minas Gerais, notably the Mobilização Democrática Mineira, protesting in particular at plans to hold in Belo Horizonte a meeting of CUTAL (Central Única de Trabajadores de América Latina), a trade union organization said to be 'Communist controlled'. The sharp, well-organized resistance to this plan from predominantly middle-class women, with usually only the most slender involvement in politics, and by poorer women brought along by their priests,[106] suggested the workings behind the scenes of those forces who in Chile at the same time were conducting massive anti-Communist campaigns among similar groups, producing demonstrations which anticipated the 'March of the Empty Pots' a decade later by ladies who had themselves rarely had to clean a pot.[107] Other demonstrations in São Paulo were infiltrated by, often mainly composed of, the police of Adhemar de Barros, but the overall effect was to create the impression of swelling public impatience with the Goulart government, and to produce public statements from the police chiefs, voicing doubts, real or otherwise, as to their ability to maintain public order for much longer.

In examining the immediate build-up to the *coup* most accounts stress what appear as two significant turning-points, the large rally of Goulart supporters in Rio de Janeiro on 13 March 1964 and the sudden mutiny of sailors from 25 to 27 March, both of which had the principal effect of further alarming and inciting the right. The rally was to be the first of several large demonstrations of support for Goulart and his reform programme, with others planned for May Day in São Paulo and for Belo Horizonte late in April. It was mainly organized by the CGT with the participation of other groups, such as the UNE, the CNTI, and the FPN. The CGT organizers seem to have been nervous about unleashing a flood of rather wild radical-sounding rhetoric, being keenly aware of the danger of a right-wing backlash. However, the rally went ahead, with Brizola, after some hesitation, included among the speakers, and on a hot Friday night there was a noisy, colourful gathering of about 150,000 people, waving banners and shouting for reform. The fears of the CGT organizers now were shown to be justified. Early in the meeting it was announced, to loud cheers and applause, that Goulart had just signed the SUPRA decree concerning the expropriation of land within ten kilometres of federal roads, railways, and water projects, and, after several other speakers, Brizola launched an attack on Congress for having failed to respond to the people's demands for reform, calling instead for a constituent assembly with more popular membership, transferring power to the people.[108] The SUPRA decree, as earlier noted, was not very radical or far-reaching, not even starting to tackle the deeper issues of land reform, but it was widely seen as the thin end of the wedge and fiercely resented by landowners throughout the country.[109] The manner in which it had now been issued seemed precisely to confirm that the shift from Congressional to popular power for which Brizola was calling was already taking place.

Goulart arrived on the platform, accompanied by his beautiful wife. Much already had been made of the fact that this was the same platform from which Vargas had spoken to the Brazilian workers, and Goulart now recalled the 'extreme sacrifice' to which Vargas was led by a false 'democracy', not the democracy of a free regime linked to the people, but the 'democracy' which was against the people, anti-reform, anti-trade union, favouring instead the privileged, the national and international monopolies, based in hatred and intolerance. His speech was a vigorous attack on those who claimed that he, by meeting the people in this way, was endangering democracy, and who used the worst kind of anti-Communist mythology, and abused Christian feeling, to mislead and deceive the people.[110] He referred to recent papal encyclicals to show another concept of Christianity and social responsibility, and to General MacArthur's efforts for land reform in Japan, rejecting the idea that land reform was always 'Communist', while also reminding his audience, both those present and those watching television, that military leaders could be associated with programmes of reform. This point, on which he ended, noting with satisfaction that 'we can count on the patriotism of the brave, glorious Armed Forces', seemed reinforced by the presence of military ministers as well as trade union leaders on the platform.

Having already noted how Goulart from late 1963 onwards was being forced into short-circuiting the formal political system and into direct appeals to the people, it is nevertheless important not to identify, even at this late date, in March 1964, Goulart's position with that expressed by Brizola in his speech on the same occasion. The overall picture is still unclear, but its interpretation may become severely distorted by seeing Goulart as now finally abandoning all hope of achieving reform through constitutional means, so appealing directly to the people for support for radical, extra-constitutional measures. Though a common view,[111] this may be going too far. The president in his speech criticized the constitution as being out of date and promised reforms, but these, including votes for illiterates, legalization of the Communist Party, wider legislative powers for the executive, and provision for holding more frequent plebiscites, were all to take the form of amendments to the constitution, which—a crucial point—he said he would lay before Congress. Nowhere in his 13 March speech did Goulart assail Congress in terms similar to those of Brizola, whose more extreme denunciations may also have been, in any case, more a means of applying pressure on Congress than an assault on its continued existence.

This difference of emphasis is critical to an understanding of Goulart's strategy in these last weeks, but, for various reasons, it seems better to see the rally of 13 March as part of a strategy still to work *within* the system than as a first step to ending it. It should be remembered, for instance, that the rally was planned to take place just three days before the opening of the regular session of Congress, that Goulart talked of referring the proposed constitutional amendments to Congress, and that he then immediately flew to Brasília to do just that. He issued new decrees on his own initiative, changing the regulations on the renting of housing, and increasing by 100 per cent the salaries of government personnel, both civilian and military; but his main effort was directed towards regaining Congressional support, trying especially to move the PSD behind a wider programme of reforms, especially agrarian reform.

This interpretation of Goulart's behaviour gives him more credit for political insight and sense of realism than does the view of him abandoning established processes and appealing wildly to the people. Both he and his advisers had enough sense to know that such appeals must be empty, since, short of producing violent demonstrations in the streets, there were no clear alternative channels for the organized expression of popular demands. He also knew well enough the reaction he might then expect from the leaders of the armed forces, whose support, as he indicated in his 13 March speech, was indispensable.

If, however, Goulart was gambling on sufficient popular pressure to push Congress into accepting further reforms, his gamble failed. The *Estado de São Paulo* carried on the same day, with heavily obvious inference, photographs of Hitler, Mussolini, and Castro speaking to mass rallies, while, even as Goulart was speaking, women in São Paulo publicly recited rosaries to keep Brazil free of communism. Goulart's critics unanimously interpreted the rally as a further step towards a 'Peronist' appeal to the people, with Lacerda attacking the meeting in *Tribuna da Imprensa* and *Jornal do Commércio* as 'an assault on the constitution, the pocket and the honour of the people'. Goulart's speech was 'subversive and provocative, as well as stupid. I believe Congress should rise to defend what remains of freedom and peace in the country. Then the Armed Forces will understand what the people already felt . . .'.[112] The SUPRA decree was interpreted as sheer 'confiscation, . . . violation of the most sacred juridical and constitutional traditions'.[113]

One immediate, but scarcely spontaneous, reaction, again categorizing the 13 March rally as a move towards communism, was an enormous march in São Paulo six days later, the feast of St Joseph. The organization was impressive,[114] mobilizing support much as in 1932 against Getúlio Vargas, resulting in a 'March of the Family with God for Liberty' in which roughly three times as many people as had attended the rally in Guanabara now marched from the Praça da República to the Praça da Sé, to the cathedral in São Paulo. It was an occasion for all anti- Goulart forces to gather, using appeals so familiar to right-wing mobilization, to country and liberty, family and God, excluding, by implication, from all such values those whose social philosophy was different from that of the demonstrators. Adhemar de Barros and his wife helped the organizers and the March was attended by, among others, Lacerda, by Moura Andrade, President of the Senate, who recently had attacked the SUPRA decree, and by Nelson de Melo, Goulart's former Minister of War, who now had turned against him. Shops were closed, the excitement intense, with the band of the Civil Guard playing 'Paris Belfort', the anthem of the 1932 constitutionalist revolt, all ending in a mass for the preservation of democracy. Other Catholic groups in the city, such as Brazilian Catholic Action, deplored the identification of Catholicism and Christianity with a particular political faction. The Cardinal of São Paulo shared this view, and many devout Christians were shocked at what they felt was the exploitation of shallow religious emotionalism by narrow political interests. But the March was seen as a great success by its organizers, and a regular series of similar demonstrations was planned for cities throughout the whole country.

Much more seriously for Goulart, the movement against him was now gathering speed, partly influenced by adverse reaction to the meeting of 13 March. Lacerda was working ceaselessly to build up the anti-Goulart alliance, holding discussions with Adhemar de Barros after the March, and reporting to journalists the closer agreement between São Paulo and his own state of Guanabara, hinting that Rio Grande do Sul, under its governor Ildo Meneghetti, would also stand firm, then leaving for Belo Horizonte to speak with the governor of Minas Gerais, Magalhães Pinto.[115] Here being rebuilt was the alliance which Vargas's enemies had sought to forge after 1930, between Rio de Janeiro, São Paulo, Minas Gerais, and Rio Grande do Sul, an alliance which then had failed when Flores da Cunha in Rio Grande do Sul had stayed loyal to Vargas, and when, above all, the federal army under the influence of Góes Monteiro had supported the central government. Now, unfortunately for Goulart, the alliance was hardening against him. Magalhães Pinto issued a statement which echoed the earlier Manifesto of the *mineiros* against Vargas, accepting now the need of reforms, but warning against using that need as a justification for disorder, and ending with a call to the armed forces: 'We expect from the Armed Forces a clear and coherent attitude. The law makes them not the defenders of factions within the country, but of the whole nation'.[116]

Already there were signs that these calls were being heeded. On 18 March ex-president Eurico Gaspar Dutra broke a long public silence to give an interview to the *Jornal do Brasil*, stressing the importance of the constitution, and warning that: 'Nothing good can come from a climate of disorder, and it is impossible to come through democratically a period of subversion'.[117] Two days later no less a figure than the Chief of General Staff, General Castello Branco, circulated a 'secret' memorandum, the contents of which were soon leaked to the press. He referred to growing anxiety following the rally of 13 March and to pressures on the armed forces to accept developments which would be against the interests of the country, the nation, and the people ('antiPátria, antiNação e antiPovo'). He warned that the armed forces could not be expected to support full power for trade union groups whose leadership lived by subversive, and expensive, agitation, or stand by and see the nation submitted to Moscow communism.[118]

This intervention by Castello Branco was a very important boost to the anti-Goulart movement. Castello Branco was one of the most respected senior officers, generally regarded as able, moderate, responsible, and a man who had always kept politically at a distance from the pro-*coup* faction within the officer corps. During the war he was Chief of Operations for the FEB. After the war he became Director of Courses at the Command and General Staff College, then in 1955 he was made Commandant of that College. In these posts, and as Subcommandant of the ESG, he carried much weight both among his military colleagues and civilians associated with the ESG. Under Goulart he took over from General Costa e Silva as Commander of the Fourth Army, till he was made Chief of Staff. What, however, was not known when his memorandum was issued in March 1964 was that already in late 1963 he had agreed to join those planning a *coup* against Goulart, on certain conditions. He had become increasingly anxious over the growth of what he believed was a movement of subversion, and more ready to listen to those already preparing to oust Goulart. These now included old friends and colleagues of Castello, such as General Golbery do Couto e Silva, who now was acting as chief of the 'research group' of IPÊS (Institute of Social Studies and Research), which already had 'dossiers . . . on all groups or public figures considered Communist or otherwise "subversive" . . .':[119]

> Marshal Adhemar de Queiroz, a close friend since academy days, and other senior officers committed to the *coup* worked hard to convince the scholarly general that the military should prepare to block subversion of the country's basic institutions . . .[120].

They found that he had been in contact with the UDN leader Bilac Pinto since the preceding March, concerned at the way Goulart was moving: 'This concern had deepened with the subsequent crises . . . and by late 1963 Castello had agreed to assume military leadership of the *coup* . . .'[121] This commitment seems to have been conditional, namely, that a move would only be made if Goulart looked like acting illegally, by closing Congress or attempting to stay in power beyond his term, or if he threatened the country's basic institutions. This memorandum of 20 March suggested that Castello Branco believed this danger was now increasing.

These press statements and the memorandum were warning shots for Goulart, who still, however, was insisting that he was simply being guided by popular democratic pressure applied on the nation's political institutions and Congress. Speaking on 18 March in Itabapoana in the state of Rio de Janeiro, the president stressed this position in reply to his critics:

> Nothing is more legitimate in an authentic, genuine democracy than that the people should exert pressure democratically on political institutions, on the President and Congress, so that these should be sensitive to their just demands and responsive to the people's feelings, because the people is the soul of democracy and the source of democratic power.[122]

A key issue was the position to be adopted by the Second Army in São Paulo. Goulart was being assured by General Argemiro Assis Brasil, the *gaúcho* chief of his military household and associate of the retired 'Red Marshal' Osvino Ferreira Alves, that his *dispositivo militar* was secure and that he could depend on the loyalty of the armed forces. But, as the Castello Branco memorandum had shown, this loyalty was not unconditional, and already the leaders of the anti-Goulart movement in São Paulo were putting strong pressure on the commander of the Second Army, General Amaury Kruel. This fell, at one level, into a general pattern in which São Paulo business and financial interests, both before and after 1964, tried to exert influence on the Second Army commander, often successfully; but now with IPÊS and other groups so active the pressure was intense, since:

> . . . The government and opposition alike realized that as long as General Kruel and his São Paulo-based Second Army remained firm for legality, the regime was essentially secure from any threat from the right, since this powerful force could not only control the situation in the country's industrial heartland, but also counter a Minas Gerais-based revolt . . .[123]

General Kruel as Minister of War had already made clear his opposition to communism and his fear, in particular, of any development which might subvert military discipline. In March and April 1963 he had disagreed openly with the commander of the First Army, Osvino Ferreira Alves, over allowing mass demonstrations in Guanabara, and had issued a memorandum warning Goulart of the direction in which Brizola and the unions were moving. Kruel was especially alarmed over the politicization of sergeants and NCOs, transferring to a remote posting in May 1963 Sergeant Gelsi Rodrigues Correia, who had played a prominent role in a large political meeting in Rio de Janeiro of NCOs, representatives of the CGT, and nationalist politicians. He had been dismissed as Minister of War in the general cabinet change in June 1963, but only to be given command of the Second Army after the short-lived general strike of October 1963. He was appointed to succeed General Pery Constant Bevilaqua, when it was thought that Bevilaqua was becoming too much influenced by anti-Goulart conspirators, including Adhemar de Barros, Nelson de Melo, and Cordeiro de Farias. Similar pressure was now being put on Kruel, whose appointment to São Paulo had been sanctioned by General Assis Brasil, who still was reassuring Goulart about the armed forces' loyalty.

By March 1964 Kruel was becoming more uneasy over the line being followed by Brizola and the CGT, expressing doubts about the rallies being planned to follow that of 13 March, especially the massive gathering which the CGT hoped to organize in São Paulo on 1 May, which they hoped might number one million. He was also critical of Goulart's plans to give the suffrage to enlisted men and to allow NCOs to be elected to political office, expressing the same fears as he had a year earlier of the danger to military structure and discipline. These fears were now greatly increased by the sailors' meeting of 25 to 27 March 1964.

Military involvement in Brazilian politics was until the Goulart administration almost exclusively limited to officers or retired officers,[124] but over the last few years pressure had been growing for a 'democratization' of the armed forces and fuller participation in national politics for sergeants and enlisted men. It had been this issue which had sparked off the sergeants' revolt in Brasília the previous September and now in March 1964 a new crisis involving military hierarchy and discipline pushed many of those officers who, like Kruel, were wavering into final opposition to Goulart. The immediate source of the trouble was the Associação dos Marinheiros e Fuzileiros Navais (Association of Sailors and Marines), a group which then was celebrating its second anniversary. The Association expressed solidarity with workers in Petrobrás, with congratulations on the recent presidential decree affecting private oil refineries, and held rallies demanding better working and living conditions and wider political rights. The demands in themselves were moderate, ranging from simple political participation to changes in the rules concerning the sailors' right to marry and wear civilian clothes when off duty.[125] The context in which these demands were made was, however, by now explosive, with echoes, deliberate or otherwise, of the sailors' participation in the Russian revolution, including the Ministry of Education's showing of *Battleship Potemkin* to a sailors' organization, with commentary to draw relevant parallels, just a few days before the mutiny broke out.[126] There was also growing liaison between the sailors and marines and the trade unions, with meetings held in Radio Mayrink Veiga, the station most used by Brizola, and in the offices of the Bank Workers' Union, seeking trade union and workers' support for the demands of the other ranks.

The Minister of the Navy, Admiral Sílvio Mota, appointed the previous June, was sympathetic to many of these demands, but alarmed at their extension into civilian politics and, still more, at the implied challenge to naval discipline.[127] On 24 March he ordered that eleven leaders of the Association should be imprisoned for ten days, but was immediately faced on Wednesday, 25 March, with a huge meeting of 2,000 sailors in the centre of the Guanabara Metalworkers' Union, a meeting supported by the CGT. This was the Wednesday of Holy Week, 1964, and Goulart was already leaving Rio de Janeiro for a break in Rio Grande do Sul, after having refused to take strong action against the sailors' Association.[128] Goulart was anxious not to have to make a public choice between support for the sailors, backed by the CGT, and their officers, now loudly insisting that military discipline be restored. At the moment of acute crisis, therefore, he left for his ranch in São Borja.

At the crowded, noisy meeting in the Metalworkers' Union building there were present five of the eleven Association leaders ordered to be imprisoned by Admiral Sílvio Mota. They included the president of the Association, Corporal (Cabo) José Anselmo dos Santos, who, despite Goulart's absence, addressed himself to the president, asking him to receive the greetings of the 'povo fardado', the 'people in uniform',[129] and stressing that it was not subversive to defy archaic regulations, ask for courses for sailors and marines, for medical and legal assistance, or visit Petrobrás. 'Is it subversive to invite the President of the Republic to meet and talk with the people in uniform?' The speech had strong echoes of Goulart's of Friday, 13 March, contrasting the alleged and the real subversives, namely, those allied to hidden forces which led one president to suicide, another to resignation, those who tried to prevent Jango from taking office and now opposed 'basic reforms'. It was a short, powerful speech, demanding social reforms, asking for Congressional support (a point worth noting), and expressing solidarity with members of other branches of the armed forces. In its contents and demands it was not a radical, still less subversive, appeal: but the fact that such a speech could be made at all, and in this particular context, brought a storm of angry reaction.

While the meeting was still in progress, it was reported that the Minister of the Navy had ordered the arrest of its leaders. On hearing this, those present decided to remain in session till the end of the month. This led to a force of forty marines being sent next day, Thursday, 26 March, to impose control, but most of these at once joined their comrades in the Metalworkers' Union centre. There seemed here to be all the elements of a major military and political confrontation. The Navy Minister at once dismissed the commander of the Marines, Admiral Cândido Aragão, who had taken a soft line with the sailors in the union centre, and the building was surrounded by several hundred soldiers backed up by tanks. There were further negotiations. The CGT declared its support for the sailors, calling for a general strike throughout the country, and Brizola on his way to Rio Grande do Sul spoke in support of the right of association for sailors and marines.[130] As the soldiers, now supported by a new contingent of marines under Admiral Luís Felipe Sinai, confronted the hundreds of sailors and marines in the union building, there seemed an imminent danger of bloodshed.

It was at this point that Goulart returned from São Borja, with General Assis Brasil, early in the morning of Good Friday. After urgent discussions in Laranjeiras Palace he ordered that no attack should be made on the assembled sailors and marines, but, when a further group of about one hundred sailors tried to leave their ships at the Ilha dos Cobras to join their companions in the union building, the order was given to open fire as they crossed the bridge opposite the navy ministry and four sailors were wounded.[131] The Naval Minister already had offered his resignation and now negotiations with the sailors were carried out by the labour leaders acting for Goulart, the Minister of Labour, Amauri Silva, and Osvaldo Pacheco and Dante Pelacani of the CGT. Shortly after midday on Friday the sailors were transported in lorries from the union building. A new Minister of the Navy had already been appointed, Admiral Paulo Mário da Cunha Rodrigues, a man acceptable to the sailors whose revolt now precipitated the final moves against the Goulart government.

The naval mutiny was exactly what was needed to dispel any further doubts and hesitations among officers of all services. It raised in the sharpest possible manner the two issues on which the officer corps was most adamant, the fundamental need to maintain military discipline and order, and the avoidance of the long-dreaded *república sindicalista*, the state in which the power of organized labour, whether officially through the trade unions or unofficially, as through the CGT, would directly determine actions and policies well outside the labour sphere. In this respect the role of CGT leaders in settling the naval mutiny was counter-productive rather than otherwise, since senior officers viewed with deepest alarm this further evidence of the influence of a body, the CGT, which was both unofficial and closely linked to the PCB, the party many officers held in deepest mistrust. This alarm was further increased by reports, well-founded or not, that the name of the new Minister of the Navy, da Cunha Rodrigues, had been proposed by the CGT in consultation with the mutinous sailors and marines.[132] Here was the tail wagging the dog with a vengeance, especially when the new minister freed the rebellious sailors and reinstated as commander of the marines Admiral Cândido Aragão.

The naval mutiny was such a well-timed, well-placed blow to Goulart that inevitably it led to speculation as to whether, as in the case of the sergeants' revolt in Brasília the previous September, it was influenced and its course directed by agents provocateurs infiltrating the ranks of the rebels.[133] Despite much rumour there seems, as in the story of the *coup* generally, no clear direct evidence of this, but for Goulart's enemies it was, indeed, just exactly the development they wanted. The active plotters against Goulart, who already had been assembling arms and were ready with a plan of action, could now claim that he had stepped outside the law by not taking much firmer action in this crisis.[134] There were in fact no good grounds for this assumption. The 'mutiny', as such, was no more than a defiant gathering of sailors and marines, staying stubbornly in a trade union centre in Rio de Janeiro and insisting on demands which could only be seen to be extreme in the context, first, of an antiquated, authoritarian tradition in the internal workings of the Brazilian navy, and, secondly, in the explosive political climate of Brazil in March 1964. Goulart's reaction, if at first apparently irresolute, was in fact conciliatory, avoiding what could easily have been a bloody outcome, and certainly not taking him outside the law. The use of labour leaders, the apparent acceptance of the sailors' nomination for Navy Minister, and the failure to side unequivocally with the naval authorities were all intensely provocative to many senior officers, but in no sense amounted to a 'sanctioning of indiscipline and disorder'.[135]

Without having to accept the rather pious explanations of some of those plotters who for years had resisted Goulart, and later claimed that the naval mutiny was the last straw,[136] there is no doubt that it provided the perfect occasion for the *coup* and did push into definite opposition some who previously had been uncertain or even loyal to Goulart.[137] The press emphasized the threat to military discipline, and so to national security, contained in the mutiny. The *Jornal do Brasil* stressed that: 'The armed forces were all—we repeat, all—damaged in that which is most essential to them, those fundamental requirements of authority, hierarchy, discipline and military respect',[138] a theme taken up by other leading papers, notably the *Estado de São Paulo*, and given a central place in a manifesto handed to the new Minister of the Navy by four admirals on Saturday, 28 March, signed by twenty-seven of the most senior officers in the navy.[139] This described the mutiny as an action by a few men unrepresentative of the majority, warned against the threat from communism,[140] and described the president's action in freeing the sailors as 'inadmissible and unequivocally illegal'. This manifesto was followed by another, from the Navy Club after an excited meeting on Easter Sunday. It, too, stressed the breach of fundamental discipline, but also rejected charges that Brazilian naval personnel were treated badly:

> Its lower ranks are treated as well as, or better than, in any other navy. Its men are generally recruited from underdeveloped parts of the country. The navy turns them into specialized technicians, useful not only to the service, but to themselves and the country, and offering them the chance to become officers, even admirals . . .[141]

The Clube Militar offered similar comment, warning against subversion from Moscow, and it now seemed that the ranks of the armed forces were closing against Goulart. Some politicians, labour leaders, and military officers still loyal to the president were keenly aware of the danger, and tried to argue that the mutiny was not primarily political;[142] but their voices were drowned in the general clamour of military indignation.

The stage was now being prepared for revolt, with Goulart's opponents coming out more openly against him. In Minas Gerais the governor, Magalhães Pinto, issued a Manifesto to the Brazilian People, backing the naval manifestos and promising the support of Minas Gerais to restore 'constitutional order'.[143] Other state governors made similar statements[144] and Goulart consulted anxiously with General Amaury Kruel on Easter Saturday, 28 March, to be told by the São Paulo commander that the government had entered the dangerous stage of disparaging military discipline, and that the president should take positive action to restore confidence.[145] The advice Goulart was receiving from other quarters was more reassuring, as General Assis Brasil still reported that the president could depend on the army,[146] which, despite the hostile noises of senior naval officers, was the service whose support was crucial to either side. Unfortunately, Assis Brasil, like some other military and civilian advisers close to Goulart, was no longer sufficiently in touch with events.[147] Plans for a *coup* were now a matter of public debate, as the leaders of the CGT pointed out, in growing alarm, on 30 March in a note of support for Goulart,[148] stressing how reactionary forces were now organizing publicly and scandalously, and pointing in particular to the state governors, Lacerda, Adhemar de Barros, Magalhães Pinto, and Ildo Meneghetti, all supported by *golpista* officers of the Second and Third Armies and the Força Pública of Minas Gerais. The note ended with an appeal to all workers, in cities and in the countryside, to be ready to launch 'a general strike in defence of democratic freedoms'.

Others close to Goulart insisted on the need for him to speak out and do something to calm military feeling. He was due to speak on 30 March at an anniversary celebration in the Automobile Club of the Association of Sergeants and Non-Commissioned Officers of the Military Police, a commitment many felt he should not now keep, or which he should at least use to heal any breach with senior officers.[149] The president was accompanied by his whole cabinet, received by an enthusiastic crowd outside and a packed gathering in the club. There were loud cheers for the Marine Commander Aragão, for Cabo Anselmo, and the elected 'Deputy-Sergeant' Antônio Garcia Filho, in a riotous meeting televised or broadcast throughout the country. Various speakers condemned the use of military discipline as 'a damned whip to enslave the Brazilian people', and the exploitation stemming from 'imperialist foreign capital and national and foreign trusts'. Deputy-Sergeant Garcia Filho proclaimed that alien and reactionary sources of control would no longer halt the 'irreversible march of progress and the establishment of social justice'.[150] It was this theme, too, which Goulart took up. He assured his audience, both in the club and listening throughout the country, that he would attend to the just demands of the sergeants, reminded them that legislation to improve their situation was already going before Congress, then emphasized that:

> the current crisis was provoked by a privileged minority which lives with its eyes turned to the past and fears to face up to the bright future which will be open to democracy by the integration of millions of our fellow countrymen into the economic, social and political life of the nation, freeing them from poverty and ignorance.[151]

Goulart attacked those who now, as in 1950, 1954, 1955, and 1961, sought to provoke a crisis, opposing reforms 'with the arms of calumny, subversion, and lies', and he stressed:

> I want, at the side of the people and the country's armed forces, to carry through these basic reforms . . . The sergeants of Brazil

> must now be more than ever united and more disciplined, in that conscious discipline which is founded in mutual respect between those who give orders and those who take them.[152]

The speech was a bold, brave effort to maintain popular support, especially that of other ranks, while offering sufficient reassurance to an officer corps concerned about military discipline and command; but it contained more concessions to reformist demand than some of his advisers cared to see. Goulart, as distinct from his performance on 13 March, seemed tired and uncertain, despite the cheers: 'On the 31st the general impression was that the speech of President Goulart . . . had not achieved its aim, namely, to rally on behalf of the government the support of the armed forces'.[153] In many cases the effect was the contrary, to present Goulart again as endorsing the challenge to discipline and the defiance of military and civil order. Among those listening to the speech on the wireless was General Olímpio Mourão Filho in Juiz de Fora. Though his plans for military action were already well developed, he was waiting for further support, both civilian and military. Now hearing Goulart's speech, he decided to wait no longer, and gambled that, once the military revolt was under way, others would follow his lead. Early in the morning of 31 March he made his move. Goulart, meanwhile, in Rio de Janeiro was gambling that in a crisis the armed forces would remain loyal to him, a gamble which the next few hours would show to be ill-advised.

The most important focus of the military revolt against Goulart had been for some time in Minas Gerais. General Carlos Luís Guedes, commander in Belo Horizonte of three infantry regiments, had been plotting to overthrow Goulart even before General Olímpio Mourão Filho was transferred to Minas to command the 4th Military Region in August 1963. Both soldiers had urged the governor, Magalhães Pinto, to declare open opposition to Goulart and Mourão Filho kept closely in touch with officers long known to be hostile to the president and the Vargista tradition he represented with, for example, Guedes's former superior, Marshal Denys, with Cordeiro de Farias, Nelson de Melo, Sílvio Heck, Grün Moss, and Rademaker. Osvaldo Cordeiro de Farias was the most senior of the eight four-star generals then in the army list,[154] the ex-*tenente* who in October 1945 had delivered to Vargas the ultimatum forcing his resignation. He was not currently in an army post, however, and did not command troops; nor did these other officers well known for their opposition in the past both to Goulart and earlier to Kubitschek. The president could afford to ignore opposition from men long known for their extreme views and with no troops under their command. Much more serious was the link with General Castello Branco, even though he too, as Chief of the Army General Staff, was not in direct command of troops. His memorandum of 20 March, mimeographed in Cordeiro de Farias's apartment in Rio de Janeiro, was an important intervention and his personal influence was a major asset to the anti-Goulart movement. Castello Branco was third in the army list of four-star generals, while the second on the list, General Artur da Costa e Silva, was also by early 1964 helping the plot against Goulart, having been removed from his previous post of commander of the Fourth Army in Recife and working now in Rio de Janeiro as head of the army's Department of Production and Works.

The really crucial figures, however, were those in direct command of men and arms. The other five four-star generals after Cordeiro de Farias, Costa e Silva, and Castello Branco had all been promoted by Goulart, and four of them commanded the four Armies, with headquarters in Rio de Janeiro, São Paulo, Pôrto Alegre, and Recife. The commanders of the First and Third Armies were known to be loyal to Goulart. General Joaquim Justino Alves Bastos in Recife was more ambiguous, though senior officers under him were known to be firmly opposed to Goulart. But the most important commander of all was General Amaury Kruel in São Paulo, both for the forces he controlled and the strategic importance of São Paulo in relation to any military advance from Minas Gerais to Guanabara. Many of the officers under him were anti-Goulart, but he was friendly with the president and had made it clear that only extreme provocation would bring him to move against Goulart, even though the conspirators sent his brother, the retired General Riograndino Kruel, to São Paulo to argue with him.

Between the rally of 13 March and Goulart's speech at the Automobile Club on 30 March the plotters tried to decide when and how the move against Goulart should be made. There was a general fear that any premature action might leave those responsible for it isolated and defeated, like São Paulo in 1932, so that the principal leaders were determined that as broad a front as possible should be achieved, both military and civilian, with, above all, São Paulo and Minas Gerais fully committed to the move. With the naval mutiny Guedes, Mourão Filho, and Magalhães Pinto believed that enough provocation had been given to produce widespread backing, and soundings were quickly taken among supporters in other states; but Castello Branco was adamant that nothing should be done without the collaboration of Amaury Kruel, who was again approached on 28 March, but still refused to commit himself. The commander of the First Army, General Armando de Morais Âncora, was known to be loyal to Goulart; the leaders of the anti-Goulart movement expected therefore that they might well have to face a prolonged fight. Preparations for this were still being made. An agreement was reached with the governor of Espírito Santo for the *mineiros* to use the port of Vitória in the event of civil war; the Minas Gerais state cabinet was strengthened, to include men such as Afonso Arinos de Melo Franco, experienced in foreign relations, who might be needed for negotiations over arms and supplies; the Minas state police was put under the command of General Guedes, who on 30 March arrested known 'pro-Communists'.[155]

There was still no commitment from Kruel and no rallying call from Magalhães Pinto, other state governors, or prominent anti-Goulart politicians.[156] Lacerda, for example, was uncharacteristically silent all through the critical weekend following the naval mutiny. Finally, the deadlock was broken by Mourão Filho early on 31 March, moving, like General Klinger in Matto Grosso in July 1932, earlier than his fellow conspirators expected, but this time to better effect.[157] He asked Guedes to send an infantry battalion to join the 'Tiradentes Column', which was to march on Rio de Janeiro. In Rio de Janeiro, Castello Branco and Carlos Lacerda were told through a federal deputy, Armando Falcão, that the movement had begun, and agreed to give it full support, even though both Castello Branco and Costa e Silva had recently made clear their belief that any premature move would be disastrous and that nothing should be done until General Kruel had given his support.[158]

Kruel was told by Mourão Filho by telephone at 9 a.m. on 31 March of the intention to move against Rio de Janeiro. For the rest of the day he was under pressure from both sides, while the column from Minas Gerais, under the command of General Antônio Carlos da Silva, crossed the Paraibuna river into the state of Rio de Janeiro. At 5 p.m. General Mourão Filho read a manifesto to the nation, accusing Goulart of collaborating with 'Communist' elements hostile to the constitution and the armed forces, and demanding his removal, a public challenge supported by governor Magalhães Pinto and General Guedes in Minas Gerais. In reply the government sent a force, commanded by General Luís Tavares da Cunha Melo, to suppress the Minas rising, and the Goulart *dispositivo militar* was strengthened by the relocation of officers known to be loyal, especially the appointment of Ladário Pereira Teles to command the Third Army and of Morais Âncora as War Minister.[159]

Throughout the day reports were reaching Rio de Janeiro of proclamations in São Paulo and elsewhere against Goulart, especially by Adhemar de Barros, whose police were already said to be arresting the president's supporters. The Minister of Justice, Abelardo Jurema, tried several times to telephone General Kruel, but without success. Goulart, however, managed to speak with him. Those close to the president, though not informed of the precise nature of the conversations, became convinced that Kruel, the man on whom everything depended, was no longer ready to stand by Goulart.[160] The general was in fact locked in discussions with senior officers immediately under him, who were still loyal to the president. He was wanting some solution in which Goulart would dissociate himself from his immediate advisers and those individuals and organizations most provocative to the armed forces, mentioning in particular Darci Ribeiro, Raul Ríff, the CGT, the PUA, and UNE.[161] In the evening of 31 March Kruel again put this proposal to Goulart, who rejected it. Kruel then told the president he could no longer support him. At 11 p.m. General Kruel published a manifesto announcing that the Second Army would fight to 'break the circle of Communism which now compromises the authority of the government of the Republic',[162] then confirmed his opposition in reply to queries from Magalhães Pinto, the commander of the Fourth Army, Justino Alves Bastos, and the commander of the military academy at Resende, in the strategically important Paraíba valley, General Emílio Garrastazú Médici.

With Kruel's support the military movement against Goulart quickly gathered pace. Before troops from Minas could clash with the government forces from Petrópolis they were joined by many officers abandoning Goulart, the most important being Colonel Raimundo Ferreira de Souza, commander of the Sampaio Regiment (1st Regiment of Infantry), who for many years had worked closely with Marshal Odílio Denys. He was contacted by telephone, through the son of Mourão Filho's chief of staff, Colonel João Baptista da Costa: he spoke with Marshal Denys and agreed not to fight for Goulart. The Goulart forces of the First Army under General Cunha Melo had, therefore, for all practical purposes fallen apart; Cunha Melo returned to Rio de Janeiro. General Mourão Filho later spoke of this support from Colonel de Souza as 'the key to the victory', since, if he had resisted the Minas forces, the rest of the army would probably have followed.[163]

The failure of military resistance to the Minas troops showed the far-reaching importance of the work done by officers and politicians who for years had opposed Goulart and the whole Vargista movement. Marshal Denys had prevented the crucial first clash.[164] Elsewhere, too, old enemies of Goulart, even of Kubitschek, came to the surface as part of the military opposition. The weakness of air force resistance reflected work done among air force officers by Grün Moss and his supporters,[165] while other old conspirators, such as Haroldo Veloso and Paulo Vitor, the leaders of the Jacareacanga revolt, and João Paulo Moreira Burnier, head of the rebellion at Aragarças, played at least minor roles, with Burnier mainly involved in preparing the defence of Guanabara Palace, where Lacerda was talking of armed resistance. But above all, the behaviour of the officer corps throughout the crisis reflected its deep hostility to the threat of 'Communism', growing anxiety over the challenge to military discipline, and even to civil order, and, at the height of the crisis, the failure of leadership on the part of Goulart's military *dispositivo*.

By the afternoon of 1 April Goulart realized that his military support had evaporated, except perhaps in the Third Army, whose new commander was only just taking up his post. The CGT's call for a general strike was meeting with little response and already it was clear that by far the most crucial factor was the support of military officers in command of troops, which Goulart no longer had in sufficient numbers. In the early afternoon of 1 April he flew to Brasília, leaving instructions that he wanted no bloodshed. Already the commander of the Fourth Army, Justino Alves Bastos, had signed a proclamation supporting Generals Kruel and Mourão Filho, so that the north-east too was on the rebels' side, with Goulart supporters swiftly put under arrest.[166]

In Brasília Goulart heard reports from Assis Brasil, who had disturbing news from the new head of the First Army, Oromar Osório, and from Rio Grande do Sul, where some troops were already in rebellion against the president. At the same time the Minister of War, Âncora, went to Resende to meet General Kruel, still hoping to reach some agreement. By the time Kruel and Âncora met in the early evening of 1 April it was clear that the armed forces right across the country were moving away from Goulart and that his cause was lost, a fact General Âncora now accepted, returning to Rio de Janeiro and telling Costa e Silva he was resigning as Minister of War. Costa e Silva now took over command of the army.

Goulart then continued his flight that same evening, leaving Brasília for Pôrto Alegre. His departure from the capital was seized on as the occasion for his opponents to move in quickly and declare the presidency vacant—which was done, amid angry protests, in the early hours of 2 April, by the President of the Senate, Auro de Moura Andrade, the man who had accompanied Lacerda and General Nelson de Melo at the 'March of the Family with God for Liberty' in São Paulo on 19 March, when he had spoken so vehemently of the dangers facing Brazil. His action in declaring the presidency vacant on 2 April, so making the president of the Chamber of Deputies, Ranieri Mazzilli, provisional president of Brazil, was unconstitutional. It merely gave legal form to the military *coup* which now was virtually complete, and Mazzilli was at once informed by Costa e Silva that effective power and all decisions now rested with the Revolutionary Supreme Command.

About two hours after Moura Andrade had declared the presidency vacant Goulart arrived in Pôrto Alegre. The new commander, General Ladário Pereira Teles, was still in control and there was still some will for resistance both among soldiers and civilians, with Brizola insisting on the need to fight. But units throughout the state were already going over to the other side and Goulart now knew that he had lost. He quickly withdrew into the interior of the state and two days later, 4 April 1964, moved to join his wife and children in Uruguay. Once again, as in so many crises in Brazil's history, the soldiers were in command.

Notes

1 Skidmore puts it well: 'What the anti-getulistas had won by the Army's intervention in 1945, lost in Vargas' election in 1950, won by the military again in 1954, lost in 1955 (both by the election and Lott's coup), and apparently won by the ballot box in 1960, was now again lost'; op. cit., 208, referring to the *Estado de São Paulo* of 26 August 1961.

2 For student, and other, reaction to the Quadros resignation, see Mário Victor, *Cinco Anos que Abalaram o Brasil* (*de Jânio Quadros ao Marechal Castelo Branco*) (Rio de Janeiro, 1965), 320–2. See. too, the statement of trade union leaders of 26 August, supporting Quadros, but making clear that if he did not return, he should be succeeded by Goulart.

3 Victor, ibid., 334 gives the full text of Lott's manifesto.

4 ibid., 334–5.

5 ibid., 336–45. Also Dulles, *Unrest in Brazil*, 145.

6 Victor, op. cit., 337.

7 The statement made by Deputado Oliveiro Brito is to be found in Victor, ibid., 345–6. Victor describes this decision as a 'crushing defeat' for the military ministers. A modified 'parliamentary' form of government had been discussed by a Congressional committee, headed by the *mineiro* politician Afonso Arinos de Melo Franco. One of its strongest supporters was the old *gaúcho* political leader, and foremost spokesman for the *Partido Libertador*, Raul Pilla. See Afonso Arinos de Melo Franco and Raul Pilla, *Presidencialismo ou Parlamentarismo* (Rio de Janeiro, 1958).

8 The Third Army was based in Rio Grande do Sul, being further divided into two Military Regions. The First Army, with its headquarters in Rio de Janeiro, and the Second Army, based in São Paulo, were also divided into two Military Regions, while the Fourth Army, centred in Recife, incorporated three Military Regions. The army was always stronger in men and materials in the south than in most of Brazil.

9 Skidmore, op. cit., 215: 'He [Goulart] probably had less voter appeal than any President elected since 1945 with the exception of Dutra. In both 1955 and 1960 he had won the vice presidency only by a narrow margin against Milton Campos, a conventional UDN candidate. In 1954 he had even been defeated in an attempt to win election as senator from Rio Grande do Sul'. Skidmore also makes the point that relatively little is known of Goulart's early career, noting that the study of him by Limeira Tejo, *Jango: Debate sôbre a crise dos nossos tempos* (Rio de Janeiro, 1957), is altogether too fulsome. It is a gap which still has not been filled and Goulart remains something of an enigma.

10 See his annual message to Congress, 1962: *Mensagem ao Congresso Nacional 1962*, XI–XII, where he speaks of the need of 'basic reforms' in response to the people's demands, but also in terms of the fullest measures of security for the future. He also speaks of the need of agrarian reform to resolve social tensions, which differ in kind from one part of the country to the other.

11 Kahil, op. cit., 317.

12 ibid., 320. See, too (ibid., 321), the table on 'Average Monthly Increases in Bank Loans to the Public and the Private Sectors, January 1960/March 1964'. Having noted the attempt to contain federal expenditure, Kahil, it may be noted, continues: 'Furthermore, the expansion of bank loans to the private sector can be seen to have been severely restricted in the latter period. This was strongly opposed, however, by the business community, which complained of the shortage of funds, and by trade union leaders, who denounced credit restriction as an unacceptable concession to the I.M.F., which could only hamper development. Nor was opposition to the stabilisation measures of January–April 1963 entirely unjustified. For they were applied immediately after minimum wages had been increased by 60 percent, that is, when labour costs were sharply rising; and, to make matters worse, they coincided with a considerable absorption of funds by the external sector. Thus the period was characterised by cost, rather than by demand, inflation'.

13 ibid., 317.

14 See his speeches in João Goulart, *Desenvolvimento e Independência: Discursos. 1962* (Brasília, 1963). Also see his *Mensagem ao Congresso Nacional 1962*, 45–7, where he stresses Brazil's commitment to continental solidarity: 'We condemn, and will condemn, every ideology which is likely to threaten . . . the integrity and security of its [the continent's] members . . .' Goulart also stressed Brazil's commitment to the Alliance for Progress, while reiterating that his country would follow an 'independent' foreign policy.

15 For San Tiago Dantas's own explanation, see San Tiago Dantas, *Política externa independente* (Rio de Janeiro, 1962). For a comment from a distinctly United States viewpoint, see V. Reisky de Dubnic, 'Trends in Brazil's Foreign Policy' in E. Baklanoff (ed.), *New Perspectives of Brazil* (Nashville, 1966), 92: 'Brazil's stand . . . at Punta del Este . . . could hardly be justified in terms of the Brazilian national interest. The Goulart government's objectives were to preserve Castro's Cuba within the O.A.S. and to oppose economic sanctions in Cuba. The latter aim was unrelated to the internal or external interests of Brazil, since there was virtually no trade between Cuba and Brazil. Goulart's opposition to isolating Cuba clashed head-on with the United States' objectives . . .'. It was precisely against such ready identification of United States and Brazilian interests that the Brazilian move was directed. In retrospect the stand of San Tiago Dantas may come to appear more statesmanlike than that of those who so readily agreed to isolate Cuba.

16 The attacks on San Tiago Dantas in the leading newspapers were increasingly severe, as seen, for example, in *Estado de São Paulo, Correio da Manhã, O Globo*, and all the papers of the Chateaubriand chain.

17 See on this the comment of Jover Telles, op. cit., 158, who, comparing this crisis with those of August 1954, November 1955, and August–September 1961, says: 'The particular feature of this occasion was the greater participation of the mass of workers in the political struggle, and the fact that this participation of the working class was more independent and the content of its action more advanced . . .'.

18 ibid., 158.

19 The most important statements in relation to the strike are given in Telles, ibid., 164–74, who sees the appointment of Moura Andrade and the new Council of Ministers as an attempt at a 'white coup' (174), to reverse policies recently followed, including foreign policy. He also speaks of an attempt to reinstate in the military ministries the *dispositivo militar* which had held power till August–September 1961 and had opposed Goulart's accession. Goulart's attempts at conciliation, seeking to halt the strike, are also described ibid., 178.

20 ibid.

21 See Afonso Arinos de Melo Franco, *Planalto: Memórias* (Rio de Janeiro 1968), 235–7.

22 Melo Franco, ibid., well conveys the heightened emotional atmosphere of this crisis, and the general feeling that government was being made impossible. See, too, Mário Victor, op. cit., 438–45. Victor gives details of Brochado da Rocha's *mensagem* to Congress on 10 August, and the text of Dantas Ribeiro's telegram to Goulart, the Prime Minister, and the Minister of War. He also lists some of the senior military officers who did not share some of Dantas Ribeiro's alleged apprehension.

23 For a useful analysis of the 1962 elections see again R. Schneider *et al*, op. cit., 58–68.

24 ibid., 68.

25 Some details are given ibid., 61. Without exaggerating this, and other, factors which gave undue weight to the more conservative groups within Brazilian society, it is important to note this persistent source of tension between a relatively conservative Congress and a president elected on a more populist, reformist vote.

26 There is a useful analysis of the elections on a state by state basis in a special issue of *Revista Brasileira de Estudos Políticos*, No. 16 (1964). Also Hélio Jaguaribe, 'As Eleições de 1962', *Tempo Brasileiro* No. 2 (Dec. 1962), 7–38.

27 *Plano Trienal de Desenvolvimento Econômico e Social, 1963–1965* (Síntese) (Rio de Janeiro, Dec. 1962).

28 For a discussion of these arguments in the *Plano Trienal* see Kahil, op. cit., 191–3. See, too, the contemporary comment in *Revista Brasileira de Economia*, XVI, 4 (Dec. 1962).

29 Skidmore, op. cit., 236.

30 João Goulart, *Mensagem ao Congresso Nacional* (Brasília, 1963).

31 ibid., 6–7.

32 ibid., 10–11.

33 ibid., 15.

34 Kahil, op. cit., 333.

35 On the nature and strength of this 'populist pact' see, in particular, the thoughtful reflection in Weffort, *Partidos, Sindicatos e Democracia*, especially 100–10 on the role of the PCB, and Castro Andrade, op. cit., 21–37.

36 Peter D. Bell, 'Brazilian–American Relations' in R. Roett (ed.), *Brazil in*

the Sixties (Nashville, 1972), 83. Bell is quoting Niles Bond, chargé d'affaires in the embassy prior to the arrival of Lincoln Gordon as ambassador.

37 ibid., 85–6.

38 Skidmore, op. cit., 239.

39 Kahil, op. cit., 321: 'Faced by a major economic and social crisis, the government abandoned in May what was to be the last attempt at stabilization'.

40 Bell, op. cit., 85–6.

41 'Negative left' was originally used by San Tiago Dantas to describe the more extreme radical and nationalist groups. It is an overdrawn distinction, but still much used. As for the 'negative right', Skidmore, though he does not use the phrase, puts his finger on it when noting how Lacerda's nomination as UDN presidential candidate boosted the UDN's right wing; op. cit., 248–9.

42 ibid.

43 Dulles, *Unrest in Brazil*, 213.

44 The complete list of new cabinet members is given ibid., 210. Justice: Abelardo Jurema; Finance: Carlos Alberto Carvalho Pinto; Labour: Amauri Silva; Foreign Affairs: Evandro Lins e Silva; Education: Paulo de Tarso; Industry and Commerce: Edídio Michaelsen; Mines and Energy: Antônio Ferreira de Oliveira Brito; Health: Wilson Fadul; Agriculture: Osvaldo Lima Filho; Transportation: Expedito Machado; War: General Jair Dantas Ribeiro; Navy: Admiral Sílvio Mota; Air: Brigadeiro Anísio Botelho.

45 Kahil, op. cit., 330.

46 ibid., 322.

47 Among accounts readily available in English see C. N. Hewitt, 'Brazil: The Peasant Movement of Pernambuco, 1961–1964' in H. A. Landsberger (ed.), *Latin American Peasant Movements* (Ithaca and London, 1969), 374–98; S. Forman, 'Disunity and Discontent: A Study of Peasant Political Movements in Brazil', *Journal of Latin American Studies*, vol. 3, No. 1, 3–24. Also C. Furtado, *Diagnosis of the Brazilian Crisis* (Berkeley and Los Angeles, 1965); and on Julião in particular, A. Leeds, 'Brazil and the Myth of Francisco Julião' in J. Meier and R. Weatherhead (eds.), *Politics of Change in Latin America* (New York, 1964), 3–24. See, too, the thoughtful London M.A. thesis, 1973, by V. R. Cadaxa, *Rural Trade Unionism and Politics in North-eastern Brazil, 1955–1964*. Also in English see F. Julião, *Cambão—The Yoke. The Hidden Face of Brazil* (London, 1972).

48 Antônio Callado, *Os Industriais da Sêca e os 'Galileus' de Pernambuco* (Rio de Janeiro, 1960), 35.

49 Forman, op. cit., 11.

50 IBRA, *Relatório* (1967), quoted Forman, op. cit., 4. Forman also notes that Gunder Frank calculated that in 1950 62 per cent of people dependent on agriculture for their living were landless labourers, and that, if one takes into account those whose land was not economically viable, this figure would amount to 81 per cent. A. Gunder Frank, *Capitalism and Underdevelopment in Latin America* (New York, 1967), 249.

51 Forman, op. cit., 7.

52 Hewitt, op. cit., 379: '. . . the *ligas* of the *agreste* were fewer, smaller, and less active than those of the *mata*'. She notes that organization of peasants in the *agreste* was mainly in the hands of Church-sponsored unions from about 1961 to 1964. 'Respondents interviewed in 1965 noted that a few peasant leagues (organised by Julião) did exist in the *agreste*, but that they were generally not active'. It is difficult to square this and similar evidence

with the statement by Forman that 'Generally, the leagues spread quickest in the *agreste* . . .', op. cit., 11.

53 Julião, op. cit., 97.

54 Forman, op. cit., 14 suggests that 'once in exile from Brazil, Julião's position became more radical'.

55 See, for example, the articles by Tad Szulc in the *New York Times*, and his comments on 'Julião and other extreme leftists of the Northeast' in *The Winds of Revolution* (London, 1964), where he argues (293) that: 'By the middle of 1963, agitation for land reform has become the central fact of Brazilian political life, with urgent warnings that a continuation of the present system of land tenure is bound to lead to a peasant Marxist–Leninist revolution'.

56 F. Julião, *¿Qué son las Ligas Campesinas?* (Montevideo, 1963), 9, quoted in Hewitt, op. cit., 384.

57 ibid., 384–5.

58 Manoel Correia de Andrade, *A Terra e o Homen no Nordeste* (Rio de Janeiro, 1963), 250–2, quoted Forman, op. cit., 12–13.

59 Hewitt, op. cit., 385.

60 On the various meanings of *cambão* see Julião, *Cambão—The Yoke*, especially 11–13. In particular: 'In the North-East, in the cassava and sugar-cane zone, *cambão* is the name given to the drying, leafless and earless maize stalk. It also refers to the piece of wood hung round an ox's neck and trailing between his legs to slow his pace. It means the yoke fixed to the shaft with raw leather thongs; the *boi-de-cambão* or yoke-ox is the one who walks in front pushing the yoke; the *boi-de-coice* follows behind holding up the shaft. Finally, *cambão* is the day's unpaid labour demanded by landowners once a week from their peasants as rent for their land—normally a miserable patch of one or two hectares if the tenant is a day labourer or hired hand. In the case of a tenant farmer, *cambão* is labour given free to the owners at certain times of the year in addition to the usual rent in money or kind. . . . *Cambão, cambaio, cambeta, cambado, cambo, cambembe, cambito, cambada:* look in the dictionary and you find that every variant signifies some misfortune—'gang', 'crippled', 'bandy-legged', 'limbless'—except the fundamental one: labour not even rewarded with bread and water. And this points sadly to the fact that even dictionaries omit things out of fear of or in league with the *latifúndio*'.

61 This point is cogently argued in Leeds, op. cit.

62 Forman, op. cit., 15.

63 Hewitt, op. cit., 391–4 for some of the tensions within Church-inspired groupings.

64 Cadaxa, op. cit., 10 makes this point well, namely, that: 'As land was virtually the only means of production, monopolisation of land made it possible to determine the conditions of the mass of poorer inhabitants by controlling their access to it. From the point of view of the landowners, as a class, it was crucial to prevent this monopoly from being disrupted as this would upset the whole of their economic power; even less could they afford to let the *latifundio* system itself be challenged by the rural poor'.

65 Hewitt, op. cit., 395.

66 ibid. Church influence, it is argued, was especially weakened by a government decision to divide the Federation into three parts: for wage-earners, sharecroppers, and small farmers. The paid workers provided funds for the Federation, but 'the small farmers and sharecroppers of the *agreste* furnished the voting strength to keep the Federation under Church control. Therefore when the Federation was divided, the Church lost substantial ground to

Goulart and the Communist unions of the *mata*. . . .'
67 ibid., 395–6.
68 Hewitt, op. cit., 396.
69 R. Price, 'Rural Unionisation in Brazil', *Land Tenure Center Research Paper*, No. 14 (Madison, 1964); Forman, op. cit., 21.
70 On this general control and manipulation of peasant and rural groups by populist governments or parties see Flynn, 'Class, Clientelism and Coercion'. See, too, J. Powell, 'Peasant Society and Clientelistic Politics', *American Political Science Review* (1970), 411–25; and on, for example, southern Italy, M. Salvati, 'The Impasse of Italian Capitalism', *New Left Review*, 76 (1972), 3–33.
71 Hewitt, op. cit., 396–7.
72 Forman, op. cit., 17–18.
73 Dulles, *Unrest in Brazil*, 206.
74 Some of the best accounts of all these moves are in: Abelardo Jurema, *Sexta-Feira, 13: Os Últimos Dias do Govêrno João Goulart*, 2nd ed. (Rio de Janeiro, 1964), and Mário Victor, op. cit.
75 José Stacchini, *Março 64: mobilização de audácia* (São Paulo, 1965), 4, emphasizes this lack of connection, speaking of an 'archipelago' of resistance, a series of parallel conspiracies throughout the country but with few effective links.
76 The most telling information on the role of IPÊS, IBAD, and ADEP (Popular Democratic Action) in the elections of 1962 is to be found in 'As sombras do IBAD', *Veja* (16 March 1977), 3–6. The article draws mainly on an interview with Lincoln Gordon, who admitted that American companies and the United States embassy contributed anything between $1 million and 5 million to help Goulart's opponents. ibid. (9 March 1977), 6.
77 Dulles, *Unrest in Brazil*, 231 says that anti-Communist infiltrators persuaded the NCOs' leaders to start the rising on 12 September instead of waiting to take part in a more co-ordinated action on the 14th.
78 See Glauco Carneiro, *História das Revoluções Brasileiras*, II, 533–50. Also Abelardo Jurema, op. cit.
79 Chilcote, op. cit., 152. Chilcote notes (321) how Pelacani had left the PCB in 1958 and says 'Cerqueira was probably a socialist, not a member of the PCB, although he served as director of the Soviet-oriented World Federation of Trade Unions'.
80 ibid., 153–4.
81 ibid., quoting Partido Comunista do Brasil 'Resolução aprovada pela reunião nacional, realizada no mês de setembro de 1959', as printed in Jover Telles: op. cit., 285–301.
82 Chilcote, op. cit., 152–3.
83 The call was first made in a pamphlet issued in Rio de Janeiro in November 1963, *Organização dos 'Grupos de Onze Companheiros' ou 'Comandos Nacionalistas'*.
84 Bell, op. cit., especially 82–92.
85 ibid., 85.
86 Arthur Byrnes, deputy director of AID/North-East 1963–63, director 1963–64, quoted Bell, ibid., 87.
87 Gordon both then and later believed that Goulart was being used by 'Communists', thinking he could control people who would certainly outwit him. See Gordon's comments during the Hearing Before the Committee on Foreign Relations, US Senate, 89th Congress, 2nd Session, 7 February 1966: *Nomination of Lincoln Gordon to be Assistant Secretary of State for Inter-American Affairs* (Washington, 1966).

88 Bell, op. cit., 91.
89 Stacchini, op. cit., 90–4.
90 ibid., 89–90. He reports a meeting between a senior Brazilian officer and a military member of the United States embassy, called at the latter's request, in which the embassy official offered to supply war material. The Brazilian officer replied that such help would not be needed, but that there might be need of fuel.
91 Schneider, op. cit., 121–4.
92 ibid., 124. Mauro Borges was governor of Goiás and was present at the governors' meeting. He gives a valuable account of the discussions over the presidency in *O Golpe em Goiás* (Rio de Janeiro, 1965).
93 Gordon claimed that the *coup* was '100 percent purely Brazilian'; Skidmore, op. cit., 325.
94 Gordon, to Senate Committee on Foreign Relations, 7 February 1966, quoted Skidmore, ibid.
95 See most notably Philip Agee, *Inside the Company. C.I.A. Diary* (Harmondsworth, 1975).
96 See the documents from the Lyndon Johnson Library, Austin, Texas, published in *Jornal do Brasil*, 18–20 December 1976.
97 ibid. (18 December 1976), 20—Directive from Admiral John L. Chew.
98 See Lincoln Gordon interview, *Veja* (9 March 1977), 7.
99 ibid.
100 ibid. Joint Chiefs of Staff (JCS).
101 ibid.
102 By 2 April a memorandum for Mr McGeorge Bundy could report that: 'Ralph [Ralph Burton, Undersecretary in the State Department] estimates that the chances of a reversal of the present situation (or a compromise with Goulart) are extremely slim', *Jornal do Brasil* (19 December 1976), 5.
103 Lincoln Gordon interview, *Veja* (9 March 1977), 4.
104 Gordon, while denying that vast sums of money were spent and emphasizing that in, for example, São Paulo there was plenty of local money to support IPÊS and similar organizations, admits that CIA funds were used, channelled in part through 'phantom companies' ('Além disso, pelo que todo mundo sabe dos métodos de operação da C.I.A., eles sempre usam companhias reais e algumas companhias fantasmas para canalizar suas operações'), ibid., 6.
105 ibid.
106 Dulles, *Unrest in Brazil*, 261–2 describes how on 25 February 1964 a meeting of the Frente de Mobilização Popular, attended by Brizola, in Belo Horizonte was disrupted, mainly by women: 'Hundreds of women came with their rosaries and umbrellas. Many were poor, brought from the *favelas* by priests'. Brizola's speech was drowned by loud chanting of prayers and the meeting ended in violent confusion, televised throughout the state.
107 In the Chilean case it was reported that many of the middle-class women demonstrators brought their maids with them, presumably to carry the pots.
108 Mário Victor, op. cit., 474–5.
109 ibid., 470–1 describes the growth of resistance to the proposed SUPRA decree, with landowners preparing for armed resistance. In the second half of March João Pinheiro Neto was prevented from speaking in the Law Faculty in São Paulo. On 11 March a national conference in Guanabara of the 'productive classes' ('classes produtoras') virtually broke with the government, issuing a public statement which warned against disorder and disrespect for the constitution and deplored the fact that Goulart was now acting more as a party leader than as head of state.

110 ibid., 475–6.
111 'The significance of the March 13 rally was unmistakable. Goulart had finally turned to the radical left for his policies'; Skidmore, op. cit., 289.
112 Victor, op. cit., 477.
113 Adhemar de Barros in *O Estado de São Paulo* (15 March 1964).
114 The groups active in this and other anti-Goulart demonstrations to mobilize, in particular, middle-class opinion included CAMDE (Women's Campaign for Democracy) and UCF (Feminine Civic Union), which were given both 'organizational and financial assistance' by IPÊS (Institute of Social Studies and Research), 'founded by Rio de Janeiro and São Paulo businessmen as their political action arm' (Schneider, op. cit., 88). There are obvious similarities between these organizations and those which in the same period were being used in Chile, with heavy foreign backing, to prevent left-wing political successes.
115 Victor, op. cit., 489.
116 ibid., 490. See, too, 482–3 for Lacerda's dealings with state governors. Meneghetti in Rio Grande do Sul was a political opponent of Brizola. All the state governors were contacted by Lacerda in a letter of 18 March.
117 ibid., 485.
118 ibid., 490–1. See, too, Alberto Dines *et al*, *Os Idos de Março e a Queda em Abril*, 2nd ed. (Rio de Janeiro, 1964), 392–3.
119 Schneider, op. cit., 89.
120 ibid.
121 ibid., 89–90.
122 Victor, op. cit., 485.
123 Schneider, op. cit., 94.
124 The role of retired officers, particularly senior officers, has not been sufficiently studied. In the build-up of opposition to Goulart they also played an important role. A manifesto signed by seventy-two retired generals argued that his government had now put itself outside the law, so that the armed forces were no longer obliged to defend the government. The manifesto, to be found in *Diário de Notícias* (22 March 1964), is quoted in A. Stepan, *The Military in Politics: changing patterns in Brazil* (Princeton, 1971), 202.
125 Mário Victor, op. cit., 495.
126 Stepan, op. cit., 205.
127 Victor, op. cit., 495.
128 It seems that he asked the Minister of Justice, Abelardo Jurema, to attend the meeting, who, however, eventually decided not to go; Jurema, op. cit.
129 This was an old, well-chosen phrase, used, too, by the 19th-century military leader and Republican Benjamin Constant (1838–91). The speech is given in full in Glauco Carneiro, *História das Revoluções Brasileiras*, II, 600–2.
130 Victor, op. cit., 497.
131 Dulles, *Unrest in Brazil*, 283–4. Dulles says the order was given by Admiral Arnold o Hasselman Fairbairn, who in the brief *Integralista* revolt of 11 May 1938 had taken over the Ministry of Navy building for the Integralists.
132 Victor, op. cit., 499–500, mentions the report that the choice of Minister of the Navy was made from a list presented by the CGT, but says that General Assis Brasil denied this, alleging the rumour was part of the campaign against Goulart. Dulles, *Unrest in Brazil*, 284, says that in an interview much later, 24 November 1968, Dante Pelacani said that 'the sailors selected Paulo Mário to take over the Navy Ministry', that Pelacani and Pacheco then informed the CGT, who, in turn, took the name of this sixty-nine-year-old retired admiral to Goulart.

133 Stepan, op. cit., 206, note 41: 'The naval mutiny was so obviously counter-productive that two generals who were later purged from the military even argue that it must have been deliberately instigated by right-wing officers. Interview with General Luiz Tavares da Cunha Mello and General Nicolau Fico, Rio de Janeiro, 10 October 1968'.

134 ibid., 206–7. For further details of armed preparations by leaders such as Magalhães Pinto, Adhemar de Barros, and other state governors, see Carneiro, op. cit., II, 563.

135 Stepan, op. cit., 207.

136 ibid. Plotters like General Mourão Filho, said to have 'acknowledged the effect of the mutiny on his resolve', were determined long before March 1964 to pull down Goulart.

137 ibid., 208.

138 Quoted Victor, op. cit., 502.

139 The Admiral's Manifesto is given in full in Carneiro, op. cit., II, 602.

140 In relation to this frequently repeated charge of 'communism' and, by implication, 'anti-Christian' content in this and other movements, charges repeated in all the carefully organized demonstrations of Catholic ladies, it is worth noticing, in passing, how, when the sailors and marines were released on the afternoon of Good Friday and celebrated noisily, one of their first stops was at Rio's famous Candelária church, to thank God for their victory, Dulles, *Unrest in Brazil*, 285.

141 Carneiro, op. cit., 603, where the full text is to be found.

142 See the statements of Deputies Vieira de Mello and Doutel de Andrade, quoted Victor, op. cit., 502–3.

143 ibid., 503.

144 ibid., 404.

145 Dulles, *Unrest in Brazil*, 289.

146 ibid. See, too, Jurema, op. cit., 170–1.

147 Stepan, op. cit., 209. This is, however, a difficult question. It seems that right up till the very eve of the *coup* Assis Brasil was still receiving assurance of loyalty and support from senior officers he consulted, especially in São Paulo, and Goulart, even at the eleventh hour, was led to believe he would be backed, for example, by the commander of the Fourth Army in Recife, Joaquim Justino Alves Bastos. Dulles, *Unrest in Brazil*, 331. Goulart's close military advisers during the confused excitement of these days had to distinguish carefully between bellicose noises and threats, preparations for revolt which they knew had long been brewing, and the real danger of imminent military revolt on a large scale.

148 Victor, op. cit., 205.

149 ibid., 506.

150 ibid., 507.

151 ibid., 507.

152 ibid., 508.

153 ibid., 509.

154 Dulles, *Unrest in Brazil*, 307–8. Dulles gives a most useful, detailed account of the build-up to the *coup* in a study which is generally full of valuable detailed information.

155 ibid., 312–13. Dulles, from a series of personal interviews, has done a very good job in piecing together the chronology of these events, which does not always emerge clearly from the other sources.

156 Mourão Filho had been working frantically to get through Magalhães Pinto a manifesto, stronger than his statement following the 13 March rally, to be signed by him and other state governors, making a definite

break with Goulart. But the governor procrastinated, partly because, as he made clear, he was unhappy about backing a distinctly right-wing *coup* (ibid., 306), and partly, like Alves Bastos in Recife, to avoid taking a stand prematurely.

157 Dulles notes that Mourão was beginning to believe that unless he started the revolt it would never take place, and that he was determined it should occur before 9 May, when he was due to retire. He was perhaps the most intransigent of all Goulart's enemies, having been fiercely committed to 'anti-communism' ever since he was a young *Integralista* officer, when he prepared the notorious 'Cohen Plan'.

158 Stacchini, op. cit., 98 describes a meeting in Rio on 30 March, which included Riograndino Kruel, Castello Branco, and Costa e Silva, who brought along General Octacílio Terra Ururahy. Costa e Silva said there was still no need for revolution, and recommended waiting. Riograndino Kruel was again sent to São Paulo, but no word came of Amaury's adherence to the movement. Costa e Silva also recommended that Cordeiro de Farias should not go again to talk to General Kruel in São Paulo.

159 General Armando de Morais Âncora was made War Minister in place of Jair Dantas Ribeiro, who for some time had been ill in hospital. Pereira Teles, Commander of the 1st Military Region, a man loyal to Goulart, went to Pôrto Alegre to replace General Benjamin Galhardo, who now took over Castello Branco's job of Army Chief of Staff.

160 Jurema, op. cit., 192–3. Jurema emphasizes that for the First Army, too, any real chance of fighting for 'legality' depended on Kruel. He says that to questions from himself, Samuel Wainer (of *Última Hora*), Raul Ríff (Presidential Press Secretary), and Jorge Serpa (speechwriter) about Kruel's position, Goulart replied that 'Kruel is fine . . . he's my friend . . . he's with me, but . . . always talking about this business of communism, of infiltration in the CGT, the PUA . . .'.

161 ibid., 193.

162 Dulles, *Unrest in Brazil*, 321. The role of the general, it must be said, is still obscure. It has been suggested that his long delay in defining his position may have been a ploy, either to secure his own position, politically and financially, both before and after the *coup*, or even to lull Goulart into a false sense of security. While, however, such allegations are commonly made, there is no firm evidence to support them.

163 Stacchini, op. cit., 43–5.

164 ibid., 45.

165 Dulles, *Unrest in Brazil*, 323.

166 General Joaquim Justino Alves Bastos gives an account in his memoirs of the build-up of events in Recife from January to April. In January he was visited by Castello Branco, and both Castello Branco and Costa e Silva maintained contact in subsequent weeks. Alves Bastos, op. cit., 348–50. He recalls a telephone call from Goulart at 2 a.m. on 1 April, when over a very bad line Goulart asked him how the Fourth Army was. 'At absolute readiness', replied the general, 'Here we are all ready'. Alves Bastos says his aides in the room laughed as they heard the conversation, and a few hours later, at about 9 a.m., he declared his support for the anti-Goulart cause; ibid., 359–60.

1964–67

9 The Shaping of the Authoritarian State

1964: A Political Watershed?

Reflecting on the behaviour of João Goulart in the weeks immediately preceding the *coup*, especially during the noisy crises and heady rallies of March 1964, his critics have portrayed him as a weak, confused president, caught up in forces he did not understand, playing a dangerous game which in the end destroyed him. It is a harsh picture, showing Goulart as at best inept and at worst as indulging in radical posturing he could not sustain, provoking his opponents to an extreme reaction which ended not just Goulart's career, but, as in the case of the abortive 'Communist' revolt of 1935, any short-term hope for left-wing advance more generally. On both the left and right of Brazilian politics the one point of agreement concerning the events of 1964 is disparagement of Goulart.

In several important respects this interpretation needs to be qualified. First, the crisis, financial, economic and, political, was not of Goulart's making. In all essentials he was presented with it as soon as he took over from Quadros, and in its most crucial dimensions it had been taking shape over many years. Fundamentally, the confrontation between Goulart and his opponents, as between Vargas and those same opponents, was about the nature, direction, and speed of change in Brazilian society and about the shaping and control of the modern Brazilian state and its relation to that process of social change. From the day he took office Goulart was surrounded by enemies, unwilling to give him even half a chance in their intransigent opposition to all they believed him to represent. The economic and financial crises which deepened during his presidency did not arise spontaneously, but, like the severe political constraints within which he had to work, reflected a system developed over many years by those who in the past had controlled Brazilian politics. In the president's struggle to meet international demands for stabilization, and to increase his government's credibility both at home and abroad, his enemies were more deeply alarmed at the possibility of his success than they were at his eventual failure. Seeking to perform the delicate balancing act of winning international confidence, preserving the essentials of democracy, and satisfying, however slowly and hesitantly, the growing popular demands for reform, Goulart and his government were faced, throughout the whole of his presidency, with immovable opposition at home and deep-rooted suspicion abroad, which also worked further on the growth of opposition, both civilian and military, within Brazil. Far from being helped in his task of government, Goulart was, in the main, opposed by representatives of Brazil's financial and business communities, mistrusted by their allies abroad, refused even small concessions by landowners outraged by the most timorous moves towards agrarian reform, and presented, both nationally and internationally, as an irresponsible demagogue appealing to the masses to pull down the whole structure of Brazilian society, in league with organized labour, in a subversive move to establish the long-dreaded *república sindicalista.*

A more detached appraisal of the president's actions, speeches, and policies does not sustain this picture, especially in two important respects, and does much to re-establish him as a serious national politician. First, his behaviour and strategy become more rational and intelligible when seen as aimed not at pulling down Brazil's democratic institutions, but rather at exerting new forms of pressure to break the deadlock which by early 1964 was so apparent. Having been refused special powers, but faced with popular demand for change, the only solution was to bring to bear on a reluctant, heavily conservative Congress, the pressure arising from the ever clearer manifestation of that popular demand. Again, in choosing this course Goulart was not entirely a free agent; but to decide to exert on such a Congress pressures and demands deliberately damped down by the party and Congressional system was, as Goulart repeatedly claimed, not so much to weaken or destroy the democratic system, but to make it more directly representative of, and more immediately responsive to, popular opinion. The alternative, as again he insisted, was not just the dangerous growth of frustrated reform demands, but the real possibility that the democratic form of government would be challenged, even destroyed, by those who over many years had made clear their lack of respect for the democratic process in Brazil, whether, in some cases, in their support for the authoritarianism of the *Estado Novo* or, in others, less frankly, while paying lip-service to democratic ideals, in calling for military intervention whenever their grip seemed to slacken. In the view of Goulart and those close to him the greater danger to democracy, as well as to reform, came from the right. His strategy can therefore better be seen as a last effort to make Congress work effectively, rather than as an attempt to destroy it.

The second point of emphasis with regard to Goulart's behaviour at this time concerns why he believed, with apparent sincerity, that he could carry his policies through, a belief which again makes his actions appear more rational than they are commonly presented. This was not just because he was carried away by the power of his own rhetoric at a few mass rallies, or because he trusted too eagerly the cheers and support he received on those occasions; but because, more simply, he was genuine in his repeatedly asserted belief that the armed forces would not only remain loyal to him as the constitutionally appointed successor to Quadros, but that the bulk of them would support his efforts for 'basic reforms'. He knew that trouble was brewing, but seems not to have known its scale, and to have believed it could be contained. He accepted the assurances of General Assis Brasil and was confident of the loyalty of his military commanders and his *dispositivo militar*, especially General Amaury Kruel in São Paulo. While these remained loyal, he rightly believed he could ignore the rumblings of the always conservative navy or of officers long regarded as somewhat eccentric. This trust was to prove in the end Goulart's greatest error of judgement; but his belief right till the eleventh hour that the armed forces' leaders would stand by him makes rational, intelligible, and indeed creditable, behaviour which otherwise seems merely erratic and suicidal.

Coming, finally, not just to the eleventh hour, but to the dying minutes of that hour, Goulart has often been charged, if sometimes only by implication, with irresponsibility and folly amounting to despair in refusing to heed or accept the warnings and ultimata of General Amaury Kruel in his telephone calls of 31 March from São Paulo. Instead, Goulart stood by his friends and advisers, broke with Kruel, and precipitated the final crisis. But, again, Goulart's behaviour was to a high degree honourable, rational, and politically perceptive. First, there seems little doubt that he probably could have saved his own skin and played out his presidency by abandoning both his political associates and his policies aimed at reform; that he refused to do so can only be counted to his credit, not least at a time when so many were turning their coats. Secondly, his refusal of Kruel's ultimata was above all a rational political act, amounting in effect to a political stand and statement of position, especially important when set alongside the president's refusal over the next few hours to inflict on the nation the incalculable costs of civil war. What was being asked of Goulart was that, to all intents and purposes, he himself should carry out the *coup* of which the next day he and his associates were to be the victims. He might indeed continue in office, but only as a puppet figure, after giving up his political programme and those with whom till then he had been working. It was here that the analogy which in recent months Goulart had been so fond of making, between himself and Getúlio Vargas, came nearest to being sustained. Essentially, he was being given the choice of being ejected from office, like Vargas in 1945, or of committing, if not physical, at least political, suicide, more closely resembling, therefore, Vargas in 1954. Kruel and by extension the mass of the armed forces would stand by Goulart, but only if he denied and dismantled the whole political structure and overall reformist commitment of the Vargista tradition, if he rejected his political associates and broke with all these organizations, such as the CGT and the UNE, which formed the bases of his popular support.

Goulart's refusal to supervise, in effect, the *coup* against himself also amounted in practice to the first political statement or overt public judgement about what the *coup* of 1964, while as yet scarcely under way, represented within the broad sweep of modern Brazilian politics. Listening to the demands made by Kruel on the telephone from São Paulo, Goulart judged that there could be no grounds for compromise, that the country had reached a political watershed greater than any in its modern history, a moment when men had to choose the side on which they stood. For Goulart and his supporters, with increasing clarity as the *coup* unfolded in the next days and weeks, the voice of Kruel and those who stood with him was the authentic voice of the established order, of those, however heterogeneous in other respects, who saw themselves challenged by what they believed Goulart and the whole Vargista *trabalhista* movement represented, a challenge which now they were determined and united to resist. For Goulart and his supporters up and down the country the social forces behind the *coup* were those which at various crises in Brazil's history, often with foreign encouragement and support, had opposed Getúlio Vargas, and resisted, for varying reasons, the reformism associated with Kubitschek and even with Quadros. They were interests deeply embedded in Brazil's long-established social system, still dominant in its financial and economic system, and tenaciously to be defended in the manipulation of national politics. The *coup* of 1964 was therefore, they believed, for both sides long dug-in to their political positions, a major watershed, not just another petty swing of the political pendulum, but, the most important, most far-reaching and decisive, confrontation in modern Brazilian politics.

The development of politics in the next decade or more was to confirm this view expressed in Goulart's refusal to seek a compromise with his opponents, that the *coup* of 1964, much more than, for example, the success of Vargas in 1930 or his deposition in 1945, marked a profound change, the repercussions of which would be felt over many years right through the political economy. Certainly this was the aim of the men who in 1964 took over control of national politics, who, no less than Goulart, saw their intervention as opening a new era, deliberately reversing trends they believed pernicious and turning the country towards new paths of national regeneration and development contained in their concept of the 'Brazilian democratic revolution'. Indeed, the principal concern of many of those involved in Goulart's removal was that this time there had to be a clean break, that by contrast, for example, with 1930 there must be no turning back and no premature handing over of power to those very civilian politicians so recently set aside. This time the job of 'cleansing' (*saneamento*) and restructuring must be thorough, even if it should require a prolonged period of 'revolutionary' control.[1]

When examining the more detailed character of politics before and after the *coup* of 1964, it is possible, and at some levels necessary, to emphasize striking elements of continuity, especially in persisting attitudes towards issues of national politics. Various writers have stressed, for example, the continuing strength of clientelist systems, a notable tendency to accept authoritarian patterns of behaviour, and many other features of national and local politics which show that in Brazil, as in most societies, old habits die hard and that a change of government at the top has only a limited, perhaps mercifully limited, impact on the way in which the majority of people conduct their lives and react to the society in which they find themselves. At the level of 'political culture', at that of simple description of political behaviour, the story is in many respects one of 'plus ça change'. In other respects, too, there is striking evidence of the long continuity of modern Brazilian politics, in the survival, already noted, of soldiers who in 1964, as in the 1920s, condemned the 'corruption' of civilian politics, or of ideologues who in 1964, as in 1937, drew up blueprints for direct authoritarian control of Brazil. The links between this 'new authoritarianism' after 1964 and that of the years preceding 1945 are easy to trace, even allowing an overall interpretation of Brazil which sees the period from 1945 to 1964 as an atypical excursion into more open, representative politics away from the more common pattern of authoritarian control.

Continuity, certainly, is there, and should indeed be argued at a more profound and important level than that of mere functionalist description. There is, for example, important continuity of social control in the reorganization of the 'bourgeois' state and the continuing defence of long-established interests, albeit in a new form. This is a question to be discussed later: but first it must be stressed that some at least of the accounts which emphasize continuity go altogether too far, while also concentrating on mere description of political behaviour rather than analysing changes in the structure and direction of the political economy. They also often give too much weight to static rather than dynamic features of Brazil's political experience, and, more particularly, to elements of conciliation and adjustment rather than to persistent conflict and apparently irreconcilable disagreement.[2]

Such judgements on the nature of Brazil's political development ignore the deep tensions, frequent violence, and bitter confrontation which often have been 'reconciled' only by the suppression and rigorous control of the losing faction. This analysis irons out and severely underrates the long history of social class conflict, expressed in both local and national politics, reducing social conflict almost to intra-class disagreement:

> of conflict, of course, there has been plenty in Brazilian society, but not along the monolithic, polarized lines of cleavage predicted by the 'classical' development syndrome. More often than not it has involved opposition between sectors of the same class, whether defined by property, status or power.[3]

Such a judgement, while rightly drawing attention to the importance of intra-class tension and disagreement, suggests a basic misunderstanding of how 'classical' theories of social class conflict are to be applied. The 'lines of cleavage', in anything but the crudest form of class analysis, are not expected to be starkly 'monolithic' or 'polarized'. More frequently the lines will be blurred by the successful working of ideological and other controls, so that some of the most fundamentally divisive issues may only rarely appear as points of open disagreement in national politics. But there are times, as in Brazil in 1964, when those issues do appear, when more 'normal' processes of control prove inadequate and the otherwise comparatively smooth surface of political life is shattered. In, however, the more exclusive forms of functionalist analysis applied to Brazil the description rarely proceeds beyond that smooth surface. The *coup* of 1964 is not, therefore, seen as a really crucial turning-point in Brazil's social and political formation, since it is not regarded, in any worthwhile sense, as being about conflicting class interests, working themselves out in a sharply different pattern of social and economic policies in the years after the *coup*, affecting the whole political economy, and changing in fundamentally important respects the workings of the modern Brazilian state. There are hints of some of these effects of the *coup*,[4] but for the most part, functionalist descriptions of Brazilian politics severely underplay the clash of social interests represented in the change of regime in 1964. Analyses of the *coup* by Brazilians themselves, whatever their political standpoint, are by contrast in broad agreement that the really important political break came in April 1964, with, by comparison, relatively little difference in fundamental priorities and commitment between the various military-led governments in the years which followed.[5] April 1964 is taken as marking the great political divide, even if in later years other notable bench-marks were also be be found, as, for example, the lurch to the right and harsher repression as expressed in Institutional Act No. 5 of December 1968.

This debate on the significance of the *coup* of April 1964 has been impassioned from the start and will continue so for a long time to come. It is, however, possible to reconcile to some extent both sides of the argument, by noting the essentially ambivalent, and still unresolved, nature of the change of regime, an interpretation which will be developed throughout this political analysis. Briefly, the line of argument is as follows. (1) At the level of 'political culture' and the description of political behaviour there is a striking degree of continuity. (2) Set in the context of the growing challenge from more popular social forces to the long-established political and social order of Brazil, the *coup* was the most important turning-point in modern Brazilian politics. The changing relations, for example, between capital and labour observable over the previous two decades or more were now brusquely altered and new political patterns introduced, to serve the purposes of those who now in an increasingly authoritarian manner directed the nation's affairs. In particular, by abruptly cutting short the emergence of more popular forces in national politics, the *coup* halted the move, however confused and often uncertain it may have been, towards the creation of a new social and political order in Brazil. (3) Examined at a much more important level than that of descriptive political behaviour, the *coup*, since it contained important elements of continuity, reasserted and re-established controls and priorities long dominant in the Brazilian system, even though these were now to be substantially modified and made to find new forms of expression. The past three decades had seen the rapid growth of the bourgeois state in Brazil, supported over the last twenty years by the political structures of a tightly controlled liberal democratic system. The crucial struggle throughout the whole modern period had been about who was to control that state, and in whose interests, and how that control should be made effective. 1964 saw a new alignment of social forces, with a different relationship between the state apparatus and the contending groups within Brazilian politics. But this again implied continuity, since essentially it was no more than a readjustment of the internal mechanisms of a capitalist economy and of a 'bourgeois' state organized to support it. In this sense, the *coup* of 1964, however sharp and important a watershed, was only a shift within the longer development of Brazil's capitalist economy, leaving still unresolved its most basic tensions or contradictions, problems still to be faced, therefore, in terms of economic, social, and political organization, long after the successful *coup* of 1964 had given power to the new rulers of Brazil. How these tensions were expressed and what efforts were made to contain them, now needs to be examined.

Preserving Democratic Forms: 1964–65

The Choice of President

By contrast with earlier episodes in Brazil's political history the *coup* of 1964 was quiet, and swift, lacking the noise and colour of Vargas's arrival in Rio de Janeiro in 1930, the high drama and intense emotion of his suicide in 1954, or even the deep sense of crisis surrounding the sudden departure of Quadros in 1961. But there was, from the start, an evident sense of purpose in those who now directed events, a clear determination to make a sharp break with the immediate past, and increasing evidence that the men now coming to power had behind them a coherent, well-elaborated overall plan of action, an alternative set of policies to offer, or impose on, Brazil. The victors of 1964 were a heterogeneous group, drawing on all elements of opposition to Goulart, but through the initial confusion came, first, a generalized commitment to put a stop to all recent 'subversion' and restore confidence in the country's economy, and, secondly, an outline of the strategy required for these purposes. This was built, as became ever clearer, on long debates and reflection in military colleges, especially the Escola Superior de Guerra, and among the new controlling group of civilians and military officers, who not only opposed Goulart, but, more importantly, had an alternative body of policies, which also had the ready, even anxious, support of the most important interests outside Brazil, especially the United States government. Hardly had Ranieri Mazzilli been sworn in as provisional president of Brazil, early on 2 April, before a telegram from Lyndon Johnson expressed the admiration and support of the American people, a recognition almost embarrassing in its speed and warmth, while Goulart was still within the country. Lincoln Gordon made equally clear his own enthusiasm for the new government, describing the *coup* as 'one of the major turning points in world history, in the middle of the twentieth century',[6] a view reflected in the swift, generous help now offered to the Brazilian regime by the United States government.

One striking feature of the *coup* was the speed with which the most prominent leaders of the older, *golpista* elements, those who had long called for military intervention and who finally had sparked off the movement against Goulart, were quietly but firmly removed from the direction of events. The new order was to be directed, not by the more eccentric, quirky military opponents of Vargas and Goulart, such as Olímpio Mourão Filho, nor even by the respectable 'elder statesmen' of military politics, such as Juarez Távora or Eduardo Gomes. These were given, at most, relatively minor jobs,[7] while the crucial posts went to the coalition of officers and civilians associated with Castello Branco and those who, though waiting on events in March 1964, now quickly asserted their leadership. In the early confused discussions over who should be chosen as president the candidacy of Castello Branco soon emerged as the strongest. There was mention of a civilian candidate, but Lacerda, in particular, was afraid that a civilian, once established as head of the new 'revolutionary' order, might be a serious challenge to his own presidential ambitions in 1965. Among the more eligible military figures were ex-president Dutra and General Amaury Kruel, whose role in the last hours of Goulart's government had been so crucial. But Dutra was unacceptable in some quarters because of his PSD connections, and Kruel because of his previously strong links with Goulart. There was also mention of Marshal Denys, who most strongly represented the 'hard core' military opposition to Goulart, men such as Cordeiro de Farias, Nelson de Melo, and Admiral Heck, but throughout the often quite heated discussions among the state governors and military leaders from 2 to 11 April support for Castello Branco became steadily stronger. He had the advantage of appearing as a soldier previously aloof from politics, involved only in a time of crisis. More positively, he had the strong support of the 'Sorbonne' group within the officer corps, a cluster of officers mostly associated with the ESG, perceived as intelligent, technically well-trained, and politically moderate.[8] This was in fact a more heterogeneous and less well-defined group than is often presented, but, for the purpose of presidential support, it was effective as a distinguishable, generally respected grouping within the officer corps. Perhaps most important of all, Castello Branco had the strong backing of Carlos Lacerda, who argued his case in the governors' meetings, and he was known to be very highly thought of by the United States embassy, especially through his links with Colonel Vernon Walters.[9] The discussions on who should be presented to Congress as the candidate backed by the 'revolutionary' leaders were sometimes stormy and left some deep personal bitterness, especially between Carlos Lacerda and General Costa e Silva, which would re-emerge in later years: but on 11 April Castello Branco received 361 votes from the members of Congress,[10] becoming the first military president of the new regime.

Defining the New Order

The assumption of the presidency by General Castello Branco meant that 'for the first time in the twentieth century an essentially military government came to power in Brazil'.[11] It also meant that there immediately arose the question of how long it would take to set the nation's house in order, what kind of institutional changes might be necessary, how the new regime should deal with former opponents, and above all how far the widely admitted requirements of economic recovery and of restoring political order could be compatible with democratic forms of government, free elections, and a political party system finding expression through Congress. There were some older military leaders who, in the light of their experience in 1930, when, as they believed, the old politicians had been allowed to return too easily, were convinced that national recovery, both political and economic, would take time. They mistrusted all politicians and called therefore for extended powers to carry the job through.[12] Others believed that in perhaps two to three years the armed forces would be able to withdraw, restoring 'normal' political life, with the crisis safely resolved.

Of these two viewpoints the old *tenente* analysis, though a minority view in 1964, among both military officers and civilians, was more realistic in its understanding of what was implied by the *coup* and the accession of a military president. Despite the initial confusion and the heterogeneity of the opposition to Goulart, already it was clear that the crisis of 1964 was more profound than on any other occasion on which the armed forces had intervened merely to arbitrate or impose a short-term solution. The issues involved in the removal of Goulart were more serious and far-reaching than on previous occasions, as when, for example, Góes Monteiro and Dutra had ushered in the *Estado Novo* or when Lott had guaranteed that Kubitschek should take office. Although important, these interventions had been, essentially, about reconciling differences within the broad ruling coalition of the dominant political class, adjustments which gave more direct influence to one fraction rather than another. The *coup* of 1964 was different. It might, indeed, represent, at a more profound level, a futher adjustment in Brazil's capitalist development, with a reorganization of power within the bourgeois state, but the crisis of 1964 was also about contending class interests and a challenge to the existing economic and political system.

Neither the heterogeneity nor the confusion of the anti-Goulart movement should be allowed to distract attention from this qualitative difference between the *coup* of 1964 and earlier military incursions into politics, one element of which was the readiness, psychologically, ideologically, and in terms of coherent if not yet fully explicit strategy, of those who now were taking power.[13] Ever since 1949 the Escola Superior de Guerra had been elaborating what in effect was an economic and political strategy for Brazil, a model of national development, closely linked to a highly refined concept of national security, which now was available to the new regime. Equally important, the college had also provided over the years a strong, well-defined group of military officers and civilians, all sharing a broadly common ideology. When, therefore, the *coup* took place, in contrast, for example, with the military seizure of power in 1889, there was already in the wings a strong team of technically able, confident men, ready to put into practice ideas and theories developed and debated over a long period. During the first twenty years of the ESG's existence about two thousand students followed the one-year course in the college,[14] which by the time of the *coup* in 1964 had become a regular element in the training of ambitious senior military officers:

> Rarely if ever has one educational institution, in less than two decades of existence, had so profound an impact upon the course of a nation's development . . . By 1955, nearly half the new general officers had been through it, and by 1962 the proportion had risen to nearly 80 per cent. At the time of the 1964 *coup* nearly two-thirds of the active-duty generals were E.S.G. graduates . . .[15]

But the course was also taken by many civilians who had reached an educational standard broadly equivalent to a university education:

> Through 1966, its nearly 1,600 alumni included 800 senior officers of the Armed Forces; 424 government officials (including 39 congressmen, 23 judges, 200 higher echelon bureaucrats from the ministries, 97 leading administrators of autonomous agencies, and 45 state officials); and 328 individuals from the private sector, chiefly businessmen and industrial managers.[16]

There was a deliberate attempt to integrate as closely as possible the military and civilian members of the College: 'All civilian graduates are incorporated into plans for mobilization in case of national emergency, in posts accorded rank of colonel and above'.[17] Former students were kept closely informed of their fellows' progress and of the intellectual and social activities of the College, partly through the *Boletim da Associação dos Diplomados da Escola Superior de Guerra*,[18] and well-attended weekly luncheons with prominent speakers were held in Rio de Janeiro, and other major cities (especially São Paulo) had similar, although less frequent, meetings. There was an official liaison officer in each major government ministry.[19] There were few other societies anywhere in the world where the intertwining of military and civilian careers, debate, and politics was so marked, and where the military were so prepared, albeit with civilian help, to take over the running of a modern state and reshape it in accordance with an already highly elaborated theory of national development. Nor, because of the strong links between the ESG and the United States military establishment and government officials, was there anywhere else a group who could command such swift, wholehearted support from the United States, as well as from other political, commercial, and financial interests, who, after having been deeply alarmed by events under Goulart, now saw the *coup* as introducing a new era of stability and prosperity within the framework of Western capitalist development.

On the other hand, while this strong group of civilian and military leaders was poised, ready to take over the running of the country, there were already apparent, even in the early days of defining the new political order, challenging questions and difficulties, which would become even sharper over the next decade or more. They were questions which, for the most part, sprang from the thinking and ideology behind the new regime, the logic of which was still in 1964 not fully clear even to those most closely involved in reshaping Brazilian politics. The key concept behind all teaching and debate in the ESG was, right from the start, that of 'national security'. This was partly derived at first from 'National Defence with a capital D', as stressed by those who in 1936 had founded a similar college in France;[20] but the preoccupation with the concept of 'national security' was much strengthened in the years of the Cold War, being elaborated with obsessive, neo-scholastic refinements throughout the 1950s and early 1960s. In the first decree establishing the college (Law No. 785. 20 August 1949) its aim was said to be to strengthen studies required to direct and plan National Security, an idea repeated and developed in later directives.[21] From this basic concept of 'national security' sprang long discussion of related issues of 'national objectives', both 'permanent' and 'current', of 'national power' and of 'national strategy', all of which were examined in detail and woven into a coherent ideology and broad overall strategy for national development.[22] Studies bearing such titles as *Planejamento Estra-*

tégico (Strategic Planning) and *Geopolítica do Brasil* (Geopolitics of Brazil)[23] reflected the content of courses taught in the ESG up to 1964, with an increasing stress on questions of national 'development' and their relation to 'security' rather than on the more technical military issues which previously had taken up so much time. These discussions were to go on long after the *coup* of 1964, but, already by the time the move against Goulart was made, there had been constructed an ideologically consistent position, shared at least in broad terms by all associated with the ESG, incorporating both a coherent economic theory of Brazilian development and a firmly held set of political views.[24]

At its most general level, and particularly in terms of its broad political analysis, there was little that was very new in ESG thinking, the most suasive of its elements being in the economic field, but, even then, as the post-*coup* years were to show, with too little attention being paid to the political dimensions of the economic policies envisaged. The two central concepts, from which all else sprang, were those of 'security' and 'development', always seen as inextricably linked. The main threat to security, both external and internal, was always perceived to be the 'subversion' associated with 'Communism'. At its most simplistic level, the main thrust of ESG thinking was towards a commitment to Western, and effectively to United States-led, capitalism, which, with elementary Cold War logic, required the concentration of all national power in an effort to produce a 'development' process which would effectively eliminate many of the pressures favourable to the growth of subversion. Lectures in the ESG stressed the inescapable fact of 'total war' and the consequent need to develop an overall 'Strategy' to safeguard national security, a 'Grand Strategy' or 'General Strategy', involving both the armed forces and civilians, to which should be subordinated 'Military', 'Economic', 'Political', and 'Psychosocial Strategy'.[25] Much attention was given to such issues as 'Brazil and the Defence of the West',[26] in which it was stressed that the West needed Brazil for its total security, a theme developed in more detail in discussion of, for example, the nature of 'revolutionary war'.[27] It was reflections such as these which caused members of the ESG, both military and civilian, to react with alarm to the move towards 'subversion' under Goulart, and which accounted for the fact that out of the 102 line generals who in 1964 were on active duty those who had been at the ESG were prominent in the plotting against Goulart, with 60 per cent of ESG graduates among them actively resisting Goulart, as compared with only 15 per cent of those who had not attended the ESG.[28]

This persistent emphasis on 'security' and the close links, personal as well as ideological, between the ESG, other Brazilian military colleges, and the United States military and political establishment can, however, easily lead to too ready an identification of the ESG with a simplistic 'Cold War' offensive and support for United States and other foreign interests in Brazil. These connections undoubtedly were important, right from the start, but, as well as the reiteration of familiar arguments in defence of the capitalist system, there were other features of military–civilian thinking which were essentially part of a longer indigenous tradition of military criticism of society, giving to certain areas of ESG argument an originality and at times an ambivalence which must not be overlooked. The ESG was not simply a foreign implant. It fitted into the pattern of military–civilian involvement in national politics, the roots of which went back well into the nineteenth century, and it represented only a further development in an already established tradition of 'intellectual' officers, involved both in theoretical critique of and active participation in national politics, of which it was difficult to find the like either in Latin America or in more 'developed' societies. Many elements in ESG thinking could be traced to the blend of military and civilian criticism which made up *tenentismo* in the 1920s and early 1930s, and, as with *tenentismo*, there was room for disagreement and dialogue within the broad range of reflection and debate to be found in the ESG. This is a large subject, but a few brief examples are worth citing, as indicative of how ESG thinking on important issues was not merely dependent on foreign influences, and how also were contained within it elements which reflected quite sharply differing views of national politics, potentially important for the future.

First was the stress on internal security, an area of concern developed and carefully analysed by Brazilian military theorists well before the 'guerrilla threat' in the early 1960s brought it to the forefront of debate in the United States and elsewhere.[29] This reflected the long preoccupation with an internal threat, already so strongly developed in the 1930s, and was one point on which Brazilian military theorists gave a lead. A second question, which reflected both the indigenous element in their thought and its frequent ambivalence, was that of nationalism. The common image of the ESG is of a centre of *entreguismo*, of support for those who were ready, even eager, to follow a development strategy which gave large concessions to foreign interests to work within and exploit the Brazilian economy: but a close reading of some of the leading military theorists modifies that image. Again there is the inheritance from the *tenentes*, with their stress on economic nationalism and a stouter defence of the national patrimony. There is, certainly, a central conviction that Brazil's development is tied to that of the 'Western' world, so closely linked to the United States, but within this broad commitment is wide room for disagreement as to what this implies in practice, how tight the links should be, and how and by whom they should be forged.[30] A third feature of ESG thinking, which perhaps most sharply differentiated it from some of its foreign exemplars, was its insistence on the vital role of the state in national development, linked to the central concept of 'national power'. Again there are direct echoes of *tenente* thinking of the early 1930s, and even traces of *Integralista* emphasis, on the need to find a *Brazilian* solution to Brazil's problems and face squarely the specific difficulties of underdevelopment, even if the concept of underdevelopment is not introduced as such. The emphasis, as in *tenentismo* and underlying the whole *Estado Novo* experiment, is on the need for a concentration of national forces, of centralization of control, and, above all, of rationality in planning and execution of national objectives, all closely tied, once again, to the perceived requirements of national security. The means by which all branches of national life can be brought together and subsumed under the broad direction of national security is the power of the state. Again this fitted into a familiar Brazilian pattern, which increasingly in the modern period, but especially since the 1930s, had been one of ever greater state control of key areas of the economy and of national planning. ESG theorists, at various levels and for various purposes, were quick to emphasize the key role of the state, not merely urging the need to defend it, but stressing its vital relevance to the related questions of security and development.[31]

> Security implies the coherent and progressive development of the normal activities of the State, following the direction and rhythm determined by national objectives, through the rational development of National Power....[32]

The role of the state is seen as especially important in the economic sphere,[33] but there is a general acceptance of the need for concentration of state power to carry through the strategy for national development which, in turn, is determined by the needs of national security. The reflection on the state, as on many other key issues, remained at a high level of abstraction and needed to be worked out in much greater detail. There was, in particular, no attempt to make clear who would exercise state power, and on whose behalf, but here again, as in the debate over nationalism, were features of ESG thinking which sharply distinguished it from that currently dominant in the United States, and which contained, at the very least, seeds of future disagreement.

This whole set of reflections on the related problems of security and development was to find clear expression in the new political and social order defined after the *coup* of 1964:[34] but at least as important in the context of the mounting economic and financial crises of late 1963 and the months before the takeover from Goulart was the body of economic thinking associated with the ESG. By comparison with the intricate refinement of concepts related to security and national power, the economic theories underlying the new regime were relatively inchoate and less explicit, but they were, at the same time, sufficiently recognizable in broad terms to appeal to many of those who were alarmed at the steadily rising inflation and the worsening crisis. For the most part, those most influential in criticizing the financial and economic policies of the Goulart government were not the military theorists of the ESG but civilians associated with it, some of whom had lectured on ESG courses, whose thinking fitted happily with the requirements of security and development as understood by the armed forces' leaders, and who now were to be given free rein in the shaping of the new economic order envisaged for Brazil. A basic commitment of all ESG thinking was to rational planning and organization of all aspects of national life. The soldiers would now guarantee the political and social 'stability' required by the economic planners, firmly controlling any opposition considered inimical to the smooth progress of the economic strategy to be adopted. How much control would be required was still not clear, but right from the start it was evident that the new regime, following the logic of ESG thinking, would impose whatever controls and introduce whatever changes might be found to be necessary.

Unambiguously clear in the broad economic theorizing associated with ESG courses and of those now taking control of Brazil was the commitment to a development strategy linked to the system of international capitalism under the hegemony, at least in the short-term, of the United States. In the economic as well as in the political sphere the *coup* of 1964 was seen as a victory over 'subversion' and 'Communism', putting Brazil firmly in line once more with the system of Western capitalism under the leadership, if not control, of the United States. This again is not to say that those who now were to shape economic policy were simply crude 'entreguistas' in the vocabulary of the debate of the 1950s and early 1960s, men ready to hand over the economy to foreign, especially United States, interests. The position was altogether more complex, as it would remain for many years to come. Some of those most closely involved in defining the new economic order had on occasion showed themselves ready to take a stand when they felt themselves pushed too hard. Roberto Campos, for example, the man now to become Minister of Planning and director of the nation's economic strategy, had shown this as recently as March 1963, when he and Dantas had seriously considered rejecting the conditions of the United States government and the IMF attached to further aid for Brazil. In line with ESG thinking on nationalism those now taking power, both soldiers and civilians, thought of themselves as interpreting the best national interests of Brazil. But it is true that their understanding of this was always within the context of a capitalist development strategy, directly opposed to socialism or 'Communism', and was further guided by an explicit pragmatism or readiness to accept what they believed was the only realistic course for Brazil, an economy firmly directed in association with the capitalist system in which the United States gave the lead. A central emphasis, therefore, was on rational planning and direction in a context of restored foreign confidence resulting from a renewed stability, both financial and political, within Brazil. What such a strategy involved, and what social and political costs it entailed, was to become clearer only after the seizure of power in April 1964 and, in some important respects, only over the next decade and more.

The economic and financial dimensions of the new strategy, especially some of the technical devices to promote stabilization, such as the 'crawling peg', a series of regular mini-devaluations, and the able use of indexation, were soon to attract widespread interest. But right from the start it became clear that the new 'model' to be followed, already seen at least in embryo in the thinking of both soldiers and civilians associated with the ESG,[35] was one which logically contained substantial social and political costs, with the political dimension being integrally linked to, even dictated by, the necessities of financial and economic strategy.[36] One central feature of the economic thinking behind the new regime was, for example, the belief that in any conflict between growth and distribution, priority should be given to growth, if only as a prerequisite of future redistribution.[37] Part of the failure of the Goulart government, it was commonly argued, sprang precisely from an unrealistic commitment to programmes of distribution, reform, and wider participation running ahead of economic performance. The economy, therefore, must first be put in order, with inflation severely cut back, foreign confidence restored, and higher growth-rates won, before there could be more talk of 'basic reforms' and costly policies in areas in which political rhetoric had previously outstripped the capacity to pay. There must also be effective fiscal reforms, to produce by much tighter taxation sufficient revenue to meet the nation's needs without merely printing more paper,[38] measures which would also commend themselves to the IMF and other influential foreign observers, who in recent months and years had begun to despair of Brazil's economy and the government's ability to contain political demands.

In its most simple form this was the classical capitalist criticism of programmes aimed at wider distribution of national wealth and resources, especially in an underdeveloped economy where, it was argued, growth must precede distribution.[39] The whole tone of the critique was, however, eminently sane, measured, judicious, and pure music to the ears of those abroad who only recently had looked for 'islands of sanity' in a society they believed to be drowning in chaos.[40] Hence the rapid, enthusiastic endorsement of the new regime by foreign financial interests, echoing the speedy congratulations of United States senior government officials.

The full political implications of the financial and economic strategy to be adopted were to become clear only after some time, as it was realized how large a monopoly of political power would be needed to impose on the nation policies which were bound to produce resentment and resistance from those social groups most severely hit by them.[41] The years ahead would see a reshaping of political institutions and an enlargement of state power in response to these demands; but even in its first few weeks of life the new regime showed that, in line with its understanding of 'national security' and 'development', it would deal severely and swiftly with those it defined as political opponents. Within a week of the *coup* Congress was being asked to grant to the Revolutionary Supreme Command special powers to remove from active political life elected officials and civil servants closely linked to Goulart, frequently referred to simply as 'Communists'.[42] UDN leaders, representatives of such bodies as the Centro Industrial do Rio de Janeiro, and more extreme military officers were loud in their demands for the 'immediate removal and exemplary punishment of all elements of antidemocratic, subversive, and left-wing agitation';[43] but the military ministers were aware that the 1946 constitution forbade the removal of elected senators and deputies,[44] requiring even under a 'state of siege' a two-thirds vote of the members of the Senate or Chamber.[45] Something therefore must be done to change this ruling, a practice to be followed repeatedly in years to come when political exigency conflicted with constitutional provision. On 8 April three deputies, Pedro Aleixo (UDN), Ulysses Guimarães (PSD), and Arnaldo Cerdeira (PSP) proposed a 'Constitutional Act' requiring the support of two-thirds of their colleagues to give the necessary powers to the Revolutionary Supreme Command:[46] but the military ministers were not entirely happy with this proposal, partly because they were reluctant to seem to be depending on Congress to legitimize their 'revolution' and the new regime. Instead, they called on Francisco Campos and

Carlos Medeiros da Silva to draw up a new formula, an Institutional Act, to amend temporarily the constitution. Campos, in the early 1930s, had been the leader of the 'Revolutionary Legion' in Minas Gerais, an organization which in many respects had echoed European fascism, while also pointing the way to the *Integralista* movement.[47] A firm advocate of authoritarian control, he had drafted the constitution of the *Estado Novo*, then, as Minister of Justice under that corporatist system, had advanced his protégé, Carlos Medeiros da Silva, also from Minas Gerais, who subsequently became Vargas's Solicitor-General, Kubitschek's Attorney-General, and a Minister of the Supreme Court, and in 1966 Minister of Justice, drafting the new centralizing, authoritarian constitution of January 1967. To raise so quickly the ghosts of the *Estado Novo* and Brazil's earlier authoritarian experience scarcely matched the firm assurances being given about the essentially democratic nature of the new political order, sharpening doubts which became still more acute as the Institutional Act was made known on 9 April, signed in the Army Ministry by the three military ministers. Most of the Act was drafted by Medeiros da Silva, with Campos providing the prologue and one or two articles. The aim of the Institutional Act was to 'ensure for the new government . . . the means necessary for the . . . economic, financial, political, and moral reconstruction of Brazil'.[48] The intention was to maintain the 1946 constitution as far as possible, but, a point to be stressed explicitly: 'The victorious revolution, as a Constituent Power, legitimizes itself . . . The revolution is not seeking to legitimize itself through Congress. Rather, it is the latter which receives its legitimacy from this Institutional Act, by means of the exercise of that Constituent Power inherent in all revolutions'.[49] The revolution had deposed the previous government and now had legitimate authority to make new provisions to carry through the necessary work of reconstruction, not on behalf of any one group, but of the whole nation. Already from the tone as well as the substance of this first Institutional Act it was clear that, while professing the fullest respect for the constitution of 1946 and the democratic institutions associated with it, the new leaders of Brazil would subordinate everything to the first priority of national recovery and of draining 'the Communist abscess, the poison of which had worked its way not only through the head of the government, but throughout the whole system . . .'[50]

The rhetoric and the colourful but sometimes mixed metaphors came mostly from Campos, but the essential provisions of the Act were crisply set out. Congress should elect a president and vice president within two days, military chiefs of staff now being declared eligible for such office. The president might now propose constitutional amendments which must be acted on by Congress within thirty days, the required vote being an absolute majority rather than two-thirds. Congress must also act within thirty days on ordinary bills sent by the president; otherwise, such bills would be considered to have been approved automatically. Other presidential powers were also greatly increased, to initiate financial bills and declare a state of siege, and, giving still more teeth to the new regime, the Act allowed the Supreme Court to cancel the mandates of congressmen and elected members of state and municipal assemblies and councils, and with the same power to be given to the president for sixty days. All the articles of the Act were to expire on 31 January 1966, with the coming to office of the new president and vice-president, to be elected on 3 October 1965, in accordance with the constitution of 1946.[51]

The length of time for which political rights should be cancelled was one of the points on which already there had been disagreement among Brazil's new rulers. There were those, such as the Minister of Justice, Gama e Silva, and Admiral Rademaker, one of the three signatories to the Act with Costa e Silva and Correia de Melo, who wanted much harsher measures, including the removal of about half the members of Congress, some Supreme Court judges, and cancellation of political rights for fifteen years. They managed to raise to ten years, from five originally in the draft, this period of *cassações*, but in general the final text reflected the more moderate line favoured by Castello Branco and Costa e Silva.[52]

Already, however, it was enough to allow swift action against old opponents. Immediately it was signed, the military ministers announced that Goulart, Quadros, and Luís Carlos Prestes were deprived of political rights for ten years, the immediate inclusion of Quadros, whose original presidential term still had one and a half years to run, reflecting a lingering animosity towards him felt by Costa e Silva. On 10 April, the day before Congress met in Brasília to 'elect' Castello Branco as president and José Maria Alkmin as vice president, the 'Supreme Command of the Revolution' had already declared forty members of Congress, one senator and thirty-nine deputies, deprived of political rights (*cassados*) and ineligible to take part in the voting. On 14 April another list was published and further lists quickly brought to several hundred the number of those removed from active politics for the next ten years.[53] They included Goulart's former ministers, Abelardo Jurema, Almino Afonso, Paulo de Tarso, Amauri Silva, Celso Furtado, Wilson Fadul, and João Pinheiro Neto; the ex-governor Miguel Arraes; close Goulart associates such as Samuel Wainer, Darci Ribeiro, and Raul Riff; congressmen of all parties, including a few from the

UDN; labour leaders such as Osvaldo Pacheco, Clodsmit Riani, and Dante Pelacani; and military personnel of ranks as diverse as Marshal Osvino Ferreira Alves, Cabo Anselmo, and Sergeant Antônio Garcia Filho. On 11 April seventy-seven army officers, fourteen naval, and thirty-one air force were transferred to the reserve. Most of the senior officers were also deprived of political rights, with additions to the lists being announced regularly over the next days and weeks,[54] all part of a general weeding-out of military personnel, especially in the officer corps. The process also quickly spread out from the political centre, with more state governors and regional and local politicians, as well as civil servants and diplomats, appearing on the new proscribed lists. Most prominent of all was Juscelino Kubitschek. A steady campaign was built up against him, especially stressing 'corruption' and the amassing of a personal fortune. As the most prominent, and still potentially the most successful, presidential candidate of the PSD, he was the greatest single challenger to the hopes of Lacerda, with whom strong elements of the 'hard line' were increasingly to be associated, just as he was to the presidential ambitions of the Minister of War, Costa e Silva.[55] On 25 May Kubitschek made a public statement, offering to be judged again by the Brazilian people in a free election, and warning that the campaign against him was not just aimed at his own personal candidature 'but at the whole democratic regime'.[56] But the attacks continued, with Costa e Silva comparing Kubitschek's tone and language with that of Goulart in his 30 March speech to the sergeants in the Automobile Club. Kubitschek defended himself vigorously, with a final speech on 4 June to a packed Senate in Brasília, attacking the Institutional Act as an assault on Brazil's freedom, and alleging that already the nation was living under the effects of terror:

> I know that in this country of Brazil tyrannies do not last . . . We are passing through a difficult time; but this is a democratic country . . . I repeat: the blow which they want to strike against me, as former Head of State, will hit at the democratic life and the free will of the people. They are not hurting me personally, but all who claim a right to choose who will direct their affairs. This act is not one of punishment, but of usurpation. It is not my political rights they cancel, but far more: they take away the political rights of Brazil.[57]

It was a powerful, highly emotional speech, but made when Kubitschek already knew that his cause was lost. It was widely believed that Castello Branco was strongly against the move to deprive Kubitschek of political rights, partly, at least, because of the high international reputation which the ex-president enjoyed, but also because of his undeniable popularity at home and, more important still, the high measure of support he commanded in the armed forces. But on 8 June it was announced that the president, on the advice of the National Security Council, was depriving Kubitschek of his political rights for ten years.

As the first phase of political redefinition drew to a close, it seemed that the 'hard line', a heterogeneous group favouring stronger measures, and already identified in some quarters with the presidential ambitions of Costa e Silva and, in others, with those of Carlos Lacerda, was emerging as the more influential force, as against the more moderate, less immediately politically ambitious, group around Castello Branco. More significantly still, the move against Kubitschek, with talk already of similar action against Adhemar de Barros in São Paulo, was the first sign of a reaction, not only against those defined as 'subversive' in the vocabulary of April 1964, those closely identified with Goulart. It was a political attack on the whole 'political class' of the post-war period, an action whose logic would carry the new regime beyond mere *saneamento* or short-term reconstruction, into a reshaping of the whole political system supported by a new state apparatus, implying, above all, a new political role for the Brazilian armed forces.

By comparison with the turbulent excitement of the first six months of 1964 the second half of the year was relatively quiet. The new government's success in restoring confidence abroad was shown in its ability within its first twelve months to gain from creditors in Europe, the United States, and Japan postponement of payment due in 1964–66 on much of the medium-term debt not covered by an earlier 1961 agreement under Quadros, and in the new loans and credits made available to it. The United States made a loan of US$453 million, by comparison with only $30 million of United States government help to Brazil in the last nine months of the Goulart government. The IMF authorized a stand-by credit of $125 million in February 1965 and the International Bank for Reconstruction and Development, after sending a twenty-man mission to Brazil in December 1964, approved two loans, totalling $79·5 million, for electrical energy projects. The Inter-American Development Bank also gave help and some renewed confidence was shown by private investors and firms who now began to return to Brazil, encouraged, in particular, by the amendment of the Profit Remittance Law of 1962. This amendment removed the 10 per cent annual limit on remittances and allowed the 'capital investment' base to be adjusted for reinvested profits and for inflation. Brazil could again be seen as a country favourable to the foreign businessman and financier. The willingness to co-operate was also indicated in October 1964, when Brazil bought the American and Foreign Power Company's ten subsidiaries for US$135 million, despite considerable protest within the country, especially from Carlos Lacerda, who was, however, at once given a firm warning from Castello Branco, supporting the economic programme of Roberto Campos. Such measures did not immediately produce a large-scale response from the international financial community, so that until 1968 the main source of finance was to remain official, especially United States government, assistance; but a clear start had been made, expressing the priorities of the new regime.

Internal policies, too, were directed not only to reduce inflation while still promoting development, but also to provide reassurance wherever necessary that the economy was being managed with complete rationality in a context of full political stability. The more strictly financial and economic features of these policies are discussed elsewhere, especially the tax incentives to industry, the methods used to encourage a rapid growth in exports, and the fiscal and other reforms aimed at promoting a higher level of internal savings.[58] In all these respects the new rulers of Brazil showed much skill, imagination, and ingenuity and were remarkably successful in achieving their aims. But the principal concern here is with the political underpinning of the new strategy, without which Campos's whole financial and economic programme would, on his own admission, have had little or no chance of success.

One of Campos's main convictions about planning was the need for a sufficiently stable context within which the planner could work, to solve 'the problem of maintaining popular communication and assuring political allegiance to the plans', and 'converting planning from the top into a more effective consensus-building instrument for political stability'.[59] His diagnosis of previous Brazilian experience stressed the failure to maintain a firm commitment especially under political pressures,[60] following a common Latin American pattern in which:

> The political system, relying on popular elections for congressional representation, proves incapable of digesting the often harsh, restrictive measures needed to curb inflation or to extract fiscal resources for resumption of development.[61]

The continuing danger, unfortunately, as he put it in a neat aphorism, was that too often: 'Latin American governments are known to want capitalism without profit, socialism without discipline, and foreign investment without the foreign investor'.[62] A vigorous development programme for Brazil must therefore deal with this essentially political problem:

> The gist of the problem is the political problem. We haven't found yet a suitable political formula, or at least as suitable a political formula as our development formula . . . We haven't yet learned how to avoid mistakes. The prospects are for a continuation of this alliance, which has worked satisfactorily in the last few years, between the military and the technocrats, with a somewhat subdued role for the politician proper, not because the politician is unimportant, but because there needs to be a re-education of the political class that unfortunately had, at a certain point of time, confused democracy with demagoguery. We visualize that democratic normalcy and restoration of full democratic procedure is an obtainable objective within 4 or 5 years; but we certainly need, for the moment, more than external formalistic manifestations of the democratic apparatus, we need the maintenance of social discipline to go on with the urgent business of growth.[63]

This emphasis on failure to control the political system, the degeneration of democracy into demagoguery, the consequent need for political re-education, guided by the military and, above all, the technocrats, so as to ensure the social discipline needed for the urgent business of growth, is technocratic thinking in its purest form. It is boldly and incorrigibly elitist, frank and unafraid, a succinct expression of a comprehensive ideology, or a philosophy of 'development' and its requirements, and of how, in particular, political or social behaviour which threatens this development must be controlled or curbed, however reluctantly, for the sake of the wider, rational development plan. Campos's attitude summed up perfectly the more rational, moderate wing of the ESG, but particularly of the civilian experts and technocrats who now after April 1964 were most directly responsible for shaping economic and social policies. His stress on the importance of 'maintaining popular communication' and 'converting planning from the top into a more effective consensus-building instrument for political stability' was on the whole less representative of technocratic thinking, since it conceived planning as an essentially political activity and implied the need for a strong measure of consensus, however unclear might remain the means to achieve that consensus. This element in his thinking fitted more closely his view that eventually a return must be made to more open political debate as a basis for genuine 'stability', a view by no means shared by all the technocrats and experts who after 1964 were to work with the armed forces leadership. But his emphasis on the overriding need for 'stability', whether democratically-based or otherwise, as a condition for economic recovery and future growth, was fundamental to his thinking, and shared by both major groupings in the armed forces, the more moderate elements associated with Castello Branco and those who favoured more severe measures in dealing with political opponents.

What was already apparent in Campos's reflections on planning and politics was a tension which would remain unresolved for many years to come, between the generally accepted need for sufficient political control to allow effective rational planning and reassure foreign investors and businessmen, and an awareness among the more politically sophisticated leaders of the regime that severe authoritarian controls could easily be self-defeating, by failing to achieve for the government over a period of years legitimacy based on popular support and consensus, so requiring even harsher controls in a vicious circle of mounting repression. This was a dilemma which would also attract interest and arouse concern abroad, but which, more important still, was rooted in the planning philosophy of Campos and his colleagues, and which had to be faced by all the military governments, coming to a head under the fourth military president, Ernesto Geisel, taking office almost exactly a decade after the *coup* of April 1964.

Political control to ensure the urgent business of growth: but what kind of control, and for how long, and with what results, social and political as well as economic? In the early days of victory, while former opponents were being stripped of their political rights, there was also evidence of a darker side to the new regime, with authenticated reports of the use of torture to extract information, a process which was to become common practice in later years,[64] and the appearance across the country of IPMs (Inquéritos Policial-Militar; Military-Police Investigations), set up to root out 'subversion', but also allowing an often indiscriminate use of authority and power and the paying-off of old scores, personal as well as political. At the government level there was evidently an awareness of how easily these investigations, headed by military officers, often those most hostile to the Vargista tradition, might degenerate into an abuse of the thousands of suspects and witnesses called before them. A General Investigations Commission (CGI), headed by Marshal Estevão Taurino de Rezende, issued rules and guidelines,[65] but, as so often in such situations, there were over-zealous, unscrupulous, or over-ambitious officers who far exceeded their authority and tarnished the reputation of the new regime. This was a feature of Brazilian politics which, if not entirely new, was to become still more prominent in subsequent years, especially after 1968, casting a shadow over the successful economic performance and raising serious doubts as to how far the post-1964 'Brazilian model' could ever be exported or imitated without its accompanying apparatus of terror and repression.

Throughout 1964 the government showed its readiness to take firm action against any perceived threat, even from those who previously had supported the *coup*. The case of the governor of Goiás, Mauro Borges Teixeira, dragged on throughout the year, as the governor found himself under suspicion for his earlier association with Goulart and his defence of colleagues in the state government who were, he argued, not Communists, but politicians committed to reform. In part the struggle was between the local UDN, anxious to break the control of the PSD in Goiás, headed by the governor's father, Senator Pedro Ludovico; but it quickly turned into a national issue between the governor and elements in the regime, such as Costa e Silva and General Ernesto Geisel, who were hostile to him. The governor questioned 'hard-line' demands and in particular the activities of the IPM in Goiás. In late November 1964 the government intervened in the state, appointing a military *interventor*, and, very significantly, managed to win substantial approval of its action from the Chamber of Deputies, so underlining, as it had in its treatment of Kubitschek, that it could brush aside any possible opposition from the most important national party, the PSD. Eventually, after much excitement and negotiation, Borges lost his governorship and the 'hard line', once again, had shown its strength within the new regime, emphasizing the dangers of open criticism, even from those most highly placed politically.[66]

Despite these demands and pressures from 'hard-line' officers and their civilian associates, and despite the readiness already shown by the regime to act swiftly, even harshly, against its opponents or critics, there was still by early 1965 a firm, unambiguous commitment to restore 'democracy' and to preserve democratic forms, a position genuinely held at least by the more moderate 'Sorbonne' group of military officers. These still saw their intervention of April 1964 as a necessary step to restore order and speed economic recovery, but believed that after that work was completed and 'distortions' corrected, they could, and should, withdraw to allow the democratic, representative process to work again. This was the position clearly set out in President Castello Branco's first *Mensagem* to Congress at the opening of its 1965 session,[67] when, after stressing the damage done in the recent past by political and social disturbance and instability,[68] the president went on to the policies of his own government, which were to include 'national reconstruction . . . by restoring order . . . and authority' and 'the elimination of deformations in the system, in order to improve the performance of existing institutions ...':[69]

> The Government has tried to create conditions for authentic representative democracy: but such a regime ... depends on the people's ability to make a good and wise choice of their representatives. That this choice be made effectively requires an electoral process cleansed of the vices which till now have marred it. ... It was for this reason that one of the first concerns of the Revolutionary Government was to set to work on electoral reform ...[70]

Castello Branco showed his own commitment to preserving some form of electoral process by allowing in March 1965 direct elections in São Paulo for the office of mayor, choosing to ignore warnings from more hard-line officers that this might afford opportunity for overt criticism of the regime, a decision which appeared justified when the elections passed quietly, bringing to office Brigadier Faria Lima, who had favoured the *coup* of 1964, in a contest in which local issues predominated rather than debate over the virtues or otherwise of the regime. The president also held out on another important question, whether or not there should be direct elections for governors in eleven states in which the term of office was expiring in 1965. Some of his advisers favoured prolonging the term of the current governors; while the more hard line of his critics favoured federal intervention and the appointment of *interventores*, rather than again risk an open electoral contest. Castello Branco was largely responsible for insisting that direct elections should be held in October, a decision for which later he was to be heavily criticized and which immediately produced some hostility, especially from the governor of Minas Gerais, Magalhães Pinto, who already had been granted a year's extension of office by the Minas state legislature. While, however, allowing the elections to go ahead, the president also put through Congress a measure which widened the grounds on which those suspect to the regime would be declared ineligible to stand in the October elections, a restrictive move which again was supported by Congress by a substantial majority.[71]

At the same time Congress was being asked to consider the measures for electoral reform and changes in the party system mentioned by the president in his *Mensagem*. Essentially, these sought to remove what theorists close to the regime and particularly to the ESG saw as the main weaknesses in the previous structure and practice of party politics, especially its alleged openness to corruption and patronage and the predominance of individual and personalist issues over those of programme or party allegiance, a feature often attributed to the large number of political parties. The proposed changes, set out by a commission of the Tribunal Superior Eleitoral (TSE), were made known in January 1965 and, after further discussion and modification, a new electoral code and political party statute were sent to Congress in April, to be followed in June by a much wider, more severe Ineligibilities Act, aimed at excluding those judged to be dangerous. It was clear that the regime was not simply seeking to improve the electoral process and produce a more smoothly working party system, but to exert direct, far-reaching control on that system, defining from the beginning the interests and opinions which might be represented in it. This time Congress was much less pliable, alarmed at what the government apparently understood by 'authentic representative democracy': but on 15 July the president promulgated the electoral code as drawn up by the executive, using the special powers given to him under the Institutional Act—to promulgate measures on which Congress had not acted within thirty days for each house. He also promulgated the Ineligibilities Act and signed the Party Statute passed by Congress, but only after rejecting modifications asked for by Congress, so that he 'in effect returned the eighty-one-article document almost to the version the executive had originally proposed'.[72]

Many of the features of the new electoral code and Party Statute could be defended as likely to bring order and coherence to the party system. There was to be, for example, a reduction in the number of parties, by imposing stricter requirements for legal status for a political party. It was also made more difficult to arrange inter-party coalitions in elections, with a view to tightening party loyalty, and in many other respects the new legislation could be seen as a positive attempt to curb abuses in the working of party politics and to strengthen the party system. The same could be said, up to a point, of the Ineligibilities Act, which greatly extended the number of posts from which a prospective candidate for public office must resign well in advance of the elections: but it was not these more positive features of the new measures which attracted most attention. More important, many believed, was the way in which the regime, through the president, could so easily override Congress on such important issues as the reshaping of Brazil's political institutions, and more particularly, the powers now made available to define as ineligible for public office anyone who fitted into the wide-sweeping provisions of the Ineligibilities Act. Was there behind the brave new structure of electoral and party legislation a genuine commitment to 'authentic representative democracy', or was the regime's understanding of this concept such as to allow the whole framework to be set aside without compunction should it seem incapable of maintaining sufficient control in the hands of the government?

The answer came in October 1965, with the elections for governors in eleven states and the reaction to the results in the shape of a second Institutional Act, Institutional Act No. 2.[73] The eleven states involved were Guanabara, Minas Gerais, Paraná, Goiás, Alagoas, Maranhão, Pará, Paraíba, Rio Grande do Norte, Santa Catarina, and Matto Grosso. Since such key states as São Paulo, Rio Grande do Sul, Rio de Janeiro, and Pernambuco were not at issue, it could be argued that the elections did not really represent a test for the regime and should not be regarded as such by either the government or the opposition: but, right from the start, they came to be seen in these terms. The principal centre of interest was Guanabara, where Carlos Lacerda, still with strong support among certain groups of officers, was increasingly critical of Castello Branco and desperately anxious to strengthen his own presidential ambitions by seeing his UDN choice of candidate succeed him as governor. After some confusion the UDN nomination went to Carlos Flexa Ribeiro, State Secretary for Education, who was to be opposed by Francisco Negrão de Lima, supported by the PSD and PTB, who under the Kubitschek government had administered the city as the federal district. From the beginning it was clear that the UDN could by no means be sure of victory, which was also the case in Minas Gerais, where Magalhães Pinto's choice, Roberto Resende, was opposed by a former associate of Kubitschek, Israel Pinheiro. In both states the opposition had had potential candidates excluded by the Ineligibilities Act, but was likely to offer a strong challenge. In the other nine states it was likely that local issues would predominate and that the pattern of the elections, often dominated by entrenched state machines, would not be markedly different from the past.

A close analysis of the results of the elections of 3 October does not suggest that they represented an unambiguous defeat for the government: but that was the interpretation which many on both sides, and particularly the more 'hard-line' and pro-Lacerda officers, chose to put on them. In both Guanabara and Minas Gerais the UDN candidates were soundly defeated, but in both cases this could be attributed as much to the greater attraction of their successful opponents, Negrão de Lima and Israel Pinheiro, as to a massive vote of no-confidence in the regime at the level of national politics. Nor was it even clear that the new governors would prove to be particularly critical of the government, as indeed they showed during their term of office, in which they worked closely and readily with the regime. Their success, in effect, could only be seen as a government defeat by those who identified government interests with those of the UDN or even with Carlos Lacerda, or who chose to see any victory for men supported by the PSD and PTB as an intolerable resurgence of the political forces defeated in April 1964.

The results in the other states made even clearer the fact that confidence in the regime was not a major issue, or that even if it were, the results would suggest a large measure of support. In Paraná, for example, where the outgoing governor was Ney Braga, his candidate, Paulo Pimentel, won a victory for the UDN–PDC as convincing as that of Negrão de Lima in Guanabara for the PSD–PTB. The PSD won in Santa Catarina and Matto Grosso, but the voting was reasonably close and reflected the traditional strength of the PSD rural vote. In the northern states the UDN won three of the five states, with the PSD and PSP one each, the defeat of the PSD in Maranhão ending three decades of PSD-machine control.[74]

With results such as these it was difficult to see the gubernatorial elections as a major humiliation for the regime, and it has even been suggested that Castello Branco and those close to him were anxious to see precisely the sort of resounding defeat for Lacerda and Magalhães Pinto which the elections provided:

> In a sophisticated strategy which very nearly was successful, the Castello Branco forces looked toward the elimination of Lacerda and Magalhães Pinto through the defeat of their hand-picked choices as successors by individuals who, although nominally from the ranks of the opposition, could be counted on to seek accommodation with the regime and hence to cause fewer problems for the government than had the politically ambitious 'revolutionary' governors...[75]

But the general interpretation of the elections throughout the country was that the regime had suffered a defeat and, most important of all, this was the meaning which the 'hard-line' officers and their civilian allies chose to read into the results. In this respect, however, the election results were less the cause of the crisis which now threatened the Castello Branco government as the occasion for his critics and enemies within the regime to attack him openly and to produce the tougher, more repressive measures which they had long been wanting. Pressure from the 'hard line', both those officers associated with Costa e Silva and those more closely linked to Carlos Lacerda, had been building up steadily ever since the *coup*. The crisis of October 1965 was produced at least in part to safeguard the presidential ambitions of the Minister of War and of the outgoing governor of Guanabara. But there were other interests and forces behind it, too, some reaching back to much earlier anti-Vargas groupings, such as the 'Lantern Club', of which Lacerda was the most prominent member, ostensibly acting like Diogenes searching with his lantern for one honest man. The members of that group, both civilian and military, were still to be found in the 'hard line', demanding tougher action against their old Vargista enemies. They also included officers, men such as General Afonso Albuquerque Lima, who, not of the Castellista, 'Sorbonne', group, disliked the more liberal economic policies of Castello Branco and Roberto Campos. These were the men who were to come to power with Costa e Silva and whose more authoritarian political position was accompanied by more 'nationalist' demands in relation to economic policy.

The crisis of October 1965 was really the first occasion on which there was evidence of substantial disagreement among different elements, both military and civilian, producing for the first time a '*coup* within the *coup*'. The group which now challenged Castello Branco was itself heterogeneous, but had certain recognizable features. It was more than just an anti-Vargas grouping or one with a preference for firmer controls. For the most part the opponents of Castello Branco, sometimes referred to as 'authoritarian nationalists',[76] were men who had not been part of the FEB,[77] the Brazilian expeditionary force in the Second World War, nor heavily involved in the ESG. They drew much of their support from more junior or middle-ranking officers, expressing their views through troop commands, especially the Vila Militar in Rio de Janeiro, while their main base of support in the military colleges was the Escola de Aperfeiçoamento de Oficiais (EsAO; the school for junior officers in Rio de Janeiro). Unlike the Castellista, ESG officers, his opponents were less favourable to the United States, urging more nationalist control, but they combined with this louder demands for social reforms at home and in particular for more attention to neglected areas such as the north-east.[78]

Although Costa e Silva did not represent this group, and did not, when president, put their policies into action, he was closer to them than was Castello Branco, and able to act as intermediary when the crisis broke in October 1965. This started on the night of 5 October, with preparations in the Vila Militar, headed by General Albuquerque Lima and some *linha dura* colonels, to move against Castello Branco and deprive him of the presidency. There was widespread discussion of this plan, also involving senior naval officers and, for example, LIDER (Radical Democratic League), a right-wing group in the army,[79] and it seemed quite probable that Castello Branco would go. The crisis was only ended when Costa e Silva went to the Vila Militar to discuss the demands of the officers opposed to Castello Branco, promising that firmer action would be taken, including if necessary a more far-reaching second Institutional Act.[80] His intervention in the crisis also made virtually certain that the Minister of War would succeed Castello Branco in 1967.

Over the next three weeks the government sought to win Congressional support for further changes to strengthen the executive and provide more power to act against alleged subversion, during which time the Minister of Justice, Milton Campos, resigned, being replaced by the old *tenente* Juracy Magalhães, just returned to Brazil after having been ambassador in Washington. It did not prove possible to get new legislation approved in time by Congress, but in any case the new measures were already being drafted. On 27 October they were announced as Institutional Act No. 2, appearing in the press on 28 October. Once again, one of the principal authors was Francisco Campos, together with Vincente Rao and Nehemias Gueiros. Its appearance abruptly ended the first phase of politics after the April *coup*, marking in effect the end of the attempt by Castello Branco to retain as much as possible of democratic politics and debate, and opening a new period of more intensified direct control with scarcely more than the appearance of representative government. The Act greatly increased the powers of the president, allowing him to suspend Congress and govern by decree, to dismiss government employees and elected officials, and suspend the political rights of citizens for ten years. Among other provisions it extended the power of military courts, allowed for further complementary acts to be issued in future, and gave the president greater control over government spending. But, most important of all, the Act dissolved Brazil's political parties and ended direct election for the presidency, stating that such election would now be indirect, by Congress. In place of the party system which had functioned for the last twenty years a new arrangement was announced in Complementary Act No. 4 of 20 November 1965. This allowed registration of political organizations which had the support of at least 20 senators and 120 federal deputies. The government put its weight behind a new grouping, ARENA (National Renovating Alliance), which was joined by more than twice the minimum number of senators and deputies, leaving possible only one alternative grouping, which came into existence as MDB, the Brazilian Democratic Movement. Within these two political bodies all previous political parties had now to come to some kind of uneasy compromise. Almost all the UDN joined ARENA, together with most of the PSD and the smaller parties. The bulk of the MDB was made up of the PTB, though already weakened by the removal from politics of some of its most active members.

Institutionalizing the Revolution: October 1965–March 1967

There needs to be some qualification of the generally accepted interpretation of Institutional Act No. 2 as an outright victory for the 'hard-line' faction. In strengthening the executive and ending the previous party system this group won its point: but, at the same time, a severe reduction in the number of political parties was generally considered to be necessary by theorists associated with the ESG, whose demand for rational planning also pointed to more executive power to resolve deadlocks in Congress. Furthermore, once Castello Branco was given further authority under Institutional Act No. 2, he did not act against the recently elected 'opposition' governors in Guanabara and Minas Gerais, as might have been expected had he been virtually under the control of the 'hard line'. Instead, he kept those governors in office, but closed LIDER, the extreme right-wing group in the army, and appointed some of the officers most critical of him to other posts.[81] In important respects, however, Institutional Act No. 2 was undoubtedly a victory for the 'hard-line' element within the regime, determined to give more teeth to their 'revolution' and produce major changes in Brazil's political institutions, so as to end what they perceived to be the most serious abuses of the old system.[82] From October 1965 to the end of his presidential term Castello Branco remained under constant pressure from this group, though never under its direction, with the story being one of steady tightening of control, which was given legal or institutional form through a series of new institutional and complementary acts, culminating in the new constitution of January 1967. The last sixteen months also saw the emergence of more vocal opposition, sometimes from within the regime, but mainly from students and groups within the Church, expressing, as best they could within a context of ever more effective control, the resentment and frustration shared by many in Brazilian society. Another reason for a quickening of legislation institutionalizing the change of regime was almost certainly a clause in Institutional Act No. 2 which prevented Castello Branco from continuing in office, though already in July 1964 he had expressed his reluctance to continue much longer. He may have feared that, unless he could define the framework of the new political order before March 1967, his successor, or successors, more directly under the influence of the 'hard line', might impose even more extreme control, a process which indeed eventually occurred despite the legislation left by Castello Branco.

Towards the end of 1965 there were rumours of yet another Institutional Act, which would impose indirect elections for state governors. This produced a vigorous press campaign against the idea and allowed Adhemar de Barros in São Paulo to pose as the defender of democracy, producing still greater strains between him and the government. But on 5 February 1966 was promulgated Institutional Act No. 3, which ordered that state governors should no longer be elected directly, but chosen by the state legislatures. This Act, which also ended direct election for mayors of capital cities, avoided the possibility of another crisis over gubernatorial elections like that of the previous October and greatly extended the government's control within the states. At the same time it was announced that direct legislative elections would be held on 15 November 1966, so going some way to reinforce the commitment to representative government at one level while restricting it at others.

In its handling of Carlos Lacerda and Magalhães Pinto the Castello Branco government already had shown its readiness to break with previously important civilian allies whose political ambitions threatened the work of the revolution. In May 1966 the president showed the same firmness with a senior military colleague, General Justino Alves Bastos, who wanted to become governor of Rio Grande do Sul, but lacked the residential qualifications demanded by the new electoral code of July 1965. Alves Bastos criticized the government's ruling on these qualifications. A recording of his speech was on Castello Branco's desk within hours and the general was summoned to appear before the president, to be informed of his replacement as commander of the Third Army in Rio Grande do Sul by General Orlando Geisel. Similar authority was shown in June, when Adhemar de Barros, controlling in São Paulo a dense network of patronage and a political machine which covered the state as well as the city, was summarily removed from office, deprived of his political rights, and replaced by a governor of Castello's choosing. The ostensible reason for moving against Adhemar was his refusal to comply with the financial restrictions imposed by the federal government,[83] but the break was much more deeply rooted. The São Paulo governor had for years been regarded as thoroughly corrupt and, simply as such, was an embarrassing ally for a government who had declared war on political and financial corruption; but more important was his continued determination to maintain a political base in São Paulo capable of challenging the Castello Branco government. Both before and after 1964 a persistent feature of Brazilian politics was the attempt by the political leaders of São Paulo, or by one or other faction in *paulista* politics, to win to their camp the head of the Second Army, often as a counterbalance to the federal government. In later years one characteristic of the *paulista* interest was a closer identification with 'hard-line' policies, a development which, ten years after Castello Branco, was to cause problems for his only Castellista successor to date, President Ernesto Geisel. But already by 1966 there were signs of a challenge centred in São Paulo, headed by Adhemar de Barros, but in association with, for example, General Amaury Kruel, who, like Alves Bastos in the south, had ambitions to be state governor. The summary removal of Adhemar de Barros in June cut short this challenge, underlined the president's authority, and marked the departure of the last of the important civilian allies of 1964 who had hoped to use the *coup* to advance their own political ambitions. Castello Branco was working easily with the new governors of Guanabara and Minas Gerais, and now had curbed the challenge from São Paulo. It was all part of a process which was building up a formidable monopoly of power in the central government, reinforced by the new legislation, which reached a crescendo in July 1966 with a stream of Complementary Acts, bringing them to No. 18, all further strengthening the federal government and the executive.

The grip of the government was in no way lessened by changes at the ministerial level at this time, even though some of the changes marked substantial political differences, such as the replacement of Marshal Cordeiro de Farias because of his opposition to the candidature of Costa e Silva for the presidency. Cordeiro de Farias was senior to both Castello Branco and Costa e Silva. He had been a leading *tenente*, prominent in the Prestes Column, and had had a distinguished military career, which included acting as the first commandant of the ESG. He had wider experience as governor of Pernambuco in 1954 and as the most senior member of the 'Sorbonne' group was widely regarded as a likely successor to Castello Branco. His resignation from the post of Minister for Co-ordination of Regional Agencies, virtually Minister of the Interior, was not merely from pique, but further evidence of the persistent tension between 'Sorbonne' officers and the 'hard line'. The departure of Marshal Cordeiro de Farias marked, therefore, another step in the advancement of Costa e Silva and those who hoped to work through him.

Other ministerial changes were simply to allow ministers to resign in time to stand in the coming elections, especially the indirect elections for state governors. One of the most important shifts was the appointment as Minister of Justice of Carlos Medeiros da Silva, co-author of Institutional Act No. 1, with special responsibility for drawing up a new constitution to pull together all the recent decree legislation. Castello Branco was now in a hurry to complete the process of institutional change and to strengthen the government's grip on the country. Sometimes he seemed in too much of a hurry, as when he involved himself directly in *gaúcho* politics by his determination to put his outgoing Minister of Labour, Peracchi Barcellos, into the job of governor of Rio Grande do Sul. There was substantial resistance to this proposal by members of ARENA in the state, who were willing to work with the MDB to push the candidature of Rui Cirne Lima. The federal government reacted vigorously to this challenge, removing state deputies in Rio Grande do Sul who supported Cirne Lima, while it further strengthened its control through more Complementary Acts, Nos. 14–17, which made it impossible for ARENA legislators in the elections for president or governor to vote for an MDB candidate, or even for MDB representatives to resign as a mark of protest, under penalty of the loss of political rights for ten years. There were also changes through Complementary Act No. 20 in the method of balloting, returning for much of the country to the *cédula avulsa*, or individual ballot sheet, to be distributed by the candidate, a change widely regarded as favouring ARENA candidates, whose names would no longer appear on the ballot sheet alongside those of their MDB opponents.[84]

The flood of Complementary Acts and the sharp involvement in Rio Grande do Sul provoked protests from those alarmed by the rigid moves towards authoritarianism, especially from opposition politicians, intellectuals, and students, but the means for peaceful protest were increasingly restricted and Castello Branco preserved, as throughout the whole of his presidency, a cool indifference, at least in public, to criticism from these quarters. Believing that, especially in the early stages of the 'revolution', painful restructuring was necessary, he did not seek to be popular or to win legitimacy for his regime through popular support. The impression he gave was of a soldier who had not sought the job in hand, but who would see it through, the whole tone of his government being one of *Oderint dum metuant*. Later presidents would feel the need to cultivate more popular support, employing public relations teams to soften their image and make controls more acceptable: Castello Branco felt no such need, preserving some democratic forms, but constructing before his term expired a formidable apparatus, of political and social control. As these controls tightened, the difference between the reputedly more liberal 'Sorbonne' group, as represented by Castello Branco, and the 'hard line', now associated with Costa e Silva, became harder to make, the distinction between different levels of authoritarianism appearing altogether too nice. That real differences did, however, exist was to become clearer again in later years, when Brazil moved even further and faster into a system which seemed to rely for its maintenance and survival on ever harsher repression and terror, to a degree not known under Castello Branco:

but by July 1966 it was already apparent that the return to any genuine form of democracy would be long and hard.

In August the disagreement between the president and General Amaury Kruel came to a head, when Kruel resigned from his command of the Second Army in São Paulo, openly criticizing Castello Branco for betraying the ideals of the revolution. His reaction in part expressed the dismay of the more 'legalist' group in the officer corps at the recent sharp move towards authoritarianism but was compounded by his failure to win nomination as governor of São Paulo.[85] Much more bitter were the attacks of Carlos Lacerda, angry at being set aside by men he had thought to manipulate and probably succeed in office. For over twenty years he had railed against one president after another, Vargas, Kubitschek, Quadros, and Goulart, often effectively, building up a strong political following, both civilian and military. Seeing now that his military allies of 1964 did not intend to step aside in his favour, he attacked Castello Branco both personally and for his handling of the government.

The role of Lacerda in this post-*coup* period still needs careful analysis, but he was a key figure in both civilian and military politics, especially in so far as one important faction, perhaps the most important, in the so-called *linha dura*, could be reduced to pro-Lacerda officers and civilians. He had acted as a leading spokesman for the *linha dura* in attacking the economic policies of Roberto Campos, over, for example, the buying of the American and Foreign Power utility company in November 1964 and in his criticism of Campos and Bulhões in relation to the PAEG, especially its severe credit restrictions, so resented, too, by the CNI (National Confederation of Industries). Thus Lacerda had powerful interests, both military and civilian, to back him in his growing opposition to the Castello Branco team. But equally the interests lined against him were not just Castello Branco and officers close to him, so that Lacerda's failure to win the role of heir-apparent was due as much to the suspicion and hostility of other civilian politicians as to any decision by military officers. A good example of this can be seen in the decision in 1964 to prolong Castello Branco's mandate till 1967, a sharp blow to Lacerda's ambitions. Military opinion was strongly in favour of Castello continuing, a view urged, for example, by General Justino Alves Bastos, General Golbery do Couta e Silva, the Minister of War, Costa e Silva, and ex-president Dutra: but it was a view shared by a number of pro-Lacerda officers, such as Deputado Costa Cavalcanti, an army colonel in March 1964.[86] Some at the time said that Congress, in voting for an extension of Castello Branco's period in office, was merely acting under orders from the military government, a view expressed by Deputado Ùltimo de Carvalho: but this underestimated the opposition to Lacerda in Congress and the continued play of party rivalries. Though most of the UDN *bancada* supported Lacerda, important representatives, such as Bilac Pinto, the national UDN leader, and Daniel Krieger, the leader of UDN in the Senate, were in favour of the absolute majority amendment and extra time for Castello.[87] The Lacerdistas, with the support of Ernani Sâtiro, the UDN leader in the Chamber of Deputies, thought they might be able to carry the party with them against the national leadership, as they did in the conference in Curitiba in 1963: but again there were important inter-party divisions. Magalhães Pinto, for example, put out of the running as UDN candidate at the Curitiba conference, also favoured postponement of presidential elections in 1965, since this would serve to weaken the Lacerdistas and allow him an extra year as governor of Minas Gerais.[88] Other governors agreed with him, including Ney Braga in Paraná and Aluísio Alves in Rio Grande do Norte. In other words, some of the blame at least for the thwarting of Lacerda's ambitions on this occasion lay with his own UDN colleagues.

It was also, in large part, fear of giving power to Lacerda which motivated members of the PSD, PTB, and PSP in Congress. The PSD was divided. Filinto Müller, leader of the majority *bancada* in the Senate, thought Castello should continue,[89] but Martins Rodrigues, the PSD leader in the Chamber of Deputies, was against it, as was the party leader, Amaral Peixoto. But for many in the PSD a prolonged term for Castello Branco was at least better than Lacerda in his place, a view widely shared by many in the PTB, especially in the Senate. They did not want Castello Branco to continue, but still less did they want to give power to Lacerda. The PSP, following Adhemar de Barros, generally favoured prolonging the term for Castello.[90] The final vote, therefore, severely curbing Lacerda's ambitions, did reflect military pressure, but equally Lacerda was the victim of the long-familiar process ot civilian political rivalries.

By 1966, however, his chances hurt still further by the gubernatorial elections of October 1965, all Lcaerda's energies were directed not at his civilian political opponents, but at the soldiers and *técnicos* associated with Castello Branco. By September 1966 he was even willing to use a long spoon and sup with men he had so recently attacked for bedevilling Brazilian politics, Juscelino Kubitschek and João Goulart, moving towards a broad alliance, or *Frente Ampla*, to oppose the Castello Branco regime. This initiative was to develop throughout the rest of the year, being highlighted by the so-called 'Lisbon Pact', when Lacerda and Kubitschek sought to reach closer agreement. From the beginning it appeared as an attempt to strengthen the position of Lacerda, especially when, for example, its long-awaited manifesto made no mention of amnesty for those deprived of political rights, including Kubitschek and Goulart,[91] which probably accounted for the failure of both Kubitschek and Goulart to sign the manifesto. It seemed that it was largely a means of winning for Lacerda the support of Kubitschek's and Goulart's following: 'And to win this support Carlos Lacerda has shown himself ready to speak in terms pleasing to Communists, leftists, liberals, reformers, and those simply nostalgic for the past'.[92] He also struck a notably anti-United States note, attacking the 'neofascist group' in the government for serving foreign rather than national interests, so that 'the American CIA governs Brazil by proxy'.[93]

There was in the heightened language of these attacks and the readiness to embrace former bitter enemies an air of mounting desperation on Lacerda's part, and, in the long run, it was a tactic which harmed rather than helped his cause, in that it smacked to many of his former supporters, especially in the officer corps, of unprincipled opportunism. It was, after all, Lacerda who was going to Canossa, speaking now of the 'semi-illiterate, but pretentious group of the Sorbonne' in a manner which largely vindicated the victims of the regime, such as Kubitschek and Goulart, and the political system which Lacerda had done much to pull down,[94] even as recently as October 1965 in his attacks on the gubernatorial elections and his appeal to the armed forces to intervene, in effect to protect his own interests.

While Lacerda was building up his attack on the Castello Branco government, with Castello astutely refusing to make a move against him, the government continued to strengthen its hold throughout the country, by making sure its own men were in positions of power, and by further changes in the process and institutions of politics. Opposition became ever more difficult and dangerous, as was seen in the harsh treatment given to student protestors. Many student leaders were arrested soon after the *coup* of April 1964 and the government attempted to curb student political activity by means of a law of 9 November 1964 bringing student organizations under government control, the so-called Suplicy Law, named after Castello Branco's Minister of Education. The new law, perceived as a crude attempt to impose government control, heightened the tension between the government and the technically illegal UNE[95] (National Union of Students), which was made worse by government intervention in the universities, most conspicuously in the University of Brasília, where the crisis ended with the closure of the university for several months. The UNE was able to hold an unofficial Congress in São Paulo in July 1965, but the organization was constantly harassed and not even the appointment of a new Minister of Education, Pedro Aleixo, helped to improve relations. Student protest now not only covered issues directly relating to their own organization and the universities, but was the most vocal expression of broader criticism of government policy on such matters as indirect elections for state governors, the choice of Costa e Silva as successor to Castello Branco, and the still wider question of the return to democratic politics. In September and October 1966 student demonstrators met with violent response as the government showed its determination to quell resistance, and officers in command, as at Praía Vermelha in Rio de Janeiro in October, over-reacted to provocation and allowed young demonstrators, some the children of military officers, to be severely battered. But the resistance from students still continued, proving a particularly sharp thorn in the side of the regime, especially since most of the youngsters involved were the sons and daughters of the middle and upper classes. Often their protest was vague and ill-defined, stirred by specific educational issues or by a general idealistic commitment to more open, representative government. The regime tended, misguidedly, to identify all such opposition as 'Communist' or 'Marxist', but while some student leaders might use the vocabulary of Marxism, relatively few in 1966, or even two or three years later, had read much if anything of authors whose names they quoted so freely. Few things, however, so quickly produced a political commitment and opposition to the new regime as experience of being on the wrong end of a baton charge backed up by firecrackers and barking dogs. For the daughter or son of a middle-class family a broken jaw or the loss of front teeth was a compelling political experience, confirming the worst impressions of a brutal soldiery: but this was a lesson of politics the regime, both in 1966 and later, was extraordinarily slow to learn. Its treatment of the universities gave the strong impression of moving in unfamiliar, alien territory, apparently unaware of how difficult it is to coerce ideas. Both in Brazil and abroad this was a sphere of government policy which did its reputation much harm, associating it with some of the most disreputable contemporary regimes.

A similar difficulty was experienced, for broadly similar reasons, in the handling of opposition and protest from the Churches, especially, granted the religious structure of Brazil, from sections of the Catholic Church. The purging of 'subversive' elements included many Christians, some associated with student movements, others with educational ventures such as MEB[96] (Movement for Basic Education), who represented a growing element within the Church, not just in Brazil, which, further encouraged by the Second Vatican

Council, stressed the social responsibilities of Christians to their fellow men in society. These were people who saw many of the most serious problems of modern society as rooted in social injustices and inequalities, which, if often opposed by individual Christians, too frequently had been accepted and condoned by the Church as a whole, especially through too easy an identification with those groups most dominant in society. Some of these Christians explicitly diagnosed much of the poverty and suffering of many of their fellow men in Latin America, and not just in Latin America, as stemming from the very structure and dynamic of capitalist society, especially in a situation of neo-colonialism. They thus argued, logically, that their Christian duty was to seek to change that society and to remove the causes of injustice, arguments which sometimes took them close to a socialist or Marxist critique. Others, however, concerned themselves less with a radical analysis of more underlying causes, and sought simply to work for better conditions of life and better opportunities for their fellow citizens, in north-east Brazil, for example, but within the existing system. Already by 1964 the dialogue within the Church was loud, often heated, as it was to continue in later years, producing a wide range of strategies and programmes of action, taking equally sincere men and women down very different paths. But, again, as in its handling of criticism from the universities and from intellectual sources generally, the new regime showed little subtlety or ability to make necessary distinctions between different sources and types of criticism, reacting, for the most part, in a heavyhanded manner, which identified virtually all criticism as hostile and subversive, and which again gave credence to those who portrayed the men behind the new government as intolerant and insensitive to arguments which, if they could not accept, they sought to repress.

This tension between the regime and groups within the Church was to grow worse in later years, turning especially on the questions of human rights, and an economic strategy whose success bore too heavily on the poorest elements of society: but already by 1966 these were straws in the wind. In July the bishops of the north-east gave public support to the claims of rural workers, so strengthening the earlier action of Catholic groups in the region, such as ACO (Catholic Workers' Action); ACR (Rural Catholic Action); and JAC (Catholic Agrarian Youth). In August the commander of the 10th Military Region, centred in Recife, General Itiberê Gouvêa do Amaral, accused Dom Helder Câmara, archbishop of Olinda and Recife, of irresponsible agitation and of preparing the ground for communism; but the protests from the Church were not confined to the north-east: they came from all parts of Brazil. In the south the archbishop of Pôrto Alegre, Dom Vicente Scherer, eventually to be named a cardinal in March 1969, had already defended members of JUC (Catholic University Youth) from serious charges of subversion, being followed in this by Dom Cândido Padim, bishop of Lorena, while the criticism of government policies in the north-east came not just from Dom Helder Câmara, but significantly from Dom Nivaldo Monte, archbishop of Natal, who not long before had supported the marches of the Family with God for Liberty.[97] Opinion in the Church generally was now, it seemed, moving against policies which threatened to support rather than remove existing social injustices, a movement which included not only members of the hierarchy, but many within the religious orders and many of the laity.[98] Unfortunately, the reaction of General Gouvêa do Amaral was typical of many associated with the regime, including on this side, too, many priests and laymen, who identified social concern with 'Communist' subversion. The immediate crisis in July and August 1966 was solved by the personal intervention of Castello Branco, who sent as commander of the Fourth Army in Recife, General Rafael Souza Aguiar, an old friend of Dom Helder Câmara from his time in Rio de Janeiro. General Souza Aguiar would also have authority over the 10th Military Region, and so be able to calm the situation: but already it was clear that the tension between the regime and some of the most important and respected elements in the Church was likely to persist, even worsen, unless more attention were paid to issues of social justice.

Despite this growing criticism both from outside the regime and from individuals, both civilian and military, formerly associated with it, the government strengthened its grip, as it clearly showed in September 1966 in the indirect elections for twelve state governors, which with good reason were likened to Vargas's appointment of state *interventores*. The new governors were nearly all of Castello Branco's choosing, carefully placing men on whose support he could rely. In São Paulo, for example, he had made clear for some months that he supported a state deputy, Roberto de Abreu Sodré. One reason for the removal of Adhemar de Barros in June was that he was trying to negotiate with supporters of ex-president Jânio Quadros to block the path of Abreu Sodré, who had been chosen as ARENA candidate in preference to Adhemar's vice-governor, Laudo Natel, who was, however, to take over the governorship on the removal of Adhemar. Castello Branco originally had seemed to prefer as his candidate Paulo Egydio Martins, but by now had decided on Abreu Sodré. Adhemar preferred a non-party man, and at first there was talk of Edmundo Monteiro of the *Diários Associados*, but eventually he was willing to accept a Jânista, such as Faria Lima, since, as he said, a defeat for Sodré was a defeat for Castello. He might have added that it would also be a defeat for Lacerda, and indeed one of Castello Branco's own reservations about Abreu Sodré was his links with Lacerda.

This whole question of the next choice of governor provided a microcosm of São Paulo politics and its intertwining with national politics, through both civilians and military officers. This 'São Paulo connection' was to continue to be vitally important, as it always had been in modern Brazilian politics, with these same political interests forming similar links in years to come, as Abreu Sodré, Laudo Natel, and Paulo Egydio Martins, all became governors of São Paulo, all deeply involved in the swirling undercurrents of civilian–military politics and the contending economic and other interests which moved them. But in 1966 the strongest contender in an open election, the former governor Carvalho Pinto, who had succeeded Jânio Quadros, was set aside, moving instead into the contest for the Senate. Other possible candidates, such as the prominent ex-UDN politician and banker Herbert Levy, were also passed over for the relatively young Abreu Sodré, who in September 1966 duly won the indirect election. The story was similar in the other states, with Colonel Walter Peracchi Barcellos taking office as a direct result of Castello's involvement in *gaúcho* politics to set aside a more popular ARENA choice. In Rio de Janeiro the president imposed the ARENA state president, Jeremias Fontes, and, in Bahia, Luíz Viana Filho, and so on in all the states in question.[99]

On 3 October, as planned, Costa e Silva was chosen by Congress as the next president of Brazil, after a prolonged tour through the country in which he spoke much of acting more democratically, of 'humanizing' the revolution, and of paying attention to the just demands of all the groups he met. The tour softened his image as the strong man of the 'hard line',[100] raising some hopes that he might be less rigid and remote than Castello Branco; but it did little to clarify the policies he might offer to the country, leading many to wonder whether he really had any coherent aim other than to succeed Castello Branco.[101]

Meanwhile the government again showed its determination to ensure the smooth transition of power and to check abruptly any move towards open opposition, a sharp disappointment to those who believed there would be no more *cassações* after 3 October, and hoped, like the leader of the Chamber of Deputies, Adaucto Lúcio Cardoso, that Institutional Act No. 2 might be revoked. Such hopes completely misread the whole shaping of politics over the last twelve months or more, as was seen on 12 October, when Castello Branco abruptly ordered the *cassação* of six opposition deputies, including two, Sebastião Paes de Almeida (ex-PSD) and Doutel de Andrade (ex-PTB), who were known to be against Lacerda's plans for a *Frente Ampla.* Paes de Almeida, from Minas Gerais, was a wealthy banker-industrialist and former Minister of Finance, well-known for his enormously high electoral expenses, especially in the 1962 Congressional campaign. Doutel de Andrade, from Santa Catarina, was currently joint vice-leader of the MDB and regarded as one of its most effective spokesmen. The president's action was a direct challenge to Congress, reaffirming that anyone judged to be corrupt or subversive would not be allowed to be a candidate in the coming Congressional elections. The leaders of Congress, Adaucto Cardoso and Auro de Moura Andrade, stood out against Castello, and the politicians whose *cassações* had been ordered remained in Brasília. But after eight days, on 20 October, Castello cut through the crisis: armed federal troops surrounded the Congress building, and marched out the senators and deputies present. Complementary Act No. 23 declared Congress closed until 22 November, after the elections for the new Congress.

For the Congressional elections of 15 November 1966 there were almost 23 million registered voters, out of a population of about 84·7 million.[102] But by comparison with previous Congressional elections there was a general air of apathy, even cynicism, among many of the electorate. This reflected widespread disenchantment at elections held under such tightly controlled conditions, which excluded so many of the most lively and exciting political figures of the past, especially since Congress by late 1966 had been purged of over 20 per cent of those elected in 1962. A striking feature of the campaign was the eagerness of many ARENA candidates to dissociate themselves from the regime, or at least from the Castello Branco government, which was constantly attacked by its previous allies, such as Lacerda and Amaury Kruel, for betraying their 'revolution' of 1964. The most lively issues were those of political freedom and freedom of expression, especially in relation to the mass of decree legislation already in force and the reported designs of the new constitution now in preparation to pull together, and confirm, the disparate decrees issued since the *coup* of 1964.

On 15 November just over 17¼ million voters went to the polls[103] in an election which, in many respects, followed patterns similar to those of earlier Congressional contests, but which was notable for the high proportion of blank or null votes, mostly meant as a gesture of protest. Null votes made up almost 7 per cent of the total; blank votes over 14 per cent,[104] which, since they mostly came from opponents of the regime, helped to strengthen ARENA.

In practice, and on the most simple analysis, the results were a victory for the regime, strengthening it further in Congress, as the earlier removal of opponents through *cassações* or the ineligibilities legislation had been intended to do, so reinforcing the control already won by the recent indirect elections of ARENA state governors. ARENA now had 277 federal deputies, as compared to 254 before the elections, while MDB now had 132 as opposed to 149 previously, though MDB did better in the elections for state assemblies. But a closer analysis of these results throughout the country, as of the results of the voting for the Senate, produces a less clear picture in terms of how and why the nation voted.

The high proportion of null or blank votes immediately produced some distortion, not least through strengthening ARENA, but it was an important gesture of derision in the face of elections which many Brazilians believed to be an empty farce. This was also a gesture which would be made still more clearly in the next Congressional elections of 1970. At the same time the heavy voting for ARENA could not be interpreted unambiguously as a vote for the regime, and still less for the Castello Branco government. Many ARENA candidates had either played down their connection with the regime or, as in the case of Carvalho Pinto in São Paulo, had even openly attacked Castello Branco. Already it was becoming clear that if a pro-ARENA vote did not necessarily imply full support for the regime, still less did it mean support for the present government, a distinction already being made in many cases between support for the *system* introduced in 1964 and for a particular president and his policies: this was a distinction which would be made ever more frequently in years to come.

A more difficult complicating factor in interpreting these election results was the play, as in previous elections, of regional, local, and personal issues as opposed to a vote for or against the government or regime.[105] In general, throughout the country, MDB did better in urban centres, not only in the industrialized centre-south, but also in the north-east, a pattern which was to be strengthened in most subsequent elections: but regional issues and the personal following of candidates often cut across party lines or national government policies. For example, looking first at the north and north-east, the victory of MDB for the Senate in Amazonas reflected the pre-1964 political situation, as did the ARENA victory in Pará, where Colonel Jarbas Passarinho, though an ARENA candidate, was at odds with the central government. In Maranhão the governor, José Sarney, won a victory in support of the government, but in Piauí, the elected ARENA senator, Petrônio Portela, again a former governor, was in 1964 a strong supporter of João Goulart, and only just survived the first wave of purges. In Rio Grande do Norte, the contest was simply between two local factions, those of Dinarte Mariz and Aluísio Alves, both of ARENA, though Aluísio Alves, a former governor, had had his candidature for Senate vetoed by the central government and was already coming under further government fire. By contrast, in Paraíba the successful MDB candidate for Senate, Rui Carneiro, spent most of his campaign expressing his support for Castello Branco and Costa e Silva. Elsewhere the fight was on purely local issues between old-established factions, as in Alagoas, Sergipe, Espírito Santo, and Matto Grosso.

In the east and south, with over 70 per cent of the electorate, the picture was scarcely less complex. Milton Campos, as candidate for Senate, won easily for ARENA in Minas Gerais, which also elected 35 ARENA deputies as against 13 MDB: but Campos, who had resigned from the government over Institutional Act No. 2, was a fierce critic of Castello Branco, as was even more so the man who won most ARENA votes, the former governor, Magalhães Pinto. In Guanabara the voting seemed more than elsewhere to have turned on support or opposition to the government, resulting in a notable victory for current or former Lacerdistas, with the new senator, Mário Martins, claiming that his success was the result of his support for the *Frente Ampla.* The three ARENA candidates who received most votes, Rafael de Almeida Magalhães, Veiga Brito, and Flexa Ribeiro, were also all close to Lacerda, so that the ARENA victory, here as elsewhere, could certainly not be seen as an endorsement of Castello Branco or his government's policies. This was certainly the case, too, in São Paulo, where Carvalho Pinto won a massive victory for senator, after having openly criticized Castello Branco throughout his campaign. Elsewhere in the centre-south the picture again reflected personal following and local issues, as in Paraná, where Ney Braga, the former governor, won an easy victory in the senate election, despite having to contend with much local resentment against the government's coffee policies; or in Santa Catarina, where the election for Senate returned Celso Ramos, reflecting the long and deeply entrenched political influence of the Ramos family. Santa Catarina also saw, however, the election to the Chamber of Deputies of the wife of Doutel de Andrade, in a direct snub to the government which so recently had removed her husband from politics.

The results of these elections of 15 November 1966, while, as planned and arranged, they immediately strengthened the government in relation to Congress, did not show widespread support for, or even indifference towards, the regime. Despite the *cassações* and ineligibilities and the pruning of the electoral process, the opposition, in so far as it could find expression through MDB, showed it had substantial support in those parts of Brazil, mainly the urban centres of the more modern sections of the economy, where the electorate was more critical and actively involved in politics. More often than not the ARENA victories there too were a vote for the government's critics more than for its supporters, while in the rural areas victory often simply followed long-established lines of entrenched political influence. If any lesson could be drawn, it was that the regime was right in the analysis implicit in its continuing attempts to establish and extend its control: in completely free and open elections it would almost certainly suffer a severe, humiliating defeat, which would, in a democratic system, sweep it from power.

The government's determination that this should not happen was seen in the speed at which it now began to issue a whole stream of decree legislation, prepared the ground for swift acceptance of the new draft constitution, and issued further lists of *cassações*, all to remove potential opposition and secure the system to be handed over to Costa e Silva in March 1967. The most conspicuous of these actions, if not the most important, was the new constitution, the draft of which was made known on 6 December 1966, followed the next day by Institutional Act No. 4, which ordered a special session of Congress to consider the new constitution and laid down strict procedures and time limits for the mixed commission of senators and deputies to do its work. From the beginning it was clear that the predictably loud opposition would be brushed aside, since the constitution had to be promulgated by 24 January 1967.[106] The new proposals were also supported by a new Press law, the Rules for the Freedom of Expression and Information of 21 December 1966, politically more important than the new constitutional formulae, which greatly extended the government's control through censorship.[107] Congress introduced hundreds of amendments in the short time available, but few were accepted and the new constitution was approved by Congress on 24 January with no sign of enthusiasm even from the members of ARENA. Essentially it pulled together the Institutional and Complementary Acts already introduced since 1964, the greatly increased power of the central government being reflected in the change of name of the country from the United States of Brazil to the Federative Republic of Brazil. The central government was now given much more extensive powers in the field of economic planning, allowing it to intervene in states which did not follow the directives of central planning. The enlarged powers of the executive in relation to Congress were confirmed, as was the power of military courts to try civilians in matters affecting national security. The exceptional powers accorded to the executive since April 1964 were now, in effect, made legal and incorporated into the new constitution.[108]

Before he left office Castello Branco was determined to finish what he regarded as the 'first phase of the Revolution', which would end on 15 March 1967 with the start of the presidency of Costa e Silva.[109] In mid-February he ordered eighteen *cassações*, on 27 February another forty-four, and on his very last day in office a further twenty-eight, so that about 250 people had now lost their political rights since Institutional Act No. 2 of October 1965.[110] On 25 February was issued Decree Law 200, spelling out major changes in the structure of the federal administration, again seeking to give the fullest priority to planning at every level, and raising now to a full ministry of first importance the Ministry of Planning and General Co-ordination, headed by Roberto Campos.[111] The new law was a clear expression of the crucial importance attached to planning by Campos and his fellow *técnicos*, just as the new constitution gave legal form to that monopoly of power in the executive and central government which was regarded by the planners, at least in the current state, as they believed, of Brazilian politics, as a necessary condition for the safe, smooth working of their economic strategies. The stability of this political context was now further guaranteed by a wide-ranging Law of National Security, which in future years was to be still further tightened, and invoked whenever the government should deem necessary.

One of the final acts of Castello Branco's government pointed to what ever since April 1964 had been its central preoccupation, to which all else had been subordinated. Just before he left the presidency, Castello ordered the publication of a new Ten-Year Economic and Social Development Plan, a sophisticated, ambitious programme drawn up by EPEA (Escritório de Pesquisa Econômica Aplicada do Ministério do Planejamento; the Office for Applied Economic Planning). The plan had been prepared with the help of foreign consultants,[112] and set out objectives to be achieved between 1967 and 1976, supported by a detailed five-year investment plan. The new programme was intended to replace the original PAEG (Programa de Ação Econômica do Govêrno), as explained by Campos:[113]

> While the PAEG was essentially strategy for the transition period, President Castello Branco felt acutely the need for a much more systematic long-term planning effort . . . with sufficient perspective and lead time to guide the decision-making process. It was hoped that the formulation of long-term development strategy and pluri-year investment budgets would help in assuring a certain degree of administrative continuity.

Hopes for the success of the Ten-Year Plan were high, with several advantages being claimed over previous efforts, such as more attention to social sectors, for example education, and to agriculture, but particularly,

> The decisive technical contribution of the Ten-Year Plan is . . . the micro-economic planning and model-building approach. Most of the earlier attempts were but collections of micro-plans. For the first time the Ten-Year Plan related the sectoral plan to a broader framework of monetary, fiscal, and foreign trade policies. Several alternative strategies were analysed and consistency tests applied to determine the compatibility of the growth objectives with the stabilization objective, the employment objective, and the preservation of balance-of-payments viability.[114]

Perhaps more than any other single initiative the Ten-Year Plan most clearly expressed the hopes and aims of Castello Branco and his government, especially the man who has often been described as virtually the prime minister within that government, Roberto Campos.[115] The ground had now been cleared, with the first stage of reorganization and reconstruction coming to an end. Some of the necessary costs and sacrifices already had been imposed and the changes which the new regime considered necessary already had been introduced. Early crises and tensions within the regime had been resolved or at least temporarily overcome. The time was now ready, under the new constitutional arrangements, making legal the extraordinary powers assumed since 1964, to push ahead with the second phase. This would see the operation of the clear, rational plans of the *técnicos*, so fully in line with the commitment to rational organization of the ESG, all in a stable social and political context where the hurly-burly of party politics before 1964 would no longer disturb the planning process. Calm and order had been restored, albeit at a cost. Stability and consequently the continuity of the planners' strategy were guaranteed. With the executive in control of a stronger centralized government machine the second phase of the 'revolution' could now begin under the new president, Costa e Silva. But ironically such a smooth transition was not to be possible. As Castello Branco left office, politics, this time the internal tensions within the regime, were already disturbing this calm rational world created by the soldiers according to the design of the *técnicos* and planners, both Brazilian and foreign. The first victim of new political pressures was precisely the Ten-Year Plan which was meant to be the product of present order and the guide to continuing future progress. As Campos himself sadly described it:

Bequeathed by Castello Branco to the Costa e Silva administration, which took over in March 1967, it was promptly consigned to oblivion as part of the image-building effort of the new government; it was replaced by a new Plano Trienal, which did little more than incorporate the first three years of the investment program, and abandoned the conceptual structure, sacrificed the long-term perspective, and blurred the compatibility tests inherent in the model-building approach of the Ten-Year Plan.

Despite all the social and political costs, the smooth working of the government's neatly dovetailed strategy was not, it seemed, as easy in practice as it appeared on paper. March 1967 was not then, after all, the end of a clearly defined first phase, as Castello Branco hoped, but only a minor shift in a longer process, already well advanced, producing something not yet fully recognized even by the president and his colleagues. What Castello Branco was in fact leaving to Brazil was not simply a more disciplined, better-ordered system to ensure economic reconstruction and development in accordance with rational aims, a system which, after this initial period, could again return to democratic government responsive to popular demands. What already was emerging was a centralized authoritarian state, largely controlled by the armed forces leaders and the *técnicos*, linked to a bureaucracy firmly committed to supporting the new state machine, the workings of which were increasingly free from public scrutiny or critique, and from popular pressures expressed through Congress, organized labour, the media, or even the ballot box. April 1964 had seen a strong, well-mounted attack on the liberal bourgeois state, as it had emerged since 1945. Already by March 1967 was well-advanced, imbued with its own logic, the process of creating a new form of state to serve that new economic model of authoritarian capitalism which was to be further refined and developed over the next few years. The hard foundations of that state, whether consciously or not, had been laid by the Castello Branco government.

Notes

1 This attitude, discussed in more detail above (pp. 327–9), was especially common among the old *tenente* group among the military opponents of Goulart, men like Juarez Távora and Cordeiro de Farias. Távora had been scornful of 'corrupt' politicians in 1930 and, when campaigning for the presidency in 1955, had resoundingly condemned the 'corrupt' political class. The *tenentes*, however, were not alone in demanding a decisive break with the past.

2 See, for example, Philippe C. Schmitter, *Interest Conflict and Political Change in Brazil* (Stanford, 1971), 368–9.

3 ibid., 374.

4 'Only after the coup of 1964 did something like a pure authoritarian bureaucracy appear with its accent on political neutrality, expertise, social and political engineering, and paramilitary command systems based on an alliance of officers and technocrats'; ibid., 380.

5 See, for example, Octavio Ianni, *Estado e Planejamento no Brasil 1930–1970* (São Paulo, 1971), discussing the relatively little difference in economic policy between the governments of Castello Branco and Costa e Silva. The more detailed differences are discussed later, but see, especially, the very useful analysis in Schneider, op. cit. and in Stepan, op. cit. Some of the more fundamental commitments of the post-1964 governments are also discussed in P. Flynn, 'The Brazilian Development Model: the Political Dimension', in *The World Today*, vol. 29, No. 11 (November 1973), and in 'Brazil: Ten Years of Military Control', *Current Affairs Bulletin*, Sydney (July 1974). See, too, F. H. Cardoso, *O Modelo Político Brasileiro*, 2nd ed. (São Paulo, 1973), especially 53–6.

6 Quoted Skidmore, op. cit., 329. Gordon later said it might have been better to wait at least until Goulart had left the country before sending Johnson's message; *Visão* (9 March 1977), 8.

7 Távora, as Minister of Transport, was probably the most senior.

8 Schneider describes them succinctly as 'composed of members of the National War College [ESG] General Staff and Command School and the Army Chief of Staff's collaborators', op. cit., 120. Schneider also has most useful discussions of the general position of this group, and how it changed over time. For a more general analysis of the ESG, its ideology, and its role in the 1964 *coup* see Stepan, op. cit., 174–87.

9 On the choice of Castello Branco see, in particular, Schneider, op. cit., 121–4 and Dulles, op. cit., 346–54. For details of the governors' meetings see, especially, Mauro Borges, *O Golpe em Goiás: História de uma Grande Traição* (Rio de Janeiro, 1965).

10 Schneider, op. cit., says there were 72 abstentions, 3 votes for Juarez Távora, and 2 for Dutra, and notes that 53 PTB congressmen voted for Castello Branco.

11 Stepan, op. cit., 210.

12 See, for example, Juarez Távora, quoted Schneider, op. cit., 122–3. At the time of the 1930 revolution Távora had expressed the strong *tenente* conviction that politicians could not be trusted. He now believed that it would take a long time to get rid of 'subversion and corruption' and urged that the lessons of 1930 should not be forgotten, and that, in particular, it was an illusion to believe that the soldiers could manipulate the politicians once restored to office.

13 In this respect Schneider seems to go rather too far in saying that: 'Of major significance for the future was the heterogeneity of the revolutionary forces, compounded by the diversity of their motives in supporting the ouster of Goulart and the inconsistencies of their future expectations . . . the developments which brought about an abrupt governmental vacuum were too sudden, and their configuration too confusing, to permit rapid definition of a new order'; ibid., 116–17. Despite this heterogeneity and confusion the emergence of the Castellista group and the definition of a new strategy were really remarkably quick.

14 ibid., 250.

15 ibid., 244. The military members of the course came from all three services,

most at the rank of colonel, or an equivalent rank; Stepan, op. cit., 176.

16 Schneider, op. cit., 250, drawing information from Glauco Carneiro, 'A Guerra da "Sorbonne"', *O Cruzeiro* (24 June 1967), 16–21. See, too, Stepan, op. cit., 177, who uses the same source, but also makes the point that the educational qualification requirement excluded almost all trade unionists, and that, in any case, there was in operation a process of recruiting like-minded, 'clubbable' types.

17 Schneider, op. cit., 250.

18 This contained not only the usual information contained in college magazines or bulletins concerning the social and intellectual activities of the college and of former members, but also substantial articles on national and international issues. In 1968 it adopted the significant title of *Segurança e Desenvolvimento: Revista da Associação dos Diplomados da Escola Superior de Guerra*, the two related concepts of 'security' and 'development' being crucial to the overall ideology elaborated within the college.

19 Stepan, op. cit., 177.

20 General Augusto Fragoso, *A E.S.G.—Origem, Evolução e Posição Atual.* Separata do Informativo da Fundação Getúlio Vargas. *Ano.* III, no. 3, Março de 1971, Rio de Janeiro, 4. Fragoso was Commandant of the ESG when on 30 September 1970 he presented this long paper to the Fundação Getúlio Vargas, explaining the origins of the ESG, the courses followed, and the basic concepts developed in ESG discussions over the years.

21 Decree 35.187, 11 March 1954, and Decree 50.352, 17 March 1961, quoted Fragoso, op. cit., 17–18.

22 ibid., 18–23.

23 General Golbery do Couto e Silva, *Planejamento Estratégico* (Rio de Janeiro, 1955); *Geopolítica do Brasil*, 2nd ed. (Rio de Janeiro, 1967). See, too, his *Aspectos Geopolíticos do Brasil* (Rio de Janeiro, 1957). Also the very influential writing of General Aurélio de Lyra Tavares, including, before the *coup: Território Nacional: Soberania e Domínio do Estados* (Rio de Janeiro, 1955); *Segurança Nacional: Antagonismos e Vulnerabilidades* (Rio de Janeiro, 1958).

24 See, for instance, Aurélio de Lyra Tavares: *Segurança Nacional: Problemas Atuais* (Rio de Janeiro, 1965); *O Exército Brasileiro visto pelo seu Ministro* (Recife, 1968); *Além dos Temas da Caserna* (Fortaleza, 1968); *Orações Cívicas e Militares* (João Pessoa, 1967); and *Por Dever do Ofício* (Rio de Janeiro, 1969). A clear outline of more recent courses can be found in *Escola Superior de Guerra: Manual Básico* (Rio de Janeiro, 1975). For a detailed post-*coup* analysis of the concept of 'national security' see the special number of *Revista Brasileira de Estudos Políticos*, No. 21 (July 1966), which devotes 286 pages to examining the concepts of 'national security' and 'national power', especially the political, psychosocial, and economic elements of 'national power'.

25 Golbery, *Geopolítica do Brasil*, 24–5. The book mainly consists of lectures given in the ESG. It is full of schematic representations of the relation between National Objectives (Permanent and Current), the various 'factors' (political, psychosocial, economic, and military), and maps showing such things as the way that national integration may be achieved, and the outline of 'Fortress America'. See particularly the definition of the key related concepts, 155–9.

26 ibid., 219–50.

27 See, for example, Lyra Tavares, *Segurança Nacional*, Part 2: 'The Revolutionary War and the Brazilian Situation'.

28 Stepan, op. cit., 183–4. Stepan argues cogently the important role of the

ESG, both in deposing Goulart and in shaping the Castello Branco government.

29 Stepan notes this point in passing (179–80), quoting Golbery. But see, too, for example, the long passages on 'revolutionary war' in Lyra Tavares, *Segurança Nacional*.

30 See, for example, Golbery's discussion of 'nationalism' and the Permanent National Objectives, *Geopolítica do Brasil*, 96–102. Out of such general discussion of 'nationalism' and 'pseudo-nationalism' came material for a wider debate.

31 Lyra Tavares, *Segurança Nacional*, 27 and especially Part 3. 'Fundamental Problems of National Security', 97–106, where he discusses 'antagonisms' within the state and its degree of vulnerability.

32 ibid., 101.

33 ibid., 105.

34 For interesting later discussion of the link between these concepts and the post-1964 pattern of national politics see two important lectures by the previous head of the ESG, General Augusto Fragoso, when minister of the Superior Military Tribunal in 1976. The first, given on 19 February 1976 to the Escola Nacional de Informações, is 'Política Nacional. Conceitos Fundamentais'. SNI/ENI. Departamento de Ensino. LS–A–01–101. The second, 'A Segurança Nacional na Atual Legislação Brasileira', was given on 19 April 1976.—SNI/ENI. Departamento de Ensino. LS–A–03–05–05.

35 Apart from civilians associated with the ESG there were other important centres advocating policies similar to those adopted after April 1964. Perhaps the most important was the strongly anti-Goulart IPÊS (Institute of Social Studies and Research), which had been so active in organizing public protests against his government, including the mass demonstrations of women. Besides developing a very effective intelligence service, directed by Golbery, IPÊS also ran a vigorous campaign of criticism of Goulart's economic policies. A similar, but smaller, pressure group was *Fundo de Ação Social*, which from March 1962 also urged an unambiguously capitalist development path for Brazil, which was defended with equal tenacity by the older IBAD (Brazilian Institute for Democratic Action).

36 Flynn, 'The Brazilian Development Model'.

37 The most useful single source for the economic critique underlying the new regime is the collection of papers by Roberto Campos, published in English as *Reflections on Latin American Development* (Austin, 1968). See, too, his elegant speech of 16 May 1972 in Lancaster House, London, noting 'premature welfare goals that promote distribution but shrink production', and stressing the need for 'a re-education of the political class' and 'the maintenance of social discipline to go on with the urgent business of growth'. Among his important publications in Portuguese are: *Economia, Planejamento e Nacionalismo* (Rio de Janeiro, 1963); *Ensaios de História Econômica e Sociologia*, 2nd ed. (Rio de Janeiro, 1964); *A Moeda, O Govêrno e O Tempo* (Rio de Janeiro, 1964); *Política Econômica e Mitos Políticos* (Rio de Janeiro, 1965); *A Técnica e o Riso* (Rio de Janeiro, 1967); *Do Outro Lado da Cêrca* (Rio de Janeiro, 1968); and *Ensaios contra a Maré* (Rio de Janeiro, 1969). See, too, the study by the regime's first Minister of Finance, Octávio Gouvêia de Bulhões, *Dois Conceitos de Lucro*, and perhaps most influential of all for its emphasis on the pursuit of growth, Antônio Delfim Neto, *Planejamento para o Desenvolvimento Econômico* (São Paulo, 1966). Also H. S. Ellis (ed.), *The Economy of Brazil* (Berkeley and Los Angeles, 1969). Introduced by Lincoln Gordon, the collection includes illuminating papers by Bulhões and Campos. The policies advocated by these theorists found

fullest expression in *Programa de Ação Econômica do Govêrno 1964–1966* (Rio de Janeiro, 1964), the course of action outlined in 1964, which, however, Campos says was not a 'plan', but an 'emergency program'; Ellis, op. cit., 318.

38 Bulhões, in particular, laid much stress on fiscal reforms. See his *Dois Conceitos do Lucro* and his paper 'Financial Recuperation for Economic Expansion'; Ellis, op. cit., 162–76.

39 This line of argument was to become increasingly common in later years, when the regime came under heavy criticism both at home and abroad for its headlong pursuit of economic growth while ignoring demands for more just distribution of the wealth and resources at its disposal, but the insistence on growth as the first priority was there from the start.

40 One such group liable to appeal to foreign financiers and businessmen was the powerful *Consultec*, headed by Roberto Campos, whose members, influentially placed in government, financial, business, and academic circles in 1962–63, were to play an important role after April 1964.

41 That severe political restraints would be needed was clear from the beginning, especially if the rational planning on which Campos and others insisted were to go on undisturbed. Campos lays particular stress on the absolute need for 'political stability' in his paper in Ellis, op. cit., 343–4. He also accepted in his Lancaster House speech that 'A certain measure of consented authoritarianism may be needed in the transitional period', though arguing that, '. . . sooner or later, economic pluralism would lead, and indeed require liberalisation and political pluralism . . .'.

42 One of the most detailed accounts of these early demands and the removal of Goulart's associates and other opponents of the victors of April 1964 is in Mário Victor, op. cit., 542–60.

43 ibid., 543–4.

44 Article 44.

45 Article 213.

46 Victor, op. cit., 546.

47 Flynn, 'The Revolutionary Legion and the Brazilian Revolution of 1930'.

48 Victor, op. cit., 547.

49 ibid.

50 ibid.

51 These and other provisions were, of course, changed by later decrees, especially Institutional Act No. 2 of October 1965, which, besides dissolving the existing political parties, put back the presidential and vice-presidential elections till October 1966, while also making them indirect elections through Congress.

52 Dulles, in his very useful account of the early moves of the new government, probably overstates the case when he says that Campos and Medeiros da Silva 'translated into legal phraseology the wishes of Costa e Silva and Castello Branco'; *Unrest in Brazil*, 355. Those who favoured more extreme measures exerted some weight, though evidently there was consideration of how foreign opinion might react, especially in the United States, still publicly wedded to Alliance for Progress reformist democracy. The more extreme authoritarian camp lived to fight, and win, another day, as Schneider notes: 'In December 1968, and January 1969, under the Fifth Institutional Act, Gama e Silva as Costa's Justice Minister would be able to reach those who had previously escaped his wrath', op. cit., 125.

53 The early list of names is given in Victor, op. cit., 548–50, while the complete listing of those removed in this first phase is to be found in Edmar Morel, *O golpe começou em Washington* (Rio de Janeiro, 1965), 248–59. Dulles,

Unrest in Brazil, 359 says that according to Ruy Mesquita 299 persons lost their political rights under Institutional Act No. 1, including 5 governors, 11 mayors, 51 federal congressmen, 2 senators, and 46 military officers.

54 Schneider gives useful information on this: op. cit., 129–30.

55 'Costa e Silva, whose presidential ambitions were ill concealed, strongly favoured the cassation of the man whose popularity was the most important single obstacle to his achieving that goal'; Schneider, op. cit., 131.

56 Victor, op. cit., 579ff., 583, laying special stress on the hostility of Lacerda, joined by Júlio de Mesquita Filho and the 'conservative classes'. In talking, however, of administrative corruption as being, in their view, the Achilles heel of the Kubitschek administration, he tends to group together too easily quite different elements of opposition to Kubitschek.

57 ibid., 585–6.

58 Useful analysis of these measures can be found in E. N. Baklanoff (ed.), *New Perspectives of Brazil* (Nashville, 1966); Ellis, op. cit.; Roett (ed.), *Brazil in the Sixties*; and A. Stepan (ed.), *Authoritarian Brazil* (New Haven, 1973). The papers in these volumes cover such topics as foreign investment, the pattern of industrialization (including the degree of success of incentives for the north-east), the handling of inflation, the role of the public sector, and the pattern of distribution of wealth.

59 Roberto Campos in Ellis, op. cit., 343.

60 To be fair, he also emphasized this failure after the *coup* of 1964 with regard to the Ten-Year Plan: 'Bequeathed by Castello Branco to the Costa e Silva administration . . . it was promptly consigned to oblivion as part of the image-building effort of the new government . . .'; ibid.

61 Lancaster House speech, 16 May 1972.

62 ibid.

63 ibid.

64 For this early repression see especially: Márcio Moreira Alves, *Torturas e Torturados* (Rio de Janeiro, 1966); Alceu Amoroso Lima, *Pelo Humanismo Ameaçado* (Rio de Janeiro, 1965); and Mário Lago, *1º de Abril: Estórias para a História* (Rio de Janeiro, 1964). References to the later, more highly organized and institutionalized, use of torture are given below.

65 For a report which well reflects the general tone and aims of an IPM see *O Comunismo no Brasil*, Inquérito Policial Militar 709 (Rio de Janeiro, 1966). See, too, the experience of the governor of Sergipe, João de Seixas Doria, with the IPM in Bahia under Colonel Hélio Ibiapina, as described in Seixas Doria, *Eu, Réu sem Crime* (Rio de Janeiro, 1965).

66 Borges's own clear account of the affair, and a valuable source for this period more generally, is his *O Golpe em Goiás* (Rio de Janeiro, 1965). There is also a good discussion of the various interests involved in Schneider, op. cit., 135, 145–9, who, in particular, notes the hostility towards Borges of General Ernesto Geisel.

67 Humberto de Alencar Castello Branco, *Mensagem ao Congresso Nacional* (Brasília, 1965). Schneider, op. cit., 108–61, speaks of 'Castelo Branco and "Manipulated Democracy"'.

68 Castello Branco, op. cit., 20–7.

69 ibid., 31.

70 ibid.

71 Schneider, op. cit., 154–5.

72 ibid., 158. Schneider gives a good account of the genesis and content of these new measures (157–61). For more detail see *Revista de Direito Público e Ciências Políticas*, vol. VIII, No. 1 (January–April 1965), and No. 3 (September–December 1965).

73 The fullest account of the gubernatorial elections and Institutional Act No. 2 is Schneider, op. cit., 162–73.
74 ibid., 168.
75 ibid., 163. See, too, 169: '. . . the inner circle around Castelo knew that the isolation and undermining of Lacerda and Magalhães Pinto were perhaps the regime's priority electoral goal . . .'.
76 The term is used by Stepan, op. cit. See especially his discussion of this group in relation to the crisis of October 1965, on which the analysis above is largely based.
77 Stepan notes that only one of the five key officers under Costa e Silva had been in Italy.
78 Stepan reproduces, op. cit., 251, a statement put out before 1964 by the *Frente Patriótica Civil-Militar*. This, *The Ten Commandments of the Law of the People*, is given in Stacchini, op. cit., 20–2 and shows the concern for reform as well as for more complete political control.
79 Schneider, op. cit., 100.
80 Stepan, op. cit., 255–6 says that 'The powerful Mechanized-Reconnaissance Regiment had its armor ready to move against Castello Branco . . .'.
81 Schneider, op. cit., 174.
82 Castello Branco's own reluctance to introduce more severe controls is stressed in Daniel Krieger, *Desde As Missões . . . Saudades, Lutas, Esperanças* (Rio de Janeiro, 1976), 198–200.
83 Schneider, op. cit., 176: 'The final straw which brought about his ouster was the São Paulo state government's insistence on issuing short-term bonds, popularly termed "*ademaretas*", which undercut federal efforts to curb inflation'.
84 The *cédula avulsa* was to be used everywhere except in capital cities and towns of over 100,000 inhabitants. It was seen as likely to strengthen the hold of *coroneis* of the interior and the grip of ARENA. Although ARENA deputies joined in the general criticism of this change, their protests were widely regarded as insincere. The government claimed to have sounded ARENA before introducing the change and to have found 80 per cent in favour of it. See *Visão* (19 August 1966), 14. The Act exacerbated the already deteriorating relations between the president and Congress.
85 ibid., 14–15. The report notes how Castello Branco played down the break with Kruel, despite his open breach of military discipline on four counts.
86 *O Cruzeiro* (15 August 1964), 122.
87 *O Cruzeiro* (1 August 1964 and 8 August 1964).
88 ibid. (8 August 1964).
89 *O Cruzeiro* (1 August 1964).
90 Within the government, Milton Campos, Juarez Távora, and Pedro Aleixo were against keeping on Castello Branco, but were outweighed.
91 *Visão* (4 November 1966), 11.
92 ibid.
93 ibid.
94 See the useful analysis in *Visão* (2 December 1966), 14–15, which also discusses earlier relations between Kubitschek and Lacerda, which really deteriorated only after August 1954.
95 The legal existence of UNE was ended by the Suplicy Law, the government's intention being to replace it by a new organization, DNE, the National Student Directorate. For a short account of student politics, especially through the UNE, see Robert O. Myhr, 'Brazil', in Donald K. Emmerson (ed.), *Students and Politics in Developing Nations* (New York, 1968), 249–85.

96 For a study of the changing position of the Church, especially in relation to the experience of MEB, see Emanuel de Kadt, *Catholic Radicals in Brazil* (London, 1970). Also Thomas C. Bruneau, *The Political Transformation of the Brazilian Catholic Church* (Cambridge, 1974).

97 *Visão* (26 August 1966), 22–5: 'Igreja militante está em campanha'. The article examines the growth of opposition from within the Church all over Brazil, even from traditionally conservative Catholic areas such as Minas Gerais.

98 The *Visão* article lists prominent Christian laymen throughout Brazil who now were more openly critical of elements of government policy, in particular of lack of attention to the problems of health, education, and widespread poverty, issues which had been recently underlined in the papal pronouncement *Gaudium et Spes*.

99 Schneider, op. cit., 181–2.

100 He was already making assiduous use of a public relations team; *Visão* (16 September 1966), 56.

101 See, in particular, the severe, but perceptive, interview with Carlos Lacerda in *Visão* (2 September 1966), 9–13. Lacerda, implacably hostile to Castello Branco, alleged that Costa e Silva's only qualification for office was that he had not deposed Castello Branco in October 1965. He argued that Castello 'detested the candidature' of his ex-Minister of War and, while allowing that the candidate might be more 'human' than Castello, noted scathingly that his candidature was not the culmination of a political career, nor the high point of long public service, but that of an unknown entity: 'What will he be? What does he think? What does he want, apart from being—at any price—the successor of Castello . . .'? The interview is a good example of how much more easily the press could carry critical articles (though *Visão* disavowed opinions expressed in this one) under Castello Branco than under his successors.

102 Schneider, op. cit., 186. Schneider has a detailed account of changes in the method of voting and the percentage of national and state populations eligible to take part in the elections.

103 ibid., 190.

104 ibid.

105 See the useful comments in *Visão* (25 November 1966), 11–15, and (2 December), 14–16. Also the analysis in the special number of *Revista Brasileira de Estudos Políticos*, No. 23/24 (July 1967–January 1968). The volume consists of analyses by different authors of the election results in eleven states, though with only limited analysis of Minas Gerais; a general essay on the elections; and studies of more specific cases, in Belo Horizonte, Uberaba, Rio Claro, and Araraquara.

106 See *Visão* (16 December 1966), 11, which notes the intention to avoid prolonged debate on the eve of change of president and sees the essence of the new proposals as introducing authoritarian presidential control with greater centralizing powers, especially to intervene directly in politics.

107 See the protest contained in the so-called 'Declaration of Brasília', resulting from the first National Meeting of the Press, Radio, and Television in Brasília, 11 and 12 January 1967. This produced some, but only minor, modifications in the new law.

108 For useful discussion of the new constitution see *Visão* (27 January 1967 and 3 February 1967). For some of Castello Branco's own comments on these changes at the time see the photocopies from his personal archive published in *Veja* (5 April 1972), which provide an illuminating insight into the importance he attached to these changes, and some of the reservations

he had about their possible abuse by a future president. Also see Oscar Dias Correia, *A Constituição de 1967* (Rio de Janeiro, 1968).

109 *Veja* (5 April 1972), 39.

110 Schneider, op. cit., 199–200. Schneider also lists 'the major purges under the original institutional act during 1964—with 116 elected mandates cancelled; 378 cases of political rights being suspended; 544 compulsory retirements for political reasons; 1,528 firings; 555 forced military retirements; 165 voluntary transfers to the reserves; and various other punitive acts, for a grand total of more than 3,500 in the federal sphere (plus at least an equal number by state and municipal authorities)'.

111 *Visão* (17 February 1967). There was also set up IPEA (Instituto de Pesquisa Econômico-Social Aplicada) to carry out detailed research related to planning.

112 Among these was a team from the University of California at Berkeley, headed by Howard B. Ellis.

113 Campos in Ellis, op. cit., 337. See his comments on the PAEG and, in particular, how it improved on the Plano Trienal of the Goulart government.

114 ibid., 339.

115 See Schneider, op. cit., 120, referring to the position of Costa e Silva after the crisis of October 1965: 'If in Planning Minister Roberto Campos Brazil had a virtual prime minister within the functioning of the Castello Branco government, it now also had an heir apparent in the person of the War Minister'. Also see Georges-André Fiechter, *Brazil since 1964: Modernisation under a Military Regime. A Study of the Interactions in a Contemporary Military Regime* (London, 1975), 58: 'Roberto Campos, who was virtually Prime Minister, later defined his strategy as "the gradual transition from the objective of warding off catastrophe to the objective of growth by applying a 'creative orthodoxy' . . ." '. Fiechter's study contains much useful information, especially textual quotation from government decrees and other documents: but it tends to accept rather too uncritically the regime's own account of its behaviour.

1967–74

10 Repression and the Politics of Growth

Divisions within the Regime

The crisis of October 1965, which virtually determined that Costa e Silva would succeed as president in March 1967, had shown that, despite the forcible removal and retirement of many officers after the *coup*, sharp divisions still existed within the armed forces. The most immediately crucial question, therefore, for Brazilian politics as the new president took office was how deeply those divisions ran and what they might mean in terms of government policy.

The months leading to the *coup* of April 1964 had produced a closing of ranks on issues on which most of the officer corps could agree, particularly the threat to national security they believed contained in the economic crisis, especially though inflation, and the challenge they saw in the growth of activities regarded as subversive. These were especially associated with the trade union movement, whose wage demands were seen as excessive and as a prime cause of inflation, but whose growing political power raised in military eyes the more serious threat of the *república sindicalista*, widely judged to be corrosive of Brazil's social and political institutions; therefore of national security and even of development, as understood by theorists and propagandists most influential among the officer corps.[1] These were basic issues on which by March 1964 there was widespread consensus, reinforced by pressure from civilian interest groups, both in Brazil and abroad, who were hostile to the wider political mobilization contained in policies associated with Vargas and most recently Goulart. Former differences were patched up as opinion in the officer corps, strongly influenced by a press repeatedly urging the armed forces to shoulder their responsibility for maintaining social order and national institutions, moved towards the idea of direct intervention to end the crisis. At the same time, the removal of officers closest to Goulart, and the widespread fear among the victors that some attempt at a counter-*coup* might still be made, not only brought more agreement among different groups supporting the new regime, but, in particular, allowed the control of affairs, at least in the short-term, to pass to that element within the armed forces which was, both by organization and strategy, most prepared to take over immediately: those most closely linked to the ESG, as represented, in its two wings, by Castello Branco and Roberto Campos. But both these features of military–civilian politics immediately before and after the *coup*, the appearance of greater unity and homogeneity, and the dominant position of the 'Sorbonne', Castellista group, were to some extent deceptive, as was seen in the opposition which produced Institutional Act No. 2 and the recurring tension between those most closely associated with Castello Branco and those loosely described as the 'hard line', part of which urged, or virtually imposed, the candidature of Costa e Silva.

Some of the most bitter criticism of the Castello Branco government from fellow military officers was certainly motivated by frustrated personal ambition or by a fear that any relaxation of control might bring back to active service more senior officers set aside after the *coup*, whose empty shoes younger officers were eager to fill. This latter motive seems to have been especially important in the 'hard-line' objection to any talk of amnesty for political opponents, military and civilian, on the part of some of the captains and majors, determined to prevent the return of senior officers:

> In many instances the most vocal advocates of the purges, and the middle-level interrogators on the severe and often arbitrary military investigating committees that meted out revolutionary justice, were only captains and majors, while their victims were senior colonels and junior generals. The possible return of the purged officers in the future presented a built-in institutional obstacle to amnesty.[2]

Shifts in national politics over the last twenty years always had been reflected in the pattern and pace of promotions in the officer corps, but 1964 had seen not only the forcible retirement of officers known to have favoured Goulart, but a much more sharply defined political test of 'revolutionary' loyalty to determine a man's chance of promotion: hence the eagerness of many junior officers who in October 1965 supported Costa e Silva to prove themselves more Catholic than the Pope. Other opposition, by contrast, often taking the shape of demands for a return to constitutional forms of government, stemmed from frustration at being passed over or excluded from higher office, as, for example, in the case of General Olímpio Mourão Filho, who, angry at his lack of recognition after April 1964, soon became a severe critic of the Castello government.

Similarly, Generals Amaury Kruel and Justino Alves Bastos also moved into opposition when their hopes for state governorships were frustrated. The main question by March 1967 was how far such divisions within the regime merely turned on personal differences, or how far they represented significantly different groupings, perhaps with different policies for the country.

Analysis of the officers close to or supporting Costa e Silva, as compared with those linked to Castello Branco, showed some quite striking differences, but none which pointed unambiguously to a probable dramatic change in overall policy.[3] In terms of social origins, for example, there was by the early 1960s little to choose between different elements in the officer corps. Several decades earlier many officers were second or younger sons of small landowning or professional families, mainly from the north-east or the far south, especially Rio Grande do Sul. Often the pattern was one of the eldest son taking over the *fazenda*, while the others were glad to enter a career which maintained a certain status, while also providing some form of education which even brought some slight remuneration to the officer cadet. Relatively few officers, by comparison, in the first three decades of the century came from the more prosperous industrializing areas of São Paulo, so that the *tenentes*, for instance, found it difficult to find a strong representative in São Paulo, especially after the untimely death of Siqueira Campos. After the Second World War the pattern altered to some degree, with more and more entrants from the expanding middle class, but still with relatively few from São Paulo, where young men of middle-class families had better fish to fry. As in most Western societies, the bulk of officer cadets came from what, broadly speaking, were middle-class homes, often from provincial towns, bringing with them many of the marks of provincial culture, not least a rather stolid suspicion of the soft, corrupting influences of the metropolis, though by at least the 1960s many were coming immediately from Guanabara.[4] Analysis of the family background of officer entrants to the military academy from 1941–43 showed 76·4 per cent with fathers in middle-class occupations; a similar analysis for 1962–66 found much the same, 78·2 per cent,[5] a readily understandable percentage when the academic qualification for entrants to the officer corps, as to the universities, could normally be met only by youngsters whose family could afford relatively expensive private secondary education. Educational requirements, again predictably, caused a drop in entrants from Brazil's poorest states, the north-east, by 1964–66, with only 14 per cent of cadet entrants,[6] though at the more politically important level of senior officers men from the north-east and the far south were still strongly represented. São Paulo, too, still remained under-represented, with only 8·3 per cent of the cadet intake for 1964–66, although the state had 18·3 per cent of the total national population in 1960.[7]

On all counts what seems to have been most important in Brazil, as elsewhere, is not so much where or *from* what the young officers have been recruited, as the culture, training, group consciousness, and ideology *into which* they have been recruited, which is also where the differences between the Castellista, or 'Sorbonne', group, and others becomes most interesting. This distinction between family and regional background as a major influence and the educational and training system into which the young cadets are absorbed may become less strong in future as there is increasing group reinforcement through the recruitment of sons of military officers, a percentage which grew from 21·2 per cent of intake in 1941–43 to 34·9 per cent in 1962–66;[8] but this background is also reinforced by the influence, not only of military colleges, but of military-supported schools, since it has been found that 'probably up to 90 per cent of the present post-war generation of army officers in Brazil entered the military academic system around the age of twelve'.[9] It is this training within the military educational system which contributes most to the shaping of young Brazilian officers, and it is within this area of training and service experience that the differences between the Castellista and other groups become most apparent.

One of the most striking features of promotion procedures in the Brazilian officer corps is the importance, in contrast to some other armed forces, of academic achievement throughout a long period of specified training, a pattern which partly reflects the lack of opportunity to win promotion in the field, but which leads to a close adherence to professional and bureaucratic norms:

> In the army, all officers who have command responsibility must attend the four-year military academy (Academia Militar das Agulhas Negras, AMAN). To be promoted to captain, all officers are obliged to attend for one year the junior officers' school (Escola de Aperfeiçoamento de Oficiais, EsAO). To be eligible for promotion to general, or for appointment to the general staff of any of the four armies or service schools, an officer must also pass the difficult entrance examination to the General Staff School (Escola de Comando e Estado Maior do Exército, ECEME) and then attend a course of three years' duration. (The comparable training period in the General Staff School in the United States is only nine months long.) Normally, less than 25 percent of the applicants pass this entrance examination.
>
> In addition, there are many specialized technical schools and

> opportunities for study abroad (mostly in the United States or France). Increasingly, a year's study at the Superior War College (Escola Superior de Guerra, ESG) is becoming the norm for senior colonels and junior generals.
>
> Since most Latin American armies have very little or no recent combat experience, academic achievement is extremely important for subsequent promotion. In Brazil, for example, 40 of the 102 army line generals on active duty in 1964 had graduated first in their class at one of the three major army service schools.[10]

Analysis of the group most closely associated with Castello Branco during his presidency shows that one shared characteristic was very high academic performance, with every one of the ten generals in the 'core group' around Castello Branco having graduated first in one of the three major army schools.[11] Nine of the ten had attended the ESG; seven had served at one time or other on its permanent staff; all had been at military school abroad, eight in the United States, and six had served together in the FEB, the Brazilian Expeditionary Force in Italy during the Second World War. Five out of the ten had been in the FEB, worked on the permanent staff of the ESG, attended courses abroad, and graduated first in one of the three major army schools, whereas of the other ninety-two generals only one had the same record.[12] Investigating more closely the significance of this training and career experience it was argued that:

> The value placed on interdependence in foreign policy, the fear of excessive nationalism, the relatively strong belief that Brazil could profit through a close relationship with the United States, the deep distrust of emotional appeals, the idea that capitalism could create a physically powerful nation, the belief that democracy was a more 'civilized' style of politics—these were attitudes that were specifically strengthened or largely created by officer participation in the Brazilian Expeditionary Force (FEB) in Italy during World War II.[13]

The experience in the FEB, backed by reflection on the failure of Mussolini and the analogy between problems of development found in Italy and Brazil, strengthened the belief in the need not only for careful organization, but for modern technology, industry, and a flexible—or, as the spokesmen of this group would say, a realistic—attitude towards foreign capital and foreign aid, avoiding the merely verbal posturing of empty nationalism.[14] The Italian experience also seems to have strengthened a preference for democratic rather than authoritarian government, the perception of the legitimate role of the armed forces being to intervene in a national crisis, but not to take control of the country for a long period. Most of these views were later developed further in the ESG, but with greater priority being given to planning and organization, democracy being seen as an ideal but not always attainable, especially when it might conflict with the more urgent needs of planning for development and security.[15] Further experience abroad strengthened the commitment to Western capitalism on the United States model, including a large role to the private sector, especially since 80 per cent of the generals closest to Castello Branco attended courses in the United States, as compared with only 24 per cent of the other generals who had taken courses anywhere abroad.[16] This experience almost certainly further modified, too, the thinking on nationalism and national development of this Castellista group, strengthening the suspicion of mere *ufanismo*, a narrow emotive nationalism, and developing a perception of the 'nation' and nationalism which later brought charges of *entreguismo*, of too readily opening the door for foreign penetration and exploitation, during the Castello Branco government. The idea of the 'nation' or 'national interest' now seemed to be extended, with application well beyond Brazil's frontiers, not only through its close association with 'national security' or 'national development', but because this thinking about 'the nation', always at the highest level of abstraction, also embraced the concept of a 'Western', 'Christian' heritage, which, in turn, was closely linked to the survival and efficient performance of a wider capitalist economy within which Brazilian development was conceived.

While such thinking on nationalism may have seemed to soldiers and civilians close to Castello Branco merely pragmatic and realistic, an acceptance of the conditions within which Brazil's development strategy could best be pursued, it seemed to many others a betrayal of even the moderately nationalist demands made throughout the 1950s, especially in relation to such sensitive issues as the exploitation of subsoil mineral wealth. The more liberal policies of the Castello Branco government, as seen, for example, in its grant of iron-ore concessions to private United States capital, produced vigorous criticism both from military officers and from many businessmen, who saw the government's policies as little more than crude *entreguismo*, albeit in more sophisticated form and supported by high-sounding theorizing on development goals and means. There was growing anger in business and financial circles at the tight credit controls which drove many businesses to bankruptcy or to selling out to United States and foreign companies, a process which many believed would end in the large-scale takeover of Brazilian firms, all in the name of Brazilian development. Businessmen, particularly in

São Paulo, found themselves less able to exert political influence on the new regime than they could previously, being more subject to government directives, but with less immediate access to power in a system where the role of the military, the *técnicos*, and the bureaucrats had so sharply increased in importance.[17] The new system, politically and economically, seemed increasingly to be shaped to promote the interests of the foreign financier or businessman as much as, or even more than, of the local Brazilian. The new system was sometimes described, though the distinction could be pressed too far, as one which favoured the international as opposed to the national bourgeoisie; but, whatever terms were used, there was a growing sense, both among military and civilians, that the Castello Branco group was soft on nationalism. Equally, in the view of many officers who supported the candidature of Costa e Silva, the government was too soft politically, too neglectful of that other military priority, security.

Among the issues which had divided the armed forces throughout the post-war period the two most important, and now the most relevant by early 1967, were, in the economic sphere, the degree and manner of foreign participation in the economy and, in national politics, the legitimate role of the armed forces, both to intervene at a time of crisis and to retain power for as long as they judged necessary. The second question had always been the most directly relevant throughout the recurrent crises of the 1950s and 1960s when the strong 'constitutionalist' group within the officer corps, most conspicuously led by Marshal Lott, had effectively contained the *golpistas*, whose spokesmen were not representative of the majority of the officer corps, even in the last months before the *coup*. The issue of nationalism was, however, even more hotly debated, being the point on which internal military politics turned in some of the most closely fought elections in the Clube Militar. In the 1950s, for example, these elections centred on the question of oil and the creation of Petrobrás, as well as on Vargas's return to national politics. The nationalist candidate for president of the Club, General Newton Estillac Leal, beat the then commandant of the ESG, General Cordeiro de Farias, and went on to become Minister of War under Vargas, but his victory was only the start of a long struggle, still not resolved by 1964, between the more nationalist camp and those more favourable to foreign intervention. Economic nationalism had deep roots in the officer corps, being an important source of the *tenente* critique in the 1920s and 1930s. Throughout the 1950s the term 'nationalist' became identified with the political left, particularly with those most sympathetic to the Vargista tradition, while the *entreguistas* were popularly seen as clustered heavily on the right, mainly round the UDN and linked to the *golpistas*. But these categories were altogether too crude. Many officers who were firmly set against a *coup* took a less rigorous line with regard to the role of the foreigner in Brazil's economy: but, no less important, some of the officers most deeply suspicious of civilian politicians were also reluctant to see the Brazilian economy exploited by foreign financial and business interests, standing firm, most particularly, on such questions as oil and mineral deposits, which also had for them strong implications for national security.[18] The terms and slogans of national politics tended to mask the existence of this right-wing authoritarian nationalism among the Brazilian military, but it persisted strongly, as one of the main sources of criticism of the softer view of nationalism held by the ESG. The other factor which tended to obscure the nationalism of the right was the predominance from 1950 to 1964 of the distinct, but always closely related, issue of security, which led many officers to give greater priority to the fight against subversion and communism as contained, they believed, in the 'nationalist' camp.[19] So, for example, in the 1952 elections in the Clube Militar the 'anti-nationalist' bloc formed a 'Democratic Crusade', to oppose Estillac Leal, a 'Crusade' in which were strongly represented men who by 1967 were closely associated with Costa e Silva. These included, for example, Lieutenant-Colonel Sizeno Sarmento, Captain Mário David Andreazza, Major Edson Figueiredo, and Lieutenant-Colonel João Bina Machado. Vargas's own position at the time, like that of many 'nationalists', was not an extreme one. He said he welcomed foreign investment and participation in Brazil s economy, but not to the point of exploitation. Brazil welcomed help, but in line with Brazilian interests:

> We are not opposed, as often is insinuated, to foreign capital coming to Brazil. On the contrary, we want it to come. But what we do oppose is the handing over of our natural resources and our reserves to the service of monopoly capitalism . . . I have said, and I solemnly repeat, that whoever hands over his petroleum hands over his own independence. Petroleum cannot be removed from the economic control of the state, so as not to compromise our political sovereignty.[20]

But by early 1952 Vargas was under increasing political pressure from the right wing and in March 1952 dismissed Estillac Leal as Minister of War, who then was heavily defeated in the Clube Militar elections in May by candidates who personally opposed the nationalist position on the control of Brazil's economy, but whose electoral support more directly reflected increased concern over 'communism' and the threat to security.[21] The Clube Militar elections of May 1954 showed this same growing concern with security, especially strengthened by Lacerda's charges in *Tribuna da Imprensa* that Vargas intended to support a *coup* to keep himself in office. The successful candidates were General Canrobert da Costa, formerly Dutra's Minister of War, and Juarez Távora, the most prominent opponent of the 'nationalists'. But, again, the move to the right of many moderate officers could be interpreted mainly as a result of the alleged plans for subversion of the constitutional process, and not as unambiguous evidence of a vote against nationalism in economic affairs.

For the next decade or more this issue of nationalism and its meaning for the direction of the economy remained at the forefront of military debate, but still obscured for many officers by what seemed the more immediate problem of a drift towards subversion, which, in turn, led to too easy an identification of nationalism and the 'Communist' menace, a tendency which was, however, only increased by the left wing's habit of describing itself simply as 'nationalist' and virtually arrogating the term for itself. The changes in senior military personnel introduced in 1961 under Quadros greatly strengthened, as seen above, the right wing of the military, putting into key positions many men who in 1964 were to move against Goulart.[22] This strengthened the *golpistas* as compared with those who might support Goulart and his policies, or even as compared with the more liberal 'Sorbonne' group, but it by no means silenced the nationalist bloc in the officer corps. In the 1962 Clube Militar elections:

> a general who had sharply defended Vice-President Goulart's right to assume the presidency in the crisis of 1961, and who had publicly applauded the nationalization of a foreign utility company and urged land reform, was narrowly defeated by 4,884 votes to 4,312. This fact illustrates that the momentary unity of the army during their overthrow of President Goulart in 1964 was not a result of permanent ideological unity but rather of their interaction with the political system in a time of crisis.[23]

Much work still needs to be done to gauge more accurately the strength of military feeling on key issues throughout the whole modern period.[24] What is already clear, however, is that strong feelings on nationalism were not confined to pro-Vargas or pro-Goulart supporters and that many officers who at various points of crisis sided against Vargas, Goulart, and the 'nationalists' did so primarily out of fear of the other features they ascribed to Vargista politics, namely the threat they believed it contained for national security, as symbolized, in part, in the left wing's exclusive use of the term 'nationalist' to describe itself. But, equally important, especially when considering the forces within the officer corps which criticized the Castello Branco government and supported Costa e Silva, and which, moreover, were to remain strong during the following ten years and more, the thinking of the Castellista group, like the training, background, and career experience of the men who made up that group, was not typical of the officer corps as a whole. Rather, the 'Sorbonne', ESG group, despite their preparedness to take over in 1964 and their dominance in the Castello Branco government, were atypical in some important respects. The coherence and homogeneity which characterized the group around Castello Branco, and which shaped the policies of his government, marked off the Castellistas by comparison with most of their fellow officers, as can clearly be seen by comparing the first group with the men most closely associated with Costa e Silva.

The best analysis of the 'hard line' younger officers who in October 1965 supported Costa e Silva, and of those closest to him in his government, says of the more junior hard-liners:

> There was a self-interested element of fear of the return of those they had helped purge. More important, however, were the twin urges to be more authoritarian—purge more politicians, disband Congress and political parties, censor the press, cancel all elections—and to be more radically reformist—expropriate large landownings, confiscate wealth of profiteering businessmen, and have more nationalistic assertive relations toward foreign capital and the United States.[25]

The pressure from these younger officers seems to have been sufficient in 1965 to have supported a successful *coup* against Castello Branco, had that been decided on, but instead it guaranteed the presidency for Costa e Silva.[26]

It has also been said of the senior officers closest to Costa e Silva in the first year of his government that

> . . . these men owed their positions . . . to the fact that they symbolically and actually represented the opposite of the ideas and career-patterns of the original core-group of officers in the 1964–1967 government. . . .[27]

This group included, most conspicuously, General Afonso Augusto de Albuquerque Lima, the Minister of the Interior; General Sizeno

Sarmento, commander of the First Army in Rio de Janeiro; General Jayme Portella, head of the Military Household and secretary-general of the National Security Council; and General Emílio Garrastazú Médici, director of the SNI, National Information Service, the man who eventually was to succeed Costa e Silva as the third president of the new regime. Of these officers, by contrast with the group around Castello Branco, only one of the five had been in Italy with the FEB, only one had graduated first in one of the major service schools, only one had been on the permanent staff of the ESG, and all had fewer contacts outside Brazil, especially in the United States.[28] What these men represented, in part at least, was a new generation of officers, men younger than themselves, but who had not shared, for example, the experience of service in Italy and who often had not been subjected to vicarious experience and the shared values of the FEB as conveyed through courses in the ESG.

Throughout much Brazilian political thinking, both civilian and military, as indeed in Latin American reflection on politics and development more generally, there runs a pattern analogous to the tension in, for example, Russian thought between the 'Westernizers' and the 'Slavophiles'. There are those whose model of development and modernization, as to both ends and means, is explicitly 'Western', seeing Brazil as part of a wider system within which its future development lies. It was into this category, broadly speaking, that the Castellista, ESG group fell most clearly, even though ESG thinking, as already argued, contained strong indigenous elements. But, though less explicit, less articulate, and less poised to step in in 1964, there was another, more indigenous tradition, particularly in military thinking, which, though masked by the political controversy of the 1950s and 1960s, still persisted strongly. This was a tradition which also went back to the *tenentes* and beyond, to writers such as Oliveira Vianna and Alberto Torres, whose ideas on the need to develop a political system suited to the specific traditions and conditions of Brazil still helped to shape political attitudes and reactions among those disposed to seek more authoritarian and more nationalist solutions to Brazil's problems. This was a strain clearly to be found in Integralism, the influence of which still persisted strongly, and it was this less cosmopolitan, less liberal, but, again like Integralism, more reformist, tradition which partly was reflected in the critique of Castello Branco and the backing for Costa e Silva.[29]

Looking at military thinking in Brazil throughout the modern period two themes had always been predominant, those of security and of nationalism. Speaking generally, the thinking of the ESG saw the relation of those two themes as extending well beyond Brazil's frontiers, since genuine national security, and genuine national development, could only be achieved in the wider context of 'Western' security and development, a view which, in itself, resulted in a 'softer' line on nationalism and nationalist controls. Especially in the period of growing 'subversion' and the threat to security of the 1950s and early 1960s the preoccupation with nationalism was subordinated to that over security. But the other school of thought, though more latent, argued in effect that nationalist concern need not be sacrificed, especially if a much more rigorous, less liberal line was taken over security. In this sense, for the 'hard-liners', as for the ESG, security and nationalist development were closely tied, in that a more genuinely nationalist, and even reformist, programme could be possible, provided that there was no back-pedalling on security.

Granted the dominant role of the ESG in the post-war period, the number of influential graduates produced, and the importance attached to it by the United States, it is at first sight rather surprising how by October 1965 the 'hard line' element in the officer corps, and the civilian pressures behind it, could be so strong as to be able to dictate terms to Castello Branco and those who thought as he did: yet this was the case, evidence of the strength of authoritarian nationalist feeling within the armed forces, raising important questions not just for the new Costa e Silva government, but for the future shaping of the post-1964 regime. Authoritarian, nationalist, but also reformist: these were the qualities attributed to the 'hard line' close to the new president. Evidence of the reformist demands was still relatively slight, but it was there, reflecting the dislike of political corruption, manipulation, and control through wealth derived from large landholdings or from big business, similar to that seen in the *tenentes*' formulations, or in, for example, the Revolutionary Legion of the early 1930s or in later Integralism. The reformist concern of the right-wing authoritarian nationalists had been seen in the demands, mentioned above, of the Frente Patriótica Civil-Militar, in which were said to be prominent such men as the former Minister of the Navy, Sílvio Heck, General José Alberto Bittencourt, and the influential journalist of the *Estado de São Paulo*, Oliveiros Ferreira.[30] Their *Ten Commandments of the Law of the People* were:

1 Dissolution of Congress in order to restructure the popular democratic base of the country by a new constituent assembly.
2 Confiscation of all fortunes acquired by shady business deals, embezzlement, administrative frauds, or any other illicit means, with the cancelling of the political rights of all involved.
3 Distribution to the peasants of all uncultivated lands with the

obligation of immediate cultivation and with direct financial and technical assistance guaranteed.

4 Energetic combating of the high cost of living and inflation by the intervention of the state in the means of production and distribution and the suppression of taxes on the basic necessities of life.

5 Eliminate excessive bureaucracy and unify the social welfare system and guarantee medical and hospital care to all workers, including rural workers.

6 Abolition of all forms of government intervention in trade unions.

7 Preferential concern for the solution to the problems of the north and the northeast and other underdeveloped areas of the country in all national development plans.

8 Defense and development of Petrobrás and of the great state industries. Control of the remission of profits abroad and the requirement that profits be reinvested in the development of the country.

9 Extension of free primary, secondary, technical, and higher education by the state for the training of poor students.

10 The pursuit of an independent foreign policy opposed to all forms of totalitarianism and imperialism, respect for the rights of self-determination and condemnation of the monstrous arms-race in accordance with the democratic and Christian principles of Brazil.[31]

It was difficult to know how widely these reformist demands were shared by the 'hard line', or how much backing they had from important civilian interest groups: but the experience of government from 1964 to 1967 at least had shown that

> the military-backed government of Castello Branco was clearly as subject to ultimatums from the military institution as civilian governments had been in the past. Castello Branco had, in fact, capitulated to the threats from the military.[32]

The main questions, therefore, as Costa e Silva took office, was how far he, too, would be moved by pressure from within the armed forces, especially from the 'hard line' younger officers who had helped him to power.

The New Government: Continuity and Change

Before taking office Costa e Silva had talked much of his desire to 'humanize' the regime and of his close identification with the sufferings and sacrifices of the Brazilian people.[33] The imminent change of presidency had also renewed debate on party politics, especially the possibility of a return to a wider representative system than that allowed through ARENA and MDB.[34] There was a general atmosphere of cautious expectancy as the new man came to office, since, while Costa e Silva was recognized as not belonging to the more liberal wing of the 'Sorbonne', he already had made clear that he personally did not endorse all the demands of the 'hard line' group which had most strongly opposed Castello Branco. He appeared, rather, as a broker between the two factions, who might under pressure move in either direction. Unfortunately for those who hoped for a liberalization of the system and a gradual return to more open political debate, the period between Costa e Silva's assumption of government and the crisis caused by his illness in September 1969, saw only an intensification of the move towards more arbitrary government, a failure to listen to reform demands, and the strengthening of a state apparatus increasingly geared to harsh repression.

Analysis of the membership of Costa e Silva's new government showed a notable representation of officers associated with the 'hard line', a hint of a possible shift towards more independent nationalist policies in certain areas, a strong representation of the armed forces, and a continuing commitment to an economic strategy perceived as pragmatic and realistic, albeit designed by *técnicos* not entirely in tune with the thinking of Roberto Campos and his team of planners.[35] There were, in other words, strong elements of continuity, but, especially in view of the regime's claims to be able to rise above the squabbles and differences of civilian politics, a surprising degree of discontinuity, uncertainty, and tension. The most conspicuous representative of the 'hard line', including its more nationalist and reformist elements, was the Minister of the Interior, Major-General Afonso Augusto de Albuquerque Lima. Over the next two years he was to emerge as a serious contender for the presidency, with strong backing from 'hard line' officers, especially from the rank of colonel downwards, and from many of the younger *técnicos*, increasingly preoccupied with the enlarged role of foreign interests in Brazil's development strategy, particularly in the matter of technology, and with the continuing neglect of reform, and of distribution of the fruits of economic growth. Albuquerque Lima, now fifty-seven, was a north-easterner, who previously had worked as head of the National Department of Anti-Drought Works (DNOCS), had been First Army Chief of Staff during the confrontation of October 1965, and most recently Director of Military Engineering. Although he had spent time in the ESG, he was firmly identified with the authoritarian nationalist wing of the officer corps and with its demands for greater priority for such issues as regional development, especially in the north-east and Amazonas, demands which pulled closely together the 'hard line' concern for both nationalist development and security by taking possession of an exploiting Brazil's resources through development of neglected territories. Another 'hard-liner' was in charge of the area in which nationalist opinion was most sensitive Mines and Energy, the new minister being Colonel José Costa Cavalcanti, who was also prominent as a 'hard-liner' on the National Security Council. Another officer generally regarded as 'hard line' was the new director of the SNI (National Information Service), a body which, created after the 1964 *coup*, was already becoming one of the most important centres of political power and a springboard to high office. The new director was, like Costa e Silva, a *gaúcho*, General Emílio Garrastazú Médici. He formerly had been Costa e Silva's chief of staff in the 3rd Military Region, then Commandant of the Military Academy in Agulhas Negras, where he had worked with Costa e Silva at the time of the 1964 *coup*. Before taking over the SNI from General Golbery do Couto e Silva he had been commander of the 3rd Military Region with the rank of major-general. The new Chief Military Aide, General Jayme Portella, was part of this same bloc, one of those who in 1955 had supported Carlos Luz against the constitutionalist General Lott. He later was to be made head of Costa e Silva's Military Household and promoted to three-star general, but already his role in the new government emphasized the prominence of the 'hard line'. So, too, did the appointment to the Ministry of Justice of Luís Antônio da Gama e Silva, who had been Minister of Justice and Education under the Revolutionary Supreme Command just after the 1964 *coup*. He had long argued the need for much tougher measures, including a longer period for the deprivation of political rights. Although a former rector of the University of São Paulo, he was well-known for his illiberal convictions, and under the new government his name was to become synonymous with severe reaction and political repression, often of men who once had been his colleagues in academic and political life. Gama e Silva, as one of eight civilian ministers and eight military in the new government, represented the civilian 'hard line'. The new Minister of Foreign Affairs, the former governor of Minas Gerais and UDN leader, Magalhães Pinto, was one of the most severe critics of Castello Branco. While having a strong vested interest, like Lacerda, in urging a return to civilian presidential government, which allowed him to appear more liberal and constitutionalist than some of his colleagues, he also reflected some of the dissatisfaction over policies too closely linked to those of foreign interests, especially the United States. He too, therefore, especially in contrast to his predecessor, Juracy Magalhães, strengthened the impression of a new team which might be expected to take a somewhat different course.

In the case of the other posts, too, the influence of the 'hard line' could be seen. Of the three service ministries, for example, that of the navy went to Admiral Augusto Hamann Rademaker Grünewald, a former member of the Revolutionary Supreme Command, who at the time of the *coup* had joined Gama e Silva in demanding sweeping purges of Congress, and who had continued as a critic of Castello Branco's allegedly soft treatment of subversive threats. The Minister of the Air Force had served briefly in Castello Branco's cabinet and, despite disagreements, was less opposed to him, but he had been a bitter enemy of Goulart and was generally regarded as a 'hard-liner'. Of the three service ministers only the new Minister of the Army, General Aurélio de Lyra Tavares, belonged squarely to the ESG, 'Sorbonne' group, being currently commandant of the ESG: but his appointment was seen as an attempt to preserve the unity of the officer corps, especially when so many senior officers were still Castello Branco men, owing their promotion to him. Legislation introduced by Castello Branco, ending some benefits and promotion procedures for officers on retirement, caused an unusually heavy number of retirements before the deadline of 10 October 1966. This allowed Castello Branco to fill an exceptionally large number of vacancies for senior officers at the end of 1966, including seven new full generals. These were Jurandir Mamede, Alvaro da Silva Braga, Rafael de Souza Aguiar, Alberto Ribeiro Paz, Antônio Carlos Muricy, and Ernesto Geisel, the last two being promoted ahead of others generally thought to be more eligible for promotion, but closer to Costa e Silva. This adroit move by Castello Branco, as well as emphasizing the extent of the divisions within the officer corps, protected and strengthened his own following and helped to shape military politics for some years to come.[36] It also largely explained the need to give the Army Ministry to a senior ESG man, however much this may have gone against the grain. Costa e Silva had relatively little opportunity to promote his own men to the most senior positions:

> Thus individuals closely linked to Castello Branco, albeit in most cases maintaining good relations with the President, remained in most important command positions down through 1969.[37]

Among others appointed to the new cabinet was General Edmundo de Macedo Soares e Silva, an old *tenente*, but one whose career mostly had been spent in developing Brazil's state-owned steel industry, mainly as director of the National Steel Company. His post of Minister of Commerce and Industry again advanced a man long associated with an area of nationalist pride and sensitivity, who also was an old colleague of Costa e Silva. Among others of the president's close associates was the new Minister of Transport, Colonel Mário David Andreazza, widely regarded as a protégé whom Costa e Silva would advance rapidly.

All these appointments marked off the new government from its predecessor, reflecting the strength of the more nationalist 'hard line' and the critics of Castello Branco: but the most crucially important posts also emphasized most clearly the essential continuity of the post-1964 regime in its commitment to an overall development model, the necessities of which overrode all others. One such necessity was that of maintaining the confidence and support of international business and finance, which, whatever the reservations of nationalists within the regime, remained under Costa e Silva a fundamental condition for the success of the urgent drive for economic growth. Hélio Beltrão now became Minister of Planning, while the Ministry of Finance went to the thirty-eight-year-old Antônio Delfim Neto, state Secretary of Finance in São Paulo under Laudo Natel. One element of change over the next six years was the relative decline of the Ministry of Planning, which Roberto Campos had built into the most important ministry of the Castello Branco government, and the re-establishment in the front rank of the Ministry of Finance under Delfim Neto.

The role of Delfim Neto is, in some respects, a key to an understanding of Brazilian politics from 1967 to 1973, the period of Brazil's so-called 'Economic Miracle'. These were years of sustained high growth-rates, rapidly expanding exports, especially of newly developed industrial products, but also of new levels of political repression and neglect of other social and economic priorities which might endanger the headlong pursuit of growth and the foreign confidence which sustained it. It is in this sphere of the political economy that one finds, behind the many shifts and changes, in tactics as well as in style, by comparison with the Castello Branco government, the strong underlying continuity, determined by an essentially identical model of rapid economic growth within the framework of Western capitalism. The long nationalist tradition within the armed forces might, indeed, be represented in the new government by men such as Albuquerque Lima. It might even remain an important, perhaps the most important, factor for future development; but, in the short term, certainly during the presidencies of Costa e Silva and his successor, the absolutely determining priority was to be that of economic growth in an ordered, stable political context, which nothing must be allowed to disturb, not even the growing dissatisfaction of nationalist 'hard line' officers. The intriguing result, therefore, was a situation in which the 'hard line', having won their victory over Castello Branco and having placed in office men loud in their criticism of policies so favourable to foreign penetration of the economy, now found that they, too, in all essentials, were confined and shaped by an economic strategy which could allow only some gestures of defiance towards the world of international finance and business, a stance mainly directed at the United States. But the unswerving economic strategy of this government, as of its predecessor, required, as an absolute condition of success, a strict curb on any real defiance, even to the extent of allowing throughout this period the greatly enlarged role of multinational corporations within Brazil's economy. The result of this tension and contradiction was a dichotomy at times between rhetoric and reality strangely reminiscent of that which the military victors of 1964 had condemned in civilian 'populist' politicians. At the same time appeared a recurring pattern in which the reformist and more nationalist priorities of the 'hard line' were neglected or muted, while, as an integral part of the 'development' process, their demands for tougher, more authoritarian control were heeded, and at times even turned against the 'hard liners' themselves. Stressing the essential continuity of economic strategy does not mean, on the other hand, that there were no important changes after March 1967: quite the contrary, since it was in the sphere of economic policy that some of the most notable differences were to be found. But these were changes not radically to alter or challenge the previous economic model, but rather to strengthen and develop it further.

It has been argued that one important curb on nationalist demands, in 1967 and again during the 'succession crisis' of September–October 1969, was the fear among senior officers that more radical nationalism could threaten the hierarchy of command: 'as well as alienate the São Paulo business community, whose cooperation they regarded as necessary for the success of the economic programs of the government'.[38] This view probably poses too sharp a distinction between the 'hard-liners' and the São Paulo business community, certainly in terms of a commitment to more severe authoritarian control, since, as was seen even more clearly from 1967 onwards, there was strong support for tougher measures from *paulista* financial and business interests, which consistently attempted to win over military commanders in São Paulo, regularly opposing them to the more liberal wing of the officer corps. This was to become one of the dominant features of military politics over the next decade, but already by 1967 it was abundantly clear that the more authoritarian political demands of the 'hard-liners' had firm backing in São Paulo.

In the sphere of economic policy the position is much more confused. There was, certainly, considerable opposition in São Paulo to the tight credit restrictions imposed by Roberto Campos, and there was undoubtedly support from some elements of business and industry for those critics of Campos's policy who feared a virtual takeover of sections of the Brazilian economy by foreign or transnational enterprises.[39] What is not yet clear, however, is just where the divisions ran and from where, in particular, came the main support for a more sharply nationalist critique. Most of the categories used hitherto have been too broad, seeing, for example, the main opposition as being between a 'national' or 'local' bourgeoisie and those groups more representative of international capitalism, especially the transnational corporations. More work still needs to be done to chart carefully these lines of division and support, and to gauge the strength of opposition, actual and potential, not only among the military but in business, financial, and professional circles in São Paulo and elsewhere, to the encroachment of foreign and transnational enterprises. What is already evident, however, is that throughout the government of Costa e Silva tension was high between the 'nationalist' bloc and those who, through conviction or expediency, feared to alarm or alienate the international business community, as can be clearly seen from the strength and speed of reaction to the nationalist critique as led by Albuquerque Lima. Equally clear is the fact that by late 1969 the nationalist camp had suffered at least a short-term defeat, and that the policies of Delfim Neto, despite considerable innovation and changes in emphasis, had pushed Brazil into still further collaboration with and dependence on the international financial and business community.

One distinction which is commonly made between economic policy under Roberto Campos and under Delfim Neto is the move to end the recession caused by the former's tough stabilization policies, a change marked by an easing of credit restrictions to industry and a sharp stimulus to economic growth, especially through government incentives to exports. In part the contrast is evidence of a changing analysis by policy-makers of the reasons for earlier and current inflation, the argument being that Brazil's inflation was by now 'cost-push', so that suppression of demand only produced stagnation without solving the inflationary problem.[40] Hence the adoption of a new economic 'heterodoxy', which pointed logically to a substantially modified economic programme.[41] It has been argued that: 'the new government embarked on almost full reversal of earlier policies'.[42] But still, it must be stressed, these changes were not to challenge or overturn the fundamental policies pursued by Campos, not even to the extent of producing a more 'nationalist' variant of Brazilian capitalism: but, rather, to strengthen that system to which Delfim Neto, like Campos, was fully committed. While therefore the changes were significant, as in Delfim Neto's easing of orthodox monetary controls which by 1966 had produced a serious industrial recession,[43] in his sharp increase in the money supply (by over 40 per cent in both 1967 and 1968), and in wage policies which kept minimum and industrial wages more closely in line with the rate of inflation, the shifts were essentially those of *tactics* within a wider strategy that remained markedly consistent.

What was the nature of this consistency and continuity? First, while it is certainly true that from 1967 onwards Brazil abandoned the broadly orthodox monetary policies of the previous three years, right from the start, the Campos programme, too, had been geared to the *eventual* achievement of economic growth, but through the gradual implementation of a stabilization programme that would take time to make itself felt. In this respect the Campos programme, however bitterly resented by industrialists and businessmen hit by the recession, laid the groundwork for the later expansion under Delfim Neto:

> . . . the Campos team appeared to lack a strategy that would guide Brazil back onto the path of growth. In part this appearance was deceptive. The relative success in controlling price increases was itself a prerequisite for renewed expansion. Inflationary distortions previously promoted by the government had to be removed. Most important, the government deficit was sharply reduced, primarily by increasing federal revenues. The extensive rationalization of the public sector, including better management of public corporations and the simplification of bureaucratic procedures in key areas such as export promotion, was indispensable. Increased efficiency in the private sector—now induced by the deflationary squeeze—was another prerequisite. Finally, the renegotiation of the large short-term foreign debt, the increase of capital inflows (private and public), and the promotion of exports all helped to strengthen Brazil's balance of payments, thus relieving external pressure on policy makers. By 1967 Brazil was ready to resume growth.[44]

Secondly, the basic purpose of both teams, whether emphasizing stabilization in one period or growth in another, was to strengthen Brazil's capitalist system,[45] the corollary of which was that both groups were willing to entail certain social and political costs, the brunt of which fell most heavily on the poorer sections of the population, and which, the important point for political analysis, directly implied and demanded a continuing, even an intensifying, pattern of direct authoritarian control.[46] In this respect the differences in Brazil's economic management under Delfim Neto and Roberto Campos are of much less significance than the basic political commitments shared by both men, and by both the military presidents they served.

The persistent nature of these costs and how they affected politics under Costa e Silva and his successors as much as, or even more than, under Castello Branco, is important evidence of the essential continuity of overall economic and social strategy. For example, despite all the protests of industrialists and businessmen against the stabilization measures of Campos, the brunt of the 'sacrifices' called for by the government fell on the poor and the working class: and it was these, once again, after 1967 as before, who were to see least benefit from a 'miracle' which to a large extent they subsidized through a deliberately restrictive wages policy. Official government explanation of wages policy was that the reduction of inflationary wage expectations, alleged to have been one of the primary causes of pre-1964 inflation, would produce a temporary lag which eventually would be overcome.[47] There is now solid evidence that wage demands were not the main cause of inflation,[48] but after the 1964 *coup* the new government, after having given large increases in salary to the armed forces (120 per cent) and to civil servants (100 per cent),[49] made severe wage control a central feature of its stabilization programme. The new wage formula was linked to the average real wage of the previous two years and to an estimate of inflation over the next twelve months:

> This so-called inflationary residual was consistently, and deliberately, under-estimated. Real wages therefore were systematically reduced between 1964 and 1967, 20 per cent in the case of the minimum wage, and somewhat less for industrial wages. Despite the theoretical niceties of the formulation, the policy as practiced became one of maximum wage containment. As a consequence, the average real minimum wage received in 1967, despite such additional current fringes as the thirteenth monthly salary, family allowances, as well as improved future claims on pension funds, was at least 5 per cent smaller than its 1955 level. Even though the income per capita was more than a third as great in 1967, twelve years of economic growth had come to naught for the unskilled wage earners of Brazil.[50]

The sharpest fall certainly came between 1964 and 1967 as a result of stabilization policies,[51] with wages picking up again after the change of government in 1967: but increases in real wages still lagged behind the cost of living, so that a continuing feature of the economic model was one of a steadily worsening pattern of distribution of income, both socially, including within the ranks of the workers themselves,[52] and regionally:

> The net result of the various shifts among and within classes appears to be a dramatic increase in the inequality of the non-agricultural income distribution between 1960 and 1970. The Gini coefficient calculated directly from the respective decennial censuses increases from ·49 to ·56, a substantial change indeed for such a short period. The extent of the growing inequality is vividly captured by the estimated share of income received in the upper reaches of the distribution: 5·8 percent of those gainfully employed in non-agricultural activities in 1960 received 29·8 percent of monetary income; in 1970, an equivalent 5·8 percent received 37·9 percent. It is difficult to hold stabilization (*and subsequent*), policies blameless for this outcome.[53]

The important point about these continuing disparities in income distribution, a question which at one point the regime forbade to be discussed openly because of its subversive overtones, is that it was both before and after 1967 a direct result of government policies aimed at stabilization and at growth, the social costs involved being seen as implicit in both the push for stabilization before 1964 and the frenetic drive for growth after 1967. Real wages in industry were dropping at a time when industrial productivity was going up. Not all the surplus went directly to the industrial capitalist, but labour was certainly receiving a declining share.[54] Those who did best out of Brazil's rapid growth, especially after 1967, were the rich and the middle classes, especially in the centre-south, where they enjoyed all the fruits of an economy geared to consumption, but which worsened rather than improved the pattern of income distribution:

> the only clear winners were the top 5 percent of wage earners whose real income rose 72 percent and whose share of the G.N.P. advanced from 27 to 36 percent. Overall, Brazil's index of income inequality . . . rose from a modest ·488 in 1960 (relatively low by Latin American standards) to a whopping ·574 in 1970 (the highest ever recorded at the national level in Latin America). . . .[55]

Nor was this simply a question of a relatively smaller share of a rapidly growing total, so that absolute levels were markedly improved. The absolute levels were extremely low in many cases, as economists were quick to point out,[56] but the most dramatic change, certainly, was in the growing relative inequality of distribution, which was found to be regional as well as social, with the north-east, for example, seeing its share of gross domestic income slipping between 1960 and 1970,[57] while within the region was to be found the same growing disparity as throughout the whole country. So, for example, research by the Bank of the Northeast showed that the percentage of total income going to the lowest 40 per cent of Recife's population fell from 16·5 per cent in 1960 to 11·5 per cent in 1967, while in Maceió the equivalent group received 15·4 per cent of total income in April 1964 and only 11·2 per cent by March 1968.[58]

What appears clearly, therefore, is that in this fundamental area of economic policy, that of wages and the relative transfer of wealth from one social group to another, there was striking continuity both before and after March 1967. Delfim Neto paid heed to the complaints of industrialists and middle-class groups, especially in São Paulo, but his complete commitment to economic growth allowed or, rather, determined a pattern of increasing inequality in the distribution of wealth, with the poorest members of Brazil's society paying the heaviest price for growth, as they had for earlier stabilization.

It is not just money wages which shows this trend, but other indicators, on, for example, health,[59] including the rise of infant mortality, even in São Paulo, the very centre of the prospering consumer boom;[60] on education, where statistics disproved the arguments of those who claimed that Brazil was experiencing indirect distribution, especially through the spread of education, which gave more job opportunities to many members of society, while also producing, as a by-product of development, a widening gap between the educated and others.[61] Having first tried to silence the debate on distribution, the regime later went into the attack, often stigmatizing those who drew attention to the social costs of their growth strategy as ill-motivated, ill-trained, or stupid: but the weight of evidence was overwhelming, however embarrassing it might be. Still more to the point, it was increasingly clear that this worsening pattern of distribution and other social and political costs were not just chance results, easily to be remedied by adjustments in immediate economic or political tactics; but, rather, that they stemmed directly and essentially from the whole capital accumulation process and the overall economic strategy, being an integral part of the political economy of the new regime.[62]

There were those on the government side who angrily denied this intrinsic connection, as, for example, Delfim Neto:

> The publication of the results of the Demografic Census made clear the growth of inequality in income distribution between 1960 and

> 1970. Some people, with little imagination and with more ideology than theory, tried to attribute to the political economy of the second half of the decade the major responsibility for what had happened . . . Langoni proves that the observed increase in inequality is a direct result of market disequilibria characteristic of the development process.[63]

But these protests were unconvincing by comparison with the mounting evidence that the majority of the Brazilian people was receiving a relatively declining share of national wealth, most of which went to a prospering minority composed of middle-class groups and above. These were not affected by the wages policy and, though the government could justifiably claim, for example, that sharp fiscal reforms after 1964 had pushed up the number of people paying income taxes, from about 470,000 in 1967 to about 4 million in 1971, doubling the amount paid in real terms between 1965 and 1971, these payments were more than offset by generous tax concessions. These included 12 per cent tax relief, and sometimes more, for buying shares on the now rapidly expanding stock market, in which for a few heady years huge profits could be had.[64] More generally, they were offset by an economy geared to satisfy these social groups, who, however unhappy some of them may have been in the 'stabilization' phase under Campos, now enjoyed the benefits of the growth economy. In the same way, those regions already most prosperous now grew relatively richer at the expense of areas, such as the north-east, which saw a brake on the trend to direct more national resources towards north-eastern development.[65] Efforts to stimulate industrial investment in the region, initiatives started before the 1964 *coup*, such as the Tax Credit Scheme of Article 34/18, proved disappointing, or of only limited success,[66] and attention was either diverted to other regions, notably to Amazonas, or more seriously, was concentrated on the already developed areas of the country. It was found, for example, by the end of 1973 that one agency of the National Development Bank (BNDE) applied only 13 per cent of its resources to the north-east, a mere 1·5 to the northern states, but 68·1 per cent to the south-east, and 47 per cent to São Paulo alone. The state savings bank showed 64·5 per cent going to the south-east (35·4 per cent to São Paulo), 9·3 to the north-east, and 1·2 to the north. Despite, again, the desperately serious housing situation of the north-east, which contains one-third of the nation's people, the National Housing Bank spent 55·7 per cent of its resources in the south-east (27·5 per cent in São Paulo), only 15·8 per cent in the north-east, and 3·2 per cent in the north. Industrial development showed the same discrepancies, with the council for industrial development applying in 1973 89·7 per cent of its resources in the south-east (77·1 in São Paulo alone) and only 3 per cent in the north-east.

That this continuity within the regime, in terms of imposing heavy burdens on the poorest social groups and regions of Brazil, stemmed directly from government policy, became increasingly clear as Delfim Neto's strategy unfolded, revealing policies which, by contrast with those of the 'populist' politicians of the pre-1964 era, rejected, as impracticable or unrealistic, efforts to achieve wider distribution in the economic sphere and fuller participation and reform in national politics and social policy. This importance of *political* decisions within the realm of planning had already been stressed by no less an observer than Delfim Neto, now Minister of Finance, an emphasis which contrasted strongly with his subsequent denial that, for example, the worsening pattern of income and distribution was directly linked to the economic strategy of the second half of the decade. In his best-known economic study published in 1966, only the year before he took office, he had emphasized the inescapable necessity of planning:

> It is an illusion to think that there is an alternative, either to plan or not to plan, since the only alternative, in fact, is to plan well or to plan badly. . . . The advantage of producing an explicit future programme ['de conscientizar o programa futuro'] lies precisely in the possibility of choosing between those alternatives which are most adequate for achieving the ends in view. . . .[67]

Delfim had already made a clear distinction between developed and developing countries in one important respect, namely, that in developed societies it was easier to reconcile two basic aims: '(i) the maximization of the rate of economic development, with as rapid a spreading as possible of the fruits of development to all citizens, and (ii) a decentralization of political power, which allows all citizens freely to enjoy those benefits'. In developing countries, by contrast, this was not the case:

> For an underdeveloped country the problem is much more complex, since its decisions cannot be restricted to the realm of distribution, but also have to include that of capital accumulation. To the degree to which it is necessary to choose between these two areas, the contradictions become more intense . . .[68]

Delfim then rejected two main sources of criticism of the kind of planning he was advocating, that of the 'conservative classes', on the one hand, with a naive belief in the 'mythical value of the market', and that of socialist, 'revolutionary' groups on the other, who for tactical reasons oppose planning as being an effective instrument for achieving social wellbeing in an open society.[69]

But, he emphasized:

> It is important that everyone should understand that planning is a simple technique for administering resources and that, in itself, it is neutral: it can be used to strengthen a market economy or to substitute it; it can be restricted to traditional areas of government activity or it can extend it; it can be used with worthy social objectives or in order to benefit one class to the detriment of another. The objectives of planning are not within its own sphere of action, but within the sphere of political power. *It is the minority which holds power in every system which decides which are to be the objectives to be achieved.*[70]

But throughout the years when Delfim Neto, more than any other single politician, determined the pattern of Brazil's economic policies it was precisely these *political* choices, made by a minority, concerning the ends to be achieved and the means to be followed, which provoked most criticism.

Others who followed Delfim Neto and, in all essentials, supported his views on the pattern of Brazil's development, were equally clear that the 'miracle' achieved in the next few years was in no sense 'miraculous'. The man who was to succeed Delfim Neto as Minister of Finance, Dr Mário Henrique Simonsen, happily quoted him to this effect:

> a miracle is an effect with no apparent cause, whereas our growth is anything but the result of sudden spontaneity. In fact, the development of Brazil in recent years is based on the application of an economic model, soundly structured in theory and accompanied by a healthy dose of pragmatism.[71]

One feature of this model, Simonsen acknowledged, was that it made clear choices:

> Speaking generally, countries which are still in a state of development must choose between two alternatives as far as economic policy is concerned: that of productivity and that of redistribution . . . in Latin America today one may say that Brazil is the country which most favours productivism.[72]

He also recognized that the Brazilian strategy: 'establishes as a basic priority the accelerated growth of the G.N.P., accepting as a short-term liability the corollary of an appreciable imbalance between individual rates of income'.[73] One source of this imbalance was recognized as being the wages policy, but Simonsen stressed the advantages of the established government-controlled system of wage adjustment: 'in the first place it has served to simplify and pacify wage-claim negotiations; these are no longer resolved by rounds of strikes, and other forms of collective pressure, but simply by rapid mathematical calculations'.[74]

The worsening pattern of distribution and the increasingly evident social and political costs were not then just random effects, dissociated from overall economic strategy, but, rather, the direct results of an overall, coherent, deliberately chosen economic model, a form of capitalist development for Brazil adopted by Campos and continued, albeit in modified form, by Delfim Neto. And, more specifically still, the basic choice was exactly that which Delfim had posed, between reconciling growth and distribution, or giving fuller priority to that other overriding need which he perceived in an underdeveloped economy, namely, capital accumulation. It was, in short, the particular pattern of capital accumulation, the headlong pursuit of rapid economic growth at all costs, which determined and shaped the pattern of Brazilian politics in these years, above all, the ineluctable drift towards greater authoritarian control, the build-up of a repressive state machine controlled by a tight coalition of soldiers and *técnicos*, and the steady erosion of civil and political liberties. The choice was an explicit one, and the model deliberately chosen. The shifts and twists on the surface of Brazilian politics over the next few years were to prove exciting, sometimes tragic, often important: but the basic pattern was set by the choice of development strategy, shaping politics under Costa e Silva, as under his predecessor, and indeed his successor, limiting real choices and providing the essential continuity between different military-led governments. This is not to say, it must be emphasized, that the whole process was a simple, deterministic one: choices were made in 1964 and reinforced in later years. But the choices contained logical implications which were played out over the years, in their turn excluding other choices and other policy options, social and political as well as economic.

The impact of Delfim Neto's strategy after 1967 was dramatic. The technical handling of the economy, by the clever use of, for example, 'monetary correction', indexation, and the 'crawling peg', a regular series of mini-devaluations, preventing speculation against the currency, provoked much interest and admiration outside as well as inside Brazil. But it was the success of economic policies which was most striking, and quickly used by the regime as a source of self-justification and legitimacy. In part this success merely seemed to confirm the arguments of those who believed that in a country of Brazil's earlier industrialization pattern, during the process of import substitution industrialization, a regressive distribution scheme would now produce most rapid growth; but certainly the results were startling, continuing over a period of about five years.[75] From a very low base exports had shot up by 1972 to about 4 billion (American billion) dollars, of which over one billion came from industrial exports, one-third of which had been developed over the previous five years. By 1973 exports had increased by 55 per cent on the previous year, to nearly 6·2 billion dollars, with industry contributing about 30 per cent of the total at US$1·841 billion and by the end of 1974 had reached 8 billion dollars, a further increase of 25·8 per cent as compared with 1973. This was, in fact, the high point of the Delfim Neto strategy, which could boast of real growth-rates from 1968 averaging about 10 per cent, with inflation allegedly contained at about 20 per cent, a surplus on the balance of payments of US$2·327 million, and foreign currency reserves of US$6·417 million, 53 per cent more than at the end of 1972, so making Brazil one of the half-dozen countries with the highest foreign-currency reserves in the world. 1974 was to see the downturn in this performance, which also, by chance, corresponded with Delfim's departure from office, but owed most to the impact of the oil crisis, pushing up dramatically the cost of imports, though the situation was also worsened by certain government measures. The 2·3 billion-dollar surplus in 1973 led the Central Bank to expand the money supply in 1973 by 47 per cent, 'a percentage too far above the one which would be consistent with the expected rate of inflation and the real growth of the G.N.P.'.[76] This produced demand inflation, aggravated by cost push resulting from the oil crisis, so that in the first six months of 1974 'the general price index increased at an average monthly rate of 3·5 percent, which would correspond to an inflation rate of 51 percent a year'.[77] At the same time, while exports rose to $8 billion, imports expanded even faster, to $12·5 billion, so leaving Brazil no longer with a balance of payments surplus, as in 1973, but with a trade deficit of $4·5 billion. Adding this to a deficit in services, there appeared a current account deficit of $6·9 billion, which, even when offset by 5 billion in loans and $900 million in direct investment, still left Brazil at the end of 1974 with a total deficit in the balance of payments of one billion dollars.[78] At the same time the total foreign debt rose to $16·7 billion, which, set against foreign reserves of $9·2 billion, meant a net foreign indebtedness of $11·5 billion.

What 1974 really marked was the end of the heady, euphoric days of the 'Brazilian miracle', marking the start of a more critical phase, which, while not immediately threatening to blow the system apart, emphasized some of its more vulnerable features. Over the next two years the trade deficit was to rise steeply as Brazil, faced with the need to import more than three-quarters of the oil it needed, and faced with very high bills for capital goods, plunged deeper into debt, its foreign debt rising by 1976 to about $25 billion, compared to $12·9 billion in 1973, and its foreign reserves dropping to around $3·5 billion, as compared to the figure, already quoted, of just under $6·5 billion in 1973. The rapid growth between 1968 and 1973 was now seen as a thing of the past, with zero or even negative growth forecast for 1976. The earlier growth had been made possible not just by rapidly expanding exports, but by a huge inflow of foreign capital, encouraged by easier repatriation of profits, the easing of restrictions on loans and imports, and, above all, a secure political context guaranteed by military force. But most of this inflow had always been in the form of loans and suppliers' credits, rather than coming from direct foreign investment: hence the rapidly rising foreign debt and service charges. By 1976, therefore, it was estimated that debt repayment and interest would consume about 44 per cent of Brazil's export revenue, which, coupled with an inflation rate of about 50 per cent and the absence of growth, posed real problems for the economic planners. Few people really doubted the vitality and dynamism of the Brazilian economy, but already the foreign creditors were charging higher interest-rates and were asking searching questions about the true nature of earlier economic performance.

But long before the appearance of these tensions and difficulties other equally important questions were being asked about the social and political costs, already observable, behind the loudly proclaimed miracle, costs which made it clear that hopes for an early return to an open political system must be ill-founded.

The most obvious political requirement of the economic strategy, particularly the wages policy, was the severe curbing of the trade unions and all organizations and political groupings which most directly expressed the demands of the working class and the poorer sections of the population. The imposition and maintenance of the *arrôcho salarial*, the tight suppression of wage-levels, could only be possible in an increasingly authoritarian system. Otherwise, it would have been impossible to lay on these groups the main burden of the stabilization programme and to keep wages behind the rise in the cost of living, even when industrial productivity was rising. Only with the backing of military force could the planners speak so confidently of wage-rates arrived at by a simple mathematical formula, without reference to the people who were to live on those wages. Moreover, in so far as the wages policy was seen as central to the whole pattern of accumulation of capital followed after 1964, there was a built-in need to maintain control not just of the trade unions, but also of groups within Congress who might challenge the sacrifices involved.

Closely linked to this demand was the urgent need to reassure the international financial and business community, especially Brazil's creditors, that the new pattern of growth and recovery would not be threatened by excessive wage demands, strikes, or indeed any political upheaval which might disturb the stable context within which the planners must work. This was seen as a particularly urgent priority in the period immediately after the *coup*, when foreigners must be convinced that the political uncertainties of the Goulart era were now a thing of the past; but the need for the regime not only to be in control, but to be seen to be in control, remained a basic requirement, most conspicuously apparent, for example, in the response to direct, armed opposition during the Costa e Silva government. This need to maintain foreign confidence was, again, not just a feature of national politics which could easily be modified, but was essential to the whole model of dependent capitalist growth in the post-*coup* period. The pattern of foreign involvement was now rather different from that of earlier years, but the need to maintain foreign confidence, especially of the financiers and bankers, was more urgent than ever. The period of really rapid growth of foreign investment in Brazil had been in the import-substitution phase in the 1950s, especially in consumer durables and motor cars (with about 25 per cent foreign investment associated with the motor industry). For the first few years after the 1964 *coup* most of the inflow came from official sources, mainly United States government assistance, and net foreign investment only picked up substantially from 1968. It was not, in fact, till 1969 that the levels of the mid-1950s were again reached, but then there was a further fall in 1970 and 1971 before renewed recovery. The nature and scale of foreign involvement, quite apart from its political implications, remained a complex and controversial issue. The total share of foreign business in industrial output in 1965 was calculated at about 33·5 per cent,[79] and even by the end of 1974 the stock of foreign-owned assets was judged to be worth about $5·5 billion, or about only 6–7 per cent of the total Brazilian capital stock.[80] This, at first sight, seems a relatively small figure, but there are important qualifications to be made. First, half this capital stock consisted of dwellings; secondly, the foreign capital was heavily concentrated in the most strategic areas of the economy; and thirdly, the figure reflected an increasing tendency in recent years for transnational corporations to prefer currency loans as the means to finance new capital outlay, since they could then repatriate both profits and the capital sum.[81] The importance of foreign participation in the dynamic sectors of the economy could be seen from the fact that in those sectors where foreign capital was most concentrated the largest firms were usually foreign-owned, so that, for example, by 1975 the top twelve largest firms (in terms of assets) in the consumer durables sector were all foreign-owned, as were thirteen of the largest twenty in the non-durable goods sector and ten of the largest eighteen in the capital goods sector.[82] The dominance of foreign interests in the capital goods and consumer durables industries was particularly striking, being also reflected in the structure of advertising in Brazil, where by as early as 1967 the top twelve advertisers were all foreign-based firms, who were able to exert a powerful influence on the media on which they spent such large sums of money.[83] With foreign capital, albeit mainly loan capital, financing so much of Brazil's development there was a persistent need for every government, whether or not it contained a high proportion of nationalist critics of earlier policy, to avoid alarming or offending creditors abroad. The fuelling of the development model required ever larger doses of foreign capital,[84] so that in practice:

> successive governments have encouraged increasing internationalization of the economy and, as things stand, the foreign enterprise at present plays an absolutely central role in the transmission of commodities and technologies to Brazil and in the reproduction there of the consumption patterns and mode of production characteristic of the advanced capitalist countries.[85]

These two fundamental requirements, wages control and the need to reassure foreign creditors, both closely connected and both stemming from the pattern of capital accumulation, determined most strongly in the post-*coup* years the shaping of national politics. Both requirements followed directly from the commitment to rapid growth and its implied relegation of other priorities, such as distribution, and both logically demanded a strengthening of authoritarian control at every level. Closely associated, too, was the need to stifle criticism and protest at the pattern which was being imposed, whether it came directly from workers' groups, through an organized opposition in Congress, or through newspapers and other media seeking to open up debate on the handling of the political economy. Gradually, therefore, but inexorably, there emerged a picture not of lessening authoritarian control, but of an ever more intense, more severe repression of all dissent and opposition, whether expressed through Congress, the media, through strikes, or even through noisy protests in the street. Here was the essential continuity and determinism in Brazilian politics, arising logically from the choice of economic model followed both before and after March 1967. To ignore these basic realities and to hope for an eventual lessening of authoritarianism and repression was to ignore the substance of politics for the more trivial movements on the surface. The arrival of Costa e Silva and Delfim Neto brought notable changes, not least in the appointment of men whose thinking on nationalism might in time introduce substantial modifications in policy: but the essential continuity of economic strategy meant that talk of 'humanizing' the system must be viewed with at best a judicious scepticism, as the shaping of authoritarian controls under both Costa e Silva and his successor was now clearly to show.

Repression and Resistance

For most of the first year of Costa e Silva's administration such political excitement as there was centred on the activities of the *Frente Ampla*, or, more specifically, on the political manoeuvres of Carlos Lacerda and the reaction they were likely to produce both in Congress and within the armed forces. There was from the start a certain element of desperation in Lacerda's approach to politicians he previously had abused and condemned, but the moves towards a united front of opposition to the regime at least provided a focus for discussion of such issues as amnesty for those proscribed since 1964 and a dismantling of the more repressive political controls. It provided a means of testing what Costa e Silva might mean by his talk of 'humanizing' the system, and a goad to make him define more sharply the position of his new government. There were various efforts to test the water, notably a series of articles in *Tribuna da Imprensa* by Hélio Fernandes, a journalist colleague of Lacerda whose political rights had been suspended just before the 1966 Congressional elections, when he seemed certain of election as a federal deputy. As one who was *cassado*, Fernandes was not allowed to write signed political articles, but the Supreme Court ruled that he had a right to exercise his only profession, that of journalism. The articles, like Lacerda's activities more generally, were merely counterproductive, especially in relation to the officer corps. Many who previously had most strongly supported Lacerda were dismayed and angry at his apparent abandonment of principle and his opportunistic courtship of men he only recently had condemned as dangerous enemies of Brazil, especially when his approaches were received so cautiously by Kubitschek and Goulart. But the opening of the debate was enough to dispel any illusions that might have existed: senior army spokesmen, including the Minister of the Army, General Lyra Tavares, made clear their views that the objectives of the revolution still remained to be achieved, and that the time was not ripe for major changes, a position which Costa e Silva, evidently under pressure from military colleagues, strongly emphasized in his first major statement on the subject, on 24 May 1967.

But through the surface excitement and manoeuvring surrounding the *Frente Ampla* there appeared the most substantial issue of national politics in Costa e Silva's whole period in office, the degree of freedom to be allowed to Congress and to opposition in any form, and the degree to which this would be decided by contending groups not so much within the regime, but, as was becoming ever more clear, within the officer corps of the armed forces, especially the army. How those groups were aligned was increasingly difficult to determine as the earlier distinctions between 'hard-liners' and the 'Sorbonne', always in any case rather fuzzy categories, became steadily more blurred; but there was no doubt as the months went by that it was primarily, at times it seemed almost exclusively, within the officer corps that the power struggle was taking place.

One factor which quickened and greatly embittered military reaction to attempts to reopen the political system was a virulent attack by Hélio Fernandes in the editorial of *Tribuna da Imprensa* of 19 July 1967 on the late Castello Branco, killed in an air crash in Ceará the previous day. The former president had had many critics both during his time in office and since handing it over, but the Fernandes article, rejecting any idea of *nil nisi bonum*, outraged military feeling and shocked, as being in thoroughly bad taste, many who otherwise had little time for either Castello Branco or the regime. The editorial refused to mourn for

> the ex-President a cold, unfeeling, vengeful, implacable, inhuman, calculating, cruel, frustrated man . . . whose life was a spiteful act of mistrust and detachment—without any gesture of courage, without an emotional content, without a moment of grandeur, an instant of piety, contemplation, or humility . . .'[86]

Whatever its taste, or however justified Fernandes may have felt in his attack on the leader of the post-1964 regime, who might be held morally responsible for the repressive apparatus already introduced by it, there was no doubt that the timing of the article was singularly maladroit. Any politician of Fernandes's, and still more Lacerda's, long experience knew very well how an attack on the reputation and honour of the military would be received: from the mid-nineteenth century onwards there were repeated precedents, all pulling together diverse or contending elements in the officer corps. At a time when there was talk and, ostensibly, hope of *détente*, the article, evidently written with the assent and very much in the style of Lacerda, could be interpreted at best as irresponsible and, more realistically, as an open challenge to the regime. The furious reaction it produced led directly to the mounting tension and crisis which came to a head only seventeen months later with Institutional Act No. 5 of December 1968. Lacerda, once the political mentor of much of the 'hard line', was now forbidden to appear on television, and was fiercely attacked, particularly by the president of the Clube Militar, General Augusto César Moniz de Aragão, who, like many of his predecessors, felt obliged to defend the honour of the officer corps.[87] In December 1968 the army was to have its revenge, when Lacerda was hoisted with his own petard and deprived of his political rights by the regime which, however he may have attacked it in the frustration of later years, he had earlier done so much to bring to power.

The mounting reaction against Lacerda was directed, in turn, against the *Frente Ampla*, which from the beginning was seen as largely an instrument to further his political aims.[88] 'Hard line' officers already had expressed their growing disquiet over the possibility of more liberal policies and had even sought reassurance with regard to the government's economic strategy by questioning Delfim Neto in a private session towards the end of June. This particular incident caused the removal from their posts of several officers, notably Colonel Boaventura Cavalcanti, commander of Fort São João in Rio de Janeiro, brother of the Minister of Mines and Energy, and Colonel Amerino Raposo, head of the SNI, National Information Service, in Rio de Janeiro; but it showed how confident were the 'hard-liners', who now, with the insult to military honour they perceived in the Fernandes article, had further support for their case against a return to more open politics. The gap between such officers and Lacerda widened further, ending any possibility of Lacerda being called in to work with Costa e Silva,[89] while, at the same time, the tension between the military and the civilian politicians was further increased, as it was made clear that there would be no immediate changes in the constitution or in wages policy, concessions which some ARENA leaders had hoped would reduce potential support for the *Frente Ampla*.[90] On 24 September Lacerda went to Montevideo, where he signed with Goulart the Pact of Montevideo, a dramatic move to strengthen the *Frente Ampla*, now described as primarily a unified movement to exert pressure for direct elections, but which served mainly to divide politicians in their reaction to this new initiative and still further to antagonize many military officers.[91] The breach between Lacerda and his former military supporters was now virtually complete, and over the next few months his attacks on the regime became ever more extreme, accusing the armed forces of corruption and of defending a decadent oligarchy.[92] His attacks brought angry replies, especially from the Minister of the Interior, Albuquerque Lima. Lacerda was forbidden access to the radio, but still pursued the same theme, losing to the *Frente* many, especially in the PSD, who feared where his attacks might lead him. At the same time the agitation over the *Frente Ampla* was accompanied by protest and opposition from other quarters, mainly from students and church leaders. There was increased pressure on Costa e Silva to move against the *Frente* and go further by issuing a new, and tougher, Institutional Act. In April 1967 he gave in to the extent that in Instruction No. 177 of 5 April he forbade any further activities of the *Frente*. In just over a year the new government had made clear that direct opposition would not be tolerated and that not even the most influential civilian leader of the 1964 *coup* could with impunity challenge the regime.

For a man of Lacerda's experience the whole opposition associated with the *Frente Ampla* was an astonishingly crude venture, which was bound to divide an opposition inspired by a lively fear of Greeks bearing gifts, and which in its bitterly vituperative style could only antagonize the regime and many of the officer corps. The breadth and basis of the *Frente* were from the start implausible and highly suspect, but any chance a broad opposition front might have had was shattered by Lacerda's hostile language of confrontation and his abuse not only of the regime, but of the armed forces in general. Far from offering the chance of reconciliation and a more open system, the *Frente Ampla* pushed more moderate officers into opposition, increased still further the 'hard line's' mistrust of civilian politicians, and justified again for Lacerda's critics his reputation as a pernicious influence in Brazilian politics. His formal exclusion from political life was now only a matter of time.

This is not to argue that, had Lacerda behaved more judiciously, the *Frente*, at least in the form it was conceived, could have succeeded, or that the regime would have been prepared, or able, to make concessions. The political and social requirements of the economic strategy did not allow a genuine opening of the system to wider participation and scrutiny, as was clearly seen in the regime's reaction to other, more effective and more authentic, opposition, which with the closing of all alternative channels was steadily forced to seek more direct means of expression. The main centres of this opposition were the Church, the universities, and groups seeking to work through or on behalf of the working class, all of which now found themselves caught up in what, in effect, was the politics of frustration, seeking to preserve some effective opposition in an ever more tightly controlled, closed political system. The remainder of Costa e Silva's period in office was to see the upsurge of this opposition, reacting to the repression already built up since 1964, but producing, in turn, an even tougher, more far-reaching repression to a degree never before witnessed in Brazil. All three of these principal centres of opposition were to some degree intertwined, with both university teachers and students and the church leaders voicing a protest which, while aimed generally at the repressive aspects of the regime, stemmed in particular from the costs it imposed on the poorer sections of Brazilian society as a direct result of the economic strategy. In the case of the Church, the protests were explicitly centred around the issues of social justice and abuse of human rights as the criticism already evident under Castello Branco now swelled into a wider movement, strengthened still further by the repression it evoked. Often, too, the immediate occasion for the Church's involvement was the harsh treatment given to students, some of them active Christians connected to Church-based student organizations, others acting from an amalgam of idealistic elements, usually not too clearly defined.

Students

Of all the opposition groups the students were the most vocal and most conspicuous. In August 1967 the twenty-ninth congress of the National Union of Students (UNE) was held in a Benedictine monastery near Campinas.[93] It came shortly after clashes between police and students in São Paulo and was in open defiance of the regime which had sought to prevent the conference. It also heightened tension between the government and the Church, since the Benedictine prior, Father Francisco Araújo, and other monks were arrested. Student discontent simmered all through the rest of the year, punctuated by small protests and demonstrations, but flared up in March 1968, when, after demonstrations had been forbidden by General Jayme Portella, an eighteen-year-old student, Edson Luís Lima Souto, was shot dead and about twenty others wounded in Rio de Janeiro.[94] The violence, denounced by the MDB in the state legislative assembly where the student's body was taken, produced large demonstrations and marches throughout Brazil, with more violence in Salvador, Belo Horizonte, Goiás, and Pôrto Alegre. Over 20,000 people attended the funeral of the student killed in Rio de Janeiro on 31 March, and in the clashes which followed, after Negrão de Lima had called in the army, at least one more person was killed, about sixty wounded, and over two hundred arrested.[95] After the seventh-day mass on 4 April in the Candelária church in the centre of Rio de Janeiro the mourners were attacked by soldiers and mounted police, backed by military vehicles, and about 700 people were said to have been arrested. The demonstrations could have been contained with much less use of force, but the police and soldiers were often ill-controlled, over-excited, and too prone to use violence, even, as in the action on 4 April, against priests and nuns totally incapable of replying in kind.

Aware that a potentially serious confrontation was building up, the government tried to placate students to some degree, especially after a report in mid-May from General Meira Mattos on the situation in the universities, half of which report was devoted to the relations between students and the government. Already, too, there had been an increase in federal funds for the universities and sweeping changes in the Ministry of Education, all supposedly to improve relations between the regime and the universities. But basically the government, and particularly the police and military leaders on the spot, regarded students and universities in terms of an enemy to be contained, or defeated, defining them in military categories, especially as centres of subversion, which left little room for more refined distinctions between different forms of student and civilian protest. The combination of crude analysis and inadequate control of the men under command caused the demonstrations to take on precisely the larger importance which the regime wished to avoid.

After a short lull there was more trouble in late May, when about 150 students were arrested in the medical school in Belo Horizonte. From 19 to 21 June there were further violent clashes in Rio de Janeiro, as students barricaded the streets, facing about 4,000 troops, as they protested against the Minister of Education. The Avenida Rio Branco was virtually a battlefield, hidden in clouds of tear-gas: more people were killed and injured and the next day about 400 students were arrested, and on 22 June courses in the Federal University of Rio de Janeiro were suspended. Yet, despite these upheavals, an enormous march to protest against police violence, the 'March of the 100,000', passed off quietly on 26 June. By now the student protests were the central issue of national politics, and were perceived by the regime as only part of a much wider network of 'subversion' and opposition, especially as the student marches coincided with a wave of bombings and explosions. There was also growing concern over the presence of workers' delegates in, for example, the march of 26 June, suggesting a growing solidarity, which some members of the regime also discerned in the appearance of strikes in São Paulo in July, marked by workers' take-overs in the factories. On 2 July Costa e Silva personally received a students' delegation, listening to demands for an end to police repression and censorship in the arts. Three days later the Minister of Justice forbade all marches and demonstrations, and the atmosphere hardened still further.

The true nature and impact of student protest by August 1968 were difficult to determine. It clearly formed part of a widespread reaction to the regime four years after the *coup*, as opposition forces mustered in the growing realization that the government, under Costa e Silva as under his predecessor, was moving steadily further away from open politics. But there is little, if any, evidence of effective collaboration between the different elements of opposition, though clearly there was mutual support and regular expressions of solidarity. Even within the students' ranks there were divisions of aims and strategy as widely heterogeneous groupings came together in common opposition on the streets. Some student leaders hoped that such opposition could bring down the government, relying on the capacity of any form of public opposition to provoke a wave of reaction against a system which had closed almost every channel of protest.[96] Others were less optimistic, or more realistic, aware of the strength of the regime and believing that student opposition would mainly point the way for others. On 5 August, for example, the principal organizer of the large, successful demonstration of 26 June was arrested in Rio de Janeiro. He was Vladimir Palmeira, son of an ARENA senator from Alagoas, Rui Palmeira, an example of how sons and daughters of men close to the regime were now often among its most severe critics. Vladimir Palmeira's arrest provoked student demonstrations, to which the government replied with a massive show of force. The streets of Rio de Janeiro were covered by tanks and the press reported that 5,000 military police were actually on duty and another 60,000 were ready should they be needed.[97] In the next day or two at least 650 people were arrested and an estimated 14,000 troops and police were needed to keep order in the centre of Rio de Janeiro, where 2,000 students, including Luís Travassos, demanded the release of Vladimir. Buses were covered with slogans denouncing 'imperialism and dictatorship'[98] and, as the crisis deepened, Palmeira himself was attacked as being a 'Marxist agitator', Costa e Silva solemnly warned of 'an international plan of subversion which takes advantage of students' idealism',[99] and the ARENA leader in Congress, Senator Daniel Krieger, replying to questions on government violence, argued that nothing justified disorder in the country when the democratic Brazilian regime had a constitution guaranteeing individual liberties.[100]

Palmeira was, in fact, a good example of a student leader, particularly of the way in which young men, often with little or no knowledge of Marxism, started by opposing the government on idealistic but rather vague grounds, but then were pushed vigorously into a much more radical and more explicitly defined position, largely by the violence of the government's reaction. In September 1969 Vladimir Palmeira was one of the prisoners released in return for the United States ambassador having to leave the country immediately. But in August 1968 his own description of his position and his analysis of the Brazilian situation were altogether less clear or radical than the government claimed or than subsequently they became. In August 1968 an interview with him was published in Brazil, shortly after he had had a full-page report in *Time Magazine*. His views, rather than showing him as a clearly committed activist with a tight Marxist philosophy, suggested instead a position typical of the great majority of the young men and women crudely labelled as 'Marxist' or 'subversive' by the government, young people who knew why they were opposed to the regime, but whose radicalism more often was born of direct experience of police violence, or of imprisonment, than of a close reading of Marxist texts. The interview is worth quoting at some length, ringing true, as it does, of many young students at the time when discussing their attitudes to national, and international, politics. Palmeira firmly refused, for example, to label himself as a Marxist, not out of political expediency, but because, in all honesty, he was not sure what the label implied:

> . . . We are all very young [Vladimir was then only twenty-three] and none of us can yet say if he is a Marxist or not, or whether he is this or the other. It's only now that we are beginning to study these things. It is only now, for instance, that I am starting to read a fraction of what there is to be read, including Marx. I still can't even honestly say whether or not I am a Marxist. But in order to fight it is not necessary to have read Marcuse. I still haven't read Marcuse and it would be dishonest if I said that I know him and that his philosophy must guide our struggles. But I guarantee that 90 per cent of those who go round here talking about Marcuse are like me and have never read him . . .[101]

What Palmeira was clear about, however, was the need to struggle, for the 'true Brazilian revolution' ('a verdadeira revolução brasileira'). He did not mind whether or not his work was known abroad: 'We don't care if our movement gets international publicity', and, still more interesting, he did not believe that the student movement could bring down the government:

> . . . It's a childish error to think that students are going to bring down the government.—France has recently given an excellent example that students never pulled down anything.—. . . Our task . . . is to open the way ['abrir caminhos']. Afterwards will come the workers, and then, yes, will come our authentic Brazilian revolution . . .[102]

Most telling of all, especially in the light of what followed in the next few months, was the way in which, according to Vladimir, and many of his fellow students, that revolution would be made:

> . . . the true Brazilian revolution, which in my view, by no stretch of the imagination, can be peaceful. I believe it will only come about by violence: not because we want it that way, but because they will not freely give up what they have . . .[103]

Comments such as these most clearly summed up the attitudes of many of the opposition. They did not want confrontation, feared open, still more armed, resistance in the streets, but saw no real alternative, feeling themselves caught up in a situation not of their making, but one which they had to face. Usually they did so with remarkably good humour, as when the students and some staff occupied the university departments in the Rua Maria Antônia in São Paulo in August 1968. Faced with growing repression and the excesses of unauthorized right-wing groups, such as the CCC (Commando for Hunting Communists), they still wore their opposition sufficiently lightly to produce improvised meals listed on the menu under such headings as' Consomé à Mao' or 'Pâté à Ho Chi Minh', partly in amused defiance of authorities seemingly so ready to label as dedicated Marxist revolutionaries young people fired more by social concern and patriotic idealism than any close attachment to Marxist orthodoxy.

The far-reaching debate as to whether social and political change was really possible except through recourse to violence became for many young, and many not so young, Brazilians at this time the key issue of national politics, imposed not by any predilection for violence but by the severe narrowing of real political options. At the end of August troops invaded the university of Brasília, killing a student and roughly ignoring protests of deputies and senators, an incident condemned even by many members of ARENA, which triggered off more protests throughout the country. The situation was now fast deteriorating. On Sunday 15 September the *Jornal do Brasil* published a document by Carlos Marighela, dedicated to Ché Guevara, advocating guerrilla warfare in Brazil, with the creation of guerrilla *focos*, arguing that the popular revolutionary movement must now take the offensive. This, however, was balanced by a report from Recife on 19 September that Dom Helder Câmara was now organizing a movement of Action: Peace and Justice, to be launched on 10 October. Here were two scarcely reconcilable strategies of opposition, but both evidence of the depth of feeling behind the broad, heterogeneous resistance to the military government. The students, too, continued their protests, despite the raid on 12 October 1968 on Itabira, where the thirtieth congress of UNE was in progress. There were more serious clashes, especially in São Paulo,[104] and, while from October onwards there seemed a falling-off in student protest, this partly reflected the conclusion of some of the most committed student opponents of the regime that only better-organized, direct armed resistance could possibly be effective in challenging the armed force of the regime.

The Church

The Church played throughout this period a less conspicuous, less dramatic, but always important role. It reflected the growing polarization of Brazilian society more generally, but couched the debate in wider, more abstract terms of Christian duty and human dignity, avoiding as far as possible open antagonism to the regime, especially through political violence, but ascribing to itself the right to set the priorities and policies of the regime alongside the body of Christian teaching on social justice and human rights. The story of Church–State relations from the start of the Costa e Silva government to the end of 1968 was one of steady deterioration,[105] the main focus of activity being in the shift within the CNBB, National Conference of Brazilian Bishops, towards a position more critical of the regime, and in increased confrontation arising from the support individual members of the hierarchy gave to clergy and laymen who fell foul of the government. The intervention of churchmen in 1966 on behalf of Catholic laymen in north-east Brazil, during the crisis involving General Gouvêa do Amaral, already had produced sharp reaction.[106] The more progressive clergy were viewed as betraying the true traditions of the Church and of supporting, however innocently, the cause of 'Communist' subversion. But from the start of Costa e Silva's presidency open criticism of social policies from church leaders was heard ever more frequently.[107] In May 1967 the CNBB sided with the call for redistribution of land to lessen social injustices and it became clear that many responsible members of the hierarchy saw the demand for social reform as entirely compatible with their pastoral duty,[108] a point Dom Helder Câmara emphasized in a speech to the legislative assembly in Pernambuco in August 1967, also arguing that only the social action of the Church could save the north-east from violent revolutionary demands. The speech was badly received by the landowners and industrialists of the north-east and particularly again by the commander of the Fourth Army, who later spoke of the agitation of 'false preachers'.[109] Dom Helder's remarks were in fact remarkably moderate, as was the whole tenor of his speaking and preaching in this period, concentrating on the need to avoid social and political violence, and the Christian duty to curb social injustice as found in regions such as the north-east.[110]

Dom Helder Câmara was rapidly becoming the main target for the indignation of right-wing Catholics, being already highly regarded abroad while bitterly opposed in Brazil. But the reaction from church groups to the results of current economic strategy was much wider than Dom Helder or the north-east. Others among the hierarchy voiced their growing concern, notably Dom Eugênio Salles, cardinal archbishop of Salvador till 1971, founder of the Natal Movement, and a powerful influence on the development of MEB and of Catholic-supported rural trade unions. There was also Dom Antônio Batista Fragoso, bishop of Crateus, and Dom Marcus Antônio Noronha, bishop of Itabira, but more generally it can be said that throughout 1967 and 1968 the questions of social reform and the nature of Brazilian development since the *coup* preöccupied all but a handful of more reactionary and stubbornly traditional members of the Brazilian hierarchy.[111] Often their direct involvement was provoked by members of their clergy or laity whose protests or activities brought a clash with the regime, but, by one means or another, the Church, in the period of about twenty-one months from Costa e Silva's assumption of the presidency to Institutional Act No. 5 in December 1968, was pulled ever more firmly into the centre of political debate. One example of how a relatively small incident could quickly provoke a major crisis came in November 1967, when four members of JOC (Young Catholic Workers) were arrested in Volta Redonda in possession of a vehicle belonging to the diocese while distributing pamphlets declared to be subversive. Two of the men involved actually lived in the bishop's house and the matter was further complicated by the fact that one of the men was a young French deacon, Guy Thibault. The arrest were made on 5 November and nine days later troops entered and searched the bishop's house. The incident quickly flared up, with the bishop, Dom Valdir Calheiros, intervening to urge that more attention should be paid to the social injustice which caused such pamphlets to be produced. This statement was read in churches and in turn distributed, which provoked the arrest of another eight priests. The presence of a foreigner, as in other cases, also allowed on the one hand the authorities to stress the foreign element in subversion and on the other attracted more attention in the international press. More seriously still, the affair showed how inflammatory the situation now was, with this incident dragging on for about two months, and how relatively moderate church leaders, like Dom Valdir Calheiros, were now linking persistent poverty and injustice to the failure of the regime to give attention to these issues.

These same problems were now being widely discussed by such groups as Catholic Workers' Action and Catholic University Youth, groups active in the prosperous centre-south of the country, serving to show that progressive Catholic movements could not be dismissed as a fundamentally north-eastern phenomenon, linked to the under-development of the north-east. The Church's criticism, to be heard now all over Brazil, was focussed directly on the regime's economic and social strategy, and it was becoming increasingly difficult to dismiss all criticism as a reflection of subversive Marxism disloyal to the central and traditional teaching of the Church. Rather the contrary, as apologists and supporters of the regime now found themselves faced with the need, both at home and abroad, to explain how strategies which imposed these heavy burdens on the poor and weaker members of society could be squared with Christian teaching, especially that emphasis in Christian teaching dominant since the Second Vatican Council in the Catholic Church,[112] and which was equally strong, and equally critical, in some of the most vital forms of Protestantism. As one member after another of the Catholic hierarchy joined in the protest, the regime, ostensibly introduced, in part at least, to defend Western, 'Christian' values, found this further ground of legitimacy cut from under its feet. Costa e Silva again tried to damp down the conflict between the Church and the regime, arguing that it was no more than a disagreement between some clergy and some members of the armed forces, but how much deeper the issues ran was symbolized in January 1968, when Dom Avelar Brandão discussed Church–State relations in a long meeting with Costa e Silva, presented him with six copies of *Populorum Progressio*, and suggested that an official government body be set up to study the encyclical and its implications.

Disagreements still broke the surface at regular intervals,[113] as in January 1968, when the bishop of Santo André in the industrial belt of São Paulo argued that armed rebellion was justified in cases of severe repression. Dom Helder Câmara continued to appeal for reforms to prevent the growth of social and political violence, a call echoed by the ninth assembly of the CNBB in July and given further impetus in October by his announcement of his movement

Action: Peace and Justice. Other bishops supported these moves, including Dom Valdir Calheiros in Volta Redonda and, very important, Dom Agnelo Rossi, cardinal archbishop of São Paulo, who supported in his archdiocese an organization linked to Action: Peace and Justice, and who pointedly refused the honour of the Grand Cross of the Order of Merit which was to be conferred on him in October by Costa e Silva.[114] This greatly heightened the tension in São Paulo, and now reprisals against the Church became more frequent. These ranged from deliberate snubs to Cardinal Rossi, to mark the armed forces' disapproval, to armed attacks on Dom Helder Câmara's residence in Recife, which was machine-gunned in October 1968 and plastered with extremist slogans. Ironically this attack occurred just as the CNBB meeting in Rio de Janeiro was agreeing on the need to reduce, wherever possible, political tension between the government and the Church. But members of the government were now more ready to take up the attack, with solemn warnings about irresponsible opposition from churchmen, who must realize that the clock could not be put back. The most explicit of these warnings came from the Minister of the Interior, Albuquerque Lima, who, with his eye fixed on the presidency, made a series of speeches, both in the south and in the north-east, about the need for the revolution to be on its guard against Communist corrosion of Brazilian society. In the weeks leading to Institutional Act No. 5, when already there were strong rumours of intervention by the 'hard line', the speeches of a minister of this seniority were a firm, clear warning that churchmen could not expect immunity from punishment, should they be involved in subversive opposition.

The message was driven home in November 1968. By now the security forces were searching furiously for Carlos Marighela, the former Communist who by this time was one of the most influential leaders of the urban guerrilla movement. On 21 November the security forces, through the Secretary of Security of Guanabara, accused Bishop Fragoso of having contact with Marighela. The evidence for the charge was extraordinarily flimsy and the incident seemed mainly to be an attempt to warn off churchmen, but it provoked a furious reaction, including a declaration by bishops in the north-east that they would go to prison along with Dom Fragoso, should he be arrested.[115] Church–State relations were now deteriorating fast and on the eve of the promulgation of Institutional Act No. 5 came the most serious crisis so far. On 28 November the security forces in Belo Horizonte arrested three French priests and a Brazilian deacon, all attached to JOC, living in one of the poorest areas of the city. They were all questioned, under torture, and eventually confessed to having been involved in subversive activities. Again the proof of their complicity was very thin. The case against the priests rested mainly on the possession of books, a letter containing criticism of the regime to superiors in Europe, but no solid proof of directly subversive activity. Notebooks said to be 'Marxist' and subversive contained little that could not be found in current church teaching.[116] There was an immediate, widespread protest from the church authorities and a hardening of attitudes on both sides. While the controversy was at its height, more priests were arrested in Santos and Recife and the government now found that it had arraigned against it the most influential elements in the Brazilian Catholic Church, not all of which, by any stretch of the imagination, could be dismissed as 'subversive' or 'Communist', a point driven home, for example, in a letter from Cardinal Dom Jaime Câmara of Rio de Janeiro, read in all the churches of the archdiocese. The whole tone of the letter, particularly the analogies used by an essentially very conservative church leader, showed how serious now was the breach with the Church and how large a problem the government had created for itself:

> The Church of Christ, here in Brazil, cannot stop being faithful to her mission especially when misunderstanding and foolishness impede her . . . Presently in our nation, the Church is undergoing tensions which include suspicions and accusations against various ministers . . . We cannot allow them to deny us the liberty of preaching and to silence the preachers of the Gospel by calling them Communists . . . Christ himself . . . the same God Jesus was punished for subversion which was the principal 'proof' in his process with the Roman attorney. We reaffirm, defend, and assert the right of the Church to organize and choose her methods of evangelization.[117]

More significantly still, by December 1968 the conflict and debate were openly reported in both the Brazilian and the international press, raising in the process issues concerning the nature of the regime and its overall strategy and philosophy which had never been so openly and fully discussed since 1964.[118] But on 13 December came Institutional Act No. 5 and a rigid tightening of censorship and control. The tension between Church and State remained as acute as ever, and its more dramatic moments continued to be reported, but the previously lively political debate on Church–State relations was, like all political debate, now severely muted, as a new period of Brazilian politics was introduced by the '*coup* within the *coup*'.

The most obvious, and at first sight rather bewildering, question about the regime's political behaviour in response to the challenge from both students and the Church is why evidently able and astute politicians should have reacted so indiscriminately and often excessively to opposition which in other societies, or in Brazil in other periods, would have been contained with altogether less noise, publicity, and the inevitable hardening of positions on both sides. Sometimes the reason, quite clearly, was the over-reaction of men on the spot, lacking the training and discipline to handle student, or other, demonstrations, so allowing soldiers or police to react too viciously, often in a state of some panic themselves. Sometimes, too, the attacks on churchmen for preaching 'subversion' reflected no more than intellectual isolation, parochialism, even sheer ignorance, on the part of men unaware of the changes taking place in Catholic and Christian thinking in the world at large, men whose instinctive reaction to talk of the Church's Christian duty to end social injustice was the same as their reaction to talk of limited land reform or peasant unionization, namely, to reach for the nearest stick. But the explanation ran much deeper, partly to the fear of raising the lid even a little in case the pot boiled over, and, further still, to the need to reassure foreign observers, especially creditors and potential investors, that Brazil's newly imposed political stability would not now be endangered. Hence the constant need not only to be in control, but, equally important, to be seen to be so. More immediately important, however, was the fact that student and church opposition was seen by the regime not as isolated phenomena, to be controlled within their own sphere, but as part of a much wider fabric of opposition, linked, at least in part, to groups who no longer believed in the possibility of a peaceful path to change, but, however reluctantly, now saw violent opposition as the only means of challenging what they regarded as the all-pervasive institutionalized violence of the regime.

Armed Opposition

In many respects, it was surprising that substantial armed resistance had not appeared sooner, but in the case of the Brazilian *coup* of 1964, unlike, for example, that of Chile almost a decade later, there was little initial recourse to violence. One evident reason was that the Brazilian opposition and more particularly the working-class organizations, were not armed and had no strategy either of violent opposition or even for resistance to violence used against them. They were for the most part surprised by the *coup* and in no way prepared to offer an armed challenge to the new regime. The armed movement only built up slowly as opposition groups realized that the regime was becoming more firmly entrenched in power and equally important, as all other channels of protest and opposition were closed. But by late 1967 and 1968 the debate on the necessity for violent resistance was growing stronger, stimulated partly by the example of guerrilla warfare in other parts of Latin America,[119] but mainly by a growing belief that the new rulers of Brazil would not willingly give ground. In this respect, it should be stressed, the swing to armed opposition was, historically, a response to the growing authoritarianism of the regime and to the closing of alternative forms of protest, rather than an initial armed resistance which made that authoritarianism necessary.[120] The opposition groups who argued the need for a strategy of violent resistance did so therefore in terms of the futility of alternative strategies, their view being that only by violence could they respond to what they regarded as the now greatly enlarged capacity for violence of the state and the security forces.

There were a few isolated cases of violent protest after the *coup*, but the movement grew only very slowly, accelerating from mid-1967 onwards. In one early clash Carlos Marighela, still a member of the Central Committee of the PCB, was shot and seriously wounded in May 1964, but the advocates of armed resistance at that time were still mainly to be found in the Partido Comunista do Brasil, a Maoist breakaway group founded in 1962 by Maurício Grabois and João Amazonas. While, however, more committed in theory to direct action than was the PCB, this group remained small and failed to organize armed resistance on any significant scale. Some of the nationalist opposition associated with Leonel Brizola also tried to offer some early resistance, forming in particular together with former soldiers the MNR (Nationalist Revolutionary Movement), attempting to set up revolutionary *focos* in rural areas, as, for example, in the Serra do Caparão in early 1967.[121] The doctrine of revolutionary action based on the rural *foco*, or nucleus, sprang mainly from a particular interpretation of the Cuban revolutionary process. This view tended to play down the role of mass organization, especially urban-based organizations, stressing rather the impact of the presence of a small group of rural guerrillas who would be the 'small motor' which would move the 'large motor' of revolution. The theory was fiercely debated on the left throughout the 1960s, being criticized as first an historical distortion of the pattern of the Cuban revolution, ignoring the contribution of mass, especially urban, organizations in the struggle against Batista, and second as a theory which might lead to disastrous results if used elsewhere as a basis for revolutionary strategy.[122] In Brazil the early efforts to establish rural *focos* were helped by some elements from AP (Popular Action), the left-wing group of the Christian student movement which from 1961 onwards was moving towards a more radical position, which, however, was mainly expressed in the organization of student protests in 1967 and 1968. Members of the PCdoB also worked to set up rural *focos*, especially from 1967 onwards.

Apart from this early attempted organization of rural *focos* there were isolated instances of violent opposition, such as the bombing of the home of the United States consul in Pôrto Alegre in February 1966, of the USIS building in Brasília in June, and, most serious of all, an attempt on the life of Costa e Silva at Recife airport in July. There were also bomb attempts against the homes of senior ministers in October. Some of the earliest groupings, in addition to the MNR, were the MAR (Armed Revolutionary Movement) and the MR–26, the 26 July Revolutionary Movement, named after Fidel Castro's 26 July movement, which in turn commemorated his attack on the Moncada barracks. Also reshaping at this time was POLOP (Política Operária; Workers' Politics), a Marxist group active among students and workers. In 1967 POLOP was severely split. One group in São Paulo became part of the first organization of VPR (Popular Revolutionary Vanguard), discussed below, joining mainly with military elements from the MNR. Most of POLOP in Minas Gerais, with others from Guanabara, formed a new organization, COLINA (Commando of National Liberation), which later formed the nucleus of yet another group, VAR-Palmares (Armed Revolutionary Vanguard), together with a splinter group of VPR. The VAR-Palmares commemorated in its name the seventeenth-century slave republic in Brazil (1630–97).[123] The main issue between it and other groups, such as, for example, the main body of VPR, was that which lay behind most of the splits and regroupings. This was essentially whether priority should be given to the more careful political organization of such sectors as workers, peasants, students, and, in some cases, even of the urban middle class, or whether there should be greater emphasis on the formation of groups which, even before this organization, would offer armed resistance. The idea behind this second line of argument was that the organization of the masses would develop at the same time as, and be associated with, the armed struggle. VAR placed much emphasis on mass organization, without abandoning the idea of armed struggle. Other groups, such as the ALN (National Liberation Action; Ação Libertadora Nacional), especially as led by Carlos Marighela, as discussed below, or the VPR, under the leadership of Carlos Lamarca, stressed more strongly the need for more spontaneous direct action and armed resistance. It was a matter of emphasis, but a crucially important one.

After the breakaway from POLOP the main POLOP group survived and in February 1968 merged with yet another dissident group, from the PCB in Rio Grande do Sul, forming a new organization,

POC (Partido Operária Comunista; Workers' Communist Party). Three years later, again over the issue of armed struggle, the main bloc of old POLOP members broke with the POC and took once again the name POLOP. Throughout 1967 and 1968 these groups were forming, splitting, and reshaping, all evidence of the intense argument on the left as to how the armed resistance should best be organized and, in particular, what relative weight—one of the oldest arguments in Marxist debate—should be given to organization and spontaneity in the shaping of opposition strategy. Sometimes the groups which were formed were made up of only a handful of men and women, sometimes they were the result of divisions within larger groups. So, for example, MRT (Tiradentes Revolutionary Movement), named after the eighteenth-century hero in Minas Gerais, was a breakaway from the so-called Ala Vermelha (Red Wing) of the Maoist PCdoB. Similarly, while most of the AP, the Catholic group mainly involved in student organization and rural unionism, moved towards the PCdoB, adopting a firmly Maoist position, a splinter group broke away to form the PRT (Revolutionary Workers' Party), claiming to adopt a Marxist-Leninist line, a position already also claimed by POC. As time went on, there was also a growing tendency for groups to work together in particular operations, perhaps in the process giving a new emphasis to their activities. From about October 1968, for example, there appeared the MR–8 (Revolutionary Movement of 8 October), named after the anniversary of the killing of Ché Guevara. This mainly concentrated, as its name implied, on establishing a rural *foco*, being composed mainly of ex-PCB and ex-POLOP members: but after a period of severe repression, lasting about six months, it established closer links with the most important of the activist groups, the ALN (National Liberating Action), the movement formed around ex-PCB members Carlos Marighela and Joaquim Câmara Ferreira. As time went on it became clear that the ALN was, in fact, the most important in promoting and shaping armed resistance. This group in particular, therefore, needs more careful analysis when evaluating the build-up of direct opposition in these years.

Of all those engaged in armed opposition in Brazil much the best known, both at home and abroad, was Carlos Marighela, and it was his break with the PCB which marked the most important step in the move towards direct opposition from 1967 onwards. Marighela was born in Bahia in 1911. He joined the PCB within five years of its foundation and for the next forty years till his expulsion from the party in September 1967 was deeply involved in its activities and organization. He helped the ANL in 1935, was subsequently imprisoned, and was on the Central Committee by 1943. In 1945 he was elected federal deputy for Bahia, together with the novelist Jorge Amado, and was a very active member of Congress till the PCB was again made illegal in 1947. He worked mainly in São Paulo and in the late 1940s was editor of the Communist journal *Problemas*. In 1957 Marighela became a member of the Executive Commission and Secretariat and from June 1966 was head of the committee of the state of São Paulo. In the intense internal debates within the party he sided in the immediate post-war years with the so-called 'Arruda group', named after another party leader, Diógenes Arruda Câmara, the group which most helped to have Luís Carlos Prestes elected as secretary-general of the PCB, and which was influential in setting aside Agildo Barata in 1957, when Marighela became a member of the party's Executive Commission and Secretariat.[124] Just prior to this, from 1953 to 1954, Marighela spent a year in China, his only prolonged period of time abroad, but his position remained generally Stalinist and from 1957 onwards he was one of the most prominent members of an inner group which came to dominate party policy, taking over from the men more closely associated with Arruda. This became known as the 'Bahia group', advocating a more aggressive political strategy, its most prominent members coming mainly from Bahia,[125] notably Marighela, Mário Alves de Souza Vieira, Giocondo Alves Dias, and one of the party's most prominent theorists, Jacob Gorender. Among these Marighela represented a link with the previously dominant 'Arruda group', but this shift in political weight within the party was eventually to lead to splits and expulsions as the members of the 'Bahia group' moved steadily towards a more militantly revolutionary position, especially in the wake of the 1964 *coup*. Giocondo Alves Dias continued as perhaps the most important party leader apart from Luís Carlos Prestes, but Mário Alves de Souza Vieira attacked the party's policy recommendations in May 1965, was removed from the Executive Commission, and in December 1967 was expelled from the party. He then founded the PCBR (Partido Comunista Brasileira Revolucionário), together with other dissident Communists, Gorender and Apolônio de Carvalho, now advocating direct action. In 1969 the members of the PCBR in Rio de Janeiro joined those remnants of MR–26 who under the name of MAR had tried to establish a *foco* in Angra dos Reis in August 1969. Mário Alves, still the leader of PCBR, was arrested and killed in 1970. Gorender was also expelled from the PCB in December 1967, having been suspended from voting in the Central Committee in September. He, too, joined in the founding of the PCBR, also arguing that effective revolutionary strategy must now include direct resistance and armed action.

The most famous convert to this line by late 1967 was Marighela, whose name was now most closely associated with criticism of the PCB for its too pacific, compromised policies of earlier years, for its rigid bureaucracy and centralization, and for its failure to understand the need to develop more militant revolutionary policies. Having served faithfully under such leaders as Astrojildo Pereira and Luís Carlos Prestes,[126] he had now become convinced of the weakness of earlier analysis and action. In December 1966, critical of the theses of the Sixth Congress approved by the Central Committee in June for the Congress in December 1967, Marighela resigned from the Executive Commission of the PCB.[127]

Although the PCB had decided to send no official delegate to the conference of OLAS (Organization of Latin American Solidarity) in Havana from 31 July to 10 August 1967, Marighela attended, together with other dissident Latin American Communists, such as Douglas Bravo from Venezuela. In reply to his persistent criticism, the Central Committee of the PCB expelled Marighela, together with Jover Telles, from the party in September, when also suspending Gorender's right to vote on the Central Committee. At the Sixth Congress in December these decisions were confirmed, with the formal expulsion now of Marighela, Telles, Alves de Souza Vieira, Joaquim Câmara Ferreira, Apolônio de Carvalho, and Miguel Batista. By the end of 1967, therefore, the split was complete, between those who favoured direct action and violent resistance and those who accepted official party policy.[128]

The reasons for Marighela's break were clearly set out in letters and interviews at the time, providing one of the most comprehensive critiques of earlier policies from a man whose whole life hitherto had been spent in the service of Brazilian communism. One of his earliest and most important statements was his letter of resignation from the Executive Committee of the PCB, dated 10 December 1966,[129] which criticized the party for its lack of mobility, lack of contact with workers, and, particularly, the peasantry, and for being frozen in bureaucratic inaction:

> All its [the Executive Committee's] activities consist in organising meetings and publishing policies and information. No action is planned, the struggle has been abandoned. And in moments of crisis, the party has no grasp on reality . . .[130]

He was scathing about the refusal to allow more vigorous debate, through an emphasis on a 'theory of unanimity', which led directly to the 'utterly un-Marxist and un-dialectical notion of a monolithic "kernel of leadership", cut off from the base' . . .[131] One of the fatal mistakes, he argued, was the emphasis on the bourgeoisie and its potential role:

> It is indeed the sheerest historical fatalism to declare that the bourgeoisie is the moving spirit of the Brazilian revolution, and that the proletariat's action must be subordinate to it—denying the people all initiative, and making them the plaything of events.[132]

This had been for some time one of Marighela's most forceful points of criticism of PCB strategy, the acceptance in practice, arising out of a particular interpretation of Brazilian society and politics, of a policy of collaboration with the 'bourgeois' politicians, men like Kubitschek, Quadros, Adhemar de Barros, even, most recently, with Lacerda, as well as military leaders like Amaury Kruel and Justino Alves Bastos, the focus of unrealistic political hopes.[133] Marighela now completely rejected any idea of working with such groups as the *Frente Ampla,* which he saw as a means to foster Lacerda's personal ambition,[134] or even with the MDB, in the hope of weakening the regime by electoral defeat. He wanted a more directly revolutionary strategy, rooted in the working class and the peasantry, open to more spontaneous influences from below rather than the exclusively centralized bureaucratic machine which, in its misreading of Brazilian society, had in effect abandoned the revolutionary struggle. The decision to break with the PCB was a hard one ('It is hateful to me to have to say these things'),[135] but, as he explained in a letter to Fidel Castro in August 1967 at the time of the OLAS conference:

> I believe that my break with the Central Committee will help to deepen the ideological struggle of the Brazilian revolutionary movement, and put a stop to all rightist and revisionist ideas . . . The way I have opted is that of guerrilla warfare, and we must set it on foot all over the countryside; only thus shall we fully become part of the Latin American revolution.[136]

For Marighela, then, as for others who broke with the PCB at this time, the choice of armed struggle was a reaction not just to the violence he saw contained in the *coup* of 1964, but a rejection of the official party strategy dominant since the mid-1930s. Other writings of his, particularly the *Handbook of Urban Guerrilla Warfare*, discussed below, and his reflections on the relation between guerrilla activity and wider revolutionary strategy, which he developed in the two years of armed struggle, brought him international prominence as a theorist and activist; but within the context of left-wing politics in Brazil, his fundamental criticism of Communist strategy, his rejection of compromise and collaboration, his call for action and for greater spontaneity in the direction of revolutionary strategy, and his emphasis on the need to work always at the grass roots, were to prove of more enduring importance in the reshaping of opposition strategy, long after the phase of direct guerrilla resistance was ended. Others at the time, both inside and outside the PCB, joined in criticizing earlier policies,[137] but by 1968 Marighela was the best-known and most influential of those who called for a radical reappraisal both of the party's strategy and its theoretical basis, convinced, as he told the Executive Committee, that:

> People have a right to expect of us as Communists and Marxist Leninist revolutionaries that we have the courage to say what we wish and believe, and also the courage to act upon it.[138]

The Coup within the Coup

Towards the end of 1968 direct armed resistance was still being organized and as yet had shown no dramatic success: there were seizures of arms and explosives, isolated bomb attacks, and bank raids to amass funds for action,[139] but no clear or effective threat to the regime. But already the evidence of gathering resistance, coupled with the student demonstrations and growing strain and confrontation between the government and members, often leaders, of the Church, was producing a forceful reaction on the right, especially in the armed forces. Already Albuquerque Lima had expressed his brusque impatience with churchmen who stepped out of line and it now was clear that no one, whatever his status or rank, would be allowed to offer serious challenge to the regime, despite earlier talk of 'humanization'. The pressure on Costa e Silva from the right was evidently growing stronger, fed still further by the resistance and opposition which it previously had provoked. What now was developing, ever more sharply and strongly, was a spiral of violence and a growing polarization of politics, a process in which dialogue was becoming steadily more difficult as the hardening of the authoritarian system and the closing of all legal forms of protest pushed the opposition into direct confrontation, which, in turn, produced still harsher reaction. The question by November 1968 was not whether there would be more repression and still more authoritarian control, but how far it would go and what possible solution there could be in terms of ending the mounting violence and re-creating a political system built on a more rational communication between contending interests.

One notable sign of 'hard line' strength within the officer corps and, as was becoming increasingly obvious, among some of the *técnicos*, was a growing, and more public, tension between Albuquerque Lima and the Ministers of Finance and Planning. The earlier attempt by 'hard line' officers to quiz and win assurances from Delfim Neto had brought a swift rebuke, but throughout the first year of Costa e Silva's administration there was persistent evidence of 'hard line' criticism of certain areas of economic policy. Albuquerque Lima, as the most prominent and most powerfully placed spokesman of this group, stressed the need for more attention to the north-east and Amazonas and for more investment, criticizing in the process certain features of the anti-inflationary policies of Delfim and Beltrão. Running what was, in effect, an unofficial campaign for the presidential succession, he attacked both Lacerda and the *Frente Ampla*, defending Brazil's transition to an 'authoritarian democratic regime',[140] but also insisting on the need for 'the real participation of the people of all socio-economic levels in the modern processes of economic development'.[141] The strength of his 'hard line' support in the army was increased by promotions and reappointments during 1968, and was reflected in the 'hard line' preparations for elections in the Clube Militar,[142] all pointing to a build-up of right-wing strength, which would be crucial in the crisis towards the end of the year. The military support for Albuquerque Lima was not matched, it seemed, among civilian politicians of ARENA,[143] but the Minister of the Interior was certainly by August 1968 much the most forceful and conspicuous critic within the regime of the priorities contained in the policies of Delfim Neto and Beltrão.[144] Mounting a campaign in many respects similar to that of Costa e Silva before he was assured of the presidency, Albuquerque Lima not only severely chided dissident students and churchmen, but highlighted his disagreement over current economic policies, as, for example, in a lecture at the ESG in October 1968, where he proposed a National Development Council, linked to the National Security Council, which would allow members of the armed forces to play a larger role in shaping development policy, as against the current system dominated by civilian *técnicos*. He also spoke now of the need for the 'revolution' to last another ten years in order to achieve all its objectives.

While the energy and controversial nature of Albuquerque Lima's campaign marked him as the leader of the 'hard line' in its attempt to exert pressure on the regime, it also reflected in part his awareness that he was still relatively poorly placed in his bid for the presidency. He was still only a three-star general, influential in the officer corps, but not as close to Costa e Silva personally as were some other presidential candidates, while still outranked by rivals, such as

General Sizeno Sarmento, who by late 1970 would be second in seniority among generals on the active list. Sarmento was currently commander of the First Army in Rio de Janeiro, a key post, in which he had strengthened his reputation among military colleagues by his firm reaction to the student demonstrations of mid-1968.[145] In an attempt to improve his relative position Albuquerque Lima proposed the creation of a new Fifth Army in Amazonas, a ploy which would confirm both his military seniority and his commitment to regions previously, as he argued, much neglected. This link between his more apparent 'hard line' activity and pressure and his evident presidential ambitions caused some observers to play down the strength of the 'hard line' faction: but this could easily be overdone, taking the reduction too far. Apart from Albuquerque Lima's more dramatic statements and confrontation there was evidence of persistent and steadily growing 'hard line', more authoritarian, and, in so far as could be judged, more nationalist opinion,[146] especially among more junior officers. Some of the reaction was evident in the increased activity of terrorist groups of the right, such as the CCC (Commando for Hunting Communists), active in São Paulo by mid-1968 and working with other groups in such wider movements as the FAAC (Anti-Communist Armed Front). A growing concern on the right could also be seen, for example, in the appearance in the press of 1 November 1968 of a manifesto signed by nearly 400 captains, attacking alleged corruption and growing subversion and demanding tougher changes.[147]

Part of the background to this right-wing reaction and the growing support for the 'hard-line' was a crisis which broke in Congress in early September, and which eventually was to provide the occasion for the most far-reaching and most repressive of government measures so far, Institutional Act No. 5. After the violent invasion of the University of Brasília by troops on 30 August 1968 there were vigorous protests in Congress, the most notable being a speech by a MDB deputy Márcio Moreira Alves, one of the most articulate members of the opposition, who, in speeches on 2 and 3 September, demanded gestures of protest against increasing militarism in Brazilian life, a plea echoed by other opposition spokesmen, including journalists.[148] The speeches and articles were immediately interpreted by military officers as a direct insult to the honour of the armed forces,[149] with the three military ministers demanding on 13 September that Costa e Silva should act against those responsible for the insults. The president wanted to find a compromise, possibly with a statement in Congress withdrawing any implied insult, but the pressure on him was too great, with the 'hard-line' Minister of Justice insisting that the deputies concerned should lose their civil rights. This immediately brought up the question of parliamentary privilege and produced a major crisis, a test of strength between the regime and Congress. After intense discussions the president of ARENA, Senator Daniel Krieger, told Costa e Silva that both the party and he personally thought the deputies were covered by parliamentary immunity and that the matter should not be pressed, but still the military high command persisted with its demands. There were, in fact, some gestures from Congress to mollify military feeling, including a massive vote of support for the armed forces in late October during 'Air Force Week', but there were too many on both sides eager to fish in troubled waters. On 29 October Carlos Lacerda, already politically out on a limb, adroitly cut it off with an article in *Tribuna da Imprensa* attacking the armed forces in his usual lurid manner, so sealing his own political future and ensuring, in effect, that the crisis should become worse. There was relative calm during the official visit to Brazil of Queen Elizabeth II in early November and the clash between the regime and Congress did not play a large part in the campaign leading to the municipal elections on 15 November. Many *municípios* were excluded from the elections on the grounds of national security, their mayors, like those of capital cities, being appointed by the state governor. The main characteristic of the elections, which gave a predictably heavy victory (about 75 per cent of votes) to ARENA, was one of popular disregard for an electoral system rigged by the regime. But the row with Congress still continued. The justice committee of the Chamber of Deputies was changed in late November to produce a decision to take action against Moreira Alves, but on 11 December the Chamber reversed this decision by a vote of 216 to 141, with fifteen abstentions, holding fast to the principle of parliamentary immunity and refusing to be intimidated. Ninety-four of these votes came from ARENA, stressing that it was not a mere tool of the regime. At the same time the judiciary showed similar independence, when on 11 December the Supreme Court issued writs for *habeas corpus* for thirty-three students, then ordered that two of the most prominent leaders, Luís Travassos and Vladimir Palmeira, should be released.

Preparations for such a crisis had already been made, especially by one of the most extreme civilian members of the 'hard line', the Minister of Justice, Gama e Silva.[150] The details of the debate within the regime are still not fully known, but the principal military spokesman urging very tough measures was evidently General Sizeno Sarmento, who also, however, seems to have been concerned not to give an opportunity to Albuquerque Lima and his supporters to use the crisis to strengthen their position.[151] It was clear, however, that the demand for more severe controls had widespread support in the armed forces, among officers of all ranks, but particularly among some of the more junior officers.[152] The crisis precipitated by Moreira Alves and Congress was, therefore, only the occasion for, not the cause of, the introduction of more fiercely repressive measures.

The government's answer to the crisis came on 13 December 1968, in Institutional Act No. 5, producing the '*coup* within the *coup*' which now introduced very much more severe measures. This new Institutional Act marked a definitive break with the attempt to maintain some form of 'controlled democracy', emphasizing, rather, the essentially authoritarian nature of the regime and its apparent inability to handle crisis and challenge other than by ever more extreme repression. The new Act declared in Article 2 that:

> The President of the Republic may decree recess of the National Congress, the state assemblies, and the municipal chambers through complementary edicts whether or not the state of siege is in force. They will be called into session again only by the President of the Republic.

Article 3:

> The President of the Republic in the national interest may decree intervention in the states and municipalities without the limitations set forth in the constitution.
>
> The *interventores* in the states and municipalities will be appointed by the President of the Republic and will exercise all functions and duties which are the respective responsibility of the Governors or Mayors and will enjoy all privileges, salaries, and benefits fixed by law.

Article 4:

> In the interest of preserving the revolution, the President of the Republic after consultation with the National Security Council and without the limitations established in the constitution will be able to suspend the political rights of any citizen for ten years, and to cassate federal, state, or municipal elective mandates.
>
> Federal, state, and municipal legislative members whose mandates are cassated will not be replaced and the parliamentary quorum will be adjusted in accord with the number of places effectively filled.

Following Institutional Act No. 5 political opposition was then further emasculated with the *cassações*, or loss of political rights, of prominent critics, the most conspicuous being Carlos Lacerda.

Congress was closed indefinitely by means of Complementary Act No. 38, again emphasizing that, in the government's view, ARENA had failed to win in Congress the pro-government support and control considered essential for the preservation of the system shaped since 1964. There was, moreover, clear evidence of disagreement between the government and ARENA. The new measures were criticized by some of the most important ARENA senators, including the ARENA president, Daniel Krieger, and such influential figures as Carvalho Pinto, Milton Campos, Mem de Sá, Ney Braga, and Arnon de Melo. Nor were ARENA members spared in the purge of political critics which now was to be introduced. When, for example, on 7 February 1969, it was announced that the mandates of 33 congressmen had been cancelled, eleven of those affected belonged to ARENA.

Most of the repression, however, fell on the MDB and opposition spokesmen more generally. On 30 December were announced the *cassações* of eleven deputies, including Mário Moreira Alves, Hermano Alves, and Renato Archer, all vocal critics of the regime. 16 January saw this process taken even further, with the removal of two senators, Aarão Steinbruch and João Abrão, together with 35 federal deputies. At the same time came a demand for the retirement of a member of the Superior Military Tribunal, General Pery Bevilaqua, and of three judges from the Supreme Court, Victor Nunes Leal, Hermes Lima, and Evandro Lins e Silva.

In early February appeared another list of those whose political rights had been suspended and electoral mandates cancelled. This included two more senators and 31 deputies, meaning that in the space of three months the MDB opposition in the Chamber had been reduced by nearly 40 per cent. At the same time important state legislatures were declared as being indefinitely in recess, including those of Guanabara, São Paulo, and Pernambuco, and on 26 February 1969, through Institutional Act No. 7, the government went even further, cancelling all elections due to be held before November 1970.

This sharp, effective shift towards more direct, much tougher authoritarianism, showed how well prepared had been the regime's contingency plans. There were also well-founded rumours of further moves to curb all potential extra-Congressional opposition, with proscription lists being drawn up of anyone perceived as dangerous, including distinguished academics, journalists, and diplomats. These lists, which eventually appeared in April, were now being drawn up in an atmosphere of increased surveillance, tension, and uncertainty, heightened by the renewed activity of a General Investigations Commission (CGI), again overseeing IPMs (Military–Police Investigations), holding inquiries throughout the country. By late April 1969 a list of several hundred prominent Brazilians was ready for publication, removing from their jobs scholars of international reputation in a wide range of academic disciplines, together with diplomats, writers, and politicians.[153] No one, it was now clear, could feel entirely safe from the government's suspicion or displeasure, a displeasure made all the more dangerous by changes in the National Security Law in March 1969. This so widened the concept of offences against national security as to allow the government virtually limitless control. Described by the International Commission of Jurists as 'a formidable weapon of repression', the modified Act developed the concept of 'adverse psychological warfare', with inciting to sedition, even in private, now defined as subject to punishment through military courts. The new legislation hit particularly hard the press and other media, with Article 34, for example, stipulating two to four years' imprisonment for 'moral offence to anyone in authority, for reasons of factionalism or socio-political differences', the sentence to be increased by half if the offence were committed by means of the press, radio, and television. Article 45 provided penalties of up to four years for the crime of 'subversive propaganda', which included the use of any means of communication as a vehicle for adverse psychological warfare, and 'abuse, calumny, or defamation directed at an organ or entity which exercises public authority or at a public official because of his functions'.

Several points emerged clearly from the crisis of December 1968 and the intensified repression of the '*coup* within the *coup*'. One was the inadequacy, or essential irrelevance, of the civilian base of the regime, especially as expressed in Congress by ARENA. This was, indeed, one of the most persistently evident features of the post-1964 regime, emphasized by every reasonable test of public opinion, even in the tightly constrained electoral system allowed after Institutional Act No. 5. Time and again it was seen that the regime had no real popular civilian basis and that it could not be sustained in any really free electoral contest. In this respect the harshly tightened controls of late 1968 and early 1969 were a logical response by those determined to maintain the system, but aware that it would not be legitimized even by an emasculated Congress.

The '*coup* within the *coup*' also emphasized the equally important fact of continuing substantial divisions within the armed forces. One of the commonly alleged justifications for military intervention was the advantage of a united government, speaking with one voice, providing a degree of stability and coherence of planning said to be lacking in previous civilian governments. The abandonment of Campos's Ten-Year Plan had already suggested that such rationale for military intervention was a myth. Now by December 1968 it was clear that Costa e Silva could command no greater unity within the armed forces than could his predecessor and, in particular, that he could not curb its right wing, demanding more direct authoritarian control. The concept of 'humanizing' the regime was, in other words, still a forlorn hope, as the weight of Brazilian politics shifted emphatically to the right.

This, undoubtedly, was the most important feature of Institutional Act No. 5, that it marked a definitive stage in the formation of Brazil's authoritarian state and its new relations with civil society, particularly the political parties and Congress. Individual members of the old political class still remained important, men such as Magalhães Pinto, for example, who, almost a decade after Institutional Act No. 5, still could hope, however unrealistically, to be the first civilian president since the *coup* of 1964. But he and other similar political survivors were exceptional rather than typical. Most of the old political class, most conspicuously exemplified in Lacerda, were now out of the game. The interests behind the new regime, the social and economic forces which sustained and required it, no longer trusted, or needed, the civilian politicians. Rather, the logic contained in the intervention of April 1964 was now being played out, with its essential political requirements becoming ever clearer. Power, it could be seen, was now being exercised ever more directly and immediately by a tightly-knit group of soldiers and *técnicos*, determined to impose their policies for Brazilian development, untroubled by protest or opposition from whatever direction it might come. By April 1969, five years after the military *coup*, the essential features of Brazil's new authoritarian state had been clearly defined.

The Struggle for Succession: Nationalism versus Internationalism

While the '*coup* within the *coup*' was being prepared and carried out, another equally important struggle was being fought, not between the government and its opponents, but inside the regime itself, between different factions of the ruling group. Partly this consisted of a struggle for power between various dominant personalities in the armed forces leadership, each backed by groups of junior officers, but, more substantially and more seriously, it turned on two of the most persistent issues of Brazilian political debate. These were, first, the relative weight to be given to policies favouring growth rather than distribution; secondly, the long, tangled question of 'nationalism' versus 'internationalism', defence of national interests versus excessive *entreguismo*. The debate over distribution had essentially two dimensions, social and regional, namely, how national wealth and resources might be distributed between different social classes or groups, and how priorities should be allocated between the different regions of Brazil, particularly the rich centre-south and the much poorer, relatively neglected areas of the north-east and Amazonas. Linked to this yet again was the closely related question of where power was to be located, whether increasingly it should be centralized in the federal government or devolved to the regions, allowing them a greater share in the direction of resources. These two central questions, how wealth and power should be distributed, and how great a role to allow to foreign interests, already had been defined sharply by 1964: from 1969 onwards they became ever more fiercely debated, the main focus of controversy within the regime. Behind all the play of personal rivalry and contending ambition they now became the most crucial and far-reaching issues in the struggle for presidential succession.

The most vocal representative by late 1968 of those who wanted tighter, if not extreme, nationalist control, and more emphasis on distribution, especially to the regions, was Albuquerque Lima. Since becoming Interior Minister at the age of fifty-seven, he had brought new vigour and greater prestige to the office and had built up a solid basis of support, particularly among *técnicos* linked to the ministry and among more junior officers, from about the rank of colonel downwards. Not only did he seem a strong contender for the presidency, but was seen as the advocate of policies significantly different from those being pursued by Delfim Neto and indeed those most firmly adopted ever since 1964. Albuquerque Lima believed strongly in the need for tough, authoritarian control and the curbing of 'subversion', taking in this respect a harder line than Castello Branco and many of the 'Sorbonne' group. He had been one of the most important leaders of the movement stemming from the Vila Militar in October 1965 to oust Castello Branco, producing the reaction which led to Institutional Act No. 2 and its insistence on tighter controls. But he was also sharply critical of certain features of social and economic policy. He belonged squarely to the more 'nationalist' wing of the armed forces leadership, so from the start had been suspicious of too ready a dependence on and welcome for economic interests based outside Brazil. This had brought him into conflict first with Roberto Campos, then with Delfim Neto, whose policies he also criticized as laying too much stress on growth without sufficient attention to distribution and the allocation of resources to neglected regions such as Amazonas and the north-east. He wanted less emphasis on rapid stabilization, the cost of which fell heaviest on weaker social groups and poorer regions, urging, instead, the need for much greater investment to develop more backward regions. Throughout 1967 and 1968, while fiercely attacking any initiative which seemed to threaten the regime, such as, for instance, Lacerda's moves to form a *Frente Ampla*, he made clear his disagreement with some central features of government policy. Having once, under Quadros, headed DNOCS, the National Department for Anti-Drought Works, Albuquerque Lima maintained an active interest in the north-east. He was convinced that, handled vigorously and imaginatively, the problems of the north-east such as drought, could be solved, but only by adopting solutions in the north-east, genuinely aimed at solving north-eastern problems. He was, however, deeply suspicious of plans hatched up outside the north-east and of central policies which had other overall priorities than the needs of troubled or neglected regions such as the north-east and Amazonas. But his stress on the need for far-reaching regional development was not merely a political tactic, but part of a coherent interpretation of 'national objectives' and national development, a view which found much sympathy in both military and civilian circles throughout 1968 and 1969, and which provoked strong reaction from others within the regime.

Having played an important role in the '*coup* within the *coup*' of December 1968, Albuquerque Lima was required to return to active service before 15 March 1969, another reason for his stress on the creation of a Fifth Army in Amazonas. By early 1969 he was insisting with Costa e Silva on the need for more resources to be assigned to the north-east and more local autonomy in deciding their use. He especially stressed the urgent problems of housing and sanitation and the need for more energetic government action to develop both agrarian and industrial activity in the north-east. When government policies seemed to contradict these priorities, he resigned as Minister of the Interior in late January, now clearly presenting himself as a potential successor to Costa e Silva, but on the basis of substantially different policies.

Among Albuquerque Lima's most conspicuous ministerial successes had been his emphasis on 'national integration', a concept for him closely linked to that of 'national security', but with distinctly nationalist overtones. His initiatives in this respect had included firm support for SUDENE, the development agency for the north-east, and SUDAM, designed to promote development in Amazonas. He had also sponsored the definition of Manaus as a 'free zone', which was supposed to act as a stimulus to industrial and other development in Amazonas, and the establishment of SUDECO (Superintendency for the Development of the Centre East), again designed to open up and 'possess' new areas. Similarly he tried to harness or stimulate youthful idealism to work for development of the interior, by launching the 'Rondon Project', named after Marshal Cândido da Silva Rondon, whose working life had been dedicated to the protection of Brazil's Indian population. The aim of this project was to take city-bound youngsters into the interior, to learn about and help to alleviate some of the acute social and economic problems which previously they had not met.

In his speech on quitting office, Albuquerque Lima himself emphasized these initiatives, all geared towards the integration of the interior and towards regional development.[154] The key phrase in his speech was, however, 'Integrar para não entregar'—'Integrate, so as not to hand over'; the term 'entregar' having rich political overtones from the popular use of *entreguismo*. His speech contained a sharp attack on the Ministers of Finance and Planning and, in particular, on recent government legislation, which, Albuquerque Lima alleged, had seriously weakened the position of *municípios* and the regions generally. The speech referred bitterly to policies of the Ministers of Finance and Planning which used:

> simplistic arguments to benefit still further the south-east and southern region, which concentrates about 75 per cent of Brazil's economic potential and where are to be found the bases of support for old, powerful economic groups insensible to the need to preserve the territorial integrity of the country.

Approving of Institutional Act No. 5, Albuquerque Lima attacked the government for legislation and policies which favoured powerful groups in the centre-south at the expense of other poorer regions, whose development should be a basic principle of 'nationalist affirmation'. He called, instead, for 'the genuine Revolution, which, by its very spirit, is opposed to men linked to economic groups without any feeling for the national reality [sem nenhuma sensibilidade para a realidade nacional]'. He appealed, too, for 'a Revolution which will carry out . . . courageously and quickly agrarian reform, in which area are grave social tensions which need to be resolved peacefully' and, above all, he argued for the integration of areas, especially Amazonas, which could more cheaply be occupied now than they could be won back in future.

Albuquerque Lima was, in effect, challenging Delfim Neto and the whole thrust of current economic and social policy, a challenge which he was to continue to make over the next two years, and which was to be taken up by others after he had been passed over for promotion to four-star general, so effectively removed from political life.[155] The call was for less centralization, less exclusive attention to the centre-south, much more emphasis on distribution, both socially and regionally, necessary reforms, especially in the agrarian sector, and, above all, a more careful definition of nationalist priorities *vis-à-vis* foreign interests, especially in such areas as Amazonas.

The challenge was not, it should be stressed, a very radical one. Albuquerque Lima himself already had business connections which excluded a thoroughly nationalist defiance of either foreign or the São Paulo and centre-south financial and business interests. If he had any hope of becoming president, he would need eventually to come to terms with those 'powerful groups' he now severely criticized. Nevertheless, his criticism of the Ministers of Finance and Planning, his appeal to regionalism and nationalism, and his demand for wider distribution of the fruits of growth, expressed an unease and dissatisfaction shared by many more junior officers concerned about the direction the revolution was taking. Equally, though the subject was rarely discussed publicly, his call for austerity and integrity echoed the concern felt by many in the armed forces at the spreading corruption which allegedly was to be found among senior military and civilian personnel close to the centre of government.

One measure of the strength of Albuquerque Lima's criticism was the reaction it produced and the concerted, ultimately successful, attempt to keep him from power. Both the São Paulo and the international financial community were deeply alarmed at the prospect of more rigorous nationalist opinion among the armed forces, perhaps finding similar expression in Brazil as in Peru since the *coup* of October 1968.[156] Albuquerque Lima himself denied that he favoured a 'Peruvian' model, rightly claiming that what he advocated had deep roots in Brazilian military thinking. But in a system so tightly enmeshed in and dependent on the world of international finance, especially through the transnational corporations, the idea of stricter nationalist controls, based on an appeal to more junior officers, was utterly unacceptable. More attention might, indeed, be paid to the regions, though not to the detriment of São Paulo and the heartlands of the 'Miracle': but nationalist defiance of international and multinational interests could not be tolerated, and produced a predictably strong reaction.

The months between the resignation of Albuquerque Lima and the crisis of Costa e Silva's illness and the presidential succession in September–October 1969 were a time of mounting tension, confusion, and a struggle for control between different factions and individuals in the armed forces' leadership. The pattern is still difficult to follow in detail, since the struggle only occasionally broke the surface of national politics; but it is clear that the biggest single issue was the determination of the interests underlying the regime and the 'Brazilian model' not to allow a more nationalist presidential candidate to win power. The interests of, and the need to woo and conciliate, multinational and international financial and business interests were seen by most Brazilian policymakers after 1964 as an essential element in the country's growth and 'development', so given full state support. Men associated with, or belonging to, powerful multinational corporations were placed in strategically important positions both military and civilian. The new state apparatus which was being shaped, now further strengthened and delimited by Institutional Act No. 5, was becoming ever more clearly an instrument working on behalf of international or multinational groups rather than of those more readily defined as a local or 'national' bourgeoisie. These interests now reacted sharply to any hint of substantial nationalist challenge, especially in the scramble for the presidency.

The impact of multinational corporations in Brazil is discussed more fully below,[157] but at this stage it is important to bear in mind at least the conclusion of the most important survey to appear so far:

> . . . U.S. MNC's in Brazil, operating in concentrated markets denationalized through acquisition and rapid internal growth, are in a structural position to wield considerable economic and non-economic power over the performance of the Brazilian economy.[158]

Precisely how this 'non-economic' power is brought to bear is still being researched, itself a rather delicate job; but it is clear that in Brazil, as elsewhere, one of the most effective ways has been for the large multinational corporations to place their men close to the centre of power, particularly in the case of Brazil, of state power.[159] Albuquerque Lima's defiance may be interpreted as in part opportunistic, or as essentially an assertion of the need for a more *diversified* dependence, less exclusively linked to United States multinationals; but even this degree of defiance was taken very seriously by those in the system committed to the defence of multinational operations in the Brazilian economy and polity.

What was equally clear by 1969 was that on this issue, as on that of corruption, of regionalism versus centralism, and distribution versus growth, the armed forces were seriously split, always a matter of concern for the high command. Albuquerque Lima not only represented a possible alternative strategy or 'model' for Brazil, but a rallying-point for disaffected junior officers and *técnicos*, with the clear possibility of an even wider appeal, which might even embrace and partly remobilize the hitherto tightly controlled trade unions.

Such a potential threat to the unity of command and solidarity of the armed forces was again perceived as highly dangerous, again jeopardizing the image of solid 'political stability' required to reassure foreign bankers and businessmen and to sustain the 'Brazilian model'. Consequently, five years after the *coup* of 1964, despite the greatly strengthened system of control produced by Institutional Act No. 5 and its aftermath, the regime showed signs of serious internal strains, which could not fully be papered over, despite the rigid censorship.

One early indication of how things might be moving was the promotion lists of 25 March, where 'nationalist' officers were conspicuous by their absence in all the more senior and key command positions.[160] The three new full generals were Augusto César Castro Moniz de Aragão, previously president of the Clube Militar; Emílio Garrastazú Médici, head of the SNI, and José Canavarro Pereira. Moniz de Aragão was soon to break with the Costa e Silva government, to be suspended from the army high command: but his quarrel was not primarily on 'nationalist' grounds, though related to the nationalist critique in that he was mainly appealing for more austerity and an end to corruption. Garrastazú Médici, by contrast, was eventually to succeed Costa e Silva in the presidency and continue for another four and a half years essentially the strategy which the nationalist officers were criticizing. His new posting in 1969 was to take over the Third Army in Rio Grande do Sul, his native state.

April 1969 saw the compulsory retirement and/or removal from political life of hundreds of prominent politicians, diplomats, academics, and writers, a further development of the moves introduced the previous December. But more indicative of tension within the regime itself was the compulsory retirement to the reserves on 19 May of Colonel Francisco Boaventura Cavalcanti, a 'hard-line' officer,[161] previously close to Lacerda, who in the crisis of late 1968 had been judged to be too sympathetic to the Congressional opposition. Boaventura Cavalcanti had earlier worked hard for Costa e Silva's candidacy and his brother, Colonel José Costa Cavalcanti, had first been appointed as Minister of Mines and Energy in Costa e Silva's government, then moved to the Ministry of the Interior on Albuquerque Lima's departure. Although 'hard line' he had expressed reservations about the regime's treatment of Congress and his abrupt removal alarmed and offended many officers uncertain as to the wisdom of keeping Congress closed and pushing the armed forces more firmly into direct control of the state and national politics.

The move against Boaventura Cavalcanti also touched the 'nationalist' bloc of military officers, whose calls for greater austerity, an end to corruption, a firmer line with the multinationals, and a clearer programme of national integration had been echoed in part at least by Boaventura. His removal also showed that the most influentially placed of officers was not immune from government disapproval and retribution. Most important of all, the affair brought into the open the whole question of military disunity and disagreement on serious issues, notably in Moniz de Aragão's attack. Government censorship was largely successful in stifling most of the criticism and disagreement, but not entirely, since publications which were officially suppressed were soon circulating unofficially, providing material for rumour, counter-rumour, and widespread discussion of the nature and even the viability of the Costa e Silva government.

One such publication, providing the most detailed account of the crisis leading to the change of president and the death of Costa e Silva, was written by his press secretary, Carlos Chagas. Some of the material appeared in articles in *O Estado de São Paulo* and *O Globo* in January 1970, but the final work, in book form, forbidden to be published, was eventually circulated, mostly in xeroxed copies, providing a sympathetic account of Costa e Silva and much useful information and documentation on the succession crisis.[162] The book contains an appendix of documents, including letters of Moniz de Aragão protesting at the treatment of Boaventura Cavalcanti and complaining of abuses within the regime. In his first letter of 22 May 1969, to General Lyra Tavares, Minister of the Army, he stresses the high reputation of Boaventura Cavalcanti, both in civilian and military circles, but, above all, emphasizes the danger to the reputation, morale, and unity of the army when action of this kind is taken against a colleague.[163] His second letter, of 17 June, is much more powerful and far-reaching. He starts with a reference to Maritain of the dangers of arbitrary government exercised on behalf of particular interests, whether family ties, friendship, or other connections, then suggests that reports and rumours, neither corrected nor denied, are leading many to believe that the 'Revolutionary Government' is on this path. He then produces a list of specific examples, mainly relating to Costa e Silva's family, such as, for example, the nomination of the president's brother to the Tribunal of Accounts of Rio Grande do Sul, the return to active service from retirement of his father-in-law, General Severo Barbosa, and similar unjustified advancement of his brother-in-law, Jair Rodrigues, a man of dubious reputation. He also condemns the abuse of public funds by a friend of the president, General Clovis Bandeira Brasil, and, in particular, the lavish funds made available to the Minister of Transport, Andreazza, to carry out questionable policies, at a time when the armed forces, especially the army, are very short of money.[164] The letter is a stern appeal for greater honesty and loyalty o the original concept of the 'Revolution', which aimed to end subversion and restore a government of national regeneration, to put an end to corruption. He asks the Army Minister to get the president 'to listen even to the rumblings of doubt and complaint from the lowest ranks of the barracks' and heed the anxieties and resentments of his soldiers. One of the key phrases in Moniz de Aragão's letter was:

> Officers of the armed forces, because they judge themselves responsible for the revolutionary regime, understand they have the right and duty not only to watch and judge the acts of the government, which they think belongs to them, but even to remove that government if they disagree with it.[165]

It was this phrase which Lyra Tavares seized on in his reply of 30 June. He said that Costa e Silva rejected and dismissed any charges not made in writing, with evidence, and duly signed; Moniz de Aragão's letter would be treated as secret; the phrase about the accountability of the government implied military control, so was totally unacceptable, and the matter was being laid before the president. On 9 July Moniz de Aragão was removed from his post as head of the Directorate of General Provisions, being also suspended from the army high command.

The whole incident of Moniz de Aragão's criticism and dismissal, and the bitter correspondence it provoked, including a further letter to Lyra Tavares of 1 July, was only the tip of the iceberg, but sufficient to indicate the deep divisions, uncertainty, confusion, and dismay to be found in the armed forces by mid-1969. Severe criticism of the government from a four-star general, criticism quickly made public, was unprecedented since 1964, as was his abrupt removal. And, as Moniz de Aragão claimed, the divisions and disenchantment ran all the way down, coming 'do fundo das casernas', from, as it were, the barrack-room floor, but found at all levels.

One feature of national politics, which further provoked disagreement within the armed forces, but eventually, in September 1969, brought a temporary closing of the ranks, was the growing challenge from urban guerrillas and others favouring direct action. January had seen the defection of Captain Carlos Lamarca and three non-commissioned officers, taking with them automatic weapons to strengthen VPR, and there had been a series of bank-raids and attacks on television stations, all bringing further publicity to underground groups. The groups were also reforming, with a new alliance established between VPR and COLINA, producing by July 1969 VAR–Palmares, which, initially at least, appeared capable of producing more effective, better-organized opposition, though soon it was to split over the question of broad strategy.[166] In its early days, however, it managed to reappropriate $2·4 million from the estate of Adhemar de Barros, a haul which many people felt showed a piquant sense of justice, even a sense of humour. But the attacks and apparently growing support for urban guerrilla movements deeply alarmed the armed forces, especially when they also sensed uncertainty and disagreement behind the Costa e Silva regime. Consequently, dramatic, if short-lived, successes, such as the seizure of Radio São Paulo on 15 August and the reading of a speech by Marighela, brought disproportionate reaction.

Guerrilla activity also made more difficult the argument of those in the armed forces who favoured a quick return to 'normalcy', with the reopening of Congress and the dismantling of Institutional Act No. 5 and its associated framework of control. Rather, there was a marked shift in the other direction, to strengthen and intensify mechanisms of control. This was particularly to be seen in the further rapid development of the use of torture as a means of extracting information and, more importantly, of terrorizing any potential opposition. Torture for political purposes was now being used systematically throughout Brazil, with generally standard practices and methods. One centre found across the country was the DOPS in every state (Department of Political and Social Order). A notorious centre in Rio de Janeiro was CENIMAR (Information Centre for the Navy) 'working' on the fifth floor of the Ministry of the Navy, next door to the United States naval mission. Also in Guanabara was Ilha das Flores and Ilha Grande, as well as other army centres. The Second Army in São Paulo had its main base for such work in the city centre, in Rua Tutoia 921, while another infamous place in São Paulo was the Tiradentes prison. There was also, as in every state, CODI (Operations Centre for Internal Defence) and, again in São Paulo, DOI (Division of Internal Operations), a mixed group of elements from the military police of São Paulo and the most vicious of all such organizations, OBAN, discussed below. Elsewhere there was the prison of the 12th Infantry Regiment in Belo Horizonte, the Linhares prison in Juiz de Fora, and other prisons where torture took place in Pôrto Alegre, Salvador, Recife, and Fortaleza.

Across the country by 1969 there were other groups working wholly or in part to eliminate anyone considered 'subversive' or even 'marginal', usually acting unofficially, as in the case of the Commando for Hunting Communists (CCC), whose victims included a young priest working as assistant to Dom Helder Câmara, and, most notoriously, the 'Death Squads'. These latter were mostly made up of off-duty policemen, often torturing their victims before killing them.[167] The São Paulo Death Squad's activities in particular were closely linked to the prodigiously profitable traffic in drugs, as well as to protection, prostitution, and organized crime in general. Very few Death Squad members were ever brought to trial, apparently having very powerful friends to protect them.

The activities of the Death Squads were not primarily political, but, rather, further evidence of social and criminal violence towards which the authorities turned a blind eye. But mid-1969 now saw the emergence of the most notorious of all the organizations employing torture for directly political purposes, OBAN (Operation Bandeirantes), a name which would sully the old title of *bandeirante* with a new association of vicious, well-organized, and well-financed torture on a large scale. OBAN was composed of members of the three services and the police, but was distinguished by drawing its main financial support from business interests, both Brazilian and multinational, which supported OBAN as a means of repressing the threat of 'subversion'.[168] Very substantial sums of money were provided for this purpose, with businessmen in some cases even directly and immediately associated with the work of OBAN. Over the next few years this organization was responsible for some of the most brutal cases of torture recorded in Brazil.[169]

Distasteful though the subject may be, it is not possible fully to understand the nature of Brazilian politics and the control exercised by the regime, especially from 1969 onwards, without appreciating the terrorizing impact of the widespread and systematic use of torture for political purposes. The subject, sadly, is well-documented with detailed accounts from many victims of how they were treated. The names of many of those responsible are known, men such as, for example, Sérgio Paranhos Fleury, *delegado* of the DOPS in São Paulo, one of the most prominent members of the Death Squad, said to be one of those most active in the brutal work of OBAN.[170] Methods of torture varied, but the same methods were used throughout the country. They included sleep-deprivation, near-drowning, beating, sexual abuse, and the use of methods developed and refined over the years, such as the *pau de arara* (parrot's perch), the 'dragon chair', and the 'operating table'. On the 'parrot's perch' the victim was handcuffed and his arms placed over his legs, which were drawn up to his chest. He then was suspended on a long pole, to be beaten or subjected to electric shocks or some form of water torture. One young man, in a long letter to the Pope, to try to get the Vatican to put pressure on the Brazilian government to stop the use of torture, described how he was subjected to this torture in OBAN headquarters:

> I was beaten as I went up the steps to a room on the top floor where they continued to slap me, hit me about the head and bang my ears with cupped hands (telephone torture); they took the handcuffs off and continued to hit me with their truncheons whilst questioning me. They ordered me to strip completely; I obeyed. They made me sit down on the ground and tied my hands with a thick rope. One of the six or seven policemen present put his foot on the rope in order to tighten it as much as possible. I lost all feeling in my hands. They put my knees up to my elbows so that my tied hands were on a level with my ankles. They then placed an iron bar about 8 cm wide between my knees and elbows and suspended me by resting the two ends of the iron bar on a wooden stand so that the top part of my body and my head were on one side and my buttocks and legs on the other, at three feet from the floor. After punching me and clubbing me, they placed a wire in the little toe of the left foot and placed the other end between my testicles and my leg. The wires were attached to a camp telephone so that the current increased or decreased according to the speed at which the handle was turned. In this way, they began to give me electric shocks and continued to beat me brutally both with their hands and with a 'palmatoria'—a plaque full of holes—which left a completely black hematome, larger in size than an outstretched palm, on one of my buttocks. The electric shocks and the beatings continued for several hours. I arrived about 14.30 and it was beginning to get dark when I practically lost consciousness. Each time that I fainted, they threw water over me to increase my sensitivity to the electric shocks. They then took the wire from my testicles and began to apply it to my face and head, giving me terrible shocks on my face, in my ears, eyes, mouth and nostrils. One of the policemen remarked 'Look, he is letting off sparks. Put it in his ear now'. The group of torturers were under the command of Captain Albernaz and consisted of about six men, amongst them sergeant Tomas, Mauricio, Chico and Paulinho.[171]

The 'dragon chair', was an electric chair, sometimes used in conjunction with a dentist's drill, while on the 'operating table' the victim was strapped to an iron table equipped with a device for stretching the body. Often, too, prisoners were terrorized still further by being made to watch the torture of relatives or friends before they themselves were treated in the same way. A Belgian priest, Father Jean Talpe, imprisoned for six months in 1969 and tortured, later recalled after being deported:

> the slightest suspicion and you are brought to the torture room . . . if the suspect cannot be located, members of their family are taken as hostages. The prisoner, whether suspect or hostage, is subjected to the most brutal torture. One of my friends, a university professor, was hung naked by the feet and was 'worked over' for two hours with baton blows and with electric shocks to the most sensitive parts of the body. A young girl, whom he did not know, was forced to watch the proceedings and later, in the presence of my friend, was treated in the same shameful manner. For weeks, my friend was forced to undergo torture of this kind. Another prisoner was interrogated whilst his wife was raped in front of his very eyes by one of his torturers. Often the victim is tortured to death.[172]

The use of torture as an instrument of terror and repression was not the result of growing guerrilla activity, since it antedated the appearance of guerrilla opposition: but it became more intense from 1968 onwards as a persistent feature of control. This increase was associated with the apparent growth of guerrilla activity, especially in 1969, which produced its most dramatic *coup* on 4 September 1969, with the kidnapping of the United States ambassador, C. Burke Elbrick. The seizure of the ambassador, with the demand for the release of fifteen political prisoners as a condition for his safe return, brought worldwide publicity to the armed opposition, but it had perhaps the more important effect of humiliating and infuriating the regime and members of the armed forces, and, most important of all, seems to have produced a drawing-together of ranks in the face of a common enemy. Those voices which had called for an early end to the exceptional form of government introduced by Institutional Act No. 5 were now silenced.

The temporarily restored unity of the armed forces was especially important in that the regime was now suffering a major crisis of leadership, which threatened to produce still further bitterness and struggle between contending groups, both military and civilian. Costa e Silva was anxious to introduce a new constitution, which was ready by late August, and to reopen Congress, still hoping to 'humanize' the regime and reconcile what seemed to be the incompatible aims of maintaining 'national security' while achieving a more open, less repressive system of government.[173] But this plan had strong, politically powerful critics, including most leaders of the armed forces, as the three military ministers made clear to Costa e Silva. The plan was particularly opposed by such influential figures within the regime as General Lyra Tavares and Admiral Rademaker,[174] and the opposition clearly ran deep, causing repeated rumours of plans to replace Costa e Silva by someone who would guarantee a much tougher line. The president himself was unwell, much upset by the letters from Moniz de Aragão,[175] and aware that he was becoming more isolated politically. He still intended, however, to introduce the new constitution on 8 September. But on 29 August Costa e Silva became seriously ill and it was announced that he had suffered a 'circulatory impediment'. His illness at once produced a major crisis. His place, according to the constitution, should have been taken by the vice president, Pedro Aleixo, a civilian, but after urgent discussions among the most senior military officers, it was decided that he should be passed over in favour of a Junta, composed of the military ministers.[176] The decision was taken by the High Command of the Armed Forces, made up of the three military ministers (Lyra Tavares, Márcio Melo, and Rademaker), the three Chiefs of General Staff of the army, navy, and air force (General Antônio Carlos Muricy, Brigadier Oliveira Sampaio, and Admiral Barros Nunes), and the Chief of General Staff of the Armed Forces (General Orlando Geisel). They also decided that the reopening of Congress and the announcement of the new constitution should be postponed. The decision of the High Command was not immediately acceptable to all senior officers, including General Sizeno Sarmento and General Afonso Albuquerque Lima,[177] but eventually they agreed to the Junta's temporary control and began serious manoeuvring for the presidential succession.

The setting-aside of the civilian vice president and the assumption of control by a markedly right-wing Junta amounted, in effect, to a further '*coup* within the *coup*', further postponing, and making more difficult, a return to constitutional government. It also meant that the armed forces had moved even further into taking direct control of government: more clearly than ever before they were seen, and perceived themselves, as masters of the country. The change also meant that the choice of president would be made entirely by the armed forces' leadership, requiring, in turn, that new procedures for this choice had to be found.

The armed forces were now, in effect, the only 'party of the revolution', so that the choice of the next military president had many of the features of the selection of a new party leader. What, however, was particularly interesting was the obviously felt need to take very wide soundings, consulting officers down to a more junior level than might have been expected, further evidence that, despite the temporary unity resulting from guerrilla opposition and the kidnapping of Ambassador Elbrick, the high command was aware of how deeply the divisions ran. The procedure decided upon was that all generals on active duty (118), admirals (6), and air-force general officers (61) should discuss the nature and direction of the revolution with their subordinate officers and sound opinion on the question of succession.[178] Each general of four-star rank would then make up a list of the three most favoured candidates in each command, which would be consolidated in a list for each service and, finally, in a list for the armed forces as a whole.

That this consultation, even down to battalion level, was not merely an internal public relations exercise on the part of the senior officers, was made clear by the liveliness and duration of the debate, lasting over one month and a half. There was intense political lobbying, with the issue of manifestos and counter-manifestos and growing evidence that 'the senior officers were barely able to carry the day and install their candidate in the presidency'.[179] The most prominent candidates among the four-star generals were soon seen to be Garrastazú Médici, Orlando Geisel, and Antônio Muricy, with the principal challenger obviously being Albuquerque Lima, who, despite being only a three-star general, had most support in the First, Second, and Third Armies. Not everyone, by any means, was happy with the process of consultation and choosing. The supporters of Albuquerque Lima wanted the consultation to be wider and reaching down to more junior ranks, and they believed that disproportionate weight was given to certain groups, such as the ESG.[180] Albuquerque Lima himself was anxious to reassure business interests, especially in São Paulo, that he was not a wild radical nationalist,[181] so indicating that while the formal, direct choice was made by the armed forces, other pressures from outside their ranks remained, as always, important. He was also being carried along by his supporters, angry at the process of selection. On 2 October he wrote to Lyra Tavares, expressing this disquiet and stressing:

> I should like to reaffirm my position within the Revolution, which in my view has not been realized, through the simple fact that it has not done what it could for the benefit of the Brazilian people within the principles of pure, and judicious, nationalism and in pursuit of development involving all Brazilians.[182]

Others, too, made strong protest, notably the ex-Navy Minister, Admiral Melo Batista, who deplored the impression which many had that the choice was being made too exclusively by the army, as the highest post in the military hierarchy, and by those who essentially were 'satisfied with the political, social, and economic[183] orientation of the present government'. But he stressed:

> Such arguments do not carry weight for those who are aware of the seriousness of the situation of the nation and who pause to

> consider it. The financial-economic crisis, the revolutionary war, the decapitalization of private initiative, the transfer abroad of our wealth, student dissatisfaction, the bitterness of the workers, the impoverishment of agriculture, the destruction of the political system.[184]

The admiral then asked whether this present government really should go on for another five years and a half, and suggested wider consultation, including with senior officers now in the reserve, such as Dutra, Denys, Pena Bôto, Sodré, Heck, Eduardo Gomes, and others.

Such a letter clearly sought to open up the most far-reaching debate about the regime's whole political, economic, and social strategy, a demand ever more loudly heard, but which threatened the already fragile unity of the armed forces and, in the view of senior officers, the whole chain of command. A few days after sending the letter Melo Batista had his answer, suspension from military activity for a year.[185] The infighting and mutual suspicion were now intense, but with evidence that Albuquerque Lima was backing off. He made a special point of reassuring General Médici that his objections were over procedure and were not directed at Médici personally.[186] It was estimated that Albuquerque Lima had overwhelming support in the navy, perhaps as much as 90 per cent of the opinion sounded, somewhat less in the army, and rather less again in the air force, but, in all, appearing as much the most popular candidate within the armed forces themselves. But the High Command of the Armed Forces was now deeply alarmed both at the strong support for more nationalist, reformist policies representing a break with post-1964 strategy, and at the threat of an open split within the armed forces. Consultation was stopped abruptly and it became known that the firm candidate of the most senior officers was Garrastazú Médici. He was an eminently safe choice, a four-star general, a friend of Costa e Silva, a former head of the SNI, and, most important, not linked to those who were urging a change of direction in national policy. Médici at first said he did not want the job,[187] but eventually he gave in to pressure.[188] On 14 October the presidency was formally declared vacant and Congress was called to meet again on 22 October with the presidential 'election' on 25 October. Seventy-six congressmen abstained, but 293 voted in favour of Garrastazú Médici and Rademaker, evidence of the degree to which the earlier purges of Congress had reduced its power to criticize or oppose decisions of the military high command.

The crisis and power struggle which for over a year had rocked the system established in 1964 was now at least temporarily settled as Garrastazú Médici took office.

Garrastazú Médici: the Logic of Authoritarian Capitalism

Reasserting Control

The whole of the presidency of Garrastazú Médici was, in effect, an anti-climax after the serious power struggle and choice of options in late 1968 and throughout 1969. The contradictions of authoritarian military control and the economic, social, and political priorities built into the system established in 1964 had now been clearly demonstrated. Costa e Silva himself had summed up the fundamental political issue in stressing the need for the regime, at some time or other, to walk on two legs, with popular as well as civilian support, but his failure to 'humanize' the regime and further sharp moves towards tighter controls had shown how difficult, perhaps impossible, was such a requirement in view of the basic social and economic priorities expressed in the 'Brazilian model', now directed by Delfim Neto, as previously by Roberto Campos. Campos, too, had stressed the need for a solid political base, without making clear how this could be achieved, but the experience of the Costa e Silva government now pointed more clearly to the organic, inescapable link between political repression, increased authoritarianism, and the intrinsic requirements of the current 'growth model' and its whole process of capital accumulation. Similarly, the reaction, both by the military high command and financial interests inside Brazil and abroad, to the more nationalist reformist demands of Albuquerque Lima and his supporters had shown the degree of dependence of the 'Brazilian model' on international capital and the degree to which international financial and business interests had penetrated not only Brazil's economy, but, more significantly, its whole social and political system. Not even substantial disenchantment and criticism from within the armed forces could now, it seemed, challenge the entrenched 'internationalized' interests which sustained the Brazilian economy in a greater degree of dependency than it had ever known in the past. The choice of Garrastazú Médici as president was in this respect, it must be emphasized, not just a recourse to a safe candidate to patch up threatened divisions in the armed forces. It represented a definitive victory for those who favoured, and needed, continuing, even intensified, authoritarianism to support this more internationalized and dependent capitalist system. The contradictions and tensions contained in this 'Brazilian model' would emerge again in time, especially when its economic performance began to falter from about 1973 onwards; but from 1969 to 1974 the Médici government essentially played out the logic of the choices made in 1964 and firmly reinforced in 1968 and 1969.

Just before he took office in October 1969 new measures further reinforced the authoritarian state. Amendment No. 1 to the constitution of 1967 was promulgated on 17 October. This further strengthened the powers of the federal government in relation to the states and significantly reduced the immunity and powers of Congress. Considerations of national security now took precedence over the rights of members of Congress, while the power of the executive to issue decree laws was strengthened. The government's power to deprive political opponents of political rights for ten years was now reinforced by much tougher provisions under a new Article 153, allowing for banishment, confiscation of property, and even the death penalty for 'intention to subvert the democratic regime or corruption'. At the same time the powers of the Superior Military Tribunal were extended and its military composition strengthened. Médici, therefore, came to office not only with a virtual mandate to maintain tight control, but with wider constitutional powers *vis-à-vis* Congress and civil society generally to allow the regime to impose its will.[189]

By comparison with his two predecessors Médici was relatively little known outside military circles. He had worked as Costa e Silva's Chief of Staff when Costa had commanded the 3rd Military Region, later became Commandant of the Military Academy of Agulhas Negras, then served as three-star general in the 3rd Military Region in Pôrto Alegre. Costa e Silva appointed him as head of the SNI, a post which was becoming increasingly important politically, then, after promotion to four-star general in 1969, to the command of the Third Army in Rio Grande do Sul. His career, in other words, like that of Costa e Silva, but in contrast to that of Médici's successor, Ernesto Geisel, had been entirely in military posts.

The team chosen by him mainly reflected an attempt to conciliate Castellista and Costista groupings, while acknowledging the power of the more right-wing elements in the armed forces and firmly excluding the nationalist officers associated with Albuquerque Lima. The post of vice president went to Admiral Rademaker, despite an initial show of reluctance on his part,[190] reflecting his important role in deciding the presidential succession. The Ministry of the Army went to Orlando Geisel, whose brother, in particular, had been close to Castello Branco. Delfim Neto continued as Minister of Finance, together with Antônio Dias Leite as Minister of Mines and Energy, while the other civilian ministers were mainly *técnicos*, the most notable for the future being João Paulo dos Reis Veloso, who as Minister of Planning for both Médici and his successor would provide an important element of continuity in the two governments. The Ministry of the Interior was still held by José Costa Cavalcanti, while Andreazza, despite recent criticism, stayed at the Ministry of Transport. The Ministry of Education was taken over by the energetic and dynamic former Minister of Labour, Jarbas Passarinho. Among military appointments the most notable were those of Lyra Tavares as Chief of the Civil Cabinet and of General João Batista de Oliveira Figueiredo as Chief of the Military Cabinet and Secretary-General of the National Security Council. The direction of the SNI stayed with General Carlos Alberto da Fontoura.

In general, while conspicuously excluding supporters of Albuquerque Lima, the stress in the new government was on essential continuity, as most clearly was to be seen in the crucial ministries of Finance and Planning. The primary emphasis was on the continuing need for cool technocratic planning, defusing the volatile situation of the last few months, and reassuring foreign observers that Brazil's growth was still going forward smoothly, in safe hands, untroubled by opposition or criticism either inside or outside Congress. The stress on centralized executive government and the general disparagement of Congress or other consultative bodies, was to be seen in a diagram of the federal administration drawn up in 1970 by the government's own Administrative Department of Civilian Personnel. The key bodies are above the ministries, in particular the Chief of Staff of the Armed Forces, the National Security Council, the SNI, and the High Command of the Armed Forces. There was no reference, however obliquely, to Congress, the model being highly elitist and closed, concentrating power at the top in relatively few hands, essentially those of the armed forces leaders.

Heightened Repression

Equally important as a means of reassuring foreign financial interests that all again was well in Brazil was the vigorous pursuit and harsh treatment of extra-Congressional opposition, especially the urban guerrillas. After the humiliation of the Elbrick affair the government was determined to show it was fully in command. Its greatest single triumph came on 4 November 1969, only days after Médici took office. The police in São Paulo ambushed Marighela and shot him dead, while also implicating in his discovery and killing two Dominican friars, so as to try to drive a wedge between guerrilla and church groups. The Dominicans were said to have revealed under torture a telephone number, that of the Dominican bookshop, Livraria Duas Cidades, which had been tapped, and which led to Marighela being trapped. Other kidnappings were still to come, notably the Japanese consul in São Paulo and the German and Swiss ambassadors, the order of the kidnappings following the ranking of those countries in investment in Brazil, but by now the level and intensity of the violence were too high for the guerrillas to match. Every success brought ever greater repression and reaction, severely weakening the guerrillas, and depriving them of important leaders, as with the killing in April 1970 of Juarez Guimarães de Brito, a leader of the ALN, and in October, in prison after his arrest, of Joaquim Câmara Ferreira, who had succeeded Marighela as leader of the ALN. Throughout 1970, for the whole first year of Médici's presidency, action against opposition, potential or real, was stepped up, with the arrest in October, for example, in São Paulo of 500 suspects, including most of the São Paulo branch of VAR-Palmares. In November just before the first anniversary of Marighela's death, the government launched a pre-emptive campaign, Operation Birdcage, with estimates of the number arrested ranging from five to ten thousand. The repression and torture became steadily worse and no one, however high his connections, could feel safe from the dangers of being caught up in it. In November a relative of Marshal Lott, the hightly respected defender of the 'constitutional' role of the army, was badly tortured. It was reported that Marshal Lott personally sought out and killed the officer responsible, and demanded a public trial to bring the whole issue out into the open. Instead the affair was hushed up: but it was widely discussed and everyone drew from it his own conclusions. The armed opposition still continued, winning, for example, the release of seventy political prisoners in exchange for the Swiss ambassador, Giovanni Bucher, in December 1970, but always there was swift reprisal, as in the police announcement on the day after the kidnapping of the deaths of three guerrillas, including a prominent former leader of VPR, now head of a splinter group, Eduardo Leite, 'Bacurí'. In January 1971 a labour leader and federal deputy, Rubens Paiva, was arrested, with his family, and reportedly died under torture. In April guerrillas killed a Scandinavian industrialist in São Paulo, Henning Albert Boilesen, because of his links with OBAN. Shortly afterwards an MRT leader, Devanir José de Carvalho, was shot dead in a battle with the police. The year brought one blow after another to the guerrilla opposition. On 18 April another MRT activist. Dimas Antônio Cassemiro, was killed. On 24 July, João Carlos dos Santos, leader of the group which captured the German ambassador, von Holleben, was arrested. On 5 August, José Raimundo Costa of VPR was shot to death, and, the hardest blow of all, as a result of information obtained under torture, Carlos Lamarca was tracked down and killed in Bahia. Although the armed resistance was to continue, Lamarca's death marked the end of the most active and challenging phase of guerrilla activity. Many of the leaders were dead, many guerrillas in prison, or forced to leave the country, their movements uncovered by the use of torture. There now came a period of reassessment of the pattern and priorities of opposition under a regime such as Brazil's. For the immediate future at least that opposition would take a different form. In the meantime the Médici government had achieved its aim of smashing effectively and quickly attempts at direct opposition to a regime which could outmatch in violence any opposition offered to it. The torture and terror were to be continued long after the main guerrilla threat was ended, just as, indeed, they had preceded and largely stimulated that opposition; but by late 1971 other means were already being sought to express protest and opposition to the regime.

Emasculated Congress

One vehicle generally considered ineffective by now was Congress, largely emasculated by *cassações* and the whole apparatus of repressive legislation, and all too obviously kept alive under the Médici government as an ever more exiguous democratic fig-leaf. The men who now ran the system made no secret of their scorn for and disparagement of civilian politicians and of their determination to nip in the bud any sign of genuine Congressional opposition, an attitude known and duly noted throughout the country. ARENA had been chastened in 1968 and 1969 and MDB, as well as being weakened by the removal of some of its most vigorous members, was divided over how it should behave in relation to the regime. After the blows of the last few months it moved cautiously, aware that it was already on a short lead. In the first relatively minor test of opinion, the municipal elections of November 1969, the position of the parties remained largely unchanged. In areas deemed important for 'national security', the most significant cities and state capitals, mayors were directly appointed by the government. Otherwise the elections followed a pattern already familiar and to be further reinforced in future, namely, of the more urban, industrial centres favouring MDB, while the *municípios* of the interior still reflected the clientelistic influences supporting ARENA.

In any case, as everyone well knew, elections, whether local or national, were no longer much of a guide to popular opinion or relative political strength. Médici's earliest pronouncements, notably his inaugural address of 30 October 1969, had been full of pious clichés about belief 'in the generous soul of youth, in my country and in my people . . . in development as a universal phenomenon'. 'I am a man of the Revolution. . . . I believe it will become more active and progressive'. But everyone knew that as a 'man of the Revolution' there was a *ne plus ultra* to the level of criticism or opposition he would allow.[191] This was expressed more clearly in Médici's speech of 10 March 1970, opening the academic session at the ESG, where he explained his concept of the 'revolutionary state', which would be maintained as long as should be necessary, implying that a return to democratic processes was an ideal which must be matched against harsh reality:

> The revolutionary state will last as long as it is necessary for the implantation of the political, administrative, legal, social and economic structures which can promote the integration of all Brazilians into a state of life that reaches at least the minimum levels of well-being.[192]

The social implications of such remarks, if they could be believed, were encouraging, as was the comment that the new president had come to 'the pungent conclusion that the economy may be getting along fine, but the majority of the people are still getting along badly'.[193] But Médici made clear that he would not give up the special powers stemming from Institutional Act No. 5, as he reiterated his belief that now had been begun:

> a new stage in our democratic evolution—which, while it is not yet perfectly defined, will mark the end of a political liberalism that is incompatible with the violent changes that are affecting the heart of our socio-economic structures.[194]

The same theme was sounded in his speech on the sixth anniversary of the *coup* of 1964, as in that of Orlando Geisel, contrasting the new democracy with the 'romantic democracy' of the past, a distinction sharpened by the concurrent *cassações* of eight distinguished scientists of the Oswaldo Cruz Institute, who, as the *Jornal do Brasil* scornfully commented, would 'shortly be in Harvard, Cambridge, or the Sorbonne and Brazil will have become poorer'.

Rather than on popular elections, more attention was focused on the presidential choice of new state governors, even though that choice had finally to be made by the existing state legislatures on 3 October. The choice was made in co-operation with the SNI, sixteen governors having been chosen 'more than four months before the scheduled ratification by ARENA majorities in state assemblies'.[195] The men designated were mainly remarkable for their proven administrative competence, being on the whole young technocrats, in line with the repeated emphasis on the need for able, technically competent professionals, though even the MDB nominees, as in the case of Guanabara, had to be sufficiently acceptable to the regime. The whole process of selection was, however, completely centralized in the hands of the executive, further clear evidence of how decisively power had shifted. Yet curiously, while exercising the most complete control of any president in Brazil's history, and leaving a record of presiding over the most repressive period of Brazilian politics yet experienced, Médici and his government shared unprecedented concern for improving the popular image of the regime, both nationally and internationally. This was in large measure an attempt at cosmetic surgery, a conscious response to mounting criticism, especially abroad, over the question of torture and of human rights generally, and over the social and political costs of the growth model. Partly it was an attempt to find the second leg which Costa e Silva had said was necessary, seeking to widen the basis of support for the regime and to produce a greater degree of legitimacy than so far had been possible. This concern was now especially seen in the attempt to reach a *rapprochement* with the Church, including with the Vatican. Colonel Miguel Pereira Manso Neto, now head of the president's special advisory staff, was sent to Rome to explain away the distorted image of the regime and in May 1970 top government ministers, notably the Minister of Justice, Alfredo Busaid, and the persuasive Minister of Education, Jarbas Passarinho, assisted by Colonel Manso Neto, carefully explained the government's position to the Eleventh General Assembly of the National Conference of Brazilian Bishops, meeting in Brasília. Their apologia was partly reflected in the bishops' subsequent statement.

The department mainly responsible for burnishing the regime's image was AERP (Assessoria Especial de Relações Públicas), headed by Colonel Otávio Costa. This was started in late 1969, producing results in 1970, particularly short films for television putting over a positive image of the regime, linked, as explained by the head of the Rio office, Professor Carlos Alberto Rabassa, to 'aspects of the daily life of the Brazilian which are dear to him, the family, work, carnival, football. . . .'[196] One such film was linked to a goal by Jairzinho in the 1970 World Cup in Mexico, with the slogan by now repeated *ad nauseam* by the government's public relations machine, 'Ninguém segura o Brasil' (No one can hold back Brazil). The form of the film was similar to advertisements for Shell, showing Pelé and Simonal: the goal was divided into nine parts, each linked to shots of present-day Brazil emphasizing its virtues and progress.

The World Cup in 1970 provided a golden opportunity for this public relations effort. Without undue prescience Médici had forecast a third Brazilian victory, so bringing the Jules Rimet trophy permanently to Brazil. In this he associated himself with the great national passion, the one national game, linking men of all social classes and acting as the most pervasive and most effective agent of national pride and identification. Brazil not only won the World Cup for the third time: they entirely dominated the competition, again raising the game to new heights. And at once the regime's public relations men worked to link soccer triumph with yet another element in which Brazil was everywhere acknowledged to be supreme, samba and pop music, especially as harnessed to preparations for the carnival of 1971, where Brazil's success in Mexico would again be celebrated riotously.[197] Already there was a tradition of sambas expressing social and political protest, despite in recent years the efforts by government censors to stop anything they understood to be subversive. Already in *Pedro Pedreiro*, Chico Buarque de Hollanda had told of Pedro:

> Waiting, waiting and hoping for the sun,
> for the train, for a rise next month,
> for the day he can return to the north,
> for a child who in turn will wait . . .

Others of his sambas, such as *Construção*, would take up similar themes. From their beginning in the *favelas* the sambas and carnival had been linked to social protest, not merely to themes of sun and sand and sex, though they, too, were always present. More recently *Opinião* had declared, and all Brazil sang and danced it for a while: 'They can take me. They can beat me. But I won't change my views'. And Gilberto Gil, on the place of carnival in contemporary Brazil, sang: 'The *bloco* of youth must come into the street, wait for what is to come—and take courage'.

Football had always had an important social and political dimension, explicitly used by populist politicians whose provision of football pitches was one sure way to win votes, and always showing those features of *panem et circenses*, as in many other societies, which served usefully, however pleasurably, to divert attention. For the regime now to link football success to samba rhythms was an evident ploy, seen, for example, in a record which had instant success, with on one side the *Marcha do Tostão* (*gool do jair*) and on the other a swinging, whistling *frevo—Pra frente Brasil*. The record opens with a breathless, unbelievably fast commentary from the World Cup, ending in the long delicious howl of 'Goal', followed by the 'march' by Nelson Castro and Alvaro Mattos. *Pra frente Brasil*, by Miguel Gustavo, incorporating yet another regime slogan—'Forward Brazil'—was soon endlessly repeated on television and radio and by military bands on ceremonial occasions. The association of football success and heroes such as Tostão (Eduardo Gonçalves de Andrade from Minas Gerais) with government propaganda slogans helped to spread throughout the country phrases and slogans often taken directly from United States campaigns—as in the case of 'Brazil, love it or leave it'. Sometimes these rebounded, with wags adding pert or obscene rejoinders, as the postscript to 'Brazil, love it or leave it', which read: 'And the last one to leave, please put out the lights'. Many cars carried these slogans throughout 1970 and 1971, though sometimes in modified form, such as 'No one can hold back my little banger'. The propaganda campaign was intense, and very expensive, using all established North American techniques to sell the regime, but to a population which, with typical humour and readiness to deflate the self-important, regularly turned aside the all too explicit and often condescending efforts to win its support.

But behind the campaigns and humour there was a serious and, since 1964, unprecedented effort to win more popular understanding and support, the winning smile behind the riot shield. The government was clearly worried by its image both at home and abroad, concerned at public protests in Europe and the inability of its ambassadors to speak about Brazil in European universities without having to face a barrage of well-informed perceptive questions about the nature of Brazil's current development model.[198] Responsible members of the regime knew full well that such questioning could not simply be attributed to ill-will or some kind of leftist conspiracy, since it came from diverse quarters and often from those most emotionally identified with and most sympathetic to Brazil and its people.

Particularly interesting in this intense propaganda campaign was the explicit attempt to win wider, more popular support lower down the social scale. The successful performance of the economy directed by Delfim Neto, meant that throughout the whole of Médici's presidency the regime could, broadly speaking, depend on the support of most middle-class groups, or at least their lack of opposition, since they so obviously stood to benefit from the 'miracle'. This was one strong reason, apart from terror and intimidation, for the relative lack of protest over torture and other abuses. Later, when the economy ran into difficulties, there would be more criticism from this quarter, but, even then, often merely contrasting high rates of inflation and falling or negative growth rates with the heady days of the Médici/Delfim era, despite the repression and political controls of the Médici period. The main thrust of the propaganda campaign was, then, at other groups, attempting essentially to convince them that policies and strategies which by most objective standards imposed the heaviest sacrifices on them, were in fact in their interest, that they too were moving 'pra frente'.

One immediate motive behind this effort was Médici's and his government's hope to transform ARENA into a party of government analogous to the PRI in Mexico, an instrument of control for the regime which could also exclude and swamp other attempts at popular mobilization, an institution to express and direct the 'revolutionary' ideals and aims as understood by the regime. This effort was to be maintained over the next few years, as seen, for example, in March 1972, when Médici instructed Senator Filinto Müller to become president of ARENA, to make of it an instrument more closely attuned to government requirements: but in 1970 there were other ends in view, especially the need to perform effectively in the scheduled Congressional and other elections in November. These were to be carried out under somewhat different rules, the number of deputies being cut from 409 to 310 and being determined by the number of voters, not by the size of the population in any given state. Every 100,000 voters would now be represented by 3 deputies, with an extra deputy for every further 100,000 up to 3 million, after which one deputy for every further 300,000 up to 6 million. In some respects this was rather a strange decision from the regime's point of view, in that it weakened the representation from more backward, more rural states in which a relatively large population, but with a high percentage of illiterates, resulted in relatively few voters electing an unduly large number of deputies. This had been designed originally to prevent the economically powerful states having disproportionate power, but had resulted in a Congress heavy with conservative members. Granted ARENA's relative advantage in rural areas still characterized by clientelistic voting patterns, the new ruling moved in favour of MDB, with its strength in more urban, more industrialized areas, especially in the centre-south. Some years later, in 1977, when the regime realized this situation, the rules were changed yet again, to restore the advantage to ARENA.

The electoral campaign was distinguished only by the apathy of both candidates and electors, with forecasts of large numbers of null and blank votes. These forecasts turned out to be more than correct, with the total of null and blank votes reaching a startling 50 per cent in many areas, mainly pointing to a deliberate rejection by the electorate of what commonly was seen as an empty farce. ARENA, predictably in such a rigorously controlled system, won more than 70 per cent of seats in the Chamber and 40 out of the 46 senate seats contested. ARENA now had 220 federal deputies, as against MDB's 90, and 59 senators, as compared to 7 for MDB. On the other hand, it was notable that, even though some of the most prominent MDB leaders lost their seats, including the party president, Oscar Passos, and vice presidents Ulysses Guimarães and Nogueira da Gama, they elected senators in São Paulo (Franco Montoro) and the state of Rio de Janeiro (Amaral Peixoto), and returned all three senators from Guanabara. In short, there appeared again the picture of MDB success in the more urban, dynamic areas which, most people believed, could be 'extended' much further, if only more people could be convinced that their vote really mattered in the overall scheme of national politics.[199]

Internationalism and New Initiatives

At the same time as elections were being held, Delfim Neto was chosen as the 'Man of Vision, 1970' by the periodical *Visão*, providing at the same time an explanation and apologia for government policy.[200] In his speech he emphasized the successes of 1970, the generally favourable performance of the economy, particularly the sharp rise in exports, especially industrial exports. He also defended government policies in relation to Amazonas and the north-east and underlined the overall theme of 'accelerated development with progressive internal stability, together with independence in relation to external decisions'.[201]

The roll call of those who joined most enthusiastically in the *homenagem* to Delfim was more illustrative of the real nature of the 'Brazilian model' than were the election results of November or Delfim's dutiful emphasis in finishing his speech of thanks that 'without social justice development is of no avail'. The audience was made up of senior government officials and above all of the representatives of foreign banks and companies and the whole 'internationalized' business world of São Paulo and Rio de Janeiro.[202] It was in these mutual congratulations and reinforcement that the real dynamic of the system was to be seen, just as its power was also demonstrated, at quite a different level, in the army promotions in late November. Albuquerque Lima was by now second in seniority among division generals, but he was deliberately and conspicuously passed over, with João Bina Machado and Humberto de Souza Mello being promoted to four-star generals over his head. This, again, was only part of the logic of the victory of the 'internationalist' camp a year before, but marked the end of Albuquerque Lima's serious political ambitions, at least for the forseeable future. The new promotions reinforced those of the previous July, as well as the results of the Clube Militar elections in May, all of which had marked the eclipse of more nationalist officers or other critics of the government.

While consolidating its position at this important level of military and intra-regime politics, the Médici government introduced various measures to demonstrate some limited commitment to redistribution, albeit indirect, and to defuse charges of altogether neglecting such priorities. An early move in this direction under the Costa e Silva government had been the creation of MOBRAL, the Brazilian Literacy Movement, headed by the able economist Mário Henrique Simonsen. The budget for 1970 was US$13 million and the stated aim was to provide basic literacy for about 4 million Brazilians in two years. The movement eventually penetrated every *município* in the country, an achievement of which Simonsen is justifiably proud, and, while many people questioned the value of providing only basic literacy, as well as asking about the nature of the material used, Simonsen spoke convincingly of the potential uses of his organization in such vitally necessary, though neglected, areas as social medicine and educational and agrarian extension courses, including birth-control programmes.

During 1970 much publicity was given to the creation of PIS, the Social Integration Programme, started in September.[203] This claimed to give workers a share in the product of industry, primarily, it was planned, through a 'participation fund' controlled by the National Savings Fund, to which over one million firms were supposed to contribute. The contributions were of two kinds, one based on the volume of profits tax, the other calculated on the gross turnover achieved. The scheme was intended to operate as a sort of mutual investment fund, with the money being distributed to workers with the amount calculated in relation to their wages and number of years worked. Members of the fund were said by 1971 to number over 13 million and were able, according to the scheme, to withdraw yearly profit and even the capital itself under certain conditions.

Another initiative was PIN (National Integration Scheme), first announced in June 1970 and starting in September. This aimed at the 'integration' of Amazonas, an idea previously urged by Albuquerque Lima and now adopted by Médici. The overall plan was to open up Amazonas to settlement and development, moving colonists from the overpopulated north-east and giving stimulus to industrial and commercial development in Amazonas, part of which involved declaring Manaus a 'free zone'. The plan hinged, in particular, on the building of two great roads, the Transamazonica, to be about 3,200 miles long, running from the coast westward to link with the road-system of Peru; the other cutting at right-angles from Cuiabá in Matto Grosso to Santarém on the Amazon. There would also be spur roads to Boa Vista near Guyana and Venezuela.[204]

The administration claimed that the Amazonas programme was an 'adventure', the phrase used by Delfim Neto, that it would incorporate this vast territory within the national economy, allowing the exploitation of its resources and the settlement of new populations, especially in the new towns to be built along the roads. It claimed to have paid sufficient attention to issues of ecology, both in terms of the possible destruction of the rain forest and of the Indian population of the region.[205] Unfortunately, these claims have not been proved valid. The main exploitation has been of the colonists persuaded to move to Amazonas and of the indigenous population. The project has allowed the entry into the region of multinational consortia, in line with the overall pattern of the 'Brazilian model',[206] groups such as Liquigas, Volkswagen, and Swift-Armour. It has also greatly helped the operations of individual entrepreneurs, such as D. K. Ludwig, a United States citizen of Austrian descent, whose projects by the River Jari in Amapá cover at least one to 2 million hectares,[207] or Donval Kniphoff, whose timber enterprise between the Rivers Juría and Bió on the south of the Amazon covers one million hectares. But there is little evidence that the scheme will to any notable degree help to solve the problems of the north-east by transferring population, or that the enormously expensive roads are producing the stimulus to the regional and national economy which was expected.

A similar judgement seems required about another much-heralded project launched in May 1971, PRORURAL, the Rural Workers' Aid Programme, the stated aim of which was to bring workers in the agrarian sector within the net of social security. This was meant to complement a revived effort to produce some effective agrarian reform, as expressed in INCRA (National Institute for Colonization and Agrarian Reform), which in July 1970 incorporated all organizations previously dealing with such matters: mainly IBRA, INDA, and GERA. In turn, these new initiatives were meant to support a further plan, introduced in July 1971, PROTERRA (Programme for the Redistribution of Land and the Stimulus of Agroindustry in the North and North-east). This whole network of programmes was offered as an attempt to tackle the massive problems of rural poverty and to give major stimulus to the hitherto woefully neglected agrarian sector, the production of which did indeed increase in 1971 by 12·2 per cent as compared with 5·6 per cent in 1970. Unfortunately, there was no real will to carry through effective, far-reaching agrarian reform, every hint of which in Brazil had always produced the most ferocious resistance from landowners. Vargas had not even attempted it. Goulart had spoken of it, and even this had proved to be one of the major causes of his downfall. The new military regime certainly had power enough to push through a full-scale agrarian reform, should it wish to do so, since it had already shown how it could move against any interests or opposition it chose to challenge. But the will was not there. What was envisaged, rather, was a rationalization of the agrarian sector similar to that which had occurred in industry. The net result of the new schemes was to do little or nothing for the peasantry and rural workers, but to allow easier entry to the rural sector for certain groups within the Brazilian bourgeoisie and, above all, the powerful multinational companies which now had further means of penetrating Brazil's economy and society.

Médici and the Miracle

At various points during their term as presidents Castello Branco and Costa e Silva had been in danger of being removed from office by a further *coup* within the *coup*, mainly stemming from more 'hard line' right-wing elements. After 1974 President Ernesto Geisel was to face the same possibility, again from more extreme right-wingers unhappy about both his political and economic strategy. There is, by contrast, no evidence that Garrastazú Médici was ever threatened in this way, the reason being simply that he was the right wing in power, the man of the 'internationalized' bourgeoisie, carrying through policies favourable to the multinationals and to those sections of the Brazilian bourgeoisie most closely associated with them. He came to power as a result of a serious power struggle, mainly on the issue of 'nationalism' versus 'internationalism' and of less rigorous versus more severe control. His 'election', though conciliating in part supporters of Castello Branco and Costa e Silva, was above all a victory for Delfim Neto and the 'miracle', for a strategy which, while it might talk of tighter controls in dealing with foreign interests, as Delfim did at his *homenagem*, in reality geared Brazil's economy intimately, and in a relation of increased dependency, to the international capitalist system. His presidency was the most repressive in Brazil's history, marred by the worst excesses of torture and abuse of human rights, yet it was the period when Brazil basked most warmly in the sun of international financial and business approval as a 'stable' system safe for investment, providing sure profits in its fast-expanding, efficiently run economy. Médici's presidency was also the heyday of the middle classes and the richer members of Brazilian society, with the fruits of the economy channelled to them, providing in the early 1970s an unprecedented standard of living for those of middle-class status and above.

The Médici regime was in full control of a state geared to the needs of the 'Brazilian model', with the president able in March 1972 effectively to forbid the opening of the debate on the presidential succession: 'Only in the second half of the year will the parties be called upon to express their opinions as to the presidential succession'.[208] The date he fixed was 1 July 1973, allowing fifteen days for candidates to give up any official posts they might then hold. Just as easily he could suddenly announce to Congress on 3 April 1972 that he had just enacted Constitutional Act No. 2, changing Article 13, Chapter 9, Paragraph 2 of the constitution. As a result, the direct election for state governors scheduled for October 1974 would no longer take place. Instead, the elections would be indirect. There were only feeble protests from MDB, reflecting the acknowledged impotence of the licensed opposition, which prompted remarks such as that when the government issued an order ARENA answered 'Yes'; MDB answered 'Yes, sir'. Some members of MDB believed it would be more honest to dissolve the party altogether and end the farce: others thought that even a limited, tightly circumscribed opposition was better than none. The only opposition voice was that of the Church, protesting at the abuse of human rights and the social priorities of the growth model;[209] but the regime simply continued to send out its apologists to explain away such criticism, attributing it to malice or deliberate misunderstanding on the part of the critics. Growing inequalities, mounting repression, a soaring foreign debt were all explained away. In his final presidential *Mensagem*, before handing over to Ernesto Geisel, Médici was able to look back with pride and complacency:

> In the period of government now coming to an end we have followed, in the financial and economic sphere, those guidelines laid down from the beginning by the March Revolution, the fundamental objective of which consists in accelerating the growth of the economy. Conducted with objectivity and firmness, this policy soon managed to transform the economic shape of the country, whose prosperity between 1969 and 1973 reached the highest levels of our history.[210]

There might already be evidence of difficulties and crises ahead, but with the help of repression and the persistent use of state power to silence or exclude their critics, Médici and Delfim Neto had achieved what they wished. Now, as they left office in March 1974, the contradictions of the 'Brazilian model' would emerge more clearly, partly exacerbated by external factors, such as the price of oil, but also made more apparent by the refusal of Médici's successor to condone the patterns of government or the level of repression of the Médici years.

Notes

1 The best discussion of this growing sense of crisis and the rising fears among the military concerning their own interests and the whole direction of national politics is Stepan, *The Military in Politics*, 134–87.
2 ibid., 224–5.
3 Much the best analysis is, again, in ibid., especially 30–56, 229–52.
4 ibid., 39 notes that in 1964–66, 223 out of 557 cadets entering the academy, 40 per cent, came from Guanabara. But a very important factor here is that many were the sons of military officers stationed or living there, Guanabara being an important military centre.
5 ibid., 33–4.
6 ibid., 37.
7 In the earlier period young men from São Paulo also had, it should be remembered, better career opportunities in the state militia, the Força Pública, than in the federal army. Stepan notes that in 1935 out of 36 generals on active duty none came from São Paulo and in 1964, of the 89 line generals on active duty whose birthplace is known (out of a total of 102), only 3 came from São Paulo, all relatively junior in ranking. For 1935 he uses the military almanaque, before which the almanaques did not list birthplace. He mentions that the 1935 figure may reflect changes after the 1932 São Paulo revolt, but he could have noted how the *tenentes* over a decade earlier found it difficult to find *paulista* officers.
8 ibid., 40–1.
9 ibid. The importance of these schools, acting as 'minor seminaries' for the military academy, has not been studied sufficiently, but the sons of military personnel receive free teaching, while those of civilians can only take up extra places which may be left, and then have to pay. Stepan also stresses the importance of curricula in these colleges, more geared to the entrance demands of the military academy than those of most secondary schools.
10 ibid., 50–1.
11 ibid., 237–42. Stepan carefully put together a 'core group' of 10 generals, those most closely identified with the policies of Castello Branco, out of the 102 active-duty line generals listed in the officers' register for 1964, then compared their training and career experience with that of the other 92 and with the group of 20 pro-Goulart generals purged after the *coup*.
12 ibid., 239–42.
13 ibid., 239–42.
14 Stepan quotes, among others, Roberto Campos in support of the view that the FEB experience, in particular, shaped the style of government under Castello Branco, stressing the emphasis on organization, the need for technology, and the avoidance of demagoguery, especially in the guise of nationalism.
15 Stepan also argues that the ESG strengthened a more sympathetic attitude towards the private sector than is commonly found among the Brazilian and Latin American military more generally, an attitude again reinforced by experience in the United States. 'To my knowledge, this institutionalized relationship between the military and the private sector is unique in Latin America. The fear shared by the military and the private sector of what they felt was the growth of a Communist threat in Brazil from the late 1950s until the 1964 revolution also served to strengthen this relationship'; ibid., 246.
16 ibid., 239–42.

17 For very interesting analysis of the perceptions of industrialists see Luciano Martins, *Industrialização, Burguesia Nacional, e Desenvolvimento* (Rio de Janeiro, 1968). For the businessman's sense of less control over policy see the useful discussion of associated interest group politics in Schmitter, op. cit.,

18 The vice president of the Clube Militar, elected in 1948, General Leitão de Carvalho, joined a group of retired generals to form the Centre for the Defence of Petroleum and the National Economy (CEDEPEN), opening up debate in the Club on the whole question of oil and nationalism, a debate largely led by General Júlio Caetano Horta Barbosa, formerly head of the National Petroleum Council, and General Juarez Távora. Horta Barbosa, supported by generals such as Leitão de Carvalho, Raimundo Sampaio, and Felicíssimo Cardoso, strongly opposed control by foreign oil companies, an opposition shared by officers who were often at odds on other political issues.

19 One of the best accounts of these disputes is in Sodré, *História Militar do Brasil*. Discussing the role of Juarez Távora, who now believed Brazilian oil development should be seen in a continental context, he quotes Távora's *O Problema Brasileiro do Petróleo. Ensaio de Solução Objetiva* (Rio de Janeiro, 1948), where the author sees such a continental oil policy as a 'reinforcement of continental security' and a defence against 'the Communist menace'; Sodré, op. cit., 308, note 447.

20 Vargas, speech of 31 December 1951, quoted in Sodré, op. cit., 321–2. The nature of Vargas's nationalism and populism has been discussed above. For a much more recent account of how the large oil companies shape national and international politics see Anthony Sampson, *The Seven Sisters. The Great Oil Companies and the World They Made* (London, 1975).

21 Skidmore, op. cit., makes a similar point when discussing the defeat of Estillac Leal in 1952. He speaks of a centre group of officers 'sympathetic to the need for a national (although not necessarily "nationalist") effort towards economic development', who were mainly concerned with preserving military unity and not 'unleashing political forces that might become uncontrollable'. But 'The defeat of Estillac Leal in May 1952 had not been an unqualified victory of the conservative faction over the nationalists'. Elsewhere Skidmore tends to make too sharp a distinction between 'the left-wing nationalist and the anti-Communist camps' (126), obscuring the fact that there were right-wing nationalists whose vote in 1952 and later was against 'subversion' rather than nationalism.

22 Sodré, op. cit., 370–1.

23 Stepan, op. cit., 45.

24 This research is now being undertaken by P. Flynn and R. Dreifuss in an SSRC supported research project: *Brazil: the State, the Armed Forces and Policy Formation: 1955–76*.

25 Stepan, op. cit., 255.

26 ibid., 257.

27 ibid., 250.

28 ibid.

29 The most readily available study in English of Brazilian nationalism, E. Bradford Burns, *Nationalism in Brazil: A Historical Survey* (New York, 1968), fails, unfortunately, to give sufficient weight to this right-wing authoritarian nationalist tradition. He briefly mentions Alberto Torres and the nationalism of the Integralists, but in the more recent period does less than justice to nationalism in the armed forces. He posits too sharp a dichotomy between 'nationalists' and the armed forces, though he mentions

a survey in 1966 in which a poll among the military showed 47 per cent declaring themselves as unreservedly nationalist (p. 118) and he notes the encouragement felt by nationalists at the succession of Costa e Silva. But he does much less than justice to right-wing nationalism.

30 Stepan, op. cit., 251.

31 ibid. Also Stacchini, op. cit., 252.

32 Stepan, op. cit., 256–7. Stepan also notes (ibid.) how one result of the crisis was a further loss of civilian support for the regime. He quotes a poll taken by the normally pro-government *Jornal do Brasil* at the time of the indirect election of Costa e Silva, which asked how people would vote in a *direct* election for president. Only 12 per cent said they would vote for Costa e Silva, while 71 per cent would have voted for either Kubitschek or Lacerda, the government's severest critics.

33 See his interview in *Visão* (12 August 1966), 12–13.

34 See, for example, the views of Senator Carvalho Pinto, recommending four parties, *Visão* (9 December 1966), 12–13.

35 The most succinct analysis of the Costa e Silva government is in Schneider, op. cit., 204–11.

36 Schneider, ibid., 210–11 makes this important point. He notes, for example, how two men passed over for appointment to full general in late 1966 were Sizeno Sarmento, a close associate of Costa e Silva, a leading figure in the 'Democratic Crusade' in 1951–52, and a former Secretary of Security of Lacerda. So, too, was Carlos Luís Guedes, a hard-liner in 1964, who now also failed to get his fourth star. Schneider stresses the general disparagement of Lacerdistas and 'hard-liners' in late 1966, and its importance for the future, as, for example, in the fact that the new full generals would mostly stay on active duty till the end of 1970, when more senior major-generals would then take precedence over the nine men now made major-general: '. . . Among these "junior" three-star generals, João Dutra de Castilho, João Bina Machado, Newton Fontoura de Oliveira Reis, Nogueira Paes, and Itiberê Gouvêa do Amaral would bear watching in the events of late 1968 and 1969'.

37 ibid., 211. Schneider explains how Sizeno Sarmento was made full general in late March 1967 by Costa e Silva, when he also advanced three officers from brigadier to major-general, but 'the opportunity for promotions on a large scale was denied him by the recent nature of advancement to the top grades within the Army'.

38 Stepan, op. cit., 264. He also notes that one reason for the choice of Garrastazú Médici to succeed Costa e Silva was that 'he was not a radical nationalist and was thus acceptable to the São Paulo and international community, which had expressed worry lest a Peruvian route be followed if nationalist candidate Lt. Gen. Affonso Albuquerque Lima were to become president'.

39 For discussion of the move towards less protectionist policies especially through changes in tariffs, under Campos, see Joel Bergsman, *Brazil: Industrialization and Trade Policies* (London, 1970). Some of the vigorous reaction to these policies from the left of the political spectrum can be seen in Fernando Gasparian, later owner and editor of *Opinião*, in *Em defesa da economia nacional* (Rio de Janeiro, 1966). For changes in economic policy generally throughout the 1960s see: Baer and Kerstenetsky, op. cit., 105–45 and, for sharply critical analysis of the assumptions on which stabilization policies were based in 1964, of the costs entailed, and, particularly, the changes in 1967, see Albert Fishlow, 'Some Reflections on Economic Policy', in Stepan (ed.), *Authoritarian Brazil*.

40 Samuel A. Morley, 'Inflation and Stagnation in Brazil', *Economic Development and Cultural Change*, 19 (2 January 1971), 184–203.

41 Fishlow, op. cit., 73: 'To understand fully the post-1967 heterodoxy, one must first appreciate the thrust of the orthodox model as applied between 1964 and 1967 . . .'

42 ibid., 72.

43 Fishlow (ibid., 78) speaks of the period from early 1966 to mid-1967 as 'one of substantial decline of industrial production. . . . Orthodoxy can apparently ultimately prevail, but only at the expense of serious reductions in economic activity . . .'

44 Thomas E. Skidmore, 'Politics and Economic Policy Making in Authoritarian Brazil, 1937–71' in Stepan, *Authoritarian Brazil*, 12. Skidmore's essay emphasizes some of the persistent themes and recurring patterns of Brazilian politics, and, perhaps because he takes a longer view, or because he more firmly stresses the political dimension of economic policy, notes the underlying continuity of aims between the Campos and Delfim Neto teams. Fishlow, by contrast, tends as an economist to lay more stress on the different economic techniques and tactics of the two government teams.

45 Fishlow, in effect, makes a similar point in discussing (op. cit., 80) 'the true priorities of the government': 'It was committed to the establishment of a functioning free market system in Brazil, perhaps even more than to the struggle against inflation. This larger objective helps to explain the apparent inconsistency of the government's policy of extensive monetary correction which necessarily reinforced inflationary forces. Even during the Castello Branco period, the principal aim was not stabilization; it was making market capitalism work. In the long run these goals were viewed as mutually compatible, indeed as indispensably linked; in the short run they might conflict—to the consistent disadvantage of stabilization'.

46 These points are well developed in Skidmore, 'Politics and Economic Policy Making'. See, too, Flynn, 'The Brazilian Development Model'.

47 See *Programa de ação econômica do govêrno, 1964–1966*, Ministério de Planejamento e Coordenação Econômica (Rio de Janeiro, 1964), 80–6.

48 Kahil, op. cit.; Fishlow, op. cit., 84–97. He notes how economists like Eugênio Gudin, whose earlier views strongly influenced policy on wage controls, later had to accept evidence that those views had been exaggerated, often through political prejudice.

49 ibid., 85.

50 ibid. See, too, Skidmore, 'Politics and Economic Policy Making', 20: 'Most unpopular, not surprisingly, was the deliberate policy of letting wage increases lag behind increases in the cost of living . . . Given the "political cover" of a military regime, the technocrats were able to carry out a stabilization policy that weighed most heavily on one social sector—the working class'.

51 ibid., 93.

52 Fishlow, op. cit., 94–5.

53 ibid. My italics. Fishlow also shows that the decline within the non-agricultural sector was not accompanied by a larger share to agricultural wages (94–5). Also on income distribution see Fishlow's earlier article: 'Brazilian Size Distribution of Income', *American Economic Review* (May 1972), and his paper in what is the most comprehensive collection of essays on the question: Ricardo Tolipan and Arthur Carlos Tinelli (eds.), *A Controvérsia sobre Distribuição de Renda e Desenvolvimento* (Rio de Janeiro, 1975). The analysis in this collection is highly critical of the government's record. For views much more sympathetic to the regime see Carlos Geraldo Langoni, *Distribuição da Renda e Desenvolvimento Econômico do Brasil* (Rio de

Janeiro, 1973), which has a preface by Delfim Neto. See, too, the more popular, but lively, study of Fausto Cupertino, *A Concentração da Renda no Brasil. O bolo está mal dividido* (Rio de Janeiro, 1976).

54 See, in particular, the article by John Wells in Tolipan and Tinelli, op. cit., especially Table I, showing the average real wages of industrial workers, deflated according to the cost of living index in Guanabara, from 1959 to 1970, set aside the rates of productivity of industrial workers. Taking 1959 as 100, the relevant figures are:

	Wages	*Productivity of Work Force*
59	= 100	100
60	—	—
61	—	—
62	104	111
63	123	122
64	119	124
65	107	120
66	111	127
67	111	135
68	116	144
69	124	150
70	126	163

See, too, John Wells, *Distribution of Earnings, Growth and Structure of Demand in Brazil, 1959–1971*. University of Cambridge, Centre of Latin American Studies, Working Paper No. 11 (1973).

55 Philippe C. Schmitter, 'The Portugalization of Brazil?' in Stepan, *Authoritarian Brazil*, 200–2.

56 See Albert Fishlow, 'Brazil's Economic Miracle', in *The World Today*, vol. 29, No. 11 (November 1973). He notes: 'About a third of the Brazilian population is to be found in families unable to attain the equivalent of the minimum wage in the north-east—less than £200 for a family of five. Yet the actual resource transfer required to bring all Brazilian families up to a minimum poverty standard is of the order of 6 per cent of the income of those above the line.'

57 Schmitter in Stepan, *Authoritarian Brazil*, 203, Table 6.7: 'Regional Distribution of Gross Domestic Income, 1939–68'. See, too, Table 66: 'Social Classes, Income Groups, and the Distribution of Wealth, 1960–1970'. This confirms the findings of other scholars, showing that between 1960 and 1970 the real income of the bottom 5 per cent of the working population went up by 1 per cent, while that of the top 5 per cent went up by 72 per cent.

58 ibid., 204.

59 See, for example, the data on federal government spending by selected ministries during 1955–69 in Schmitter's Table 6.4 in ibid., 195–6. In 1955 the Ministry of Health spent 4·1 per cent of federal expenditure; in 1970 1·1 per cent. See, too, the evidence for declining consumption of meat and sugar among the poorer sections of the population; ibid., 201; '. . . families were compelled to spend more proportionately on merely staying alive. Like Alice, they were running harder simply to stay in the same place . . .'; ibid., 203. On education see particularly José Serra, 'A Reconcentração da Renda: Justificações, Explicações, Dúvidas', in Tolipan and Tinelli, op. cit., 263–88.

60 *Infant mortality per 1,000 live births moved in the municipality of São Paulo as follows:* *In Greater São Paulo, excluding São Paulo city, it went:*

1940	123·99	1940	227·24
1950	89·71	1950	147·88
1960	62·94	1960	72·73
1961	60·21	1961	64·79
1962	64·42	1962	67·21
1963	69·80	1963	67·72
1964	67·75	1964	59·51
1965	69·38	1965	66·46
1966	73·80	1966	74·50
1967	74·39	1967	77·10
1968	76·61	1968	74·44
1969	84·34	1969	88·49
1970	88·35	1970	99·12

See Lúcio Kowarick, *The Logic of Disorder. Capitalist Expansion in the Metropolitan Area of Greater São Paulo* (São Paulo, 1976), Table 8.

61 On this issue of indirect distribution, especially through education, see the arguments of Langoni, especially a paper given in London in July 1973 at a conference where, among others, Langoni and Dr Mário Henrique Simonsen, then director of MOBRAL (Brazilian Literacy Movement), defended the regime's record on distribution. The regime by then had accepted that the debate on distribution could not be stifled, so sent abroad apologists, especially to audiences of bankers and businessmen. See especially Langoni's paper 'The Brazilian Alternative—Either to Distribute Income or to Distribute Opportunities'. This reflected a common line of argument of some Chicago economists, Langoni having written his Ph.D. thesis in Chicago in 1970.

62 Flynn, 'The Brazilian Development Model'.

63 Delfim Neto in his introduction to Langoni, op. cit. Delfim continued by asserting that Langoni had shown that the relative behaviour of prices reflected, first and foremost, the intense differentiation within the labour force caused by the rapid expansion of the modern sectors, within which, he argued, a highly productive workforce received relatively high wages. Within this context, therefore, it was meaningless to use this growing inequality as an indicator of worsening welfare. Rather, Langoni had shown that rapid growth was the most powerful means of 'redistributing opportunities'. But, of course, those who criticized the regime's record on growing inequality did not claim that money wages were the only, still less the perfect, criterion. They claimed it as a significant one, but always pointed to other indicators, too, including educational opportunity, where they also rejected Langoni's arguments on the role played by education in present-day Brazilian society.

64 For a brief note on taxation see Schmitter in Stepan, *Authoritarian Brazil*, 193–4. He quotes Andrea Maneschi from R. Roett (ed.), *Brazil in the Sixties*, where, writing on the public sector, Maneschi shows that total taxes as percentage of GDP went up from 15·8 in 1955, 17·8 in 1962, 19·4 in 1964, to 26·7 in 1968. Schmitter acknowledges the very sharp rise in income tax revenue (by as much as 70 per cent in 1968 alone), and the importance of making *all* Brazilians register. But he also stresses the regressive nature of the tax system. 'The highly touted "squeezing" of the rich must be placed in context—the poor have been squeezed even harder'.

65 ibid., 203–4.

66 See Albert O. Hirschman, 'Industrial Development in the Brazilian North-East and the Tax Credit Scheme of Article 34/18', *Journal of Development Studies*, vol. 5 (October 1968). Also David E. Goodman, 'Industrial Development in the Brazilian Northeast: An Interim Assessment of the Tax Credit Scheme of Article 34/18' in R. Roett (ed.), op. cit., 231–72.

67 Antônio Delfim Neto, *Planejamento para o Desenvolvimento Econômico* (São Paulo, 1966), 14. The book was published with the collaboration of the University of São Paulo, the rector of which at the time was Professor Luís Antônio da Gama e Silva, who in 1967 was to be Minister of Justice in the same government as Delfim.

68 ibid., 11.

69 ibid., 12.

70 ibid., 13–14. Italics in the original text of Delfim.

71 Mário Henrique Simonsen, 'The Brazilian Model for Development', a paper given in the London conference of July 1973 (above, note 61).

72 ibid.

73 ibid., 7.

74 ibid., 8. It is interesting that almost two years later, on 3 March 1975, now Minister of Finance, Simonsen was still willing to stress this same point in almost identical words, again to a conference made up mostly of bankers and businessmen, in a paper entitled 'Current Aspects of the Brazilian Economy': 'Our wage policy is used today for the calculation of all adjustments in collective bargaining. . . . The importance of this formula within the present Brazilian development model should be particularly stressed. In the first place, it serves to simplify and detraumatise collective bargaining for salary adjustments: these are no longer decided on the basis of strikes and pressures but rather by a simple and rapid mathematical calculation'. On neither occasion did Simonsen question the cost to the political process of unilateral decisions affecting workers' wages, or the wisdom of excluding strikes or 'pressures'. The language throughout was that of the technocrat, and banker, safely installed in power, planning from above.

75 For the relation between distribution and growth see especially Samuel A. Morley and Gordon W. Smith, 'The Effect of Changes in the Distribution of Income on Labor, Foreign Investment, and Growth in Brazil', in Stepan, *Authoritarian Brazil*, 119–41. Also their 'Import Substitution and Foreign Investment in Brazil', *Oxford Economic Papers*, 23 (March 1971), 120–35. One of the most coherent arguments linking regressive distribution and growth is that of Nicholas Georgescu-Roegen, 'Structural Inflation—Lock and Balanced Growth', *Economie et Sociétés, Cahier de L'I.S.E.A.*, 4, No. 3 (March 1970). Morley and Smith (120) present this hypothesis as follows: '. . . the pattern of growth through import substitution has led to an industrial structure producing goods for the rich. Any equalization in the distribution of income would lead to underutilization of capacity in luxury goods industry and consequently a low rate of industrial growth. According to this argument, since the regime is basing its claim for support on its ability to guarantee a high rate of growth, it is forced to follow an income distribution policy favoring the rich'. Their findings support this view, ibid., 129.

76 Simonsen, op. cit., 1–2.

77 ibid., 2.

78 ibid., 8–9. Simonsen notes, when discussing the trade deficit of $4·5 million: 'The increase in oil prices justified a deficit of 2 billion dollars, but the additional 2·5 billion dollars can be classified in the I.M.F. language as non-oil deficit'.

79 Morley and Smith, 'Import Substitution and Foreign Investment'. See, too, their discussion of foreign investment in Stepan, *Authoritarian Brazil*, 133–7.

80 John A. Wells, 'Industrialisation and Foreign Capital', in *Foreign Investment in Brazil: The Political Climate, Focus Research* (London, 1976), 14–22.

81 ibid., 15. See also Albert Fishlow, 'Foreign Capital and the Economy', in *Investment in Brazil: The Political Climate, Focus Research* (London, 1972), 15–27. He notes that 'Capital is entering as supplier's credits and loans to banks to be reloaned to domestic borrowers. Direct foreign investment has been notably limited as a vehicle for resource transference' (19).

82 ibid., 16, quoting *Visão: Quem é Quem* (31 August 1975).

83 See Fernando Henrique Cardoso, 'Associated-Dependent Development: Theoretical and Practical Implications', in Stepan, *Authoritarian Brazil*, 144–6. See especially his Table 5.2, on Source of Capital for the Ten Largest Firms in Each Economic Sector in Brazil, 1968. In the capital goods sector foreign capital accounts for 72·6 per cent; in durable consumer goods 78·3 per cent; and in non-durable consumer goods 53·4 per cent. Cardoso also lists the twelve major advertisers.

84 Fishlow, 'Foreign Capital and the Economy', 19, discusses the growth of capital inflow from $625 million in 1968 to $1·3 billion in just the first six months of 1972. He points out that not all this inflow was to finance the current account deficit, since much went to augment reserves: 'Thus the government seems to be willing to accept more capital than is actually required to supplement domestic savings requirements. The logic of such a policy is intimately related to the strategy as a whole. It rests on the desirability of cultivating ties on the international capital market. Brazil, now attracting funds from abroad on its own at favourable interest rates, is creating conditions of future access that can be subsequently relied on'.

85 Wells, 'Industrialisation and Foreign Capital', 16. He also notes: 'In recent years, with the rapid expansion of the world economy, such internationalization has gone a stage further with foreign enterprises investing in Brazil with the aim of exporting their output back to the markets of the advanced countries. While it is true that local capitalist groups have successfully exported traditional manufactured products, the penetration of the markets of the advanced countries by technologically more sophisticated products has been one of the important "contributions" made by foreign capital'.

86 Quoted Schneider, op. cit., 220–1.

87 See his articles in *O Globo*. Schneider notes (op. cit., 221) how Aragão was forbidden to continue these attacks by General Orlando Geisel, Army Chief of Staff, because the affair was attracting too much attention to the *Frente Ampla*.

88 See the article in *Visão* (7 April 1967), 12–14, 'A saida? Onde fica a saida da "frente"?'. This emphasizes the dominant role of Lacerda and the reservations of others, notably Kubitschek and PTB leaders, such as Yvete Vargas. It also notes the growing tension between Lacerda and members of the new government who previously were so close to him, such as Costa Cavalcanti, Albuquerque Lima, Hélio Beltrão, and Sizeno Sarmento.

89 There was speculation earlier that Lacerda might use the *Frente* to offer an alternative form of support to Costa e Silva. See *Visão* (19 May 1967), 14, 'O que traz a frente de volta'.

90 The Minister of Labour, Jarbas Passarinho, wanted an easing of wages policy, but was overruled by Delfim Neto. See *Visão* (12 May 1967), 'Trabalhador une Govêrno e oposição', 12–13, which also discusses Passarinho's views with regard to the restoration of a more genuinely independent trade

union movement. Also *Visão* (12 October 1967), 12–13, 'O salario das divergências'.

91 See *Visão* (19 October 1967), 9–13, 'As perspectivas para a Frente'.

92 *Jornal do Brasil* (17 December 1967), quoted Schneider, op. cit., 226.

93 The previous conference in 1966 had been held in a Franciscan priory in Belo Horizonte, one result being an organized protest against the reform of higher education in collaboration with USAID. See Roberto O. Myhr in Emmerson, op. cit., 272.

94 The original protest was over the closing of a student restaurant, but was turned into a major confrontation through the over-reaction of an ill-disciplined police force.

95 See the special number of *Jornal do Brasil* (31 March 1968).

96 See the interview with Luís Travassos, president of UNE, in *Realidade* (July 1968).

97 *Última Hora* (7 August 1968).

98 *Le Monde* (9 August 1968).

99 ibid. (6 August 1968).

100 ibid. (9 August 1968).

101 *Realidade* (April 1968), 65. Marcuse was at this time the theorist most in vogue in Rio de Janeiro and São Paulo, as elsewhere, but he was a name to quote at second-hand, rather than a writer carefully studied and immediately influential. Foreign visitors were closely quizzed as to their interpretation of Marcuse, often to their distinct embarrassment, and the interest in his views is clearly reflected in, for example, *Visão* (30 August 1968), 303–8, 'Marcuse para principiantes', especially the short piece by Nelson Rodrigues, 'Marcuse em sociedade', describing the alleged impact of Marcuse on *carioca* high society!

102 ibid., 56.

103 '. . . que no meu modo do ver não tem jeito de ser pacifica, não. Acho que ela so virá mesmo pela violência. Não por nossa vontade, mas porque êles não vão querer entregar de graça a "rapadura" . . .'; ibid., 49.

104 *Veja* (9 October 1968), 'A Incrível Batalha dos Estudantes', 14–21, describing fighting which led to the death of the young student, José Guimarães, shot in the head during the demonstration. For a broader analysis of the problems of education, especially in the universities, see *Visão* (16 August 1968), 55–66.

105 For general reflection on the issues involved see Ivan Vallier, *Catholicism, Social Control, and Modernization in Latin America* (Englewood Cliffs, 1970). His information on Brazil draws heavily on a doctoral thesis which later appeared as the most comprehensive account of the Church and politics in Brazil: Thomas C. Bruneau, *The Political Transformation of the Brazilian Catholic Church* (Cambridge, 1974). See, too, de Kadt, op. cit.; Thomas Sanders, 'Catholicism and Development: The Catholic Left in Brazil', in Kalman Silvert (ed.), *Churches and States: The Religious Institution and Modernization* (New York, 1967); and Rowan Ireland, 'The Catholic Church and Social Change in Brazil: An Evaluation', in Roett (ed.), op. cit., 345–71.

106 Bruneau, op. cit., 183–4. This included a severe attack on Dom Helder Câmara by the sociologist Gilberto Freyre, who at the same time labelled Dom Helder as a fascist and a tool of Communists. See, too, the remarks of the *Estado de São Paulo* in support of Dom Castro Mayer of Campos (Rio de Janeiro), a member of the conservative Tradition, Family and Property group, who also criticized the north-eastern bishops.

107 In an audience with Pope Paul VI in the Vatican in January 1967 Costa e

Silva had spoken confidently about good future relations between the regime and the Church. His confidence was obviously misplaced.

108 Dom Vincente Scherer, for example, archbishop of Pôrto Alegre, said of the north-eastern bishops' documents: 'Personally I would have no difficulty at all in signing the document which is entirely in conformity with the religious and social doctrine of the Church in all its parts'; *Paz e Terra*, 2, 264, quoted Bruneau, op. cit., 185. This was also the view of Protestant spokesmen.

109 ibid., 188.

110 The development of his thought, leading to the launching of the Action: Peace and Justice movement, and initiatives such as *Operação Esperança* (Operation Hope), can be traced in one of the best sources for church thinking and debate more generally in this period, *Paz e Terra* from No. 1 (July 1966) onwards. See, too, his *Revolução dentro da Paz* (Rio de Janeiro, 1968); *Church and Colonialism* (London, 1969); and *Spiral of Violence* (London, 1971). See, too, the study by José de Broucker, *Dom Helder Câmara: the Violence of a Peacemaker* (Maryknoll, 1970).

111 On the growing involvement of the hierarchy and clergy, especially in the wake of *Populorum Progressio*, see for example *Visão* (14 December 1967), 9, 'A ponte oferecida'.

112 Bruneau, op. cit., 190–1 quotes a number of statements by churchmen in support of Bishop Calheiros, all of which stress the greater need of the Church, especially since Vatican II, to emphasize its social mission. Other commentators, such as an ARENA spokesman in Congress, Clovis Stenzel, would have none of this, stressing rather that the kingdom of God is not of this world; ibid., 194. For more on Stenzel's views see *Visão* (14 December 1967), 12–13, 'Stenzel: arauto de nova revoluçao'.

113 Bruneau, op. cit., 198–200.

114 This was the culmination of a crisis which broke out in July, when a priest, in effect, supported strikers in a factory in Osasco, was imprisoned, then put under house arrest in Dom Agnelo's house and deported during the cardinal's absence abroad; ibid., 199–201.

115 ibid., 202–3.

116 ibid., 203–9.

117 ibid., 207–8, quoting *O Globo* (14 December 1968).

118 A useful analysis of the issues facing the Church, both in Brazil and in Latin America more generally, is in *Visão* (16 August 1968), 48–54, 'Paulo VI e as Duas Posições da Igreja no Brasil'. See also ibid., 56–66, 'A Universidade: Solução ou Subversão'.

119 For a general survey of guerrilla movements elsewhere in Latin America see Richard Gott, *Guerrilla Movements in Latin America* (London, 1970). Unfortunately this study neglects Brazil almost entirely, having only a few passing references, mainly to Brizola and Julião, neither of whom was involved in armed resistance. There is no mention of Marighela or other advocates of guerrilla action in Brazil: but there is much information on guerrilla movements in Spanish America.

120 This point is persistently stressed by those involved in armed opposition. See, for example, the interview given in 1970 by four militants released in exchange for the West German ambassador, after reaching Algeria. Asked why and when armed resistance developed, one man, Fernando Nagle Gabeira, answered: 'We did not choose this way of fighting . . . Before 1964, we thought change might come in Brazil through peaceful means, but with the right-wing military coup, *the only way left to us* was armed struggle'. Another interviewee, Ladislaw Dobor, asked how the armed struggle started,

emphasized: 'In the first year after the *coup*, we had many discussions and splits. By 1967 only a few small groups had taken up arms . . . But then in 1968, very large mass movements among the students and workers erupted . . . Many were killed . . . *Since the government had closed off the peaceful forms*, they came into the armed organizations. It was then that the urban guerrilla commandos really began. Our organizations grew tremendously . . .' The interviews are printed in what is the best single source in English on the urban guerrillas: James Kohl and John Litt, *Urban Guerrilla Warfare in Latin America* (Cambridge, Mass., 1974), 136–48 (my italics).

121 The most suasive proponents of *foco* theory were Ché Guevara and Regis Débray. Débray especially stressed the role of the *foco* in stimulating wider revolution. See, for example, Regis Débray, *Revolution in the Revolution?* (New York, 1967). Guevara also emphasized its probable effect in producing United States intervention, a 'new Vietnam'. See especially Ché Guevara, *Guerrilla Warfare* (New York, 1961); 'Cuba: Exceptional Case or Vanguard in the Struggle for Colonialism?', *Monthly Review* (July–August 1961); *Obra Revolucionária* (Mexico City, 1967); *Testamento Político* (Lima, 1967); and David James (ed.), *The Complete Bolivian Diaries of Ché Guevara and other captured documents* (New York, 1968). For criticism of the *foco* theory see especially Leo Hubermann and Paul Sweezy (eds.), *Regis Débray and the Latin American Revolution* (New York, 1968). Also see the discussion of Marighela above, pp. 414–18.

122 There is interesting analysis of the failure of the attempt to start a *foco* in the Serra do Caparão by Carlos Marighela. See 'Los Tupamaros en Uruguay y Marighella en Brasil' in the Chilean journal *Punto Final*, 87 (September 1968).

123 The most succinct and, on the whole, most accurate explanation of these various groups is given in Kohl and Litt, op. cit., 167–70. The account given here is based partly, but not mainly, on this source. There are particular points on which Kohl and Litt would seem to be wrong, as, for example, in saying that POC (see below) was later absorbed into VAR-Palmares (119). For more general discussion of these new formations see, too, Chilcote, op. cit., especially 165–70.

124 For details of the 'Arruda group' see ibid., 120–2. See, too, his discussion of divisions within the party (ibid., 66–73), especially between the more 'conservative', or 'closed', group (*fechadistas*) and those who favoured more open debate and a new, more independent, strategy, less tied to the Soviet Union. Barata's faction was part of this second group, with Marighela a representative of the first. Later Barata and other *renovadores* broke away to form the Corrente Renovadora do Movimento Marxista Brasileiro, taking a more nationalist line expressed in its weekly *O Nacional*, of which eventually Agildo Barata became editor.

125 For discussion of this 'Bahia' or *Pantano* group and its success in 1957, see ibid., 66–8, 122–4.

126 Pereira was Secretary General from the founding of the party in 1932 to the Third Congress in 1929. Prestes held the post from the Second National Conference (the Conference of Mantiqueira) of 1943 till the Sixth Congress in 1967.

127 The previous Congresses has been in 1922, 1925, 1928–29, 1954, and 1960. There also had been meetings of the National Conference, called on specific issues, in 1934, 1943, 1961, and 1962.

128 In an interview some years later one of the leading dissidents stressed how Luís Carlos Prestes, the dominant figure in the Executive Committee, had believed all through the early 1960s that a section of the armed forces, led

by officers sympathetic to the PCB, would eventually stage a *coup*, taking units with them. They would also provide arms for the workers. Prestes was the only military man on the Executive Commission, but emphasis was laid on the influence of military men on the PCB in the Goulart period; 'os operários subiam pela escada, os militares pelo elevador'. ('The workers went up by the staircase, the soldiers in the lift'.) The official thesis, right up to 1967, was the Prestes thesis that the army was democratic.

129 The letter can most conveniently be found in Carlos Marighela, *For the Liberation of Brazil* (London, 1971), 183–91, and Carlos Marighela, *Pour la Libération du Brésil* (Paris, 1970), 47–59. The French edition, presented by Conrad Detrez, contains letters from Marighela and two important interviews, as well as the *Manuel de guérillero urbain*. Unfortunately it is marred by a weak and historically inaccurate introduction, particularly as it describes the shaping of left-wing politics in Brazil. The English text is fuller and contains, in particular, essays written by Marighela before his break with the PCB, mostly from 1966.

130 Marighela, *For the Liberation of Brazil*, 183–4.

131 ibid., 185.

132 ibid.

133 See, too, for example, ibid., 137–43, 'Causes of the Defeat and Present Outlook', where he attacks past dependence on the leadership of the bourgeoisie and the resultant abandoning of revolutionary Marxism–Leninism, with a 'loss . . . of a clear sense of the class basis of the revolutionary struggle . . . The party must cease to be a sort of appendix to the bourgeois parties . . . For Brazilian revolutionaries there is no alternative but to prepare for combat'. He also noted elsewhere that 'the bourgeoisie has shown itself incapable of managing the political processes of Brazil . . . the hegemony of the bourgeoisie is not a historical inevitability, and there is nothing to indicate that the proletariat is obliged to adopt a conformist position and subject itself indefinitely to bourgeois leadership . . . we who follow Marxism–Leninism have no alternative but to build proletarian strength in order not to remain subordinated to the bourgeoisie . . .' (ibid., 147, 149, 150). See, too, 'Against Tactics which Subordinate Proletariat to Bourgeoisie', ibid., 164–9.

134 ibid., 186.

135 ibid., 190.

136 ibid., 125.

137 One of the most cogent critiques came from the distinguished *paulista* economic historian Caio Prado Júnior, *A Revolução Brasileira* (São Paulo, 1966), again emphasizing how inadequate social and political analysis had led to a misguided strategy for action. See, too, the rich, though slightly earlier, debate in the journal founded by Caio Prado: *Revista Brasiliense* (1956–64) edited by Èlias Chaves Neto.

138 Marighela, op. cit., 191.

139 Kohl and Litt, op. cit., 64–5 give a chronology of the most important raids and seizures of arms.

140 *Jornal do Brasil* (27 December 1967).

141 *Jornal do Brasil* (16 July 1968), quoted Schneider, op. cit., 258.

142 ibid., 259.

143 Schneider (ibid., 258) quotes an unofficial poll at an ARENA convention as to the delegates' preference for presidential candidate in 1970. 60 favoured Magalhães Pinto; 36 Andreazza; 35 Jarbas Passarinho; 31 Carvalho Pinto; 26 Abreu Sodré; 23 Daniel Krieger. Only seven preferred Albuquerque Lima, putting him in thirteenth place.

144 ibid., 260–1 mentions a sharp disagreement in a meeting of the National Security Council of 23 August, in a discussion of a draft paper on 'National Strategic Concept'. Though there was agreement in principle on Permanent National Objectives, it was not clear how these should be translated into policies, with two rival groups at loggerheads, led by Albuquerque Lima and the Minister of Finance and Planning.

145 Sarmento had been made commander of the Second Army in São Paulo in March 1967. His appointment to head the First Army in 1968 seemed strongly to indicate a move towards still higher office.

146 See *Visão* (11 October 1968), 21–3, 'A corrente inconformada do Govêrno'.

147 *Correio da Manhã* (1 November 1968); *Jornal do Brasil* (2 November 1968); also *Visão* (28 November 1968), 25–6, 'Críticas sérias de jovens oficiais'.

148 See, in particular, the articles by Hermano Alves in *Correio da Manhã* of the period.

149 Among the proposed gestures of disapproval were that parents should not allow their children to take part in the Independence Day celebrations of 7 September and that Brazilian girls should refuse to go out with officers, scarcely very radical measures, but enough to incense military feeling.

150 The important role of Gama e Silva and his insistence on strong measures in relation to Congress are stressed in Krieger, op. cit., 327–45.

151 Schneider, op. cit., 273, drawing partly on interviews with senior officers and partly on published accounts. See, in particular, *Visão* (6 December 1968), 102–6, 'A crise de expectiva', which catches the mood of pending crisis. Schneider notes, in particular, the pressure on the First Army Commander, Sarmento, from some of his subordinates, Dutra de Castilho of the Vila Militar, Ramiro Conçalves of the Armoured Division, and Câmara Sena of the Coastal Artillery.

152 Stepan, *The Military in Politics*, 259–60, stresses the growing dissatisfaction of younger officers, partly over salary and what they regarded as their declining status. He also sees a growing demand to do away with the whole process of political bargaining, for the military to restructure the whole political system once and for all. 'This restructuring was seen as simultaneously *less* political and *more* revolutionary'. See too *Jornal do Brasil* (8 December 1968), 'Capitães começam vida política com Manifesto da ESAO'.

153 Schneider, op. cit., 285 lists some of the most prominent victims of this action.

154 *Discurso proferido pelo General Afonso de Albuquerque Lima na ocasião da transmissão do cargo de Ministro do Interior* (January 1969).

155 See, in particular, his paper on *O Nacionalismo como força imanente da Revolução e do Desenvolvimento* and his speech of 14 July 1970: *O Desenvolvimento Regional como Fator da Unidade Nacional*.

156 Stepan, *The Military in Politics*, 264, speaks of the worry of the 'São Paulo and international financial community . . . lest a Peruvian route be followed if nationalist candidate Lt. Gen. Alfonso Albuquerque Lima were to become president . . .' There is no doubt that the new 'Peruvian' model was causing widespread alarm.

157 Two of the most important sources already available are Marcos Arruda, Herbet de Souza, and Carlos Afonso, *Multinationals in Brazil. The Impact of Multinational Corporations in Contemporary Brazil* (Toronto, 1975) and *Multinational Corporations in Brazil and Mexico: Structural Sources of Economic and Non-economic Power: Report to the Subcommittee on Multinational Corporations of the Committee on Foreign Relations of the United States Senate*, by Richard S. Newfarmer and Willard F. Mueller (Washing-

ton DC, August 1975). Much detailed information on the working of multinational companies in Brazil can also be found in *Interinvest Guide: Brazil and International Capital* (Rio de Janeiro, 1973).

158 US Senate Report, 144.

159 The best-documented cases of large corporations building up an international network of agents for the use of 'slush funds' come from the arms industry, especially the cases of Lockheed and Northrop: but work is now being done in other areas. On the arms industry see, in particular, the fascinating study by Anthony Sampson, *The Arms Bazaar* (London, 1977).

160 The most important changes are listed in Schneider, op. cit., 282–3, but without interpretation as to their significance in the internal power struggle.

161 The term 'hard-line' at this stage is notoriously difficult and confusing. To give one example: Schneider, op. cit., 258 speaks of 'duros' associated with Albuquerque Lima in mid-1968. He names sixteen colonels as 'duros'. But there are important distinctions to be made between them. Five were 'duros' mainly in that they were associated with the seamier side of the regions' repressive activities, namely Tarcísio Nunes, Sebastião Chaves, Gustavo Coutinho de Farias, Igrejas Lopes, and José Carlos Amazonas. Seven were 'hard-line' principally in that they believed in the strengthening of authoritarian controls in relation to efforts to reopen the system: Hélio Lemos, Hélio Mendes, Caracas Linhares, Walter Baere, Anselmo Lira, Antônio Morais, and Marcelino Rufina. On the other hand, the other four in the list were substantially different. They eventually opposed Institutional Act No. 5 and, more important still, they had by this period a well-articulated alternative project or strategy for Brazilian development, wanting in particular a tougher line with the multinationals. These were Boaventura Cavalcanti, Amerino Rapôso, Ruy de Castro, and Luiz Alencar Araripe. It was this group which was potentially most important as a challenge to the system of Delfim and Beltrão, but which was to be defeated in the crisis of 1969. (The other officer in the list, Air Force Brigadier João Paulo Burnier, was more clearly a fascist, an admirer of Mussolini.) This one list alone stresses the care to be taken with comprehensive labels.

162 Carlos Chagas, *113 Dias de Angustia. Impedimento e Morte de um Presidente* (Rio de Janeiro, 1971).

163 ibid., 241–2.

164 ibid., 243–6.

165 ibid., 244.

166 For details see Kohl and Litt, op. cit., 48, 67, 161.

167 *Jornal do Brasil* (20 April 1970): 'In Guanabara and in the state of Rio alone, the number of deaths attributed to the Death Squad is more than 1000, i.e., almost 400 a year. The victims show signs of unnecessary cruelty. For example, between 11 January and 2 July 1969, 40 bodies were found in the waters of the Macacu river, buried in the mud near the bridge between Maje and Itaborai. All of the bodies, in an advanced state of decomposition, still showed the marks of handcuffs and burns caused by cigarettes or cigars and multiple bruising; some of them were still handcuffed. According to the findings of the autopsy, it was noted that many had been tortured, shot, and then drowned'.

168 A list of some of the companies alleged to have 'contributed to official bodies of repression' from 1968 and 1969 is to be found in Moniz Bandeira, *Cartéis e Desnacionalização. A Experiencia Brasileira: 1964–1974*, 2nd ed. (Rio de Janeiro, 1975), 204.

169 See Amnesty International Report on Allegations of Torture in Brazil (London, 1973), 61–9, 'Torture techniques at Operação Bandeirantes'.

170 The Amnesty *Report*, 75–80, discusses Fleury and his work and gives the names of eighty-six people said to have been tortured by him. See also Paulo Freire (ed.), *Memórias do Exílio* (Lisbon, 1976).
171 Amnesty International *Report*, 62–3.
172 ibid., 58.
173 He said that military support was only 'one leg' and that two were needed to walk normally, the second being popular support; Chagas, op. cit., 33.
174 ibid., 25.
175 ibid., 32–4.
176 The best account of these discussions is Chagas, op. cit., 73–4. One reason for passing over Pedro Aleixo, as explained to him by Admiral Rademaker, was his commitment to reopen Congress and introduce the new constitutional arrangements; ibid., 89–90.
177 ibid., 82, 93–4. They accepted it to preserve the appearance of unity at a time of crisis.
178 Schneider, op. cit., 298–9.
179 Stepan, *The Military in Brazil*, 264. He also notes that 'Ranks were finally closed behind the choice of the senior generals, but only because of the specter of complete military fragmentation'.
180 Chagas, op. cit., 182.
181 Schneider, op. cit., 300.
182 Chagas, op. cit., 191.
183 ibid., 194.
184 ibid.
185 ibid., 193.
186 ibid., 195.
187 See his telegram to Albuquerque Lima of 4 October 1969; ibid., 198.
188 ibid., 199.
189 See 'Os Novos Limites do Congresso', *Veja* (22 October 1969) and 'Médici e o Govêrno de participação', *Visão* (24 October 1969).
190 Chagas, op. cit., 207–8.
191 The degree to which the 'new' Congress was scarcely new is stressed in *Visão* (11 April 1970), 'Seis anos de Revolução', 17–18, which also notes how many members of Congress welcomed the new period of quiet and 'stability'.
192 *Latin America* (London, 20 March 1970), 94.
193 ibid.
194 ibid.
195 Schneider, op. cit., 321 provides a clear and useful account of the choice of the new governors.
196 'A batalha da imagem', *Visão* (10 October 1970).
197 See P. Flynn, 'Sambas, Soccer and Nationalism', *New Society* (19 August 1971), 327–30.
198 See, for example, 'O retrato sem resposta', *Visão* (24 October 1970), 17–18, which discusses frankly the declining image of Brazil abroad.
199 For comment on the artificiality of the current two-party system, see *Visão* (7 November 1970), 19–20, 'Avanço apesar do ato'. See too the analysis, ibid. (5 December 1970), 23–4, 'MDB perdeu. Quem ganhou?'. This particular article ends with the telling quotation: 'Whoever is afraid of prison can hardly offer effective opposition'.
200 See *Visão* (21 November 1970), especially 'A longa luta de Delfim', 35–44. Also ibid. (5 December 1970), 'Uma festa medita para Delfim', 24–8.
201 ibid., 28.
202 See too the list of outstanding people and achievements of 1970 drawn up

by *Revista Propaganda* and reported in *Visão* (19 December 1970), 15–16. Prizes went to AERP, especially for its work on television; to the government for its slogan 'Ninguém segura êste pais', and to Miguel Gustavo for the best 'jingle' of the year, 'Pra frente, Brasil'.

203 Supplementary Law No. 7 (7 September 1970).

204 There is a clear short description of this scheme in *Transamazonian Highways* (Montreal, 1970), a report by the Brazilian Ministry of Transport to the VI World Meeting of the International Road Federation. The most complete study of the whole Amazonas programme and its successes and failures is Richard Bourne, *Assault on the Amazon* (London, 1978).

205 Bourne, op. cit., chapters 7 and 8.

206 Arruda and de Souza, op. cit.; and see, in particular, Bourne, op. cit., chapter 5.

207 Ludwig began accumulating land on the River Jari in 1964. Estimates of his holdings now range from one to 2 or even 4 million hectares.

208 Médici, television speech to celebrate the 8th Anniversary of the *coup* of 1964.

209 See, for example, the charges made by the conference of bishops in July 1973, specifically referring to torture of priests. This period also saw the first trial of police officers accused of torture. See *Latin America* (3 August 1973).

210 Emílio Garrastazú Médici, *Mensagem ao Congresso Nacional* (1974).

1974–77

11 The Contradictions of Authoritarian Control

A Change of Style?

General Ernesto Geisel, who took over the presidency almost exactly ten years after the *coup* of 1964, was widely regarded as one of the most able officers in the Brazilian army with a reputation for austerity and honesty generally associated with the German immigrant community of southern Brazil from which he came. Born in 1908, his career experience had been more varied than that of Médici, following a pattern often found in Brazilian officers, a mixture of military and quasi-civilian posts. In the 1950s he had served on the staff of the National Security Council, but from 1955 to 1956 was Superintendent of the President Bernardes Refinery. In 1957 he was named to represent the War Ministry on the National Petroleum Council, later headed the intelligence section of the army general staff, and subsequently became Director of Petrobrás until his selection as federal president.

As a close friend of Castello Branco and an officer who had played an important role in the development of the ESG, Geisel was very much a man of the Castellista 'Sorbonne' group. At the same time he had been on good terms both with Costa e Silva and Médici. Geisel had served as Chief Military Aide to Castello Branco, but then had been appointed to the Superior Military Tribunal by Costa e Silva: his brother, General Orlando Geisel, had served as Médici's Minister of the Army. To this degree he might be expected to conciliate the Castellista and Costista factions in the armed forces. Moreover, his association with Petrobrás and the state oil industry, always a focus for economic nationalism, might be expected to have enlarged his sympathy for the more nationalist camp, as should his record of austerity and personal dislike of corruption and dishonesty. Politically, it was known that he could take a hard line when necessary, as he had shown in his attitude to the governor of Goiás, Mauro Borges Teixeira, during the crisis in Goiás following the 1964 *coup* and in his earlier hostility to Goulart, having been one of that group of officers who had never accepted Goulart in the place of Quadros. But he was in no sense identified with the 'hard line' and reports of his views before he took office raised hopes of a much less repressive period of government after the excesses of the Médici years. Finally, as a man experienced in running the largest enterprise in Brazil not only was Geisel a proven administrator of real ability, but one used to dealing with *técnicos* and professional men outside military circles, above all in the oil industry. This, it seemed, should allow both easy relations with the bureaucrats and *técnicos* in government, and should provide, most fortunately, a man at the helm familiar with problems of oil and energy at just the time when soaring oil prices represented the most serious external threat to the balance of payments and the continued success of the 'Brazilian model'. For all these reasons Geisel seemed as good a presidential candidate as might be found in the senior ranks of the officer corps.

Geisel's choice of cabinet also suggested a new approach and a possible break with the policies of the Médici administration. The only element of continuity was the former Minister of Planning, Reis Velloso. Otherwise, there was a clean break. Two appointments, in particular, seemed to hint at a more flexible political style, perhaps with a new opening to the civilian politicians. These were the Ministry of Justice, which went to Armando Falcão, and Education, to Ney Braga. Falcão was a man of long political experience, serving previously under Vargas, Dutra, and Kubitschek. A member of the former PSD, he had been Minister of Justice under Kubitschek and seemed the sort of man who could most easily negotiate with the former political leaders, Kubitschek, Quadros, and Goulart. Ney Braga's appointment also suggested a new approach. Previously governor of Paraná, he was a member of the Christian Democratic Party before the 1964 *coup*. He was also a retired general, with good links with both military and civilian political groups, especially in the UDN, through his close connection in the past with Marshal Juarez Távora. These appointments also caused speculation as to a possible *rapprochement* with the Church, relations with which had deteriorated badly under the Médici government. Some indication of Geisel's anxiety to patch up this quarrel had been seen in an early meeting between his close associate, General Golbery do Couto e Silva, now evidently raised to the position of Geisel's most influential political adviser, and appointed as head of the president's civilian household, and Cardinal Paulo Evaristo Arns, archbishop of São Paulo. There had been much recent tension between the cardinal and the regime and shortly after this meeting the cardinal issued a pastoral letter listing the names of all those who had of late been arrested and tortured: but the meeting was at least a straw in the wind, indicative of the new government's readiness to open a dialogue.

Golbery's role seemed particularly significant. He too was a *gaúcho*, perhaps the leading intellectual of the armed forces, with his influential books on geopolitics. He had an outstanding academic record, had studied in the United States, served in the FEB in Italy, and had started his intelligence career in the Army General Staff in 1950. From March 1952 to November 1955 he served on the staff of the ESG, headed the National Security Council under Quadros, working closely with General Geisel. Rather than serve under Goulart as president he resigned from active service and headed the research office of IPÊS, the actively anti-Goulart movement linked to business interests, helping also to establish closer contacts between IPÊS and the ESG. He was virtually the founder and subsequently director of the SNI, working closely with Castello Branco, and having almost daily meetings with Ernesto Geisel, when the latter was Castello's Chief Military Aide. As a high-ranking intelligence officer he also worked closely with a mutual friend of Castello Branco and himself, General Vernon Walters, United States military attaché and subsequently assistant director of the CIA, and he was perhaps the most important single influence on Castello Branco's political strategy, being firmly opposed to the choice of Costa e Silva as his successor. Golbery do Couto e Silva had also been president of Dow Chemicals of Brazil, so was himself linked to multinational interests. The influence of this cool, rational, professional intelligence officer on Geisel's policies was certain to be considerable.

The key appointment of Minister of Finance, to replace Delfim Neto, went to the thirty-eight-year-old economist Mário Henrique Simonsen. He was a banker who previously had combined the direction of MOBRAL with the vice-presidency of the Bozano-Simonsen investment bank. At public conferences in recent years, Simonsen had strongly defended the handling of the economy under Delfim Neto, but there were also reasons for thinking he might introduce changes, perhaps with a more nationalist emphasis in policy, though much clearly would depend on external or international factors influencing Brazil's economy and on how much freedom of action Simonsen consequently would have. The appointment to the Itamaraty of Antônio Azeredo da Silveira, previously ambassador to Argentina, also suggested a possible change of emphasis in foreign affairs. He had been prominent in the first UNCTAD conference in Geneva, and was a man of known sympathies for the 'Third World', particularly interested in Asia and Africa. His appointment raised speculation as to how far might be seen a return to the less dependent, more pragmatic line of the period of Quadros and Goulart, rather than the close following of United States interests experienced since 1964.

Other posts seemed less interesting and hinted less at change. Some simply promoted former colleagues of Geisel, such as Shigeaki Ueki, who had worked with Geisel in Petrobrás. Others suggested concessions to the right wing of the armed forces, as in the appointment as head of the SNI of General João Batista de Figueiredo. He had been talked of as a possible contender for the presidency and his political ambitions, at the age now of fifty-five, were still far from over. He was a man of the right, who in the key post of head of SNI was both politically powerful and a reminder that the line followed under Médici could be renewed. A similar reminder came with the appointment as Minister of the Army of General Vicente Dale Coutinho. He was a relatively undistinguished officer, now suffering from poor health. He had some reputation as a theorist of 'national security' and his appointment, together with that of Figueiredo, suggested a need on Geisel's part to conciliate more right-wing groups. Consequently, as the new president took office there was much speculation as to how far he might want to introduce changes, and how much freedom he would be allowed, should he wish to do so. More basically, it was asked how far the system built up since 1964, especially the authoritarian state, with its entrenched social and economic interests and its basis in the repressive, exceptional powers accumulated over the years, was capable of substantial modification. Already serious question marks hung over the economic system bequeathed by Delfim Neto: how far could the repressive political system now be modified?

Economic Problems and Early Initiatives

Some of the sharpest constraints on Geisel and his ministers came from the downturn in the economy already discussed in the previous chapter. Strains and difficulties were appearing before Delfim Neto left office, but, nevertheless, he was able to leave with a record of having guided Brazil's economy through the years of rapid growth, swelling currency reserves, steadily rising exports, and inflation contained within what was regarded as acceptable limits. In his New Year 1974 speech to the nation Médici had stressed these successes, noting an 11·4 per cent expansion of GDP in 1973, the highest growth-rate of any major country in the world, with an increase in the last five years of 63 per cent, claimed by Médici as the fastest growth-rate in modern history. Exports had reached a record $6,600 million; there was a balance of payments surplus of 2,100 million and foreign reserves of 6,400 million. Though inflation had not been kept to the projected figure of 12 per cent, the president claimed it was less than 16 per cent. From 1969 to 1973 the picture was:

Estimated Annual Increases in GDP[1]

	1969	*1970*	*1971*	*1972*	*1973*
Agriculture	6·0	5·6	11·4	4·1	3·5
Industry	10·8	11·1	11·2	13·9	15·0
Commerce	8·8	9·0	12·8	11·6	12·5
Transport and Communications	11·7	3·4	8·4	8·1	14·0
Other Services	8·8	10·5	11·3	—	—
Gross domestic product	9·0	9·5	11·3	10·4	11·4

But already, too, there were signs of concern about the prospects for 1974, mainly surrounding the problems of 'imported inflation', especially through increased import prices for oil and foodstuffs, particularly wheat, with predictions that the trade deficit in 1974 might be as high as $3,500 million. It soon became clear that these gloomy forecasts were more than accurate, especially as Brazil was hit more than most countries by the rapid rise in oil prices. By 1974 about 45 per cent of Brazil's energy consumption came from oil, requiring about 900,000 barrels a day, of which the domestic oil industry produced only about 180,000 barrels daily. The petroleum council therefore estimated that on current prices the oil bill for 1974 could be as high as $4,000 million, which, combined with price rises on wheat, capital goods, and steel imports, would seriously deplete the foreign reserves. This, as already seen, was precisely what happened. Throughout 1974 imports increased rapidly, reaching $12·5 billion and producing a trade deficit of $4·5 billion. It was also found that the real rate of inflation was considerably higher than the 16 per cent claimed by Delfim Neto and that an expansion of the money supply by 47 per cent by the Central Bank in 1973 had contributed to a swift acceleration of the inflation rate, so that, as the Minister of Finance reported: 'in the first six months of the year the general price index increased at an average monthly rate of 3·5 percent, which would correspond to an inflation rate of 51 percent a year'[2]. By the end of 1975 the total foreign debt had also risen to $22 billion, as compared to $12·8 billion at the end of 1973.

In their public speeches government spokesmen tended to play down the sharp decline in economic performance, emphasizing the continued success of exports[3] and Brazil's generally stable system, as when Minister Reis Velloso emphasized in June 1976, discussing Brazil's soaring debt: 'We are speaking of the foreign debt of one of the ten largest economies in the world, not a small country nor a medium country. In relative terms the size of the debt is not excessive'.[4] The stress, rather, was on Brazil's continuing attraction for the foreign investor:

> I can think of very sound reasons for putting Brazil among the five top countries for international investment in the world, including both the industrialized and developing nations. . . . Brazil has no difficulty in assimilating foreign investment, thanks to the size of its economy and also to its stable and rational approach to foreign capital, particularly since 1964, within the context of an economic model based on private enterprise. We shall be able to go on maintaining the social and political stability achieved over the last ten years.[5]

Such sanguine assurances were not entirely convincing, especially when by the end of 1976 the foreign debt was around $25 billion, rising to about 30 billion in 1977, with an inflation rate approaching 50 per cent. Estimates towards the end of 1976 suggested that debt repayment and interest would be equal to about 44 per cent of Brazil's export revenues, with foreign reserves down to about $3,500 million, as compared with $6,400 million in 1973. Measures were being taken to cut back imports, such as the requirement, for example, in late 1975 that importers should deposit with the Central Bank for 360 days an amount equal to the full value of the goods to be imported, with no interest or monetary correction. The percentage of commercial bank deposits that must be kept at the Central Bank was increased several times. Interest-rate ceilings on commercial loans were removed and interest rates quickly climbed to between 45 to 55 per cent, though still there were plenty of customers for such expensive money. Because of Brazil's great natural wealth, its mineral resources and agriculture, foreign capital was still forthcoming, reinforced by the fact that those who had already loaned so much to Brazil now had to lend more to prevent a crisis.[6] But there were signs of growing anxiety: at a seminar organized in Rio de Janeiro by the *Financial Times* in March 1976, James Greene, the senior vice-president of the Manufacturers' Hanover Trust commented:

> Commercial bankers are exhibiting growing concern at the rapid rise of the Brazilian external debt in the past five or six years . . . a 30 percent rise, in one year, of $5,000 m., from $17,000 m. to $22,000 m., admittedly put us on edge. We, of necessity, keep very much in mind the official (Brazilian) forecast of an additional increase of $4,200 m. in 1976.[7]

No one was suggesting that the Brazilian economy was about to collapse, but with talk of the need to renegotiate the debt, it was clear that the heady years of the 'miracle' were over and that the dangerously dependent nature of Brazil's capitalist development since 1964, above all the heavy reliance on foreign loans, was now more evident than ever before. New strategies were now required, particularly more attention to the agrarian sector and to primary products for export, a line the government was anxious to develop faster, though this, too, had its problems as farmers made large profits from soya, sugar, coffee, and cocoa, but at the neglect of basic foodstuffs such as beans, manioc, and vegetables.

It was precisely this search for a new line, a different 'project' for Brazil, which most fuelled speculation about the Geisel government right from the start, with expectations of a different approach both to the economy and to politics. Early analysis of his cabinet had quickened this discussion[8] and much was made of the phrase used by Geisel in his first speech to his ministers: 'Continuity does not imply immobility' ('continuidade não significa imobilismo'), a phrase then echoed by several of the new ministers, threatening to become the slogan of the new government. Geisel also spoke of the need for 'gradual, but sure, democratic improvement' and his hope that the exceptional instruments of control, namely the powers stemming from Institutional Act No. 5, would be superseded by means of 'creative political imagination' with 'efficient safeguards and ready and really efficient remedies within a constitutional context'; but he also warned that: 'This does not only depend on the will of the federal executive power, since it demands in large measure the sincere, effective collaboration of other powers in the nation . . .'[9]

It was at once noted that Geisel came not with promises but plans, a clear outline of what he intended to do, as seen in some of the changes he immediately introduced into the machinery of government. He created two new bodies, the Secretariat for Planning and the Council for Economic Development, and introduced a new Ministry of Social Welfare and Assistance (Ministério da Previdencia Social), taking it out of the Ministry of Labour, together with its budget of 28 million cruzeiros, and more than 100,000 people working with it.[10] The Secretariat for Planning strengthened the Ministry of Planning, making it directly subordinate to the president. The Council for Economic Development was also to be presided over by Geisel himself, with the Secretary of Planning as its Secretary-General and the Ministers of Finance, Agriculture, Industry and Commerce, and the Interior as members.[11]

These, and other related, changes marked right from the beginning one of the features of Geisel's government which distinguished it from that of Médici. This was the much more prominent, direct role of the president himself. Médici had been content, broadly speaking, to leave the direction of the economy to Delfim Neto, the handling of the army and security to Orlando Geisel, and publicity and various other initiatives to Andreazza. The new president wanted to be much more directly, personally involved in government, bringing with him the experience and qualities of his years as an administrator, especially in Petrobrás. Above all, he was expected to show a quality regularly repeated of him in his previous work, an imaginative pragmatism:

> It may be expected that Geisel will make use of power as one uses a precision instrument, on the basis of exact information, without permitting himself to be either blinded or dominated by it. His style of governing is likely to be authoritarian rather than liberal, but without pretentiousness or a sense of majesty.[12]

His handling of Brazil's oil policies at Petrobrás had been described as 'state control without state dirigism and nationalism without chauvinism'.[13] The distribution of petrol, which had remained in the hands of the international companies, was largely brought under the control of Petrobrás petrol stations, but without closing down the stations of the international companies. In building up the petrochemicals industry he had allowed foreign private investments, but acquired the necessary holdings for Petrobrás, so that it retained control of the production of the raw materials needed by the petrochemicals industry. He also created Braspetro, an international subsidiary of Petrobrás, reaching oil production agreements with producing countries that found themselves in conflict with the international oil companies.

> Geisel proceeded completely free of ideological considerations, for example, he concluded an oil prospecting agreement with the Socialist Baath government in Iraq just one week after Baghdad had expropriated the British firm Iraq Petroleum company. Thanks to the policy, initiated long before the present oil crisis, Brazil today has oil agreements with most Arab states (Libya, Iraq, Egypt, Saudi Arabia) and also with the new oil producers of Latin America, such as Ecuador, Colombia and Bolivia.[14]

His overall policy was described as 'aimed at securing independence and state control for Brazil'. His first major speech and his quick reorganization of certain branches of government, his reference to moves towards democracy, his aim, as he claimed, to 'strengthen trade union power, in the city and in the countryside, to allow the appearance of an authentic leadership', all suggested that a change of substance as well as style in national politics might now be a real possibility.

Distensão and Opposition

Among the words most frequently used both before and after Geisel took office were *distensão, descompressão*, and other phrases connoting a relaxation and easing of the political system, with a move away from the brutal repression and abuses of the previous government. In his general political perception Geisel was evidently much nearer to Castello Branco than to Médici and it was notable how many of those who in one form or another had served under Castello were now to be found around Geisel, particularly Golbery do Couto e Silva. Both Golbery and Geisel now seemed convinced that the more extreme methods of control under Médici needed to be relaxed, in part, it seems, influenced by the lessons drawn from Portugal. Here, some argued, possibly Vernon Walters among them, the danger could be seen of too sharp a backlash after a long period of repressive control. Portugal and its experience became an important factor in Brazilian national politics. Some people urged the danger of lifting the lid, even a little, with fears growing in some quarters that Geisel might prove to be a Brazilian General Spinola. Others took the opposite line, the need to ease controls to avoid extreme reaction; while others, particularly those deeply involved in political torture, looked fearfully on the possibility of a day of reckoning should Brazil go the way of Portugal.

The whole question of *distensão* obviously touched a sensitive nerve, raising again, on the one hand, the question of finding the 'second leg' of wider popular support, but seeming to the more extreme right-wingers to threaten national security and the whole fabric of control built up since 1964.[15] It was known that the main body of opposition to the choice of Geisel as president had come from those close to Médici who wanted the continuation of rigid controls, as well as from those supporters or clients of Delfim Neto who either wanted him to continue in office or become governor of São Paulo as a springboard to still higher things, and who wanted essentially a continuation of his policies. It was difficult to follow the precise contours or fully gauge the strength of this opposition and intra-regime factionalism, but it was clearly there as a threat to Geisel just as it had been to Castello Branco and to Costa e Silva. A key question, therefore, was how strong was Geisel and how secure his position as he talked of *distensão* and hinted at further changes.

The appointment of Dale Coutinho as Minister of the Army in place of Orlando Geisel was interpreted as a possible sign of weakness and concession to the right, especially when combined with the appointment of Figueiredo as head of SNI. Geisel was said to have wanted to appoint a different officer to the army post: the appointment of Dale Coutinho suggested that he had been overruled, while the SNI post for Figueiredo seemed also out of tune with moves towards *distensão*. Figueiredo had been close to Médici, serving as his Chief of Staff both in the SNI and in the Third Army; then, when Médici was president, as his Chief of the Military Cabinet and Secretary-General of the National Security Council. His appointment to this politically sensitive post, now becoming a stepping-stone for those with presidential ambitions, suggested a concession wrung from Geisel by the right wing associated with Médici. The evidence was not, however, conclusive, since Figueiredo, as a senior intelligence officer, had also worked closely with Golbery, so that his new appointment might owe as much to Golbery as to Médici. He had worked closely with the SNI from its beginning, after having been an instructor at both EsAO and ECEME, teaching at the latter school during the crucial period 1961–64. He was, therefore, a relatively obvious choice as head of SNI.

Other lines of speculation as to the weakness of Geisel's position also seemed poorly based. The president was said to have been forced to give way in agreeing to the prosecution, under the law of National Security, of a deputy from Bahia, Francisco Pinto, who had criticized the presence of Chile's General Pinochet at the ceremonies in Brasília to mark Geisel's inauguration. On the other hand, in what was a much more substantial test of strength, on a far more important issue, Geisel was able to block Delfim Neto's ambitions to become governor of São Paulo, putting in his own man, again previously associated with Castello Branco, Paulo Egydio Martins. Egydio Martins had been Minister of Industry and Commerce under Castello Branco, but was not by 1974 a figure of the same national and international stature as Delfim Neto. Delfim had the backing of the São Paulo industrial, business, and financial community, whose dense net of power and patronage included the São Paulo ARENA party. He was supported, too, by the current governor, Laudo Natel, who in turn was linked to such immensely rich and politically influential groups as *Bradesco* (Banco Brasileiro de Descontos) headed by Amador Aguiar, who had flourished mightily in the years of the 'miracle'. For Geisel to take on such opposition required nerve and confidence, but he was determined to keep out Delfim Neto and, most important, he was backed in this by senior officers who shared his dislike and distrust of the former Finance Minister. The grounds for this mistrust were never set out publicly, but at the time it was credibly reported that:

> Geisel has forbidden Delfim's candidacy because he, and other high ranking officers, believe the former minister to have been corrupt. This has not been the subject of public debate because the Brazilian military are extremely unwilling to have their dirty linen washed in public. In fact there was a gentleman's agreement between Médici and Geisel that there would not be any investigation or recriminations concerning the activities of the outgoing administration. The mantle of immunity was extended to cover Delfim, as well as two of his closest associates José Maria Vilar de Queiroz and Carlos Alberto Andrade Pinto.[16]

It had always required a strong president to take on São Paulo successfully, as Vargas had discovered in 1932. Vargas had succeeded then because of the support of the army high command, notably of Góes Monteiro. Now in 1974 another *gaúcho* imposed his will, again because he had sufficient support at the top of the armed forces: but again, like Vargas, Geisel made enemies in the process and left bitterness and resentment which could be important in later years.

Some evidence of opposition to Geisel from more junior officers came in reports of a manifesto from officers in EsAO (Escola de Aperfeiçoamento de Oficiais), opposing any moves to open up the system. Such reports, however, needed to be examined carefully. Granted the structure of command and the shape of military politics, a manifesto from young captains, even if it existed, would not carry much weight, unless it was another case of more senior and influential officers using the old ploy of claiming that the young men were becoming restless. What was perhaps more important was the continued speculation over Geisel's position, with rumours that the replacement in April of General Dilermando Gomes Monteiro as chief of his military household by General Hugo de Abreu was a further concession to the right, offset by the appointment to the command of the First Army of General Reinaldo de Almeida, a Geisel man. Neither of these appointments was terribly significant, but the speculation they provoked was itself evidence of the general tension, the awareness that beneath the surface of military politics a real struggle was in progress. It also suggested that in some quarters there was hope that enough speculation over Geisel's weakness might have the quality of a self-fulfilling prophecy.

The sudden arrest in São Paulo on the night of 3 April of about sixty intellectuals, professors, and students was interpreted less as a sign of the government tightening its control as of the local São Paulo security forces showing their strength, largely in defiance of the central government. This was a pattern which would continue for a long time to come, evidence of the autonomy and entrenched power of the repressive apparatus in São Paulo, also shown by the fact that Sérgio Fleury, who was meant to be under house arrest for his activities with the Death Squad, took an active part in interrogating those arrested in early April. The continued reports of the use of torture in São Paulo also showed that it would be no easy job to put an end to a system of repression now apparently carried along by its own momentum.

The big test of *distensão* and *normalisação*, as everyone knew, would be the Congressional and other elections scheduled for November 1974. The last Congressional elections in November 1970 had been a cynical farce, held in the shadow of the *cassações* and repression of 1969 and treated with due contempt by opponents of the regime, but by August 1974 a conference of lawyers could protest publicly over the continued suspension of *habeas corpus*, and the maintenance of Institutional Act No. 5, while, as the elections approached, it became clear that the government was willing to allow far freer debate than at any time since 1964. Opponents of the regime were allowed television time and uncensored press coverage for the expression of their views on such previously forbidden topics as human rights, especially in relation to the use of torture, the worsening pattern of the distribution of wealth, the rise in infant mortality, and the role of multinational corporations in Brazil. At first there was evidence of widespread cynicism or indifference on the part of the electorate,[17] but the campaign began to warm up right across the country[18] as the day came nearer for the 36,121,319 Brazilian electors to vote for 22 senators (one third of the Senate), 364 federal deputies, and 787 state deputies, with evidence appearing that there might, in fact, be a fairly massive opposition vote,[19] and far less abstentions and spoiled votes than in 1970.

The results more than bore out this evidence. Instead of spoiling their papers Brazil's electors voted heavily for MDB, taking advantage of the first chance in years to express their views. Of the 22 senate seats contested, MDB won 16 giving them 20 seats in the new Senate (61 per cent of the votes in the senate elections were for MDB candidates; 39 per cent for ARENA). MDB also elected 172 deputies to the lower house, as against 192 for ARENA, compared to only 87 MDB deputies before the elections. The voting for state assemblies was equally startling. Whereas previously MDB had controlled only Guanabara, the party was now successful in six states, including São Paulo, Rio Grande do Sul, and what was to become in March

1975 the new state of Rio de Janeiro, formed through the combination of Guanabara and the state of Rio de Janeiro to produce Brazil's second most important industrial state. The results of these state assembly elections were not to be underestimated, since, though state governors were in effect appointed by the federal government, they could only carry through programmes initiated by their state assemblies. Also noteworthy was the disappearance of some of the major political figures of recent years, men like Carvalho Pinto in São Paulo and João Cleofas in Pernambuco, again contributing to the sense of change and movement in national politics.

The elections of November 1974 were carefully scrutinized and analysed.[20] The conclusions were simple, but important. They showed that, despite years of repression, lack of electoral experience, and many other disadvantages, there was, broadly but clearly, a definite if not exclusive correlation between the poorer most disadvantaged social groups in Brazil and the vote for MDB. The vote in the more urban, industrial, and on the whole more clearly informed areas of Brazil was an opposition vote, with ARENA making more ground among sections of the electorate still more subject to clientelistic controls. Those who were now to represent the electorate scarcely reflected their hopes and aspirations, not surprisingly in view of the degree of interference in past years and the removal or exclusion of those who might have been the most effective spokesmen of the people. But, as was emphasized in the most perceptive of these electoral studies, the people of Brazil had shown on 15 November, however inadequate the means at their disposal, their desire for change.[21] Even among rural voters, with all their well-founded suspicion of the electoral system as yet another way of doing them down, there was, it seemed, a perception of MDB as the party of the poor (dos pobres) and of ARENA as a party of 'the others'. Similarly in São Paulo MDB was perceived as the 'party of popular interests', which in turn was defined as being against the government, to the extent that, justly or not, as the editors said, the government appeared to embody established interests and social exploitation.

The elections of November 1974 were a resounding refutation for all those, whether privileged groups in Brazil or sophisticated social scientists abroad, defending consciously or otherwise the interests of those groups, who denied the capacity of the Brazilian people to vote shrewdly and responsibly within a sensitively elaborated political system. In November 1970 they had voted with their feet, by staying away from the polls, or had deliberately spoiled their ballot papers as a gesture of protest and derision. Now in 1974, given only half a chance, they had used their vote to make clear their opposition to a system which had been imposed on them. Those who argued, with whatever brutal logic, that only by repression could the Brazilian people be controlled for the sake of narrow social and economic interests now had further justification for stifling freedom of expression: those who, sincerely if mistakenly, looked for a 'second leg' to support an essentially unpopular system now found that that second leg ended in a boot, to be applied in the most appropriate manner.

Opposition leaders, themselves surprised and rather taken aback by the extent of their success, were the first to acknowledge the importance of President Geisel's role in allowing the elections to take place smoothly.[22] The government, in turn, was quick to take due credit for a successful move to reopen political debate, interpreting the result of the election as a setback, admittedly, but not a disaster, arguing that the system could absorb and survive the result of the polls.[23] There seemed now a chance that in 1975 Congress might play a fuller part in shaping national policy, moving from the grey obscurity of the last six years or more.[24] Even the more radical wing of MDB, the so-called *autênticos*, now spoke of working towards a possible agreement, towards 'slow and certain relaxation' ('lenta e segura distensão'). Unlike October 1965 or December 1968 there was no sharp repressive reaction to a setback for the regime. Some 'hard-line' officers were obviously unhappy at the results, but Geisel was strong and confident enough to stand his ground. But the pressures were still there, as was shown most clearly in Geisel's broadcast to the nation on New Year's eve. Although a rather improbable time for concentrating one's mind on serious political matters, this was traditionally an occasion for a survey of achievements in the dying year. Geisel in a major speech emphasized his acceptance of a more open system, allowing room for public disagreement, but stressed, too, the need for an overriding consensus. In particular, he handed off the demand of one of his senior army colleagues, General Rodrigo Octávio, for a repeal of Institutional Act No. 5 and other special powers. Some relaxation, yes: but not too much, too quickly.[25] At the same time, seeking to hold the middle ground, Geisel was also warning those on the right who wanted to push him too hard: the special powers might also be used against them.

The end-of-year speech was reputedly drafted with the help of Golbery and Professor Heitor de Aquino Ferreira, but it was a fair and honest statement of Geisel's position since he took office. Indeed, fairness and honesty, frankness and probity, were the terms one reached for in describing Geisel, in refreshing contrast to many of those who opposed him for being too liberal. He had no time for corruption, for torture, or for many of the features of the previous administration, living up to his reputation as an austere, straight soldier and administrator, albeit, as some believed, saddled with an impossible task. There were persistent reports that he and those close to him, General Ednardo D'Avila Melo in São Paulo, Humberto Barreto, and even Golbery, were powerless to control continuing excesses and abuse of human rights, especially in São Paulo;[26] but there seemed no doubt of Geisel's personal antipathy to the institutionalized violence and terror licensed under Médici and all too ready to re-emerge should his own grip slacken.

The first months of 1975 brought continuous reports that Geisel's control was, indeed, slackening under repeated pressure from critics within the armed forces angry at his moves towards *distensão* and the alleged threat to the whole post-1964 system. Opposition success in the November elections was attributed to Communist influence and much was made of the discovery in late January of the source of a PCB publication. The security forces had certainly known of this earlier, but now felt it opportune to make a case of it, to underline the persistent danger of subversion. The discovery was announced on television by the Minister of Justice, Armando Falcão, with hints at tighter controls in future.[27] There was still optimistic comment on the realignment of ARENA and MDB in Congress, still clinging to the goal of 'lenta e segura distensão',[28] and 'descompressão gradual', with renewed emphasis on the need, as Geisel said at the opening of the new session of Congress on 1 March, for the political system to keep pace with the development of the economic system.[29] There was talk of a 'master plan' involving substantial changes, with frank debate over the future of Congress and the whole reshaping of Brazilian politics.[30] Censorship was evidently less strict, with Chico Buarque de Hollanda, for example, discussing how his best work had been censored and his hopes for better times to come.[31]

But there was also disturbing evidence running in the other direction. Speeches to mark the eleventh anniversary of the *coup* of 1964 took a harder line, accompanied by rumours of the government's intention to suppress both ARENA and MDB, because of its fear of a MDB victory in the next Congressional elections in 1978.[32] To mark the anniversary it was reported that Geisel had planned an important speech on the theme of *distensão*, but had been put under pressure by the army high command and forced to cut down the speech. He formally denied rumours of changes in the party structure in his short speech to the Senate,[33] but there were well-substantiated reports that during its meeting on 26 March in Brasília the high command, meeting to consider the current promotion lists, had expressed concern over threats to the reputation of the armed forces and to the maintenance of discipline and order. Part of the discussion centred around a letter written earlier in the month by a retired general, Pedro Celestino da Silva Pereira, who had protested that his son had been tortured for over two weeks by members of the First Army in Rio de Janeiro. The letter, given much attention in the press, implied that both Golbery and the commander of the First Army, General Reinaldo Melo de Almeida, knew of the torture, but had not intervened. The reaction of the high command was that there was altogether too much talk of torture and too many reports besmirching the reputation of the armed forces, and that it was time to clamp down. At the anniversary celebrations in São Paulo, General Ednardo D'Avila Melo deliberately stressed the unity of the army: 'The Brazilian army is one unity in which there is neither a hard group nor a soft group . . . a cohesive unity under the orders of General Geisel'.[34] He strongly attacked those who suggested that 'we are disobeying the will or orders of our president'. Nevertheless, the need to deny so emphatically reports of serious disagreement, themselves lent credence to the reports. It was said that key figures, such as the Minister of the Army, General Sílvio Coelho da Frota, were joining the president's critics and that, in particular, opinion was hardening against him in the SNI. Some of his most prominent opponents, men of the SNI and close to Médici, had been isolated to some degree, notably General Carlos Alberto da Fontoura, sent as ambassador to Portugal, but the SNI, with its own Siemens communications system, different from the Bell systems of the army, navy, air force, and police intelligence services, was a world of its own and a formidable centre of opposition to moves towards a more genuinely open political process.

This period also saw the first appearance of the so-called *Novela da Traição à Revolução de 1964*. This was a series of scurrilous broadsheets attacking Geisel and his government and the whole policy of 'abertura'. 'Opening of what and for what?', asked the first 'Chapter': 'From 1964 onwards Brazil never had need of any kind of "opening" and did not for any lack of it cease to go on developing. . . .' The authors then charged Golbery, in particular, with trying to reach agreement with politicians of the past, seeking to form a 'Brazilian Labour Union' (União Trabalhista Brasileira). They upbraided Congress, the National Conference of Brazilian Bishops, and the press for: 'insisting that an inquiry should be opened to find subversive elements who have disappeared. They even want an inquiry into our brave security forces, the unsleeping sentinels of our country . . .'. People with Communist sympathies, they said, or hostile to the Revolution of 1964, and with opinions contrary to those of the security forces, were being appointed to high government office. Five of these were named, but the bitterest attack was reserved for Golbery, who, after having worked for the Revolution, then, allegedly, took $30,000 a month from Dow Chemicals and now was betraying the Revolution.

These bitter attacks were to appear regularly over the coming months, abusing Geisel's team and anyone apparently sympathetic to *distensão*: Senator Petrônio Portela of ARENA; Célio Borja, president of the Chamber of Deputies; Manuel Diegues Júnior, a sociologist and director of the Cultural Department of the Ministry of Education and Culture; Dirceu Nogueira; Maurício Rangel Reis; Ney Braga; Arnaldo Prieto; Severo Gomes; Alisson Paulinelli; and Azeredo da Silveira. The lists went on and on,[35] with accusations against 'bloodsuckers of the nation', Communists, or the 'esquerda festiva', 'unprepared provincial nonentities', 'homosexuals', and 'traitors'. These attacks were associated with other manifestos and protests in, for example, the EsAO, but could not be shrugged off simply as the wild excesses of silly young officers on the right. A concerted attack on efforts to liberalize and open Brazilian politics was being mounted, backed by powerful industrial and financial interests, both national and international, afraid of a threat to the profitable workings of the system built up since 1964 and, in their terms, so admirably successful under Médici. Speculation now began to grow that *distensão* was finished and that Geisel might not long survive opposition within the armed forces, which were said to want to replace him by his vice president, General Adalberto Pereira dos Santos.

Nationalism versus Internationalism

The other major issue running parallel to the struggle over *distensão* was the old debate, now renewed, over the relative weight of nationalist and internationalist interests in Brazil's economy and development more generally. In April 1975 a parliamentary committee of inquiry was set up to look into the role of multinational corporations in Brazil. It was composed of thirteen deputies (seven ARENA, six from MDB), presided over by the opposition deputy Alencar Furtado, with another MDB deputy as vice president, Wellington Moreira Franco of Rio de Janeiro. Prominent from the start in this debate was the Minister of Industry and Commerce, Severo Gomes, who almost two years later would have to resign his post precisely because of his stand on this issue and because of his attempt to widen the internal market, however slightly, so urging nationalist priorities as against those of the multinationals.

The question of the role of multinational or transnational corporations in Brazil's economy and politics was, and still remains, the most hotly debated and far-reaching issue of national politics. It was one which particularly exercised the armed forces, because of its implications for national sovereignty and security, because of the challenge it contained for the traditionally strong nationalist sentiment of the armed forces, and because of the vested interest which many senior officers had as clients and, in effect, representatives, of different multinational groups, all of which had their highly paid placemen to promote their interests within the post-1964 political system. The new parliamentary committee of inquiry was meant to examine closely for the first time how the power of multinational interests worked, how it was articulated, where it was most effectively located, and what implications, at every level, it had for Brazil.

The debate on the role of multinational corporations since 1964 is still very much in progress and it would be wrong to anticipate the conclusions of current analysis and research. Some things, however, are already clear. First, as the report of the CPI (Parliamentary Committee of Inquiry) emphasized,[36] much more work needs to be done on the whole problem of multinational corporations in Brazil, and not just in Brazil. Secondly, the report showed that in dealing with foreign capital and multinational corporations the Brazilian government was still lamentably short of information and seriously lacking in coherent policy: no one, for example, had calculated as yet the social costs of foreign capital: the multinational firms seemed to have altogether better information and intelligence than the federal government. As one government official put it: 'I believe there is nothing worse for a country than that it should find itself defenceless in relation to the workings of international firms either through administrative incompetence or lack of administrative resources. . . .' Concern was also expressed as to the political and socio-cultural aspects of the heavy involvement of foreign capital in a country such as Brazil.

One important conclusion of the report was that the positive contribution of foreign and multinational capital was less than commonly supposed: the CPI raised again a question already posed by President Geisel: were these corporations a force for good or ill? Above all, what steps was the government taking, bearing in mind the overall nature of the 'Brazilian model' and the 'miracle', to increase its bargaining power in relation to the multinational corporations? The corporations, clearly, were profiting from Brazil's openness to foreign involvement, its low wage-rates, its absence of strikes, and its political stability, but this maximization of profits should also be geared to the development of the country, especially social development. It was simply not enough, the report argued, to go 'cap in hand' ('chapeu na mão') to multinational corporations.

The general conclusion of the report was that the Brazilian government should look again, very closely, at its relations with the world of international capital and the large multinational corporations, to see whether in fact it was not faring very badly, and with it Brazilian society as a whole, in relation to multinational interests. The debate on multinationals and foreign capital also ran in tandem with that on 'statism' versus less state involvement, one side of this argument being that only a very strong state could stand up to the multinationals and internationalized interests, while the other, very different, view was that the modern Brazilian, or post-1964, state could scarcely do that, since it was itself the creature of those internationalized interests.

Probably the most important feature of the parliamentary inquiry was to bring the whole question of foreign capital into the forefront of national debate, pinpointing its merits and demerits for both military and civilian politicians. The report showed that the share of foreign investments in all investment in industry had risen from 11 per cent in 1963, to 14 in 1964, 16 in 1965, 14 in 1966, 26 in 1967, 20 in 1968, and 35 per cent in 1969.[37] In certain key sectors, such as electrical industry and transport material, it was as high as 76·16 and 96·44 per cent. Foreign capital was especially concentrated in the most crucial productive sectors of industry and its share in the total sales of different sectors had risen steadily from 1966 to 1970. Noting the difficulty of calculating precisely the level of profits enjoyed by the multinationals, the report concluded, on the basis of, for example, the eleven multinational firms classified by the Central Bank as the biggest in each productive sector, that each of them without exception remitted abroad an amount of capital greater than they had invested. In the period under scrutiny multinational firms had brought in an estimated $298·8 million and had taken out something of the order of $774·5 million, a difference over the last ten years only of about half a billion dollars, though even these figures were said to be an underestimation.

The insistence in the report that multinational firms and multinational capital were playing the key role in the most crucial and sensitive areas of Brazil's economy; the figures on the levels of profit; the debate on the whole pattern of the import of technology, and on the overall lack of government control gave stimulus to still further analysis. The findings of the report also coincided with other work already done or in progress. In particular they complemented the 1975 report of the Subcommittee on Multinational Corporations of the United States Senate, already quoted, in its examination of *Multinational Corporations in Brazil and Mexico; Structural Sources of Economic and Noneconomic Power*. That report, too, emphasized the problem for any single nation of controlling the workings of multinational corporations, as Senator Church said in his introduction: 'The international nature of the M.N.C. limits the capability of present institutional structures to guide and direct them in a manner perceived as maximizing the public good'. This was particularly a problem when, as the report noted:

> . . . $150 billion, or well over one-third of the total $350 billion aggregate world G.N.P. is produced by international firms . . . The relative growth rates of nations and multinationals indicate that this role is increasing. . . . Some projections predict that 'in another 20 years 600 or 700 corporations will control most of the business in the non-Communist world'. . . . Present trends could produce a regime of 300 or 400 multinational corporations controlling 60 to 70 percent of the world industrial output . . .[38]

The Senate report rightly stressed the size of MNCs:

> Many of the MNCs have total sales three to five times greater than the gross products of the countries in which they operate. By 1972 fully 57 of the 100 largest economic entities were MNCs. This comparison includes only industrial corporations; had banks and other nonmanufacturers been included, another dozen or more MNCs would have joined the list of the world's top economic entities.[39]

In the table in question the United Kingdom lay fifth, with a gross product of $153 billion; Brazil was eighth with 50·7 billion, and General Motors was sixteenth with 30·4 billion, just between Belgium (35·6) and Argentina (29·7).

Turning to Latin America the Senate report noted that for the period 1960 to 1972 the net outflow of funds was $9·2 billion.[40] Looking at Brazil it calculated that by 1972 total foreign investment was about $7 billion, with 68 per cent concentrated in manufacturing, the next largest sector being public utilities, 16 per cent.[41] The United States controlled 36 per cent of the total foreign capital stock, with the rate of United States investment quickening from a 4 per cent annual rate of expansion during 1950–60, to about 5 per cent in 1960–66, and around 12 per cent in 1966–72.

One striking feature of the Brazilian economy stressed by the Senate report was its 'denationalization'. Among the largest 50 non-financial corporations in 1972, 14 were foreign multinationals: among Brazilian-controlled firms most were state-owned. Only 8 of the largest 50 firms were controlled by private Brazilian citizens.[42]

Of the largest hundred firms, 77 were either foreign- or government-owned. In the manufacturing sector almost half (49 per cent) of the largest 300 manufacturing enterprises were foreign-controlled: the Brazilian private sector accounted for 46 per cent and the state controlled the other 5 per cent. 59 of the top hundred were foreign-controlled, 19 being United States based. The overall trend was for the largest enterprises in key industries to be controlled by multinational corporations, with a notable increase in non-United States MNCs.[43] The report also estimated that 'United States and other foreign multinationals together produce roughly 50 percent of all local sales in Brazil'.[44]

The finding that almost half Brazil's industry was under foreign control[45] had further implications for what the Senate report called 'considerable potential noneconomic power',[46] a potential the authors of the report wished to see curbed. But it was also a power which seriously exercised Brazilian nationalists, both civilian and military. What the reports did not analyse sufficiently, however, was how precisely that power was articulated in the Brazilian political system, particularly in the use of highly paid placemen operating on behalf of multinational corporations, moving the levers of power when their interests demanded it. This research into the politics of the multinationals is now going on, accompanied in particular by theoretical analysis of the nature of the post-1964 Brazilian state and its organic links with the international capitalist system.[47]

Quis custodiet . . . ?

One important feature of the debate on the multinationals was that it necessarily went beyond mere scrutiny of the role of foreign capital, the economic impact of 'denationalization', or other related economic issues. It opened up the whole question of the nature of the 'Brazilian model' and the 'miracle' and the whole pattern of policy formation in a semi-closed system in which public debate was stifled, so that too often it was impossible for alternative models to be examined carefully, whether in the press or other media, in Congress, in the universities, or any other public forum. Too often, it seemed, key decisions on national policy, not always wise decisions, were 'taken in technocratic offices, surrounded by the secrecy of a pseudo-national security'.[48] This narrowness of the debate and the restricted, self-selecting, circle of decision-makers were alarming. In this respect the growing public concern over the multinationals was directly linked to the other key issue of Geisel's presidency, the search for a viable, flexible, more open, and more genuinely democratic political system, which not only would end the abuses and excesses of earlier years, but provide a more efficient, more sensitive process for shaping national decisions in line with more clearly defined and more rigorously and widely argued national priorities. In other words, what was now being called in question was not just the violence and abuse of human rights associated with recent government in Brazil, nor its openness to corruption or its tendency to dangerous infighting and consequent compromise in choice and decision. All these features, described by some social scientists and spokesmen for military regimes as weaknesses of civilian politics which military control would avoid, were to be found in recent Brazilian experience. But now, particularly in relation to the multinationals, the argument went further, again not just stressing the social costs of recent policy, or the benefits flowing to only a small minority of Brazil's people, but questioning the whole effectiveness and ultimate viability of a system which persistently and systematically removed from public scrutiny and debate the most far-reaching decisions concerning national policy. In this sense *distensão* was not just a more pleasing, perhaps less offensive, option for national politics, but, if genuinely carried through, a return to a more effective system of government in the national interest. The real question at issue was the will of the regime to carry it through.

May 1975 saw a substantial rise in the minimum wage, of the order of 41·4 per cent, to 532 cruzeiros a month. This was the first time since 1964 that the wage increase had exceeded the rise in the cost of living, which accounted for estimates from DIEESE (Trade Union Department of Statistics and Socio-Economic Studies) that by April 1974 the minimum wage was worth only 44 per cent of its real value in 1964. The question of wage adjustment had provoked sharp disagreement. Those, such as Minister Severo Gomes, who wanted to expand the internal market, were firmly in favour of a substantial rise. Others, like Mário Henrique Simonsen, wanted a smaller increase, but, with the sharply climbing inflation, there was an increasing problem sheerly in terms of reproduction of the labour force which the government had to face.[49] The new increase also reflected the public debate, no longer a forbidden subject, of the relation between growth and distribution and the subsequent criticism of the regime both at home and abroad. In his 1 May speech at Joinville, Geisel emphasized his government's hope to establish closer dialogue with the workers.[50] Some lessons from the previous November's elections seemed to have been learned.

In relations between the state and the working class, as seen in this slight shift in government policy, the initiative and control was firmly on the side of the government and the state. The degree of state involvement and control in every area of national life was also by now one of the major issues of discussion, the power and degree of penetration by the state being ever more apparent as the debate went on.[51] Recognition of this was reflected in June 1975 in tentative moves by the leaders of MDB to woo the armed forces. Many members of the armed forces had evidently voted for MDB the previous November and new overtures on the part of the opposition were now explained as a logical acceptance of the fact that the armed forces as an institution claimed to be above party politics. The aim of MDB was simply to attract them as individual citizens, in support of opposition policies.[52] Nevertheless, the move brought predictable reaction from those who saw it as essentially an attempt to infiltrate the armed forces, and one which neither Geisel nor Golbery regarded with favour. Later in the month Geisel showed that Institutional Act No. 5 was not dead, using it to intervene in the state of Acre, while a speech by José Bonifacio, leader of the government in the Chamber of Deputies, provided a clear, obviously government-inspired warning that *distensão* had very definite limits.[53] Geisel showed this yet again in July, by using his powers under Institutional Act No. 5 to take away the senate seat of an ARENA senator, Wilson Campos, cleared of corruption by the Senate, but now removed by Geisel in a swift action which showed not only his strong dislike of corruption, but his readiness to move against members of the government party when necessary.

There were now increasing signs of government anxiety over public discussion of torture, corruption, the nature and direction of the economy, and over the violent expression of popular resentment, as seen, for example, in July 1975, in riots by frustrated travellers on the Central do Brasil railway linking working-class areas to the centre of Rio de Janeiro. There continued to be discussion of a reformulation of politics on a wider basis,[54] but the tone of military pronouncements was far from encouraging, with repeated emphasis on the continuing threat of subversion and the danger of infiltration, as D'Avila Melo stressed to a packed audience in São Paulo on 18 July, an audience made up of members of the state government, senior military officers, businessmen, and members of the ADESG (Association of Graduates of the ESG).[55]

The most formal warning came in a speech by Geisel on 1 August speaking, on television, on the eve of the reopening of Congress after its mid-term recess. Speeches in July had sustained the idea of *distensão*, apparently supported by key governors, such as Paulo Egydio Martins in São Paulo, Aureliano Chaves in Minas Gerais, and Sinval Guazelli in Rio Grande do Sul.[56] Geisel's long speech, the longest he had made as president, seemed to most observers, especially in MDB, to mark the end of *distensão*.[57] This judgement was, in fact, premature and partly hinged on a misinterpretation of Geisel's remarks. Speaking of *distensão*, he commented on speculation, especially since the November elections, attributing to the government, especially to himself, intentions, aims, successes, failures, submissions to pressure, all mainly the product of the imagination of those indulging in such unfounded comment. His persistent aim, he repeated, was for a 'humane, integrated development'.

One important result of the speech, whether misinterpretation or not, was a further demoralization in the ranks of MDB. Officially, their spokesmen reacted defiantly, notably the party chairman, Ulysses Guimarães, in a statement on 5 August,[58] but subsequent evidence was to indicate that Geisel's speech had a considerable impact on recruitment to and participation in MDB in the months which followed, persuading many, who otherwise might have worked for the opposition, to proceed more cautiously. The speech pricked the bubble of opposition euphoria at a time when party organization and future planning should have been at their height. There was, in fact, talk of splitting MDB, perhaps with the right-wing of the movement joining groups now in ARENA, while those more to the left, the so-called *autênticos* and *renovadores*, might form a more vigorous opposition body. The disadvantage of this plan, however, was that the loss of the more right-wing elements in MDB, sometimes called the *adhesionistas*, might well serve both to strengthen the government, working with ARENA, and isolate and make more vulnerable those further to the left. This hesitancy was also encouraged by reports in late September that Geisel was again losing ground with strong supporters in command of troops in only General Reinaldo Melo de Almeida in Rio de Janeiro and General Moacir Potiguara in the Fourth Army at Recife. Geisel was said to be trying to improve his position by moving Reinaldo Melo de Almeida to the job of Minister of the Army, replacing him with a man again closer to himself, General Euler Bentes Ribeiro. Such reports, well-founded or not, coupled with further rumour of the growing influence of the SNI and, in particular, of Figueiredo, all gave further cause for concern to MDB in its moves towards party reorganization and its plans for the future.[59]

In October 1975 Geisel showed both his flexible pragmatism and his ability to survive by first accepting, then pushing through against opposition, a decision to allow 'risk contracts' to foreign oil companies to search for oil in Brazil. Such a decision, although the details were not yet known, was a major break with past policy, which had always accepted Brazilian claims to its oil as a touchstone of nationalist loyalty. The decision was particularly interesting, in that former prominent nationalist spokesmen, such as Albuquerque Lima, now supported it. In the long run it seemed probable that the debate and decision might prove important more for their symbolic value than for any real substance, but, compared with the furore of past years over oil, it was a notable straw in the wind.

Far more attention was given to an altogether different event in late September, one which was also to have a more important political impact. This was the death under torture in São Paulo of one of the city's best-known journalists, Vladimir Herzog. He worked for TV Cultura and had also worked for *O Estado de São Paulo, Visão,* the BBC, and in films. He had reported, as asked, to the security authorities and his body was returned next day to his wife. Herzog's death caused a major scandal for the regime, being associated with an intensification of repression more generally in São Paulo, carrying overtones of anti-semitism and producing a swift angry public reaction, most clearly demonstrated at an ecumenical service in São Paulo in his memory. The authorities tried to prevent a public show of sympathy on this occasion, but without success, so that the torture and death of Herzog became a major source of embarrassment, both nationally and internationally. D'Avila Melo was summoned from São Paulo to Brasília to explain the disastrous mistake and there was a wave of disgust against the repressive apparatus in São Paulo. For perhaps the first time middle-class opinion was deeply stirred, or at least publicly mobilized, over abuses already long entrenched in the Brazilian political process, and there was a notable reaction of sympathy for Geisel and for Egydio Martins in São Paulo, in so far as they were perceived as representing a line within the regime opposed to such excesses.

By the start of 1976 Geisel was in a stronger position than he had been for many months. His stand over the Herzog affair had done him credit and had allowed him to stamp firmly on some of the most repressive elements in São Paulo. He had been able, for example, to transfer to Matto Grosso Colonel José Barros Paes, head of the *Segunda Secção* in São Paulo, the man held directly responsible for Herzog's death, and one who was said to have been influential with D'Avila Melo, head of the Second Army, who, starting as a pro-Geisel man, committed to curbing torture and other excesses in São Paulo, was now widely regarded as having followed the established pattern of having been 'won over' by an important sector of the São Paulo financial and political establishment. This was a pattern discernible from at least the days of General Isidoro Dias Lopes in the 1920s, or João Alberto in the early 1930s, but was still as vigorous as ever. There were rumours that the scandal over Herzog's death had in fact caused a move to replace Geisel to be called off, a move allegedly involving D'Avila Melo in São Paulo, with the complicity, among others, of the Army Minister, General Coelho da Frota, and of Delfim Neto from his comfortable base in Paris. There was, it was said, much more to the death of Herzog than the over-zealous activity of soldiers and strong-arm thugs on the spot, pushing one man, among others, beyond his endurance. Herzog, according to one report, was associated with José Mindlin, a man of substantial commercial interests in São Paulo and a member of the São Paulo state government. He, in turn, had connections with Geisel's most important representative in São Paulo, Egydio Martins, who, again, was involved with a man who eventually had followed him in the federal Industry and Commerce Ministry, Severo Gomes. The linkage, in this case, involved a cluster of interests, liberalization and *distensão*, commerce and smaller industry in São Paulo, and the build-up of a project to expand the internal market. In São Paulo, in particular, these interests were also associated with such figures as Lafer and Klabin, all pointing to a relatively coherent picture. On the other side, linked in one form or another to the whole repressive apparatus, was an equivalent cluster. At one extreme in São Paulo this had been seen in the death of Vladimir Herzog, but from there it was articulated to wider São Paulo interests, through Maluf, Salim, Lutfallah, Laudo Natel, Aguiar (*Bradesco*), Atalla (*Copersucar*), and on to Delfim in Paris and the whole Médici, anti-*distensão*, pro-multinational enterprises, seeking to remove and replace Geisel and return to the more untrammelled days of the 'Brazilian model' and its associated 'miracle'. The torture and death of Herzog, in other words (however coded), were only the tip of the iceberg: the scandal his death generated had, therefore, widespread repercussions.

One immediate change came later in January 1976, when yet another prisoner was known to have died under torture, a metal-worker, Manoel Fiel Filho.[60] Geisel hesitated no longer, dismissing D'Avila Melo and replacing him by another general reputedly close to the president, Dilermando Gomes Monteiro, who had figured prominently in Geisel's first appointments in 1974. Influential in this dismissal was a letter published on 13 January, in which many of Brazil's leading journalists had expressed their dissatisfaction at the lack of more careful, public inquiry into the circumstances of Herzog's death. They included Prudente de Morais, chairman of ABI (Brazilian Press Association), Carlos Castello Branco of the *Jornal do Brasil*, and Carlos Chagas, press officer of Costa e Silva and author of the most perceptive study of the succession crisis leading to the takeover by Médici.

With Geisel now firmly in the saddle the early months of 1976 were relatively quiet. In his speech to Congress in March, marking the start of the new legislative session, Geisel reaffirmed his commitment to improving the democratic process, reassuring members of Congress that the municipal elections would take place as scheduled in November.[61] At the same time, however, the Minister of Justice, Armando Falcão, speaking only a week later to a conference of states' secretaries of security in Brasília, strongly emphasized the need to keep up the fight against subversion, a concern seen, too, in a renewed wave of arrests, involving in March alone over one hundred prominent people associated with MDB, mainly journalists and intellectuals. It was estimated that over the previous two years of Geisel's presidency more than 2,000 people had been arrested[62] and it was also regarded as significant that the new army commander in São Paulo, General Dilermando, refused to reopen the inquiry into Herzog's death and forbade the disclosure of the results of the inquiry into the case of Manoel Fiel Filho. At the same time Geisel strengthened his position still further by dismissing the head of CIEX (Centro de Informações do Exército), General Danton de Paula Avelino, having previously dismissed his deputy, Colonel Rui Cavalcanti. Both had been involved in an attempt to cover up the death of Manoel Fiel Filho and the president's action was again a salutary warning to others.

But still the *cassações* and curbing of politicians critical of the regime continued. In January Geisel had suspended the political rights of a federal deputy, Marcelo Gatto, and a São Paulo state deputy, Nelson Fabiano, both of MDB. Gatto was one of the most outspoken new members of the *autênticos* and was removed after having been accused by Colonel Erasmo Dias and Major Ismael Armond of the DOPS in São Paulo of having Communist connections. Now Geisel acted in the same way in reply to speeches made on 20 March in Palmeira das Missões (Rio Grande do Sul) by two state deputies, Nadyr Rosseti and Amaury Müller. Rosseti had claimed that: 'The fall of the regime is certain, if not through its own rottenness, because of corruption', and Müller had declared: 'The time has now come to put an end to the dictatorship'.[63] Geisel at once ordered the *cassações* of both state deputies and a few days later acted in the same way against one of the most prominent MDB federal deputies, Lysâneas Maciel of Rio de Janeiro, because of his speech in Congress condemning the earlier *cassações*. The air was thick with rumour of further lists of 'cassáveis' and the MDB was more angry and alarmed than at any time since the elections of November 1974.[64] Maciel was now the sixteenth opposition member to lose his mandate in the last two years. The national directorate of MDB, made up of 71 members, 24 of them from the *autêntico* group, met to discuss what should be done. The *autênticos* at first wanted to issue their own vigorous protest, but were told quite unambiguously by the president's press secretary, Humberto Esmeraldo Barreto, that anyone signing such a statement would join the list of *cassados*. A compromise statement was at last agreed on, published in the press, but not allowed to be broadcast on radio or television. The whole affair showed clearly that the opposition was strictly under licence, which went only so far.

The list of military promotions announced at this time also strengthened Geisel's hand and favoured men who had previously worked with him. There were three new *generais de exército:* eight were promoted as *generais de divisão* and eleven to the rank of *general de brigada*. The three four-star generals were Ayrton Pereira Tourinho, Ariel Pacca da Fonseca, and Fernando Belforth Bethlem. Tourinho had served with Geisel in Brasília in the early 1960s, Fonseca had run the secretariat of the National Security Council in 1964, when Geisel was chief of the Military Cabinet of Castello Branco, and Bethlem had headed the cabinet of the late Dale Coutinho, Geisel's Minister of the Army. Geisel was able to leave for his official visits to France and Great Britain confident that he was stronger than at any time since taking office.

One important issue on which divisions within the regime were discernible was, yet again, that of the degree of state and nationalist control of the economy. During a visit to Brazil, Henry Kissinger had made clear his reservations about the extent of state involvement in the economy and the discussion ran on warmly throughout the year, becoming the main subject of political debate.[65] Some government officials favoured selling large state-owned companies, such as Petrobrás and Companhia Vale do Rio Doce (CVRD), as a means of reducing the large foreign debt. The campaign against *estatização* was orchestrated by the conservative economist Eugênio Gudin and had support in the government, notably from Shigeaki Ueki, Minister of Mines and Energy. It was strongly opposed, on the other hand, by the Minister of Industry and Commerce, Severo Gomes, who was by now the main government spokesman for the camp whose main aim seemed to be to build up a stronger internal market than had been thought necessary by policy-makers since 1964.[66] There were powerful voices urging the case for *desestatização*, such as the chairman of the Banco Nacional de Desenvolvimento, Marcos Pereira Viana, and the campaign had especially strong support in São Paulo, particularly in *O Estado de São Paulo*. In July 1976 it suffered a temporary setback, when Delfim Neto, on a visit to Brazil, spoke against the idea of handing over the key state firms to private ownership. This seemed mainly, if somewhat improbably, a tactic to win favour with Geisel and further Delfim's hopes of standing as governor of São Paulo in 1978, itself further evidence of Geisel's strong position. At the same time it was a blow to those who looked for a clear lead from Delfim in the debate over state control. Some evidence of how Giesel himself saw this debate seemed to appear in July. On 14 July, *Veja*[67] carried an interview with a retired admiral, José Celso de Macedo Soares Guimarães. This followed the appearance of a series of articles on Fridays in *Jornal do Brasil*, all arguing the case for taking state companies into private control. Macedo Soares was well connected, now working as an engineering consultant. He was the nephew of a former governor of São Paulo, of a former Minister of Industry and Commerce in the government of São Paulo, and of a journalist and owner of the now defunct *Diário Carioca*. He was not, as he said himself, just a recent convert to the cause of private control. He had been director, under Médici, of the Superintendência Nacional de Marinha Mercante (*Sunamam*) and had broken the monopoly of Lloyd as an act, as he said, of *desestatização*. He had also headed a committee of businessmen to discuss how state control might be reduced. His latest series of articles were a strong frontal attack on the government. They were followed by the announcement that Macedo Soares was being charged under the law of national security. This at once became a major talking-point. Eventually, however, it seemed that the main source of government indignation was a remark about Reis Velloso. Tempers cooled and the storm was found to have blown over.

Meanwhile, Geisel further demonstrated confidence in his ability to maintain his policy of a cautious move towards more open politics by resisting demands, especially from Figueiredo and the SNI, to cancel the municipal elections planned for November. The campaign began to grow in volume, though reduced by a ruling that excluded the use of radio and television except in a few carefully defined cases. It further stimulated the debate on state control, and the elections were evidently going to become precisely that major test of support for the government which the right-wing military and their civilian supporters feared. In this context a speech by ex-president Médici in July, his first since leaving office, was regarded as particularly important. He took a typically illiberal line, publicly siding in effect with those who opposed *distensão* and the decision to hold elections in November.[68]

Despite opposition and criticism Geisel continued to strengthen his position. In late July he moved General Moacir Barcellos Potiguara from his command of the Fourth Army in Recife to be Chief of the General Staff of the Armed Forces. Potiguara was an old associate of the president's brother, Orlando Geisel, and his transfer meant that the president would now have in three armies a commander close to himself in the months leading to the November elections. The list of promotions at the same time showed important developments, with the promotion to four-star general of Tácito Teóphilo Gaspar de Oliveira and Argus Lima.[69] That more support was still welcome was seen in mounting criticism, particularly in *O Estado de São Paulo*, over alleged corruption among government ministers and those close to the centre of power. The articles in *O Estado* fiercely attacked the perks and life-style of government ministers, altogether different from the austere personal image of Geisel. The president at once ordered an inquiry and acted swiftly against the ex-governor of Rio Grande do Norte, Cortez Pereira, suspending his political rights and those of four of his associates, including two of his brothers. It was an adroit move and a quick recovery, since Cortez Pereira had originally been governor under Médici and was still an admirer and associate of the previous president.[70] Nevertheless, the series of articles, associated with renewed attacks on the role of the state and reports of growing dissatisfaction among junior officers, all showed how carefully Geisel still had to tread.

Some measure of the degree of repression which had been experienced over the last two years was contained in a report from the PCB in its paper *Voz Operária* that the party had lost over the past two years half of its leaders, killed or imprisoned by the security forces.[71] In a long article of self-criticism the paper urged the opposition to use the weapon of the vote in the coming November elections to protest against the regime, at the same time acknowledging the failures in strategy and tactics on its own side in recent years. Such appeals, coupled to exaggerated claims by prominent Communists, such as Luís Carlos Prestes, about the party's role in the elections of November 1974, tended to play into the hands of those who identified democratic opposition with a Communist plot. But in late August came a further reminder of the days of more genuinely democratic government, with the death on 22 August in a motor accident of ex-president Juscelino Kubitschek. The former president had wanted his funeral service to be held in Brasília and about 60,000 people accompanied his coffin, with widespread demonstrations of affection and respect being repeated throughout the nation during the three days of mourning which the government reluctantly decreed.

On 15 August the election campaign was formally opened, at once dominating the media and swamping all other issues.[72] The start of the campaign was marked by the bombing of offices belonging to such groups as the Brazilian Press Association, the Order of

Brazilian Lawyers, CEBRAP, and the National Council of Brazilian Bishops. There was also an assault on the bishop of Nova Iguaçú, Adriano Mandarino Hypólito, in late September, the bishop being seized, stripped, painted red, then later released. All these actions seemed to be the work of the Aliança Anticomunista Brasileira (AAB), as was a bomb attack on the home of Roberto Marinho, publisher of the daily *O Globo*.[73] The municipal elections were obviously causing much concern, even though there would be no real contest in key *municípios* defined as important for national security, where mayors would be appointed by the government, and even though MDB would not be contesting about 1,500 *municípios* because of lack of local support. The polling would, in effect, be restricted to about 3,750 *municípios*, for mayors and councillors, and for councillors only, in another 175 *municípios*, including the 22 state capitals and the *municípios de segurança nacional*.

The MDB attitude, from the start, was reminiscent of Augustine's prayer, for chastity: but not yet. The MDB wanted victory, but not too much, in case a too resounding defeat for the government should result in the cancellation of the still more important Congressional elections due to be held in 1978. In any case there was much ground to be made up, since in 1972 ARENA had elected 3,349 mayors and 29,331 *vereadores* (councillors) as against MDB's 436 mayors and 5,936 *vereadores*. The difference in 1976, however, was not just the much more open debate, or the opposition victory in the November 1974 elections, but the fact that in approaching these elections the government, notably Geisel himself, had become directly involved, so that the elections inevitably were seen as a test of government support and popularity. Most of the debate in the campaign therefore centred on national rather than narrowly local issues, especially in the larger towns and cities, where MDB could offer most effective opposition. The campaign began to build up strongly throughout October with packed meetings as evidence of popular interest and involvement.[74] Geisel, stressing to ARENA that the elections were not restricted 'only to local interests', encouraged the party's candidates to push forward with a campaign which was 'attacking, even aggressive'. MDB leaders, such as Franco Montoro and Ulysses Guimarães, recommended their opponents to remember 1974 and claimed growing support, not only in the big cities, but also in medium-sized and small *municípios*.

Geisel was undoubtedly right to emphasize that these were not merely parish-pump elections except perhaps in those rural *municípios*, in any case dominated by ARENA, where clientelistic patterns of control still persisted. The November elections were being held at a time when the economy was looking less impressive than at any time in the last decade. The rapidly rising inflation and neglect, or mishandling, of certain areas of the economy were now not only hitting the poorer sections of society. These were, indeed, still doing badly, hit for example by such measures as the shift towards the production of soya beans for export, resulting in a serious lack of black beans, *feijão*, one of the basic staple foods, which now had to be imported from Chile, and which were fast becoming so expensive as to be out of the reach of the poor and many working people. But the crisis in the economy, by late 1976, was also hitting the middle class and those who most had benefited in the past from the 'miracle'. As inflation reached over 40 per cent and as a limit seemed to have been reached in the degree to which the sacrifices could be imposed on those lower down the social scale, the burden had inevitably to be spread out further, extended logically to the middle-class and still richer groups. These were already irked by such restrictions as having to deposit money with the Banco do Brasil before they could travel abroad, except on business; they felt especially keenly the rapid rise in the price of petrol, and generally were more discontented, more critical of the government, and more sceptical about the Brazilian model than at any time since 1964. The model, therefore, became one of the issues in the elections, even though these were ostensibly for local offices. Much attention was given in the Brazilian press to repeated doubts abroad as to the viability of the Brazilian model as handled in recent years, doubts expressed in October, for example, in *The Times* and in the *Wall Street Journal.* Already in August an article in *The Times* had suggested that dissatisfaction over the handling of the economy could cause trouble for Geisel in the November elections.[75] Now it was quoted again, as evidence of widespread unease abroad over Brazil's economy.[76] The president of Chase Manhattan Bank, David Rockefeller, regarded as a great enthusiast for the Brazilian model, which he had helped to create, was quoted as issuing in Hong Kong a warning that the pattern of increasing loans by bankers to developing countries, such as Mexico, Brazil, the Philippines, and Indonesia, could not go on indefinitely.

The *Wall Street Journal* upbraided 'Brazilian bureaucrats' for panicking and trying to blame multinational corporations for their problems, especially in the balance of payments. Such comment naturally provoked irritation, and gave further stimulus to those, such as Severo Gomes, who favoured a sufficiently different strategy for Brazil. Speaking in São Paulo in October, he urged that the country should take positive advantage of its difficulties, by choosing a different option—strengthening substantially its internal market and seeking to reduce socio-economic inequalities. One necessary condition for doing this, he stressed, was a new *political* alignment, seeking a pattern of development in tune 'with the most legitimate and authentic characteristics and aspirations of the Brazilian people'. In other words, while the problem was basically economic, the solution would have to be found at the political level.[77] Others wanted a different approach, with some industrialists arguing that both state and multinational companies were given privileged treatment, which should be curtailed, as Senator Magalhães Pinto now reported to Geisel.

There was, it soon appeared, much sympathy for the views expressed by Severo Gomes, but also strong opposition. There were those, such as the president of the Federation of Industries of Pernambuco, who favoured both Severo's defence of Brazilian business and industry and his stress on distribution, a view echoed by the head of the same federation in Rio Grande do Sul. Others regarded his views as dangerously socialistic and statist, while another interpretation was that all that Severo Gomes was wanting was a flexible adjustment in the current economic model, switching emphasis, as the international situation changed, from the export sector to production for consumption in an expanded internal market.[78] This last interpretation was probably nearest the mark. Severo Gomes seemed mainly to want a readjustment in the pattern of Brazil's recent development, while also expressing the concern of many smaller industrialists and businessmen at the weight of transnational interests in the present model. To that extent he was the spokesman for a fraction of the industrial and commercial bourgeoisie different from that dominant in recent years—those more 'internationalized' elements in the bourgeoisie. His shift in emphasis towards expanding the internal market necessarily implied an increase in salaries and more attention to distribution generally, but it was scarcely a radical or socialist demand. Nevertheless, in the heightened debate leading to the November elections he could appear as the most forceful critic from within the regime, whose calls for even moderate change of emphasis could also win support from more nationalist and, on certain points, more radical critics of the system.

One sign of the caution of all opposition, or potential opposition, groups was the decision by the National Conference of Brazilian Bishops not to publish a report prepared on violence against the Church until after the elections. The report reflected concern over a number of killings and acts of violence in recent months, especially the shooting of a Jesuit priest, João Bosco Penido Burnier in October. Burnier, whose family was well connected in both military and church circles, had protested against the torture of three women held by the police (PM)[79] in the settlement of Ribeirão Bonito in Matto

Grosso. Burnier and the local bishop were in the village by chance, heard of the torture, and protested. They were accused of being 'subversives' and 'Communists', and Burnier was beaten with rifle butts and shot in the head.

Burnier's death, preceded by the killing of another priest in Matto Grosso, Rudolfo Lubenkein, was an acute embarrassment to the government, which at once condemned the outrage and the torture which had led to it. Geisel personally condemned it in conversation with a relative of Burnier, the archbishop of Juiz de Fora.[80] The incident not only illustrated, however, the persistent friction between Church and State; it also reopened discussion about the violent behaviour of *fazendeiros* against *posseiros* (squatters) in Brazil's interior in the rush to open up new land. The bishop who had accompanied Burnier alleged that 'the Church of the people is being persecuted'.[81] The women who were being tortured were related to *posseiros*, one of whom was being sought for murder; but the incident brought more public attention to violence against *posseiros* in areas such as Matto Grosso.[82] This, in turn, brought to the forefront of attention the government's whole policy for developing the interior, particularly Amazonas, raising sharp, often embarrassing questions on the eve of elections.[83]

The election campaign[84] was followed by a large turn-out in the elections themselves on 15 November. The results were something of a stalemate, with both sides claiming victory, if for rather different reasons. As expected, ARENA did much the best in rural areas, while MDB was clearly ahead in the larger urban centres. There were unexpected losses in some cases, such as Curitiba, but, by and large, the opposition was happy with its success in the most dynamic centres of high urban and industrial concentration, or those in which the electorate, as in Rio Grande do Sul, traditionally played a vigorous role in politics.[85] The press acknowledged victory for the regime, which the opposition, contented with its own performance, was wise enough not to deny. The most important thing about these elections was quite clearly the fact that they had been held. Opportunity had been given, and duly taken, for wide-ranging debate on the economic, social, and political priorities of the regime, for examination of alternative strategies, for discussion about the gains and losses of the last thirteen years, for comparison with earlier performance under, for example, Kubitschek, and for a finer awareness of how far the present system could be stretched. Both Geisel, to whom all credit should be, and was, given, and the opposition had explored the limits of *distensão*, and found that, despite an aggressive, even vicious, right wing in the army and the state, those limits could be extended.

After the excitement of the municipal elections the year closed with something of a whimper. Geisel had not only survived the public scrutiny of the elections, but had emerged stronger for the experience. The end-of-year promotions further strengthened his position, notably by the advancement to four-star general of Carlos Alberto Cabral Ribeiro and José Pinto de Araujo Rabelo.[86] There were rumours already of possible presidential aspirants, with talk, as indeed there had been on every occasion since 1967, of Ney Braga as a possible successor able to reconcile, as former general and civilian state governor, the contending claim of military and civilian interests. More substantially, perhaps, there was speculation as to the chances of Figueiredo, the most likely candidate of the SNI, the pro-Médici, and, scarcely by now a secret, the anti-Geisel team. All, however, remained at the level of political speculation. Geisel at the end of 1976 seemed firmly in control, able to take away the political rights of Leonel Júlio, president of the São Paulo legislative assembly,[87] the seventh elected deputy to be *cassado* by Geisel in 1976.

Probably the most notable event of December 1976, though recorded with much reluctance and little magnanimity by the regime, was the death of João Goulart, at the age of fifty-eight. He died, still in exile, in Uruguay and a categorical order was issued that only a simple note of his death should appear in the press. There should be no extensive comment on his life or career, no repetition of the wave of sympathy and respect which had followed the death of Kubitschek. The enforced silence was eerie and ear-splitting. More than 20,000 mourners filled the town of São Borja, permission having been refused for more formal ceremony elsewhere. The seventh-day Mass in the Candelária in Rio de Janeiro provided a roll-call of those who had supported and remained loyal to Goulart and the Vargista tradition. Shops and businesses quietly closed in the centre of Rio de Janeiro and curious questioners were told, once credentials were established, that this was out of respect, 'because the president has died'.

The Way Ahead?

Throughout his presidency Geisel was consistent in seeking a new political formula, not only to curb the viciousness of the repression under Médici, nor simply to refurbish the image of Brazil, so badly tarnished by the time of his succession, though both these aims had priority in his schemes. More positively, like Castello Branco and, in a different manner, Costa e Silva, he wanted to find that 'second leg' of which Costa e Silva had spoken, a sufficient measure of popular support both to legitimize and to stabilize the system introduced in 1964. It was not that he was unwilling to use coercion, though he had a cultivated distaste for the cruder excesses previously practised in the name of 'national security' and licensed as a necessary condition for the success of the 'Brazilian model'. Geisel's liberalism had sharply defined limits: what he wanted was a 'controlled' democracy, within rules and boundaries defined by his own perception of national interest, which, in turn, reflected fairly closely the thinking of the ESG. But within these limits, as in the doctrine of the ESG and of the post-1964 regime generally, there was considerable room for disagreement. At the very least there were different strands, or themes, to be emphasized or played down as circumstances required. What those circumstances were, and who decided on the theme to be followed at any given time, was, however, another matter.

Despite all the careful scrutiny of ESG doctrine and military thinking more generally, it was not, at the end of the day, the armed forces' leaders who made the key decisions. They were not, on the one hand, simply a sword, even a two-edged sword, to be drawn from a scabbard. They were not merely instrumental either before or after 1964, but a body with views and a will of their own. But always they worked hand in glove with different civilian groups, whose economic interests, social priorities, and political theories carried, at the end of the day, more weight than the exquisitely refined, neo-scholastic, and highly abstract theorizing of the soldiers on 'national security', 'national objectives', or the dynamics of geopolitics.

An example of this was given in February 1977 with the removal from ministerial office of the most provocative and challenging member of Geisel's government, Severo Gomes. His demand for somewhat different priorities, notably an expansion of the internal market and a consequent raising of wage-levels, had won him many friends, but more enemies, particularly among the transnationals and among bankers. He was now replaced by a banker, Angelo Calmon de Sá, a former head of the Banco do Brasil, who was the nominee to the post of Industry and Commerce of Mário Henrique Simonsen. It was now noted that, with the exception of Reis Velloso, Brazil's economic management was dominated by bankers, perhaps not inappropriately, in view of the country's ever mounting foreign debt and its dependence on the confidence of bankers abroad.

But how completely dependent was Brazil, or how dependent need it be? The answer to that question still lies in the future, despite easy, over-confident assurances on both sides of the political fence. In March 1977 Geisel showed that in certain directions at least dependency had its limits, breaking with an agreement on military aid signed with the United States in 1952. In part this was seen as a reaction to President Carter's stand on human rights and the subsequent pressure on Brazil. There was comment that the tension, therefore, was not with the United States government, not even with the Pentagon or the State Department, but simply with the Carter administration. But the issue ran deeper than this. A constant theme of government spokesmen over the past few years had been that a stronger, more powerful Brazil could take a more independent, or interdependent, stand, or could at least ring the changes on dependency. This view echoed the old argument in military thinking that real 'security' was a necessary condition for genuinely 'nationalist' development, while, equally, national control of basic resources, such as oil or steel, was a necessary component of effective security. Even in the 1930s, when discussing control of the steel industry, military spokesmen had had in mind a future arms industry in Brazil, to avoid too great a dependence on foreign supplies. Forty years later this was still a theme, though linked to the idea of a more flexible pattern of buying material wherever seemed most appropriate.[88] The ending of the agreement with the United States had substantial support, not only in the armed forces, but in both parties in Congress. The same theme, of a more flexible, pragmatic, and independent policy in relation to the import of technology, underlay the massive nuclear deal with West Germany worth $4·7 billion, which again the United States, maladroitly, tried to stop. The issue had many facets, but in particular it again highlighted the potential strength of nationalist reaction in Brazil to any form of foreign pressure regarded as illegitimate. Those who had pretensions to shape United States policy should have learned over the years that the military leaders of Brazil, like its politicians, more generally, might be led, but could not be pushed.

That the military themselves could, and would, still push was also seen at the time of the thirteenth anniversary of the 1964 *coup*. Faced with a refusal by Congress to provide a two-thirds majority required for a judicial reform bill, Geisel summarily closed Congress. Later in the month, while excitement was still running high, he put through new measures calculated to improve the position of ARENA between April 1977 and the end of his presidency. One of the most important was the decision not to allow direct elections for state governors in 1978. Instead, these would be chosen by electoral colleges, made up of state deputies and delegates from municipal councils. Since these would provide a weighting in favour of ARENA, the new ruling meant the virtual exclusion of the opposition in this key area of national politics. Similarly, the new decree changed the pattern of voting in Congressional elections, returning to the old rule whereby the number of deputies was determined not by the number of voters, but in relation to the total population. This meant, once again, that in states with a relatively high population, but a large percentage of illiterates, mostly the more backward states of the interior, relatively few voters would return a substantial number of deputies, weighting Congress in favour of the more backward, conservative, and pro-ARENA areas. Also now enforced was the *Lei Falcão*, introduced for the municipal elections of November 1976, now extended to other elections, excluding the use of radio and television in electoral campaigns. Finally, from the end of Geisel's term of office, the presidency would be held for six years rather than five, reducing the frenzied period of debate over presidential succession, but also providing a longer breathing-space for any military successor to Geisel. At the same time the date for the nomination of the next president was brought forward from January 1979 to October 1978. These measures seemed strongly to suggest not only that Geisel now knew that in an open and completely free election ARENA and his regime would be defeated, but that, just as much as his predecessors, he was determined that this must not happen. His methods might be blander, but the message was much the same.

One reaction on the part of the opposition was to call for a constituent assembly, a call which fell on deaf ears. More significantly in May 1977 there were large, enthusiastic demonstrations of students in Brazil's largest cities, the first since 1968, but this time joined by bystanders and cheered on by office workers and other onlookers. By comparison with 1968 the police and security forces behaved calmly, but there were also senior military officers ready to ascribe the protest of youngsters, still infants in 1964, as part of a general subversive plot against the regime. The government now forbade student demonstrations, a ruling roundly condemned by the leader of MDB in the Chamber of Deputies, Alencar Furtado.

On 21 May 1977 came news of the death of another former political leader, Carlos Lacerda. Deprived of his political rights in 1968, he had tried in 1975 to make a final, unsuccessful appeal to the 'hard line' of the armed forces, drawing parallels between events in Portugal and possible developments in Brazil. His death was a reminder of how prominent civilian politicians had used military leaders before 1964 and had hoped to use the *coup* as a stepping-stone to high office, only to be disabused as the soldiers tightened their control. Lacerda had helped to pull down civilian presidents, only to find, in his turn, how difficult it was to ride the tiger.

By late May 1977 all the signs were that Brazil was heading for further confrontation and, ultimately, further repression. Student protests were becoming louder and there was increasing evidence of serious disagreement within the armed forces. Geisel's highhanded treatment of Congress in April had produced criticism from men at about the rank of colonel, deploring his action and urging a return to the barracks for the armed forces. There were reports that this group, said to number about 110, had taken the name of Movimento Militar Democrático Constitutionalista (MMDC), reminiscent of the 'constitutionalist' opposition to Vargas in 1932.

How serious was this opposition was difficult to gauge, since by definition any serious challenge to the government would need to tread cautiously. The position was further complicated by manoeuvring for the presidential succession, with reports that the most prominent contender, Figueiredo, was now being undermined by the head of Geisel's military household, General Hugo de Abreu, and by the army minister, General Sílvio da Frota. Nevertheless, the movement of colonels had to be taken seriously, especially once their manifesto was made public. Dated 21 April, the holiday in honour of Tiradentes, hailed as a hero for opposing the Portuguese before independence, the manifesto made an appeal for some immediate, and some far-reaching, changes.[89]

The colonels proclaimed their loyalty to the *coup* of 1964 'which resulted in the salvation of our democratic institutions'. Now, however, they felt betrayed: 'The army, air force, and navy have become praetorian guards of the technocrats who were not part of the revolution, but remained comfortably seated in their offices. . . .' The colonels stressed particularly how 'ambitious people':

> infiltrated our community, creating an entire system for the perpetuation of their own power . . . Forever proclaiming an alleged communist threat, and allied to the group at the top of the armed forces [cúpula], which is as corrupt as in Goulart's times, they are set on maintaining the Armed Forces in a permanent state of war . . .

The colonels, said to include about ten from the air force, all in command of troops or staff officers, said that their aims: '. . . are the same as those of the great majority of people, as evidenced by the massive participation in the elections, in the declarations of intellectuals, in the stands taken by the Church, judges, the press and parliament'. They then asked

> For the complete re-establishment of democracy, we demand in the name of the traditions and principles of the Armed Forces which we are sworn to obey: the immediate formation of a constitutional assembly, to be freely and directly elected with all candidates guaranteed full access to the media.

Immediate amnesty for all those accused or condemned for political crimes.

Reintroduction of judges' guarantees [prerrogativas da magistratura] and full rights of defence for those accused of crimes.

Re-establishment of the right of habeas corpus. Abolition of Institutional Act No. 5 and all the other exceptional legislation.

The formation of a provisional government, chaired by the president of the Supremo Tribunal Federal, and including representatives of the Armed Forces, the Ordem dos Advogados do Brasil [the bar association] and the two political parties at present in existence. This will hand over power to those duly elected according to the rules laid down by the constitutional assembly.

'It is time for peace and harmony . . . we must restore, without delay, a government of law and order'.

By late June 1977 it seemed that at no time since the *coup* of 1964 had there been so much movement, uncertainty, and excitement in Brazilian politics. Student demonstrations were continuing, there were mass demonstrations on human rights, one organized in São Paulo by Archbishop Evaristo Arns, and manifestos from journalists and intellectuals arguing for change. Congress was in full cry, with demands for a constituent assembly, often quoting the manifesto of the colonels. With new Congressional elections scheduled for 1978 and a change of president also just round the corner, there seemed some reason to believe that the political lid, once raised though not taken off by Geisel, could not be screwed down as firmly again.

But still there was reason to pause. Geisel had recently ordered the *cassação* of a federal deputy, Marcos Tito, and there were rumours of a pending 'ideological purge' of Congress.[90] There was evidently, too, severe tension among senior military officers, all linked to the question of presidential succession, but crystallizing around now familiar themes. These still included the role of foreign interests in the shaping of Brazil's economy and the relative degree of state control which should be allowed: but equally important, especially in view of the rising wave of protest, both military and civilian, was the question of the degree to which such opposition should be given free expression. The situation seemed ripe for the sort of backlash seen on numerous occasions since 1964, most notably in October

1965 and December 1968, but also, though to a lesser extent, in Geisel's intervention as recently as April 1977. On 27 June MDB was allowed a television programme to discuss national political issues. Both Ulysses Guimarães and the leader of the party in the Chamber of Deputies, Alencar Furtado, strongly attacked the government. Many who saw the programme, though sympathetic to the points being made, wondered how judicious was this frontal assault. The opposition leaders clearly felt it their duty to speak plainly, joining their voice to the many now being raised not only against the current government but against the whole regime installed in 1964. As in the past, reaction was swift. Just as Congress was closing for its July recess came the news that Alencar Furtado had been deprived of his political rights. MDB members left Brasília still fiercely debating this most recent move, again forced to examine their role as a licensed opposition.

Meanwhile, it was clear that opposition to the regime was strong and growing stronger, as every test of strength in recent years had shown. Workers, students, intellectuals, churchmen, and, most recently, even officers of the armed forces, had voiced their discontent; but the opposition came not only from a few more articulate groups. It ran much deeper, as the regime's fearful attitude to completely free elections clearly showed. After more than thirteen years of coercion and control the Brazilian people refused to provide for the regime that 'second leg' the soldiers and technocrats wanted. It was an appeal for popular support which Brazilians would not give.

Notes

1 'Brazil. Performance and Prospects', *Bolsa Review*, vol. 8 (July 1974), 387. The GDP per head for 1973 was estimated at $565 (equivalent), a rise of 8 per cent over the 1972 figure.
2 Mário Henrique Simonsen, 'Current Aspects of the Brazilian Economy', mimeo (3 March 1975), 2.
3 ibid., 7–8.
4 João Paulo dos Reis Velloso, 'The Development of Brazil: Priorities and Opportunities', speech given at Canning House, London (21 June 1976), 4.
5 ibid., 1.
6 David Uren, 'Brazil. Credits of headier days obstacle to deflation', *The Times* (4 October 1976).
7 Quoted Gersan Toller Gomes, 'Brasil casts round for a new "miracle"', *The Times* (21 April 1976).
8 See the useful analysis in 'Últimas vagas para o poder', *Veja* (20 February 1974), 19–22.

9 ibid., 22.
10 The structure of the new ministry is explained and set out in a diagram; ibid., 23.
11 For a diagram of the new structure of government see ibid., 24. See, too, *Bolsa Review*, vol. 8 (July 1974), 386–7.
12 A 'Correspondent', 'Brazil: A New Chapter', *Swiss Review of World Affairs* (March 1974), 20.
13 ibid.
14 ibid.
15 For contemporary discussion of 'national security' as expressed in Brazilian legislation and of the fundamental concepts of national security as elaborated over the years, see the two conferences given by General Augusto Fragoso in the Escola Nacional de Informações on 19 February and 19 April 1976. *Política Nacional. Conceitos Fundamentais*, SNI, Departmento do Ensino (1976) and *A Segurança Nacional Na Atual Legislação Brasileira*, SNI (1976).
16 *Latin America* (5 April 1974), 110.
17 See 'Eleições. A oportunidade desperdiçada', *Visão* (7 October 1974), 19–21.
18 'Um certo calor em Pernambuco', *Visão* (21 October 1974), 20–2.
19 'Os inesperados votos contra', *Visão* (4 November 1974), 23–6. See too the perceptive article 'ARENA e MDB na hora de vota', *Veja* (13 November 1974), 20–4.
20 See, for example, 'A ARENA no dia do M.D.B.', *Veja* (20 November 1974), 20–7 and 'A reabilitação do voto', ibid., 28–33. Also, 'Os caminhos do M.D.B.', *Veja* (28 November 1974), 3–50. For more detailed analysis see the special number of *Revista Brasileira de Estudos Políticos*, 43 (July 1976). This devotes the whole volume to analysis of the elections. But, in particular, see the careful study edited by Fernando Henrique Cardoso and Bolívar Lamounier, *Os Partidos e as Eleições no Brasil* (Rio de Janeiro, 1975). This contains a general essay by the editors, studies of São Paulo by Lamounier and Cardoso, an overview by Carlos Estevan Martins, analysis of Minas Gerais by Fábio Wanderley Reis, of Rio Grande do Sul by Hélgio Trindade, and a provocative contribution by Verena Martinez-Alier and Armando Boito Júnior on '1974: Enxada e Voto'.
21 Cardoso and Lamounier, op. cit., 11.
22 See *Le Monde* (19 November 1974): 'Brésil. L'opposition remporte un succès sans précédent aux elections parlementaires'.
23 See 'Os resultados antes das eleições', *Visão* (18 November 1974), 20–5, and 'O Brasil depois da eleição', *Visão* (2 December 1974), 17–27.
24 'Em 1975, a tarefa do Congresso: remover o entulho', *Visão* (30 December 1974), 16–18.
25 There is a very good analysis of the speech in *Visão*: 'A coerência das palavras e a permanência dos Atos' (13 January 1975), 14–19. The article opens with a quotation from Castello Branco, which exactly sums up Geisel's position, from a speech of Castello in the ESG of 13 March 1967: 'For a society to be democratic, it must have free expression for disagreement; for it to be viable, it is necessary that the areas of agreement outweigh those of disagreement'.
26 *Latin America*, IX, No. 3 (17 January 1975).
27 'Agora, regras para a política de segurança', *Visão* (10 February 1975).
28 'Os caminhos para o avanço da distensão política', *Visão* (24 February 1975), 16–17.
29 Geisel noted the attempts at liberalization under Costa e Silva ('perhaps prematurely') and the need under Médici to maintain internal security, and of his own hopes for a 'full, humanistic development'. See Ernesto Geisel,

Mensagem ao Congresso Nacional (Brasília, March 1975), 7–13. See also 'A esperança dos políticos e o plano do Palácio', *Visão* (10 March 1975), 14–19.

30 See the frank discussion and interviews in *Visão* (24 March 1975).
31 ibid., 94.
32 'Sentença de morte ameaça ARENA e M.D.B.', *Visão* (7 April 1975), 13–14.
33 See 'A Aliança para salvar o M.D.B.', *Veja* (9 April 1975), 12–14.
34 Quoted *Veja* (9 April 1975), 17.
35 Those listed are a selection from chapter 1 and chapter 8.
36 The report contains general analysis of multinationals and foreign capital, a special chapter on multinationals and the balance of payments, general conclusions and suggestions, and a long appendix of some of the evidence given.
37 Quoting Álvaro A. G. Pignaton, *Capital Estrangeiro e Expansão Industrial no Brasil* (Brasília, 1973), 104.
38 US Senate Report, 5.
39 ibid., 6.
40 ibid., 10.
41 ibid., 101–2.
42 ibid., 106.
43 ibid., 108–9. See, in particular, Table 5–7, 'Ownership of Brazilian Economy by United States, Other Foreign and National Firms, Year Ended 1969', p. 112. and Table 5–8, 'Brazil: U.S. MNC. Proportion of Manufacturing Sales, 1966, 1970', p. 113.
44 ibid., 113.
45 ibid., 117.
46 ibid., 151.
47 Among seminal work in this area see Arruda and de Souza, op. cit. See also Herbet de Souza, *An Overview of Multinationa ιCorporations and the Quest of the State* (February 1977) (mimeo) and *Internationalisation of Capital and the Role of the Brazilian State* (1977) (mimeo).
4 Fernando Henrique Cardoso, 'As multinacionais e a democratização', *Opinião* (2 May 1975), 9.
49 See 'Salário maior: o que muda nos preços e no mercado', *Visão* (12 May 1975), 40–50. This long, useful discussion should also be set alongside the previous number of *Visão*, a special number on finance in Brazil.
50 'Diálogo só com os trabalhadores', *Veja* (7 May 1975), 17–18.
51 See, for one example, 'Brasil: capitalismo de Estado?', *Visão* (26 May 1975), 43-97.
52 'M.D.B. A questão militar', *Veja* (11 June 1975), 17.
53 'Uma pausa na marcha da distensão', *Visão* (23 June 1975), 17–18.
54 See, for example, José Alvaro Moisés, 'SABs, uma nova força', *Opinião* (25 July 1975), 5.
55 The long speech is reported in detail in *Movimento* (28 July 1975), 3.
56 See *Veja* (18 June, 25 June, 2 July 1975).
57 'Um requiem para a distensão', *Veja* (6 August 1975).
58 *Veja* (13 August 1975), 21.
59 There is useful discussion of the different groupings in MDB in 'A partilha de cargos no M.D.B.' in *Veja* (27 August 1975), 17–18.
60 Fiel Filho was one of fourteen workers secretly arrested on 16 January, and died under torture next day. Many others had suffered the same fate, but Geisel on this occasion was determined to act firmly, not least as a means of removing Ednardo D'Avila. On the replacement of D'Avila, see the bland account 'Novo comando em São Paulo', *Veja* (28 January 1976), 20–3.

61 See 'Um compromisso reaffirmado', *Veja* (10 March 1976).
62 *Le Monde* (4–5 April 1976).
63 *Veja* (31 March 1976), 24.
64 See 'Das *cassações* ao tumulto', *Veja* (7 April 1976), 26–7. The article and photographs capture well the confusion and anger of the opposition in Brasília.
65 See the important discussion 'Até onde vai o Estado?', in *Veja* (19 May 1976), 20–5.
66 See 'Desestatização: Temperatura em elevação', *Veja* (2 June 1976), 21–2.
67 *Veja* (14 July 1976), 22–3. See too *Veja* (21 July 1976), 22.
68 See 'De volta aos palanques', *Veja* (21 July 1976).
69 *Veja* (4 August 1976), 22–3.
70 'As ameaças de Agosto', *Veja* (11 August 1976).
71 *Le Monde* (20 August 1976).
72 See 'O Corpo-A-Corpo Eleitoral', *Veja* (18 August 1976), 20–4. See also the interview with the MDB leader, Ulysses Guimarães, ibid., 25–6.
73 See *Veja* (29 September 1976), 20–3.
74 See 'A caça ao voto urbano', *Veja* (20 October 1976), 20–32.
75 Patrick Knight, 'The Brazilian "miracle" may backfire on President Geisel at the polls', *The Times* (25 August 1976).
76 'O Modelo. Qual a trajetória a seguir?', *Veja* (13 October 1976), quoting *The Times* (4 October 1976), 100–1.
77 ibid., 101.
78 See the long analysis in 'Um começo de carreira?', *Veja* (27 October 1976).
79 Polícia Militar. This is the state police, under army command. Details of the killings are given in 'A morte do padre', *Veja* (20 October 1976), 33.
80 *Veja* (3 November 1976), 26.
81 ibid., 33. In a later interview—*Veja* (27 October 1976), 34–5—he also noted that 'The words with which they insulted Father Burnier and me—"Communist, subversive"—didn't come from the mouths of the soldiers: they are words they have heard from their superiors'.
82 See particularly 'Matto Grosso: As terras da discórdia', *Veja* (27 October 1976), 34–6.
83 'A Amazónia agüentará?', ibid., 86–91.
84 There are good detailed accounts in *Veja* (3 November and 10 November 1976).
85 See 'Uma liderança em julgamento', *Veja* (24 November 1976), 20–3; also 'Primeiros nomes para 1978', 24–6. The elections, as always, were not without their lighter moments. In Bom Jesus, a town on the border of Paraíba and Ceará, one candidate for *vereador* ended up without a single vote from the 590 electors. The unfortunate candidate, Francisco Carlos de Morais, explained: 'All my friends promised to vote for me, so I voted for my brother-in-law'. Another ARENA candidate was in an even more delicate position. José Tomaz got only one vote: he had voted for his brother of MDB, as had his wife. Asked about his one vote, he replied that he 'would rather not reveal the name of the person, since my wife doesn't like her', *Veja* (1 December 1976), 20.
86 *Veja* (1 December 1976), 28.
87 *Veja* (8 December 1976).
88 See 'Uma diplomacia de golpes e contragolpes', *Veja* (16 March 1977), 20–3. It should also be remembered that in 1975 Brazil exported 66 million dollars'-worth of arms (at 1974 prices). See *Latin America* (8 April 1977), 107. Brazil has much the most advanced arms industry in Latin America.
89 It is summarized in *Latin America* (27 May 1977), 155.
90 *Le Monde* (8 June 1977).

12 Conclusion: the Armed Forces, the State, and Class Control

Shortly before he died in 1976 Juscelino Kubitschek talked to MDB leaders about the present regime and his own time in office, commenting that under his presidency economic growth had been maintained without the loss of political freedoms, that there had been no political prisoners, no one was deprived of political rights, and yet progress was made and the economy grew. In similar vein, João Goulart, again not long before his death in 1976, remarked wryly that one of the main justifications for removing him by force had been the rate of inflation, yet at no time during his presidency had the actual rate of inflation been as high as it was at that period of 1976. Both these points could be parried, but they raised one of the key issues of Brazilian politics, and a question the relevance of which extends well beyond Brazil. The argument in this book has been that there is no necessary correlation between economic growth, the containment of inflation, and the imposition of a rigid authoritarian political system as found in Brazil since 1964. The economy can grow and inflation be contained while maintaining political freedoms and open democratic processes. From 1945 to 1964, as both Kubitschek and Goulart rightly claimed, the Brazilian economy continued to grow, though never, as in any society, free from problems. At the same time, economic and all other policies were scrutinized in public forum, with the decision-makers answerable to an electorate. No one claimed that the party system was perfect or that Congress was as representative as it might have been. Important social groups were still in effect excluded. The political system was still weighed down with corporatist social and labour legislation from the days of the *Estado Novo*, with the trade unions still weakly organized politically. Only by the early 1960s was the working class movement showing signs of escaping from controls contained in Vargista populism, even though that populism had itself helped to mobilize and organize Brazil's urban, if scarcely yet its rural, workers. Populism was still strong by the early 1960s, but already there was clear evidence of new, more vigorous, more clear-sighted movements, seeking far-reaching changes in Brazil's social and political system, with more emphasis on the wider distribution of national wealth, with all that implied in terms of necessary structural reforms, especially in the agrarian sector. No one denied that Brazil's political system could be improved: but it was viable, still lively, still overcoming the problems inherited from earlier decades, including those of public health and popular education as well as a structure of wealth and power slow to give way to popular demand for change. Certainly it was not a system ready to collapse, ripe for military intervention and the imposition of repressive controls. Nor was this justified by the financial and economic crisis of the early 1960s. This in part was associated with a faltering of import-substitution industrialization, so that new strategies needed to be tried, but equally it was associated with and largely caused by the fear of change generated in financial and business circles, both in Brazil and abroad, at the sudden departure of Quadros and the succession of Goulart.

This leads into the second main theme of this book: that while economic growth and the containment of inflation do not require rigid authoritarian control, there is at the same time an organic link between the economic model pursued after 1964 and the repressive political system built up in the same period. This springs from the nature and pattern of economic strategy after 1964, the whole process of capital accumulation which imposed explicitly accepted social and political costs, accepted, that is, by those who imposed them, not by those on whom they were imposed, since this, too, was part of the total 'development model'. Among those social costs were the direction of resources, not to weaker or poorer sections of Brazilian society, but rather to the middle and upper classes, with the pattern of distribution of wealth worsening over the years, both as between classes and between regions, the rich becoming richer, the poor, poorer. This was the direct result of social and economic planning which believed that rapid capitalist growth must always, at least in the short term, produce a worsening pattern of distribution, and which, acknowledging that, broadly speaking, different strategies emphasized either distribution or growth, firmly and unequivocally chose the latter.

But this choice also involved political costs. Sacrifices could only be imposed on others through a monopoly of power in the hands of the decision-makers. After 1964 this monopoly was seized, then ruthlessly maintained, by those who controlled Brazil. This required not only purging the trade unions and universities, censoring the media, and emasculating Congress, but the creation of a wider apparatus of repression and control, which might at certain times be made more bland, but which ultimately had to be maintained.

And this introduces the third, most fundamental, theme of this present analysis, that the heart of the story, in Brazil as elsewhere, is not about the capacity of political institutions to carry the load required of them, but about contending social class interests which shape and maintain those institutions. Political institutions are shaped, or misshaped, by men in line with certain interests. Not only is this true of the political parties, Congress, the trade unions, but also of the armed forces. Analysis of the Brazilian experience does not support the view that the armed forces intervene because political institutions in some version of a 'praetorian society' are weak. Or, if to any extent it does support this interpretation, it raises starkly the question of why they are weaker than they might be, and in whose interests were they prevented from being stronger? Similarly, analysis of the Brazilian case does not support the comfortable view that the armed forces intervene as being more united, more efficient, more able to give a clear lead and maintain continuity of planning and overall policy. There were sharp discontinuities after 1964, as seen in the abandonment of Campos's Ten-Year Plan. There was, and remains, disunity and disagreement, even over quite fundamental issues, such as, for example, the degree of foreign involvement to be allowed in the economy, or the role to be played by state companies as compared with private enterprise. Nor has there been freedom from the pattern of ragged compromise allegedly characteristic of civilian politics, but mercifully absent after military intervention. All three of the first military presidents were compromise choices, arrived at after severe, even bitter, disagreement, and the political stability of the system has been threatened and the tone of politics embittered by severe rivalries between senior officers, not only on personal grounds, but as representatives of substantially different interests, both inside and outside Brazil. Finally, the claim that government after a military *coup* is less corrupt and more efficient than under civilian rule, a claim often made in relation to the 'Third World', is again scarcely substantiated by Brazil's experience since 1964. Time and again the government and the system have been rocked by revelations of corruption, sometimes on a grand scale and at times very close to the heart of government. Geisel, it must be said, has always reacted quickly and forcibly in such cases, responding in particular to accusations concerning corruption stemming from disaffected and disillusioned members of the armed forces themselves, as in the case of the Colonels' Manifesto of 1977. But there have been too many cases of corruption, involving military personnel as well as civilian, within the regime, to sustain the idea of a process markedly better in this respect than that which it replaced. Nor, a related point, is it clearly more efficient, despite, or perhaps because of, its rigid centralization and tight restriction of decision-making to a narrow governing group of soldiers and *técnicos*. Mention has already been made of the dangers and weaknesses of a process by which, in the name of some spurious concept of national security, major decisions of government policy are taken behind closed doors, removed from public scrutiny, a system which also more readily lays open those who make these decisions to charges of being influenced by undue pressures not always in the national interest.

Why, then, did the armed forces intervene in 1964, what has been the nature of the regime which then was established, how does it relate to the longer sweep of earlier political development in Brazil, and what chances are there for substantial change in the future? The principal argument of this book has been that the *coup* of 1964 and the regime to which it gave birth can only be understood in terms of the relations between social classes, the contending interests of those classes, and sometimes of fractions of classes, and of the way in which that process of competing interests finds expression in the change from 'Old Republic' to *Estado Novo*, in the party system after 1945, and finally in the *coup* of 1964. The argument has been that the revolution of 1930 marked a transition from the 'Old Republic', dominated by the coffee oligarchy, to another system in which during the 1930s, particularly under the *Estado Novo*, the industrializing bourgeoisie, especially in São Paulo, were predominant. It was these relatively new industrialists, working with Vargas, who shaped Brazil's modern state under the *Estado Novo*, controlling that new state apparatus, while also making skilful use of the ideologies of corporatism and nationalism, to exercise the fullest control of Brazilian society yet achieved in the twentieth century. But it was a control which from the start had in it the seeds of its own decay, failing to survive sufficiently the change in the pattern of politics introduced in 1945. In this respect it is possible to trace from at least 1930 onwards a crisis of hegemony which was never resolved right up to 1964.

The main challenge for the system after 1954, or rather for the classes who controlled it, was how to absorb and satisfy the demands of social groups previously excluded from any effective share in national wealth and power, the mass of urban and later of rural population. The main means of control was the usual one—the bourgeois state. Within this, control was exercised through the party system; the machinery of populism, first urban, then rural; and, in particular, through the ideological controls of corporatism and nationalism, effectively used to mobilize support and damp down further demand. Had this system been allowed to continue and change over time, the *coup* of 1964 need never have occurred. But the dominant elements in Brazilian society refused to widen sufficiently the political process, so as to allow fuller participation by new contending groups. Instead they excluded, for example, the PCB and branded as dangerously subversive many who might most effectively have exercised control for them. Then they cried alarm, calling in the armed forces to impose a new system of controls on their behalf, even though in the process the bourgeoisie had to give up direct command of the state and the political system. In this sense, the 'Bonapartist' intervention of the armed forces directly served the interests of certain narrow social groups, as was clearly seen in the social and economic policies followed after the *coup* and the costs these entailed for some social classes to the benefit of others. The leaders of the armed forces were the first to deny that their intervention was class-based, claiming that they were above such interests, acting on behalf of the nation, as 'the people in uniform'. Unfortunately, the ideology by which they had been shaped in schools such as the ESG, and throughout their careers, was itself a class-based ideology, now simply finding expression in policies chosen after 1964.

Again, the main instrument of control was the state, the new authoritarian state forged after 1964, its power steadily strengthened under successive military presidents. But now the main instrument of state control was not ideology, but direct coercion and repression, used as deemed necessary to defend 'national security' and 'development' and the interests of the Brazilian model. But what were those interests? Increasingly it appeared that not only were they not the interests of the mass of the Brazilian people, but not even of many sections of Brazilian commerce and industry. Rather, they were the interests of international finance and multinational, or transnational, corporations and those groups in Brazil most closely associated with them. The power of the Brazilian state, based on the strength of the armed forces and on the apparatus of repression, was being used essentially to maintain a pattern of 'development' heavily dependent on foreign finance and foreign capital, whose confidence must at all costs be sustained. This pattern was seen most vividly and most viciously under Médici, after Costa e Silva had failed to 'humanize' the system or to find the 'second leg' of popular support he believed necessary for the regime's survival.

The key question under Geisel was: could the system be changed, humanized, opened up, perhaps with a different emphasis in social and economic priorities? The answer seemed to be: yes, but only to a certain degree. Some move politically could be made away from the worst excesses of the Médici period, with free discussion and free elections. But always there was a *ne plus ultra.* After a certain point the brakes were put on. In economic policy, too, there seemed to be strict limits. Flexible pragmatism made sensible an attempt to expand the internal market when the international picture looked bleak. But when Severo Gomes too sharply offended the sensibilities of multinational interests, he had to go.

One of the most crucial questions still to be answered concerns the future role of the armed forces, as the key element in the state apparatus. There is evidence that in some important areas the Brazilian regime both can and will take a more independent line than in the past, as seen, for example, in its revoking of the arms agreement with the United States and in its nuclear deal with West Germany. But how far does this autonomy extend? One line of thought on the nature and role of the state, the more determinist one, would argue that the post-1964 Brazilian state is so much the creature of international capital, the multinational corporations, and the social groupings in Brazil which are tied to them, that independent challenge and action is out of the question. At any sign of real defiance, therefore, a clamp-down will come, with whatever degree of repression may be considered necessary. Another view, equally well-founded theoretically, sees more possible autonomy in the state and state apparatus, particularly through the armed forces. The empirical evidence from Brazil, examination of the shaping of the Brazilian state over several decades, and analysis of the different currents which in the past have been found in the armed forces, would point to the possibility of some degree of autonomy. There may, in short, be more room for change than commonly supposed, and perhaps at a faster rather than a slower pace. Deterministic interpretations of Portugal and its armed forces before 1974 were, after all, found to be too rigid. The Colonels' Manifesto of 1977 in Brazil is more than a straw in the wind, not to be dismissed as the untypical reaction of a few unimportant officers.

Perhaps, however, the most important feature of that manifesto was its declaration that the aims of the colonels were the same as those of the great majority of the people, with the stress on a constituent assembly and a freely elected Congress. In all the political and economic debate of the last thirteen years the most neglected and disparaged element has been the people of Brazil. Too often the soldiers in their refined theorizing on geopolitics and national objectives have spoken of the people of Brazil only in the vocabulary of warfare, as though their own people were an enemy to contain and conquer, the main threat to national security. This was not always the language of the armed forces in Brazil. The Colonels' Manifesto and other evidence now stemming from the armed forces suggests the tide may again be turning. March 1979 will see a new president in Brazil, possibly General João Batista de Oliveira Figueiredo, current head of the SNI. As always, a new presidency will bring an opportunity for fresh initiatives and changes of direction. Whether these opportunities will be taken remains to be seen, but high on any list of priorities must be the search for a more flexible, more humane, and more legitimate political system, with careful reflection on the experience of recent years. Certainly, if nothing else, in terms of this search the political experience of the last thirteen years, indeed the whole long experience of modern Brazilian politics, has shown that no political solution can be lasting and ultimately successful which disparages or despises the people of Brazil. In a country rightly proud of its rich natural resources the richest resource is the Brazilian people.

Abbreviations and Glossary

All abbreviations and terms used are explained in full in the text.

ABI	Brazilian Press Association.
AC	Catholic Action.
ACO	Catholic Workers' Action.
ACR	Rural Catholic Action.
ADEP	Popular Democratic Action.
ADESG	Graduates' Association of the Escola Superior de Guerra.
adhesionistas	Group within the MDB more closely associated with the regime.
AERP	Special Department for Public Relations.
agreste	Zone of north-east Brazil. Transitional zone between more fertile coastal *zona da mata* and more arid *sertão*.
AID	Agency for International Development (USAID)
Ala Vermelha	Red Wing. Guerrilla group within PCdo B.
ALN	National Liberating Action (urban guerrilla group).
Alvorada Palace	The presidential residence in Brasília.
AMAN	Military Academy of Agulhas Negras.
AMFORP	American and Foreign Power Company.
ANL	National Liberation Alliance (Popular Front organization in 1935).
AP	Popular Action.
apuração	The checking of votes in an election.
ARENA	National Renovating Alliance.
ARPA	Revolutionary Parliamentary Action.
autênticos	'Authentics'.—Somewhat more radical group within MDB.
bacharel	Graduate. Usually a law graduate in nineteenth-century Brazil.
bico de pena	Literally, 'pen nib', a form of electoral corruption by writing in fake results.

bilhetinos	Short notes.
BNDE	National Bank for Economic Development.
Brigada	The state armed forces of Rio Grande do Sul.
cabo	Corporal.
caciquismo	Political system dominated by rural bosses.
CAEM	Centre for Advanced Military Studies.
café com leite	Literally, coffee with milk. Used to describe political domination in 'Old Republic' of São Paulo (coffee) and Minas Gerais (cattle).
cambão	Literally, a yoke. Often a day's unpaid labour every week, demanded by landowners in the north-east from their peasants as rent for their land.
CAMDE	Women's Campaign for Democracy.
Campos Elísios	Palace of governor of São Paulo.
Carioca	Native of, or appertaining to, the city of Rio de Janeiro.
Casa Militar	Military Household.
cassação	Deprivation of political rights. Those who suffer this are *cassados*.
Castellista	Supporter of Castello Branco.
CCC	Commando for Hunting Communists.
CD	Democratic Crusade.
CEDP	Centre for the Study and Defence of Petroleum
cédula avulsa	Ballot sheet containing name of only one candidate, as distinct from *cédula única*, a ballot sheet containing all the names.
CENIMAR	Information Centre for the Navy.
CGG	General Strike Commando. Later became the CGT (General Commando of Workers).
CGI	General Investigations Commission.
CGT	General Commando of Workers.
CIA	Central Intelligence Agency.
CIEX	Army Centre of Information
Clube da Lanterna	Lantern Club. An anti-Getulista 'club', in which Lacerda was particularly prominent.
Clube Militar	The Military Club.
CNBB	National Conference of Brazilian Bishops.
CNI	National Confederation of Industry.
CNP	National Petroleum Council.
CNTC	National Confederation of Workers in Commerce
CNTI	National Confederation of Workers in Industry.
CNTTMFA	National Confederation of Workers in Sea, River, and Air Transport.
CNTTT	National Confederation of Land Transport Workers.
CODI	Operations Centre for Internal Defence.
Colégio Militar	Prestigious Military College in Rio de Janeiro.

COLINA	Commando of National Liberation.
Comintern	Executive Committee of the Communist International.
CONTAG	National Confederation of Workers in Agriculture.
CONTEC	National Confederation of Workers in Credit Establishments.
coronelismo	The domination of rural politics by 'colonels', essentially political bosses. Brazilian term for more general *caciquismo*, or clientelistic politics.
CPI	Parliamentary Committee of Inquiry.
CPOS	Permanent Committee for Trade Union Organizations.
DASP	Administrative Department of Public Service.
descompressão	Literally, decompression. Move towards less repressive forms of government and control. Also see use, in same context, of *distensão*, a relaxing or easing of controls.
desestatização	A process of reducing state control.
DIEESE	Trade Union Department of Statistics and Socio-Economic Studies
DIP	Department of Press and Propaganda
dispositivo	Support or backing. Particularly used in *dispositivo militar* (military support) or *dispositivo sindical* (trade union support).
DNOCS	National Department of Anti-Drought Works.
DOI	Division of Internal Operations.
DOPS	Department of Political and Social Order.
ECEME	Army General Staff and Command School.
ECLA	Economic Commission for Latin America.
Electrobrás	State-owned and controlled electric-power corporation.
EMFA	The General Staff of the Armed Forces.
engenho	Sugar estate.
entreguismo	Term used to describe readiness of certain groups in Brazilian society and politics (*entreguistas*) to 'hand over' to foreign interests.
ESA	Sergeants' School.
EsAO	Officer Specialization School. School for junior officers before promotion to captain.
Escola Naval	Naval Academy.
ESG	National War College.
Esquadrão da Morte	Death Squad.
Estado Novo	Literally, New State, the corporatist system lasting from 1937 to 1945.
FAAC	Anti-Communist Armed Front.
FAB	Brazilian Air Force
FAS	Social Action Fund.—Anti-Communist organization in São Paulo, supported by Brazilian and

	foreign business interests.
favela	Shanty town. Essentially an area of low-cost housing, usually built and occupied by internal migrants.
fazenda	An estate. See, too, *fazendeiro*, estate-owner. Also treasury or finance, as in Ministro de Fazenda, Minister of Finance.
FEB	Brazilian Expeditionary Force in Second World War.
filhotismo	Part of duty of political boss or *patrão* to look after the interests of his clients.
FMP	Popular Mobilization Front.
FPN	Nationalist Parliamentary Front.
Força Pública	State armed force. Later state police force.
FRN	Front of National Renovation.
gaúcho	Native of, or appertaining to, Rio Grande do Sul.
GERA	Executive Group for Agrarian Reform.
getulismo	Political philosophy and policies of Getúlio Vargas.—Also *getulista*: supporter of Getúlio Vargas.
golpe	Military *coup*. *Golpista:* one who favours or supports a *coup*.
Grupo da Sorbonne	Particular group of officers linked to ESG.
Grupos de Onze Companheiros	Groups of Eleven Comrades. Attempt at cell organization in support of Brizola.
Guanabara	State formed out of the old Federal District, including city of Rio de Janeiro, after move of national capital and federal district to Brasília in 1960. In 1975 fused with state of Rio de Janeiro to form new super-state of Rio de Janeiro.
Guanabara Palace	Former presidential palace in Rio de Janeiro, taken over by governor of Guanabara in 1960.
homenagem	Ceremony, often at a formal dinner, to honour someone.
IBAD	Brazilian Institute for Democratic Action.
IBRA	Brazilian Institute of Agrarian Reform.
ICFTU	International Confederation of Free Trade Unions.
ICT	Cultural Institute of Labour.
IMF	International Monetary Fund
impôsto	Tax. Especially see *impôsto de renda*, income tax, and *impôsto sindical*, trade union tax.
INCRA	National Institute for Colonization and Agrarian Reform.
INDA	National Institute of Agricultural Development.
Integralista	Member of AIB (Brazilian Integralist Action), the Brazilian variant of international fascism, founded in 1932.

IPEA	Institute of Applied Social and Economic Research.
IPÊS	Institute of Social Studies and Research.
IPM	Military-Police Investigations.
ISEB	Institute of Advanced Brazilian Studies.
JAC	Catholic Agrarian Youth.
janguista	Supporter of Jango Goulart.
jânista	Supporter of Jânio Quadros.
JEC	Catholic Student Youth.
JOC	Young Catholic Workers.
JUC	Catholic University Youth.
Lacerdista	Supporter of Carlos Lacerda.
Laranjeiras Palace	Presidential palace in city of Rio de Janeiro.
latifúndio	Very large holding of land. Usually as contrasted within the same land-tenure system with *minifúndio*, land divided into very small holdings.
Lei Falcão	A ruling limiting the use of television in electoral campaigns.
Lei Suplicy	A law attempting to control student organizations.
LIDER	Radical Democratic League.
ligas camponesas	Peasant Leagues.
linha dura	Hard line.
machismo	Value system emphasizing allegedly masculine qualities.
mandonismo	Term referring to some of the duties of a rural political boss, mainly to control political opponents.
MAR	Armed Revolutionary Movement.
MDB	Brazilian Democratic Movement.
MEB	Movement for Basic Education.
mensagem	Presidential or ministerial report.
mineiro	Native of, or appertaining to, state of Minas Gerais.
MMC	Constitutionalist Military Movement.
MNF	Women's Nationalist Movement.
MNPT	National Popular Labour Movement.
MNR	Nationalist Revolutionary Movement.
MOBRAL	Brazilian Literacy Movement.
MRT	Tiradentes' Revolutionary Movement.
MR–8	Revolutionary Movement of 8 October.
MR–26	Revolutionary Movement of 26 July.
MSD	Democratic Trade Union Movement.
município	Municipality. An administrative and political district.
NOVACAP	Urban Authority for the New Capital (Brasília).
OBAN	Operation Bandeirantes. One of the most repressive elements of the security apparatus, working in São Paulo and largely financed by

	business interests, Brazilian and multinational.
OLAS	Organization of Latin American Solidarity.
PAC	Pact of United Action
PAEG	Government Programme for Economic Action.
parentela	Extended family.
patrão	Patron, boss. Often political patron.
pau de arara	Parrot perch, a frequently used instrument of torture. Also a type of lorry.
paulista	A native of, or appertaining to, the state of São Paulo.
paulistano	Someone from the city of São Paulo.
PCB	Brazilian Communist Party.
PCB Revolucionário	Revolutionary Brazilian Communist Party.
PCdoB	Communist Party of Brazil.
PCPR	Popular Revolutionary Communist Party.
PDC	Christian Democratic Party.
pelego	Literally, a sheepskin to go between the saddle and the horse. As a political term, a trade union leader in the official trade union, corporatist-inspired system, who represents government or the bosses rather than the workers, so making their ride more comfortable. Working in system of *peleguismo*.
Petrobrás	State-owned and directed petroleum company.
PIN	National Integration Scheme.
PIS	Social Integration Programme.
POC	Workers' Communist Party.
politicagem	Political manipulation.
POLOP	Workers' Politics.
posseiros	Certain kind of rural squatters, mainly in newly exploited land in interior.
Programa de Metas	Target Programme under Kubitschek.
PRORURAL	Rural Workers' Aid Programme.
PROTERRA	Programme for the Redistribution of Land and the Stimulus of Agroindustry in the North and North-east.
provisórios	'Provisional' armed forces in state of Rio Grande do Sul.
PRP	São Paulo Republican Party.
PRP	Party of Popular Representation.
PRT	Revolutionary Workers' Party.
PSB	Brazilian Socialist Party.
PSD	Social Democratic Party.
PSP	Social Progressive Party.
PTB	Brazilian Labour Party.
PUA	Pact for Unity and Action.
PUI	Pact of Unity between Trade Unions.
República Sindicalista	Republic which allegedly would be run or dominated by the trade unions.

SALTE	A plan for federal government expenditure, the word being composed of first letter of Portuguese for health (*saúde*), food (*alimentação*), transport (*transporte*), and energy (*energia*).
saneamento	'Cleansing', in a political context, often found in military vocabulary.
sertão	Arid region of the North-east.
sindicato	Trade union.
SNI	National Information Service [Intelligence].
SUDAM	Superintendency for the Development of Amazonas.
SUDECO	Superintendency for the Development of the Centre-East.
SUDENE	Superintendency for the Development of the North-east.
SUMOC	Superintendency of Money and Credit.
SUPRA	Superintendency of Agrarian Policy.
tenente	Lieutenant. More specifically, a member of a civilian–military opposition movement (*tenentismo*) in the 1920s.
TSE	Superior Electoral Tribunal.
TSM	Superior Military Tribunal.
UCF	Women's Civic Union.
UDN	National Democratic Union.
UNE	National Union of Students.
usina	Sugar mill.
UST	United Trade Union Workers.
VAR-Palmares	Armed Revolutionary Vanguard (Palmares).
Vila Militar	Important military complex near Rio de Janeiro.
voto do cabresto	Literally, 'herd vote', referring to control and manipulation of electorate within the *coronelismo* system.
VPR	Popular Revolutionary Vanguard.
zona da mata	Fertile coastal region in North-east Brazil.

Brazilian Emperors and Presidents

Pedro I	1822–31
Pedro II	1840–89
Manoel Deodoro da Fonseca	1889–91
Floriano Peixoto	1891–94
Prudente José de Moraes Barros	1894–98
Manoel Ferraz de Campos Salles	1898–1902
Francisco de Paula Rodrigues Alves	1902–06
Affonso Penna	1906–09
Hermes da Fonseca	1910–14
Wenceslau Braz	1914–18
Epitácio da Silva Pessoa	1919–22
Artur da Silva Bernardes	1922–26
Washington Luís Pereira de Souza	1926–30
Getúlio Dorneles Vargas	1930–45
Eurico Gaspar Dutra	1946–50
Getúlio Dorneles Vargas	1950–54
João Café Filho	1954–56
Juscelino Kubitschek de Oliveira	1956–61
Jânio Quadros	1961
João Belchior Marques Goulart	1961–64
Humberto Castello Branco	1964–67
Artur da Costa e Silva	1967–69
Emílio Garrastazú Médici	1969–74
Ernesto Geisel	1974–

Bibliography

This bibliography is restricted to books to which reference has been made. All other sources, from newspapers, journals, or other material, are cited in the end of chapter notes.

Abranches, Dunshee de: *A revolta da armada e a revolução Rio Grandense: Correspondência entre Saldanha da Gama e Silveira Martins*, Rio de Janeiro, 1955.

Agee, Philip: *Inside the Company: C,I.A. Diary*, Harmondsworth, 1975.

Alexander, Robert Jackson: *Labor relations in Argentina, Brazil, and Chile*, New York, 1962.

Almeida, José Américo de: *A bagaceira, romance*, Parahyba, 1928.

Almeida, José Américo de: *A Parahyba e seus problemas*, Parahyba, 1923.

Alves, Marcio Moreira: *Torturas e torturados*, Rio de Janeiro, 1966.

Amado, Jorge: *O cavaleiro da esperança: Vida de Luiz Carlos Prestes.* 10th ed., Rio de Janeiro, 1956.

Amado, Jorge: *Gabriela, cravo e canela: crônica de uma cidade do interior*, 10th ed., São Paulo, 1959.

Amora, Paulo: *Bernardes, O estadista de Minas na República*, São Paulo, 1964.

Andrade, Manuel Correia de: *A terra e o homen no Nordeste*, São Paulo, 1963.

Anselmo, Octacílio: *Padre Cícero, mito e realidade*, Rio de Janeiro, 1968.

Armitage, John: *The History of Brazil* (2 vols.), London, 1836.

Arruda, Marcos; Souza, Herbert de; Afonso, Carlos: *Multinationals and Brazil. The Impact of Multinational Corporations in Contemporary Brazil*, Toronto, 1975.

Avila, Fernando Bastos de: *Economic impacts of immigration: the Brazilian immigration problem*, The Hague, 1954.

Azevedo, Antonio José Amaral: *O Estado autoritario e a realidade nacional*, Rio de Janeiro, 1938.

Baer, Werner: *Industrialization and economic development in Brazil*, Irwin, 1965.

Baklanoff, Eric N.: *New perspectives of Brazil*, Nashville, 1966.

Bandeira Júnior, Antônio Francisco: *A indústria no estado de São Paulo*, São Paulo, 1901.

Bandeira, Moniz: *Cartéis e Desnacionalização. A experiencia Brasileira: 1964–1974*, 2nd ed., Rio de Janeiro, 1975.

Barata, Agildo: *Vida de um revolucionário*, Rio de Janeiro, 1962.

Barbosa, Francisco de Assis: *Juscelino Kubitschek: uma revisão na política brasileira*, Rio de Janeiro, 1960.

Barros, João Alberto Lins de: *Memorias de um revolucionário*, 2nd ed., Rio de Janeiro, 1954.

Barroso, Gustavo: *Brazil, colony of bankers*, 2nd ed., Rio de Janeiro, 1934.

Barroso, Gustavo: *Roosevelt is Jewish*, Rio de Janeiro, n.d.

Barroso, Gustavo: *The São Paulo synagogue*, 2nd ed., Rio de Janeiro, 1937.

Barroso, Gustavo: *What the Integralist should know*, Rio de Janeiro, n.d.

Basbaum, Leoncio: *História sincera da República*, São Paulo, 1962.

Bastos, Joaquim Justino Alves: *Encontro com o tempo*, Rio/Pôrto Alegre, 1965.

Bello, José Maria: *A History of modern Brazil, 1889–1964*, trans. James L. Taylor, Stanford, 1966.

Benevides, Maria Victoria de Mesquita: *O Governo Kubitschek. Desenvolvimento econômico e estabilidade política*, Rio de Janeiro, 1976.

Bergsman, Joel: *Brazil: industrialisation and trade policies*, London and New York, 1970.

Bethell, Leslie: *The Abolition of the Brazilian slave trade: Britain, Brazil and the slave trade question, 1807–1869*, London, 1970.

Bicudo, Hélio Pereira: *Meu depoimento sôbre o esquadrão da morte*, 2nd ed., São Paulo, 1976.

Bigg-Wither, Thomas Plantagenet: *Pioneering in South Brazil. Three years of forest and prairie life in the province of Paraná*, 2 vols., London, 1878.

Borges, Mauro: *O golpe em Goiás: história de uma grande traição*, Rio de Janeiro, 1965.

Boucas, Valentina F.: *História de dívida externa*, 2nd ed., Rio de Janeiro, 1950.

Bourne, Richard: *Getúlio Vargas of Brazil, 1883–1954: sphinx of the pampas*, London, 1974.

Boxer, Charles Ralph: *The Golden Age of Brazil, 1695–1750: growing pains of a colonial society*, Berkeley and Los Angeles, 1962.

Brasil, Conselho do Desenvolvimento: *Programa de metas 1958*, 3 vols., Rio de Janeiro.

Brazil, Constitution 1891: *Constituição da República dos Estados Unidos do Brasil*, Rio de Janeiro, 1891.

Brazil, Constitution 1946: *Constituição dos Estados Unidos do Brasil*, Rio de Janeiro, 1946.

Brasil, Instituto Brasileiro de Geografia e Estatística: *Recenseamento geral do Brasil (1 de Setembro 1940): Sinopse do censo agrícola, dados gerais*, Rio de Janeiro, 1941.

Brasil, Instituto Brasileiro de Geografia e Estatística: *Recenseamento geral do Brasil, 6, 1950 VI recenseamento geral da República*, Rio de Janeiro, 1950.

Brasil, Ministério das Relações Exteriores: *O Brasil e a segunda guerra mundial*, 2 vols., Rio de Janeiro, 1944.

Brazil, Ministry of External Relations: *The Brazilian Green Book, con-*

sisting of Diplomatic Documents relating to Brazil's attitude with regard to the European War, 1914–1917, London, 1918.

Brasil: Presidência: *Plano trienal de desenvolvimento econômico e social, 1963–1965 (síntese) Dezembro de 1962*, Rio de Janeiro, 1963.

Brasil, Presidente: *Mensagens presidenciais*, Rio de Janeiro, 1912—vol. I 1891–1910; vol. II 1910–14, etc.

Brasil, Presidente: *Mensagem ao Congresso Nacional apresentada pelo presidente João Goulart por ocasião da abertura da sessão legislativa de 1962*, Rio de Janeiro, 1962.

Brasil, Presidente, 1964–67: *Humberto de Alencar Castello Branco, Mensagem do Presidente da República ao Congresso Nacional*, Brasília, 1965.

Brito, Mário da Silva: *História do modernismo brasileiro*, Rio de Janeiro, 1964.

Bruneau, Thomas C.: *The Political transformation of the Brazilian Catholic Church*, London, 1974.

Bryce, James: *South America: observations and impressions*, London, 1912.

Bulhões, Augusto de: *Ministros de Fazenda do Brasil, 1808–1954*, Rio de Janeiro, 1954.

Burden, William: *The Struggle for airways in Latin America*, New York, 1943.

Burns, E. Bradford: *Nationalism in Brazil: a historical survey*, New York, 1968.

Burton, Sir Richard Francis: *Explorations of the highlands of Brazil*, 2 vols., London, 1869.

Cabanas, João: *A columna da morte, sob o comando do tenente Cabanas*, 6th ed., Rio de Janeiro, 1928.

Cadernos do Povo Brasileiro: Instituto Superior de Estudos Brasileiros, Rio de Janeiro, 1962.

Café Filho, João: *Do sindicato ao Catete: memórias políticas e confissões humanas*, 2 vols., Rio de Janeiro, 1966.

Callado, Antônio: *Os industriais da sêca e os 'Galileus' de Pernambuco: aspectos da luta pela reforma agrária no Brasil*, Rio de Janeiro, 1960.

Calmon, Pedro: *Vida de d. Pedro I, o rei cavaleiro*, 3rd ed., Pôrto, 1952.

Calógeras, João Pandia: *A History of Brazil*, trans., and ed., Percy Alvin Martin, Chapel Hill, 1939.

Calógeras, João Pandia: *A política monetária do Brasil*, trans. Thomas Newlands Neto, São Paulo, 1960.

Câmara, Helder: *Church and colonialism*, London, 1969.

Campos, Francisco: *O estado nacional, sua estructura, seu conteudo ideológico*, Rio de Janeiro, 1940.

Campos, Roberto de Oliveira: *Reflections on Latin American development*, Austin, 1967.

Caó, José Dutra: *O presidente e a restauração democrática*, São Paulo, 1949.

Cardoso, Fernando Henrique: *O modelo político brasileiro e outros ensaios*, São Paulo, 1972.

Carneiro, Edison: *A insurreição praieira 1848–1849*, Rio de Janeiro, 1960.

Carneiro, Glauco: *História das revoluções brasileiras*, 2 vols., Rio de Janeiro, 1965.
Carneiro, Glauco: *O revolucionário Siqueira Campos*, 2 vols., Rio de Janeiro, 1966.
Carneiro, José Fernando: *Imigração e colonização do Brasil*, Rio de Janeiro, 1950.
Carone, Edgard: *A Primeira República, 1889–1930*, São Paulo, 1969.
Carone, Edgard: *A República velha: instituições e classes sociais*, São Paulo, 1970.
Carone, Edgard: *O Estado Novo (1937–1945)*, Rio de Janeiro, 1976.
Carone, Edgard: *A Terceira República (1937–1945)*, Rio de Janeiro, 1976.
Carqueja, Bento: *O povo portuguez, aspectos sociais e economicos*, Oporto, 1916.
Carr, Raymond (ed.): *Latin American Affairs*, London, 1970.
Carr, Raymond: *Spain, 1808–1939*, Oxford, 1966.
Carvalho, Fernando de: *O Comunismo no Brasil*, Rio de Janeiro, 1966–67.
Castello Branco, Humberto de Alencar: *A diplomacia da revolução brasileira*, Rio de Janeiro, 1964.
Castro, José Viriato de: *Espada x vassoura: Marechal Lott*, São Paulo, 1959.
Castro, José Viriato de: *O fenômeno Jânio Quadros*, 3rd rev. ed., São Paulo, 1959.
Castro, Josué de: *The Geography of Hunger*, Boston, 1952.
Cava, Ralph della: *Miracle at Joaseiro*, New York, 1970.
César, Afonso: *Política, cifrão e sangue: documentário do 24 agosto*, Rio de Janeiro, 1955.
Chagas, Carlos: *113 Dias de Angustia. Impedimento e morte de um presidente*, Rio de Janeiro, 1971.
Chilcote, Ronald H.: *The Brazilian Communist Party: conflict and integration, 1922–1972*, New York, 1974.
Clissold, Stephen: *Soviet relations with Latin America, 1918–68*, London, 1970.
Collor, Lindolfo: *Garibaldi e a guerra dos farrapos*, 2nd ed., Pôrto Alegre, 1958.
Conn, Stetson: *The Framework of Hemisphere defense*, Washington, DC, 1960.
Conrad, Robert: *The Destruction of Brazilian slavery 1850–1888*, Berkeley and Los Angeles, 1972.
Cooke, Morris Llewellyn: *Brazil on the march*, New York, 1944.
Corrêa, Oscar Dias: *A constituição de 1967, contribuição crítica*, Rio de Janeiro, 1969.
Costa, Sérgio Corrêa da: *Every inch a King, a biography of Dom Pedro I, first Emperor of Brazil*, New York, 1950.
Coutinho, Lourival: *O General Góes depõe*, 2nd ed., Rio de Janeiro, 1956.
Cunha, Euclides da: *Rebellion in the backlands*, Chicago, 1944.
Cupertino, Fausto: *A Concentração da Renda no Brasil. O bolo está mal dividido*, Rio de Janeiro, 1976.
Dantas, San Tiago: *Política externa independente*, Rio de Janeiro, 1962.
Dean, Warren: *The Industrialization of São Paulo*, Austin, 1969.

Debret, Jean Baptiste: *Viagem pitoresca e histórica ao Brasil*, trans. Sérgio Milliet, 2 vols. in 1, 3rd ed., São Paulo, 1954.

A Década republicana, 8 vols., Rio de Janeiro, 1899.

Delfim Neto, Antônio: *Planejamento para o desenvolvimento econômico*, São Paulo, 1966.

Dent, Charles Hastings: *A Year in Brazil*, London, 1886.

Deodato, Alberto: *Nos tempos do João Goulart*, Belo Horizonte, 1965.

Dias, Everardo: *História das lutas sociais no Brasil*, Rio de Janeiro, 1962.

Dias, Manuel Nunes (ed.): *Brasil em perspectiva*, São Paulo, 1968.

Dines, Alberto, *et al.*: *Os idos de março e a queda em abril*, 2nd ed., Rio de Janeiro, 1964.

Doria Seixas, João de: *Eu, réu sem crime*, Rio de Janeiro, 1965.

Dulles, John W. Foster: *Vargas of Brazil: A political biography*, Austin, 1967.

Dulles, John W. Foster: *Unrest in Brazil: political-military crises 1955–1964*, Austin, 1970.

Dulles, John W. Foster: *Anarchists and communists in Brazil, 1900–1935*, Austin, 1973.

Dutra, Eurico Gaspar: *O govêrno Dutra: algumas realizações, diretrizes doutrinárias, um período de paz*, Rio de Janeiro, 1956.

Ellis, Howard Sylvester: *The Economy of Brazil*, Berkeley and Los Angeles, 1969.

Emmerson, Donald K. (ed.): *Students and Politics in Developing Nations*, New York, 1968.

Epstein, David G.: *Brasília, plan and reality*, Berkeley and Los Angeles, and London, 1973.

Faoro, Raymundo: *Os donos do poder: formação do patronato político brasileiro*, Pôrto Alegre, 1958.

Fernandes, Florestan: *The Negro in Brazilian society*, New York, 1969.

Fernandes, Florestan: *A revolução burguesa no Brasil. Ensaio de interpretação sociológica*, Rio de Janeiro, 1975.

Fernandes, Heloisa Rodrigues: *Política e segurança. Força Pública do Estado de São Paulo: Fundamentos Histórico-Sociais*, São Paulo, 1974.

Fiechter, Georges André: *Brazil since 1964—Modernisation under a military regime*, London, 1975.

Figueiredo, Affonso Celso de Assis, Viscount Ouro Preto: *Advento da dictadura militar no Brasil*, Paris, 1891.

Figueiredo, Euclydes: *Contribuição para a história da revolução constitucionalista de 1932*, São Paulo, 1954.

Fleiuss, Max: *História administrativa do Brasil*, 2nd ed., Rio de Janeiro, 1923.

Foerster, Robert Franz: *The Italian emigration of our times*, Cambridge, Mass., 1919.

Fontoura, João Neves da: *Memórias*, vol. I: *Borges de Medeiros e seu tempo*; vol. II: *A aliança liberal e a revolução de 1930*, Rio de Janeiro, 1958, 1963.

Franco, Afonso Arinos de Melo: *A escalada: memórias*, Rio de Janeiro, 1965.

Franco, Afonso Arïnos de Melo: *Um estadista da República: Afrânio de Melo Franco e seu tempo*, 3 vols., Rio de Janeiro, 1955.

Franco, Afonso Arinos de Melo: *Planalto* (memórias), Rio de Janeiro, 1968.

Franco, Afonso Arinos de Melo: *Presidencialismo ou parlamentarismo?*, Rio de Janeiro, 1958.

Franco, Virgílio Alvim de Mello: *A campanha da U.D.N.*, Rio de Janeiro, 1946.

Franco, Virgílio Alvim de Mello: *Outubro, 1930*, 2nd ed., Rio de Janeiro, 1931.

Freyre, Gilberto: *Casa grande e senzala: formação da família brasileira sob o regime de economia patriarcal*, Rio de Janeiro, 9th ed., 2 vols., 1933.

Freyre, Gilberto, *Ingleses no Brasil: aspectos de influência britânica sôbre a vida, a paisagem e a cultura do Brasil*, Rio de Janeiro, 1948.

Freyre, Gilberto: *The Masters and the slaves: a study in the development of Brazilian civilization*, trans. Samuel Putnam, 2nd Eng. lang. ed., rev., New York, 1956. (*Casa grande e senzala*)

Freyre, Gilberto: *Ordem e progresso: processo de desintegração das sociedades patriarcal e semi-patriarcal no Brasil . . . e da monarquia para a república*, 2 vols., Rio de Janeiro, 1959.

Freyre, Gilberto: *The Mansions and the shanties: the making of modern Brazil*, trans. Harriet de Onis, New York, 1963. (*Sobrados e mucambos*)

Freyre, Gilberto: *Sobrados e mucambos: decadencia do patriarcado rural e desenvolvimento do urbano*, 2nd ed., 1951, 3rd ed., 1961. Rio de Janeiro.

Fulbright, James William: *The Arrogance of power*, London, 1967.

Furtado, Celso: *Análise do 'modelo' brasileiro*, 4th ed., Rio de Janeiro, 1973.

Furtado, Celso: *Diagnosis of the Brazilian crisis*, Berkeley and Los Angeles, 1966.

Furtado, Celso: *The Economic growth of Brazil: a survey from colonial to modern times*, trans. Ricardo W. de Aguiar and Eric C. Drysdale, Berkeley and Los Angeles, 1963.

Gardner, George: *Travels in the interior of Brazil, 1836–1841*, London, 1846.

Gauld, Charles Anderson: *The Last Titan: Percival Farquhar, American entrepreneur in Latin America*, Stanford, 1964.

Gordon, Lincoln: *United States manufacturing investment in Brazil: the impact of Brazilian government policies, 1946–60*, Boston, 1962.

Goulart, João Belchior Marques: *Desenvolvimento e independência: discursos 1962*, Brasília, 1963.

Graham, Maria: *Journal of a voyage to Brazil*, London, 1824.

Graham, Richard: *Britain and the onset of modernisation in Brazil, 1850–1914*, London, 1968.

Gramsci, Antonio: *Selections from the prison notebooks of Antonio Gramsci*, London, 1971.

Great Britain, Commercial Relations and Exports Dept: *Brazil: Economic and commercial conditions in Brazil*, 1919.

Griffin, Keith Broadwell (ed.): *Financing development in Latin America*, London, 1970.

Gudin, Eugenio: *Rumos de política econômica: relatório apresentado á commisão de planejamento econômica sôbre a planificação da economia brasileira,* Rio de Janeiro, 1945.

Guimarães, Alberto Passos: *Quatro séculos de latifúndio*, Sao Paulo, 1963.

Haar, Jerry: *The Politics of higher education in Brazil*, New York, 1977.

Hahner, June Edith: *Civilian-military relations in Brazil, 1889–1898*, New York, 1969.

Hambloch, Ernest: *His Majesty the President: a study of constitutional Brazil*, London, 1935.

Harris, Marvin: *Town and country in Brazil*, New York, 1956.

Henderson, James (1783–1848): *A History of Brazil; comprising its geography, commerce, colonisation, aboriginal inhabitants . . .*, London, 1821.

Henriques, Affonso: *Ascensão e queda de Getúlio Vargas*, 3 vols., Rio de Janeiro, 1966.

Henriques, Affonso: *Vargas, O maquiavélico*, São Paulo, 1961.

Herman, Donald: *The Communist tide in Latin America: a selected treatment*, Austin, 1973.

Hilton, Stanley E.: *Brazil and the Great Powers, 1930–1939. The politics of trade rivalry*, Austin and London, 1975.

Hirschman, Albert O.: *Journeys towards progress: studies of economic policy-making in Latin America*, New York, 1963.

Holanda, Sérgio Buarque de (ed.): *Historia geral da civilização brasileira*, 2nd ed., 2 vols., São Paulo, 1963–67.

Houston, John Albert: *Latin America in the United Nations*, New York, 1956.

Humboldt, Alexander von: *Personal narrative of travels to the Equinoctial Regions of the New Continent during the years 1799–1804*, 7 vols., London, 1814–26.

Huntington, Samuel P.: *Political order in changing societies*, New Haven, 1968.

Ianni, Octávio: *As metamorfoses do escravo; apogeu e crise da escravatura no Brasil Meridional*, São Paulo, 1962.

Ianni, Octávio: *Estado e capitalismo: estructura social e industrialização no Brasil*, Rio de Janeiro, 1965.

Ianni, Octávio: *Crisis in Brazil*, New York, 1970.

Ianni, Octávio: *Estado e planejamento no Brasil (1930–1970)*, Rio de Janeiro, 1971.

Ianni, Octávio, *et al.*: *Política e revolução social no Brasil*, Rio de Janeiro, 1965.

Institute for the Comparative Study of Political Systems: *Brazil: election factbook No. 2. September 1965*, Washington DC, 1965.

Interinvest Guide: *Brazil and international capital*, Rio de Janeiro, 1973.

Jaguaribe, Hélio: *Economic and political development: a theoretical approach and a Brazilian case study*, Cambridge, Mass., 1968.

James, Herman Gerlach: *The Constitutional system of Brazil*, Washington DC, 1923.

James, Preston E.: *Latin America*, 3rd ed., New York, 1959.

Jesus, Carolina Maria de: *Child of the dark*, New York, 1962.

Julião, Francisco: *Cambão—the yoke: the hidden face of Brazil*, Harmondsworth 1972.

Julião, Francisco: *¿Qué son las ligas campesinas?* trad. de Ana María Chiesa de Ramo, Montevideo, 1963.

Jurema, Abelardo: *Sexta-Feira, 13; os últimos dias do govêrno João Goulart*, 2nd ed., Rio de Janeiro, 1964.

Kadt, Emanuel de: *Catholic radicals in Brazil*, London, 1970.

Kahil, Raouf: *Inflation and Economic Development in Brazil, 1946–1963*, Oxford, 1973.

Kelchner, Warren H.: *Latin American relations with the League of Nations*, Boston, 1930.

Kohl, James and Litt, John: *Urban guerrilla warfare in Latin America*, Cambridge, Mass., 1974.

Kowarick, Lúcio: *Capitalismo e marginalidade na América Latina*, Rio de Janeiro, 1975.

Krieger, Daniel: *Desde as missões. Saudades, lutas, esperanças*, Rio de Janeiro, 1976.

Lago, Mário: *1° de Abril: Estórias para a História*, Rio de Janeiro, 1964

Lambert, Jacques: *Latin America: social structure and political institutions*, Berkeley and Los Angeles, 1967.

Landsberger, Henry A. (ed.): *Latin American peasant movements*, Ithaca, 1969.

Langoni, Carlos Geraldo: *Distribuição de Renda e Desenvolvimento Econômico do Brasil*, Rio de Janeiro, 1973.

Leal, Victor Nunes: *Coronelismo, enxada e voto; o município e o regime representativo no Brasil*, Rio de Janeiro, 1948.

Leff, Nathaniel H.: *Economic policy-making and development in Brazil, 1947–1964*, New York, 1968.

Leuenroth, Edgard (ed.): *Anarquismo roteiro da libertação social: antologia de doutrina crítica, história, informações*, Rio de Janeiro, 1963.

Levine, Robert M.: *The Vargas regime: the critical years, 1934–1938*, New York, 1970

Lima, Afonso de Albuquerque: *Discurso proferido na ocasião da transmissão de Ministro do Interior*, Rio de Janeiro, 1969.

Lima, Alceu Amoroso: *Pelo humanismo ameaçado*, Rio de Janeiro, 1965.

Lima, Cláudio de Araujo: *Mito e realidade de Vargas*, 2nd ed., Rio de Janeiro, 1955.

Lima, Lourenço Moreira: *A coluna Prestes* (*marchas e combates*), 2nd ed., São Paulo, 1945.

Lima, Manuel de Oliveira: *O império brasileiro, 1822–1889*, 2nd ed., São Paulo, n.d.

Lima Sobrinho, Alexandre José Barbosa: *A verdade sôbre a revolução de outubro*, São Paulo, 1933.

Lins, Alvaro: *Rio Branco* (*O barão do Rio Branco*) *biografia pessoal e história política*, 2nd ed., São Paulo, 1965.

Lisboa, Rosalina Coelho: *A seara de Caim: romance de revolução no Brasil*, 2nd ed., Rio de Janeiro, 1952.

Lobo, Hélio: *O Brasil e seus princípios de neutralidade*, Rio de Janeiro, 1914.

Loewenstein, Karl: *Brazil under Vargas*, New York, 1942.

Lopes, Juarez Rubens Brandão: *Sociedade industrial no Brasil*, São Paulo, 1964.

Lopes, Theodorico: *Ministros da guerra do Brasil, 1808–1950*, 4th ed., Rio de Janeiro, 1950.

Loureiro, Júnior, José: *O golpe de novembro e outros discursos*, Rio de Janeiro, 1957.

Love, Joseph Leroy: *Rio Grande do Sul and Brazilian regionalism, 1882–1930*, Stanford, 1971.

Luccock, John: *Notes on Rio de Janeiro and the southern parts of Brazil*, London, 1820.

Luz, Nícia Vilela: *A luta pela industrialização do Brasil, 1808–1930*, São Paulo, 1961.

Lyra, Heitor: *História da queda do império*, 2 vols., São Paulo, 1964.

McCann, Frank D.: *The Brazilian-American alliance, 1937–1945*, Princeton, 1973.

Macaulay, Neill: *The Prestes column: revolution in Brazil*, New York, 1974.

Magalhães Júnior, Raymundo: *Deodoro, a espada contra o império*, 2 vols., São Paulo, 1957.

Magalhães Júnior, Raymundo: *Ruí, o homen e o mito*, 2nd ed., Rio de Janeiro, 1965.

Maine, John: *Travels in the interior of Brazil*, London, 1812.

Malloy, James M.: *Authoritarianism and corporatism in Latin America*, Pittsburgh, 1977.

Manchester, Alan Krebs: *British preeminence in Brazil, its rise and decline: A study in European expansion*, Chapel Hill, 1933.

Martins, Luciano: *Pouvoir et développement économique: formation et évolution des structures politiques au Brésil*, Paris, 1976.

Maxwell, Kenneth Robert: *Conflicts and conspiracies: Brazil and Portugal, 1750–1808*, London, 1973.

Medeiros, Mauricio de: *Outras revoluções virão*, Rio de Janeiro, 1932.

Melo, Olbiano de: *A marcha da revolução social no Brasil: ensaio histórico-sociológico do período 1922 à 1954*, Rio de Janeiro, 1957.

Mercadante, Paulo: *A consciência conservadora no Brasil: contribuição ao estudo da formação brasileira*, Rio de Janeiro, 1965.

Miliband, Ralph: *The State in capitalist society*, London, 1969.

Monbeig, Pierre: *Pionniers et planteurs de São Paulo*, Paris, 1952.

Moraes, João Baptista Mascarenhas de: *A F.E.B. pelo seu comandante*, Rio de Janeiro, 1960.

Moraes, João Baptista Mascarenhas de: *Memórias*, 2 vols., Rio de Janeiro, 1969.

Moraes, José: *Juscelino: o homen, a candidatura, a campanha*, Belo Horizonte, 1955.

Morazé, Charles: *Les trois âges du Brésil: essai de politique*, Paris, 1954.

Morel, Edmar: *O golpe começou em Washington*, Rio de Janeiro, 1965.

Nabuco, Carolina: *A vida de Virgílio Melo Franco*, Rio de Janeiro, 1962.

Nash, Roy: *The Conquest of Brazil*, London, 1926.

Newfarmer, Richard S. and Mueller, Willard F. (eds.): *Multinational corporations in Brazil and Mexico: structural sources of economic and non-economic power, report to the subcommittee on multinational corporations of the Committee on Foreign Relations of the United States Senate*, August 1975.

Niemeyer, Oscar: *Minha experiencia em Brasília*, Rio de Janeiro, 1961.

Nogueira Filho, Paulo: *Ideais e Lutas de um burguês progressista: o Partido Democrático e a revolução de 1930*, 2 vols., 2nd ed., Rio de Janeiro, 1965.

Normano, João Frederico: *Brazil: a study of economic types*, Chapel Hill, 1935.

Ó, Manoel do: *100 anos de suor e sangue: homens e jornadas da luta operária do Nordeste*, Petrópolis, 1971.

Oiticica, José: *Ação direita* (*meio século de pregação libertária*), Rio de Janeiro, 1970.

Oliveira, Clovis de: *A indústria e o movimento constitucionalista de 1932*, São Paulo, 1956.

Oliveira, Francisco de: *A economia brasileira: crítica à razão dualista*, São Paulo, 1962.

Oliveira, José Teixeira: *O governo Dutra*, Rio de Janeiro, 1956.

Oliveira, Nelson Tabajara de: *1924: a revolução de Isidoro*, São Paulo, 1956.

Pedreira, Fernando: *Março 31. Civis e militares no processo da crise brasileira*, Rio de Janeiro, 1964.

Peixoto, Alzira Vargas do Amaral: *Getúlio Vargas, meu pai*, Pôrto Alegre, 1960.

Pelaez, Carlos Manuel: *História da industrialização brasileira: crítica à teoria estructuralista no Brasil*, Rio de Janeiro, 1972.

Peralva, Oswaldo: *O retrato: depoimento sôbre o comunismo no Brasil*, Rio de Janeiro, 1962.

Pereira, Astrojildo: *Formação do PCB, 1922–1928: notas e documentos*, Rio de Janeiro, 1962.

Perlman, Janice E.: *The Myth of marginality*, Berkeley and Los Angeles, and London, 1977.

Pessoa, Epitácio: *Na política da Paraíba, 2a fase: 1912–1935*, Rio de Janeiro, 1962.

Pessoa, Epitácio: *Pela verdade*, 2 vols., Rio de Janeiro, 1957.

Pimentel, Osmar (ed.): *São Paulo, espírito, povo, instituições*, São Paulo, 1968.

Pinto, Adolfo Augusto: *As estradas de ferro de São Paulo*, São Paulo, 1916.

Pinto, Luís Augusto de Aguiar: *Lutas de famílias no Brasil: introdução ao seu estudo*, São Paulo, 1949.

Poppino, Rollie E.: *Brazil: the land and people*, New York, 1968.

Poulantzas, Nicos: *Political power and social classes*, London, 1973.

Poulantzas, Nicos: *Fascism and dictatorship: the Third International and the problem of fascism*, London, 1974 (trans. Judith White).

Prado Júnior, Caio: *The colonial background of modern Brazil*, Berkeley and Los Angeles, 1967 (trans. Suzette Macedo).

Prado Júnior, Caio: *História econômica do Brasil*, 9th ed., São Paulo, 1965.

Price, R.: *Rural unionization in Brazil*, Madison, 1964.

Quadros, Jânio: *Mensagem ao Congresso Nacional*, Brasília, 1961.

Quartim, João: *Dictatorship and armed struggle in Brazil*, New York, 1971.

Queiroz, José (Jr): *222 anedotas de Getúlio Vargas: anedotário popular, irreverente e pitoresco. Getúlio no inferno. Getúlio no céu.* Rio de Janeiro, 1955.

Ramos, Plínio de Abreu: *Brasil, 11 de novembro*, São Paulo, 1960.

Reisky-Dubnic, Vladimir: *Political trends in Brazil*, Washington, 1968.

Robock, Stefan Hyman: *Brazil's developing Northeast: a study of regional planning and foreign aid*, Washington, DC, 1963.

Rocha, Bento Munhoz da: *Radiografia de novembro*, 2nd ed., Rio de Janeiro, 1961.

Rodrigues, Edgar: *Socialismo e sindicalismo no Brasil*, Rio de Janeiro, 1969.

Rodrigues, José Albertino: *Sindicato e desenvolvimento no Brasil*, São Paulo, 1968.

Rodrigues, José Honório: *Brasil e Africa: outro horizonte: relações e política brasileiro-africana*, Rio de Janeiro, 1961.

Rodrigues, José Honório, *et al.*: *Política externa independente: a crise do Pan Americanismo*, Rio de Janeiro, 1965.

Rodrigues, Leôncio Martins: *Conflito industrial e sindicalismo no Brasil*, São Paulo, 1966.

Roett, Riordan (ed.): *Brazil in the sixties*, Nashville, 1972.

Rosa, Othello: *Júlio de Castilhos*, Pôrto Alegre, 1928.

Rosenbaum, Harris Jon, and Tyler, W. G. (eds.): *Contemporary Brazil: issues in economic and political development*, New York, 1972.

Rowe, John Wilkinson Foster: *The World's coffee: a study of the economics and politics of the coffee industries of certain countries and of the international problem*, London, 1963.

Rugendas, Johann Moritz: *Viagem pitoresca através do Brasil*, trans. Sérgio Milliet, 1st ed., São Paulo, 1940; 5th ed., São Paulo, 1954.

Salgado, Plínio: *Enciclopédia do integralismo*, 11 vols., Rio de Janeiro, 1958–61.

Salgado, Plínio: *O integralismo perante a Nação*, 3rd ed., Rio de Janeiro, 1955.

Salles, Alberto: *A pátria paulista*, Campinas, 1887.

Salles, Manuel Ferraz de Campos: *Da propaganda á presidencia*, São Paulo, 1908.

Sampson, Anthony: *The Arms Bazaar*, London, 1977.

Santos, José Maria dos: *Bernardino de Campos e o partido republicano paulista*, Rio de Janeiro, 1960.

Sayers, Raymond S. (ed.): *Portugal and Brazil in transition*, London, 1968.

Schmitter, Philippe C.: *Interest conflict and political change in Brazil*, Stanford, 1971.

Schneider, Ronald M.: *The Political system of Brazil: emergence of a 'modernizing' authoritarian regime, 1964–1970*, New York, 1971.

Schwartzmann, Simon: *São Paulo e o Estado Nacional*, São Paulo, 1975.

Scott, James C.: *Comparative Political Corruption*, Englewood Cliffs, 1972.

Sette, Adyr Pontes: *A verdade sôbre a deposição de Getúlio Vargas: documentário contendo a íntegra do famoso discurso do senador Getúlio*

Vargas, proferido no senado a 13 de dezembro de 1946, e um extrato do discurso de Pôrto Alegre, Juiz de Fora, MG, 1947.

Siegal, Gilbert Byron: *The Vicissitudes of government reform in Brazil: a study of the DASP*, Los Angeles, 1966.

Silva, Golbery do Couto e: *Planejamento estratégico*, Rio de Janeiro, 1955.

Silva, Golbery do Couto e: *Aspectos geopolíticos do Brasil*, Rio de Janeiro, 1957.

Silva, Golbery do Couto e: *Geopolítica do Brasil*, 2nd ed., Rio de Janeiro, 1967.

Silva, Hélio: *O ciclo de Vargas*, Rio de Janeiro, 1964.

Silva, Hélio: *1964: Golpe ou Contragolpe?*, Rio de Janeiro, 1975.

Simmons, Charles Willis: *Marshal Deodoro and the Fall of Dom Pedro II*, Durham, N.C., 1966.

Simonsen, Roberto Cochrane: *Brazil's industrial evolution*, São Paulo, 1939.

Simonsen, Roberto Cochrane: *História econômica do Brasil, 1500–1820*, 3rd ed., São Paulo, 1957.

Simonsen, Roberto Cochrane: *A indústria em face da economia nacional*, São Paulo, 1937.

Simonsen, Roberto Cochrane: *O planejamento da economia brasileira: réplica ao Sr. Eugênio Gudin, na comissão de planejamento econômico*, São Paulo, 1945.

Skidmore, Thomas E.: *Politics in Brazil, 1930–1964: an experiment in democracy*, New York, 1967.

Smith, Thomas Lynn: *Brazil: people and institutions*, rev. ed., Baton Rouge, 1954.

Smith, Thomas Lynn (ed.): *Brazil: portrait of half a continent*, New York, 1957.

Sodré, Nelson Werneck: *Introdução à revolução brasileira*, Rio de Janeiro, 1958.

Sodré, Nelson Werneck: *História militar do Brasil*, Rio de Janeiro, 1965.

Sodré, Nelson Werneck: *História da burguesia brasileira*, 2nd ed., Rio de Janeiro, 1967.

Southey, Robert: *History of Brazil*, 3 vols., London, 1817–22.

Stacchini, José: *Março 64: mobilização da audácia*, São Paulo, 1965.

Stein, Stanley J.: *The Brazilian cotton manufacture; textile enterprise in an underdeveloped area, 1850–1950*, Cambridge, Mass., 1957.

Stein, Stanley J.: *Vassouras, a Brazilian coffee county, 1850–1900*, Cambridge, Mass., 1957.

Stepan, Alfred: *The Military in politics: changing patterns in Brazil*, Princeton, 1971.

Stepan, Alfred (ed.): *Authoritarian Brazil: origins, policies and future*, New Haven, 1973.

Szulc, Tad: *The winds of revolution: Latin America today and tomorrow*, London, 1964.

Taunay, Affonso d' Escragnolle: *História do café no Brasil*, Rio de Janeiro, 1939–43.

Taunay, Affonso d'Escragnolle: *Pequena história do café no Brasil*, Rio de Janeiro, 1945.

Tavares, Aurélio de Lyra: *Além dos temas da caserna*, Fortaleza, 1968.
Tavares, Aurélio de Lyra: *O exército brasileiro visto pelo seu ministro*, Recife, 1968.
Tavares, Aurélio de Lyra: *Orações cívicas e militares*, João Pessoa, 1967.
Tavares, Aurélio de Lyra: *Segurança nacional: antagonismos e vulnerabilidades*, Rio de Janeiro, 1958.
Tavares, Aurélio de Lyra: *Segurança nacional: problemas atuais*, Rio de Janeiro, 1965.
Tavares, Aurélio de Lyra: *Território nacional: soberania e domínio do estado*, Rio de Janeiro 1955.
Tavares Aurélio de Lyra: *Por dever do ofício*, Rio de Janeiro, 1969.
Távora, Juarez: *A guisa de depoimento sôbre a revolução brasileira de 1924*, 3 vols., Rio de Janeiro/São Paulo, 1927–28.
Távora, Juarez: *Petróleo para o Brasil*, Rio de Janeiro, 1955.
Tejo, Aurelio de Limeira: *Jango, debate sôbre a crise dos nossos tempos*, Rio de Janeiro, 1957.
Telles, Jover: *O movimento sindical no Brasil*, Rio de Janeiro, 1962.
Tinoco, Brígido: *A vida de Nilo Peçanha*, Rio de Janeiro, 1962.
Tolipan, Ricardo and Tinelli, Arthur Carlos (eds.): *A Controvérsia sôbre Distribuição de Renda e Desenvolvimento*, Rio de Janeiro, 1975.
Toplin, Robert Brent: *The Abolition of slavery in Brazil, 1880–1888*, New York, 1972.
Torres, João Camillo de Oliveira: *A democracia coroada: teoria política do império do Brasil*, 2nd rev. ed., Petrópolis, 1964.
Torres, João Camillo de Oliveira: *O presidencialismo no Brasil*, Rio de Janeiro, 1962.
Trigueiros, Florisvaldo dos Santos: *Dinheiro no Brasil*, Rio de Janeiro, 1966.
Valladares, Benedicto: *Tempos idos e vividos: memórias*, Rio de Janeiro, 1966.
Vargas, Getúlio: *A campanha presidencial* (*discursos*), Rio de Janeiro, 1951.
Vargas, Getúlio: *O govêrno trabalhista do Brasil*, 2 vols., Rio de Janeiro, 1952.
Vargas, Getúlio: *A nova política do Brasil*, 11 vols., Rio de Janeiro, 1938–47.
Vargas, Getúlio: *A política nacionalista do petróleo no Brasil*, Rio de Janeiro, 1964.
Vergara, Luiz: *Fui secretário de Getúlio Vargas: memórias dos anos de 1926–1954*, Rio de Janeiro, 1960.
Viana Filho, Luís: *A vida de Rui Barbosa*, 6th ed., São Paulo, 1960.
Vianna, Francisco José de Oliveira: *O ocaso do império*, 3rd ed., Rio de Janeiro, 1959.
Victor, Mário: *Cinco anos que abalaram o Brasil (de Jânio Quadros ao Marechal Castello Branco)*, Rio de Janeiro, 1965.
Vidal, Olmio Barros: *Um destino a serviço do Brasil*, Rio de Janeiro, 1945.
Vieira, Dorival Teixeira: *O desenvolvimento econômico do Brasil e a inflação*, São Paulo, 1962.
Vinhas, M.: *Estudos sôbre o proletariado brasileiro*, Rio de Janeiro, 1970.

Vita, Luís Washington: *Alberto Salles, ideólogo da República*, São Paulo, 1965.

Wagley, Charles: *An introduction to Brazil*, New York, 1963.

Williams, Mary Wilhelmine: *Dom Pedro the Magnanimous, second emperor of Brazil*, Chapel Hill, 1937.

Winpenny, James Thomas: *Brazil—Manufactured exports and government policy: Brazil's experience since 1939*, London, 1972.

Wirth, John D.: *The Politics of Brazilian development, 1930–1954*, Stanford, 1970.

Young, Jordan M.: *The Brazilian revolution of 1930 and the aftermath*, New Brunswick, 1967.

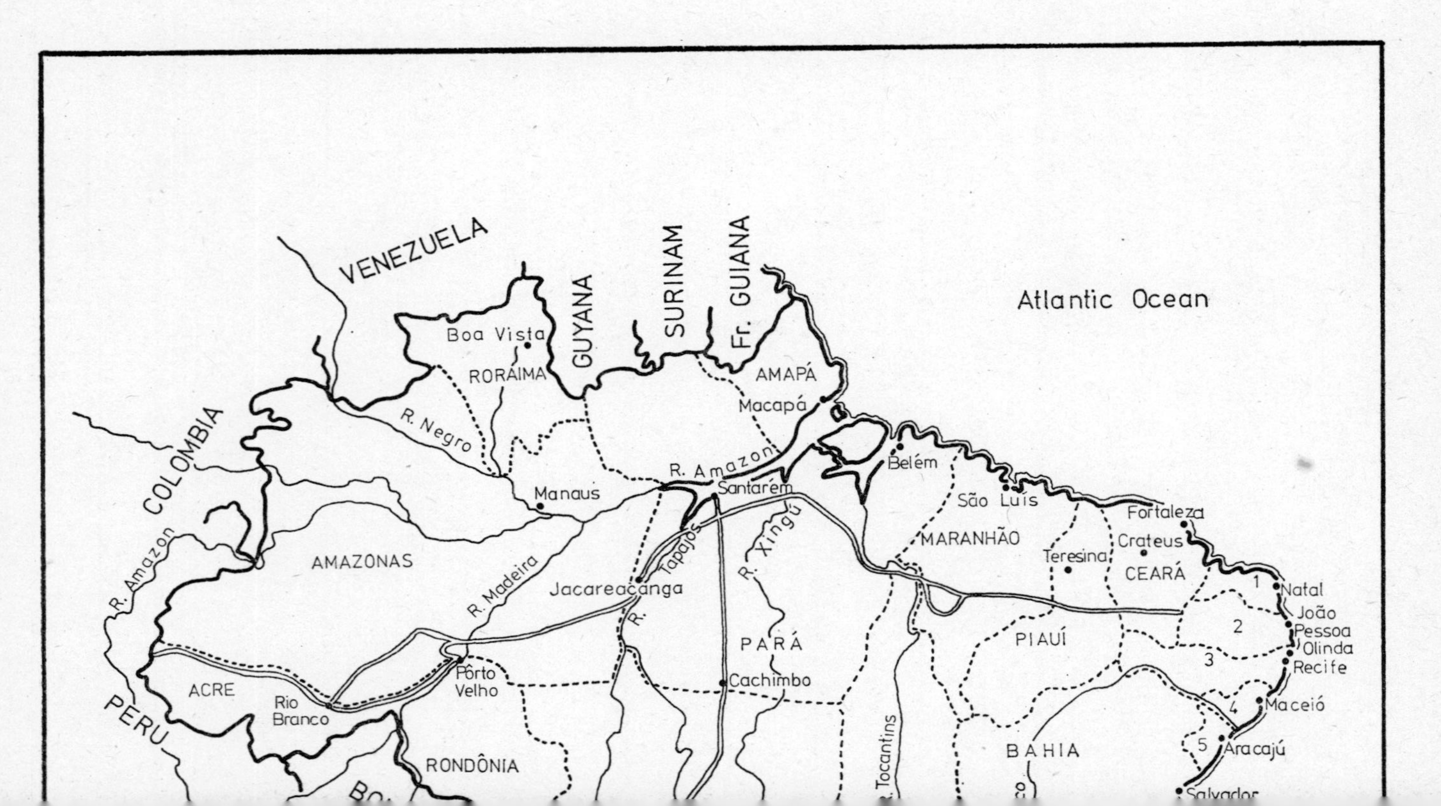
Atlantic Ocean
VENEZUELA
GUYANA
SURINAM
Fr. GUIANA
COLOMBIA
PERU
Boa Vista
RORAIMA
AMAPÁ
Macapá
R. Negro
R. Amazon
Belém
São Luís
Fortaleza
Manaus
Santarém
MARANHÃO
Crateus
Teresina
CEARÁ
AMAZONAS
R. Xingu
R. Tapajós
R. Madeira
Jacareacanga
R. Amazon
Natal
João Pessoa
Olinda
Recife
PIAUÍ
PARÁ
Pôrto Velho
Cachimbo
ACRE
Rio Branco
RONDÔNIA
R. Tocantins
BAHIA
Maceió
Aracajú
Salvador
1
2
3
4
5

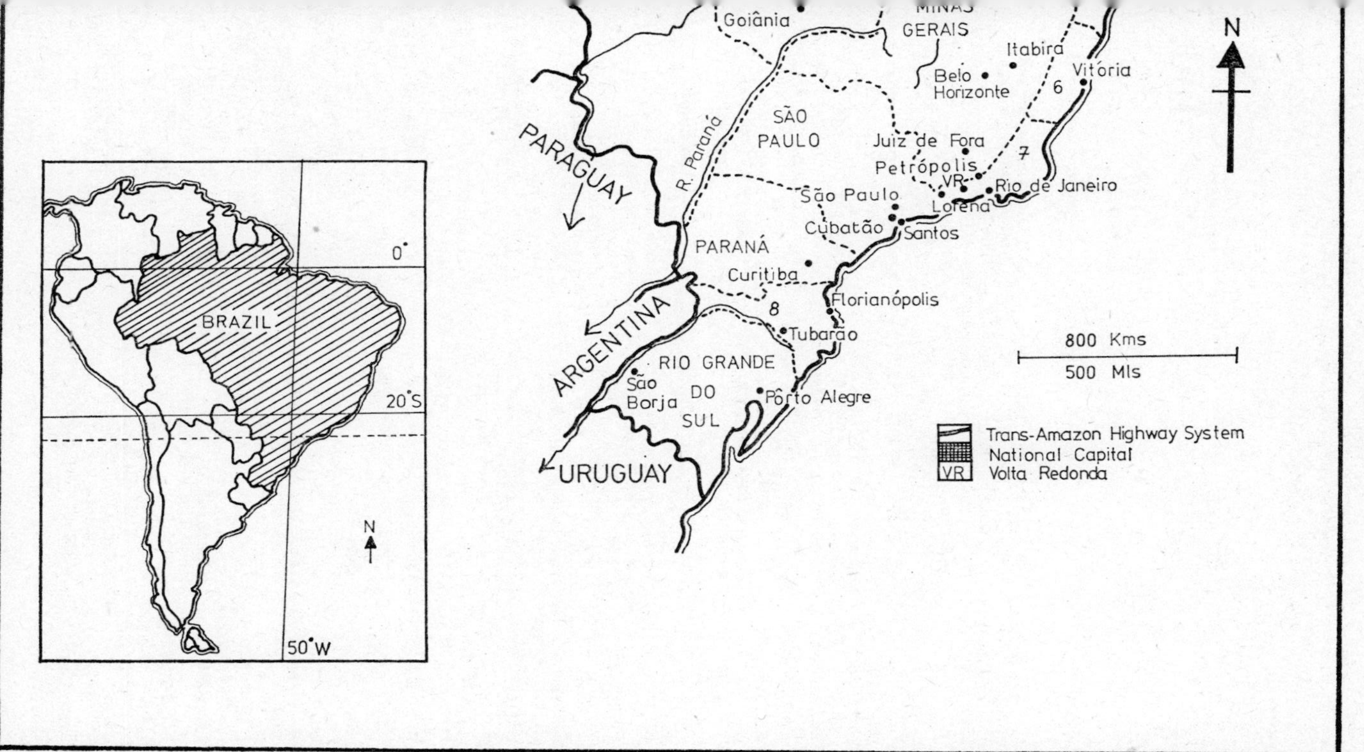

BRAZIL: General Map
1 Rio Grande do Norte. 2 Paraíba. 3 Pernambuco. 4 Alagôas. 5 Sergipe. 6 Espírito Santo.
7 Rio de Janeiro (inc. former state of Guanabara). 8 Santa Catarina.

Index

Index

303282838.